Classic and Contemporary
Perspectives in Social Psychology

Classic and Contemporary Perspectives in Social Psychology: A Reader

Sharon E. Preves

Hamline University

Jeylan T. Mortimer

University of Minnesota

New York   Oxford

OXFORD UNIVERSITY PRESS

2011

Oxford University Press, Inc., publishes works that further
Oxford University's objective of excellence
in research, scholarship, and education.

Oxford New York
Auckland Cape Town Dar es Salaam Hong Kong Karachi
Kuala Lumpur Madrid Melbourne Mexico City Nairobi
New Delhi Shanghai Taipei Toronto

With offices in
Argentina Austria Brazil Chile Czech Republic France Greece
Guatemala Hungary Italy Japan Poland Portugal Singapore
South Korea Switzerland Thailand Turkey Ukraine Vietnam

Published by Oxford University Press, Inc.
198 Madison Avenue, New York, New York 10016
http://www.oup.com

Oxford is a registered trademark of Oxford University Press

Library of Congress Cataloging-in-Publication Data
Classic and contemporary perspectives in social psychology : a reader /
    [edited by] Sharon E. Preves, Jeylan T. Mortimer.
p. cm.
ISBN 978-0-19-973399-6 (pbk.)
1. Social psychology.   I. Preves, Sharon E.,   II. Mortimer, Jeylan T., 1943–
HM1033.C596 2011
302–dc22
2010003113

ISBN 978-0-19-973399-6

Printed in the United States of America
on acid-free paper

To the remarkable children who came into our lives during the creation
of this book: Jessica, Cheyenne, and Eileen.
We love you.

ACKNOWLEDGMENTS

This book has been actively supported by many players. From Hamline University, we gratefully acknowledge the able research assistance of Aaron Wahlstrom, Robyn Miller, Wendy Werdin, Jackie Austin, and Kelly Dahlman (our queen of copyright permissions). Matt James and Mark Wierzenski at the IKON Copy Center and Christiane Reilly and Laura Kroft from the Center for Academic Technology did much of the heavy lifting with regard to reproducing and safe keeping of our documents. Steve Dondelinger, of Information Technology Services, created a safe harbor for their storage.

From the University of Minnesota, Ross Macmillan and Holly Schoonover of the Life Course Center and Karl Krohn of the Department of Sociology provided space and additional resources to sustain this project.

Rosanne Bane and the members of the Loft Literary Center's Woodbury Library Writer's Habit Class provided helpful structure for the final writing in the summer of 2009.

Claude Teweles gave us the impetus for the book. Our fabulous editor at Oxford, Sherith Pankratz, provided us with unwavering support, encouragement, patience, and insight. Taylor Pilkington, editorial assistant at Oxford, was of tremendous help as the book went to press.

We would also like to thank the reviewers who formally commented on the manuscript for Oxford University Press: Janelle Wilson, University of Minnesota—Duluth; Timothy B. Gongaware, University of Wisconsin—La Crosse; Norman Goodman, Stony Brook University; Bruce K. Friesen, University of Tampa; Christopher Bradley, Indiana-Purdue University—Fort Wayne; David Daniel Bogumil, California State Polytechnic University—Pomona; Monika Ardelt, University of Florida; John Eric Baugher, University of Southern Maine; Tiffani Everett, University of Georgia; David A. Gay, University of Central Florida; Terri L. Orbuch, University of Michigan; and Rebecca F. Plante, Ithaca College.

Our social psychology students gave us the inspiration to write this book. We look forward to and welcome your feedback!

Our families, Nico, Jessica, Cheyenne, and Jeff: We love you. We couldn't have done it without you. Your humor, love, and faith in us and in this project kept us afloat.

ANNOTATED CONTENTS

Press as "one of the most accurate descriptions available of an often misunderstood subculture" when it published the paperback edition of Shared Fantasy *in 2002. Fine's research, conducted nearly 30 years ago, provides considerable insight into today's wildly popular leisure activity of FRP games.*

IV. Constructing a Social Self 219

Comic Strip: F Minus, "Cell Block D"

A. THE SOCIAL SELF 221

Classic:

31. Charles Horton Cooley, "The Social Self"   222
    Cooley outlines his theory of "the looking-glass self," a self that is experienced in one's imagined reflected appraisal from others.

32. George Herbert Mead, "Play, the Game, and the Generalized Other"   225
    Several of Mead's key contributions are contained within this brief selection including his discussion of the "play" and "game" stages of self-development, his concept of "the generalized other," and the "I" and the "me."

Contemporary:

33. Kate Hellenga, "Social Space, the Final Frontier: Adolescents on the Internet"   228
    Adolescents prefer computers to other media and spend an increasing amount of their social time interacting online in "virtual" communication with others who are often unknown to them. Hellenga discusses how online social interactions are changing the very experience of adolescence and development of the sense of self.

B. DEVIANCE AND LABELING 237

Classic:

34. David L. Rosenhan, "On Being Sane in Insane Places"   238
    Rosenhan (and his colleagues) discovered the "stickiness" of labels when they sought admission to (and release from) a dozen U.S. psychiatric institutions in the early 1970s. In the context of hospital psychiatric wards, their everyday behaviors and personal histories were interpreted as evidence of their mental illness.

35. Peter Conrad, "The Discovery of Hyperkinesis: Notes on the Medicalization of Deviant Behavior"   243
    Conrad explores how medicine acts as an agent of social control by diagnosing and treating hyperkinesis in children, illustrating how children's "deviant" behavior became defined as the concern of medical doctors, pharmacists, teachers, and politicians in the second half of the twentieth century.

Contemporary:

36. Patricia Gagné, Richard Tewksbury and Deanna McGaughey, "Coming out and Crossing Over: Identity Formation and Proclamation in a Transgender Community"   248
    In their study of 65 male-to-female transsexuals, Gagné and her colleagues explore the continued expansion of medical social control over behavior and identity into the twenty-first century.

C. STIGMA 254

Classic:

37. Mary K. Zimmerman, "Passage Through Abortion: The Personal and Social Reality of Women's Experiences"   255
    Zimmerman documents the long-term experiences of 40 women who have an abortion, from the point at which they decide to have the procedure to how their identities and relationships are affected long after their pregnancy is aborted.

Contemporary:

38. Spencer E. Cahill and Robin Eggleston, "Managing Emotions in Public: The Case of Wheelchair Users"   269
    Cahill and Eggleston report findings from their fascinating ethnographic study of how wheelchair users cope with having a visible stigma.

39. Kent L. Sandstrom, "Confronting Deadly Disease: The Drama of Identity Construction among Gay Men with AIDS"   280
    In this moving piece written close to the onset of HIV infection and AIDS in the United States, Sandstrom draws on 56 interviews with 19 gay men who are HIV positive or who have AIDS.

V. Social Structure and Social Psychology 291

Boy Toys, Shapiro conducted field research and interviews with 28 of its members.

PART I

Understanding and Studying Social Life

The Social Construction of Reality

In 1928, Dorothy and William Thomas published their book *The Child in America: Behavior Problems and Programs*. In it, they penned one of the most famous and often cited propositions in social psychology: "If men [sic] define situations as real, they are real in their consequences" (p. 572). Over time, their proposition became known as the Thomas theorem. According to this principle, an individual's beliefs shape interpersonal behavior, relationships, and ultimately social institutions. This occurs even if those beliefs are not factually correct.

The selections in this section recall the Thomas theorem as they emphasize the power of belief in structuring everyday social interactions and rituals. Miner's classic ethnographic research on the Nacirema gives us an insider's view of a culture seemingly obsessed with bodily imperfections. Turner and Edgley give us "backstage" access to the delicate performances conducted by morticians at funeral parlors. Van Maanen looks behind the smile at one of the world's best-known amusement parks to reveal a rigid power structure and the need for intensive emotional labor on the part of employees.

All three pieces speak to the construction of realities that serve to distance people from the discomforts of daily life. Whether trying to distance oneself from decay (Nacirema), death (funerals), or complexity (Disneyland), each of these cultural productions reveals a social construction of a reality that is orderly, clean, and predictable. A complex set of rules separate frontstage and backstage regions, thereby "covering up" natural bodily functions, death and decay, or frustration at work. As a result, the unsightly and unseemly are hidden from public consumption.

REFERENCES

Thomas, William I. and Dorothy Swaine Thomas. 1928. *The Child in America: Behavior Problems and Programs*. New York: Knopf.

1. Body Ritual among the Nacirema

HORACE MINER

In his brilliant anthropological account, Miner critically explores the taken-for-granted daily rituals and beliefs of a "tribal Other"—the Nacirema. Taking on the scientific gaze of the "Other" casts a critical awareness on even the most mundane tasks.

The anthropologist has become so familiar with the diversity of ways in which different peoples behave in similar situations that he is not apt to be surprised by even the most exotic customs. In fact, if all of the logically possible combinations of behavior have not been found somewhere in the world, he is apt to suspect that they must be present in some yet undescribed tribe. In this light, the magical beliefs and practices of the Nacirema present such unusual aspects that it seems desirable to describe them as an example of the extremes to which human behavior can go.

Professor Linton first brought the ritual of the Nacirema to the attention of anthropologists twenty years ago, but the culture of this people is still very poorly understood. They are a North American group living in the territory between the Canadian Cree, the Yaqui and Tarahumare of Mexico, and the Carib and Arawak of the Antilles.

Little is known of their origin, although tradition states that they came from the east. According to Nacirema mythology, their nation was originated by a culture hero, Notgnihsaw, who is otherwise known for two great feats of strength—the throwing of a piece of wampum across the river Pa-To-Mac and the chopping down of a cherry tree in which the Spirit of Truth resided.

Nacirema culture is characterized by a highly developed market economy which has evolved in a rich natural habitat. While much of the people's time is devoted to economic pursuits, a large part of the fruits of these labors and a considerable portion of the day are spent in ritual activity. The focus of this activity is the human body, the appearance and health of which loom as a dominant concern in the ethos of the people. While such a concern is certainly not unusual, its ceremonial aspects and associated philosophy are unique.

Miner, Horace. 1956. "Body Ritual among the Nacirema." *American Anthropologist*, 53(3): 503–7.

The fundamental belief underlying the whole system appears to be that the human body is ugly and that its natural tendency is to debility and disease. Incarcerated in such a body, man's only hope is to avert these characteristics through the use of the powerful influences of ritual and ceremony. Every household has one or more shrines devoted to this purpose. The more powerful individuals in the society have several shrines in their houses and, in fact, the opulence of a house is often referred to in terms of the number of such ritual centers it possesses. Most houses are of wattle and daub construction, but the shrine rooms of the more wealthy are walled with stone. Poorer families imitate the rich by applying pottery plaques to their shrine walls.

While each family has at least one such shrine, the rituals associated with it are not family ceremonies but are private and secret. The rites are normally only discussed with children, and then only during the period when they are being initiated into these mysteries. I was able, however, to establish sufficient rapport with the natives to examine these shrines and to have the rituals described to me.

The focal point of the shrine is a box or chest which is built into the wall. In this chest are kept the many charms and magical potions without which no native believes he could live. These preparations are secured from a variety of specialized practitioners. The most powerful of these are the medicine men, whose assistance must be rewarded with substantial gifts. However, the medicine men do not provide the curative potions for their clients, but decide what the ingredients should be and then write them down in an ancient and secret language. This writing is understood only by the medicine men and by the herbalists who, for another gift, provide the required charm.

The charm is not disposed of after it has served its purpose, but is placed in the charm-box of the household shrine. As these magical materials are specific for certain ills, and the real or imagined maladies of the people are many, the charm-box is usually full to overflowing.

The magical packets are so numerous that people forget what their purposes were and fear to use them again. While the natives are very vague on this point, we can only assume that the idea in retaining all the old magical materials is that their presence in the charm-box, before which the body rituals are conducted, will in some way protect the worshipper.

Beneath the charm box is a small font. Each day every member of the family, in succession, enters the shrine room, bows his head before the charm-box, mingles different sorts of holy water in the font, and proceeds with a brief rite of ablution. The holy waters are secured from the Water Temple of the community, where the priests conduct elaborate ceremonies to make the liquid ritually pure.

In the hierarchy of magical practitioners, and below the medicine men in prestige, are specialists whose designation is best translated "holy-mouth-men." The Nacirema have an almost pathological horror of and fascination with the mouth, the condition of which is believed to have a supernatural influence on all social relationships. Were it not for the rituals of the mouth, they believe that their teeth would fall out, their gums bleed, their jaws shrink, their friends desert them, and their lovers reject them. They also believe that a strong relationship exists between oral and moral characteristics.

The daily body ritual performed by everyone includes a mouth-rite. Despite the fact that these people are so punctilious about care of the mouth, this rite involves a practice which strikes the uninitiated stranger as revolting. It was reported to me that the ritual consists of inserting a small bundle of hog hairs into the mouth, along with certain magical powders, and then moving the bundle in a highly formalized series of gestures.

In addition to the private mouth-rite, the people seek out a holy-mouth-man once or twice a year. These practitioners have an impressive set of paraphernalia, consisting of a variety of augers, awls, probes, and prods. The use of these objects in the exorcism of the evils of the mouth involves almost unbelievable ritual torture of the client. The holy-mouth-man opens the client's mouth and, using the above mentioned tools, enlarges any holes which decay may have created in the teeth. Magical materials are put into these holes. If there are no naturally occurring holes in the teeth, large sections of one or more teeth are gouged out so that the supernatural substance can be applied. In the client's view, the purpose of these ministrations is to arrest decay and to draw friends. The extremely sacred and traditional character of the rite is evident in the fact that the natives return to the holy-mouth-men year after year, despite the fact that their teeth continue to decay.

It is to be hoped that, when a thorough study of the Nacirema is made, there will be careful inquiry into the personality structure of these people. Most of the population shows definite masochistic tendencies. It was to these that Professor Linton referred in discussing a distinctive part of the daily body ritual which is performed only by men. This part of the rite involves scraping and lacerating the surface of the face with a sharp instrument. Special women's rites are performed only four times during each lunar month, but what they lack in frequency is made up in barbarity. As part of this ceremony, women bake their heads in small ovens for about an hour. The theoretically interesting point is that what seems to be a preponderantly masochistic people have developed sadistic specialists.

The medicine men have an imposing temple, or *lati pso*, in every community of any size. The more elaborate ceremonies required to treat very sick patients can only be performed at this temple. These ceremonies involve not only the thaumaturge but also a permanent group of vestal maidens who move sedately about the temple chambers in distinctive costume and headdress.

The *lati pso* ceremonies are so harsh that it is phenomenal that a fair proportion of the really sick natives who enter the temple ever recover. Small children whose indoctrination is still incomplete have been known to resist attempts

to take them to the temple because "that is where you go to die." Despite this fact, sick adults are not only willing but eager to undergo the protracted ritual purification, if they can afford to do so. No matter how ill the supplicant or how grave the emergency, the guardians of many temples will not admit a client if he cannot give a rich gift to the custodian. Even after one has gained admission and survived the ceremonies, the guardians will not permit the neophyte to leave until he makes still another gift.

The supplicant entering the temple is first stripped of all his or her clothes. In every-day life, the Nacirema avoids exposure of his body and its natural functions. Bathing and excretory acts are performed only in the secrecy of the household shrine, where they are ritualized as part of the body-rites. Psychological shock results from the fact that body secrecy is suddenly lost upon entry into the *lati pso*. A man, whose own wife has never seen him in an excretory act, suddenly finds himself naked and assisted by a vestal maiden while he performs his natural functions into a sacred vessel. This sort of ceremonial treatment is necessitated by the fact that the excreta are used by a diviner to ascertain the course and nature of the client's sickness. Female clients, on the other hand, find their naked bodies are subjected to the scrutiny, manipulation, and prodding of the medicine men.

Few supplicants in the temple are well enough to do anything but lie on their hard beds. The daily ceremonies, like the rites of the holy-mouth-men, involve discomfort and torture. With ritual precision, the vestals awaken their miserable charges each dawn and roll them about on their beds of pain while performing ablutions, in the formal movements of which the maidens are highly trained. At other times they insert magic wands in the supplicant's mouth or force him to eat substances which are supposed to be healing. From time to time the medicine men come to their clients and jab magically treated needles into their flesh. The fact that these temple ceremonies may not cure, and may even kill the neophyte, in no way decreases the people's faith in the medicine men.

There remains one other kind of practitioner, known as a "listener." This witch-doctor has the power to exorcise the devils that lodge in the heads of people who have been bewitched. The Nacirema believe that parents bewitch their own children. Mothers are particularly suspected of putting a curse on children while teaching them the secret body rituals. The counter-magic of the witch-doctor is unusual in its lack of ritual. The patient simply tells the "listener" all his troubles and fears, beginning with the earliest difficulties he can remember. The memory displayed by the Nacirema in these exorcism sessions is truly remarkable. It is not uncommon for the patient to bemoan the rejection he felt upon being weaned as a babe, and a few individuals even see their troubles going back to the traumatic effects of their own birth.

In conclusion, mention must be made of certain practices which have their base in native esthetics but which depend upon the pervasive aversion to the natural body and its functions. There are ritual fasts to make fat people thin and ceremonial feasts to make thin people fat. Still other rites are used to make women's breasts larger if they are small, and smaller if they are large. General dissatisfaction with breast shape is symbolized in the fact that the ideal form is virtually outside the range of human variation. A few women afflicted with almost inhuman hypermammary development are so idolized that they make a handsome living by simply going from village to village and permitting the natives to stare at them for a fee.

Reference has already been made to the fact that excretory functions are ritualized, routinized, and relegated to secrecy. Natural reproductive functions are similarly distorted. Intercourse is taboo as a topic and scheduled as an act. Efforts are made to avoid pregnancy by the use of magical materials or by limiting intercourse to certain phases of the moon. Conception is actually very infrequent. When pregnant, women dress so as to hide their condition. Parturition takes place in secret, without friends or relatives to assist, and the majority of women do not nurse their infants.

Our review of the ritual life of the Nacirema has certainly shown them to be a magic-ridden people. It is hard to understand how they have managed to exist so long under the burdens which they have imposed upon themselves. But even such exotic customs as these take on real meaning when they are viewed with insight.

DISCUSSION QUESTIONS
1. What parallels do you see between the Nacirema culture and your own, if any?
2. Miner does not overtly address issues of race, class, or gender in Nacireman society. What evidence do you see of such a power structure?
3. How might an anthropologist describe contemporary American society? How is it similar or different from Miner's description of the Nacirema in the 1950s?

ADDITIONAL RESOURCES

Internet
http://www.anthropology.pomona.edu/html/Faculty/1thomas/Thomas_1994-Body%20ritual-long%20version.pdf. A summary of research conducted by Lynn Thomas documenting "Student Reaction to Horace Miner's Body Ritual among the Nacirema."

FURTHER READING

Ellin, Nan. 2008. "Life Support: Nacirema Redux." *Journal of Urbanism: International Research on Placemaking and Urban Sustainability*, 1(1): 47–55.

Kimmel, Michael. 2006. "Ritualized Homosexuality in a Nacirema Subculture." *Sexualities*, 9(1): 95–105.

Murphy, Robert. 1987. *The Body Silent*. New York: Henry Holt.

Schopmeyer, Kim D. and Bradley J. Fisher. 1993. "Insiders and Outsiders: Exploring Ethnocentrism and Cultural Relativity in Sociology Courses." *Teaching Sociology*, 12(2): 148–53.

2. Death as Theater: A Dramaturgical Analysis of the American Funeral

RONNY E. TURNER AND CHARLES EDGLEY

Turner and Edgley describe the complexities of the funeral industry. Most notably, they discuss the role conflict encountered by funeral directors who must care for the deceased as well as their grieving family and friends. In a beautiful application of Erving Goffman's dramaturgical metaphor, Turner and Edgley provide a detailed account based on field research conducted in funeral parlors.

The notion that life is rather like a theater, of actors playing their parts to audiences, sometimes within the bounds of roles, and sometimes with considerable distance from them, is an ancient metaphor recently resurrected by social psychology as a device for analyzing behavior. Our study uses the dramaturgical metaphor to understand some of the relationships and interactions that comprise the American funeral.

The study is based on unobtrusive observations of and information obtained from fifteen mortuaries in three cities. Funeral directors were interviewed, "in-house" manuals on how to successfully perform a funeral were subjected to content analysis, and both national and local advertising material were studied. Only funeral services performed in mortuary chapels (a growing trend) were studied; however, the techniques we describe are probably also applicable to services held in churches of various denominations.

No memorial services in which the deceased had been cremated were included in our observations, and all of the funerals we observed were open-casket.

THE PERFORMATIVE NATURE OF FUNERAL DIRECTING

Funeral directors and allied members of their team may be seen as actors whose job is to stage a performance in such a way so that the audience to it (the bereaved family and friends) will impute

Turner, Ronny E. and Charles Edgley. 1976. "Death as Theater: A Dramaturgical Analysis of the American Funeral." *Sociology and Social Research*, 60(4): 377–92.

competence, sincerity, dignity, respect, and concern to their actions. Given the one-shot nature of the funeral service, and the impossibility of doing it over in the event of mistakes, the funeral director must necessarily be concerned with those performative aspects of his business which will lead the audience to be impressed favorably by his effective staging of the show. As in any other performance, the concern is likely to be with whether the show comes off or falls flat, and consequently, to use Goffman's phrase, the expressions given off must be arranged in such a way so that the images and impressions formed are favorable ones.

From the standpoint of the sociology of work, the funeral director is in a unique business. He draws his living from a relatively fixed resource, the death rate in a community. He cannot increase the amount of business available to him by increasing the number of deaths in the community, and he must be very careful of how he advertises lest someone gain the impression that he wants more people to die. (One does not, for example, see funeral homes sponsoring such risky events as the Indianapolis 500). His choices for increasing the flow of money, then, are limited and center basically around two options: 1) Getting more than his share of the business from deaths that do occur in the community; and 2) merchandizing up, so that the average cost of a funeral rises. In short, his opportunities to make money stem from his performative ability to stage dramas which are meaningful to his audience, and will leave them with an impression favorable enough to contribute to the all-important "reputation" which funeral homes find is in many respects their most marketable, if not tangible, quality.

ROLE-DISTANCE: THE SACRED AND THE PROFANE

The performative necessities of his work are, however, made more difficult by another aspect of the relationship between the funeral director and his audience which has been pointed out repeatedly by various studies: the amount of social distance that exists both between him and his clients and between the object of his work (death), and the public he undertakes to perform before. He deals with objects which are both sacred and profane; simultaneously loved and loathed. As a result, the funeral director often attempts to separate the body work from the directive work, thereby putting distance between himself and his traditionally assigned role. Sometimes this is accomplished in the same routine as when he dresses out differently for embalming and for directing; at other times role-distance is accomplished by simply hiring separate functionaries to do the body work so that he can concentrate on staging the show without being seen as someone who has been contaminated by contact with the dead. What is separated here by the funeral director is not so much himself from his role, but rather himself from a loathsomeness ordinarily attributed to certain aspects of that role by his audience.

As in other occupations (the medical profession being the most salient example), some emotional detachment from the objects one is manipulating is desirable. Funeral directors and their staff, therefore, tend to separate their own personal identity from the task of embalming bodies. The language and non-verbal conduct in the preparation room, then, demonstrate a type of role distance which effectively communicates detachment and sometimes even disdainful alienation from the role one is performing.

BACKSTAGE REGIONS: PREPARATION AND REHEARSAL

A successful funeral is a sequence of activities performed by the funeral director and his staff that are later seen by the bereaved as a respectful, appropriate tribute to the life and memory of the deceased. It requires an extensive series of preparations backstage, or behind the scene that will later be used for the performance. A backregion or backstage is simply the space and the enclosed activities strategically hidden from the audience. It is ordinarily a place, but it may also be constituted simply by the shielding and masking of information in an interpersonal situation so that the audience does not realize certain things which would conflict with the performance as staged.

The necessity of backregions is due, obviously, to the fact that preparations for performances, if seen, may contradict, alter, qualify, or destroy the impressions fostered frontstage. Because people seem to have a limited capacity for seeing ritual as ritual, and since funerals, like any other drama, are prepared for, the viewing of the preparations may undercut the impressions fostered frontstage. Similarly, those who have worked in the backregions of a restaurant, in the kitchen or after hours, and have participated in the preparation of food, the classification of customers by the staff, and so forth, may have difficulty seeing the frontstage performances in the same manner again.

In the backstage, equipment and props used to produce the performance are stored, the behavior within the area is considered "private" and the scenes that go on are protected from public observance by various territorial imperatives socially constructed and enforced: doors, curtains, locks, and "employees only" signs.

THE BACKSTAGE SETTING

What we have said about backstage regions are generally applicable with few qualifications to the dramas of the American funeral. The preparation room, referred to by some morticians as a "medical laboratory," is spatially segregated from the funeral chapel, visitation rooms, viewing rooms, offices, and other regions the public frequents. It may be noted that the awesome and sacrosanct qualities of such places may be heightened by successfully identifying them with medicine, a line of endeavor which seems to establish particularly esoteric meanings for the bulk of Americans.

The social and physical boundaries that separate the preparation room from other parts of the home are essential to the ceremonial performances that will be given later. Here the corpse is washed, shaved, sprayed with disinfectant, sliced, pierced, creamed, powdered, waxed, stitched, painted, manicured, dressed, and positioned in a casket. Embalming involves the draining of blood via the major arteries while simultaneously refilling them through an injection point in the neck or armpit with fluid. Through the use of other chemicals the flesh is softened, stretched, shrunk, restored, colored, and even replaced.

Obviously, these procedures would be likely to shock the friends and family of the deceased. But more than that, such viewing would tend to present the audience with an impression that would contradict that being fostered frontstage. In the presence of family and friends the casketed body is never touched by mortuary personnel; they honor a distance of two to three feet from the body. However, the preparation room is characterized by handling of the body (a naked body in some procedures) in ways that would appear disrespectful and even inhuman, even if one were unaware of the identity of the deceased. One might respond to all of these by asking just how it is possible to talk about inhumanity when the object is a corpse, and yet it is precisely this "human identity" conception of the enterprise that supports the funeral profession, and indeed, becomes the basic polarity between which the mortician must balance his act. At any rate, the embalming, restoration, and other preparatory procedures requiring manual labor might appear to the layman as morbidly intimate, repulsive, and a violation of dignity, even to the dead. Virtually all of the amenities persons accord to each other in everyday life are violated by the attendants who prepare a corpse for the service.

In order to maintain the historically hard-won image as a legitimate professional and counselor rather than an "undertaker" with all of its attendant morbid stereotypes, a funeral director must seclude the backstage by utilizing rhetoric less suggestive of what transpires behind closed doors. Here we come to the interpersonal shielding we discussed earlier which is at least

The grieving family also can have a backstage in the funeral home

as important as the barriers formed by physical space. It should be noted that backstage regions are protected not only by the funeral director, but also by others; most people, except some curious sociologists of everyday life, voluntarily avoid areas where they are uninvited. In this sense, the audience actively, rather than passively, participates in the distinctions we have drawn. They want to be put on by the show as much as the producers of it, and they seem to recognize that part of the meaning of any performance will be diluted with disenchantment if one knows too much.

Even though the specifics of the preparation room are a mystery, most people know enough to choose acceptable ignorance and avoid trespassing into the region. Once again, the audience is a party to the stage production, avoiding asking questions about embalming procedures, and generally managing their behavior in such a way as to suggest they know nothing of such preparations, and want to keep it that way.

THE RHETORIC OF BACKSTAGE REGIONS

Both the technical and the informal nomenclature which mark the universe of discourse of backstage regions serve a number of functions, but they are sufficiently different from the language characterizing the frontstage production itself that they must be segregated from clients who seek funeral services. There exists quite clearly in the funeral business a backstage language and another rubric entirely for those occasions in which the performance that has been so laboriously prepared is being staged. A superb example of frontstage rhetoric is a sign on the door of the embalming room at one of the establishments we studied:

Remember

This preparation room become sacred when a family entrusts us with one of its most precious possessions. Keep faith with them by conducting yourself as though the family were present. The body is dear to them.... Treat it reverently.

Backstage, however, morticians develop a very different set of behaviors toward their activities. Rather than being a person, the body becomes an object upon which one performs restorative art. And while the deceased is a dearly beloved, Mr. Doe, a father, loved one, etc., during front-stage encounters with the bereaved family, backstage references to various types of bodies such as "floaters" (one who has drowned and was not recovered until the body floated to the surface), "Mr. Crispy" (one who burned to death in an airplane crash), a "fresh" or "warm" one (a body received shortly after death), a "cold" one (a frozen body) are encountered in the conversations of the backstage crew. References to restorative art in the information materials given the public may in fact be referred to in the preparation room as "pickling" or "curing a ham." The use of "bod" instead of "body," especially with younger female corpses, is not uncommon. Joking, singing, the discussion of political issues, and (infrequently) open sexual remarks, racial slurs, complaints about the size of some bodies, profanity, and other rhetoric inconsistent with the frontstage regions are employed as ways of distancing the embalmer from the role he is performing.

Similarly, frontstage references to the burial containers such as casket, gift to the deceased, home, place of rest, and so on, are referred backstage as coffins, stuffing boxes, tin cans, containers, stove pipes (a cheap metal over wood casket), or brand names given to caskets by manufacturers.

The preparation room is a scene constructed in such a way as to establish the impression of a sterile medical atmosphere. Even though the backstage crew may humorously refer to themselves as a "bod squad," they more often refer to themselves and their behavior in medical rhetoric, thereby borrowing credence and legitimacy from that professional most esteemed in American society: the medical doctor. The medical atmosphere and terminology is also a part of on-going role-distance; the white surgical garb, the white walls, and the operating table help the practitioner to see and present himself as at least a quasi-medical professional rather than simply a handler of corpses.

Just as theaters have their make-up rooms, the preparation room serves as a setting for the cosmetology that will turn the corpse into the star of the show. As make-up artists, morticians are unsurpassed, and have elevated their skill to a high art. Given the various causes of death and subsequent kinds of bodily disfigurement, "restorative art" is designed to make the deceased look natural and, in a sense, "alive." Cosmetics in the hands of a skilled mortician can cover a multitude of wounds, bruises, ravages of long-term disease and discoloration, and even major forms of disfigurement. (One funeral director told us with pride of a suicide he had reconstructed, even though the man had succeeded in blowing the top of his head off.) When successful, an unblemished star is born for a magnificent final performance.

As with other performers, the actor is not supposed to appear "made up," but rather the make-up is applied to convey "natural" impressions rather than the artificiality the make-up room as a backstage region implies. (One is reminded of the cosmetic company that advertises that women can achieve the "natural look" only by using their new line of cosmetics.) Funeral directors take as a compliment remarks that the deceased looked natural, at peace, younger than before, asleep, etc., apparently because his art is being validated by the very audience at which it is directed.

FRONTSTAGE PERFORMANCES: BRINGING OFF THE SHOW

The change of titles from "undertaker" to "funeral director" has been perhaps the largest single clue to the dramaturgical functions the industry now sees itself as performing. He is indeed a "director," controlling a dramatic production. The staged performance is supported by elaborate backstage preparations of the body, equipment, and props, and the immediate family is rehearsed as to the schedule of events and protocol. In order to preclude any miscues in the performance, the rehearsal covers entrance cues, exit, places to sit, and timing of events; special requests by the family can also be included in the script and program.

The funeral director and his crew continue backstage activities during the funeral service: automobile drivers, pallbearers, ministers, and musicians must all be orchestrated in a smooth and uninterrupted performance. As a skilled director, the mortician is available but largely unnoticed, particularly by the audience of friends and acquaintances who come to pay their respects.

In addition, he constantly checks the floral pieces for placement, fallen petals, water leakage, and all such tidying is made prior to the family's arrival.

CONTROLLING THE SITUATION: THE CAST OF CHARACTERS

The funeral as a staged performance features a marquee listing a well-respected director affiliated with National Funeral Directors Association; a star, the deceased, whose life and attributes comprise the plot; a supporting cast of the bereaved (one of whom usually takes charge of managing details); supporters of the bereaved; ministers; musicians; and pallbearers; and, of course, the audience of friends and acquaintances. The bereaved are themselves supporting actors and actresses, for they too are part of the performance. They are "on-stage" in that their behavior is reviewed and judged by others whose comments on how well the family "held up" at the funeral will later be taken into account. Observations of funerals and especially post-funeral gatherings show that such evaluations comprise much of the conversation, and the bereaved who shows too little emotion for the audience's conception of their relationship to the deceased, or those who show too much when it is known that the relationship did not warrant it, are likely to be judged negatively. Mourners are aware of this, and may construct their performances accordingly. Sometimes, in fact, part of the directing task is coaching mourners on how to act.

Cast members must also be controlled: one of the most potentially troublesome of these is the minister. As such, he may, if not carefully managed, act in such a way as to construct a counterreality that can cast doubt on the entire show. With the emergence of the professional "funeral director," the minister has been increasingly shunted to the background, and now it may be properly said that he is the minor functionary. The counterreality the minister may establish is the idea that all of this funeral business is really nonsense because the body is a shell and the "soul" has departed. In addition, he may feel that there is too much emphasis on rituals involving the body, and that these smack of paganism and status seeking, as well as being a waste of money. The minister may have long years of close association with the family, and if allowed to operate unmanaged, can be a significantly moderating influence on the family's choice. Consequently, trade journals devote occasional space to giving helpful advice on how to control this potentially truculent member of the cast.

THE FUNERAL HOME AS THEATER AND STAGE

Seldom are funeral homes space-age in architectural design; rather they present themselves with traditional white columns, Colonial style, or even proudly as older structures. They are usually decorated profusely with flowers, the walkways are carefully landscaped, the grass must be sprayed green during the winter months and of course the interiors are meticulously decorated. Such appearances are ways of establishing other meanings besides the usual ones of death and morbidity. Brightly colored drapes, curtains, and fixtures seem to breathe life; black hues are out, for they conspicuously betray the image of "undertaker." Even the traditional black limousine is no longer fashionable among more modern funeral homes; colors such as grey, white, and blue are now seen as more appropriate to death-free imagery.

The stage itself, the funeral chapel, is a model of theatrical perfection; many chapels would make a Broadway star envious. The chapel is usually arranged with ample entrances and exits, and may be served by back-doors, halls, tunnels, and passageways that lead from the preparation room without ever trespassing frontstage areas. Equipment and props such as flower holders, religious symbols and decorative roping are used to set the stage for the performance. In addition, the basic stage area is often neutral so that appropriate props can be used to establish the correct symbols for the various religious types of funerals common in our society.

If all of this background is successfully arranged, the funeral director—like other persons responsible for the direction of performances in our society—is in a position to control the kind of definitions that arise in the situation. Having had little opportunity to rehearse for such rituals, the majority of mourners face a highly problematic, tense, and relatively undefined situation. Consequently, monitoring the director's cues become a way of apprehending what the situation calls for.

Despite the best of scheduling, however, the inevitable "mistakes at work" occur. But while every funeral director can unreel a series of atrocity stories about things that go wrong, ordinarily his recovery techniques are successful in salvaging the show. Caskets are rarely dropped, leak, or have their contents spilled onto the floor, especially since the troublesome role of "pallbearer" has been successfully turned into an honorary position, with the actual carrying of the casket done by members of the staff.

ESTABLISHING THE MOOD

A crucial, and therefore precarious, feature of virtually all human affairs is mood. And it is important to remember that actions establish mood. The putting on of certain conduct will lead the reviewer to feel this way or that; and, as we have already shown, the review of the funeral director's show is in many ways the most tangible product he sells.

Probably the single most effective way of establishing the right mood for a funeral is the judicious use of music. Emanating usually from a veiled location, "appropriate" organ music (as opposed to "inappropriate" music such as amplified guitar) is the vital medium through which the atmosphere of the funeral is created. In counsel with the family, the musical selections are planned to set the mood for serenity, beauty, respect, or whatever values are desired. Many mortuaries offer lists of musicians upon which the family can call, and who will perform for a fee; other establishments have their own musicians available for hire. As in other shows, the selection, volume, tone, and timing of the music provide cues for the series of events or acts that are presented. With the aid of a printed program, music cues the audience in sequence: be respectfully quiet; the service is beginning; the choir is about to sing; a prayer is forthcoming; a minister is about to speak; the eulogy is being delivered; it is time for the processional view of the deceased; the service is over—you may leave. Mood management, then, is a major means by which the director controls the situation.

FRONTSTAGE RHETORIC AND THE DENIAL OF DEATH

Although one of the consensually stated objectives of funerals is the acceptance of death by the family, the rhetoric of the frontstage as well as the social and physical setting of the funeral service itself tends to contradict such claims. Despite the many criticisms and subsequent industry denials and changes in procedure, the metaphors used in the American funeral continue to be those of sleep, transition to other worlds, and eternal life, rather than death. Much of this denial, of course, stems from religious traditions which tend to treat death as a kind of minor nuisance on the way to glory. And there is little in the funeral to contradict such ideas. "Mr. Jones" reposes in a "Slumber room" in a casket whose mattress rivals the posturepedics designed for those of us still alive but suffering from back trouble. The titles and words of songs frequently sung at a funeral ("Death Is Only a Dream," "Asleep in Jesus," "It Is Not Death to Die") pointedly do not say "death has occurred, I am sorry" but rather "he or she is still with us."

In addition to this socially established denial of death, funerals serve as morality plays which weave social commentary into the ritual. Eulogies to the deceased will ordinarily contain references to his community service, character, righteousness, and approved identities. Certain behaviors are validated as noble, while others are by implication denounced. The audience is thereby advised to take note, for they too will someday be reviewed in such a public ceremony. One comforting aspect of such eulogizing, however, is that the deceased is usually given the benefit of the doubt; the eulogizer selectively parades his various careers. The dramaturgical necessity of such selectivity, of course, makes for considerable juggling of the available facts of a person's life, especially when dealing with those whose lives have been less than sterling. When mentioned at all, such elements will almost always be placed in contexts that were not used while he was alive: recalcitrance being redefined as "independence," or purposelessness as a "restless spirit," for example.

CONCLUSION

The dramaturgical metaphor we have employed in this paper offers an alternative way of viewing the interactions and relationships comprising the American funeral. Death and dying obviously involve ritual and ceremony; without these much of what we take for granted among the living such as respect, character, and substance would likely vanish. Nevertheless, because social relationships involve ritual communication, much of it of a covert nature, care must be taken that performances be given "in character."

We also wish to enter a caveat regarding our use of a metaphorical argument. To say that funerals may be seen as performances does not suggest that they are performances. Rather, the dramaturgical metaphor offers an interpretive framework that serves to illuminate what is often obscured by those perspectives that center on either the structural apparatus of the society in which death occurs or on the alleged psychological characteristics and states of the participants. Dramas can, of course, be viewed as expressions of either psychological or social determinants, but what we have suggested here is that there may be value in viewing them as fundamental realities in their own right. For no matter how standard the ritual expression becomes, each drama must still be brought off on its own with all the attendant opportunities for error. It is this possibility that makes our dramas at once precarious and satisfying.

DISCUSSION QUESTIONS

1. Turner and Edgley describe an industry that requires employees to emotionally detach from their work. What other types of work might necessitate such emotional detachment?
2. Turner and Edgley describe a clear distinction between frontstage and backstage regions in the funeral industry. What are some of your own experiences in keeping frontstage and backstage regions at work separate?
3. Turner and Edgley refer to the medical doctor as the most esteemed profession in American society. How does this relate to Miner's article on the Nacirema? Does this professional distinction still hold today?

ADDITIONAL RESOURCES

Film

"My Girl." 1991. A Columbia Pictures movie starring Dan Aykroyd as a widowed undertaker and Jamie Lee Curtis as his love interest. The film does an excellent job of representing the stigma of being a funeral director and the importance of keeping frontstages and backstages separate.

Internet

http://www.abfse.org/. The website for the American Board of Funeral Service Education. This site provides a fascinating look at the professional presentation of the funeral industry and the process of becoming a funeral director.

http://www.fnacademy.com/. The website for the Fountain National Academy of Professional Embalming Skills. This website documents the significance of highly skilled embalming to loved ones' grieving process.

Radio

"Morticians and the Emotional Toll of Youth Violence." August 6, 2007. A Tell Me More program produced by National Public Radio about the emotional labor involved in being a funeral director for youth killed by gang violence: http://www.npr.org/templates/player/mediaPlayer.html?action=l&t=l&islist=false&id=12525744&m=12525745.

FURTHER READING

Garden, Pam. 2001. "Rising from the Dead: Delimiting Stigma in the Australian Funeral Industry." *Health Sociology Review*, 10(2): 79–87.

Levine, Robert. 1997. *A Geography of Time*. New York: Basic Books.

Marks, Stephen R. 1977. "Multiple Roles and Role Strain." *American Sociological Review*, 42(6): 921–36.

3. The Smile Factory: Work at Disneyland

JOHN VAN MAANEN

Van Maanen provides us with a fascinating "backstage" view of life at Disneyland. His field research gives us access to the hierarchy of the workplace, the special organization of the park, and the various methods that lead customers to believe in the show produced by the Happiest Place on Earth.

Part of Walt Disney Enterprises includes the theme park Disneyland. In its pioneering form in Anaheim, California, this amusement center has been a consistent money maker since the gates were first opened in 1955. Apart from its sociological charm, it has, of late, become something of an exemplar for culture vultures and has been held up for public acclaim in several best-selling publications as one of America's top companies. To outsiders, the cheerful demeanor of its employees, the seemingly inexhaustible repeat business it generates from its customers, the immaculate condition of park grounds, and, more generally, the intricate physical and social order of the business itself appear wondrous.

Disneyland as the self-proclaimed "Happiest Place on Earth" certainly occupies an enviable position in the amusement and entertainment worlds as well as the commercial world in general. Its product, it seems, is emotion—"laughter and well being."

The "feeling business" does not operate, however, by management decree alone. The happiness trade is an interactional one. It rests partly on the symbolic resources put into place by history and park design but it also rests on an animated workforce that is more or less eager to greet the guests, pack the trams, push the buttons, deliver the food, dump the garbage, clean the streets, and, in general, marshal the will to meet and perhaps exceed customer expectations. False moves, rude words, careless disregard, detected insincerity, or a sleepy and bored presence can all undermine the enterprise and ruin a sale. The smile factory has its rules.

IT'S A SMALL WORLD

The writing that follows represents Disneyland as a workplace. It is organized roughly as an old-fashioned realist ethnography that tells of a culture in native categories. The culture of interest is the Disneyland culture but it is not necessarily the same one invented, authorized, codified, or otherwise approved by park management. Thus the culture I portray here is more of an occupational than a strictly organizational one.

This rendition is of course abbreviated and selective. I focus primarily on such matters as the stock appearance (vanilla), status order (rigid), and social life (full), and swiftly learned codes of conduct (formal and informal) that are associated with Disneyland ride operators. These employees comprise the largest category of hourly workers on the payroll. During the summer months, they number close to four thousand and run the 60-odd rides and attractions in the park.

They are also a well-screened bunch. There is—among insiders and outsiders alike—a rather fixed view about the social attributes carried by the standard-make Disneyland ride operator. Single, white males and females in their early twenties, without facial blemish, of above average

Van Maanen, John. 1991. "The Smile Factory: Work at Disneyland," in Peter J. Frost, Larry F. Moore, Meryl Reis Louis, Craig C. Lundberg, and Joanne Martin (eds.). *Reframing Organizational Culture*, 58–76. Newbury Park, CA: Sage Publications.

height and below average weight, with straight teeth, conservative grooming standards, and a chin-up, shoulder-back posture radiating the sort of good health suggestive of a recent history in sports are typical of these social identifiers. There are representative minorities on the payroll but because ethnic displays are sternly discouraged by management, minority employees are rather close copies of the standard model Disneylander, albeit in different colors.

This Disneyland look is often a source of some amusement to employees who delight in pointing out that even the patron saint, Walt himself, could not be hired today without shaving off his trademark pencil-thin mustache. But, to get a job in Disneyland and keep it means conforming to a rather exacting set of appearance rules. These rules are put forth in a handbook on the Disney image in which readers learn, for example, that facial hair or long hair is banned for men as are aviator glasses and earrings and that women must not tease their hair, wear fancy jewelry, or apply more than a modest dab of makeup. Both men and women are to look neat and prim, keep their uniforms fresh, polish their shoes, and maintain an upbeat countenance and light dignity to complement their appearance—no low spirits or cornball raffishness at Disneyland.

The legendary "people skills" of park employees, so often mentioned in Disneyland publicity and training materials, do not amount to very much according to ride operators. Most tasks require little interaction with customers and are physically designed to practically insure that is the case. The contact that does occur typically is fleeting and swift, a matter usually of only a few seconds. In the rare event sustained interaction with customers might be required, employees are taught to deflect potential exchanges to area supervisors or security. A Training Manual offers the proper procedure: "On misunderstandings, guests should be told to call City Hall...In everything from damaged cameras to physical injuries, don't discuss anything with guests...there will

always be one of us nearby." Employees learn quickly that security is hidden but everywhere. On Main Street, security cops are Keystone Kops; in Frontierland, they are Town Marshalls; on Tom Sawyer's Island, they are Cavalry Officers, and so on.

Where one works in the park carries much social weight. Postings are consequential because the ride and area a person is assigned provide rewards and benefits of wages.

Ride operators, as a large but distinctly middle-class group of hourly employees on the floor of the organization, compete for status not only with each other but also with other employee groupings whose members are hired for the season from the same applicant pool. A loose approximation of the rank ordering among these groups can be constructed as follows:

1. The upper-class prestigious Disneyland Ambassadors and Tour Guides (bilingual young women in charge of ushering—some say rushing—little bands of tourists through the park);
2. Ride operators performing coveting "skilled work" such as live narrations or tricky transportation tasks like those who symbolically control customer access to the park and drive, the costly entry vehicles such as the antique trains, horse-drawn carriages, and Monorail);
3. All other ride operators;
4. The proletarian Sweepers (keepers of the concrete grounds);
5. The sub-prole or peasant status Food and Concession workers.

Pay differentials are slight among these employee groups. As the rank order suggests, most employee status goes to those who work jobs that require higher degrees of special skill, relative freedom from constant and direct supervision, and provide the opportunity to organize and direct customer desires and behavior rather than to merely respond to them as spontaneously expressed.

The basis for sorting individuals into these various broad bands of job categories is often unknown to employees—a sort of deep, dark secret of the casting directors in personnel. When prospective employees are interviewed, they interview for "a job at Disneyland," not a specific one. Personnel decides what particular job they will eventually occupy. Personal contacts are considered by employees as crucial in this job-assignment process as they are in the hiring decision. Some employees, especially those who wind up in the lower ranking jobs, are quite disappointed with their assignments as is the case when, for example, a would-be Adventure-land guide is posted to a New Orleans Square restaurant as a pot scrubber. Although many of the outside acquaintances of our pot scrubber may know only that he works at Disneyland, rest assured, insiders will know immediately where he works and judge him accordingly.

Uniforms are crucial in this regard for they provide instant communication about the social merits or demerits of the wearer within the little world of Disneyland workers. Uniforms also correspond to a wider status ranking that casts a significant shadow on employees of all types. Male ride operators on the Autopia wear, for example, untailored jump-suits similar to pit mechanics and consequently generate about as much respect from peers as the grease-stained outfits worn by pump jockeys generate from real motorists in gas stations. The ill-fitting and homogeneous "whites" worn by Sweepers signify lowly institutional work tinged, perhaps, with a reminder of hospital orderlies rather than street cleanup crews. On the other hand, for males, the crisp, officer-like Monorail operator stands alongside the swashbuckling Pirate of the Caribbean, the casual cowpoke of Big Thunder Mountain, or the smartly vested Riverboat pilot as carriers of valued symbols in and outside the park. Employees lust for these higher status positions and the rights to small advantages such uniforms provide. A lively internal labor market exists wherein there is much scheming for the more prestigious assignments.

For women, a similar market exists although the perceived "sexiness" of uniforms, rather than social rank, seems to play a larger role. To wit, the rather heated antagonisms that developed years ago when the ride "It's a Small World" first opened and began outfitting the ride operators with what were felt to be the shortest skirts and most revealing blouses in the park. Tour Guides, who traditionally headed the fashion vanguard at Disneyland in their above-the-knee kilts, knee socks, tailored vests, black English hats, and smart riding crops were apparently appalled at being upstaged by their social inferiors and lobbied actively (and, judging by the results, successfully) to lower the skirts, raise the necklines, and generally remake their Small World rivals.

Movement across jobs is not encouraged by park management but some does occur (mostly within an area and job category). Employees claim that a sort of "once a sweeper, always a sweeper" rule obtains but all know of at least a few exceptions to prove the rule. The exceptions offer some (not much) hope for those working at the social margins of the park and perhaps keep them on the job longer than might otherwise be expected. Dishwashers can dream of becoming Pirates, and with persistence and a little help from their friends, such dreams just might come true next season (or the next).

These examples are precious, perhaps, but they are also important. There is an intricate pecking order among very similar categories of employees. Attributes of reward and status tend to cluster, and there is intense concern about the cluster to which one belongs (or would like to belong). To a degree, form follows function in Disneyland because the jobs requiring the most abilities and offering the most interest also offer the most status and social reward. Interaction patterns reflect and sustain this order. Few Ambassadors or Tour Guides, for instance, will stoop to speak at length with Sweepers who speak mostly among themselves or to Food workers. Ride operators, between the poles, line up in ways referred to above with only ride proximity (i.e., sharing a break area) representing a potentially significant intervening variable in the interaction calculation.

Paid employment at Disneyland begins with the much renowned University of Disneyland whose faculty runs a day-long orientation program as part of a 40-hour apprenticeship program, most of which takes place on the rides. In the classroom, however, newly hired ride operators are given a very thorough introduction to matters of managerial concern and are tested on their absorption of famous Disneyland fact, lore, and procedure. Employee demeanor is governed, for example, by three rules:

First, we practice the friendly smile.
Second, we use only friendly and courteous phrases.
Third, we are not stuffy—the only Misters in Disneyland are Mr. Toad and Mr. Smee.

Employees learn too that the Disneyland culture is officially defined. The employee handbook put it in this format:

Dis-ney Cor-po-rate Cul-ture (diz'ne kor'pr'it kul' cher) n 1. Of or pertaining to the Disney organization, as a: the philosophy underlying all business decisions; b: the commitment of top leadership and management to that philosophy; c: the actions taken by individual cast members that reinforce the image.

Language is also a central feature of university life and new employees are schooled in its proper use. Customers at Disneyland are, for instance, never referred to as such, they are "guests." There are no rides at Disneyland, only "attractions." Disneyland itself is a "Park," not an amusement center, and it is divided into "back-stage," "on-stage," and "staging" regions. Law enforcement personnel hired by the park are not policemen, but "security hosts." Employees do not wear uniforms but check out fresh "costumes" each working day from "wardrobe." And, of course, there are no accidents at Disneyland, only "incidents."

Classes are organized and designed by professional Disneyland trainers who also instruct a well-screened group of representative hourly employees straight from park operations on the approved newcomer training methods and materials. New-hires seldom see professional trainers in class but are brought on board by enthusiastic peers who concentrate on those aspects of park procedure thought highly general matters to be learned by all employees. Particular skill training (and "reality shock") is reserved for the second wave of socialization occurring on the rides themselves as operators are taught, for example, how and when to send a mock bobsled caroming down the track or, more delicately, the proper ways to stuff an obese adult customer into the midst of children riding the Monkey car on the Casey Jones Circus Train or, most problematically, what exactly to tell an irate customer standing in the rain who, in no uncertain terms, wants his or her money back and wants it back now.

During orientation, considerable concern is placed on particular values the Disney organization considers central to its operations. These values range from the "customer is king" verities to the more or less unique kind, of which "everyone is a child at heart when at Disneyland" is a decent example. Elaborate checklists of appearance standards are learned and gone over in the classroom and great efforts are spent trying to bring employee emotional responses in line with such standards. Employees are told repeatedly that if they are happy and cheerful at work, so, too, will the guests at play. Inspirational films, hearty pep talks, family imagery, and exemplars of corporate performance are all representative of the strong symbolic stuff of these training rites.

Another example, perhaps extreme, concerns the symbolic role of the canonized founder in the corporate mythology. When Walt Disney was alive, newcomers and veterans alike were told how much he enjoyed coming to the park and just how exacting he was about the conditions he observed. For employees, the cautionary whoop, "Walt's in the park," could often bring forth additional energy and care for one's part in the production. Upon his death, trainers at the University were said to be telling recruits to mind their manners because, "Walt's in the park all the time now."

Yet, like employees everywhere, there is a limit to which such overt company propaganda can be effective. Students and trainers both seem to agree on where the line is drawn for there is much satirical banter, mischievous winking, and playful exaggeration in the classroom. As young seasonal employees note, it is difficult to take seriously an organization that provides its retirees "Golden Ears" instead of gold watches after 20 or more years of service. All newcomers are aware that the label "Disneyland" has both an unserious and artificial connotation and that a full embrace of the Disneyland role would be as deviant as its full rejection.

Employees are also subject to what might be regarded as remote controls. These stem not from supervisors or peers but from thousands of paying guests who parade daily through the park. The public, for the most part, wants Disneyland employees to play only the roles for which they are hired and costumed. If, for instance, Judy of the Jets is feeling tired, grouchy, or bored, few customers want to know about it. Disneyland employees are expected to be sunny and helpful; and the job, with its limited opportunities for sustained interaction, is designed to support such a stance. Thus, if a ride operator's behavior drifts noticeably away from the norm, customers are sure to point it out—"Why aren't you smiling?" "What's wrong with you?" "Having a bad day? Did Goofy step on your foot?" Ride operators learn swiftly from the constant hints, glances, glares, and tactful (and tactless) cues sent by their audience what their role in the park is to be, and as long as they keep to it, there will be no objections from those passing by.

> I can remember being out on the river looking at the people on the Mark Twain looking down on the people in the Keel Boats who are looking up at them. I'd come by on my raft and they'd all turn and stare at me. If I gave them a little wave and a grin, they'd all wave back and smile;

all ten thousand of them. I always wondered what would happen if I gave them the finger? (Ex-ride operator, 1988).

Ride operators also learn how different categories of customers respond to them and the parts they are playing on-stage. For example, infants and small children are generally timid, if not frightened, in their presence. School-age children are somewhat curious, aware that the operator is at work playing a role but sometimes in awe of the role itself. Nonetheless, these children can be quite critical of any flaw in the operator's performance. Teenagers, especially males in groups, present problems because they sometimes go to great lengths to embarrass, challenge, ridicule, or outwit an operator. Adults are generally appreciative and approving of an operator's conduct provided it meets their rather minimal standards, but they sometimes overreact to the part an operator is playing (positively) if accompanied by small children.

By and large, however, the people-processing tasks of ride operators pass good naturedly and smoothly, with operators hardly noticing much more than the bodies passing in front of view. Yet, sometimes, more than a body becomes visible, as happens when customers overstep their roles and challenge employee authority, insult an operator, or otherwise disrupt the routines of the job. In the process, guests become "dufusses," "ducks," and "assholes" (just three of many derisive terms used by ride operators to label those customers they believe to have gone beyond the pale). Normally, these characters are brought to the attention of park security officers, ride foremen, or area supervisors who, in turn, decide how they are to be disciplined (usually expulsion from the park).

Occasionally, however, the alleged slight is too personal or simply too extraordinary for a ride operator to let it pass unnoticed or merely inform others and allow them to decide what, if anything, is to be done. Restoration of one's respect is called for and routine practices have been developed for these circumstances. For example, common remedies include: the "seatbelt squeeze," a small token of appreciation given to a deviant customer consisting of the rapid cinching-up of a required seatbelt such that the passenger is doubled-over at the point of departure and left gasping for the duration of the trip; the "break-toss," an acrobatic gesture of the Autopia trade whereby operators jump on the outside of a norm violator's car, stealthily unhitching the safety belt, then slamming on the brakes, bringing the car to an almost instant stop while the driver flies on the hood of the car (or beyond); the "seatbelt slap," an equally distinguished (if primitive) gesture by which an offending customer receives a sharp, quick snap of a hard plastic belt across the face (or other parts of the body) when entering or exiting a seat-belted ride; the "break-up-the-party" gambit, a queuing device put to use in officious fashion whereby bothersome pairs are separated at the last minute into different units, thus forcing on them the pain of strange companions for the duration of a ride through the Haunted Mansion or a ramble on Mr. Toad's Wild Ride; the "hatch-cover ploy," a much beloved practice of Submarine pilots who, in collusion with mates on the loading dock, are able to drench offensive guests with water as their units pass under a waterfall; and, lastly, the rather ignoble variants of the "Sorry-I-didn't-see-your-hand" tactic, a savage move designed to crunch a particularly irksome customer's hand (foot, finger, arm, leg, etc.) by bringing a piece of Disneyland property to bear on the appendage, such as the door of a Thunder Mountain railroad car or the starboard side of a Jungle Cruise boat. This latter remedy is, most often, a "near miss" designed to startle the little criminals of Disneyland.

All of these unofficial procedures (and many more) are learned on the job. Although they are used sparingly, they are used. Occasions of use provide a continual stream of sweet revenge talk to enliven and enrich colleague conversation at break time or after work.

In general, Disneyland employees are remarkable for their forbearance and polite good manners even under trying conditions. They are taught, and some come to believe, for a while at least, that they are really "on stage" at work. And, as noted, surveillance by supervisory personnel certainly fades in light of the unceasing glances an employee receives from the paying guests who tromp daily through the park in the summer. Disneyland employees know well that they are part of the product being sold and learn to check their more discriminating manners in favor of the generalized countenance of a cheerful lad or lassie whose enthusiasm and dedication is obvious to all.

THE DISNEY WAY

Four features alluded to in this unofficial guide to Disneyland seem to account for a good deal of the social order that obtains within the park. First, socialization, although costly, is of a most selective, collective, intensive, serial, sequential, and closed sort. These tactics are notable for their penetration into the private spheres of individual thought and feeling. Incoming identities are not so much dismantled as they are set aside as employees are schooled in the use of new identities of the situational sort. Many of these are symbolically powerful and, for some, laden with social approval. It is hardly surprising that some of the more problematic positions in terms of turnover during the summer occur in the food and concession domains where employees apparently find little to identify with on the job. Cowpokes on Big Thunder Mountain, Jet Pilots, Storybook Princesses, Tour Guides, Space Cadets, Jungle Boat Skippers, or Southern Belles of New Orleans Square have less difficulty on this score. Disneyland, by design, bestows identity through a process carefully set up to strip away the job relevance of other sources of identity and learned response and replace them with others of organizational relevance. It works.

Second, this is a work culture whose designers have left little room for individual experimentation. Supervisors, as apparent in their focused wandering and attentive looks, keep very close tabs on what is going on at any moment in all the lands. Every bush, rock, and tree in Disneyland is numbered and checked continually as to the part it is playing in the park. So too are employees. Discretion of a personal sort is quite limited while employees are "on-stage." Even "back-stage" and certain "off-stage" domains have their corporate monitors. Employees are indeed aware that their "off-stage" life beyond the picnics, parties, and softball games is subject to some scrutiny for police checks are made on potential and current employees. Nor do all employees discount the rumors that park officials make periodic inquiries on their own as to a person's habits concerning sex and drugs. Moreover, the sheer number of rules and regulations is striking, thus making the grounds for dismissal a matter of multiple choice for supervisors who discover a target for the use of such grounds. The feeling of being watched is, unsurprisingly, a rather prevalent complaint among Disneyland people and it is one that employees must live with if they are to remain at Disneyland.

Third, emotional management occurs in the park in a number of quite distinct ways. From the instructors at the university who beseech recruits to "wish every guest a pleasant good day," to the foremen who plead with their charges to, "say thank you when you herd them through the gate," to the impish customer who seductively licks her lips and asks, "what does Tom Sawyer want for Christmas?" appearance, demeanor, and etiquette have special meanings at Disneyland. Because these are prized personal attributes over which we normally feel in control, making them commodities can be unnerving. Much self-monitoring is involved, of course, but even here self-management has an organizational side. Consider ride operators who may complain of being "too tired to smile" but, at the same time, feel a little guilty for uttering such a confession. Ride operators who have worked an early morning shift on the Matterhorn (or other popular rides) tell of a queasy feeling they get when the park is opened for business and they suddenly feel the ground begin to shake under their feet and hear the low thunder of the hordes of customers coming at them, oblivious of civil restraint and the small children who might be among them. Consider, too, the discomforting pressures of being "on-stage" all day and the cumulative annoyance of having adults ask permission to leave a line to go to the bathroom, whether the water in the lagoon is real, where the well-marked entrances might be, where Walt Disney's cryogenic tomb is to be found, or—the real clincher—whether or not one is "really real."

Finally, taking these three points together, it seems that even when people are trained, paid, and told to be nice, it is hard for them to do so all of the time. But, when efforts to be nice have succeeded to the degree that is true of Disneyland, it appears as a rather towering (if not always admirable) achievement. It works at the collective level by virtue of elaborate direction. Employees—at all ranks—are stage-managed by higher ranking employees who, having come through themselves, hire, train, and closely supervise those who have replaced them below. Expression rules are laid out in corporate manuals. Employee time-outs intensify work experience. Social exchanges are forced into narrow bands of interacting groups. Training and retraining programs are continual. Hiding places are few. Although little sore spots and irritations remain for each individual, it is difficult to imagine work roles being more defined (and accepted) than those at Disneyland. Here, it seems, is a work culture worthy of the name.

DISCUSSION QUESTIONS

1. Van Maanen describes the process of employees "learning the ropes" at Disneyland as one of acculturation. Give an example from your own experiences of learning the lay of the land at a new job or in another new setting.

2. What tactics have you used in your own work to keep customers or clients "in line"? Have you used such tactics in other settings as well?
3. Van Maanen describes various ways Disneyland employees seek revenge against customers as a form of social control. What might happen if the Mark Twain ride operator did give customers "the finger," as he so desires, instead of the expected wave of the hand?

ADDITIONAL RESOURCES

Film
"A Time to Reflect, The History of Whalom Park." A 34-minute documentary about the rise and fall of a small-town Massachusetts amusement park.

Internet
http://www.der.orq'films/whalom-park.html. The website for the documentary "A Time to Reflect, The History of Whalom Park."

http://home.disney.go.com/travel/. One of Disney's many websites. This site features its travel destinations, including its theme parks.

http://www.pbs.org/wgbh/theymadeamerica/whomade/disney_lo.html. Part of PBS's Innovators of America series, featuring Walt Disney.

http://www.pbs.org/wgbh/pages/frontline/shows/cool/giants/disney.html. A summary of the Disney conglomerate.

FURTHER READING

Charon, Joel. 1998. "The Nature of Perspective." *Symbolic Interactionism*, 1–3.

Lofland, John and Norman Skonovd. 1981. "Conversion Motifs." *Journal for the Scientific Study of Religion*, 20(4): 373–85.

Marling, Karal Ann (ed). 1997. *Designing Disney's Theme Parks: The Architecture of Reassurance*. Milan: Flammarion.

Middaugh, Donna J., Neena Grissom, and Tricia Satkowski. 2008. "Goofy Management: Taking the Magic to the Workplace." *MEDSURG Nursing*, 17(2): 131–2.

Raz, Aviad E. 2003. "The Slanted Smile Factory: Emotion Management in Tokyo Disneyland," in Douglas Harper and Helene M. Lawson (eds.). *The Cultural Study of Work*. 210–27. Lanham, NJ: Rowman & Littlefield.

SECTION I.B

Studying Social Life

Social psychology is an interdisciplinary social science that is dominated by psychologists and sociologists. Multiple methods of research used by social psychologists are represented in this volume. These methods include laboratory experiments, quantitative surveys, and qualitative field research. All research methods are valuable ways of knowing, each providing a different way to view the same phenomena.

The selections we include here explore a particular approach and critique within the field of social psychology that highlight healthy tensions within the field and within broader social science. Historically, social psychologists valued the scientific method and laboratory experiments above other ways of knowing. In the scientific method, a scholar develops a hypothesis about the relationship between key variables of study and then tests that hypothesis via data collection. A key aspect of the scientific method is scholars' ability to maintain an objective distance from their subject of study to avoid introducing bias into their research. Social scientists walk a tight line between taking on the perspective of the people they study and maintaining a nonbiased stance.

In his 1966 presidential address to the Society for the Scientific Study of Social Problems, Howard Becker laid the groundwork for a major challenge to traditional social science research methods. In his speech, Becker urged researchers to give up their attempts to be objective in research, claiming that conducting "value-free" research is impossible, let alone dangerous to the integrity of research findings. He argued that acknowledging one's values and their impact on one's research design and findings leads to scholarship that is less rather than more biased. Moreover, Becker noted that studying human attitudes and behaviors is notably different from studying nonhuman subject matter in biology or physics. Human subjects respond to and interact with the researchers and their instruments—often changing their behavior or attitudes simply because they are aware that they are the subjects of study.

The contributions of Morris Zelditch, in 1969, and Fine, House, and Cook, more recently, illustrate the continued shifting terrain of research methods in social psychology. Zelditch examines the possibility of using experimentation to study large social organizations, such as the military, in a laboratory setting, and Fine, House, and Cook trace sociological social psychologists' shift away from experimentation to survey and field research methods over the past forty years.

4. Whose Side Are We On?*

HOWARD S. BECKER

In his 1966 presidential address to the Society for the Scientific Study of Social Problems, Becker proposed what was at the time a radical idea: that objectivity in research is impossible. He suggested that researchers not only identify with their research subjects but also that it is imperative to admit that they do. Becker claimed that such awareness is one's best defense against bias in research.

To have values or not to have values: the question is always with us. When sociologists undertake to study problems that have relevance to the world we live in, they find themselves caught in a crossfire. Some urge them not to take sides, to be neutral and do research that is technically correct and value free. Others tell them their work is shallow and useless if it does not express a deep commitment to a value position.

This dilemma, which seems so painful to so many, actually does not exist, for one of its horns is imaginary. For it to exist, one would have to assume, as some apparently do, that it is indeed possible to do research that is uncontaminated by personal and political sympathies. I propose to argue that it is not possible and, therefore, that the question is not whether we should take sides, since we inevitably will, but rather whose side we are on.

---

* Presidential address, delivered at the annual meeting of the Society for the Study of Social Problems, Miami Beach, August, 1966.
Becker, Howard S. 1967. "Whose Side Are We On?" *Social Problems*, 14(3): 239–47.

I will begin by considering the problem of taking sides as it arises in the study of deviance.

We may sometimes feel that studies of deviance exhibit too great a sympathy with the people studied. This feeling, I suspect, is entertained off and on both by those of us who do such research and by those of us who, our work lying in other areas, only read the results. Will the research, we wonder, be distorted by that sympathy? Will it be of use in the construction of scientific theory or in the application of scientific knowledge to the practical problems of society? Or will the bias introduced by taking sides spoil it for those uses?

We seldom make the feeling explicit. Instead, it appears as a lingering worry for sociological readers, who would like to be sure they can trust what they read, and a troublesome area of self-doubt for those who do the research, who would like to be sure that whatever sympathies they feel are not professionally unseemly and will not, in any case, seriously flaw their work. That the worry affects both readers and researchers indicates that it lies deeper than the superficial differences that divide sociological schools of thought, and that its roots must be sought in characteristics of society that affect us all, whatever our methodological or theoretical persuasion. If the feeling were made explicit, it would take the form of an accusation that the sympathies of the researcher have biased his work and distorted his findings.

It might mean that we have acquired some sympathy with the group we study sufficient to deter us from publishing those of our results which might prove damaging to them. One can imagine a liberal sociologist who set out to disprove some of the common stereotypes held about a minority group. To his dismay, his investigation reveals that some of the stereotypes are unfortunately true. In the interests of justice and liberalism, he might well be tempted, and might even succumb to the temptation, to suppress those findings, publishing with scientific candor the other results which confirmed his beliefs.

But this seems not really to be the heart of the charge, because sociologists who study deviance do not typically hide things about the people they study. They are mostly willing to grant that there is something going on that put the deviants in the position they are in, even if they are not willing to grant that it is what the people they studied were originally accused of.

A more likely meaning of the charge, I think, is this. In the course of our work and for who knows what private reasons, we fall into deep sympathy with the people we are studying, so that while the rest of the society views them as unfit in one or another respect for the deference ordinarily accorded a fellow citizen, we believe that they are at least as good as anyone else, more sinned against than sinning. Because of this, we do not give a balanced picture. We neglect to ask those questions whose answers would show that the deviant, after all, has done something pretty rotten and, indeed, pretty much deserves what he gets. In consequence, our overall assessment of the problem being studied is one-sided. What we produce is a whitewash of the deviant and a condemnation, if only by implication, of those respectable citizens who, we think, have made the deviant what he is.

When do we accuse ourselves and our fellow sociologists of bias? I think an inspection of representative instances would show that the accusation arises, in one important class of cases, when the research gives credence, in any serious way, to the perspective of the subordinate group in some hierarchical relationship. In the case of deviance, the hierarchical relationship is a moral one. The superordinate parties in the relationship are those who represent the forces of approved and official morality; the subordinate parties are those who, it is alleged, have violated that morality.

Similar situations, and similar feelings that our work is biased, occur in the study of schools, hospitals, asylums and prisons, in the study of physical as well as mental illness, in the study of both "normal" and delinquent youth. In these situations, the superordinate parties are usually the official and professional authorities in charge of some important institution, while the subordinates are those who make use of the services of that institution. Thus, the police are the superordinates, drug addicts are the subordinates; professors and administrators, principals and teachers, are the superordinates, while students and pupils are the subordinates; physicians are the superordinates, their patients the subordinates.

All of these cases represent one of the typical situations in which researchers accuse themselves and are accused of bias. It is a situation in which, while conflict and tension exist in the hierarchy, the conflict has not become openly political. The conflicting segments or ranks are not organized for conflict; no one attempts to alter the shape of the hierarchy. While subordinates may complain about the treatment they receive from those above them, they do not propose to move to a position of equality with them, or to reverse positions in the hierarchy. Thus, no one proposes that addicts should make and enforce laws for policemen, that patients should prescribe for doctors, or that adolescents should give orders to adults. We can call this the *apolitical* case.

In the second case, the accusation of bias is made in a situation that is frankly political. The parties to the hierarchical relationship engage in organized conflict, attempting either to maintain or change existing relations of power and authority. Whereas in the first case subordinates are typically unorganized and thus have, as we shall see, little to fear from a researcher, subordinate parties in a political situation may have much to lose. When the situation is political, the researcher may accuse himself or be accused of bias by someone else when he gives credence to the perspective of either party to the political conflict.

We provoke the suspicion that we are biased in favor of the subordinate parties in an apolitical arrangement when we tell the story from their point of view. We may, for instance, investigate their complaints, even though they are subordinates, about the way things are run just as though one ought to give their complaints as much credence as the statements of responsible officials.

We provoke the charge when we assume, for the purposes of our research, that subordinates have as much right to be heard as superordinates, that they are as likely to be telling the truth as they see it as superordinates, that what they say about the institution has a right to be investigated and have its truth or falsity established, even though responsible officials assure us that it is unnecessary because the charges are false.

As sociologists, we provoke the charge of bias, in ourselves and others, by refusing to give credence and deference to an established status order, in which knowledge of truth and the right to be heard are not equally distributed. "Everyone knows" that responsible professionals know more about things than laymen, that police are more respectable and their words ought to be taken more seriously than those of the deviants and criminals with whom they deal. By refusing to accept the hierarchy of credibility, we express disrespect for the entire established order.

We compound our sin and further provoke charges of bias by not giving immediate attention and "equal time" to the apologies and explanations of official authority. If, for instance, we are concerned with studying the way of life inmates in a mental hospital build up for themselves, we will naturally be concerned with the constraints and conditions created by the actions of the administrators and physicians who run the hospital. But, unless we also make the administrators and physicians the object of our study, we will not inquire into why those conditions and constraints are present. We will not give responsible officials a chance to explain themselves and give their reasons for acting as they do, a chance to show why the complaints of inmates are not justified.

It is odd that, when we perceive bias, we usually see it in these circumstances. It is odd because it is easily ascertained that a great many more studies are biased in the direction of the interests of responsible officials than the other way around. We may accuse an occasional student of medical sociology of having given too much emphasis to the complaints of patients. But it is not obvious that most medical sociologists look at things from the point of view of the doctors? A few sociologists may be sufficiently biased in favor of youth to grant credibility to their account of how the adult world treats them. But why do we not accuse other sociologists who study youth of being biased in favor of adults? Most research on youth, after all, is clearly designed to find out why youth are so troublesome for adults, rather than asking the equally interesting sociological question: "Why do adults make so much trouble for youth?" Similarly, we accuse those who take the complaints of mental patients seriously of bias; what about those sociologists who only take seriously the complaints of physicians, families and others about mental patients?

Why this disproportion in the direction of accusations of bias? Why do we more often accuse those who are on the side of subordinates than those who are on the side of superordinates? Because, when we make the former accusation, we have, like the well socialized members of our society most of us are, accepted the hierarchy of credibility and taken over the accusation made by responsible officials.

And thus we see why we accuse ourselves of bias only when we take the side of the subordinate. It is because, in a situation that is not openly political, with the major issues defined as arguable, we join responsible officials and the man in the street in an unthinking acceptance of the hierarchy of credibility. We assume with them that the man at the top knows best. We do not realize that there are sides to be taken and that we are taking one of them.

The same reasoning allows us to understand why the researcher has the same worry about the effect of his sympathies on his work as his uninvolved colleague. The hierarchy of credibility is a feature of society whose existence we cannot deny, even if we disagree with its injunction to believe the man at the top. When we acquire sufficient sympathy with subordinates to see things from their perspective, we know that we are

flying in the face of what "everyone knows." The knowledge gives us pause and causes us to share, however briefly, the doubt of our colleagues.

When a situation has been defined politically, matters are quite different. Subordinates have some degree of organization and, with that, spokesmen, their equivalent of responsible officials. Spokesmen, while they cannot actually be held responsible for what members of their group do, make assertions on their behalf and are held responsible for the truth of those assertions. The group engages in political activity designed to change existing hierarchical relationships and the credibility of its spokesmen directly affects its political fortunes.

Superordinate groups have their spokesmen too, and they are confronted with the same problem: to make statements about reality that are politically effective without being easily discredited.

When we do research in a political situation we are in double jeopardy, for the spokesmen of both involved groups will be sensitive to the implications of our work. Since they propose openly conflicting definitions of reality, our statement of our problem is in itself likely to call into question and make problematic, at least for the purposes of our research, one or the other definition. And our results will do the same.

The hierarchy of credibility operates in a different way in the political situation than it does in the apolitical one. In the political situation, it is precisely one of the things at issue. Since the political struggle calls into question the legitimacy of the existing rank system, it necessarily calls into question at the same time the legitimacy of the associated judgments credibility. Judgments of who has a right to define the nature of reality that are taken for granted in an apolitical situation become matters of argument.

Oddly enough, we are, I think, less likely to accuse ourselves and one another of bias in a political than in an apolitical situation, for at least two reasons. First, because the hierarchy of credibility has been openly called into question, we are aware that there are at least two sides to the story and so do not think it unseemly to investigate the situation from one or another of the contending points of view. We know, for instance, that we must grasp the perspectives of both the resident of Watts and of the Los Angeles policeman if we are to understand what went on in that outbreak.

Second, it is no secret that most sociologists are politically liberal to one degree or another. Our political preferences dictate the side we will be on and, since those preferences are shared by most of our colleagues, few are ready to throw the first stone or are even aware that stone-throwing is a possibility. We usually take the side of the underdog.

We must always look at the matter from someone's point of view. The scientist who proposes to understand society must, as Mead long ago pointed out, get into the situation enough to have a perspective on it. And it is likely that his perspective will be greatly affected by whatever positions are taken by any or all of the other participants in that varied situation. Even if his participation is limited to reading in the field, he will necessarily read the arguments of partisans of one or another side to a relationship and will thus be affected, at least, by having suggested to him what the relevant arguments and issues are. A student of medical sociology may decide that he will take neither the perspective of the patient nor the perspective of the physician, but he will necessarily take a perspective that impinges on the many questions that arise between physicians and patients; no matter what perspective he takes, his work either will take into account the attitude of subordinates, or it will not. If he fails to consider the questions they raise, he will be working on the side of the officials. If he does raise those questions seriously and does find, as he may, that there is some merit in them, he will then expose himself to the outrage of the officials and of all those sociologists who award them the top spot in the hierarchy of credibility.

There is another possibility. We may, in some cases, take the point of view of some third party not directly implicated in the hierarchy we are investigating. This would indeed make us neutral with respect to the two groups at hand, but would only mean that we had enlarged the scope of the political conflict to include a party not ordinarily brought in whose view the sociologist was taking.

We can never avoid taking sides. So we are left with the question of whether taking sides means that some distortion is introduced into our work so great as to make it useless. Or, less drastically, whether some distortion is introduced that must be taken into account before the results of our work can be used. Our problem is to make sure that, whatever point of view we take, our research meets the standards of good scientific work, that our unavoidable sympathies do not render our results invalid.

We might distort our findings, because of our sympathy with one of the parties in the relationship we are studying, by misusing the tools and techniques of our discipline. We might introduce loaded questions into a questionnaire, or act in some way in a field situation such that people would be constrained to tell us only the kind of thing we are already in sympathy with.

But the question may be precisely this. Given all our techniques of theoretical and technical control, how can we be sure that we will apply them impartially and across the board as they need to be applied? Our textbooks in methodology are no help here. They tell us how to guard against error, but they do not tell us how to make sure that we will use all the safeguards available to us. We can, for a start, try to avoid sentimentality. We are sentimental when we refuse, for whatever reason, to investigate some matter that should properly be regarded as problematic. We are sentimental, especially, when our reason is that we would prefer not to know what is going on, if to know would be to violate some sympathy whose existence we may not even be aware of. Whatever side we are on, we must use our techniques impartially enough that a belief to which we are especially sympathetic could be proved untrue. We must always inspect our work carefully enough to know whether our techniques and theories are open enough to allow that possibility.

We can, I think, satisfy the demands of our science by always making clear the limits of what we have studied, marking the boundaries beyond which our findings cannot be safely applied. Not just the conventional disclaimer, in which we warn that we have only studied a prison in New York or California and the findings may not hold in the other forty-nine states—which is not a useful procedure anyway, since the findings may very well hold if the conditions are the same elsewhere. I refer to a more sociological disclaimer in which we say, for instance, that we have studied the prison through the eyes of the inmates and not through the eyes of the guards or other involved parties. We warn people, thus, that our study tells us only how things look from that vantage point—what kinds of objects guards are in the prisoners' world—and does not attempt to explain why guards do what they do or to absolve the guards of what may seem, from the prisoners' side, morally unacceptable behavior. This will not protect us from accusations of bias, however, for the guards will still be outraged by the unbalanced picture. If we implicitly accept the conventional hierarchy of credibility, we will feel the sting in that accusation.

It is something of a solution to say that over the years each "one-sided" study will provoke further studies that gradually enlarge our grasp of all the relevant facets of an institution's operation. But that is a long-term solution, and not much help to the individual researcher who has to contend with the anger of officials who feel he has done them wrong, the criticism of those of his colleagues who think he is presenting a one-sided view, and his own worries.

What do we do in the meantime? I suppose the answers are more or less obvious. We take sides as our personal and political commitments dictate, use our theoretical and technical resources to avoid the distortions that might introduce into our work, limit our conclusions carefully, recognize the hierarchy of credibility for what it is, and field as best we can the accusations and doubts that will surely be our fate.

DISCUSSION QUESTIONS

1. Becker notes that we are more likely to notice a researcher's bias when she/he takes the side of the underdog. Do you agree with this view? Do you think we are less likely to notice bias when a researcher sides with those in a position of authority? Why?
2. What methods does Becker recommend to avoid bias in research? What methods might help a researcher avoid "sentimentality" and become open to hearing both sides of a conflict?
3. Do you think it is possible to be value-free when conducting research? How does your answer relate to Becker's speech?

ADDITIONAL RESOURCES

Internet
http://home.earthlink.net/~hsbecker/. Howard Becker's website. A fascinating look into Becker's professional contributions, networks, and personal interests.

FURTHER READING
Acker, Joan, Kate Barry, and Joke Esseveld. 1983. "Objectivity and Truth: Problems in Doing Feminist Research." *Women's Studies International Forum*, 6(4):423–35.

Babbie, Earl. 1998 [1986]. *Observing Ourselves*. Long Grove, IL: Waveland Press.

Blumer, Herbert. 1969. *Symbolic Interactionism: Perspective and Method*. Upper Saddle River, NJ: Prentice-Hall.

Hammersly, Martyn. 2001. "Which Side Was Becker On? Questioning Political and Epistemological Radicalism." *Qualitative Research*, 1(1): 91–110.

Liebling, Alison. 2001. "Whose Side Are We On? Theory, Practice and Allegiances in Prison Research." *British Journal of Criminology*, 41: 472–84.

Longino, Helen E. 1990. *Science as Knowledge: Science and Objectivity in Scientific Inquiry*. Princeton, NJ: Princeton University Press.

5. Can You Really Study an Army in the Laboratory?

MORRIS ZELDITCH, JR.

Zelditch questions the notion that experimental research is intended solely for understanding the workings of small groups and organizations. He poses this question by asking whether we can effectively study a large organization, such as the army, in a laboratory.

No method has more influenced our conception of science than the experimental method; no method makes the contemporary sociologist more suspicious. The rapid and prolific development of the small groups field seems to argue a contrary thesis. But there is no sounder evidence of the way in which sociologists regard the experiment than the habit of calling them all "small groups" research. And because they think the laboratory group is a small group, many sociologists think that larger organizations cannot be studied in the laboratory.

If the idea is that the laboratory group resembles the smaller kinds of groups found in natural settings, then the idea is wrong. For the laboratory group, though usually small, is no more like small groups found in natural settings than it is like a formal organization. In fact, the laboratory group is not like *any* concrete setting in society.

The fact is that laboratory investigations are seldom efforts to study the small group *per se*, and even when they *are*, the groups studied are not often like small groups found in natural settings. But if the purpose of experiments is not to study the kinds of groups found in natural settings, just what *is* their purpose? The answer has a deceptive simplicity: *The purpose of the laboratory experiment is to create certain theoretically relevant aspects of social situations under controlled conditions.* Though the point looks simple, it has fairly profound implications for most of the issues that are most controversial about the experimental method in sociology.

The purpose of experiments is mainly to construct and test theories; theories are necessarily abstract; and therefore experiments are also necessarily abstract. Consequently, the answer to

Zelditch, Morris. [1969] 1980. "Can You Really Study an Army in the Laboratory?" in Amitai Etzioni and Edward W. Lehman (eds.). *A Sociological Reader on Complex Organizations*, 3rd edition, 531–9. New York: Holt, Rinehart and Winston.

the question which gives this paper its title is that one would not even *try* to study an army in the laboratory, if by that one means an army in the concrete sense of the term. One would try only to create those aspects of an army that were relevant to some theory.

CAN YOU REALLY STUDY AN ARMY IN THE LABORATORY?

If no theory can be concrete, and experiments are for the purpose of constructing theory, there is no basis for the common argument that an experiment ought to be as close as possible to the concrete entity it most nearly represents. Therefore, we do not even *try* to study armies in the laboratory, if by that is meant an army in the concrete sense of the word. We try only to create those aspects of armies relevant to some theory.

A process that can be studied in quite small laboratory "organizations" is the way in which stability is built into the status hierarchy of an organization. Complex organizations typically consist of at least three status classes, such as officers, noncommissioned officers, and other enlisted men in the army; or executives, supervisors, and workers in a factory. Of each status class beliefs are held about their relative abilities to perform organizational tasks. Based on these beliefs, opportunities to actually perform, evaluations of performance, and rights to influence decisions are distributed. Because it accords with the status structure, the distribution of opportunities, evaluations, and rights to exercise influence also tends to perpetuate that structure. Of particular importance to the stability of the status structure is the fact that expectations embodied in status are expansive; that is, confronting a new task or activity, one not previously associated in anyone's mind with statuses in the organization, members of the organization will often behave as if superiors in the status structure were superior at the new task—providing superiority in the new activity is something the organization positively values.

BRIDGING THE GAP

If armies are not really brought into the laboratory, what can be said about an army as a result of a laboratory experiment? Or, to put the question as it has been put several times in the past, how does one bridge the gap between experiment and natural setting?

Usually the problem is thought to be one of *generalizing* from the experiment, and by "generalizing" people often mean equating concrete features of the experiment with concrete features of the natural setting. But almost certainly it will not.

If generalization meant equating concrete features of experiment and natural setting, no bridge between the two would ever be built. But it is not concrete similarities that form the basis of generalization. One generalizes from one situation to another when both situations are described by the same abstract properties and satisfy the same conditions.

SUMMARY

Experiments are mainly for the purpose of building and testing theories; theories are necessarily abstract; therefore, experiments too are abstract. Neither the organizational experiment, nor any other kind of experiment, attempts to recreate a completely "real" instance of any concrete organization in the laboratory. One would not even want to bring an army into the laboratory, much less defend the possibility of actually doing so.

If the laboratory organization creates only the aspects of an organization relevant to some theory, then only a theory can bridge the gap between experiment and natural setting. Experiments are relevant to theory, and theory is applied to natural settings. Two interesting consequences follow: First, if an experiment is informative for a theory, and the theory applicable in a given setting, the findings of an experiment are "generalizable" even if they bear little resemblance to the typical findings in the natural setting. For if theory is thought of as a bridge, the main requirement of the bridge is that it span both settings, not that the two settings be identical.

DISCUSSION QUESTIONS

1. What answer does Zelditch give to his own question, "Can you really study an army in the laboratory?" What is the reasoning he gives for this answer?
2. According to this article, how do sociologists typically define the focus of experimental research?
3. According to Zelditch, what is the primary purpose of conducting laboratory experiments?

ADDITIONAL RESOURCES

Internet

http://www.army.mil/-news/2009/06/26/23511-army-lab-works-to-improve-soldier-health-performance/index.html. The United States Army's website presents a laboratory designed to improve soldiers' health and work performance.

http://www.sesp.org/. The website for the Society for Experimental Social Psychology. This professional association publishes two journals: the *Journal of Experimental Social Psychology* and *Social Psychological and Personality Science*.

http://www.spsp.org/. The website for the Society for Personality and Social Psychology, a professional organization that consults with the American Psychological Association and the Association for Psychological Services.

FURTHER READING

Berger, Joseph, Bernard P. Cohen, and Morris Zelditch. 1972. "Status Characteristics and Social Interaction." *American Sociological Review*, 37(3): 241–55.

Correll, Shelley J., Stephen Benard, and In Paik. 2007. "Getting a Job: Is There a Motherhood Penalty?" *American Journal of Sociology*, 112(5): 1297–338.

Cover, Dan. 1995. "Teaching Sociology as a Science: A Laboratory Reinforcement of the Sociological Heritage." *Teaching Sociology*, 23(3): 226–33.

Guetzkow, Harold. 1962. *Simulation in Social Science: Readings*. Upper Saddle River, NJ: Prentice-Hall.

6. Methodological Approach to Social Psychology

GARY ALAN FINE, JAMES S. HOUSE, AND KAREN S. COOK

Fine, House, and Cook succinctly outline three key methodologies employed by sociological social psychologists. They distinguish naturalistic inquiry from research that uses the scientific method, while highlighting the value of multimethod research to gain a more comprehensive approach.

Fine, Gary Alan, James S. House, and Karen S. Cook. 1995. "Methodological Approach to Social Psychology," in Cook, Fine, and House (eds.). *Sociological Perspectives on Social Psychology*, 601–3. Upper Saddle River, NJ: Allyn and Bacon.

INTRODUCTION: INVITATION TO METHODOLOGY

All social scientists, whether they describe themselves as empirical social scientists, social theorists, or some other way, believe ideas need to be systematically examined *in the context* of the world. To be sure, theorists are more likely to extrapolate from limited observations, but there remains a claim that any theory corresponds to the "natural world."

Methodological approaches can be categorized in various ways; we have selected three of the more prominent models of how to conduct research: qualitative field methods, experimental methods, and nonexperimental quantitative research.

The traditional approach associated with social psychology, and still dominant among psychological social psychologists, is experimentation. The experiment wrapped us in the mantle of science and made us believe we were reaching for an essential truth that is invariant over time and space.

Experimental research seeks to test or validate theoretically posited causal relationships between variables; its major strength is its ability to draw causal influences, due in most cases to experimenters' ability to manipulate or control the independent variable(s) of interest and to assign the persons or entities being studied randomly to the varying conditions or levels of the independent variable(s). Casual inferences remain inferences and can be incorrectly drawn, yet the experiment remains the strongest basis for drawing such inferences. But in many instances, for practical or ethical reasons, the phenomena of interest to social psychologists cannot be manipulated or controlled by the researcher. A major agenda of social psychologists is to understand the impact of race, gender, or socioeconomic position on individuals' life chances, behavior, thoughts, or feelings. We cannot, however, manipulate or control race or gender, and though we can to some degree alter a person's level of education, income, or occupational status, for practical and ethical reasons we cannot assign people randomly to levels of these variables. Thus, social psychologists, along with other social scientists, have played a major role in developing nonexperimental methods for observing the naturally occurring social world and formulating causal understandings of it-just as astronomers, meteorologists, and geologists have done for the physical world.

One body of techniques seeks to make and analyze quantitative observations of the social world to develop and test causal theories or models of how it operates. Nonexperimental quantitative data can come from many sources, including administrative records, systematic observation, and, most commonly, sample surveys and censuses. The associations among variables and their reliability and, to some extent, validity can be summarized via a range of statistical methods. The greatest problems are drawing causal inferences in the absence of experimental control and randomization. Advances in methods of statistical analysis and research design—especially the development of longitudinal design and analysis techniques—have played a major role in stimulating the development of quantitative nonexperimental social psychology on topics ranging from cognition, attitudes, emotions, or the self to the functioning of groups and networks and the relationships between individuals and macrosocial structures, institutions, and processes.

Since the emergence of experimental and quantitative nonexperimental social science in the first several decades of the twentieth century, many social scientists, especially in anthropology, sociology, and sociological social psychology, have been concerned that these methods are not adequate to understand the full nature and meaning of social life and individuals' lived experience. Sociological social psychologists, particularly the Chicago school of symbolic interactionism, played a major role in the development of qualitative field methods focused on illuminating the full complexity of social action and interaction, and the ways in which it is constructed by actors giving meaning to their social worlds and selves. To some degree these methods trade off the reliability, strength of causal inference, and breadth of coverage of populations found in experimental or quantitative nonexperimental methods for greater depth and richness of observation and understanding of particular individuals and social contexts, though qualitative methods also seek to achieve causal understanding of broad or even universal social phenomena and processes.

Methodologically, as well as substantively, social psychology has become less divided and more whole recently. We and most other social psychologists now agree that no method provides a royal road to truth. Each has been and will continue to be useful in providing fuller and more adequate social psychological understanding of the social world. Since the strengths and limitations of the methods reviewed in [this] chapter are largely complementary, we find [it important] to increase [the] use of multiple methods to understand important social phenomena.

DISCUSSION QUESTIONS

1. What three primary research methods do social psychologists use?
2. Which method is considered traditional in social psychology and is employed most frequently today by psychological social psychologists?
3. What do the concepts "reliability" and "validity" mean? What do the authors mean when they say that you typically sacrifice reliability for validity in research and vice versa? Why do these tradeoffs occur?

ADDITIONAL RESOURCES

Internet

http://www.ssc.wisc.edu/socpsych/ASA/. The website for the American Sociological Association's Social Psychology Section. The American Sociological Association publishes the journal *Social Psychology Quarterly*.

http://www.apa.org/journals/psp/description.html. The website for the American Psychological Association's *Journal of Personality and Social Psychology*.

http://www.espach.salford.ac.uk/sssi/. The website for the Society for the Study of Symbolic Interactionism. This professional association publishes the journal *Symbolic Interaction*.

FURTHER READING

DeLamater, John (ed). 2006. *Handbook of Social Psychology*. New York: Springer.

Denzin, Norman K. 1997. *Interpretive Ethnography: Ethnographic Practices for the 21st Century*. Newbury Park: Sage Publications.

Fine, Gary Alan, James S. House, and Karen S. Cook (eds.). 1995. *Sociological Perspectives on Social Psychology*. Upper Saddle River, NJ: Allyn and Bacon.

House, James S. 1977. "The Three Faces of Social Psychology." *Sociometry*, 40(2): 161–77.

House, James S. 2008. "Social Psychology, Social Science, and Economics: Twentieth Century Progress and Problems and Twenty-First Century Prospects." *Social Psychology Quarterly*, 71(3): 232–56.

Sandstrom, Kent L., Daniel D. Martin, and Gary Alan Fine. 2006. *Symbols, Selves, and Social Reality: A Symbolic Interactionist Approach to Social Psychology and Sociology.* Sweet Springs, MO: Roxbury Press.

Witt, G. Evans. 1999. "Say What You Mean." *American Demographics*, February 1.

The Person in Society

"YOU CAN BORROW MY DAD'S 'LECTRIC SHAVER
IF YOU WANT TO GET RID OF THAT MUSTACHE."

Socialization

Classic

These next selections explore the process of socialization that occurs throughout a person's life. Together they illustrate how grade-school children, adolescents, and adults come to learn new social norms and values. A main tenet running throughout the selections is that socialization does not just occur in infancy or childhood; rather, people continue to be socialized throughout the life course, especially when encountering new social situations or cultures.

Lareau's article analyzes social class differences in parenting third-grade children. Mortimer's piece addresses social class and gender differences in adolescents' work experience, exploring the significance of work to becoming an adult. In research published 50 years earlier, Becker's study lacks demographic comparisons but still conveys a rich ethnographic description of the process by which one becomes a "successful" marijuana user.

The selections have clear methodological similarities and differences. Both contemporary authors use a combination of research methods. For example, Mortimer relies most heavily on surveys to understand adolescents' work patterns and transition to adulthood but supplements her quantitative data with in-depth interviews. Lareau conducts field research, spending ample time observing, interviewing, and interacting with the families she studied. She augments her qualitative data with surveys. Becker's methodology is most similar to Lareau's, in that he conducts field research on marijuana users, yet he uses only qualitative methods. This classic-versus-contemporary difference in methodology represents a paradigm shift within social science: using a combination of qualitative and quantitative methods is quite common in contemporary research, whereas such a blending of methodology was rare 50 years ago.

7. Becoming a Marihuana User

HOWARD S. BECKER

Studies conducted before Becker's in-depth interviews with 50 marijuana users concluded that people became frequent drug users because of some inherent predisposition. Becker's research challenged prior findings by suggesting that a person becomes a "successful" marijuana user only as a result of a sequence of particular social experiences.

This paper seeks to describe the sequence of changes in attitude and experience which lead to *the use of marihuana for pleasure*. Marihuana does not produce addiction, as do alcohol and the opiate drugs; there is no withdrawal sickness and no ineradicable craving for the drug. The most frequent pattern of use might be termed "recreational." The drug is used occasionally for the pleasure the user finds in it, a relatively casual kind of behavior in comparison with that connected with the use of addicting drugs. The term "use for pleasure" is meant to emphasize the non-compulsive and casual character of the behavior. It is also meant to eliminate from consideration here those few cases in which marihuana is used for its prestige value only, as a symbol that one is a certain kind of person, with no pleasure at all being derived from its use.

Fifty interviews with marihuana users from a variety of social backgrounds and present positions in society constitute the data from which the generalization was constructed and against which it was tested. The interviews focused on the history of the person's experience with the drug, seeking major changes in his attitude toward it and in his actual use of it and the reasons for these changes. The final generalization is a statement of that sequence of changes in attitude which occurred in every case known to me in which the person came to use marihuana for pleasure.

This paper covers only a portion of the natural history of an individual's use of marihuana starting with the person having arrived at the point of willingness to try marihuana. He knows that others use it to "get high," but he does not know what this means in concrete terms. He is curious about the experience, ignorant of what it may turn out to be, and afraid that it may be more than he has bargained for. The steps outlined below, if he undergoes them all and maintains the attitudes developed in them, leave him willing and able to use the drug for pleasure when the opportunity presents itself.

Becker, Howard S. 1953. "Becoming a Marihuana User." *American Journal of Sociology*, 59(3), 235–42.

I

The novice does not ordinarily get high the first time he smokes marihuana, and several attempts are usually necessary to induce this state. One explanation of this may be that the drug is not smoked "properly," that is, in a way that ensures sufficient dosage to produce real symptoms of intoxication. Most users agree that it cannot be smoked like tobacco if one is to get high:

> Take in a lot of air, you know, and...I don't know how to describe it, you don't smoke it like a cigarette, you draw in a lot of air and get it deep down in your system and then keep it there. Keep it there as long as you can.

Without the use of some such technique the drug will produce no effects, and the user will be unable to get high:

> The trouble with people like that [who are not able to get high] is that they're just not smoking it right, that's all there is to it. Either they're not holding it down long enough, or they're getting too much air and not enough smoke, or the other way around or something like that. A lot of people just don't smoke it right, so naturally nothing's gonna happen.

If nothing happens, it is manifestly impossible for the user to develop a conception of the drug as an object which can be used for pleasure, and use will therefore not continue. The first step in the sequence of events that must occur if the person is to become a user is that he must learn to use the proper smoking technique in order that his use of the drug will produce some effects in terms of which his conception of it can change.

Such a change is, as might be expected, a result of the individual's participation in groups in which marihuana is used. In them the individual learns the proper way to smoke the drug. This may occur through direct teaching:

> I was smoking like I did an ordinary cigarette. He said, "No, don't do it like that." He said, "Suck it, you know, draw in and hold it in your lungs till you...for a period of time."
>
> I said, "Is there any limit of time to hold it?"
>
> He said, "No, just till you feel that you want to let it out, let it out." So I did that three or four times.

Many new users are ashamed to admit ignorance and, pretending to know already, must learn through the more indirect means of observation and imitation:

> I came on like I had turned on [smoked marihuana] many times before, you know. I didn't want to seem like a punk to this cat. See, like I didn't know the first thing about it—how to smoke it, or what was going to happen, or what. I just watched him like a hawk—I didn't take my eyes off him for a second, because I wanted to do everything just as he did it. I watched how he held it, how he smoked it, and everything. Then when he gave it to me I just came on cool, as though I knew exactly what the score was. I held it like he did and took a poke just the way he did.

No person continued marihuana use for pleasure without learning a technique that supplied sufficient dosage for the effects of the drug to appear. Only when this was learned was it possible for a conception of the drug as an object which could be used for pleasure to emerge. Without such a conception marihuana use was considered meaningless and did not continue.

II

Even after he learns the proper smoking technique, the new user may not get high and thus not form a conception of the drug as something which can be used for pleasure. A remark made by a user suggested the reason for this difficulty in getting high and pointed to the next necessary step on the road to being a user:

> I was told during an interview, "As a matter of fact, I've seen a guy who was high out of his mind and didn't know it."

I expressed disbelief: "How can that be, man?"

The interviewee said, "Well, it's pretty strange, I'll grant you that, but I've seen it. This guy got on with me, claiming that he'd never got high, one of those guys, and he got completely stoned. And he kept insisting that he wasn't high. So I had to prove to him that he was."

What does this mean? It suggests that being high consists of two elements: the presence of symptoms caused by marihuana use and the recognition of these symptoms and their connection by the user with his use of the drug. It is not enough, that is, that the effects be present; they alone do not automatically provide the experience of being high. The user must be able to point them out to himself and consciously connect them with his having smoked marihuana before he can have this experience. Otherwise, regardless of the actual effects produced, he considers that the drug has had no effect on him: "I figured it either had no effect on me or other people were exaggerating its effect on them, you know. I thought it was probably psychological, see." Such persons believe that the whole thing is an illusion and that the wish to be high leads the user to deceive himself into believing that something is happening when, in fact, nothing is. They do not continue marihuana use, feeling that "it does nothing" for them.

Typically, however, the novice has faith (developed from his observation of users who do get high) that the drug actually will produce some new experience and continues to experiment with it until it does. His failure to get high worries him, and he is likely to ask more experienced users or provoke comments from them about it. In such conversations he is made aware of specific details of his experience which he may not have noticed or may have noticed but failed to identify as symptoms of being high:

I didn't get high the first time....I don't think I held it in long enough. I probably let it out, you know, you're a little afraid. The second time I wasn't sure, and he [smoking companion] told me, like I asked him for some of the symptoms or something, how would I know, you know....

And I started feeling it, you know. That was the first time. And then about a week after that, sometime pretty close to it, I really got on. That was the first time I got on a big laughing kick, you know. Then I really knew I was on.

One symptom of being high is an intense hunger. In the next case the novice becomes aware of this and gets high for the first time:

They were just laughing the hell out of me because like I was eating so much. I just scoffed [ate] so much food, and they were just laughing at me, you know. Sometimes I'd be looking at them, you know, wondering why they're laughing, you know, not knowing what I was doing. [Well, did they tell you why they were laughing eventually?] Yeah, yeah, I come back, "Hey, man, what's happening?" Like, you know, like I'd ask, "What's happening?" and all of a sudden I feel weird, you know. "Man, you're on, you know. You're on pot [high on marihuana]." I said, "No, am I?" Like I don't know what's happening.

The novice, then, eager to have this feeling, picks up from other users some concrete referents of the term "high" and applies these notions to his own experience. The new concepts make it possible for him to locate these symptoms among his own sensations and to point out to himself a "something different" in his experience that he connects with drug use. It is only when he can do this that he is high. In the next case, the contrast between two successive experiences of a user makes clear the crucial importance of the awareness of the symptoms in being high and re-emphasizes the important role of interaction with other users in acquiring the concepts that make this awareness possible:

[Did you get high the first time you turned on?] Yeah, sure. Although, come to think of it, I guess I really didn't. I mean, like that first time it was more or less of a mild drunk. I was happy, I guess, you know what I mean. But I didn't really know I was high, you know what I mean. It was only after the second time I got high that I realized I was high the first time. Then I knew that something different was happening.

[How did you know that?] How did I know? If what happened to me that night would of happened to you, you would've known, believe me. We played the first tune for almost two hours—one tune! Imagine, man! We got on the stand and played this one tune, we started at nine o'clock. When we got finished I looked at my watch, it's a quarter to eleven. Almost two hours on one tune. And it didn't seem like anything.

I mean, you know, it does that to you. It's like you have much more time or something. Any way, when I saw that, man, it was too much. I knew I must really be high or something if anything like that could happen. See, and then they explained to me that that's what it did to you, you had a different sense of time and everything. So I realized that that's what it was. I knew then. Like the first time, I prob ably felt that way, you know, but I didn't know what's happening.

It is only when the novice becomes able to get high in this sense that he will continue to use marihuana for pleasure. In every case in which use continued, the user had acquired the necessary concepts with which to express to himself the fact that he was experiencing new sensations caused by the drug. That is, for use to continue, it is necessary not only to use the drug so as to produce effects but also to learn to perceive these effects when they occur. In this way marihuana acquires meaning for the user as an object which can be used for pleasure.

With increasing experience the user develops a greater appreciation of the drug's effects; he continues to learn to get high. He examines succeeding experiences closely, looking for new effects, making sure the old ones are still there.

The ability to perceive the drug's effects must be maintained if use is to continue; if it is lost, marihuana use ceases. Two kinds of evidence support this statement. First, people who become heavy users of alcohol, barbiturates, or opiates do not continue to smoke marihuana, largely because they lose the ability to distinguish between its effects and those of the other drugs. They no longer know whether the marihuana gets them high. Second, in those few cases in which an individual uses marihuana in such quantities that he is always high, he is apt to get this same feeling that the drug has no effect on him, since the essential element of a noticeable difference between feeling high and feeling normal is missing. In such a situation, use is likely to be given up completely, but temporarily, in order that the user may once again be able to perceive the difference.

III

One more step is necessary if the user who has now learned to get high is to continue use. He must learn to enjoy the effects he has just learned to experience. Marihuana-produced sensations are not automatically or necessarily pleasurable. The taste for such experience is a socially acquired one, not different in kind from acquired tastes for oysters or dry martinis. The user feels dizzy, thirsty; his scalp tingles; he misjudges time and distances; and so on. Are these things pleasurable? He isn't sure. If he is to continue marihuana use, he must decide that they are. Otherwise, getting high, while a real enough experience, will be an unpleasant one he would rather avoid.

The effects of the drug, when first perceived, may be physically unpleasant or at least ambiguous:

It started taking effect, and I didn't know what was happening, you know, what it was, and I was very sick. I walked around the room, walking around the room trying to get off, you know; it just scared me at first, you know. I wasn't used to that kind of feeling.

In addition, the novice's naive interpretation of what is happening to him may further confuse and frighten him, particularly if he decides, as many do, that he is going insane:

> I felt I was insane, you know. Everything people done to me just wigged me. I couldn't hold a conversation, and my mind would be wandering, and I was always thinking, oh, I don't know, weird things, like hearing music different....I get the feeling that I can't talk to anyone. I'll goof completely.

Given these typically frightening and unpleasant first experiences, the beginner will not continue use unless he learns to redefine the sensations as pleasurable:

> It was offered to me, and I tried it. I'll tell you one thing. I never did enjoy it at all. I mean it was just nothing that I could enjoy. [Well, did you get high when you turned on?] Oh, yeah, I got definite feelings from it. But I didn't enjoy them. I mean I got plenty of reactions, but they were mostly reactions of fear. [You were frightened?] Yes. I didn't enjoy it. I couldn't seem to relax with it, you know. If you can't relax with a thing, you can't enjoy it, I don't think.

In other cases the first experiences were also definitely unpleasant, but the person did become a marihuana user. This occurred, however, only after a later experience enabled him to redefine the sensations as pleasurable:

> [This man's first experience was extremely unpleasant, involving distortion of spatial relationships and sounds, violent thirst, and panic produced by these symptoms.] After the first time I didn't turn on for about, I'd say, ten months to a year....It wasn't a moral thing; it was because I'd gotten so frightened, bein' so high. An' I didn't want to go through that again, I mean, my reaction was, "Well, if this is what they call bein' high, I don't dig [like] it."...So I didn't turn on for a year almost, accounta that....
>
> Well, my friends started, an' consequently I started again. But I didn't have any more, I

didn't have that same initial reaction, after I started turning on again.

> [In interaction with his friends he became able to find pleasure in the effects of the drug and eventually became a regular user.]

In no case will use continue without such a redefinition of the effects as enjoyable.

This redefinition occurs, typically, in interaction with more experienced users who, in a number of ways, teach the novice to find pleasure in this experience which is at first so frightening. They may reassure him as to the temporary character of the unpleasant sensations and minimize their seriousness, at the same time calling attention to the more enjoyable aspects. An experienced user describes how he handles newcomers to marihuana use:

> Well, they get pretty high sometimes. The average person isn't ready for that, and it is a little frightening to them sometimes. I mean, they've been high on lush [alcohol], and they get higher that way than they've ever been before, and they don't know what's happening to them. Because they think they're going to keep going up, up, up till they lose their minds or begin doing weird things or something. You have to like reassure them, explain to them that they're not really flipping or anything, that they're gonna be all right. You have to just talk them out of being afraid. Keep talking to them, reassuring, telling them it's all right. And come on with your own story, you know: "The same thing happened to me. You'll get to like that after awhile." Keep coming on like that; pretty soon you talk them out of being scared. And besides they see you doing it and nothing horrible is happening to you, so that gives them more confidence.

The more experienced user may also teach the novice to regulate the amount he smokes more carefully, so as to avoid any severely uncomfortable symptoms while retaining the pleasant ones. Finally, he teaches the new user that he can "get to like it after awhile." He teaches him to regard those ambiguous experiences formerly defined as unpleasant as enjoyable. The older user in the following incident is a person whose tastes have shifted in this way, and his remarks have the effect of helping others to make a similar redefinition.

A new user had her first experience of the effects of marihuana and became frightened and hysterical. She "felt like she was half in and half out of the room" and experienced a number of alarming physical symptoms. One of the more experienced users present said, "She's dragged because she's high like that. I'd give anything to get that high myself. I haven't been that high in years."

In short, what was once frightening and distasteful becomes, after a taste for it is built up, pleasant, desired, and sought after. Enjoyment is introduced by the favorable definition of the experience that one acquires from others. Without this, use will not continue, for marihuana will not be for the user an object he can use for pleasure.

In addition to being a necessary step in becoming a user, this represents an important condition for continued use. It is quite common for experienced users suddenly to have an unpleasant or frightening experience, which they cannot define as pleasurable, either because they have used a larger amount of marihuana than usual or because it turns out to be a higher-quality marihuana than they expected. The user has sensations which go beyond any conception he has of what being high is and is in much the same situation as the novice, uncomfortable and frightened. He may blame it on an overdose and simply be more careful in the future. But he may make this the occasion for a rethinking of his attitude toward the drug and decide that it no longer can give him pleasure. When this occurs and is not followed by a redefinition of the drug as capable of producing pleasure, use will cease.

The likelihood of such a redefinition occurring depends on the degree of the individual's participation with other users. Where this participation is intensive, the individual is quickly talked out of his feeling against marihuana use. In the next case, on the other hand, the experience was

very disturbing, and the aftermath of the incident cut the person's participation with other users to almost zero. Use stopped for three years and began again only when a combination of circumstances, important among which was a resumption of ties with users, made possible a redefinition of the nature of the drug:

> It was too much, like I only made about four pokes, and I couldn't even get it out of my mouth, I was so high, and I got real flipped. In the basement, you know, I just couldn't stay in there anymore. My heart was pounding real hard, you know, and I was going out of my mind; I thought I was losing my mind completely. So I cut out of this basement, and this other guy, he's out of his mind, told me, "Don't, don't leave me, man. Stay here." And I couldn't.
>
> I walked outside, and it was five below zero, and I thought I was dying, and I had my coat open; I was sweating, I was perspiring. My whole insides were all..., and I walked about two blocks away, and I fainted behind a bush. I don't know how long I laid there. I woke up, and I was feeling the worst, I can't describe it at all, so I made it to a bowling alley, man, and I was trying to act normal, I was trying to shoot pool, you know, trying to act real normal, and I couldn't lay and I couldn't stand up and I couldn't sit down, and I went up and laid down where some guys that spot pins lay down, and that didn't help me, and I went down to a doctor's office. I was going to go in there and tell the doctor to put me out of my misery...because my heart was pounding so hard, you know....So then all week end I started flipping, seeing things there and going through hell, you know, all kinds of abnormal things....I just quit for a long time then.

[He went to a doctor who defined the symptoms for him as those of a nervous breakdown caused by "nerves" and "worries." Although he was no longer using marihuana, he had some recurrences of the symptoms which led him to suspect that "it was all his nerves."]

So I just stopped worrying, you know; so it was about thirty-six months later I started making it again. I'd just take a few pokes, you know. [He first resumed use in the company of the same user-friend with whom he had been involved in the original incident.]

A person, then, cannot begin to use marihuana for pleasure, or continue its use for pleasure, unless he learns to define its effects as enjoyable, unless it becomes and remains an object which he conceives of as capable of producing pleasure.

IV

In summary, an individual will be able to use marihuana for pleasure only when he goes through a process of learning to conceive of it as an object which can be used in this way. No one becomes a user without (1) learning to smoke the drug in a way which will produce real effects; (2) learning to recognize the effects and connect them with drug use (learning, in other words, to get high); and (3) learning to enjoy the sensations he perceives. In the course of this process he develops a disposition or motivation to use marihuana which was not and could not have been present when he began use, for it involves and depends on conceptions of the drug which could only grow out of the kind of actual experience detailed above. On completion of this process he is willing and able to use marihuana for pleasure.

He has learned, in short, to answer "Yes" to the question: "Is it fun?" The direction his further use of the drug takes depends on his being able to continue to answer "Yes" to this question and, in addition, on his being able to answer "Yes" to other questions which arise as he becomes aware of the implications of the fact that the society as a whole disapproves of the practice: "Is it expedient?" "Is it moral?" Once he has acquired the ability to get enjoyment out of the drug, use will continue to be possible for him. Considerations of morality and expediency, occasioned by the reactions of society, may interfere and inhibit use, but use continues to be a possibility in terms of his conception of the drug. The act becomes impossible only when the ability to enjoy the experience of being high is lost, through a change in the user's conception of the drug occasioned by certain kinds of experience with it.

This analysis of the genesis of marihuana use shows that the individuals who come in contact with a given object may respond to it at first in a great variety of ways. If a stable form of new behavior toward the object is to emerge, a transformation of meanings must occur, in which the person develops a new conception of the nature of the object. This happens in a series of communicative acts in which others point out new aspects of his experience to him, present him with new interpretations of events, and help him achieve a new conceptual organization of his world, without which the new behavior is not possible. Persons who do not achieve the proper kind of conceptualization are unable to engage in the given behavior and turn off in the direction of some other relationship to the object or activity.

This suggests that behavior of any kind might fruitfully be studied developmentally, in terms of changes in meanings and concepts, their organization and reorganization, and the way they channel behavior, making some acts possible while excluding others.

DISCUSSION QUESTIONS

1. What is the threefold process that Becker describes as necessary to become a marijuana user?
2. Becker describes novice marijuana users as presenting themselves as high, even when they are not. In what other contexts might a novice be tempted to "fake it" so that they fit in?

3. Taken out of context, Becker's description of being high sounds very unpleasant. Why would a loss of control over oneself be perceived as enjoyable? What other social phenomena are experiences that are perceived as unpleasurable at first and later become redefined as pleasurable over repeated social exposure?
4. Based on Becker's article, do you think it would be possible to "get high" using marijuana without the proper socialization? If, for example, someone were to acquire and smoke marijuana in a social vacuum, would they be able to "get high"?

ADDITIONAL RESOURCES

Film

"Bigger, Stronger, Faster." May 2008. A documentary about steroid use. The connections to Becker's three premises for becoming a successful marijuana user are clear.

Internet

http://biggerstrongerfastermovie.com/. The website for the film "Bigger, Stronger, Faster."

http://www.nida.nih.gov/MarijBroch/Marijteens.html. The "Marijuana: Facts for Teens" website of the National Institute on Drug Abuse. This site is sponsored by the National Institutes of Health.

http://monitoringthefuture.org. This website presents a wealth of information about current trends in teen substance use from annual surveys of U.S. high school seniors.

FURTHER READING

Carroll, Jamuna (ed.). 2006. *Marijuana: Opposing Viewpoints.* Detroit: Greenhaven Press.

Free, Marvin D., Jr. 1993. "Stages of Drug Use: A Social Control Perspective." *Youth & Society*, 25(2): 251–71.

Orenstein, Peggy. 1994. "Fear of Falling: Sluts," in *School Girls: Young Women, Self-Esteem and the Confidence Gap*, 51–66. New York: Doubleday.

8. Invisible Inequality: Social Class and Childrearing in Black Families and White Families

ANNETTE LAREAU

Lareau's research presents a fascinating in-depth comparison of parenting styles between middle-class and working-class families. Her findings indicate that there are very few differences in parenting styles between white and black families of the same social class. Social class differences in upbringing have long-term implications for children's skills in communication, education, and self-advocacy.

Lareau, Annette. 2002. "Invisible Inequality: Social Class and Childrearing in Black Families and White Families." *American Sociological Review*, 67(5): 747–76.

I draw on findings from a small, intensive data set collected using ethnographic methods. I map the connections between parents' resources and their children's daily lives. I seek to show empirically that social class does indeed create distinctive parenting styles. I demonstrate that parents differ by class in the ways they define their own roles in their children's lives as well as in how they perceive the nature of childhood. The middle-class parents, both white *and* black, tend to conform to a cultural logic of childrearing I call "concerted cultivation." They enroll their children in numerous age-specific organized activities that dominate family life and create enormous labor, particularly for mothers. The parents view these activities as transmitting important life skills to children. Middle-class parents also stress language use and the development of reasoning and employ talking as their preferred form of discipline. This "cultivation" approach results in a wider range of experiences for children but also creates a frenetic pace for parents, a cult of individualism within the family, and an emphasis on children's performance.

The childrearing strategies of white and black working-class and poor parents emphasize the "accomplishment of natural growth." These parents believe that as long as they provide love, food, and safety, their children will grow and thrive. They do not focus on developing their children's special talents. Compared to the middle-class children, working-class and poor children participate in few organized activities and have more free time and deeper, richer ties within their extended families. Working-class and poor parents issue many more directives to their children and, in some households, place more emphasis on physical discipline than do the middle-class parents.

I trace the connections between the class position of family members—including children—and the uneven outcomes of their experiences outside the home as they interact with professionals in dominant institutions. The pattern of concerted cultivation encourages an *emerging sense of entitlement* in children. All parents and children are not equally assertive, but the pattern of questioning and intervening among the white and black middle-class parents contrasts sharply with the definitions of how to be helpful and effective observed among the white and black working-class and poor adults. The pattern of the accomplishment of natural growth encourages an *emerging sense of constraint*. Adults as well as children in these social classes tend to be deferential and outwardly accepting in their interactions with professionals such as doctors and educators. At the same time, however, compared to their middle-class counterparts, white and black working-class and poor family members are more distrustful of professionals. These are differences with potential long-term consequences. In an historical moment when the dominant society privileges active, informed, assertive clients of health and educational services, the strategies employed by children and parents are not equally effective across classes. In sum, differences in family life lie not only in the advantages parents obtain for their children, but also in the skills they transmit to children for negotiating their own life paths.

METHODOLOGY

Study Participants

This study is based on interviews and observations of children, aged 8 to 10, and their families. The data were collected over time in three research phases. Phase one involved observations in two third-grade classrooms in a public school in the Midwestern community of "Lawrenceville."* After conducting observations for two months, I grouped the families into social class (and race) categories based on information provided by educators. I then chose every third name, and

---

* All names of people and places are pseudonyms. The Lawrenceville school was in a white suburban neighborhood in a university community a few hours from a metropolitan area. The student population was about half white and half black; the (disproportionately poor) black children were bused from other neighborhoods.

sent a letter to the child's home asking the mother and father to participate in separate interviews. Over 90 percent of parents agreed, for a total of 32 children (16 white and 16 African American). A black graduate student and I interviewed all mothers and most fathers (or guardians) of the children. Each interview lasted 90 to 120 minutes, and all took place in 1989–1990.

Phase two took place at two sites in a northeastern metropolitan area. One school, "Lower Richmond," although located in a predominantly white, working-class urban neighborhood, drew about half of its students from a nearby all-black housing project. I observed one third-grade class at Lower Richmond about twice a week for almost six months. The second site, "Swan," was located in a suburban neighborhood about 45 minutes from the city center. It was 90 percent white; most of the remaining 10 percent were middle-class black children. There, I observed twice a week for two months at the end of the third grade; a research assistant then observed weekly for four more months in the fourth grade. At each site, teachers and parents described their school in positive terms. The observations took place between September 1992 and January 1994. In the fall of 1993, I drew an interview sample from Lower Richmond and Swan, following the same method of selection used for Lawrenceville. A team of research assistants and I interviewed the parents and guardians of 39 children. Again, the response rate was over 90 percent but because the classrooms did not generate enough black middle-class children and white poor children to fill the analytical categories, interviews were also conducted with 17 families with children aged 8 to 10. (Most of these interviews took place during the summers of 1996 and 1997.) Thus, the total number of children who participated in the study was 88 (32 from the Midwest and 56 from the Northeast).

Family Observations

Phase three, the most intensive research phase of the study, involved home observations of 12 children and their families in the Northeast who had been previously interviewed. Some themes, such as language use and families' social connections, surfaced mainly during this phase. Although I entered the field interested in examining the influence of social class on children's daily lives, I incorporated new themes as they "bubbled up" from the field observations. The evidence presented here comes mainly from the family observations, but I also use interview findings from the full sample of 88 children where appropriate.

Nine of the 12 families came from the Northeastern classroom sample. The home observations took place, one family at a time, from December 1993 to August 1994. Three 10-year-olds (a black middle-class boy and girl and a white poor boy) who were not part of the classroom sample were observed in their homes during the summer of 1995.

The research assistants and I took turns visiting the participating families daily, for a total of about 20 visits to each home, often in the space of one month. The observations went beyond the home: Fieldworkers followed children and parents as they participated in school activities, church services and events, organized play, visits to relatives, and medical appointments. Observations typically lasted three hours, but sometimes much longer (e.g., when we observed an out-of-town funeral, a special extended family event, or a long shopping trip). Most cases also involved one overnight visit. We often carried tape recorders and used the audiotapes for reference in writing field notes. Writing field notes usually required 8 to 12 hours for each two- or three-hour home visit. Participating families each were paid $350, usually at the end of the visits.

We worked in teams of three. One fieldworker visited three to four times per week; another visited one to two times per week; and I visited once or twice per week, except for the two families for which I was lead fieldworker. The research teams' composition varied with the race of the family. Two white graduate students and I (a middle-aged white woman) visited the white families; for the black families, the teams included one white graduate student, one black graduate student, and me. All black families with male children were visited by teams that included a black male fieldworker. A white male fieldworker observed the poor family with the white boy; the remaining white fieldworkers were female. Team members met regularly to discuss the families and to review the emerging analytic themes.

Our presence altered family dynamics, especially at first. Over time, however, we saw signs of adjustment (e.g., yelling and cursing increased on the third day and again on the tenth). The children, especially, seemed to enjoy participating in the project. They reported it made them feel "special." They were visibly happy to see the fieldworkers arrive and reluctant to let them leave. The working-class and poor black boys were more comfortable with the black male fieldworkers than with the white female ones, especially at first. Overall, however, family members reported in exit interviews that they had not changed their behavior significantly, or they mentioned very specific alterations (e.g., "the house got cleaner").

A Note on Class

I undertook field observations to develop an intensive, realistic portrait of family life. Although I deliberately focused on only 12 families, I wanted to compare children across gender and race. I assigned the families to a working-class or middle-class category based on detailed information that each of the employed adults provided about the work they did, the nature of the organization that employed them, and their educational credentials. In the first school I studied, many children were from households supported by public assistance.

The three class categories conceal important internal variations. The Williams family (black) and the Tallinger family (white) have very high incomes, both in excess of $175,000; the median income among the middle-class parents was much lower. Income differences among the middle-class

families were not associated with differences in childrearing methods.

CONCERTED CULTIVATION AND NATURAL GROWTH

The interviews and observations suggested that crucial aspects of family life *cohered*. Within the concerted cultivation and accomplishment of natural growth approaches, three key dimensions may be distinguished: the organization of daily life, the use of language, and social connections. These dimensions do not capture all important parts of family life, but they do incorporate core aspects of childrearing. Moreover, our field observations revealed that behaviors and activities related to these dimensions dominated the rhythms of family life.

I now examine two families in terms of these three key dimensions. I "control" for race and gender and contrast the lives of two black boys—one from an (upper) middle-class family and one from a family on public assistance. I could have focused on almost any of the other 12 children, but this pair seemed optimal, given the limited number of studies reporting on black middle-class families, as well as the aspect of my argument that suggests that race is less important than class in shaping childrearing patterns.

Developing Alexander Williams

Alexander Williams and his parents live in a predominantly black middle-class neighborhood. Their six-bedroom house is worth about $150,000. Alexander is an only child. Both parents grew up in small towns in the South, and both are from large families. His father, a tall, handsome man, is a very successful trial lawyer who earns about $125,000 annually in a small firm specializing in medical malpractice cases. Two weeks each month, he works very long hours (from about 5:30 A.M. until midnight) preparing for trials. The other two weeks, his workday ends around 6:00 P.M. He rarely travels out of town. Alexander's mother, Christina, is a positive, bubbly woman with freckles and long, black, wavy hair. A high-level manager in a major corporation, she has a corner office, a personal secretary, and responsibilities for other offices across the nation. She tries to limit her travel, but at least once a month she takes an overnight trip.

Alexander is a charming, inquisitive boy with a winsome smile. Ms. Williams is pleased that Alexander seems interested in so many things:

> Alexander is a joy. He's a gift to me. He's very energetic, very curious, loving, caring person, that, um…is outgoing and who, uh, really loves to be with people. And who loves to explore, and loves to read and…just do a lot of fun things.

The private school Alexander attends has an on-site after-school program. There, he participates in several activities and receives guitar lessons and photography instruction.

Organization of Daily Life

Alexander is busy with activities during the week and on weekends. His mother describes their Saturday morning routine. The day starts early with a private piano lesson for Alexander downtown, a 20-minute drive from the house:

> It's an 8:15 class. But for me, it was a tradeoff. I am very adamant about Saturday morning TV. I don't know what it contributes. So…it was…um…either stay at home and fight on a Saturday morning [laughs] or go do something constructive…Now Saturday mornings are pretty booked up. You know, the piano lesson, and then straight to choir for a couple of hours. So, he has a very full schedule.

Ms. Williams's vehement opposition to television is based on her view of what Alexander needs to grow and thrive. She objects to TV's passivity and feels it is her obligation to help her son cultivate his talents.

Sometimes Alexander complains that "my mother signs me up for everything!" Generally, however, he likes his activities. He says they make him feel "special," and without them life would be "boring." His sense of time is thoroughly entwined with his activities: He feels disoriented when his schedule is not full.

Alexander's parents believe his activities provide a wide range of benefits important for his development. In discussing Alexander's piano lessons, Mr. Williams notes that as a Suzuki student, Alexander is already able to read music. Speculating about more diffuse benefits of Alexander's involvement with piano, he says:

> I don't see how any kid's adolescence and adulthood could not but be enhanced by an awareness of who Beethoven was. And is that Bach or Mozart? I don't know the difference between the two! I don't know Baroque from Classical—but he does. How can that not be a benefit in later life? I'm convinced that this rich experience will make him a better person, a better citizen, a better husband, a better father—certainly a better student.

Given the sheer number of Alexander's activities, events inevitably overlap. Some activities, though short-lived, are extremely time consuming. Alexander's school play, for example, requires rehearsals three nights the week before the opening. In addition, in choosing activities, the Williamses have an added concern—the group's racial balance. Ms. Williams prefers that Alexander not be the only black child at events. Typically, one or two other black boys are involved, but the groups are predominantly white and the activities take place in predominantly white residential neighborhoods. Alexander is, however, part of his church's youth choir and Sunday School, activities in which all participants are black.

Many activities involve competition. Alexander must audition for his solo performance in the school play, for example. Similarly, parents and children alike understand that participation on "A," "B," or "All-Star" sports teams signal different skill levels. Like other middle-class children in the study, Alexander seems to enjoy public performance.

Alexander's commitments do not consume *all* his free time. Still, his life is defined by a series of deadlines and schedules interwoven with a series of activities that are organized and controlled by adults rather than children. Neither he nor his parents see this as troublesome.

Language Use

Like other middle-class families, the Williamses often engage in conversation that promotes reasoning and negotiation.

Expressions of interest in children's activities often lead to negotiations over small, home-based matters. During a car ride, Ms. Williams tries to adjust the dinner menu to suit Alexander:

> Alexander says, "I don't want hot dogs tonight."
> MOM: "Oh? Because you had them for lunch."
> ALEXANDER NODS.
> MOM: "Well, I can fix something else and save the hot dogs for tomorrow night."
> ALEX: "But I don't want any pork chops either."
> MOM: "Well, Alexander, we need to eat something. Why didn't you have hamburgers today?"
> ALEX: "They don't have them any more at the snack bar."
> Mom asks Alexander if he's ok, if he wants a snack. Alexander says he's ok. Mom asks if he's sure he doesn't want a bag of chips?

Not all middle-class parents are as attentive to their children's needs as this mother, and none are *always* interested in negotiating. But a general pattern of reasoning and accommodating is common.

Social Connections

Mr. and Ms. Williams consider themselves very close to their extended families. Because the Williams's aging parents live in the South, visiting requires a plane trip. Ms. Williams takes Alexander with her to see his grandparents twice a year. She speaks on the phone with her parents at least once a week and also calls her siblings several times a week. Mr. Williams talks with his mother regularly by phone. With pride, he also mentions his niece, whose Ivy League education he is helping to finance.

Interactions with cousins are not normally a part of Alexander's leisure time. (As I explain below, other middle-class children did not see cousins routinely either, even when they lived nearby.) Nor does he often play with neighborhood children. The huge homes on the Williams's street are occupied mainly by couples without children. Most of Alexander's playmates come from his classroom or his organized activities. Because most of his school events, church life, and assorted activities are organized by the age (and sometimes gender) of the participants, Alexander interacts almost exclusively with children his own age, usually boys. Adult-organized activities thus define the context of his social life.

Summary

Overall, Alexander's parents engaged in concerted cultivation. They fostered their son's growth through involvement in music, church, athletics, and academics. They talked with him at length, seeking his opinions and encouraging his ideas. Their approach involved considerable direct expenses (e.g., the cost of lessons and equipment) and large indirect expenses (e.g., the cost of taking time off from work, driving to practices, and foregoing adult leisure activities). Although Mr. and Ms. Williams acknowledged the importance of extended family, Alexander spent relatively little time with relatives. His social interactions occurred almost exclusively with children his own age and with adults. Alexander's many activities significantly shaped the organization of daily life in the family. Both parents' leisure time was tailored to their son's commitments. Mr. and Ms. Williams felt that the strategies they cultivated with Alexander would result in his having the best possible chance at a happy and productive life. They couldn't imagine themselves *not* investing large amounts of time and energy in their son's life. But, as I explain in the next section, which focuses on a black boy from a poor family, other parents held a different view.

Supporting the Natural Growth of Harold McAllister

Harold McAllister, a large, stocky boy with a big smile, is from a poor black family. He lives with his mother and his 8-year-old sister, Alexis, in a large apartment. Two cousins often stay overnight. Harold's 16-year-old sister and 18-year-old brother usually live with their grandmother, but sometimes they stay at the McAllister's home. Ms. McAllister, a high school graduate, relies on public assistance (AFDC). Hank, Harold and Alexis's father, is a mechanic. He and Ms. McAllister have never married. He visits regularly, sometimes weekly, stopping by after work to watch television or nap. Harold (but not Alexis) sometimes travels across town by bus to spend the weekend with Hank.

The McAllister's apartment is in a public housing project near a busy street. The complex consists of rows of two and three story brick units. The buildings, blocky and brown, have small yards enclosed by concrete and wood fences. Large floodlights are mounted on the corners of the buildings, and wide concrete sidewalks cut through the spaces between units. The ground is bare in many places; paper wrappers and glass litter the area.

Inside the apartment, life is humorous and lively, with family members and kin sharing in the daily routines. Ms. McAllister discussed, disdainfully, mothers who are on drugs or who abuse alcohol and do not "look after" their children. Indeed, the previous year Ms. McAllister called Child Protective Services to report her twin sister, a cocaine addict, because she was neglecting her children. Ms. McAllister is actively involved in her twin's daughters' lives. Her two nephews also frequently stay with her. Overall, she sees herself as a capable mother who takes care of her children and her extended family.

Organization of Daily Life

Much of Harold's life and the lives of his family members revolve around home. Project residents often sit outside in lawn chairs or on front stoops, drinking beer, talking, and watching children play. During summer, windows are frequently left open, allowing breezes to waft through the units and providing vantage points from which residents can survey the neighborhood.

Harold loves sports. He is particularly fond of basketball, but he also enjoys football, and he follows televised professional sports closely. Most afternoons, he is either inside watching television or outside playing ball. He tosses a football with cousins and boys from the neighboring units and organizes pick-up basketball games. Sometimes he and his friends use a rusty, bare hoop hanging from a telephone pole in the housing project; other times, they string up an old, blue plastic crate as a makeshift hoop. One obstacle to playing sports, however, is a shortage of equipment. Balls are costly to replace, especially given the rate at which they disappear theft of children's play equipment, including balls and bicycles, is an ongoing problem.

The pace of life for Harold and his friends ebbs and flows with the children's interests and family obligations. For example, after spending time listening to music and looking at baseball cards, the children join a water fight Tyrice instigates. It is a lively game, filled with laughter and with efforts to get the adults next door wet (against their wishes). When the game winds down, the kids ask their mother for money, receive it, and then walk to a store to buy chips and soda. They chat with another young boy and then amble back to the apartment, eating as they walk.

Thus, Harold's life is more free-flowing and more child-directed than is Alexander Williams's. The pace of any given day is not so much planned as emergent, reflecting child-based interests and activities. Parents intervene in specific areas, such as personal grooming, meals, and occasional chores, but they do not continuously direct and monitor their children's leisure activities. Moreover, the leisure activities Harold and other working-class and poor children pursue require them to develop a repertoire of skills for dealing with much older and much younger children as well as with neighbors and relatives.

Language Use

Life in the working-class and poor families in the study flows smoothly without extended verbal discussions. The amount of talking varies, but overall, it is considerably less than occurs in the middle-class homes. Ms. McAllister jokes with the children and discusses what is on television. But she does not appear to cultivate conversation by asking the children questions or by drawing them out. Often she is brief and direct in her remarks. For instance, she coordinates the use of the apartment's only bathroom by using one-word directives. She sends the children (there are almost always at least four children home at once) to wash up by pointing to a child, saying one word, "bathroom," and handing him or her a washcloth. Wordlessly, the designated child gets up and goes to the bathroom to take a shower.

Similarly, although Ms. McAllister will listen to the children's complaints about school, she does not draw them out on these issues or seek to determine details, as Ms. Williams would. For instance, at the start of the new school year, when I ask Harold about his teacher, he tells me she is "mean" and that "she lies." Ms. McAllister, washing dishes, listens to her son, but she does not encourage Harold to support his opinion about his new teacher with more examples, nor does she mention any concerns of her own. Instead, she asks about last year's teacher, "What was the name of that man teacher?" Harold says, "Mr. Lindsey?" She says, "No, the other one." He says, "Mr. Terrene." Ms. McAllister smiles and says, "Yeah. I liked him." Unlike Alexander's mother, she seems content with a brief exchange of information.

Social Connections

Children, especially boys, frequently play outside. The number of potential playmates in Harold's world is vastly higher than the number in Alexander's neighborhood. When a field-worker stops to count heads, she finds 40 children of elementary school age residing in the nearby rows of apartments. With so many children nearby, Harold could choose to play only with others his own age. In fact, though, he often hangs out with older and younger children and with his cousins (who are close to his age).

The McAllister family, like other poor and working-class families, is involved in a web of extended kin. As noted earlier, Harold's older siblings and his two male cousins often spend the night at the McAllister home. Celebrations such as birthdays involve relatives almost exclusively. Party guests are not, as in middle-class families, friends from school or from extracurricular activities. Birthdays are celebrated enthusiastically, with cake and special food to mark the occasion; presents, however, are not offered. Similarly, Christmas at Harold's house featured a tree and special food but no presents. At these and other family events, the older children voluntarily look after the younger ones: Harold plays with his 16-month-old niece, and his cousins carry around the younger babies.

The importance of family ties—and the contingent nature of life in the McAllister's world—is clear in the response Alexis offers when asked what she would do if she were given a million dollars:

> Oh, boy! I'd buy my brother, my sister, my uncle, my aunt, my nieces and my nephews, and my grandpop, and my grandmom, and my mom, and my dad, and my friends, not my friends, but mostly my best friend—I'd buy them all clothes…and sneakers. And I'd buy some food, and I'd buy my mom some food, and I'd get my brothers and my sisters gifts for their birthdays.

Summary

In a setting where everyone, including the children, was acutely aware of the lack of money, the McAllister family made do. Ms. McAllister rightfully saw herself as a very capable mother. She was a strong, positive influence in the lives of the children she looked after. Still, the contrast with Ms. Williams is striking. Ms. McAllister did not seem to think that Harold's opinions needed to be cultivated and developed. She, like most parents in the working-class and poor families, drew strong and clear boundaries between adults and children. Adults gave directions to children. Children were given freedom to play informally unless they were needed for chores. Extended family networks were deemed important and trustworthy.

The Intersection of Race and Class in Family Life

I expected race to powerfully shape children's daily schedules, but this was not evident. This is not to say that race is unimportant. Black parents were particularly concerned with monitoring their children's lives outside the home for signs of racial problems. Black middle-class fathers, especially, were likely to stress the importance of their sons understanding "what it means to be a black man in this society." Mr. Williams, in summarizing how he and his wife orient Alexander, said:

[We try to] teach him that race unfortunately is the most important aspect of our national life. I mean people look at other people and they see a color first. But that isn't going to define who he is. He will do his best. He will succeed, despite racism. And I think he lives his life that way.

Alexander's parents were acutely aware of the potential significance of race in his life. Both were adamant, however, that race should not be used as "an excuse" for not striving to succeed. Mr. Williams put it this way:

I discuss how race impacts on my life as an attorney, and I discuss how race will impact on his life. The one teaching that he takes away from this is that he is never to use discrimination as an excuse for not doing his best.

Thus far, few incidents of overt racism had occurred in Alexander's life, as his mother noted:

Those situations have been far and few between....I mean, I can count them on my fingers.

Still, Ms. Williams recounted with obvious pain an incident at a birthday party Alexander had attended as a preschooler. The grandparents of the birthday child repeatedly asked, "Who is that boy?" and exclaimed, "He's so dark!" Such experiences fueled the Williams's resolve always to be "cautious":

We've never been, uh, parents who drop off their kid anywhere. We've always gone with him. And even now, I go in and—to school in the morning—and check [in]....The school environment, we've watched very closely.

Alexander's parents were not equally optimistic about the chances for racial equality in this country. Ms. Williams felt strongly that, especially while Alexander was young, his father should not voice his pessimism. Mr. Williams complained that this meant he had to "watch" what he said to Alexander about race relations. Still, both parents agreed about the need to be vigilant regarding potential racial problems in Alexander's life. Other black parents reported experiencing racial prejudice and expressed a similar commitment to vigilance.

Issues surrounding the prospect of growing up black and male in this society were threaded through Alexander's life in ways that had no equivalent among his middle-class, white male peers. Still, in fourth grade there were no signs of racial experiences having "taken hold" the way that they might as Alexander ages. In terms of the number and kind of activities he participated in, his life was very similar to that of Garrett Tallinger, his white counterpart. That both sets of parents were fully committed to a strategy of concentrated cultivation was apparent in the number of adult-organized activities the boys were enrolled in, the hectic pace of family life, and the stress on reasoning in parent-child negotiations. Likewise, the research assistants and I saw no striking differences in the ways in which white parents and black parents in the working-class and poor homes socialized their children.

Others have found that in middle school and high school, adolescent peer groups often draw sharp racial boundaries, a pattern not evident among this study's third- and fourth-grade participants (but sometimes present among their older siblings). In sum, in the broader society, key aspects of daily life were shaped by racial segregation and discrimination. But in terms of enrollment in organized activities, language use, and social connections, the largest differences between the families we observed were across social class, not racial groups.

Differences in Cultural Practices Across the Total Sample

The patterns observed among the Williams and McAllister families occurred among others in the 12-family subsample and across the larger group of 88 children. Frequently, they also echoed established patterns in the literature. These patterns highlight not only the amount of time spent on activities but also the quality of family life and the ways in which key dimensions of childrearing intertwine.

Organization of Daily Life

In the study as a whole, the rhythms of family life differed by social class. Working-class and poor children spent most of their free time in informal play; middle-class children took part in many adult-organized activities designed to develop their individual talents and interests. For the 88 children, I calculated an average score for the most common adult-directed, organized activities, based on parents' answers to interview questions. Middle-class children averaged 4.9 current activities (N = 36), working-class children averaged 2.5 activities (N = 26), and poor children averaged 1.5 (N = 26). Black middle-class children had slightly more activities than white middle-class children, largely connected to more church involvement, with an average of 5.2 (N = 18) compared with 4.6 activities for whites (N = 18). The racial difference was very modest in the working-class group (2.8 activities for black children [N = 12] and 2.3 for white children [N = 14]) and the poor group (1.6 activities for black children [N = 14] and 1.4 for white children [N = 12]). Middle-class boys had slightly more activities than middle-class girls (5.1 vs. 4.7, N = 18 for both) but gender did not make a difference for the other classes. The type of activity did however. Girls tended to participate in dance, music, and Scouts, and to be less active in sports. This pattern of social class differences in activities is comparable to other, earlier reports.

The dollar cost of children's organized activities was significant, particularly when families had more than one child. Cash outlays included paying the instructors and coaches who gave lessons, purchasing uniforms and performance attire, paying for tournament admission and travel to and from tournaments, and covering hotel and food costs for overnight stays. Summer camps also were expensive. At my request, the Tallingers added up the costs for Garrett's organized activities. The total was over $4,000 per year. Recent reports of parents' expenditures for children's involvement in a single sport (e.g., hockey) are comparably high. Children's activities consumed time as well as money, co-opting parents' limited leisure hours.

The study also uncovered differences in how much time children spent in activities controlled by adults. Take the schedule of Melanie Handlon, a white middle-class girl in the fourth grade. Between December 8 and December 24, Melanie had a piano lesson each Monday, Girl Scouts each Thursday, a special Girl Scout event one Monday night, a special holiday musical performance at school one Tuesday night, two orthodontist appointments, five special rehearsals for the church Christmas pageant, and regular Sunday commitments (an early church service, Sunday school, and youth choir). On weekdays she spent several hours after school struggling with her home-work as her mother coached her step-by-step through the worksheets. The amount of time Melanie spent in situations where her movements were controlled by adults was typical of middle-class children in the study.

The schedule of Katie Brindle, a white fourth-grader from a poor family, contrasts sharply, showing few organized activities between December 2 and 24. She sang in the school choir. This involved one after-school rehearsal on Wednesdays; she walked home by herself after these rehearsals. Occasionally, Katie attended a Christian youth group on Friday nights (i.e., December 3). Significantly, all her activities were free. She wanted to enroll in ballet classes, but they were prohibitively expensive. What Katie did have was unstructured leisure time. Usually, she came home after school and then played outside with other children in the neighborhood or watched television. She also regularly visited her grandmother and her cousins, who lived a few minutes away by bus or car. She often spent weekend nights at her grandmother's house. Overall, Katie's life was centered in and around home. Compared with the middle-class children in the study, her life moved at a dramatically less hectic pace. This pattern was characteristic of the other working-class and poor families we interviewed.

In addition to these activities, television provided a major source of leisure entertainment. All children in the study spent at least some free time watching TV, but there were differences in when, what, and how much they watched. Most middle-class parents we interviewed characterized television as actually or potentially harmful to children; many stressed that they preferred their children to read for entertainment. Middle-class parents often had rules about the amount of time children could spend watching television. These concerns did not surface in interviews with working-class and poor parents. Indeed, Ms. Yanelli, a white working-class mother, objected to restricting a child's access to television, noting, "You know, you learn so much from television." Working-class and poor parents did monitor the content of programs and made some shows off-limits for children. The television itself, however, was left on almost continuously.

Language Use

The social class differences in language use we observed were similar to those reported by others. In middle-class homes, parents placed a tremendous emphasis on reasoning. They also drew out their children's views on specific subjects. Middle-class parents relied on directives for matters of health and safety, but most other aspects of daily life were potentially open to negotiation: Discussions arose over what children wore in the morning, what they ate, where they sat, and how they spent their time. Not all middle-class children were equally talkative, however. In addition, in observations, mothers exhibited more willingness to engage children in prolonged discussions than did fathers. The latter tended to be less engaged with children overall and less accepting of disruptions.

In working-class and poor homes, most parents did not focus on developing their children's opinions, judgments, and observations. When children volunteered information, parents would listen, but typically they did not follow up with questions or comments.

Negotiations between parents and children in working-class and poor families were infrequent. Parents tended to use firm directives and they expected prompt, positive responses. Children who ignored parental instructions could expect physical punishment.

Social Connections

We also observed class differences in the context of children's social relations. Across the sample of 88 families, middle-class children's involvement in adult-organized activities led to mainly weak social ties. Soccer, photography classes, swim team, and so on typically take place in 6 to 8 week blocks, and participant turnover rates are relatively high. Equally important, middle-class children's commitment to organized activities generally pre-empted visits with extended family. Some did not have relatives who lived nearby, but even among those who did, children's schedules made it difficult to organize and attend regular extended-family gatherings. Many of the middle-class children visited with relatives only on major holidays.

Similarly, middle-class parents tended to forge weak rather than strong ties. Most reported having social networks that included professionals: 93 percent of the sample of middle-class parents had a friend or relative who was a teacher, compared with 43 percent of working-class parents and 36 percent of poor families. Relationships such as these are not as deep as family ties, but they are a valuable resource when parents face a challenge in childrearing.

Working-class and poor families were much less likely to include professionals in their social networks but were much more likely than their middle-class counterparts to see or speak with kin daily. Children regularly interacted in casually assembled, heterogeneous age groups that included cousins as well as neighborhood children. As others have shown, we observed gender differences in children's activities. Although girls sometimes ventured outside to ride bikes and play ball games, compared with boys they were more likely to stay inside the house to play. Whether inside or outside, the girls, like the boys, played in loose coalitions of kin and neighbors and created their own activities.

Interactions with representatives of major social institutions (the police, courts, schools, and government agencies) also appeared significantly shaped by social class. Members of white *and* black working-class and poor families offered spontaneous comments about their distrust of these officials. For example, one white working-class mother described an episode in which the police had come to her home looking for her ex-husband (a drug user). She recalled officers "breaking down the door" and terrifying her eldest son, then only three years old. Another white working-class mother reported that her father had been arrested. Although by all accounts in good spirits, he had been found dead in the city jail, an alleged suicide. Children listened to and appeared to absorb remarks such as these.

Fear was a key reason for the unease with which working-class and poor families approached formal (and some informal) encounters with officials. Some parents worried that authorities would "come and take [our] kids away." One black mother on public assistance interviewed as part of the larger study was outraged that school personnel had allowed her daughter to come home from school one winter day without her coat. She noted that if *she* had allowed that to happen, "the school" would have reported her to Child Protective Services for child abuse. Wendy Driver's mother (white working-class) complained that she felt obligated to take Wendy to the doctor, even when she knew nothing was wrong, because Wendy had gone to see the school nurse. Ms. Driver felt she had to be extra careful because she didn't want "them" to come and take her kids away. Strikingly, no middle-class parents mention similar fears about the power of dominant institutions.

Obviously, these three dimensions of childrearing patterns—the organization of daily life, language use, and social connections—do not capture all the class advantages parents pass to their children. The middle-class children in the study enjoyed relatively privileged lives. They lived in large houses, some had swimming pools in their backyards, most had bedrooms of their own, all had many toys, and computers were common. These children also had broad horizons. They flew in airplanes, they traveled out of state for vacations, they often traveled an hour or two from home to take part in their activities, and they knew older children whose extracurricular activities involved international travel.

Still, in some important areas, variations among families did *not* appear to be linked to social class. Some of the middle-class children had learning problems. And, despite their relatively privileged social-class position, neither middle-class children nor their parents were insulated from the realities of serious illness and premature death among family and friends. In addition, some elements of family life seemed relatively immune to social class, including how orderly and tidy the households were. In one white middle-class family, the house was regularly in a state of disarray. The house was cleaned and tidied for a Christmas Eve gathering, but it returned to its normal state shortly thereafter. By contrast, a black middle-class family's home was always extremely tidy, as were some, but not all, of the working-class and poor homes. Nor did certain aspects of parenting, particularly the degree to which mothers appeared to "mean what they said," seem linked to social class. Families also differed with respect to the presence or absence of a sense of humor among individual members, levels of anxiety, and signs of stress-related illnesses they exhibited. Finally, there were significant differences in temperament and disposition among children in the same family. These variations are useful reminders that social class is not fully a determinant of the character of children's lives.

IMPACT OF CHILDREARING STRATEGIES ON INTERACTIONS WITH INSTITUTIONS

Social scientists sometimes emphasize the importance of reshaping parenting practices to improve children's chances of success.

I now follow the families out of their homes and into encounters with representatives of dominant institutions—institutions that are directed by middle-class professionals. Again, I focus on Alexander Williams and Harold McAllister. Across all social classes, parents and children interacted with teachers and school officials, healthcare professionals, and assorted government officials. Although they often addressed similar problems (e.g., learning disabilities, asthma, traffic violations), they typically did not achieve similar resolutions. The pattern of concerted cultivation fostered an *emerging sense of entitlement* in the life of Alexander Williams and other middle-class children. By contrast, the commitment to nurturing children's natural growth fostered an *emerging sense of constraint* in the life of Harold McAllister and other working-class or poor children.

Both parents and children drew on the resources associated with these two child-rearing approaches during their interactions with officials. Middle-class parents and children often customized these interactions; working-class and poor parents were more likely to have a "generic" relationship. When faced with problems, middle-class parents also appeared better equipped to exert influence over other adults compared with working-class and poor parents. Nor did middle-class parents or children display the intimidation or confusion we witnessed among many working-class and poor families when they faced a problem in their children's school experience.

Emerging Signs of Entitlement

Alexander Williams's mother, like many middle-class mothers, explicitly teaches her son to be an informed, assertive client in interactions with professionals. For example, as she drives Alexander to a routine doctor's appointment, she coaches him in the art of communicating effectively in healthcare settings:

> ALEXANDER ASKS IF HE NEEDS TO GET ANY SHOTS TODAY AT THE DOCTOR'S. MS. WILLIAMS SAYS HE'LL NEED TO ASK THE DOCTOR....AS WE ENTER PARK LANE, MOM SAYS QUIETLY TO ALEX: "Alexander, you should be thinking of questions you might want to ask the doctor. You can ask him anything you want. Don't be shy. You can ask anything."
>
> ALEX THINKS FOR A MINUTE, THEN: "I have some bumps under my arms from my deodorant."
>
> MOM: "Really? You mean from your new deodorant?"
>
> ALEX: "Yes."
>
> MOM: "Well, you should ask the doctor."

Alexander learns that he has the right to speak up (e.g., "don't be shy") and that he should prepare for an encounter with a person in a position of authority by gathering his thoughts in advance.

These class resources are subsequently *activated* in the encounter with the doctor (a jovial white man in his late thirties or early forties). The examination begins this way:

> DOCTOR: "Okay, as usual, I'd like to go through the routine questions with you. And if you have any questions for me, just fire away." Doctor examines Alex's chart: "Height-wise, as usual, Alexander's in the ninety-fifth percentile."

Although the physician is talking to Ms. Williams, Alexander interrupts him:

> ALEX: "I'm in the what?" Doctor: "It means that you're taller than more than ninety-five out of a hundred young men when they're, uh, ten years old."
> ALEX: "I'm not ten."
> DOCTOR: "Well, they graphed you at ten ... they usually take the closest year to get that graph."
> ALEX: "Alright."

interpretation
acquiescence
?

Alexander's "Alright" reveals that he feels entitled to weigh-in with his own judgment.

Class resources are again activated when Alexander's mother reveals she "gave up" on a medication. The doctor pleasantly but clearly instructs her to continue the medication. Again, though, he receives accurate information rather than facing silent resistance or defiance, as occurred in encounters between healthcare professionals and other (primarily working-class and poor) families.

Middle-class parents and children were also very assertive in situations at the public elementary school most of the middle-class children in the study attended. There were numerous conflicts during the year over matters small and large. For example, parents complained to one another and to the teachers about the amount of homework the children were assigned. A black middle-class mother whose daughters had not tested into the school's gifted program negotiated with officials to have the girls' (higher) results from a private

testing company accepted instead. The parents of a fourth-grade boy drew the school superintendent into a battle over religious lyrics in a song scheduled to be sung as part of the holiday program. The superintendent consulted the district lawyer and ultimately "counseled" the principal to be more sensitive, and the song was dropped.

Children, too, asserted themselves at school. Examples include requesting that the classroom's blinds be lowered so the sun wasn't in their eyes, badgering the teacher for permission to retake a math test for a higher grade, and demanding to know why no cupcake had been saved when an absence prevented attendance at a classroom party. In these encounters, children were not simply complying with adults' requests or asking for a repeat of an earlier experience. They were displaying an emerging sense of entitlement by urging adults to permit a customized accommodation of institutional processes to suit their preferences.

Emerging Signs of Constraint

The interactions the research assistants and I observed between professionals and working-class and poor parents frequently seemed cautious and constrained. This unease is evident, for example, during a physical Harold McAllister has before going to Bible camp. Harold's mother, normally boisterous and talkative at home, is quiet. Unlike Ms. Williams, she seems wary of supplying the doctor with accurate information:

> DOCTOR: "Does he eat something each day— either fish, meat, or egg?"
> MOM, RESPONSE IS LOW AND MUFFLED: "Yes."
> DOCTOR, ATTEMPTING TO MAKE EYE CONTACT BUT MOM STARES INTENTLY AT PAPER: "A yellow vegetable?"
> MOM, STILL NO EYE CONTACT, LOOKING AT THE FLOOR: "Yeah."
> DOCTOR: "A green vegetable?" Mom, looking at the doctor: "Not all the time." [Fieldworker has not seen any of the children eat a green or yellow vegetable since visits began.]
> DOCTOR: "No. Fruit or juice?"

MOM, LOW VOICE, LITTLE OR NO EYE CONTACT, LOOKS AT THE DOCTOR'S SCRIBBLES ON THE PAPER HE IS FILLING OUT: "Ummh humn."

DOCTOR: "Does he drink milk every day?"

MOM, ABRUPTLY, IN CONSIDERABLY LOUDER VOICE: "Yeah."

DOCTOR: "Cereal, bread, rice, potato, anything like that?"

MOM, SHAKES HER HEAD: "Yes, definitely." [Looks at doctor.]

Ms. McAllister's knowledge of developmental events in Harold's life is uneven. She is not sure when he learned to walk and cannot recall the name of his previous doctor. And when the doctor asks, "When was the last time he had a tetanus shot?" she counters, gruffly, "What's a tetanus shot?"

Unlike Ms. Williams, who urged Alexander to share information with the doctor, Ms. McAllister squelches eight-year-old Alexis's overtures:

DOCTOR: "Any birth mark?"

Mom looks at doctor, shakes her head no.

ALEXIS, RAISING HER LEFT ARM, SAYS EXCITEDLY: "I have a birth mark under my arm!"

MOM, RAISING HER VOICE AND LOOKING STERN: "Will you cool out a minute?" Mom, again answering the doctor's question: "No."

Despite Ms. McAllister's tension and the marked change in her everyday demeanor, Harold's whole exam is not uncomfortable. There are moments of laughter. Moreover, Harold's mother is not consistently shy or passive.

Still, neither Harold nor his mother seemed as comfortable as Alexander had been. Alexander was used to extensive conversation at home; with the doctor, he was at ease initiating questions. Harold, who was used to responding to directives at home, primarily answered questions from the doctor, rather than posing his own. Alexander, encouraged by his mother, was assertive and confident with the doctor. Harold was reserved. Absorbing his mother's apparent need to conceal the truth about the range of foods he ate, he appeared cautious, displaying an emerging sense of constraint.

We observed a similar pattern in school interactions. Overall, the working-class and poor adults had much more distance or separation from the school than their middle-class counterparts. Ms. McAllister, for example, could be quite assertive in some settings. But throughout the fourth-grade parent-teacher conference, she kept her winter jacket zipped up, sat hunched over in her chair, and spoke in barely audible tones. She was stunned when the teacher said that Harold did not do homework. Sounding dumbfounded, she said, "He does it at home." The teacher denied it and continued talking. Ms. McAllister made no further comments and did not probe for more information. The conference ended, having yielded Ms. McAllister few insights into Harold's educational experience.

Other working-class and poor parents also appeared baffled, intimidated, and subdued in parent-teacher conferences. Ms. Driver, who was extremely worried about her fourth-grader's inability to read, kept these concerns to herself. She explained to us, "I don't want to jump into anything and find it is the wrong thing." When working-class and poor parents did try to intervene in their children's educational experiences, they often felt ineffectual. Billy Yanelli's mother appeared relaxed and chatty in many of her interactions with other adults. With "the school," however, she was very apprehensive. She distrusted school personnel. She felt bullied and powerless.

Working-class and poor children seemed aware of their parents' frustration and witnessed their powerlessness. Billy Yanelli, for example, asserted in an interview that his mother "hate[d]" school officials.

In classroom observations, working-class and poor children could be quite lively and energetic, but we did not observe them try to customize their environments. They tended to react to adults' offers or, at times, to plead with educators to repeat previous experiences, such as reading a particular story, watching a movie, or going to the computer room. Compared to middle-class classroom interactions, the boundaries between adults and children seemed firmer and clearer. Although the children often resisted and tested school rules, they did not seem to be seeking to get educators to accommodate their own *individual* preferences.

Overall, then, the behavior of working-class and poor parents cannot be explained as a manifestation of their temperaments or of overall passivity; parents were quite energetic in intervening in their children's lives in other spheres. Rather, working-class and poor parents generally appeared to depend on the school even as they were dubious of the trustworthiness of the professionals. This suspicion of professionals in dominant institutions is, at least in some instances, a reasonable response. Middle-class children and parents often (but not always) accrued advantages or profits from their efforts. Alexander Williams succeeded in having the doctor take his medical concerns seriously. Ms. Marshall's children ended up in the gifted program, even though they did not technically qualify. Middle-class children expect institutions to be responsive to *them* and to accommodate their individual needs. By contrast, when Wendy Driver is told to hit the boy who is pestering her (when the teacher isn't looking) or Billy Yanelli is told to physically defend himself, despite school rules, they are not learning how to make bureaucratic institutions work to their advantage. Instead, they are being given lessons in frustration and powerlessness.

WHY DOES SOCIAL CLASS MATTER?

Parents' economic resources helped create the observed class differences in childrearing practices. Enrollment fees that middle-class parents dismissed as "negligible" were formidable expenses for less affluent families. Parents also paid for clothing, equipment, hotel stays, fast food meals, summer camps, and fundraisers. Moreover, families needed reliable private transportation and flexible work schedules to get children to and from events. These resources were disproportionately concentrated in middle-class families.

Differences in educational resources also are important. Middle-class parents' superior levels of education gave them larger vocabularies that facilitated concerted cultivation, particularly in institutional interventions. Poor and working-class parents were not familiar with key terms professionals used, such as "tetanus shot." Furthermore, middle-class parents' educational backgrounds gave them confidence when criticizing educational professionals and intervening in school matters. Working-class and poor parents viewed educators as their social superiors.

We found that parents' work mattered, but also saw signs that the experience of adulthood itself influenced conceptions of childhood. Middle-class parents often were preoccupied with the pleasures and challenges of their work lives. They tended to view childhood as a dual opportunity: a chance for play, and for developing talents and skills of value later in life. Mr. Tallinger noted that playing soccer taught Garrett to be "hard nosed" and "competitive," valuable workplace skills. Ms. Williams mentioned the value of Alexander learning to work with others by playing on a sports team. Middle-class parents, aware of the "declining fortunes" of the middle class, worried about their own economic futures and those of their children. This uncertainty increased their commitment to helping their children develop broad skills to enhance their future possibilities.

Working-class and poor parents' conceptions of adulthood and childhood also appeared to be closely connected to their lived experiences. For the working class, it was the deadening quality of work and the press of economic shortages that defined their experience of adulthood and influenced their vision of childhood. It was dependence on public assistance and severe economic shortages that most shaped poor parents' views. Families in both classes had many worries about basic issues: food shortages, limited access to healthcare, physical safety, unreliable transportation, insufficient clothing. Thinking back over their childhoods, these parents remembered hardship but also recalled times without the anxieties they now faced. Many appeared to want their own youngsters to concentrate on being happy and relaxed, keeping the burdens of life at bay until they were older.

Thus, childrearing strategies are influenced by more than parents' education. It is the interweaving of life experiences and resources, including parents' economic resources, occupational conditions, and educational backgrounds, that appears to be most important in leading middle-class parents to engage in concerted cultivation and working-class and poor parents to engage in the accomplishment of natural growth.

DISCUSSION

The evidence shows that class position influences critical aspects of family life: time use, language use, and kin ties. Not all aspects of family life are affected by social class, and there is variability within class. Still, parents do transmit advantages to their children in patterns that are sufficiently consistent and identifiable to be described as a "cultural logic" of childrearing. The white and black middle-class parents engaged in practices I have termed "concerted cultivation"—they made a deliberate and sustained effort to stimulate children's development and to cultivate their cognitive and social skills. The working-class and poor parents viewed children's development as spontaneously unfolding, as long as they were provided with comfort, food, shelter, and other basic support. This commitment, too, required ongoing effort; sustaining children's natural growth despite formidable life challenges is properly viewed as an accomplishment.

In daily life, the patterns associated with each of these approaches were interwoven and mutually reinforcing. Nine-year-old middle-class children already had developed a clear sense of their own talents and skills, and they differentiated themselves from siblings and friends. They were also learning to think of themselves as special and worthy of having adults devote time and energy to promoting them and their leisure activities. In the process, the boundaries between adults and children sometimes blurred; adults'

leisure preferences became subordinate to 1 children's. The strong emphasis on reasonii middle-class families had similar, diffuse effects. Children used their formidable reasoning skills to persuade adults to acquiesce to their wishes. The idea that children's desires should be taken seriously was routinely realized in the middle-class families we interviewed and observed. In many subtle ways, children were taught that they were entitled. Finally, the commitment to cultivating children resulted in family schedules so crowded with activities there was little time left for visiting relatives.

In working-class and poor families, parents established limits; within those limits, children were free to fashion their own pastimes. Children's wishes did not guide adults' actions as frequently or as decisively as they did in middle-class homes. Children were viewed as subordinate to adults. Parents tended to issue directives rather than to negotiate. Frequent interactions with relatives rather than acquaintances or strangers created a thicker divide between families and the outside world. Implicitly and explicitly, parents taught their children to keep their distance from people in positions of authority, to be distrustful of institutions, and, at times, to resist officials' authority. Children seemed to absorb the adults' feelings of powerlessness in their institutional relationships. As with the middle class, there were important variations among working-class and poor families, and some critical aspects of family life, such as the use of humor, were immune to social class.

The role of race in children's daily lives was less powerful than I had expected. The middle-class black children's parents were alert to the potential effects of institutional discrimination on their children. Middle-class black parents also took steps to help their children develop a positive racial identity. Still, in terms of how children spend their time, the way parents use language and discipline in the home, the nature of the families' social connections, and the strategies used for intervening in institutions, white and black middle-class parents engaged in very similar, often identical, practices with their children. A similar pattern was observed in white and black working-class homes as well as in white and black poor families. Thus my data indicate that on the childrearing dynamics studied here, compared with social class, race was less important in children's daily lives. As they enter the racially segregated words of dating, marriage, and housing markets, and as they encounter more racism in their interpersonal contact with whites, the relative importance of race in the children's daily lives is likely to increase.

Differences in family dynamics and the logic of childrearing across social classes have long-term consequences. As family members moved out of the home and interacted with representatives of formal institutions, middle-class parents and children were able to negotiate more valuable outcomes than their working-class and poor counterparts. In interactions with agents of dominant institutions, working-class and poor children were learning lessons in constraint while middle-class children were developing a sense of entitlement.

It is a mistake to see either concerted cultivation or the accomplishment of natural growth as an intrinsically desirable approach. Drawbacks to middle-class childrearing, including the exhaustion associated with intensive mothering and frenetic family schedules and a sapping of children's naiveté that leaves them feeling too sophisticated for simple games and toys, remain insufficiently highlighted.

Another drawback is that middle-class children are less likely to learn how to fill "empty time" with their own creative play, leading to a dependence on their parents to solve experiences of boredom. Sociologists need to more clearly differentiate between standards that are intrinsically desirable and standards that facilitate success in dominant institutions. A more critical, and historically sensitive, vision is needed.

DISCUSSION QUESTIONS

1. Compare and contrast Lareau's "concerted cultivation" and "natural growth" parenting styles. What are key differences? Are there any similarities?
2. Do the patterns of your own upbringing most closely resemble "concerted cultivation" or "natural growth"? How so?
3. What are the costs and benefits of "concerted cultivation" and "natural growth" parenting? Do they help to prepare middle-class and working-class children for their future roles in adulthood?

ADDITIONAL RESOURCES

Internet

http://www.epi.orq/content.cfm/issueguides_poverty_poverty. The Economic Policy Institute's web resource for poverty and family budgeting.

http://www.pbs.org/pov/pov2003/loveanddiane/index.html. The interactive website for the PBS documentary "Love & Dianne."

http://www.parenting.org/. A resource for parents to support their children's development.

http://www.time.com/time/photogallery/O,29307,1626519,00.html. "What the World Eats." Featuring photographs from *Hungry Planet* author Peter Menzel, this site shows what 15 families from around the world eat in one week's time. An excellent source for a discussion of social class issues.

Film

    "Love & Dianne." A 2004 Point of View PBS documentary by Jennifer Dworkin filmed over the course of 10 years. The film follows impoverished urban single-mom Dianne and her daughter, Jennifer, as they struggle through Dianne's drug addiction and recovery.

FURTHER READING

Hill, Nancy E. 1997. "Does Parenting Differ Based on Social Class? African American Women's Perceived Socialization for Achievement." *American Journal of Community Psychology*, 25(5): 675–97.

Kohn, Melvin L. 1963. "Social Class and Parent-Child Relationships: An Interpretation." *American Journal of Sociology*, 68(4): 471–80.

9. Working and Becoming Adult

JEYLAN T. MORTIMER

Mortimer presents findings from the Youth Development Study (YDS)—a project that explores the transition from adolescence to adulthood in a panel of children raised in St. Paul, Minnesota. This longitudinal research project began studying a cohort of ninth-graders in 1987, exploring key issues affecting their transition to adulthood. This particular article addresses how paid work during adolescence can influence future employment success.

Each older generation debates the proper ways to prepare young people for adulthood. The objective, most would agree, is to help youth to become well-functioning adults, able to take responsibility for themselves as well as for others and to find some degree of personal fulfillment in doing so. How are youth to be prepared for their futures? We have considered two general answers to this question.

    On the one hand, it is argued that the young must be protected and removed from the social worlds of adulthood. Following G. Stanley Hall, developmental psychologists have long emphasized that optimal development necessitates a lengthy moratorium on the cares and responsibilities of adult roles. Youth must be allowed to entertain new interests and identities in a tentative fashion, without enduring commitment or serious consequence.

    On the other hand, it is contended that to be able to find their proper niche in the adult world, the young must first be exposed to, and meaningfully incorporated into, adult institutions. Only by interacting with adults in real-world contexts can youth develop the values, interests, and perspectives that will equip them to make critical choices as they navigate their pathways to adulthood. More pragmatically, they will acquire the

Mortimer, Jeylan T. 2003. "Working and Becoming Adult," in *Working and Growing Up in America*, 206–36. Cambridge, MA: Harvard University Press.

habits of mind and behavior, the information, and the skills they will need for adequate performance of adult roles in the future.

This debate takes on special meaning in contemporary America. During the past half-century the transition to adulthood has become prolonged; in more recent decades, the timing and sequencing of transition markers have become more variable and unpredictable as well. Indeed, it is contended that "pre-adulthood" should no longer be conceptualized as simply an extension of adolescence; some commentators suggest that a new life phase has arisen, extending well into the third decade of life, variously called "post-adolescence," "youth," "young adulthood," and "emerging adulthood."

What place does, and should, work have in adolescents' preparation for their futures? Given its longitudinal scope and comprehensive measurement of teenage work investment, its attention to the quality of work experience, and its monitoring of adolescent involvement in diverse activities, the Youth Development Study is uniquely suited to address the debate over whether adolescents should be "protected" from or "incorporated" into the world of work.

THE CHARACTER OF YOUTHWORK

Young people's paid work changes as they move through high school. Initial jobs, in the early teens, are informal—babysitting and yardwork. As they grow older, adolescents move into more formal employment, first in the fast-food industry and subsequently in a wider range of settings. They move from simple jobs to more complex ones requiring further training and involving greater supervisory responsibility.

Paid jobs during high school are nearly universal: 93 percent of the YDS participants were employed for at least some time while school was in session. But youthwork is far from homogeneous. As in the adult workforce, there are distinct, gender-linked patterns of working. Adolescent girls are more likely than boys to hold paid jobs during each year of high school, but boys work longer hours than girls.

The desirable qualities of productive activities other than paid employment are widely recognized. Being unpaid, they are not motivated by and do not foster materialistic values. Household work is an outgrowth of family membership as well as a contributor to family cohesion. While ninth-grade boys and girls do similar amounts of housework, boys' contributions to family labor decline markedly during the ensuing four years. Girls' housework likewise declines initially, but levels off after ninth grade at a much higher level than that of boys. Thus the sex-typing of family work increases during high school. This pattern may prepare young women for later juggling of work and family roles, given women's substantial responsibility for the "second shift" of family work.

Volunteer work gives youth experiences outside their usual surroundings, and, in some circumstances, encourages a broad civic identity and empathy with the less fortunate. Volunteer work fosters intrinsic and altruistic work motivations—desires for work that involves helping others and community service, as well as the capacity to express one's interests. Although they differed in regard to paid work and housework, boys and girls in the YDS had similar patterns of participation in volunteering.

Most significantly, the YDS shows that there is no empirically discernible tradeoff between paid work and these other valuable youth activities; in fact, most youth who are employed during high school participate simultaneously in a broad range of other settings. Workers and nonworkers are highly similar with respect to their other uses of time. Employed youth differed hardly at all from those who did not have paid work. Despite averaging close to 20 hours per week on the job, "active" employed youth spent as much time as their nonworking counterparts doing homework, engaged in extracurricular pursuits, helping their families with housework, and spending time with friends. Tellingly, the background and attitudinal precursors of these two active patterns were much the same, and youth readily moved between the two patterns from one year to the next.

It can be concluded that most working youth, especially when they limit their hours of work, do not sacrifice involvement in distinctly "adolescent" activities. Low-intensity workers may be "protected," given their high levels of participation in school, in extracurricular activities, and in their families, yet still "incorporated," albeit to a limited degree, in the world of work.

Given its apparent benefits, it is important to know what enables teenagers to pursue low-intensity employment. High-intensity work is more prevalent among boys and among the less advantaged teenagers. Minority youth, those whose parents had less formal education, and those from non-intact families had relatively little propensity for the "steady" (high duration, low intensity) pattern of work.

The "most invested" workers during high school, who worked at both high duration and high intensity, exhibited relatively little interest in their schoolwork in ninth grade (in comparison with those who were to pursue the "steady" work pattern), relatively low academic performance, and high orientation toward peers. "Sporadic" employment, high in intensity but low in duration, was also more prevalent among youth who, as ninth graders, had lower levels of academic performance, lower educational aspirations, more frequent problem behavior, and strong peer orientation.

Consistently, those ninth graders who were to pursue the "steady" pattern of employment had relatively high educational aspirations early on. During high school they were especially likely to seek early jobs to save money for their future educations. Those with the "most invested" pattern of employment were distinguished by their interest in acquiring skills.

Thus the more advantaged youngsters, whose parents have more education and who themselves have greater intellectual interest, higher academic performance, and stronger ambitions, limit their hours of work so as to allow paid employment as well as other activities.

In contrast, ninth graders who had lower grades either selected themselves or were selected by employers for jobs that may be more conducive to the acquisition of human capital through work. In general, teenagers from lower socioeconomic backgrounds, those who were less engaged in school, and those whose early school performance indicated less promising academic careers followed a strategy of intensive investment in work—work that involved more chances for advancement, more learning opportunities, and higher earnings, but also more demands. They steered themselves toward the more rewarding but also more stressful "adultlike" jobs.

The YDS thus demonstrates two pathways of preparation for adulthood, one involving limitation of paid work and balancing of employment and other activities; the second involving more intensive investment in paid work, more adultlike jobs, and more focused time-use patterns in general. The well-rounded, active teenagers, the majority of youth in the YDS panel, are those who participate in the distinctively youthful arenas of school and extracurricular activities as well as in the family. However, these active teenagers are also likely to be incorporated into the adult world of employment, holding time-limited jobs. The active, well-rounded adolescent lifestyle entails flexible movement in and out of the labor force, needed to accommodate diverse obligations and activities.

PSYCHO-SOCIAL CONSEQUENCES

Work in adolescence may have both contemporaneous and longer-term outcomes; given the highly formative character of this time of life, it is reasonable to suppose that any contemporaneous influences of youthwork on mental health, values, self-concepts, and identities will have lasting consequences in subsequent developmental phases. Does employment during high school make youth's movement through the increasingly protracted phase of "emerging adulthood" easier or more difficult? How does it influence educational attainment and establishment in work? Does its influence vary depending on the degree of investment in employment or on its quality?

Contemporaneous Outcomes

YDS participants who worked longer hours exhibited more problem behavior during high school and drank more alcohol; these may be considered defiant and "adultlike" behaviors in accord with the "precocious maturity" thesis.

Despite the clear link between work hours and problem behaviors, the quality of work appears to matter far more than its quantity for adolescent mental health and development. Whereas the YDS teenagers generally perceived their work experiences as positive and reported high levels of job satisfaction, their descriptions were not wholly favorable. Girls described their jobs in more desirable terms than boys—as involving more opportunities for learning and service to others, as well as fewer noxious and stressful work conditions. Boys engaged in more supervision of other workers and had higher earnings and more frequent opportunities for advancement. Boys also thought their work gave them more status in the eyes of their peers.

In general, youth whose jobs signify successful movement toward adulthood express more confidence, have more strongly crystallized work values, and show less depressive affect. Those who perceive their work as stressful manifest more depressed mood than other employed youth. Depressive affect is also linked to perceptions of incompatibility between work and school. Rather ominously, in light of the prevalent critique of youthwork, many adolescents report strain in balancing their part-time jobs with the demands of schoolwork.

What is especially important is the developmental specificity of the association between work and mental health. Our analyses suggest that the freedom to make one's own decisions at work is not conducive to young people's mental health. In fact, adolescents reported more depressed mood as their degree of control in the workplace increased. Adolescents, relative newcomers on the job scene, do not appear to react well to autonomy.

Youth whose experiences in the workplace are positive come to think of themselves as more likely to be successful adult workers—to obtain work that brings them satisfaction, is well paid, and allows them to live in the locations they prefer. Confidence about work is especially conducive to educationally successful behavior—getting good grades, actively seeking information about college, consulting with counselors, taking admittance tests, and achieving postsecondary educational attainment.

Youth whose jobs provided learning opportunities developed more strongly crystallized work values of both an intrinsic and extrinsic character. Being able to learn new skills in the work environment may convey the message that they will be able to succeed, and to obtain diverse occupational rewards in the future.

Occupational values are predictive of both college majors and eventual occupational destinations. Those youth who have more well-formed notions about what they want in their adult work are likely to have a stronger sense of direction and be better equipped to choose educational programs and further work and nonwork experiences that will enable them to realize their goals.

Influence on Other Developmental Contexts

Despite grave warnings that adolescents' most intimate ties and sources of social support are threatened by paid work, we found no evidence that this is the case. While working adolescents spent less time with their families, there was little indication that the quality of their relations with their parents suffered as a result of increasing investment in work. In fact, positive experiences at work appeared to draw adolescent boys and their fathers closer together. Similarly, there was no evidence that working disrupts supportive bonds between peers.

In regard to balancing the demands of work with those of school, there appears to be a gap between perception and reality. Many teenagers reported that balancing work and school was difficult. Although few parents mentioned any "costs" of work, those who did also highlighted this difficulty. But at the same time, the accumulated objective evidence does not show that employment jeopardizes students' grades.

The Transition to Adulthood

Some commentators, including the critics of youthwork, maintain that the transition to adulthood often occurs too rapidly, with problems arising from the absence of a lengthy "moratorium" on adultlike responsibilities. Others warn that the transition takes too long—as youth move between school and work, change educational programs and schools, and explore various occupational niches.

The effects of youthwork on this transition cannot be fully assessed here, since many YDS panel members, as gauged by standard "markers of adulthood," had not yet completed this process by 1998. Seven years after most graduated from high school, about one of four had still been attending school for at least part of the prior year. Only 27 percent had married; close to a third had become parents. As might be expected, most had left school before having children: only one in five had become parents while still attending school.

With this caveat in mind, let us address some central concerns of the critics of youthwork. What influence does early work have on educational attainment during the seven years after high school? Is there any evidence from the YDS that young people who invest more time in employment during high school have a precocious transition to adulthood?

The "steady" pattern of work appears especially conducive to postsecondary educational attainment: youth who pursued this pattern of nearly continuous employment completed the most months of postsecondary education during the four years following high school. While for the girls this pattern could be attributable to prior characteristics—family social background and earlier academic propensity—for the boys, differences between the work-investment groups persisted even after application of numerous controls.

What is particularly interesting is the strong influence of the "steady" pattern among youth with little educational promise. Ninth-grade intrinsic motivation toward school, higher grade-point average, and high educational aspirations were significantly predictive of the work investment patterns. Those with little promise were decidedly unlikely to pursue the "steady" work pattern. However, those who somehow managed to maintain this pattern were much more likely to achieve the B.A., even after a wide range of background and achievement-related precursors were controlled.

YDS youth who pursued the more intensive teenage work patterns had higher earnings immediately following high school. By 1997, however, six years after high school, the earnings profiles were very similar across the work-investment groups. Still, teenage nonworkers were at a distinct disadvantage. It is expected that those who pursued low-intensity work during high school and subsequently invested more time in postsecondary education will eventually surpass their less-educated peers in earnings.

In addition to early school-leaving and entry into full-time work, childbearing is a central component of the "precocious maturity" syndrome. More youth in the high-intensity work categories had married and had children by seven years after high school. However, few of the births to those who pursued high-intensity work occurred at a time that would be considered "precocious." Young people who worked more intensively during high school moved toward marriage and parenthood faster than other youth, but at an age that may still be considered "normative," in their early to mid-twenties. Meanwhile, the youth who pursued the "steady" work pattern and those who did little or no work during high school appear to be delaying family formation past the averages for their age group.

Whereas the YDS research team is continuing to investigate the longer-term consequences of adolescent investment in work and of work quality, the analyses thus far suggest that negative behavioral consequences of employment are not lasting. For example, four years after high school, we find no differences in alcohol use among adolescents who manifested varying levels of investment in high school work. Moreover, recent assessment of the effects of the quality of youth-work on depressive affect four years after high school revealed few long-term effects.

Young people who have greater initial advantages, in the form of family resources or their own educational ambitions, come to have "active" lifestyles—with or without paid work—that predict higher educational attainment. Young people with less educational ambition and fewer family resources tend to pursue more intensive employment during high school, work that is both more demanding and more stressful. However, they also describe their jobs as giving them more opportunities for learning and advancement, and choose their early jobs for their learning potential. These youth may also be considered purposeful—taking advantage of an alternative source of human capital formation, work experience. They reap the benefits of this strategy in higher earnings immediately after high school. However, this is not the optimal strategy with respect to lifetime earnings attainment, since they will soon be surpassed by their more highly educated former schoolmates.

IMPLICATIONS FOR FUTURE STUDIES

Lacking national scope, the YDS has obvious limitations. It cannot address regional variations in youth employment, particularly rural-urban differences and the circumstances in the poorest urban enclaves. As it focuses on a single mid-western city, it is unlikely to be exactly replicated elsewhere in America. Still, the YDS panel members' labor force participation rates and types of employment are quite similar to national profiles. The findings replicate some relationships noted in prior studies (such as associations between hours of employment and problem behavior).

Future studies should address the longer-term consequences of early paid jobs, as young people complete the transition to adulthood. This is particularly important given the prolonged

character of this transition. Our analyses indicate that steady work during adolescence does not lead to any disadvantage in higher educational attainment, as measured seven years beyond high school, in comparison to young people who had more limited or no investment in paid work. Given lengthening periods of higher education, it is possible that youth who pursued more intensive work as teenagers will eventually catch up to the steady workers, as they continue taking courses, going to night school, and attaining further degrees. Young people who restricted their labor force participation during high school might eventually surpass the steady workers in educational attainment. As noted at the beginning of this chapter, the extended period of exploration allows some youth to pursue higher education sporadically. The longer-term benefits or disadvantages of slower vs. faster completion of education, in the present context, are not known.

Research should also be undertaken over more extended periods of time to more fully comprehend the consequences of youth employment. As both the economy and youth labor markets change, it is important to continue to examine both investment and quality of work in diverse settings, their effects on adolescents, and their implications for successful passage to adulthood.

IMPLICATIONS FOR POLICY

Adolescence and the transition to adulthood are highly formative phases of the life course; the values, self-concepts and identities, and behavioral patterns that develop at this time have lasting consequences. As one young woman commented: "I feel like you sort of become sort of the person you are, while you're a teenager. Not that everything is set in stone from that point, but...I feel like the core of who I am is pretty much the same...since high school." Choices and commitments are made at this time that launch youth onto more or less rewarding, beneficial, and health-promoting trajectories—in higher education, family life, and work. How can adults help youth to make this momentous transition?

As the transition to adulthood is elongated, the need for serious consideration of future work is effectively postponed. For most high school students, work is a distant prospect. When we asked an attorney in her twenties whether she had ever thought about working after high school, she replied: "No, for me it was just automatic college. So, no matter what we did or no matter what I wanted to do, college was just like an extension of high school. It wasn't like a choice at all." Similarly, an accountant reported: "In high school, I guess I did think about things, but I didn't think real far out. It was more like, geez, what do you want to major in in college?" Expectations and institutional supports for continuing education (scholarships and loans, night classes, employer-paid certification or degree programs) foster more lengthy postsecondary schooling.

Some of our young adult interviewees indicated that they were less motivated when they got to college because of the lack of clear connection between their education and future work prospects. For example, a young woman who had dropped out of college and then returned told us:

> I went to school two and a half years and then I stopped going to school because I knew I didn't want to do accounting, but did not know what I wanted to do, so I basically had all of my generals and all of my electives done and didn't want a degree in something that I didn't want to do...I didn't do so well in school. And part of that was because I didn't know what I wanted to do, so therefore I didn't really feel like certain classes I was in were worth my time.

Even in their mid-twenties, many young people have not yet settled on an area of work that might constitute a career. As one young woman who had completed high school and was attending "night school" put it,

> I feel as if everything interests me. I start taking a class and it interests me and I'm like, well, maybe I'll do that...For example, my first class was Intro to Psychology, which I took because I enjoyed psychology classes in high school,

so I thought, well, maybe I'll do something in that field, maybe being a counselor, maybe not being an actual psychiatrist, because that would require me going to school for the rest of my life...Then I took an English Comp class because I always enjoyed English, and I was like, well, maybe I'll do something in the English field, or in writing, or something like that. So I feel in a way as if I'm still in high school because I don't know really what I want to do when I grow up.

Another, who had a B.A. but at the time of the interview was pursuing two additional B.A.'s in other subjects, said: "Everything looks good. It's like the kid in a candy store type attitude. I have never been particularly focused on one thing...I've never been very good at picking one thing out and following it. So afraid of not liking what I pick and then getting stuck."

Even with a B.A. in hand, there may be difficulty establishing oneself in careerlike employment without a clear occupational direction. When asked "What did you think you'd do once you left college?" a female graduate student replied:

> I don't think I had a concrete idea of—I mean I knew I would work, I knew I would live on my own and support myself, but I didn't have—I didn't have an idea of what—what that was going to be. And then when I graduated, I couldn't find a full-time job, so I worked several part-time jobs for the first year, year and a half...it was a really hard time for me because I was really looking for full-time employment, and even though I had my undergraduate degree, it took me a college year, year and a half, to find a full-time job.

A central conclusion from the YDS is that more limited investment in work during high school has more beneficial educational consequences. Those who guide teenagers—teachers, counselors, parents—should be aware of the benefits of multifaceted patterns of time use and lifestyles. The well-rounded adolescent has been found to achieve the highest educational credentials and to postpone full-time work and parenthood.

Of course, most teenagers who work are employed in the labor market, not in school-supervised programs, such as internships, job shadowing, or other "school-to-work" initiatives. Not surprisingly, research has demonstrated that school-supervised work is of higher quality than other work.

Employers should be encouraged to join schools in cooperative program. Such early encounters in the workplace pave the way for more intensive service learning and unpaid internships and for cooperative learning programs and paid internships. Through these experiences, young people move from tentative and short-term involvements to greater investment and commitment; from initial exploration, to gaining personal and social competence as they perform routine tasks, to greater technical competence as they learn to plan, perform, and evaluate more complex job tasks. After high school, some youth move on to college with a greater sense of career direction thanks to their work-based learning. Others continue work-based learning in the form of longer-term apprenticeships leading to certification.

Because programs such as these require considerable commitment of staff and time on the part of both schools and employers, they are difficult to initiate and sustain. Most young people participate in the naturally occurring labor market, without such institutional connections between school and work.

Teachers, counselors, and parents should be aware of the benefits of holding different kinds of jobs, and of moving from those involving simple tasks and limited experiences to those involving more learning-rich environments and possibilities for career exploration. They should help young people to formulate more specific visions of their occupational futures. It is important that these programs not be construed as deflecting youth from college or as constraining their opportunities, but instead as expanding their options.

Educators may not be taking full advantage of the fact that most students do participate in the labor market at least some time during high school. This provides an opportunity to demonstrate the relevance of schooling to "real life." We asked the seniors, "In class discussions at school, do the students ever talk about their jobs or get ideas about how to do their jobs better?" Only half responded affirmatively. Only 17 percent agreed that "I contribute more to class discussions because of what I learn at work." Still, 54 percent agreed that "My job has taught me the importance of getting a good education." Employed students recognize the connections between school and work, and they may therefore be responsive to teachers' efforts to better integrate these aspects of their lives.

Youth should be encouraged to talk about their work experiences in class or write about them in term papers and other assignments. Teachers can then help them to become aware of the kinds of opportunities, problems, and constraints in their jobs that are generalizable to other workplace settings, and encourage them to think about the kind of employment they would like to have in the future and the credentials they would need to obtain it. Through class discussions, reflection, and writing, youth can learn about the broader moral, social, and even political implications of their observations and volunteer experiences. It is these reflections and messages that have the strongest impact on their development.

Similarly, experiences in babysitting, yard-work, and fast-food jobs, as well as in clerical employment and manual labor, may have lessons to teach that are not immediately evident to teenage workers. Encouraging youth to exchange information about their jobs in school could also increase their awareness of new opportunities in the labor market, fostering productive exploration of vocational goals.

At the least, educators, parents, and others entrusted with the care of youth are urged to be more sensitive to teenagers' work experiences—the amount of time they work, their learning opportunities, their exposure to stress, and the compatibility of their work with other activities constructed for the purpose of educating youth and guiding them to adulthood. The YDS reveals that most employed adolescents find combining work and school to be stressful. Greater awareness of such stress could lead to changes, in both paid work and school settings, to foster greater compatibility between them.

Surely the goal is not to encourage young people to make firm and lasting occupational commitments while they are still in high school. Still, teenage work can have lasting consequences. Three YDS interviewees noted explicit connections between their adolescent and early adult jobs. A young man who was working as a care manager for adults with disabilities said: "In high school, when I was just a lifeguard, I would lifeguard for a...program for adults with disabilities, so I started working with people with disabilities in tenth grade and I've done that ever since." A photographer recalled her high school job in a photo shop: "It helped me learn a lot more about photography and printing on a basic level. I learned about overexposure and underexposure. I learned what the different film speeds did. I learned a lot more about customer service. I learned how to work the printing machine. I learned what was up in the film developing machine and stuff like that, so I learned a little bit more of the technical stuff." A police officer told us:

> When I was seventeen in high school, I went on a ride-along...and I liked it, liked what I saw, good exposure to different types of things, and it was pretty much the day that I decided that this was what I wanted to do and carried on from there...I became a community service officer here in this department...I applied for it as a part-time position...work on the streets also to help out the cops and more of your minor calls, your animal complaints, your parking complaints, to help out on accidents, that kind of a thing, so I did that for three years while I was going to school and that gave the good final exposure that I needed to really determine if this is what I wanted to do.

More typically, employment during high school helps to indicate congenial, or uncongenial, vocational directions, thus promoting exploration. A young woman looked back on her high school jobs in retail sales and fast food: "I realized then that I really liked to be around people. I think that was probably the first thing, is that I would not be happy working at a desk job where I'm not ever around anybody else." An accountant commented on his early job in a fast-food outlet: "It gave me my first real experience with how a business works, paperwork, inventory, accounting-wise...It kind of helped me have an idea, when I was trying to decide later, what I wanted to do, types of careers. When I saw the paperwork that the store had to do in the accounting, just the minimal stuff that had to be done in there, it was one of the things that gave me an inclination toward doing what I do now."

It is likely that today's young people would benefit from more serious early engagement with their occupational futures. For occupational choice is not a one-time decision but rather a process of exploration and discovery. As a social worker told us:

> Probably all of my jobs that I've had have really pushed me toward social work, even in a round-about way. I mean even working at the drug store really involved me in working with people...trying to help someone find what they want in a drug store, which is, even as dull as that sounds, sort of helping people, sort of moves in the direction of helping people get what they need, which is what I think...social work is about.

The recommendations set forth here are built on the premise that this exploratory process is likely to be more successful if it begins at a time when young people are still under the auspices of "protected" institutions, and when the best opportunity to pursue higher education—before the onset of parental and other adultlike responsibilities—still lies before, not behind, them.

Working has clearly become an integral part of growing up in America. The large service sector of our economy benefits much from the flexibility in young people's hours of work. Parents are enthusiastic about their children's employment and about their own early jobs, and teenagers want paid work that enables them to try out future "possible selves." Thus it is unlikely that employment of adolescents will be restricted in the future, either by law or because of employers', parents', or teenagers' preferences. Given that youthwork is probably here to stay, let us build on its potentials and help parents, educators, and teenagers themselves to identify, and thereby avoid, the more deleterious patterns and conditions of paid work. Doing so will enable adolescents to be more effectively incorporated, as well as protected, as they make their initial forays into the adult world.

DISCUSSION QUESTIONS

1. According to Mortimer, what place does work have in adolescents' preparedness for their futures? What place did work play in your own adolescence? How has work prepared you or left you ill-prepared for "adulthood"?
2. When is a person considered an adult? How does one (or how do others) know that one is an adult?
3. As an adolescent, what attitudes and values did you learn from your parents or caregivers about work? In what ways did they socialize you to have particular ideas about work? After you held your first job, did you acquire any other ideas about working?

ADDITIONAL RESOURCES

Film
"Waging a Living." A PBS "Point of View" film about the "working poor" originally broadcast in 2006.

Internet
http://www.soc.umn.edu/research/lcc/pubpaper.html. A website providing a brief background on the YDS and a list of its many publications and papers.

http://www.pbs.org/pov/pov2006/wagingaliving/index.html. The interactive website for the "Point of View" film "Waging a Living."

FURTHER READING

Lutfey, Karen and Jeylan T. Mortimer. 2003. "Development and Socialization through the Adult Life Course," in John DeLamater (ed.). *Handbook of Social Psychology*, 183–202. New York: Kluwer Academic/Plenum Publishers.

Mortimer, Jeylan T. and Jeremy Staff. Forthcoming. "The Transition from School to Work," in *Encyclopedia of the Life Course and Human Development*. Farmington Hills, MI: Gale Cengage.

Staff, Jeremy, Emily E. Messersmith, and John E. Schulenberg. Forthcoming. "Adolescents and the World of Work," in Richard Lerner and Laurence Steinberg (eds.). *Handbook of Adolescent Psychology*. New York: John Wiley and Sons.

Mortimer, Jeylan T. 2003. *Working and Growing Up in America*. Cambridge, MA: Harvard University Press.

Symbolic Communication and Language

These next selections show how language both shapes and reflects culture. Anthropologists Edward Sapir (1929) and Benjamin Whorf (1956) hypothesized years ago that much is to be learned about a society's values and beliefs by exploring its spoken language system. They believed that language not only reflects social values but also socializes people to have the very interests and values reflected in that language system. For example, the Japanese language reflects the hierarchical nature and deference relations between groups, while Eskimos have many words to reflect the different forms and textures of snow. This theory, known as the Sapir-Whorf hypothesis, became widely known and cited and is still commonly taught today.

The selections we have chosen for this section convey the social nature and power of symbolic communication and language. Davis' article about severely neglected, confined children illustrates the profound social aspects of language acquisition. O'Barr's piece provides insight into power differences in verbal and nonverbal communication.

As you read these selections, see what insights you glean about the taken-for-granted assumptions and power relations embedded in your own culture. Also reflect on whether Davis and O'Barr's work challenges or supports the Sapir-Whorf hypothesis.

REFERENCES

Sapir, Edward. 1929. "The Status of Linguistics as a Science." *Language*, 5: 207–14.

Whorf, Benjamin. 1956. "The Name of the Situation as Affecting Behavior," in *Language Thought and Reality*, 135–7. Cambridge, MA: MIT Press.

10. Final Note on a Case of Extreme Isolation

KINGSLEY DAVIS

In this classic article, Davis presents two cases of confined and severely neglected American children who have remarkable similarities. When both girls were discovered at age 6, neither of them had developed spoken English-language skills. Davis compares and contrasts their remarkable language acquisition and other changes once their social isolation came to an end.

Early in 1940 there appeared in this *journal* an account of a girl called Anna. She had been deprived of normal contact and had received a minimum of human care for almost the whole of her first six years of life. At that time observations were not complete and the report had a tentative character. Now, however, the girl is dead, and, with more information available, it is possible to give a fuller and more definitive description of the case from a sociological point of view.

Anna's death, caused by hemorrhagic jaundice, occurred on August 6, 1942. Having been born on March 1 or 6, 1932, she was approximately ten and a half years of age when she died. The previous report covered her development up to the age of almost eight years; the present one recapitulates the earlier period on the basis of new evidence and then covers the last two and a half years of her life.

EARLY HISTORY

The first few days and weeks of Anna's life were complicated by frequent changes of domicile.

It will be recalled that she was an illegitimate child, the second such child born to her mother, and that her grandfather, a widowed farmer in whose house her mother lived, strongly disapproved of this new evidence of the mother's indiscretion. This fact led to the baby's being shifted about.

Two weeks after being born in a nurse's private home, Anna was brought to the family farm, but the grandfather's antagonism was so great that she was shortly taken to the house of one of her mother's friends. At this time a local minister became interested in her and took her to his house with an idea of possible adoption. He decided against adoption, however, when he discovered that she had vaginitis. The infant was then taken to a children's home in the nearest large city. This agency found that at the age of only three weeks she was already in a miserable condition, being "terribly galled and otherwise in very bad shape." It did not regard her as a likely subject for adoption but took her in for a while anyway, hoping to benefit her. After Anna

Davis, Kingsley. 1947. "Final Note on a Case of Extreme Isolation." *American Journal of Sociology*, 52(5): 432–7.

had spent nearly eight weeks in this place, the agency notified her mother to come to get her. The mother responded by sending a man and his wife to the children's home with a view to their adopting Anna, but they made such a poor impression on the agency that permission was refused. Later the mother came herself and took the child out of the home and then gave her to this couple. It was in the home of this pair that a social worker found the girl a short time thereafter. The social worker went to the mother's home and pleaded with Anna's grandfather to allow the mother to bring the child home. In spite of threats, he refused. The child, by then more than four months old, was next taken to another children's home in a near-by town. A medical examination at this time revealed that she had impetigo, vaginitis, umbilical hernia, and a skin rash.

Anna remained in this second children's home for nearly three weeks, at the end of which time she was transferred to a private foster-home. Since, however, the grandfather would not, and the mother could not, pay for the child's care, she was finally taken back as a last resort to the grandfather's house (at the age of five and a half months). There she remained, kept on the second floor in an attic-like room because her mother hesitated to incur the grandfather's wrath by bringing her downstairs.

Ordinarily, it seems, Anna received only enough care to keep her barely alive. She appears to have been seldom moved from one position to another. Her clothing and bedding were filthy. She apparently had no instruction, no friendly attention.

It is little wonder that, when finally found and removed from the room in the grandfather's house at the age of nearly six years, the child could not talk, walk, or do anything that showed intelligence. She was in an extremely emaciated and undernourished condition, with skeleton-like legs and a bloated abdomen. She had been fed on virtually nothing except cow's milk during the years under her mother's care.

LATER HISTORY

In 1939, nearly two years after being discovered, Anna had progressed, as previously reported, to the point where she could walk, understand simple commands, feed herself, achieve some neatness, remember people, etc. But she still did not speak, and, though she was much more like a normal infant of something over one year of age in mentality, she was far from normal for her age.

On August 30, 1939, she was taken to a private home for retarded children, leaving the county home where she had been for more than a year and a half. In her new setting she made some further progress, but not a great deal. In a report of an examination made November 6 of the same year, the head of the institution pictured the child as follows:

> Anna walks about aimlessly, makes periodic rhythmic motions of her hands, and, at intervals, makes guttural and sucking noises. She regards her hands as if she had seen them for the first time. It was impossible to hold her attention for more than a few seconds at a time—not because of distraction due to external stimuli but because of her inability to concentrate. She ignored the task in hand to gaze vacantly about the room. Speech is entirely lacking. Numerous unsuccessful attempts have been made with her in the hope of developing initial sounds. I do not believe that this failure is due to negativism or deafness but that she is not sufficiently developed to accept speech at this time.... The prognosis is not favorable....

More than five months later, on April 25, 1940, a clinical psychologist, the late Professor Francis N. Maxfield, examined Anna and reported the following: large for her age; hearing "entirely normal"; vision apparently normal; able to climb stairs; speech in the "babbling stage" and "promise for developing intelligible speech later seems to be good." He said further that "on the Merrill-Palmer scale she made a mental score of 19 months. On the Vineland social maturity scale she made a score of 23 months."

The school for retarded children, on July 1, 1941, reported that Anna had reached 46 inches in height and weighed 60 pounds. She could bounce and catch a ball and was said to conform to group socialization, though as a follower rather than a leader. Toilet habits were firmly established. Food habits were normal, except that she still used a spoon as her sole implement. She could dress herself except for fastening her clothes. Most remarkable of all, she had finally begun to develop speech. She was characterized as being at about the two-year level in this regard. She could call attendants by name and bring in one when she was asked to. She had a few complete sentences to express her wants. The report concluded that there was nothing peculiar about her.

A final report from the school, made on June 22, 1942, and evidently the last report before the girl's death, pictured only a slight advance over that given above. It said that Anna could follow directions, string beads, identify a few colors, build with blocks, and differentiate between attractive and unattractive pictures. She had a good sense of rhythm and loved a doll. She talked mainly in phrases but would repeat words and try to carry on a conversation. She was clean about clothing. She habitually washed her hands and brushed her teeth. She would try to help other children. She walked well and could run fairly well, though clumsily. Although easily excited, she had a pleasant disposition.

INTERPRETATION

Such was Anna's condition just before her death. It may seem as if she had not made much progress, but one must remember the condition in which she had been found. One must recall that she had no glimmering of speech, absolutely no ability to walk, no sense of gesture, not the least capacity to feed herself even when the food was put in front of her, and no comprehension of cleanliness. She was so apathetic that it was hard to tell whether or not she could hear. And all this at the age of nearly six years. Compared with this condition, her capacities at the time of her death seem striking

indeed, though they do not amount to much more than a two-and-a-half-year mental level. One conclusion therefore seems safe, namely, that her isolation prevented a considerable amount of mental development that was undoubtedly part of her capacity. Just what her original capacity was, of course, is hard to say; but her development after her period of confinement (including the ability to walk and run, to play, dress, fit into a social situation, and, above all, to speak) shows that she had at least this much capacity—capacity that never could have been realized in her original condition of isolation.

A further question is this: What would she have been like if she had received a normal upbringing from the moment of birth? A definitive answer would have been impossible in any case, but even an approximate answer is made difficult by her early death. If one assumes, as was tentatively surmised in the previous report, that it is "almost impossible for any child to learn to speak, think, and act like a normal person after a long period of early isolation," it seems likely that Anna might have had a normal or near-normal capacity, genetically speaking.

COMPARISON WITH ANOTHER CASE

Perhaps more to the point than speculations about Anna's ancestry would be a case for comparison. If a child could be discovered who had been isolated about the same length of time as Anna but had achieved a much quicker recovery and a greater mental development, it would be a stronger indication that Anna was deficient to start with.

Such a case does exist. It is the case of a girl found at about the same time as Anna and under strikingly similar circumstances.

Born apparently one month later than Anna, the girl in question, who has been given the pseudonym Isabelle, was discovered in November, 1938, nine months after the discovery of Anna. At the time she was found she was approximately six and a half years of age. Like Anna, she was an illegitimate child and had been kept in seclusion for that reason. Her mother was a deaf-mute, having become so at the age of two, and it appears that she and Isabelle had spent most of their time together in a dark room shut off from the rest of the mother's family. As a result Isabelle had no chance to develop speech; when she communicated with her mother, it was by means of gestures. Lack of sunshine and inadequacy of diet had caused Isabelle to become rachitic. Her legs in particular were affected. Her behavior toward strangers, especially men, was almost that of a wild animal, manifesting much fear and hostility. In lieu of speech she made only a strange croaking sound. In many ways she acted like an infant. At first it was even hard to tell whether or not she could hear, so unused were her senses. Many of her actions resembled those of deaf children.

It is small wonder that, once it was established that she could hear, specialists working with her believed her to be feeble minded. Even on nonverbal tests her performance was so low as to promise little for the future. Her first score on the Stanford-Binet was 19 months, practically at the zero point of the scale. On the Vineland social maturity scale her first score was 39, representing an age level of two and a half years.

In spite of this interpretation, the individuals in charge of Isabelle launched a systematic and skilful program of training. It seemed hopeless at first. The approach had to be through pantomime and dramatization, suitable to an infant. It required one week of intensive effort before she even made her first attempt at vocalization. Gradually she began to respond, however, and, after the first hurdles had at last been overcome, a curious thing happened. She went through the usual stages of learning characteristic of the years from one to six not only in proper succession but far more rapidly than normal. In a little over two months after her first vocalization she was putting sentences together. Nine months after that she could identify words and sentences on the printed page, could write well, could add to ten, and could retell a story after hearing it. Seven months beyond this point she had a vocabulary of 1,500–2,000 words and was asking complicated

questions. Starting from an educational level of between one and three years, she had reached a normal level by the time she was eight and a half years old. In short, she covered in two years the stages of learning that ordinarily require six. The speed with which she reached the normal level of mental development seems analogous to the recovery of body weight in a growing child after an illness, the recovery being achieved by an extra fast rate of growth for a period after the illness until normal weight for the given age is again attained.

When the writer saw Isabelle a year and a half after her discovery, she gave him the impression of being a very bright, cheerful, energetic little girl. She spoke well, walked and ran without trouble, and sang with gusto and accuracy. Today she is over fourteen years old and has passed the sixth grade in a public school. Her teachers say that she participates in all school activities as normally as other children. Though older than her classmates, she has fortunately not physically matured too far beyond their level.

Clearly the history of Isabelle's development is different from that of Anna's. In both cases there was an exceedingly low, or rather blank, intellectual level to begin with. In both cases it seemed that the girl might be congenitally feeble minded. In both a considerably higher level was reached later on. But the Ohio girl achieved a normal mentality within two years, whereas Anna was still marked inadequate at the end of four and a half years. This difference in achievement may suggest that Anna had less initial capacity. But an alternative hypothesis is possible.

One should remember that Anna never received the prolonged and expert attention that Isabelle received. The result of such attention, in the case of the Ohio girl, was to give her speech at an early stage, and her subsequent rapid development seems to have been a consequence of that. Had Anna, who, from the standpoint of psychometric tests and early history, closely resembled this girl at the start, been given a mastery of speech at an earlier point by intensive training, her subsequent development might have been much more rapid.

The hypothesis that Anna began with a sharply inferior mental capacity is therefore not established. Even if she were deficient to start with, we have no way of knowing how much so. Under ordinary conditions she might have been a dull normal or, like her mother, a moron. Even after the blight of her isolation, if she had lived to maturity, she might have finally reached virtually the full level of her capacity, whatever it may have been. That her isolation did have a profound effect upon her mentality, there can be no doubt. This is proved by the substantial degree of change during the four and a half years following her rescue.

Consideration of Isabelle's case serves to show, as Anna's case does not clearly show, that isolation up to the age of six, with failure to acquire any form of speech and hence failure to grasp nearly the whole world of cultural meaning, does not preclude the subsequent acquisition of these. Indeed, there seems to be a process of accelerated recovery in which the child goes through the mental stages at a more rapid rate than would be the case in normal development. Just what would be the maximum age at which a person could remain isolated and still retain the capacity for full cultural acquisition is hard to say. Almost certainly it would not be as high as age fifteen; it might possibly be as low as age ten. Undoubtedly various individuals would differ considerably as to the exact age.

Anna's is not an ideal case for showing the effects of extreme isolation, partly because she was possibly deficient to begin with, partly because she did not receive the best training available, and partly because she did not live long enough. Nevertheless, her case is instructive when placed in the record with numerous other cases of extreme isolation.

DISCUSSION QUESTIONS

1. What do you think Anna or Isabella's life would have been like if they were not isolated in their early years? Would they have had typical language and other social skills? Do you think their overall physical health and well-being would have been different?

2. When they were first "discovered," Anna and Isabella both displayed symbolic communication skills that were relevant only to their own social worlds. What elements of symbolic communication, such as gestures, nicknames, inside jokes, songs, etc., are meaningful only to your own social networks?

3. Why did Isabella reach more language capacity than Anna? Is it because of an inherent difference in their intelligence or because of differences in their socialization before and after their "discovery"?

ADDITIONAL RESOURCES

Film

"Secret of the Wild Child." A PBS "Nova" program about Genie, a severely neglected child who was discovered in 1970 after 10 years of being locked away from social contact. This program originally aired in 1994: http://www.pbs.org/wgbh/nova/teachers/programs/2112_wildchild.html.

Internet

http://www.youtube.com/watch?v=iptOpjzomwg&NR=1. A three-part video featuring news stories about Genie, a severely neglected child who was discovered in 1970 after 10 years of being locked away from social contact.

http://www.youtube.com/watch? v=WBahDmCG3Bo&feature=related. A video featuring Oxana Malaya, a Ukrainian girl who was severely neglected by her parents and lived among dogs for the first 8 years of her life.

FURTHER READING

Curtiss, Susan. 1977. *Genie: A Psycholinguistic Study of a Modern Day "Wild Child."* New York: Academic Press.

Davis, Kingsley. 1940. "Extreme Social Isolation of a Child." *American Journal of Sociology*, 45(4): 554–65.

Mason, Marie K. 1942. "Learning to Speak After Six and One-Half Years of Silence." *Journal of Speech Disorders*, 7: 295–304.

Sapir, Edward. 1929. "The Status of Linguistics as a Science." *Language*, 5: 207–14.

Scovel, Thomas. 1988. *A Time to Speak: A Psycholinguistic Inquiry into the Critical Period for Human Speech.* East Windsor, CT: Wadsworth Press.

Whorf, Benjamin. 1956. "The Name of the Situation as Affecting Behavior." *Language Thought and Reality*, 135–7. Cambridge, MA: MIT Press.

11. Language and Patriarchy

WILLIAM M. O'BARR

O'Barr presents fascinating research findings about disempowered versus empowered speech patterns. His research on court testimony illustrates the impact speech delivery has on the perceived credibility of the speaker. The implications of his research extend further than gender differences in language to those of race, social class, and beyond.

SOCIOLINGUISTICS

Sociolinguistics is the academic field that investigates language variation that is socially conditioned. For example, there are two ways that the words *either* and *aunt* are pronounced in the United States. Their pronunciation provides important clues as to the social background of the speakers—that they may come from a particular region of the country, that they are more upper class or more educated than those who pronounce them differently, or vice versa. We may even find if we listen carefully that some individuals pronounce these words both ways, but which pronunciation they use on any specific occasion depends on the social context. These language variations are sociolinguistic variations. In other words, these differences in language reflect social distinctions.

LANGUAGE AND GENDER

Since the emergence of the field of sociolinguistics in the 1970s, considerable attention has been devoted to the study of gender differences in

O'Barr, William M. 2001. "Language and Patriarchy," in Dana Vannoy (ed.). *Gender Mosaics: Social Perspectives*, 106–13. Roxbury (Los Angeles, CA): Roxbury Publishing Company.

language. It took the work of the linguist Robin Lakoff to call direct attention to the possibility that speech variation follows gender lines along many specific dimensions. In *Language and Woman's Place* (1975), she proposed several characteristics that described—at that time in America—the way women spoke.

1. *Hedges:* It's sort of hot in here; I'd kind of like to go; I guess...; It seems like...

2. *Super polite forms:* I'd really appreciate it if...; Would you please open the door, if you don't mind?

3. *Tag questions:* John is here, isn't he? (Instead of, is John here?)

4. *Speaking emphatically as if in italics:* He's so wonderful; It's *very* difficult.

5. *Empty adjectives:* Divine, charming, cute, sweet, adorable, lovely, and others like them.

6. *Hypercorrect grammar and careful enunciation:* Comply with the instructions at the earliest opportunity (instead of, Do it now).

7. *Lack of a sense of humor:* Inability to tell a joke; frequently "missing the point" in jokes told by men.

8. *Direct quotations:* (instead of paraphrases).

9. *Special lexicon:* Magenta and chartreuse (instead of reddish purple and yellowish green).

10. *Question intonation in declarative contexts:* In response to question, "When will dinner be ready?" "Around six o'clock?" as though seeking approval and asking whether that time will be acceptable.

Since Lakoff first brought the gendered nature of language differences squarely into view, many other researchers have studied differences between the speech of women and that of men. It is important to understand how researchers have come to understand the nature and origins of gendered differences in language use. First, they are careful not to *essentialize* these differences, to make them irrevocably associated with being male or female. That is, they make it clear that not every male and not every female speaks in a particular way. Rather, these are tendencies that apply in a general way to men as distinct from women. Second, they emphasize the learned nature of gendered language. It is language socialization, not biology, that gives rise to the differences between male and female patterns in language.

Some researchers, myself included, have decided that naming the patterns first and then linking them to social structure is a better approach. For example, understanding hedging in language (one of the characteristics Lakoff attributed to women) would be the first task. Asking whether there are socially patterned differences (as opposed to, say, the personal, idiosyncratic habits of individuals) in the degree to which people hedge is a second step. In this way, any tendency to essentialize is avoided and focus is placed instead on how a particular linguistic practice may be distributed socially.

WHAT KIND OF DIFFERENCE DO LANGUAGE DIFFERENCES MAKE?

It is well and good, indeed quite interesting to many people, to learn about differences in language use that operate along lines of gender. But do these differences have any real consequences? For example, do they help perpetuate differences between men and women with regard to power, influence, and income? Evidence from studies of language in the arena of law gives provocative answers.

Studies of language and law owe much to the development of sociolinguistics. Paralleling the interest in language variation related to class, race, and gender are studies of contextual variation in language—formal versus informal, school versus home, and particular institutions such as courts, hospitals, and business. The language used in legal documents differs markedly from ordinary English, as anyone who has tried to read a deed, contract, or statute knows. The spoken language used in legal contexts (lawyers' offices, courtrooms, mediation sessions, etc.) is also different, especially in its formality and rules of communication.

POWERLESS LANGUAGE

How might gendered language be related to what occurs in legal contexts? In court, for example, would it make any difference if men and women talked differently from the way they do? I set out in the 1970s to answer this question by putting together a team of researchers (linguists, anthropologists, psychologists, and lawyers) to investigate gendered differences in courtroom language. We began by asking whether the kinds of things Lakoff had noted in women's language also occur in court. In careful and repeated listening to trials we had tape recorded, we found that many of the characteristics Lakoff had noted do indeed occur in court, but they did not characterize the speech of all women, nor were they limited to women.

We reformulated the phenomenon and called it *powerless language* to describe its deferential nature. These are its characteristics in courts of law:

1. *Abundant use of hedges:* Prefatory remarks such as "I think..." and "It seems like..."; appended remarks such as "you know"; and modifiers such as "kind of" and "sort of."
2. *Hesitation forms:* Words and phrases that carry no substantive meaning but only fill possible speech pauses such as "uh, um," or "well."
3. *Overuse of polite forms:* For example, "sir" and "please."
4. *Question intonation in declarative contexts:* Such use conveys uncertainty, as in, "Q: How fast was the car going?" and the reply, "A: Thirty-five?"
5. *Frequent use of intensifiers:* Words such as "very," "definitely," or "surely" that, although they normally increase the force of an assertion, may be so overused that they suggest that the speaker is not to be taken seriously.

Next we located powerless language socially. It was indeed more often found among women than men but also more often among people of all sorts who were in relatively powerless social situations such as being poorly educated or occupying low-status jobs. We concluded that powerless, deferential language is related to gender because women tend to occupy relatively powerless positions in society, not because of their biology or some essential characteristic of women.

A third phase of our research examined powerless language in courtroom simulations. We wanted to know whether legal decision makers (that is, juries and judges) respond to powerless and powerful language differently. We suspected for several reasons that they might. We were also mindful of the truism often stated in our society that how something is said may matter as much as what is said. We wanted to know the degree to which linguistic form mattered in the courtroom and if such differences were related to how people fare in court.

To understand our approach, imagine this model of a court trial: Many people, perhaps 10 or more, give their versions of what happened. At the end of the trial, the judge charges the jury to decide the case and, in doing so, to decide how much credibility to accord to each witness. Since the overlapping stories may be contradictory, the jury must decide which ones to believe more than others. We wanted to know whether the linguistic style in which testimony is presented is related to credibility.

Following the conventions of experimental social psychology, we conducted controlled experiments in which the same factual information was presented in a powerless or powerful style. We did this for both male and female witnesses. Then we examined credibility ratings of the testimony presented in different styles. We found strong and significant differences between the credibility of powerful versus powerless versions of the same testimony.

What all this says about language and the courtroom is that *the form of presenting information can make huge differences in the way that information is evaluated and believed.* This alone is a serious flaw in the way justice is delivered in the United States. After all, one of the highest ideals of the American legal system is equality under the law. This ideal is symbolized in the figure of Justice, who stands blindfolded holding scales so as to weigh the two sides of the case impartially and to rule out extraneous prejudices. This powerful symbol, one that is known and valued widely, fails to take language into account. The figure of Justice is blindfolded, but her ears remain uncovered. Social differences in talk are left unexamined.

The problem becomes even more complicated as we remember who it is that is more likely to use powerless language; that is, powerless language is used by socially powerless people, of whom women are a prime example. Thus, powerless language and gender are connected, and the evidence is thus that women's testimony is often devalued because of its style.

Both men and women jurors reached similar conclusions about stylistically powerless testimony. Even those who speak in powerless language devalue it in others. These prejudices run deep in the social fabric. Understanding how they work helps explain some of the mechanisms whereby men and women receive different treatment by the law. And for sociolinguistics, these studies demonstrate that variations in speech styles are not mere artifacts of social life but have real consequences with regard to power, influence, and even financial well-being.

RULES AND RELATIONSHIPS

A second research project, conducted a decade later at the end of the 1980s, further illuminates the consequences of gendered language in the law. The field of linguistics refocused interest in the 1980s on the study of larger units of speech as opposed to micro-level linguistic phenomena such as style. Influenced by this theoretical shift, my research team turned its attention to *discourse*. In our case, this meant focusing on the narratives or accounts that people give as testimony in court instead of on the linguistic style of their speech. We had another reason as well that had emerged in our previous studies of language in court. Over

and over witnesses had told us that they had disliked testifying in court. The reason they usually gave was that they felt they never got a chance to tell their story.

We decided to figure out how their unrealized stories might differ from testimony given as answers to questions posed by lawyers. We turned to small-claims courts where witnesses testify without lawyers and where the rules of legal procedure are greatly relaxed. We wanted to know how people structure their narratives and just what they include when small-claims magistrates ask them why they have come to court.

We studied more than 150 trials in three states and found provocative differences in the stories small-claims litigants tell. Some witnesses stated their claims directly (e.g., "He owes me money") and gave their reasons why (e.g., "Because he violated the terms of the rental agreement"). By contrast, others made more general claims (e.g., "She's not being a good neighbor") in the context of litanies of complaints (e.g., "She plays her radio too loud"; "her leaves blow into my yard"; "her roses grew on my side of the fence"). We termed this contrast between accounts *rule-oriented* versus *relational*. In rule-oriented accounts, litigants state claims, explain the laws they consider violated, and present evidence in support of their claims. In relational accounts, the claims are stated more broadly, may have dubious connection to the law, and are often poorly supported with adequate evidence.

Rule-oriented accounts were more common for men, whereas relational accounts were more common for women. Again, these differences seemed to be products of living and working in a business world as opposed to managing domestic situations and neighborly relations. Different conventions apply in these contexts. Domesticity and neighborliness are not reducible to rules, hence, the differences in the kinds of accounts we heard in court.

Both powerless style and relational accounts are thus more characteristic of women than men. And the law devalues both. This devaluation is not overt or even recognized. Rather, the law works through the people who make it up and functions through the behaviors of judges, lawyers, and jurors. As decisions favor powerful litigants rather than powerless ones and as judges express preferences for rule-oriented over relational accounts, the law does its work. The preferences for linguistic forms more typical of men than of women reinforce the patriarchal nature of law.

POSSIBILITIES FOR CHANGE

Can these problems be solved? Are there ways for law to filter the linguistic biases so as to better reach its goal of equal treatment under the law? Unfortunately, there are no simple answers.

Speech style (like powerless language) is not something that is easily controlled by speakers. It is not a simple matter to point out aspects of powerless language to a speaker and ask her to eliminate them from her speech. If she could do so,

she might be taken more seriously and accorded more credibility in court. But language style is the product of social conditioning as well as social position and cannot be changed overnight. The best hope to fix this problem is to alter the place of powerless people in society.

Relational narratives are associated with domesticity as distinguished from public and business life. Similarly, as long as culture links domesticity and women, ways of talking will be strongly gendered. And as long as the law—through the preferences of judges for rule-oriented talk—expresses institutional preferences, then patriarchy will find expression through this linguistic form as well.

In short, one sees gender and language in the institutions of law in such ways as to reinscribe patriarchy and to disempower women. These ways are subtle and often outside the range of conscious attention, but their very subtlety enhances their power.

DISCUSSION QUESTIONS

1. Name and discuss the patterns of disempowered speech identified by Lakoff (1975) and O'Barr (2001) in this article.

2. What other disempowered groups, besides women, might use similar linguistic forms of deferential speech?

3. O'Barr discusses the impact of disempowered versus empowered speech in the social institution of law. In what other social institutions might we see similar linguistic differences? Can you give some examples of disempowered and empowered speech in the contexts of the family, school, or workplace?

4. Have you noticed patterns of disempowered and empowered speech in your own relationships? In public discourse (e.g., political speeches)? In what contexts have you noticed these differences? Can you provide some examples?

ADDITIONAL RESOURCES

Internet

http://nonverbal.ucsc.edu/. University of California Sociologist Dane Archer's website about nonverbal communication. This highly interactive site contains terrific resources about empowered and disempowered communication.

Film

"Gender and Communication: Male-Female Differences in Language and Nonverbal Behavior." 2001. Berkeley Media. A humorous and insightful video by Professor Dane Archer, who created a 12-film series on nonverbal communication produced by the University of California: http://www.berkeleymedia.com/catalog/berkeleymedia/producers/dane_archer.

FURTHER READING

Brantenberg, Gerd. 1995. *Egalia's Daughters: A Satire of the Sexes.* Berkeley, CA: Seal Press.

Henley, Nancy. 1973. "Power, Sex, and Nonverbal Communication." *Berkeley Journal of Sociology*, 18: 1–26.

Lakoff, Robin. 1975. *Language and Women's Place.* New York: Harper & Row.

O'Barr, William M. 1982. *Language, Power, and Strategy in the Courtroom.* New York: Academic Press.

Tannen, Deborah. 1990. *You Just Don't Understand: Men and Women in Conversation.* New York: Morrow.

Ridgeway, Cecilia, Joseph Berger, and Leroy Smith. 1985. "Nonverbal Cues and Status: An Expectation States Approach." *American Journal of Sociology*, 90: 955–78.

Social Perception and Cognition

These authors explore several key cognitive processes: how we form impressions of others, how we make decisions based on the ways we categorize information, and how we experience and express emotions to maximize desirable social outcomes.

The classic 1946 article by Solomon Asch is an exemplar of early research on impression formation, which fostered the development of the field known as cognitive psychology. Over the past half-century, social psychologists have come to rely on key concepts of cognitive social psychology that teach us how we simplify, order, and understand a complex social world.

Asch's work on impression formation provides a foundation for Langer and Rosenberg's research, which illuminates the cognitive processes of stereotyping and the problem of being "trapped by categories."

As you read these articles, pay attention to the ways that social perception and cognition exaggerate similarities within categories and differences between them (e.g., *all women are alike* and *women and men are so very different from one another*). By reading these pieces, you will gain insight into the relationship between our perception of someone or something and our expectations related to that person or thing.

12. Forming Impressions of Personalities

SOLOMON E. ASCH

In his study of more than 1,000 psychology undergraduate students, Solomon Asch identifies specific principles that regulate impression formation. His research helps us understand the ways we simplify and generalize highly complex and varied bits of information to make quick, rapid judgments.

We look at a person and immediately a certain impression of his character forms itself in us. A glance, a few spoken words are sufficient to tell us a story about a highly complex matter. We know that such impressions form with remarkable rapidity and with great ease. Subsequent observation may enrich or upset our first view, but we can no more prevent its rapid growth than we can avoid perceiving a given visual object or hearing a melody.

This remarkable capacity we possess to understand something of the character of another person, to form a conception of him as a human being, as a center of life and striving, with particular characteristics forming a distinct individuality, is a precondition of social life. In what manner are these impressions established? Are there lawful principles regulating their formation?

Each person confronts us with a large number of diverse characteristics. This man is courageous, intelligent, with a ready sense of humor, quick in his movements, but he is also serious, energetic, patient under stress, not to mention his politeness and punctuality. These characteristics and many others enter into the formation of our view. Yet our impression is from the start unified; it is the impression of *one* person. We ask: How do the several characteristics function together to produce an impression of one person? What principles regulate this process?

We have mentioned earlier that the impression of a person grows quickly and easily. Yet our minds falter when we face the far simpler task of mastering a series of disconnected numbers or words. And it is quite hard to forget our view of a person once it has formed. Similarly, we do not easily confuse the half of one person with the half of another.

There are a number of theoretical possibilities for describing the process of forming an impression. Yet no argument should be needed to support the statement that our view of a person necessarily involves a certain orientation to, and ordering of, objectively given, observable characteristics. It is this aspect of the problem that we propose to study.

FORMING A UNIFIED IMPRESSION: PROCEDURE

The plan followed in the experiments to be reported was to read to the subject a number of discrete characteristics, said to belong to a person, with the instruction to describe the impression he formed. The subjects were all college students, most of whom were women. They were mostly beginners in psychology. Though they expressed genuine interest in the tasks, the subjects were not aware of the nature of the problem until it was explained to them. We illustrate our procedure with one concrete

Asch, Solomon E. 1946. "Forming Impressions of Personalities." *Journal of Abnormal and Social Psychology,* 41: 258–90.

instance. The following list of terms was read: *energetic—assured—talkative—cold—ironical— inquisitive—persuasive.* The reading of the list was preceded by the following instructions:

> I shall read to you a number of characteristics that belong to a particular person. Please listen to them carefully and try to form an impression of the kind of person described. You will later be asked to give a brief characterization of the person in just a few sentences. I will read the list slowly and will repeat it once.

The list was read with an interval of approximately five seconds between the terms. When the first reading was completed, the experimenter said, "I will now read the list again," and proceeded to do so. We reproduce below a few typical sketches written by subjects after they heard the list of terms:

> He seems to be the kind of person who would make a great impression upon others at a first meeting. However, as time went by, his acquaintances would easily come to see through the mask. Underneath would be revealed his arrogance and selfishness.

> He is the type of person you meet all too often: sure of himself, talks too much, always trying to bring you around to his way of thinking, and with not much feeling for the other fellow.

All subjects in the following experiments, of whom there were over 1,000, fulfilled the task in the manner described. No one proceeded by reproducing the given list of terms, as one would in a rote memory experiment; nor did any of the subjects reply merely with synonyms of the given terms.

The procedure here employed is clearly different from the everyday situation in which we follow the concrete actions of an actual person. We have chosen to work with weak, incipient impressions, based on abbreviated descriptions of personal qualities. Nevertheless, this procedure has some merit for purposes of investigation, especially in observing the change of impressions,

and is, we hope to show, relevant to more natural judgment.

I. CENTRAL AND PERIPHERAL CHARACTERISTICS

A. Variation of a Central Quality

Observation suggests that not all qualities have the same weight in establishing the view of a person. Some are felt to be basic, others secondary. In the following experiments we sought for a demonstration of this process in the course of the formation of an impression.

Experiment I

Two groups, A and B, heard a list of character-qualities, identical save for one term. The list follows:

> **A.** intelligent–skillful–industrious–*warm*–determined–practical–cautious
> **B.** intelligent–skillful–industrious–*cold*–determined–practical–cautious

Group A heard the person described as "warm"; Group B, as "cold."

Technique

The instructions were as described above. Following the reading, each subject wrote a brief sketch.

The sketches furnish concrete evidence of the impressions formed. Their exact analysis involves, however, serious technical difficulties. It seemed, therefore, desirable to add a somewhat simpler procedure for the determination of the content of the impression and for the purpose of group comparisons. To this end we constructed a check list consisting of pairs of traits, mostly opposites. From each pair of terms in this list, which the reader will find reproduced in Table I, the subject was instructed to select the one that was most in accordance with the view he had formed.

There were 90 subjects in Group A (comprising four separate classroom groups), 76 subjects

Table I Check List I

1. generous–ungenerous	7. popular–unpopular	13. frivolous–serious
2. shrewd–wise	8. unreliable–reliable	14. restrained–talkative
3. unhappy–happy	9. important–insignificant	15. self-centered–altruistic
4. irritable–good-natured	10. ruthless–humane	16. imaginative–hard-headed
5. humorous–humorless	11. good-looking–unattractive	17. strong–weak
6. sociable–unsociable	12. persistent–unstable	18. dishonest–honest

in Group B (comprising four separate classroom groups).

Results

We note first that the characteristic "warm-cold" produces striking and consistent differences of impression. In general, the A-impressions are far more positive than the B-impressions. We cite a few representative examples:

Series A ("warm")

A person who believes certain things to be right, wants others to see his point, would be sincere in an argument and would like to see his point won.

Series B ("cold")

A very ambitious and talented person who would not let anyone or anything stand in the way of achieving his goal. Wants his own way, he is determined not to give in, no matter what happens.

This trend is fully confirmed in the check-list choices. In Table II we report the frequency (in terms of percentages) with which each term in the check list was selected. For the sake of brevity of presentation we state the results for the positive term in each pair; the reader may determine the percentage of choices for the other term in each pair by subtracting the given figure from 100.

We find:

1. There are extreme reversals between Groups A and B in the choice of fitting characteristics. Certain qualities are preponderantly assigned to the "warm" person, while the opposing qualities are equally prominent in the "cold" person. This holds for the qualities of (1) generosity, (2) shrewdness, (3) happiness, (4) irritability, (5) humor, (6) sociability, (7) popularity, (10) ruthlessness, (15) self-centeredness, (16) imaginativeness.

2. There is another group of qualities which is *not* affected by the transition from "warm" to "cold," or only slightly affected. These are: (8) reliability, (9) importance, (11) physical attractiveness, (12) persistence, (13) seriousness, (14) restraint, (17) strength, (18) honesty.

These results show that a change in one character-quality has produced a widespread change in the entire impression. Further, the written sketches show that the terms "warm-cold" did not simply add a new quality, but to some extent transformed the other characteristics. With this point we shall deal more explicitly in the experiments to follow.

That such transformations take place is also a matter of everyday experience. If a man is intelligent, this has an effect on the way in which we perceive his playfulness, happiness, friendliness. At the same time, this extensive change does not function indiscriminately. The "warm" person is not seen more favorably in all respects. There is a range of qualities, among them a number that are basic, which are not touched by the distinction between "warm" and "cold." Both remain equally honest, strong, serious, reliable, etc.

The latter result is of interest with reference to one possible interpretation of the findings. It might be supposed that the category "warm-cold" aroused a "mental set" or established a halo tending toward a consistently plus or minus

Table II Choice of Fitting Qualities (Percentages)

	Experiment I		Experiment II			Experiment III	
	"Warm"	"Cold"	Total	"Warm"	"Cold"	"Polite"	"Blunt"
	N = 90	N = 76	N = 56	N = 23	N = 33	N = 20	N = 26
1. generous	91	8	55	87	33	56	58
2. wise	65	25	49	73	33	30	50
3. happy	90	34	71	91	58	75	65
4. good-natured	94	17	69	91	55	87	56
5. humorous	77	13	36	76	12	71	48
6. sociable	91	38	71	91	55	83	68
7. popular	84	28	57	83	39	94	56
8. reliable	94	99	96	96	97	95	100
9. important	88	99	88	87	88	94	96
10. humane	86	31	64	91	45	59	77
11. good-looking	77	69	58	71	53	93	79
12. persistent	100	97	98	96	100	100	100
13. serious	100	99	96	91	100	100	100
14. restrained	77	89	82	67	94	82	77
15. altruistic	69	18	44	68	27	29	46
16. imaginative	51	19	24	45	9	33	31
17. strong	98	95	95	94	96	100	100
18. honest	98	94	95	100	92	87	100

evaluation. We observe here that this trend did not work in an indiscriminate manner, but was decisively limited at certain points.

B. Omission of a Central Quality

That the category "warm-cold" is significant for the total impression may be demonstrated also by omitting it from the series. This we do in the following experiment.

Experiment 11

The procedure was identical with that of Experiment I, except that the terms "warm" and "cold" were omitted from the list read to the subject (intelligent–skillful–industrious–determined–practical–cautious). Also the check list was identical with that of Experiment I, save that "warm-cold" was added as the last pair. There

were three groups, consisting of a total of 56 subjects.

An examination of the check-list choices of the subjects quickly revealed strong and consistent individual differences. They tended to be consistently positive or negative in their evaluations. It will be recalled that the terms "warm-cold" were added to the check list. This permitted us to subdivide the total group according to whether they judged the described person on the check list as "warm" or "cold." Of the entire group, 23 subjects (or 41%) fell into the "warm" category. Our next step was to study the distribution of choices in the two subgroups. The results are clear: the two subgroups diverge consistently in the direction of the "warm" and the "cold" groups, respectively, of Experiment I (see Table II). This is especially the case with the two "warm" series, which are virtually identical.

It is of interest that the omission of a term from the experimental list did not function entirely as an omission. Instead, the subjects inferred the corresponding quality in either the positive or negative direction. While not entirely conclusive, the results suggest that a full impression of a person cannot remain indifferent to a category as fundamental as the one in question, and that a trend is set up to include it in the impression on the basis of the given data.

C. Variation of a Peripheral Quality

Would a change of *any* character-quality produce an effect as strong as that observed above? We turn to this question in the following experiment.

Experiment III

The following lists were read, each to a different group:

> **A.** intelligent–skillful–industrious–*polite*–determined–practical–cautious
> **B.** intelligent–skillful–industrious–*blunt*–determined–practical–cautious

The A group contained 20, the B group 26 subjects.

The changes introduced into the selection of fitting characteristics in the transition from "polite" to "blunt" were far weaker than those found in Experiment I (see Table II). There is further evidence that the subjects themselves regarded these characteristics as relatively peripheral, especially the characteristic "polite." If we may take the rankings as an index, then we may conclude that a change in a peripheral trait produces a weaker effect on the total impression than does a change in a central trait.

D. Transformation from a Central to a Peripheral Quality

The preceding experiments have demonstrated a process of discrimination between central and peripheral qualities. We ask: Are certain qualities constantly central? Or is their functional value, too, dependent on the other characteristics?

Experiment IV

We selected for observation the quality "warm," which was demonstrated to exert a powerful effect on the total impression (Experiments I and II). The effect of the term was studied in the following two series:

> **A.** obedient–weak–shallow–*warm*–unambitious–vain
> **B.** vain–shrewd–unscrupulous–*warm*–shallow–envious

Immediately "warm" drops as a significant characteristic in relation to the others.

More enlightening are the subjects' comments. In Series A the quality "warm" is now seen as wholly dependent, dominated by others far more decisive.

The term "warm" strikes one as being a dog-like affection rather than a bright friendliness. It is passive and without strength.

His submissiveness may lead people to think he is kind and warm.

A more extreme transformation is observed in Series B. In most instances the warmth of this person is felt to lack sincerity, as appears in the following protocols:

I assumed the person to appear warm rather than really to be warm.

He was warm only when it worked in with his scheme to get others over to his side. His warmth is not sincere.

We conclude that a quality, central in one person, may undergo a change of content in another person, and become subsidiary. When central, the quality has a different content and weight than when it is subsidiary.

Here we observe directly a process of grouping in the course of which the content of a trait changes in relation to its surroundings. Second, we observe that the functional value of a trait, too—whether, for example, it becomes central or not—is a consequence of its relation to the set of surrounding traits. At the same time we are able to see more clearly the distinction between central and peripheral traits. It is inadequate to say that a central trait is more important, contributes more quantitatively to, or is more highly correlated with, the final impression than a peripheral trait. The latter formulations are true, but they fail to consider the qualitative process of mutual determination between traits, namely, that a central trait determines the content and the functional place of peripheral traits within the entire impression. In Series A, for example, the quality "warm" does not control the meaning of "weak," but is controlled by it.

The evidence may seem to support the conclusion that the same quality which is central in one impression becomes peripheral in another. Such an interpretation would, however, contain an ambiguity. While we may speak of relativity in the functional value of a trait within a person, in a deeper sense we have here the opposite of relativity. For the sense of "warm" (or "cold") of Experiment I has not suffered a change of evaluation under the present conditions. Quite the contrary; the terms in question change precisely because the subject does not see the possibility of finding in this person the same warmth he values so highly when he does meet it (correspondingly for coldness).

Experiment V

The preceding experiments have shown that the characteristics forming the basis of an impression do not contribute each a fixed, independent meaning, but that their content is itself partly a function of the environment of the other characteristics, of their mutual relations. We propose now to investigate more directly the manner in which the content of a given characteristic may undergo change.

Lists A and B were read to two separate groups (including 38 and 41 subjects respectively). The

Table III Synonyms of "Calm": Experiment V

	"Kind" Series	"Cruel" Series
serene	18	3
cold, frigid, icy, cool, calculating, shrewd, nervy, scheming, conscienceless	0	20
soothing, peaceful, gentle, tolerant, good-natured, mild-mannered	11 / 11	0 / 0
poised, reserved, restful, unexcitable, unshakable	18	7
deliberate, silent, unperturbed, masterful, impassive, collected, confident, relaxed, emotionless, steady, impassive, composed	11	26

first three terms of the two lists are opposites; the final two terms are identical.

A. kind–wise–honest–*calm–strong*
B. cruel–shrewd–unscrupulous–*calm–strong*

The instructions were to write down synonyms for the given terms. The instructions read: "Suppose you had to describe this person in the same manner, but without using the terms you heard, what other terms would you use?" We are concerned with the synonyms given to the two final terms.

In Table III we list those synonyms of "calm" which occurred with different frequencies in the two groups. It will be seen that terms appear in one group which are not at all to be found in the other; further, some terms appear with considerably different frequencies under the two conditions.

We may conclude that the quality "calm" did not, at least in some cases, function as an independent, fixed trait, but that its content was determined by its relation to the other terms. As a consequence, the quality "calm" was not the same under the two experimental conditions. In Series

A it possessed an aspect of gentleness, while a grimmer side became prominent in Series B.

Essentially the same may be said of the final term, "strong." Again, some synonyms appear exclusively in one or the other groups, and in the expected directions. Among these are:

SERIES A: fearless–helpful–just–forceful–courageous—reliable
SERIES B: ruthless–overbearing–overpowering–
hard–inflexible–unbending–dominant

DISCUSSION

The investigations here reported converge on one basic conclusion. In different ways the observations have demonstrated that forming an impression is an organized process; that characteristics are perceived in their dynamic relations; that central qualities are discovered, leading to the distinction between them and peripheral qualities; that relations of harmony and contradiction are observed. To know a person is to have a grasp of a particular structure.

Let us briefly reformulate the main points in the procedure of our subjects:

1. There is an attempt to form an impression of the *entire* person. The subject can see the person only as a unit; he cannot form an impression of one-half or one-quarter of the person. This is the case even when the factual basis is meager; the impression then strives to become complete, reaching out toward other compatible qualities. The subject seeks to reach the core of the person *through* the trait or traits.

2. As soon as two or more traits are understood to belong to one person, they cease to exist as isolated traits, and come into immediate dynamic interaction. The subject perceives not this *and* that quality, but the two entering a particular relation. There takes place a process of organization in the course of which the traits order themselves into a structure. It may be said that the traits lead an intensely social life, striving to join each other in a closely organized system.

3. In the course of this process some characteristics are discovered to be central. The whole system of relations determines which will become central. These set the direction for the further view of the person and for the concretization of the dependent traits. As a rule the several traits do not have equal weight. And it is not until we have found the center that we experience the assurance of having come near to an understanding of the person.

4. The single trait possesses the property of a part in a whole. A change in a single trait may alter not that aspect alone, but many others—at times all. As soon as we isolate a trait we not only lose the distinctive organization of the person; the trait itself becomes abstract. The trait develops its full content and weight only when it finds its place within the whole impression.

5. Each trait is a trait of the entire person. It refers to a characteristic form of action or attitude which belongs to the person as a whole.

6. Each trait functions as a *representative* of the person. We do not experience anonymous traits the particular organization of which constitutes the identity of the person. Rather the entire person speaks through each of his qualities, though not with the same clearness.

7. In the process of mutual interaction the concrete character of each trait is developed in accordance with the dynamic requirements set for it by its environment. There is involved an understanding of necessary consequences following from certain given characteristics for others. The envy of a proud man is, for example, seen to have a different basis from the envy of a modest man.

8. On this basis consistencies and contradictions are discovered. Certain qualities are seen to cooperate; others to negate each other. But we are not content simply to note inconsistencies or to let them sit where they are. The contradiction is puzzling, and prompts us to look more deeply. Disturbing factors arouse a trend to maintain the unity of the impression, to search for the most sensible way in which the characteristics could exist together, or to decide that we have not found the key to the person.

9. It follows that the content and functional value of a trait changes with the given context.

A trait central in one person may be seen as secondary in another. Or a quality which is now referred to the person may in another case be referred to outer conditions.

We conclude that the formation and change of impressions consist of specific processes of organization. Further, it seems probable that these processes are not specific to impressions of persons alone. It is a task for future investigation to determine whether processes of this order are at work in other important regions of psychology, such as in forming the view of a group, or of the relations between one person and another.

DISCUSSION QUESTIONS

1. Asch demonstrates the importance of first impressions. Once we form an impression of someone, we seek to uphold that impression despite evidence that may challenge our initial perception. Have you ever formed an impression that turned out to be false? What challenged or altered your initial impression? Did you seek to confirm your initial impression despite discrediting evidence, as Asch would argue?

2. Asch claims that traits are not equally valued and that we tend to search for the "center" of a person (looking for their "central traits") in forming impressions. What are examples of "central" and "peripheral" traits used to form impressions? Would traits considered "central" remain the same or vary by social situation? That is, would a person's "master status" always be race or gender, or might it change from one situation to another?

3. Based on Asch's research, do you think there are ways to make impression formation more accurate and flexible?

ADDITIONAL RESOURCES

Film
"Social Cognition." 2001. A 30-minute program exploring impression formation and the impact attitude has on behavior. Insight Media.

Internet
http://aschcenter.blogs.brynmawr.edu/about/. The website of the Solomon Asch Center for the Study of Ethnopolitical Conflict at Bryn Mawr College.

http://www.brynmawr.edu/aschcenter/asch908/about/aschbio. A website featuring a brief biography of Solomon Asch.

FURTHER READING

Katz, Daniel. 1960. "The Functional Approach to the Study of Attitudes." *The Public Opinion Quarterly*, 24(2): 163–204.

Zerubavel, Eviatar. 1996. "Lumping and Splitting: Notes on Social Classification." *Sociological Forum*, 11: 421–33.

13. When the Light's On and Nobody's Home

ELLEN J. LANGER

Langer explores how "mindlessly" we act in our daily lives. Such mindlessness is rooted in the cognitive functions of categorization and routinization. Langer calls on us to act more mindfully, illustrating several benefits of doing so.

Imagine that it's two o'clock in the morning. Your doorbell rings; you get up, startled, and make your way downstairs. You open the door and see a man standing before you. He wears two diamond rings and a fur coat, and there's a Rolls Royce behind him. He's sorry to wake you at this ridiculous hour, he tells you, but he's in the middle of a scavenger hunt. His ex-wife is in the same contest, which makes it very important to him that he win. He needs a piece of wood about three feet by seven feet. Can you help him? In order to make it worthwhile he'll give you $10,000. You believe him. He's obviously rich. And so you say to yourself, how in the world can I get this piece of wood for him? You think of the lumber yard; you don't know who owns the lumber yard; in fact you're not even sure where the lumber yard is. It would be closed at two o'clock in the morning anyway. You struggle but you can't come up with anything. Reluctantly, you tell him, "Gee, I'm sorry."

The next day, when passing a construction site near a friend's house, you see a piece of wood that's just about the right size, three feet by seven feet—a door. You could have just taken a door off its hinges and given it to him, for $10,000.

Why on earth, you say to yourself, didn't it occur to you to do that? It didn't occur to you because yesterday your door was not a piece of wood. The seven-by-three foot piece of wood was hidden from you, stuck in the category called "door."

This kind of mindlessness could be called "entrapment by category." It is one of three definitions that can help us understand the nature of mindlessness. The other two, which we will also explain, are automatic behavior and acting from a single perspective.

TRAPPED BY CATEGORIES

We experience the world by creating categories and making distinctions among them.

The creation of new categories is a mindful activity. Mindlessness sets in when we rely too rigidly on categories and distinctions created in

Langer, Ellen J. 1989. Abridged from "When the Light's On and Nobody's Home" and "Decreasing Prejudice by Increasing Discrimination," in *Mindfulness*. New York: Perseus Books.

the past (masculine/feminine, old/young, success/failure). Once distinctions are created, they take on a life of their own. The categories we make gather momentum and are very hard to overthrow. We build our own and our shared realities and then we become victims of them—blind to the fact that they are constructs, ideas.

AUTOMATIC BEHAVIOR

Have you ever said "excuse me" to a store mannequin or written a check in January with the previous year's date? When in this mode, we take in and use limited signals from the world around us (the female form, the familiar face of the check) without letting other signals (the motionless pose, a calendar) penetrate as well.

Once, in a small department store, I gave a cashier a new credit card. Noticing that I hadn't signed it, she handed it back to me to sign. Then she took my card, passed it through her machine, handed me the resulting form, and asked me to sign it. I did as I was told. The cashier then held the form next to the newly signed card to see if the signatures matched.

An experiment I conducted with fellow psychologists Benzion Chanowitz and Arthur Blank explored this kind of mindlessness.

We sent an interdepartmental memo around some university offices. The message either requested or demanded the return of the memo to a designated room—and that was all it said. ("Please return this immediately to Room 247," or "This memo is to be returned to Room 247.") Anyone who read such a memo mindfully would ask, "If whoever sent the memo wanted it, why did he or she send it?" and therefore would not return the memo. Half of the memos were designed to look exactly like those usually sent between departments. The other half were made to look in some way different. When the memo looked like those they were used to, 90 percent of the recipients actually returned it. When the memo looked different, 60 percent returned it.

When I was discussing these studies at a university colloquium, a member of the audience told me about a little con game that operated along the same lines. Someone placed an ad in a Los Angeles newspaper that read, "It's not too late to send $1 to _____," and gave the person's own name and address. The reader was promised nothing in return. Many people replied, enclosing a dollar. The person who wrote the ad apparently earned a good sum.

The automatic behavior in evidence in these examples has much in common with habit. Habit, or the tendency to keep on with behavior that has been repeated over time, naturally implies mindlessness. However, as we will see in the following chapter, mindless behavior can arise without a long history of repetition, almost instantaneously, in fact.

ACTING FROM A SINGLE PERSPECTIVE

So often in our lives, we act as though there were only one set of rules. For instance, in cooking we tend to follow recipes with dutiful precision. We add ingredients as though by official decree. If the recipe calls for a pinch of salt and four pinches fall in, panic strikes, as though the bowl might now explode. Thinking of a recipe only as a rule, we often do not consider how people's tastes vary, or what fun it might be to make up a new dish.

The first experiment I conducted in graduate school explored this problem of the single perspective. It was a pilot study to examine the effectiveness of different requests for help. A fellow investigator stood on a busy sidewalk and told people passing by that she had sprained her knee and needed help. If someone stopped she asked him or her to get an Ace bandage from the nearby drugstore. I stood inside the store and listened while the helpful person gave the request to the pharmacist, who had agreed earlier to say that he was out of Ace bandages. After being told this, not one subject, out of the twenty-five we studied, thought to ask if the pharmacist could recommend something else. People left the drugstore and returned empty-handed to the "victim" and told her the news. We speculated that had she asked for less specific help, she might have received it. But, acting on the single thought that a sprained knee needs an Ace bandage, no one tried to find other kinds of help.

As a little test of how a narrow perspective can dominate our thinking, read the following sentence:

FINAL FOLIOS SEEM TO RESULT FROM YEARS OF DUTIFUL STUDY OF TEXTS ALONG WITH YEARS OF SCIENTIFIC EXPERIENCE.

Now count how many Fs there are, reading only once more through the sentence.

If you find fewer than there actually are, your counting was probably influenced by the fact that the first two words in the sentence begin with F. In counting, your mind would tend to cling to this clue, or single perspective, and miss some of the Fs hidden within and at the end of words.

Highly specific instructions such as these or the request for an Ace bandage encourage mindlessness. Once we let them in, our minds snap shut like a clam on ice and do not let in new signals.

DECREASING PREJUDICE BY INCREASING DISCRIMINATION

Most attempts to combat prejudice have been aimed at reducing our tendency to categorize other people. These efforts are based on the view that, in an ideal world, everyone should be considered equal, falling under the single category of "human being." Yet categorizing is a fundamental and natural human activity. It is the way we come to know the world. Any attempt to eliminate bias by attempting to eliminate the perception of differences may be doomed to fail. We will not surrender our categories easily. When we cease (for whatever reason) to make any particular distinction among people, we will probably make another.

An understanding of the nature of mindfulness suggests a different approach to combating prejudice—one in which we learn to make more, rather than fewer, distinctions among people. Such

awareness prevents us from regarding a handicap as a person's identity. Instead of a "cripple" or a "diabetic" or an "epileptic," we would see a man with a lame leg, a woman with diabetes, or an adolescent with seizures. These distinctions become more useful when further refined, for example: a person with 70 percent hearing instead of a deaf person, someone with non-insulin-dependent diabetes instead of diabetes.

Because most of us grow up and spend our time with people like ourselves, we tend to assume uniformities and commonalities. When confronted with someone who is clearly different in one specific way, we drop that assumption and instead look for more differences. Often these perceived differences bear no logical relation to the observable difference. For instance, because of the unusual gestures of a person with cerebral palsy, we might assume a difference in intelligence. Such faulty assumptions tend to exaggerate the perceived gap between "deviants" and "normal people."

The very definition of *deviance* may of course be misleading in the first place. Any categorical distinction can be broken down into farther distinctions. Once we are aware of these distinctions and make enough of them, it may no longer be possible to view the world in terms of large polarized categories such as black and white, normal and disabled, gay and straight. With skin color, this difficulty is pretty obvious. But take the distinction between homosexuals and heterosexuals. These categories do not seem to overlap; there are people who prefer sexual behavior with their own sex and they are called homosexuals, and there are people who engage in sexual behavior with members of the opposite sex and they are called heterosexuals. Surely this is clear.

The bisexual who enjoys sex with both genders is the first, obvious exception to this distinction. Next, where do we put a man who prefers to fantasize about men while making love to women? Then, what about a completely celibate person; or the married transvestite; or the person who makes love with a transsexual presently of the opposite sex; or the person who was heterosexual, had one homosexual experience, and is now without a partner?

For even more obvious reasons it makes no sense to speak of physically handicapped people as a category. Describing particular activities for which a person with a particular disability might be less competent reduces the global quality of the handicap label and thus, as we said before, makes it only an aspect of that person instead of a whole identity. This mindful perspective should reduce the importance of deviance for both actor and observer, for we would soon see that we are all "handicapped." Deviance as a category relies for its definition on another category, "normal,"

with which it is mutually exclusive. To define "normal" necessitates evaluative judgments. To be a "paraplegic" or a "diabetic," or to be "too fat" or "too thin," suggests that there is one ideal way to be a human being. To be "deviant" means that one does not belong to this so-called "normal" group. In itself, the notion of deviance has no meaning.

A mindful outlook recognizes that we are all deviant from the majority with respect to some of our attributes, and also that each attribute or skill lies on a continuum. Such an awareness leads to *more* categorizing and consequently fewer global stereotypes, or, increasing discrimination can reduce prejudice.

DISCUSSION QUESTIONS

1. Langer identifies three main types of mindlessness in her article. What are they?
2. Provide examples of how these three types of mindlessness are apparent in your own thoughts, actions, or experiences.
3. Langer argues that one way to decrease prejudice is by increasing discrimination. What does she mean by this? Are there benefits, besides decreasing prejudice, to being more mindful?

ADDITIONAL RESOURCES

Film

"Hoop Dreams." 1994. A three-hour award-winning documentary directed by Steve James about racial and class divisions in high school basketball.

"Wide Eyed." 2008. The most recent of antiracism educator Jane Elliot's "blue eyes, brown eyes" 12 documentaries. This 57-minute film is a compilation of excerpts from Elliot's previous documentaries, including "Eye of the Storm" and "A Class Divided."

Internet

http://www.documentaryfilms.net/index.php/hoop-dreams/. A documentary film website with a synopsis of "Hoop Dreams."

http://www.janeelliott.com/. The website for renowned educator Jane Elliot, featuring her "blue eyes, brown eyes exercise."

FURTHER READING

Langer, Ellen J. 1989. *Mindfulness*. New York: Perseus Books.

Snyder, Mark, Elizabeth D. Tanke, and Ellen Berscheid. 1977. "Social Perception and Interpersonal Behavior: On the Self-Fulfilling Nature of Social Stereotypes." *Journal of Personality and Social Psychology*, 35(9): September, 656–66.

Zerubavel, Eviatar. 1993. *The Fine Line: Making Distinctions in Everyday Life*. Chicago: University of Chicago Press.

14. Self-Processes and Emotional Experiences

MORRIS ROSENBERG

Rosenberg contends that emotions are central to social interaction and social structure. His work highlights the vast cultural differences in emotional norms as well as the ways cognitive schema influence our attempts to derive pleasure rather than pain from our emotions.

In recent years, there has been a veritable explosion of interest in the emotions among social scientists. Sociocultural processes have been shown to play a major role in the formation and expression of the emotions.

IMPORTANCE OF EMOTIONAL SELF-REGULATION

There are at least three major reasons why emotions are important to individuals. Emotions can enable people to get what they want out to life (instrumental), emotions can be pleasurable (hedonic), and some emotions are socially appropriate (normative).

Instrumental Reasons

The regulation of emotional *intensity* has instrumental relevance. Emotional intensity can have a major impact on performance. Someone who can remain calm during a job interview is likely to perform better than someone who is extremely nervous. Intense emotions can also interfere with motor control. They may impair manual performance by producing hand trembling, disturbances in hand–eye coordination, and so on. Intense emotions can also exercise a disorganizing effect on thought processes. Under the influence of powerful internal turmoil, concentration may be lost, thoughts may become jumbled, racing ideas and random, irrelevant associations may come to dominate the mind.

Although excessively intense emotions may interfere with the attainment of one's goals, insufficiently intense emotions may be equally damaging. Flat affect, ennui, and lack of interest tend to be enervating, and can seriously impair performance. Consider an athlete preparing for an athletic contest. Athletes know that there is an optimal level of arousal for the most effective performance. Total relaxation is apt to produce a lackluster performance. For this reason, athletes may attempt to "psych themselves up" by engaging in certain mental or physical activities.

Insufficiently intense emotions may also sap creativity. It appears to be part of the conventional wisdom to assume that intellectual challenges are best mastered by the application of cold, dispassionate reason, shorn of emotional charge. I believe that is a gross misconception. Indeed, it is difficult to think of any creative work—singing, dancing, writing, composing, painting—that is the product of pure dispassionate cognition. In the absence of such feelings, there is no drive, no spirit, no inspiration. Such work may be competent but it is likely to be flat, uncreative, pedestrian.

Emotions may hamper, restrict, or harm the individual in various ways. A dramatic example is the feeling of terror or panic associated with the phobias. From an instrumental viewpoint, the consequences today of being afraid to fly in an airplane, ride in an elevator, or walk in a crowded

Rosenberg, Morris. 1991. "Self-Processes and Emotional Experiences," in Judith Howard (ed.). *The Self-Society Dynamic: Cognition, Emotion and Action,* 123–42. New York: Cambridge University Press.

street may range from mild inconvenience to the frustration of important life goals.

Because emotions affect behavior, they may also lead to impulsive actions that the individual may have later cause to regret. In a towering rage, one person quits his job, a second drops out of graduate school, a third walks out on her husband, a fourth punches a policeman in the nose, and so on. The practical consequences of such impulsive behavior are obvious.

Of particular importance to people are emotions that affect their interpersonal relations. Much of what we want out of life depends on the goodwill of others, and this goodwill is significantly affected by emotions. For example, to express one's anger is to risk the danger of being fired, disliked, divorced, subjected to physical attack, rejected socially, evaluated negatively, and much more. In general, the person who exhibits love, warmth, respect, admiration, and so on is more likely to elicit the desired response from other people than the one who displays hostility, contempt, boredom, irritation, and the like. This is especially true of role-related interpersonal emotions. Other things equal, a good-natured salesman, a kindly doctor, a cheerful girl will sell more goods, see more patients, and receive more marriage proposals than their peers with unattractive emotions.

Emotions thus have major consequences for the lives of people. They may make the difference between success and failure, between the realization or frustration of one's goals. The ability to experience the desired emotions has monumental effects on the individual's life.

Hedonic reasons

Emotions are also central to the hedonic concerns of human beings. Some emotions are experienced as pleasurable, others as painful. It is interesting to note that in the English language, negative emotions greatly outnumber positive ones, raising the possibility that emotional self-regulation may focus more on avoiding or eliminating negative feelings than on eliciting positive ones.

But whether positive or negative emotions are involved, it is clear that the search for human happiness is at bottom a striving to maximize positive and minimize negative affect.

Normative Reasons

Finally, emotional self-regulation plays an important part in producing adherence to the emotional norms of society. Sociologists and anthropologists have provided abundant evidence showing that every society is characterized by a distinctive system of emotional norms.

Emotional norms are also attached to *social roles* or positions. In our society, a familiar example of such role-related feeling rules is the system of gender-based emotional norms. Early in life males are taught that "big boys don't cry," whereas such behavior is tolerated among girls. Among adults, men may condemn themselves (and be condemned by others) for emotional experiences that would be perfectly acceptable in a woman. Fear is a familiar example. Though a man may be quaking in his boots, it is normatively prescribed that he not experience or express such feelings, whereas for a woman the expression of such emotions may be perfectly acceptable.

Emotional norms may also be prescribed for various *situations*. Through instruction or example, society teaches children that different situations call for different emotions. At a funeral one is expected to be sad; at a party, happy; at an athletic contest, excited; and so on.

Because people have different "role-sets," they are socially expected to experience different emotions toward different *categories of others*. Thus, it is socially appropriate to hate an enemy or a renegade but not appropriate to hate one's parents, one's country, or one's family. It is all right to feel sexual desire toward one's spouse but not toward one's parent, child, sibling, or pet.

INVOLUNTARY NATURE OF EMOTIONAL EXPERIENCES

Human beings thus have ample incentive to take charge of their emotional experiences. But when

different personality types

they attempt to do so, they come squarely up against a peculiar feature of the human organism, namely, that *people lack direct control over their emotional experiences.* In contrast to emotional *display*, which is largely under voluntary control, emotional *experience* is not. I may be able to make myself *look* interested but I cannot make myself *feel* interested. I can keep myself from showing anger but I cannot keep myself from feeling anger. The emotions I show and the emotions I feel may be poles apart.

The involuntary nature of the emotions tends to be taken for granted by both professional and layperson. People say that they were *overcome* by sadness, that they were *gripped* by feelings of panic, that they were *seized* by fear, that they were *swept along* by the excitement, that they *fell* hopelessly in love, and so on. So viewed, the emotion is not seen as something that the individual controls; it is seen as something that controls the individual.

There is an idea that the emotions are spontaneous and involuntary reactions to stimulus events. Thus, if I see a car bearing down at me at high speed, I feel fear. If I see a baby sleeping peacefully in a crib, I feel affection. If I am subjected to a gratuitous insult, I feel anger. These emotional responses appear to be things that "happen" to us. They are not part of our plan or intention. We play no part in eliciting them.

There is also the familiar idea that emotions are not responsive to our volitional control. I cannot, through a simple act of will, call forth a desired emotional experience. I may want to feel loving toward a child, cheerful at a party, or sad at a funeral, but I cannot simply will these feelings into existence. Nor can I readily discard unwanted emotions. It is not within my power to eliminate feelings of rage, love, or fear by fiat.

The key problem of emotional self-control, then, is that emotional experience appears to be subject to the control of the autonomic rather than the central nervous system. Emotions are seen as biologically primitive, instinctive features of the organism. In general, people appear to have no more control over their emotional experiences than they have over their digestion, metabolism, or filtering of body wastes.

Given the importance of emotional control for the individual and society, and given the fact that emotional experiences appear to be outside the individual's control, what can be done about it? The solution that people usually adopt, is not to attempt to control the emotional experiences directly but to attempt to control the *causes* of the emotional experiences.

Since the chief causes of emotions are mental events, the main way of controlling one's emotions is to exercise control over one's thoughts. This means that people must be able to observe and recognize their thoughts and must figure out ways to regulate those thoughts in a manner best calculated to produce the intended emotional effects. They must, in other words, draw upon the self-processes that are features of human reflexivity.

That's a key issue/on!

The self-regulation of emotional experiences is strewn with obstacles and pitfalls. The basic reason is that the process is essentially indirect. People rarely, if ever, are able to produce emotional effects at will. They must depend on a series of devices (perhaps one should call them tricks) of mental self-manipulation to produce the desired emotional results. Nevertheless, it is the method on which they most depend. And what makes it possible is the phenomenon of reflexivity—the human being's virtually unique ability to stand outside the self, to observe and reflect on it (including such internal features as thoughts and feelings), and to produce intentional effects upon these internal processes. Despite the limited effectiveness of mental self-manipulation devices, the importance of emotional self-control for both the individual and society is profound.

DISCUSSION QUESTIONS

1. Rosenberg identifies three major reasons why emotions are important. What are they?

2. In exploring emotional norms, Rosenberg suggests that norms vary by culture and by social status within a given culture. Give examples of two or three social situations in which emotional norms differ despite similar objectives (e.g., the social recognition of major life transitions at both weddings and funerals). How do emotional norms in these situations differ by race, class, gender, or other social characteristics?

3. Rosenberg argues that we frequently engage in mental self-deception to bring about socially appropriate emotions. What does he mean by this? Have you ever exercised this process of "mental control"? Give an example.

ADDITIONAL RESOURCES

Film

"Emotion." 2006. A 30-minute film exploring the relationship between thought and emotion and how emotions vary by gender and culture. Insight Media.

Internet

http://www2.asanet.org/emotions/. The website for the American Sociological Association's Section on the Sociology of Emotions.

FURTHER READING

Denzin, Norman K. 2007. *On Understanding Emotion*. Edison, NJ: Transaction Publishers.

Grandey, Alicia A. 2003. "When 'The Show Must Go On': Surface Acting and Deep Acting as Determinants of Emotional Exhaustion and Peer-Rated Service Delivery." *Academy of Management Journal*, 46(1): 86–96.

Hocschild, Arlie Russell. 2003 (1983). *The Managed Heart: Commercialization of Human Feeling*, 2nd edition. Berkeley/Los Angeles/London: University of California Press.

Self-Presentation and Impression Management

The next two selections explore self-presentation and impression management. Erving Goffman's classic work on impression management was published 34 years before David Kinney's study of identity work among American middle and high school students. Both selections detail the complexities of soliciting favorable outcomes to our daily social "performances." Taken together, these articles also illustrate variation in impression management across historical time and through the life course.

Drawing on his theoretical framework of dramaturgy, Goffman uses the metaphor of the theater to explore social interaction: people become "actors" who "perform" for social "audiences." Goffman's analysis of the social stage is complete with a veil of sorts that is intended to block off the "backstage" preparatory region from audience view.

Goffman gives examples of the shop worker who engages in "make-work" (or looking busy) when the boss walks by, even if the labor is actually meaningless, like cleaning a surface that has already been cleaned. Similarly, Goffman notes that persons of high social status may attempt to "make-no-work" by hiding the work they were engaged in when visitors drop by, in order to appear to others as though they have the ability to spend their time in leisure.

In Kinney's more contemporary application of impression management, he explores the all too often grueling social hierarchy of middle-schoolers. Kinney details the two-tiered classification of popular and unpopular kids, exploring how this power structure is created and maintained. His research reveals a more complex and varied social structure in the high school realm, which brings great opportunity and relief to those who were perceived as nerds in middle school.

15. Regions and Region Behavior

ERVING GOFFMAN

In his classic book, *Presentation of Self in Everyday Life*, Goffman details the intricacies of impression management. In this selection from that text, Goffman describes a key element in giving off successful social "performances": a clear distinction between performative (front) spaces and preparatory (back) spaces.

A region may be defined as any place that is bounded to some degree by barriers to perception. Regions vary, of course, in the degree to which they are bounded and according to the media of communication in which the barriers to perception occur. Thus thick glass panels, such as are found in broadcasting control rooms, can isolate a region aurally but not visually, while an office bounded by beaver-board partitions is closed off in the opposite way.

In our Anglo-American society—a relatively indoor one—when a performance is given it is usually given in a highly bounded region, to which boundaries with respect to time are often added.

Given a particular performance as a point of reference, it will sometimes be convenient to use the term "front region" to refer to the place where the performance is given.

We are accustomed to assuming that the rules of decorum that prevail in sacred establishments, such as churches, will be much different from the ones that prevail in everyday places of work. We ought not to assume from this that the standards in sacred places are more numerous and more strict than those we find in work establishments. While in church, a woman may be permitted to sit, daydream, and even doze. However, as a saleswoman on the floor of a dress shop, she may be required to stand, keep alert, refrain from chewing gum, keep a fixed smile on her face even when not talking to anyone, and wear clothes she can ill afford.

One form of decorum that has been studied in social establishments is what is called "make-work." It is understood in many establishments that not only will workers be required to produce a certain amount after a certain length of time but also that they will be ready, when called upon, to give the impression that they are working hard at the moment. Of a shipyard we learn the following:

It was amusing to watch the sudden transformation whenever word got round that the

Goffman, Erving. 1959. "Regions and Region Behavior," in *Presentation of Self in Everyday Life*. Woodston, Peterborough, UK: Anchor Books (Forward Press).

foreman was on the hull or in the shop or that a front-office superintendent was coming by. Quartermen and leadermen would rush to their groups of workers and stir them to obvious activity. "Don't let him catch you sitting down," was the universal admonition, and where no work existed a pipe was busily bent and threaded, or a bolt which was already firmly in place was subjected to further and unnecessary tightening. This was the formal tribute invariably attending a visitation by the boss, and its conventions were as familiar to both sides as those surrounding a five-star general's inspection. To have neglected any detail of the false and empty show would have been interpreted as a mark of singular disrespect.

From a consideration of make-work it is only a step to consideration of other standards of work activity for which appearances must be maintained, such as pace, personal interest, economy, accuracy, etc. And from a consideration of work standards in general it is only a step to consideration of other major aspects of decorum, instrumental and moral, in work places, such as: mode of dress; permissible sound levels; proscribed diversions, indulgences, and affective expressions.

It was suggested earlier that when one's activity occurs in the presence of other persons, some aspects of the activity are expressively accentuated and other aspects, which might discredit the fostered impression, are suppressed. It is clear that accentuated facts make their appearance in what I have called a front region; it should be just as clear that there may be another region—a "back region" or "backstage"—where the suppressed facts make an appearance.

A back region or backstage may be defined as a place, relative to a given performance, where the impression fostered by the performance is knowingly contradicted as a matter of course. It is here that the capacity of a performance to express something beyond itself may be painstakingly fabricated; it is here that illusions and impressions are openly constructed. Here stage props and items of personal front can be stored in a kind of compact collapsing of whole repertoires of actions and characters. Here devices such as the telephone are sequestered so that they can be used "privately." Here costumes and other parts of personal front may be adjusted and scrutinized for flaws. Here the team can run through its performance, checking for offending expressions when no audience is present to be affronted by them. Here the performer can relax; he can drop his front, forgo speaking his lines, and step out of character.

Very commonly the back region of a performance is located at one end of the place where the performance is presented, being cut off from it by a partition and guarded passageway. In general, of course, the back region will be the place where the performer can reliably expect that no member of the audience will intrude.

Since the vital secrets of a show are visible backstage and since performers behave out of character while there, it is natural to expect that the passage from the front region to the back region will be kept closed to members of the audience or that the entire back region will be kept hidden from them. This is a widely practiced technique of impression management.

An interesting example of backstage difficulties is found in radio and television broadcasting work. In these situations, back region tends to be defined as all places where the camera is not focused at the moment or all places out of range of "live" microphones. Professionals, of course, tell many exemplary tales of how persons who thought they were backstage were in fact on the air and how this backstage conduct discredited the definition of the situation being maintained on the air. For technical reasons, then, the walls that broadcasters have to hide behind can be very treacherous, tending to fall at the flick of a switch or a turn of the camera. Broadcasting artists must live with this staging contingency.

One of the most interesting times to observe impression management is the moment when a performer leaves the back region and enters the place where the audience is to be found, or when he returns therefrom, for at these moments one can detect a wonderful putting on and taking off of character.

The line dividing front and back regions is illustrated everywhere in our society. As suggested, the bathroom and bedroom, in all but lower-class homes, are places from which the downstairs audience can be excluded. Bodies that are cleansed, clothed, and made up in these rooms can be presented to friends in others. It is, in fact, the presence of these staging devices that distinguishes middle-class living from lower-class living. But in all classes in our society there is a tendency to make a division between the front and back parts of residential exteriors. The front tends to be relatively well decorated, well repaired, and tidy; the rear tends to be relatively unprepossessing. Correspondingly, social adults enter through the front, and often the socially incomplete domestics, delivery men, and children—enter through the rear.

Throughout Western society there tends to be one informal or backstage language of behavior, and another language of behavior for occasions when a performance is being presented. The backstage language consists of reciprocal first-naming, co-operative decision-making, profanity, open sexual remarks, elaborate griping, smoking, rough informal dress, "sloppy" sitting and standing posture, use of dialect or sub-standard speech, mumbling and shouting, playful aggressivity and "kidding," inconsiderateness for the other in minor but potentially symbolic acts, minor physical self-involvements such as humming, whistling, chewing, nibbling, belching, and flatulence. The frontstage behavior language can be taken as the absence (and in some sense the opposite) of this.

By invoking a backstage style, individuals can transform any region into a backstage. Thus we find that in many social establishments the performers will appropriate a section of the front region and by acting there in a familiar fashion symbolically cut it off from the rest of the region. For instance, in some restaurants in America,

especially those called "one-arm joints," the staff will hold court in the booth farthest from the door or closest to the kitchen, and there conduct themselves, at least in some respects, as if they were backstage. Similarly, on uncrowded evening airline flights, after their initial duties have been performed, stewardesses may settle down in the rearmost seat, change from regulation pumps into loafers, light up a cigarette, and there create a muted circle of non-service relaxation, even at times extending this to include the one or two closest passengers.

In saying that performers act in a relatively informal, familiar, relaxed way while backstage and are on their guard when giving a performance, it should not be assumed that the pleasant interpersonal things of life—courtesy, warmth, generosity, and pleasure in the company of others—are always reserved for those backstage and that suspiciousness, snobbishness, and a show of authority are reserved for front region activity. Often it seems that whatever enthusiasm and lively interest we have at our disposal we reserve for those before whom we are putting on a show and that the surest sign of backstage solidarity is to feel that it is safe to lapse into an a sociable mood of sullen, silent irritability.

It should be clear that just as it is useful for the performer to exclude persons from the audience who see him in another and inconsistent presentation, so also is it useful for the performer to exclude from the audience those before whom he performed in the past a show inconsistent with the current one.

By proper scheduling of one's performances, it is possible not only to keep one's audiences separated from each other (by appearing before them in different front regions or sequentially in the same region) but also to allow a few moments in between performances so as to extricate oneself psychologically and physically from one personal front, while taking on another. Problems sometimes arise, however, in those social establishments where the same or different members of the team must handle different audiences at the same time. If the different audiences come within hearing distance of each other, it will be difficult to sustain the impression that each is receiving special and unique services. Thus, if a hostess wishes to give each of her guests a warm special greeting or farewell—a special performance, in fact—then she will have to arrange to do this in an anteroom that is separated from the room containing the other guests. Similarly, in cases where a firm of undertakers is required to conduct two services on the same day, it will be necessary to route the two audiences through the establishment in such a way that their paths will not cross, lest the feeling that the funeral home is a home away from home be destroyed.

DISCUSSION QUESTIONS

1. Goffman notes that a clear separation between front and back regions is essential to upholding the impression of authentic performances in the front region. Can you think of examples from your own life of boundary *blurring* between front and back regions (such as the Dennis the Menace cartoon illustrates)?

2. Goffman notes social class distinctions in the availability of back region space. What are these distinctions? What are the implications of having more or less back region available?

3. In his 1959 discussion of back region, Goffman says that telephones are kept in the back region to permit private conversations. How has the pervasive use of cell phones in public spaces challenged or upheld the division between front and back regions?

4. Do you think that individuals of high status today would be more or less likely to conceal work-related activities than in Goffman's time? Why?

5. Is there a "back region" in Internet impression management and performance space? How have social networking sites, such as Facebook and MySpace, altered the distinction between public (front) and private (back) worlds?

ADDITIONAL RESOURCES

Internet

http://www.blackwood.org/Erving.htm. A nicely detailed biographical site about Erving Goffman.

http://people.brandeis.edu/~teuber/goffmanbio.html. Another biographical site dedicated to the work of Erving Goffman.

FURTHER READING

Freidson, Elliot. 1983. "Celebrating Erving Goffman." *Contemporary Sociology*, 12(4): 359–62.

Goffman, Erving. 1959. *Presentation of Self in Everyday Life*. Woodston, Peterborough, UK: Anchor Books (Forward Press).

Hochschild, Arlie. 1983. *The Managed Heart: Commercialization of Human Feeling*. Berkeley: University of California Press.

16. From "Nerds" to "Normals": The Recovery of Identity among Adolescents from Middle School to High School

DAVID A. KINNEY

Based on interview and observation data with high school students, Kinney compares the rigidly hierarchical social world of middle school to the more forgiving setting of high school. Kinney documents students' transitions from "geek" to "chic" as they grow older.

Popular films and television shows about adolescents and schools usually include a certain type of teenager who is frequently ridiculed and rejected by his or her peers. These adolescents are often portrayed as awkward, intelligent, shy, unattractive social outcasts with unfashionable hair and dress styles who sometimes attempt to get revenge on their peers who shun them. They are called "nerds," "dweebs," "dorks," "geeks," "brainiacs," and "computer jocks." Although these stereotypical nerds appear in films and on television, do American secondary school students use such terms to label their peers? If so, what is life like for teenagers who are so labeled? And if this experience is distressing, as many people believe, how do teenagers deal with the stigma of being labeled nerds? Since social scientists have characterized the teenage years as a crucial time for the formation of identity, it is important to investigate the extent to which teenagers use these social type labels and the impact these labels have on adolescents' self-perceptions.

I used observations and in-depth interviews with teenagers in different grades and at different times to collect information regarding the everyday experiences that shape the trajectories of their concerns and identities. A recurrent theme in the data indicated that some adolescents who were labeled by their peers as unpopular nerds in middle school were able to embrace a more positive self-perception in high school that centered on defining themselves as "normal."

Specifically, the data show that adolescents' daily negotiation of the school social scene within and between groups produced powerful emotions that had a significant and ongoing impact on their perceptions of themselves and others. Moreover, adolescents with the opportunities and resources to take advantage of specialized high school-sponsored activities were actively able to affirm a positive personal identity.

To extend the findings of earlier studies, I observed and interviewed students over a two-year period to investigate the nature of their school social experiences and perceptions of self, others, and the school social structure over time.

SETTING AND METHODS

The research was conducted at a high school that enrolled students from a wide range of socioeconomic backgrounds, including a large group of students from working- and lower-class families. The school is located in a small Midwestern city (population about 60,000) and is attended by students from the city and surrounding rural areas. Although most of the students are white, a small number of African Americans also attend. The school itself is relatively large, with approximately 400 students in each grade (9–12).

Kinney, David A. 1993. "From 'Nerds' to 'Normals': The Recovery of Identity among Adolescents from Middle School to High School." *Sociology of Education*, 66: 21–40.

Beginning in March 1987, I observed social interaction at the school between classes, at lunch, and after school. I also attended the various after-school extracurricular activities to observe peer relations among the participants and fans. These activities included football games; cross-country meets; girls' volleyball games, gymnastics, and swimming meets; boys' and girls' basketball games; wrestling and tennis matches; baseball games; academic decathlon competitions; academic- and athletic-award banquets; musical and theatrical performances; talent shows; and "battles of the bands." These frequent observations of adolescents in natural settings provided information about everyday social interactions and behavior at various events that served as data to be compared with material from the in-depth interviews.

Overall, I conducted and audiotaped 81 interviews with both male and female members of all the peer groups that the students perceived to exist at the school. About half these interviews occurred with individuals and the rest with small groups. Altogether, through the interviews and social encounters at school and at their hangouts, I had contact with approximately 120 adolescents. The interviews ranged in length from 40 to 120 minutes and took place in natural settings that the adolescents normally frequented after school and on the weekends, such as pizza and fast-food restaurants or coffeehouses in the community. Several interviews were conducted in a conference room in the school library, and some took place at local parks during April and May.

I attempted to carve out a neutral identity for myself at the school by making and maintaining connections with students in a wide variety of peer groups and by being open to their different viewpoints. By showing my genuine interest in their daily lives and distancing myself from adults, I developed a high level of rapport with these adolescents, which was reflected in the students' willingness to discuss discrediting information about themselves and to invite me to their private activities. The following sections represent recurrent themes from the overall data base that delineate how mostly middle-class teenagers who were labeled nerds came to view themselves as normals. About one-third of the interviewees fit this pattern.

RECURRENT THEMES

Interview data from members of all the different peer groups indicated that the adolescents consistently and vividly recalled their middle school experience as being divided into two distinct crowds: the unpopular nerds or dweebs and the popular trendies. Members of the trendy crowd were also referred to as the preppies, jocks, or the in-crowd and consisted of roughly 20 percent of the middle school population. Male athletes, cheerleaders, and their best friends make up the vast majority of the trendy crowd and are the most popular among their peers in the school because of their visibility.

This visibility is generated and maintained by athletes' and cheerleaders' frequent public performances at well-attended school sports contests and pep rallies. For example, many teenagers noted that "everybody knows" who the popular people are and what they do; they are the ones who are "noticed" or "recognized" by everybody. Teenagers who were unpopular in middle school described their popular counterparts as having "the ability to gain recognition from everybody else, and you more or less get your choice of what to do or who to go out with. It's just, everybody would like to be like that." In addition to having a choice of activities and dating partners, both trendies and nerds noted that popular people "have the most fun" and are always invited to private parties on weekends. These teenagers emphasized traditional gender roles (achievement, competition, and toughness for boys; attractiveness, appearance, and interpersonal relations for girls) and maintaining their high peer status, which required limiting the size of their group by excluding peers who did not meet their standards.

is it that bifurcated?

Nerds in Middle School

Adolescents who were not trendies ended up by default in a large mass of students who were labeled "unpopular."

For example, two former unpopular young men said:

Ross: And middle school—.
TED: We were just *nerds*. I mean—.
Ross: Yeah—
TED: People hated us.
Ross: Well, they didn't hate us, but we weren't—
TED: Popular. Which was either you were popular or you weren't.
Ross: In middle school it's very defined. There's popular people and unpopular people. It's just very—rigid. You were popular or unpopular. That's it.
TED: And there wasn't people that were in between.
Ross: Oh no!
TED: You just had one route [to becoming popular], and then there was the other. And we were the other, and—basically you were afraid of getting laughed at about anything you did because if you did one thing that was out of the ordinary, and you weren't expected to do anything out of the ordinary, then you were laughed at and made fun of, and you wouldn't fit the group at all, and then, of course, you were excluded and then you didn't even exist.
Ross: You got "nuked," so to speak.

Ross and Ted used the label nerd in retrospect and clearly perceived "very rigid" boundaries between popular and unpopular youths in middle school. Independent data from some trendy young men about Ted corroborate Ted's recollection of himself as a nerd. These popular athletes excitedly described him in the following terms: "He had real short hair like a nerd. He was the biggest nerd of the school." These trendies also expressed the importance of avoiding unpopular students in middle school, saying:

> [We] always had that one group—we had all the good-looking girls and that is the one [group] that everybody wanted to be in. At lunch we sit at our own table [but] if you go out to lunch with the wrong person, rumors would go around that you went to lunch with a *geek*!

Since the popular crowd served as a reference group for many of the unpopular students, the ridicule and rejection that the nerds experienced from the trendies was highly salient.

Nerds' Transition to High School

Although the nerds reported having troubling social experiences in middle school, they viewed their transition to high school as being accompanied by some positive changes. Along with the transition came increased opportunities for membership in a greater variety of groups and a lessening of the desire for achieving schoolwide popularity that was so pervasive in middle school. These themes are illustrated in the following comments by two juniors, Bob and Ellen:

Bob: You had popular people—
Ellen: And unpopular people—in middle school—either you were considered a nerd and nobody liked you or else you were hanging out with the cheerleaders and the football players and stuff like that, and that was the most important…and then when you get into high school, it really doesn't matter anymore because people don't care [whether they're not in the popular crowd]—
Bob: And there's more groups [in high school]….

As these students observed, the transition to high school was characterized by a more highly differentiated social scene, based on a larger number and greater variety of groups and students. Many students commented on the diversity of the high school, noting the existence of groups like the headbangers and punk rockers—two groups that did not exist at the middle school. Moreover, other interviews and observations indicated that the trendies felt challenged by members of these new groups, who were visible (because of their "outrageous" appearance and "rowdy" behavior) at the school. In general, students entering high school confronted a more diverse social structure that consisted of a greater number of peer cultures and peer groups and in which the trendies' earlier monopoly on visibility and popularity was diminishing.

Juniors and seniors discussed this change in terms of the "disintegration" of earlier "rigid" group boundaries and that things "evened out" between crowds as they moved through high school; freshmen and sophomores did not note such changes, but expressed how "happy," "glad," and "relieved" they were to be in high school.

Nerds' Increased Confidence
Along with the more open and diverse social structure, another recurrent pattern in the data was some adolescents' lessening concern with obtaining school-wide popularity, which was facilitated by their involvement in school-sponsored activities in which participation by juniors and seniors created a supportive social environment. Many noted that as freshmen and sophomores, they had the opportunity to feel secure and gain confidence in themselves because of their acceptance by and approval from their older teammates. Regarding this theme, Ross and Ted stated:

Ross: We were goons in middle school—We're not as shy [anymore]—.
TED: Exactly. I got the attitude when I moved from middle school to high school that I don't give a damn what people are gonna think. Because in middle school you're always afraid of offending someone.
Ross: And there wasn't any way for us to get out of it anyway—.
TED: And once you get to high school, if you can find some crazier upper-class people

and hang around with them, the possibilities are limitless. I mean we got here; we met some crazier upper-class people [through participating in a "minor" sport], who just basically gave us the idea, "Go ahead. Go for it!"
Ross: …Don't worry about it so much. Stop being so self-conscious!

Making new friends through participation in a school activity provided both a supportive group and a new reference group that served as a haven from the trendies' expectations and evaluations, where these former nerds did not have to be "so self-conscious" or "give a damn what people are gonna think."

These social changes appear to parallel the psychological growth in adolescents' cognitive capacities. Developmental psychologists have suggested that early adolescence (roughly the middle school years) is characterized by an increased ability to reflect about oneself and to take the perspective of others. However, these new skills may not be used effectively or controlled adequately.

With continued cognitive development and the transition to high school, the nerds' relevant social and psychological reality changed because they were able to surround themselves with peers who provided positive reflected appraisals and more favorable social comparisons. These supportive relationships were the basis for the nerds' construction of more positive self-conceptions, since they collectively reduced the contextual dissonance that earlier had a negative effect on their self-perceptions.

Other students also recalled that the transition to high school allowed them to explore a number of activities, such as journalism, the yearbook, music, theater, the chess club, academic competition teams, science and language clubs, tennis, and cross-country and swimming teams, that were not offered at the middle school. These activities provided alternative domains to achieving school-wide popularity in which students could feel adequate and successful. Specifically, many students who participated in these activities said that they had "more confidence" in themselves and felt less "self-conscious" about how the popular people viewed them.

Along with becoming members of stable peer groups, some of these young men talked about losing weight and growing substantially taller, which enhanced their overall well-being.

Nerds Going Mainstream or Their Own Way

Although this constellation of social, psychological, and physical changes that occur during the transition to and early years of high school provide a fertile ground for progressive changes in social relations and feelings of self-efficacy, the data also indicate that teenagers experience significant shifts in their personal identity. These changes in self-attributions revolve around their assertion that they are becoming "normal" after a period of being frequently stigmatized as nerds.

Other nerds followed a different path to becoming normal. Rather than adopt mainstream characteristics and behaviors, they essentially rejected the trendies' values to develop a more positive sense of self.

This process is also captured in the following comments by Susan, a young woman who was a high school junior:

Example 15
If you have confidence, you can overlook people who put you down 'cause there are always people who are going to put you down. And [when you have confidence], you don't have to worry about what I tend to think are the more trivial things in life like appearance or being trendy.

An unpopular middle school student, Susan became independent from the trendies' evaluations as she went her own way by working on the high school newspaper and developing strong ties with several other student journalists who are interested in current social issues and reading the classics. She viewed confidence as the key to not worrying about the trendies' evaluations.

Specifically, her statement that "you don't have to worry about…the more trivial things in life like appearance or being trendy" suggests that she is shifting the identities in her salience hierarchy around to align them with her social relationships. In short, during middle school, they wanted to be popular, but in high school they devalue the trendies' attitudes and activities and go their own way.

Overall, the recurrent patterns in the data indicate two distinct processes that facilitate a change in these adolescents' identity from nerds to normals. One path centers on embracing behaviors and appearances that are respected by high-status peers, while the other path hinges on one's emancipation from popular peers' expectations and invidious comparisons. The young men were more likely to choose the first path and to use school activities as an arena in which they could adopt mainstream interests and develop rewarding relationships with peers to feel good about themselves. Similarly, the young women developed supportive friendships through participation in school activities, but they were more likely than were the young men to follow the second path by enhancing their self-perceptions through close relationships that neither centered on school-sponsored activities nor connected them to the mainstream of the school.

DISCUSSION
The transition to high school was characterized by an increasing number of students and groups who formed more diverse peer cultures that were organized into a less hierarchical social structure. The normals' emergence as visible group of confident happy individuals provided a new model for the development of a positive identity within the changing social system. These teenagers made sense of things by saying: "I'm not a nerd anymore! Now I'm *normal!*" So historically these adolescents were developing more positive self-perceptions as the immediate social structure of the peer groups changed.

Increasing peer acceptance and social confidence characterizes normals' patterns of interpersonal interactions that dovetail with the more diverse and less hierarchical social structure of the high school. The social side of high school allows these teenagers, most of whom are competent students, a chance to become competent social actors as they learn how to manage their impressions and overcome stigma within the friendly confines of their peer group. Overall, whether *going mainstream or going their own way*, within the social reality they constructed, the normals took over the position formerly attributed to the trendies.

The normals' vivid and emotional descriptions of their social experiences in school in their everyday conversations and small-group interviews revealed that they brought about the more positive and orderly nature of their high school world through the accounting practices (e.g., developing conversational skills with allies) that they lacked in middle school. In middle school the future normals were situationally and developmentally constrained because they lacked close friends and self-confidence in contrast to the social and vocal trendies. They did not become competent performers of accounting practices until they had trusted and sympathetic friends in high school. In addition to the significance of their "accounting" conversations, my observations of them in natural settings indicated that just being in each other's physical presence was an important interpersonal process of identity formation.

Their occasional glances and winks of the eye while walking closely together emboldened and reminded them that they were "somebodies." In sum, the shifting nature of interpersonal interactions and the concomitant changes in their immediate social structure and peer culture facilitated and reflected the nerds' recovery from their earlier distressing social experiences and attendant low self-evaluations.

Through their everyday experiences, the nerds gradually realize (with the help of the trendies' expectations and evaluations) that the adult world demands social skills, close friends, and self-confidence. This realization and their appropriation of key features of the adult world (e.g., self-presentation techniques) allow them to gain more control over others' evaluations of them and delimit which others matter to them and thus helps them adapt to their immediate social world.

Although the study reported here was not designed to examine such a process among White students, it should be noted that the vast majority of the normals at this school were high academic achievers and thus that their social efforts did not seem to affect their academic pursuits negatively. Future research should follow cohorts of African American and White students through secondary schools with different racial compositions to compare systematically high achievers who use strategies to downplay their academic excellence with those who do not to further our understanding of the interplay between the social and academic sides of schooling.

DISCUSSION QUESTIONS

1. According to Kinney, what makes middle school more miserable for misfits than high school?
2. What techniques do the popular kids use in both middle and high school to gain and maintain their high social status?
3. How do your own middle and high school experiences compare with the findings of Kinney's research?
4. Extending Kinney's analysis to college life, how does the social structure in college differ from that of middle or high school?

ADDITIONAL RESOURCES

Film

"Romy and Michele's High School Reunion." A 1997 mainstream popular film about impression management at high school reunions. 92 minutes.

"49 Up." A 2005 coming-of-age documentary by Michael Apted that is the seventh installment in the "Up" series, which began with a group of 7-year-old British children ("Seven Up") in 1964. The children are now 49 years old. 135 minutes.

Internet

http://www.firstrunfeatures.com/49up_home.html. The website for 49 Up.

FURTHER READING

Goto, Stanford T. 1997. "Nerds, Normal People, and Homeboys: Accommodation and Resistance among Chinese American Students." *Anthropology & Education Quarterly,* 28(1): 70–84.

Markus, Hazel and Paula Nurius. 1986. "Possible Selves." *American Psychologist,* 41: 954–69.

Snyder, Mark, Elizabeth D. Tanke, and Ellen Berscheid. 1977. "Social Perception and Interpersonal Behavior: On the Self-Fulfilling Nature of Social Stereotypes." *Journal of Personality and Social Psychology,* 35(9): September, 656–66.

Vinitzky-Seroussi, Vered. 1998. *After Pomp and Circumstance: High School Reunion as an Autobiographical Occasion.* Chicago: University of Chicago Press.

in the new setting they have a choice of significant others; in MS, the sign. others were defined for everyone

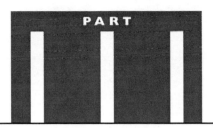

PART III

Interaction in Groups

"It's getting late, Neal."

Interpersonal Attraction and Relationships

Taken together, these three articles explore the complex yet familiar process of "hooking up," coupling, and telling stories about one's relationship to others. The authors explore when and how we find others attractive and the processes by which we come together and stay together and what makes for a happy or unhappy union.

Readers will no doubt recognize themselves and their own intimate relationship history as they read about the differences between "liking" and "loving" someone, pick-up lines and rejection in singles bars, and the retrospective narrative accounts of intimate relationships.

While there are clear similarities in these selections, the authors' research methods differ considerably. Rubin primarily used quantitative measures, such as scales and surveys, to assess liking and loving. Snow et al.'s methods were qualitative, relying primarily on participant observation at nightclubs. Holmberg et al.'s methods were qualitative as well, using in-depth interviews and analysis of couples' narratives to assess the way they construct stories about their relationships. How might the authors' research questions and findings differ if they had used other research methods? That is, what if

Snow et al. surveyed bar patrons about pick-up lines and Holmberg et al. conducted participant observation in divorce court? How do the questions scholars ask influence their research methods? What impact do research methods have on the data scholars analyze and the character of their findings?

17. The Nature of Love: A Researcher's Odyssey

ZICK RUBIN

In his early research on loving, Rubin discovered a major void in the literature. In an attempt to move beyond research on "liking" alone, Rubin empirically distinguishes the concepts of "liking" and "loving," and examines the linkages between them. The state of our current knowledge on intimacy owes much to Rubin's early contributions.

A RESEARCHER'S ODYSSEY

The state of our knowledge about interpersonal attraction has advanced considerably in the past two decades, but primarily through research on liking rather than research directly concerned with love. And while liking and loving are surely close relatives, they are by no means identical. The bridge between research on liking and the extensive writings on love remains to be built.

In this chapter I will report on my own initial endeavor to help build this bridge.

Like love itself, the course of research on love—and, indeed, of social-psychological research more generally—seldom runs smooth. There are numerous pitfalls, bumps in the road, sharp turns, and detours. These rough spots are carefully smoothed out in most research reports, presumably to spare editors and readers the shakes and jostles that the investigator had to endure. In this report, though, I should like to share at least some of the bumps with you. I hope that by doing so I will be able to convey some of the flavor of conducting research in a largely uncharted area.

To anchor my attempt to measure love at one end with the work of the "liking researchers," I decided from the start to conceptualize love as an attitude that a person holds toward a particular other person. As such, love—like liking—is an invisible package of feelings, thoughts, and behavioral predispositions within an individual. But I also assumed that the content of this attitude is not the same as that of liking, even extremely strong liking, nor could it be equated with the sentiments described as affection and respect.

What would we expect to be the empirical relationships between one person's love and his liking for another person? One would certainly expect at least a moderately positive evaluation of another person to be a prerequisite for the establishment of attachment, caring, and intimacy. Thus, it would be surprising if liking and loving were not at least moderately correlated with one another. But whereas liking and loving may have much in common, we would hesitate to equate the two phenomena. People often express liking for a person whom they would not claim to love

Rubin, Zick. 1973. "The Nature of Love: A Researcher's Odyssey," in *Liking and Loving: An Invitation to Social-Psychology*, 211–25. New York: Holt, Rinehart and Winston.

in the least. In other instances they may declare their love for someone whom they cannot reasonably be said to like very well.

A starting assumption in my attempt to develop self-report scales of liking and loving, therefore, was that they should represent moderately correlated, but nevertheless distinct, dimensions of one person's attitude toward another person. My study consisted of three stages. First, I constructed parallel self-report scales of liking and loving that met the requirements of the starting assumption. Second, I examined the ways in which the scores of members of dating couples on each of the two scales related to a variety of other things about them, including their plans for marriage. Third, I proceeded to assess the usefulness of the love scale in predicting people's subsequent behavior and the course of their relationships.

PUTTING LOVE ON A SCALE

The first step in scale construction was to make up about eighty items reflecting aspects of one person's attitudes toward a particular other person. The items spanned a wide range of thoughts, feelings, and behavioral predispositions—for example, "How much fun is _____ to be with?" "How much do you trust _____?" "To what extent are you physically attracted to _____?" "How much does _____ get on your nerves?" As a check upon my own initial intuitions, I asked a number of friends and acquaintances of both sexes to sort the items into "liking" and "loving" sets, based on their own understandings of the meaning of the two terms. After making revisions suggested by these raters' judgments, I presented a new pool of seventy items to 198 undergraduates at the University of Michigan and asked them to respond to each in terms of their feelings toward their boyfriend or girlfriend (if they had one), and again in terms of their feelings toward a "platonic friend" of the opposite sex. I then subjected these ratings to a statistical technique called factor analysis, which serves to indicate which sets of items form internally consistent

Table1 Love-Scale and Liking-Scale Items

Love Scale

1. If _____ were feeling bad, my first duty would be to cheer him (her) up.
2. I feel that I can confide in _____ about virtually everything.
3. I find it easy to ignore _____'s faults.
4. I would do almost anything for_____
5. I feel very possessive toward _____.
6. If I could never be with _____, I would feel miserable.
7. If I were lonely, my first thought would be to seek _____ out.
8. One of my primary concerns is _____'s welfare.
9. I would forgive _____ for practically anything.
10. I feel responsible for _____'s well-being.
11. When I am with _____, I spend a good deal of time just looking at him (her).
12. I would greatly enjoy being confided in by _____.
13. It would be hard for me to get along without _____.

Liking Scale

1. When I am with _____, we almost always are in the same mood.
2. I think that _____ is unusually well-adjusted.
3. I would highly recommend _____ for a responsible job.
4. In my opinion, _____ is an exceptionally mature person.
5. I have great confidence in _____'s good judgment.
6. Most people would react favorably to _____ after a brief acquaintance.
7. I think that _____ and I are quite similar to one another.
8. I would vote for _____ in a class or group election.
9. I think that _____ is one of those people who quickly wins respect.
10. I feel that _____ is an extremely intelligent person.
11. _____ is one of the most likable people I know.
12. _____ is the sort of person whom I myself would like to be.
13. It seems to me that it is very easy for _____ to gain admiration.

clusters. This procedure led to the specification of two thirteen-item scales, one of love and the other of liking (see Table I).

Some of the scale items may strike you as misplaced because they do not correspond to your own personal definition of love or of liking. In several cases I have been led to the same conclusion. On the whole, however, the content of the two scales corresponds closely to the conceptions of liking and loving outlined in the previous section. The love scale includes items that seem to tap the postulated components of attachment (e.g., "If I were lonely, my first thought would be to seek _____ out"); caring (e.g., "If _____ were feeling bad, my first duty would be to cheer him (her) up"); and intimacy (e.g., "I feel that I can confide in _____ about virtually everything"). The items on the liking scale focus on the favorable evaluation of the other person on such dimensions as adjustment, maturity, good judgment, and intelligence, and on the associated tendency to view the other person as similar to oneself. The close fit between the scales and the preceding conceptual discussion is not accidental. Rather, my own working definitions of liking and loving were to a large extent given focus by the results of the scale-development procedure.

"ONLY DATING COUPLES CAN DO IT"

My subjects for this trial run were dating couples at the University of Michigan. Trying to make use of the lessons I had learned during my college summer as a Madison Avenue copywriter, I enticed the couples to take part in the study with a saturation campaign of posters and advertisements.

The one-dollar inducement proved to be more than enough to attract throngs of couples to my questionnaire sessions. On each of the two evenings, long lines of couples started forming outside Auditorium C by 7:00, and by 7:30 they were winding completely around the ground floor of the auditorium complex, outdoing even the most popular features of the student cinema league. Approximately 400 couples showed up to take part, and they were clearly motivated more by curiosity and the hope of learning something about themselves than by the token payment. I had prepared questionnaires for about 180 couples, thinking that this would be sufficient for the maximum conceivable turnout. As a result, on each of the two successive evenings I had to make profuse apologies and send about 100 couples home.

My sample of 182 couples comprised a wide cross-section of Michigan student couples. The modal couple consisted of a junior man and a sophomore woman who had been dating for about one year. Some of the couples had been going together for as long as six or seven years, however, while others had been dating for only a few weeks. About 20 percent of the couples reported that they were engaged. Of the total sample, 52 percent of the women and 29 percent of the men lived in dormitories; 31 percent of the women and 60 percent of the men lived in their own apartments; and over 10 percent of each sex lived in fraternities or sororities. The religious background of slightly over 50 percent of the students was Protestant; 17 percent, Catholic; and 25 percent, Jewish. The remainder belonged to other religions or claimed no religious background.

During the sessions, boyfriends and girlfriends were asked not to sit near one another. Each partner filled out the questionnaire individually. They were assured that their responses would be kept confidential, and that their partners would not be given access to their responses. The questionnaire included the love and liking scales, to be completed first with respect to one's partner and later with respect to a close same-sex friend. In each case the respondent indicated how much he agreed or disagreed with each item by placing a check on the continuous scale. For example:

1. When I am with _____, we are almost always in the same mood.

Not at all true; disagree completely	Moderately true; agree to some extent	Definitely true; agree completely

With the help of a clear plastic ruler these responses were later converted to numbers from 1 to 9, to be used in analyzing the data. The questionnaire also called for a variety of other pieces of information about the subjects and their relationships, which I will say more about as I present some results.

LOVE'S CORRELATES

The statistical analysis of the questionnaire data began with an examination of the internal structure of the liking and love scales. As desired, each of the two scales proved to be internally consistent; that is, in each case its component items were highly intercorrelated. Also in accord with my starting assumption, the correlation between liking and loving scores was only moderate. The correlation between men's love and liking scores for their girlfriends was 0.56, and the correlation between women's love and liking scores for their boyfriends was 0.36.

Although the general pattern of intrascale versus interscale correlations emerged as I had hoped it would, the finding that love and liking were more highly related to one another among men than among women was unexpected. It is possible that this difference is a consequence of the distinctive specializations of the two sexes. In most societies, men tend to be the task specialists, while women tend to be the social–emotional specialists. By virtue of their specialization in matters involving interpersonal feelings, women may develop a more finely tuned and more discriminating set of interpersonal sentiments than men do. Whereas men may often blur such fine distinctions as the one between liking and loving, women may be more likely to experience and express the two sentiments as being distinct from one another.

Further insight into the nature of liking and loving for the two sexes was derived from a comparison of their average love and liking scores for their dating partners and their same-sex friends. Unsurprisingly, the students reported loving their partners much more than their friends, while the gap between liking for partners and liking for friends was narrower. Less obvious and more informative are the comparisons between

the scores of men and women. The average love scores of men for their girlfriends and of women for their boyfriends were virtually identical. But women *liked* their boyfriends significantly more than they were liked in return. The liking scale is "sex-biased" in that it asks the respondent to size up his partner on such stereotypically male characteristics as maturity, intelligence, and good judgment. It asks whether the respondent would vote for his partner in an election, and whether he would recommend the partner for a responsible job. It seems, in other words, to be getting at that task-related sort of liking that we have referred to as respect. It is doubtful that the men in our sample were in fact more responsible, more intelligent, or endowed with better judgment than their girlfriends. Nevertheless, it is generally considered to be more appropriate for men than for women to excel on these dimensions, and the obtained results conform precisely to these cultural expectations.

When respondents evaluated their same-sex friends, there was no tendency for men to be liked more than women. Thus, the data do not support the conclusion that men are generally more "likable" than women, but only that they are liked more in the context of dating relationships. The pattern of liking scores suggests that the dating relationship, instead of obliterating stereotypical differences between the sexes, may in fact perpetuate them by emphasizing role and status discrepancies. This pattern is in accord with the feminist critique of traditionally structured male–female relationships as fortifying the favored position of the male and reemphasizing the subservient position of the female.

Women tended to love their same-sex friends more than men did. It is indeed more common for female friends than for male friends to speak of themselves as "loving" one another, a linguistic fact that may reflect substantive differences in the nature of men's and women's same-sex friendships. Evidence from several surveys suggests that while women do not typically have more same-sex friends than men, women's friendships tend to be more intimate, involving more spontaneous joint activities and more exchanging of confidences. Men's special difficulties in establishing intimate relationships with other men are underlined by the love-scale results. The male role, for all its task-related "likability," may limit the ability to love. Loving for men may often be channeled into a single opposite-sex relationship, whereas women may be more able to experience and express attachment, caring, and intimacy in other relationships as well.

Another approach toward assessing the validity of the love and liking scales was to examine their correlations with other measures. One of the items included on the questionnaire was "Would you say that you and _____ are in love?" to be answered by circling "yes," "no," or "uncertain." Slightly over two-thirds of both men and women answered affirmatively, with only about 10 percent of each sex reporting that they were not in love and the remaining 22 percent of each sex pleading uncertainty. The correlations between love scores and this "in love" index were reasonably high: 0.61 for women and 0.53 for men. The correlations between liking scores and the "in love" index were considerably lower: 0.29 for women and 0.36 for men. Thus, the love scale, even though it nowhere includes the word "love" itself, tapped a sentiment that was distinctively related to the students' own categorization of their relationships.

The partners were also asked to estimate the likelihood they would eventually marry one another, on a probability scale ranging from 0 to 100 percent. The average estimate by women was about 50 percent and by men 45 percent. The correlations between love scores and estimates of marriage likelihood were substantial: 0.60 for women and 0.59 for men. The correlations between liking scores and marriage likelihood estimates were much lower: 0.33 for women and 0.35 for men. Once again the obtained pattern of correlations is reasonable. In societies like our own with a "love pattern" of mate selection, the link between love and marriage is strongly emphasized by parents, mass media, and other socializing agents. The link between liking and marriage, on the other hand, is too often a well-kept secret.

DISCUSSION QUESTIONS

1. Rubin's research was conducted during the sexual and gender revolutions of the late 1960s. Do you think that the meanings of "coupling" and "love" have changed for many people since that era?
2. Rubin's research relies on couples' willingness to open up their own relationships to the researcher's gaze. Would you be willing to participate in Rubin's research with your significant other? Why or why not?
3. How do you define "liking" and "loving"? How do your definitions differ from Rubin's?

ADDITIONAL RESOURCES

Film
"Kinsey: Let's Talk about Sex." 2004. Fox Searchlight Pictures.
"Kinsey." A 2005 American Experience documentary about the life and research of Alfred Kinsey.

Internet
http://www2.foxsearchlight.com/kinsey/site/. The official website for writer and director Bill Condon's award winning 2004 feature film "Kinsey: Let's Talk about Sex."

http://www.pbs.org/wgbh/amex/kinsey/filmmore/fd.html. The interactive website for the American Experience documentary about Alfred Kinsey.

FURTHER READING

Delaney, Tim. 2006. "Socialization and Personal Relationships," in *Seinology: The Sociology of Seinfeld*, 49–69. Amherst, MA: Prometheus Books.

Liebow, Elliott. 1967. "Friends and Networks," in *Tally's Corner: A Study of Negro Streetcorner Men*, 161–207. Boston: Little, Brown & Co.

Rubin, Zick. 1973. *Liking and Loving: An Invitation to Social Psychology.* New York: Holt, Rinehart and Winston.

Schwartz, Pepper. 2006. *Finding Your Perfect Match: 8 Keys to Finding Lasting Love through True Compatibility.* New York: Penguin.

18. "Cooling Out" Men in Singles Bars and Night Clubs: Observations on the Interpersonal Survival Strategies of Women in Public Places

DAVID A. SNOW, CHERYLON ROBINSON, AND PATRICIA L. McCALL

Snow and colleagues apply Erving Goffman's concept of "cooling the mark out" to women's rejections of men's advances in nightclubs. Using data collected from participant observation and interviews at several nightclubs, the authors describe the complex yet routine social dance visible in nightclub pickups and rejections. While they describe face-to-face encounters, the same techniques could be applied to online interactions. How might the cooling-out process differ in virtual encounters?

Urban areas provide numerous public places with the potential for interaction between unacquainted and semi-acquainted men and women. One of the characteristic features of interaction in public places is that it is laden with a range of threats to the bodies and selves of those individuals who frequent them. These threats are not randomly experienced, however. Women are particularly vulnerable to being hassled in one form or another. It thus follows that the successful negotiation of public places by women is frequently contingent on their ability to fend off men and parry their advances, whether direct or indirect. It is clear that many women are indeed accomplished at this. But how it is done and the reasons underlying the manner in which it is done are not well understood. Our aim in this article is to further empirical and theoretical understanding of these two interconnected questions by examining the strategies and practices employed

Snow, David A., Cherylon Robinson, and Patricia L. McCall. 1991. "'Cooling Out' Men in Singles Bars and Night Clubs: Observations on the Interpersonal Survival Strategies of Women in Public Places." *Journal of Contemporary Ethnography*, 19(4): 423–49.

by women in dealing with the unwanted advances of men in singles bars and other nightclub settings. Our focus is neither on the structure or culture of these settings nor on the range of encounters that occur in them involving men and women but, rather, on those encounters which women seek to avoid or from which they attempt to extricate themselves. We thus attend to the interpersonal lines and practices employed by women for such purposes.

We ask, in short, how do women "cool out" men in singles bars and nightclubs, and what factors shape the nature of this cooling-out process?

CONTEXT AND PROCEDURES

The data were collected by three means: participant observation in a number of different nightclubs, informal conversational interviews with patrons and employees in those settings, and semistructured interviews with a small nonrandom sample of bar patrons and employees and university students. The participant observation was conducted during the course of a 3-month period in which two of the authors visited, on one or more occasions, nine different nightclubs and drinking establishments. Four of the establishments were singles bars, two were country-western dance clubs, another two were disco and rock clubs, and one was a topless club.

On each occasion, the participant observer always stood or sat where she could hear or see other women. Such strategic positioning enabled the researcher to simultaneously observe and eavesdrop. The eavesdropping tactic was frequently impeded by the din of the music in several settings. As a consequence, it was often necessary to engage in informal, conversational interviews as a supplemental strategy. These interviews were typically occasioned by the observation of a cooling-out exchange that could not be overheard. In such instances, the researcher would attempt to elicit commentary from the female cooler by asking direct questions, such as "What was going on with that guy?" or by interviewing by comment, that is, by making

declarative statements, such as "That guy sure is persistent!" Every now and then, their conversations were continued or initiated in the women's restroom. Interestingly, the rest-room was found to be a particularly fruitful context for drawing out detailed commentary on cooling-out episodes, particularly when the exchange preceded the restroom excursion.

To supplement and complement the ethnographic data, we also conducted semi-structured interviews with 6 bar patrons, 6 bar employees, and 21 university students. While the majority of respondents were female (70%), we did interview 10 males in order to acquire some sense of the male perspective on the cooling-out process. Following a brief explanation of our research interests to each respondent, we asked them a number of questions aimed at getting them to discuss the cooling-out process as they had experienced it. We were particularly interested in learning about the cooling-out tactics which they had either employed or encountered, and the degree to which their experiences dovetailed with our observations. These data thus provided a kind of "validity check" for our ethnographic observations.

WOMEN'S PROTECTIVE STRATEGIES

Our research found abundant evidence of three sets of strategic practices associated with actual or anticipated cooling-out encounters. The first set includes all cooling-out lines or tactics typically triggered by initial face-to-face requests or overtures. The second set comprises more defensive and assertive tactics activated by the more persistent and obstinate males. And the third set consists of various practices employed in hopes of avoiding the cooling-out role and encounter altogether.

INITIAL COOLING-OUT TACTICS

Initial cooling-out tactics constituted the first line of defense employed by females when confronted by unsolicited or undesired advances by males. They comprised any combination of verbal and nonverbal lines employed in dyadic face-to-face encounters with men for the purpose of expressing disinterest in dancing, conversing, or continuing the encounter, at least for the moment. These tactics were typically elicited by initial advances and tended to be relatively inoffensive, as if the aim were "to let the man down easily."

Polite Refusal

A number of students of social interaction have noted that individuals who are cast or pulled into the role of an interactant are normatively obligated to respond to queries or responses directed toward them. Since male advances in nightclubs were most often initiated by questions—such as "Would you like to dance?" or "Can I buy you a drink?"—women who were the objects of such interrogative overtures had little choice but to respond. They might choose to ignore the initial inquiry by acting as if they did not hear it, but such a response only invited repetition of the question. Thus an answer was socially obligated.

The most frequently observed response was the polite refusal, the generic form being "No, thank you." Nearly all the women with whom we spoke considered such a response to be quite appropriate, especially in the face of initial advances that were courteous and inoffensive. In such instances, one 25-year-old female noted, "I try not to embarrass them or humiliate them. I just let them know very honestly and try not to lead them on."

But even more provocative and aggressive advances often elicited a polite response. In the words of one topless dancer, who routinely received sexually explicit offers during the course of her work, "I simply say 'thank you, but no thank you,' and I am as cordial as can be."

Our conversations and observations revealed further that polite and cordial cooling-out lines were often accompanied by a conscious attempt to soften or mute the rejection. One way this appeared to be done was by smiling and maintaining eye contact during the encounter. As one cocktail waitress noted when commenting about her dealings with the suggestive advances of a male customer:

> I'd go to his table to see if he needed a drink and say, "Would you like another drink?" and he'd say, "No, but I'd like something else," and I'd say, "Sorry, that's all I sell" and then smile my plastic smile.

Polite refusals were also softened on occasion by articulating them in a fashion that did not imply finality or a permanent lack of interest, as reflected in the comment "not right now, but maybe another time." By leaving the door ajar, so to speak, the female cooler provided the male with some psychic elbowroom so that while he returned to his table or bar stool empty-handed, he was at least left with a ray of hope that things would turn out differently the next time. He thus suffered a loss of sorts, but the prospect of humiliation was postponed, at least for the moment.

Excuses

Excuses comprise a second set of commonly observed cooling-out lines. Excuses can be invoked not only to exempt actors from responsibility for past action but to release them from ongoing role obligations and tacit understandings regarding situation-specific action by referring to some culpable or countervailing agent or agency. Such was the case with the use of excuses by women to cool out men in the settings we observed.

Over and over again, we heard women disengage themselves from nascent encounters with men by making excuses. The most common excuse entailed the verbalization of commitment to extant personal relationships, particularly to husbands and boyfriends.

The following comments are illustrative:

> "I'm married!"
> "I'm waiting for my boyfriend."
> "No, I really can't. My date will be back in a minute."
> "I'm with someone."

Consistent with such excuses, a cocktail waitress interviewed in a singles bar indicated that it was her sense that appeals to interpersonal attachments constituted "the greatest excuse for everybody." In fact, she related that she has used these very excuses on numerous occasions herself.

Excuses were also invoked that involved commitments to other responsibilities, such as work and family. One topless dancer explained that her work provided her with a handy excuse: "It's easy for me. I just look them in the eye and tell them that I don't date customers." A cocktail waitress was overheard responding to a male customer in a similar fashion: "I have to work and I really don't have time to socialize. I can't make any money sitting here, and you probably don't want to tip me anyway." On occasion, children were even used as an excuse. And sometimes, a challenged female would parry advances by invoking multiple commitments, as in the case of one female patron who was overheard saying during a cooling-out encounter: "You don't want to pick me up. I'm a married woman and I've got kids, and I'm too busy working."

Normative constraints were also employed as excuses, including references to race, size, and age differences. An especially tall female, who reported using her size to cool out men, recalled the following episode: "We were sitting down, and these guys kept coming over to talk with us and bother us.…They were all really short, so I just stood up. That's all I had to do." Age stereotypes were also employed, as when one 38-year-old respondent recalled cooling out a 19-year-old by simply saying, "Hey, I'm an older woman. I'm much older than you."

Finally, some women were heard to invoke excuses based on physiological considerations, such as refusing a drink by pleading, "I've had my limit." Physiological excuses were also useful in refusing a dance. For example, when queried about why she did not want to dance, one 19-year-old female simply said, "[B]ecause I can't dance in these shoes." Other excuses of this same genre included "I'm too tired" and "I can't dance to this song."

In sum, excuses seemed to be a particularly effective cooling-out tactic. Although excuses based on interpersonal commitments appeared the most compelling, each variety of excuse seemed to work more often than not. We suspect that the reason for their effectiveness was that they performed two important functions simultaneously. On one hand, excuses facilitated disengagement from encounters with men because they were grounded in factors that had generalized cultural currency and were therefore external to the men being cooled out; on the other hand, they provided men with a socially acceptable explanation for their foiled efforts. Excuses thus enabled women to rebuff unwanted advances without impugning the character of their pursuers. The male suitor left with no serious loss of face.

Joking

In addition to polite refusals and excuses, we also overheard cooling-out lines that had something of the flavor of jokes. Broadly defined, jokes are slices of action or talk which suggest that some exchange, encounter, or topic of conversation is not to be taken seriously. The following comments are illustrative of this jocular banter:

> "You've got to be kidding. You wanta dance with me?"
> "No way! We'd both look like fools."
> "No, I can't dance. My feet are too big, and I'd step all over you."
> "Sorry, but I don't drink, and if I did, I'd probably get sick. You probably wouldn't like that! So you better find someone else."

While such comments sounded a bit like excuses, they were more appropriately conceptualized as jokes in that they made light of the encounter and humorously brushed aside the serious intent of the overture. By redefining the encounter as a humorous misunderstanding, the man's advance was reframed as a deliberate but nonserious overture. Although such a cooling-out tactic ran the risk of offending the initiator of the encounter, it

altercasting

was equally likely to prevent or diffuse tension by transforming a situation of seriousness into one of levity. And, in doing so, the man was allowed to bow out without a serious loss of face, for the failed approach could be seen as a humorous misunderstanding or as the jocular contrivance of the clever man. In either case, the rebuffed suitor was likely to leave, shrouded with the illusion that he had not suffered an unmistakable rejection. It was perhaps because of these considerations that some women employed joking almost routinely as a cooling-out tactic. As one 20-year-old informant noted after having successfully parried an advance by reframing it as a joke, "I usually try to make these situations into a joke. Ya know, I just joke around." Likewise, a cocktail waitress informed us that joking was part of her standard repertoire for dealing with zealous male customers:

> If you're somebody that works with people…well, you've got to deal with them coming on to you. But you usually have to be more polite about putting them off and joke about it…. That's what I do.

DEFENSIVE, NONEMPATHETIC COOLING-OUT TACTICS

We have elaborated several ways in which women initially attempted to cool out men in nightclubs of various sorts. We have also suggested that these tactics were often quite successful, as the majority of cooling-out encounters that we observed ended without incidence, that is, without argumentation or aggressive posturing on behalf of the rebuffed male. But not all men left the encounters quietly or as inconspicuously as possible. Some simply refused to be cooled out. As one male bartender observed, "They don't get violent about it, but some get pretty irritated" and become more aggressive. The question thus arises: How did women deal with men who refused to be cooled out, at least initially? In other words, how did they counter the persistence of men who failed to acknowledge or accept their

initial rejection and the opportunity to leave the encounter with their face intact, thus creating a scene or violating, however momentarily, the interaction order?

Our observations suggest that such interactionally "deviant" persistence invited tactics of defensive assertiveness that showed little of the earlier regard for salvaging the aggressor's initial presentation of self. More specifically, humor was displaced by studied seriousness, politeness gave way to a kind of defensive incivility, and excuses were either embellished and strengthened or jettisoned in favor of justifications. Although these tactical responses were hardly mutually exclusive, we consider them separately for analytical purposes.

Studied Seriousness

By studied seriousness, we refer to the focusing of attention and energy on an immediate, pressing task. In the case of some men, the task was to avoid the personal embarrassment that may be associated with rejection and attempt to snatch victory from the jaws of defeat by trying once again. From the standpoint of the woman, it was to chase off the persistent man and thus dissolve the threatening encounter. In contrast to the initial exchange, typically characterized by seemingly ritualized civility and playfulness, this form of exchange was decidedly somber and potentially combative, as indicated by the interactants' stiffened postures, sharpened voices, and seriousness of expression. This transformation or reframing of the encounter was typically "keyed" by questions or comments offered by the male in response to initial cooling-out lines. Overheard comments and questions that served this keying function included the following:

> "Why not?" (in response to a polite refusal to dance)
> "You've gotta be kiddin'!" (in response to a jocular refusal to accept a drink)
> "Oh, come on…you can dance with me!" (in response to an excuse about being attached)

"No! What do you mean, no?" (in response to a
polite refusal)

Such questions and comments not only begged
for further response but, coming on the heel of
parried advances, they seemed to invite interpersonal lines that resonated with and reflected the
new ethos of the encounter and that were thus
different from the initial cooling-out lines.

Defensive Incivility

The generic response seemed to be characterized
by a kind of defensive incivility. Gone was the
earlier apparent concern with softening the blow
of rejection. Far more salient was the woman's
concern with extricating herself from the now
menacing encounter by making unmistakably
clear her lack of interest in the man's advance.
If she appeared rude and he was personally
embarrassed in the process, so be it. Sometimes,
the response was bold and straightforward, as
illustrated in the case of one respondent who
described how she finally cooled out a man
who persisted in asking her to dance: "I finally
pointed my finger at him as if I was scolding him
and said, 'Listen to what I'm saying. I do not want
to dance.'" She added that "there were some men
standing at the bar nearby who could overhear
the encounter" and that the persistent man left
immediately when he realized this, "probably to
avoid further embarrassment."

Self-Evident Justifications

A sense of this more defensively assertive and
nonempathetic attitude is reflected further in the
following cooling-out lines that we overheard:

> "Look, I don't want to dance with you!"
> "Just leave me alone!"
> I just told you, I'm not interested!"
> "Back off!!"
> "I don't want anything to do with you!"
> "Get control of yourself!"

There was no reference to some external constraint or countervailing agency as in the case of

an excuse. The female cooler accepted responsibility for rejecting the overture. She was just plainly
uninterested. Moreover, she acted as if there were
nothing inappropriate or pejorative about her
defensive incivility. After all, she had been pushed
into a corner. Her initial cooling-out lines had
been rejected themselves in an act of incivility by
her prospective suitor. Consequently, her more
defensive and assertive posture was situationally
commanded. As one informant mused when
explaining this switch in frame and attendant
action:

> If men come up nicely, you know, I try to be as
> nice as I can. But if somebody comes up and
> they really think they're Casanova…and they
> just are overbearing in their attitude and do
> not accept no for an answer…I just spurt out
> something like "I wouldn't want to dance with
> you"…to put him down, ya know, put him in
> his place.

While this general response seemed to be most
commonplace in the face of persistent males, we
sometimes overheard women laminate their selfjustified incivility with an embellished excuse, as
if to strengthen the force and credibility of their
claim of disinterest. To illustrate, consider the
comments of one cocktail waitress:

> Sometimes they aggravate me, and I just tell
> them flat out, "Hey, I don't want nothing to do
> with you!" Usually, it's persistence that aggravates me—the ones that say, "Oh, come on, you
> can go out."…So I also tell them a lot that I'm
> working and I'm trying to get my shit together
> and that I really don't have time to go out partying with them.

In a similar vein, a topless dancer explained how
she had used an embellished excuse to drive off a
particularly persistent client:

> I had one guy last week who wanted to follow
> me home [after work] and I said, "Well, you
> can go ahead and follow me home, but I'm not
> responsible for the actions of all six bikers that
> live with me."

Taken together, the above observations suggest that women often became noticeably more assertive when confronted by persistent males who flaunted or disregarded the initial cooling-out lines directed toward them. In such situations, women stepped out of role in the sense that their cooling-out posture became strikingly inconsistent with the more deferential behavior stereotypically associated with them and reflected in their initial response to unwanted male overtures. Such observations do not suggest that women enjoyed or relished this stance of defensive assertiveness and incivility, however. But as one woman asked rhetorically, "How else do you get them off your back?"

AVOIDANCE TACTICS

Many women often attempted to avoid the cooling-out process altogether. One tack was to avoid those public settings where women were most likely to be approached interactionally, as in the case of singles bars and nightclubs. Another possibility for women who chose to frequent such settings was to employ safeguards and strategies that signaled unavailability or disinterest, thereby lessening the likelihood of being drawn into cooling-out encounters. It is this latter tack that is of interest here. Three such sets of avoidance tactics were discernible during our research.

Tie Signs

The most reliable avoidance strategy was to provide evidence of attachment or commitment to one or more individuals. Although the copresence of signified others did not appear to be a necessary condition for keeping males at bay, it seemed to strengthen the message of unavailability. Thus our informants reported that the best way to avoid cooling-out encounters was to be in the company of a male friend or several female friends and to provide unmistakable evidence of involvement or bondedness.

Direct experiential validation of the reliability of ties with copresent others was provided on a number of occasions when one of the female authors was accompanied by a male friend during several field observations. When the male friend was visibly present, the female researcher received no overtures from other males. But when the friend drifted off from time to time, so that there was no clear-cut evidence of interactional commitment to some proximate other, then the woman became the object of advances by other male patrons.

In the absence of the protective shield provided by proximate others to whom there was indication of some attachment, there were other strategic options that could be employed to symbolize interpersonal commitments, on one hand, and unavailability, on the other. Conspicuously worn or placed jewelry, such as rings, could serve this function. As one 24-year-old female informant noted, "I have a friend who swivels her ring around so it looks like a wedding band. They [the men] really do notice, and when they do, they leave her alone."

The problem with such tie signs in the absence of the signified other is that they frequently went unnoticed. Additionally, they were sometimes ignored or taken to be indicative of a lukewarm relationship at best. Consequently, they were less likely to ensure avoidance of the cooling-out process.

Nonverbal Cues of Disinterest

A second avoidance strategy was to communicate nonverbally a lack of interest in being approached. Since sustained eye contact was perceived as a way to invite an overture, fleeting eye contact was taken as a sign of disinterest. One female respondent reported that she routinely resorted to this ploy. "I look away a lot," she said. "Eye contact is the key." A male informant agreed, noting that he took his cues from a woman's eyes: "[E]yes are very important. If you stare at someone, then it means you're more interested, and vice-versa." Other facial gestures, such as a frown, were also consciously used on occasion to signal lack of interest, sometimes in conjunction with fleeting glances and sometimes independently. One female respondent noted that "a lot of times I'll give a mean look...[I]t's not so much aimed at [any one individual], it's just a look like 'I'm a bitch, leave me alone...you don't even want to say "hi" to me.'"

Flight

Should tie signs or gestures of disinterest fail to keep men at a distance, then women occasionally resorted to flight or escape. They might leave the premises, relocate themselves in another sector of the club, or frequent the restroom. In commenting on this pattern to a woman who had just evaded an advancing man, one of the researchers suggested that perhaps a lot of movement that takes place in singles bars reflects efforts to escape undesired encounters. "Sure," the "informant responded,"...there's just so much you can do. You turn your back on some guy, and he doesn't take the hint that you aren't interested. All you can do then is walk away."

The most common refuge for escape from unsolicited encounters appeared to be the women's restroom. One of the authors tested this observation by remarking to a queue of women in a restroom that she guessed she wasn't the only one avoiding a man. She was answered by an affirmative nod by a number of women. This tack was also confirmed by several male informants who noted that they had been the objects of such evasive action on more than one occasion, as well as by a male bartender who referred to this ploy as "the duck out."

Through tie signs, cues of disinterest, or flight, then, women reduced the prospect of being approached by men. But the relative freedom secured did not come without a cost, for those who wished to avoid contact had to be constantly on guard and ever conscious of the signs they exuded, especially when not in the company of protective others.

SUMMARY AND DISCUSSION

In focusing on the matter of how women fend off and parry the unsolicited advances of men in public contexts, we did not fully attend to questions concerning the shape or form of the cooling-out process as we observed it. Why, for example, are initial advances parried in a polite and nonthreatening manner rather than in the more defensive and assertive fashion that characterizes the way in which women deal with the second and third advances of the more persistent men? Although such questions were not so much the focus of our inquiry, it is our sense that the women we observed and interviewed were very much concerned with not offending the men attempting to engage them initially in one way or another. This was indicated, in part, by the expression of wariness about insulting and humiliating the men being cooled out and, in part, by the very nature of the initial cooling-out tactics observed. A number of women indicated that they did not want to anger their pursuers out of fear that these men might retaliate with public embarrassment or perhaps even physical abuse. This, then, suggests one reason why the initial cooling-out tactics we observed tended to be polite, civil, and fairly stereotypic: They provided men with reasons for their rejection that did not impugn their character. Such tactics were, in short, relatively nonthreatening and civil.

DISCUSSION QUESTIONS

1. Snow and colleagues suggest that women's gender places them in the "cooler" role because they are "objects of satisfaction and predation" (p. 426). Do you agree or disagree with their claim?

2. Snow et al. discovered three types of cooling out techniques in their research. What are they?

3. Have you ever been a "cooler" or a "coolee"? Did you use any of the techniques described by Snow et al.?

ADDITIONAL RESOURCES

Internet

http://8minutedating.com/. An online system meant to link people to face-to-face speed dating events. Their tagline is: "8 Minute Dating, 8 Great Dates = 1 Fun Night!"

www.eharmony.com. A popular online dating site.

www.match.com. A popular online dating site.

www.relationshipobit.com. A website where those suffering bereavement from a recent breakup can post a relationship obituary.

Radio

"Neil Clark Warren on Finding EHarmony." August 17, 2005. A highly entertaining "Fresh Air" interview produced by National Public Radio featuring Terry Gross and the founder of eharmony.com: http://www.npr.org/templates/story/story.php?storyId=4803877.

"Speed Dating with Yaacov and Sue Deyo." August 17, 2005. The second part of this highly entertaining interview produced by National Public Radio featuring the founder of Speed Dating: http://www.npr.org/templates/story/story.php?storyId=4803880.

FURTHER READING

Goffman, Erving. 1952. "On Cooling the Mark Out: Some Aspects of Adaptation to Failure." *Psychiatry,* 15: 451–63.

Hobbs, Roger. Sunday, May 25, 2008. "Modern Love: Instant Message, Instant Girlfriend." *The New York Times.* http://www.nytimes.com/2008/05/25/fashion/25love.html?partner= rssnyt&emc=rss.

Horan, Kathleen. 2009. *Relationship Obits: The Final Resting Place for Love Gone Wrong.* London: HarperCollins.

Lofland, Lyn H. 1973. *A World of Strangers: Order and Action in Urban Public Space.* New York: Basic Books.

19. Changing Our Yesterdays: Reconstruction of Early Relationship Memories

DIANE HOLMBERG, TERRI L. ORBUCH, AND JOSEPH VEROFF

Holmberg et al. provide an in-depth analysis of marital narratives as told by 144 couples in the Detroit, Michigan area. Considered one of the most significant studies about marriage and family life in America, the ongoing Early Years of Marriage longitudinal research project, begun in 1986 and directed by Terri Orbuch, collects narratives of couples when they are in years one, three, and seven of marriage.

Holmberg, Diane, Terri L. Orbuch, and Joseph Veroff. 2003. "Changing Our Yesterdays: Reconstruction of Early Relationship Memories," in *Thrice Told Tales: Married Couples Tell Their Stories.* Mahwah, NJ: Lawrence Erlbaum.

Spouses' evaluations of their own marital happiness had much to do with how couples construct their relationship story. As we are all aware, memories do not always provide a complete and accurate record of past experiences. Memories show a general pattern of fading over time, such that most adults find retrieving even a dozen distinct memories of their childhood to be a relatively difficult task. People do not simply let go of faded past memories, however. Instead, they seem to unconsciously fill in any gaps they may experience with their beliefs regarding what might have happened. This tendency results in memories that appear clear and detailed to an outside observer and are held with a high degree of confidence by the person doing the remembering. And yet these memories can be shown to contain major inaccuracies, when compared with respondents' initial reports of the events.

LISTENING TO OUR COUPLES' NARRATIVES

Their stories show very clear and recognizable similarities from Years 1 through 7. Frequently, the same cherished events and key anecdotes are relayed each year. Each couple has their favored stories and their individual style. We have no doubt that even if we removed all identifying information, coders fresh to the narratives could come in, read the transcripts, and immediately match up couples' Year 1 stories with their Year 3 and 7 stories, with a high degree of accuracy.

What we do see in our narratives, however, are shifts in tone and emphasis. The same anecdotes may be told, but they may be detailed at one time and brief at another. One year, a particular incident may appear charged with affect and emotion; another time, it may be reported in an offhand manner. Individuals construct their stories to give appropriate meaning to a set of events, given the particular storytelling context, and their needs and desires at the time of the telling. Thus, individuals' current issues and concerns will shape

and mold their stories of the past. This process is largely unconscious. Thus, we would expect couples' current feelings and attitudes toward their relationship at the time of telling their story to color their reported memories of early relationship events.

Some of our own earlier work using Year 1 and Year 3 data from the current study also speaks to the issue of how memories for earlier events are shaped by current relationship feelings. For example, we compared a set of 13 couples who were high in marital happiness in both Years 1 and 3 to another group of 13 couples who were equally happy in Year 1 but much less happy by Year 3. The two groups' narratives looked similar in Year 1. However, by Year 3 the group who was less happy had imbued their memories for earlier stages of the relationship with more negative affect and more statements expressing ambivalence toward the relationship (see Holmberg & Holmes, 1994).

Our readings of the narratives suggests that couples could be remembering specific events relatively accurately but through a process of selective attention discuss only those particular events that fit well with their current relationship perspectives. As noted earlier, some events were described in detail at one point but were mentioned only in passing at another. The events that are more likely to be dwelt on in recall might be those events that best fit with current relationship feelings.

Couples could in fact be recalling exactly the same set of events, in the same amount of detail, at two different times. Their stories would still sound quite different, however, if their evaluations and perspectives on those events had changed. Wedding disagreements might be acknowledged, but described as "no big deal" at one point in time. At a later point in time, those same disagreements might be presented as problematic. Through shifts in tone and emphasis, the meaning presented by the narrative could change, even if the underlying events had remained relatively stable.

We explore how our couples' current attitudes toward their relationship might affect their stories of the early stages of their relationship. We look at how individuals' relationship feelings change across all 7 years, and see whether those changes in feelings predict particular changes in how their relationship story is remembered and told.

GLOBAL EFFECTS: CHANGES IN MARITAL HAPPINESS AS PREDICTORS OF CHANGES IN AFFECTIVE TONE

Motivation of Affective Statements

We found changes in marital well-being over time that predicted changes in the affective tone of the stories, at least for husbands. The happiest husbands were those who were in couples where themes of maintaining individual goals and desires over time, continued to be emphasized. Furthermore, there was also an effect of ethnicity. The effects were particularly strong for African-American husbands.

We see a picture of those husbands who maintain higher well-being over time participating in narratives that place relatively more emphasis on meeting individual needs and goals and relatively less emphasis on merging, or submerging, in the couple.

Consider Troy and Denise's Year 7 story, for example. Their courtship, by this point, is portrayed as logical and goal-oriented. As Troy put it:

> When we got together the second time, we knew that either we were going to be real serious, or not do it. And we decided to do it, so it was at that point that we knew we were a couple for life. I graduated. Denise had another year of school left, so I came home for a year, got an apartment, and lived in the apartment for about 3 months. Then I moved home with my parents, deciding to save some money, because at that time I think we had actually determined we were going to get married....So at that point, we knew what we wanted to do. Denise graduated the following April. She came home,

moved in with her parents, saved quite a bit of money toward the wedding, and then we had...the wedding.

Troy's story may not be excessively romantic, but it illustrates what may be a comfortable tale for many males, one where the couple got together and decided what they wanted to do, carefully completed their individual needs and goals first, then proceeded forward to marriage when the time was right. Both husband and wife were then emotionally and financially prepared to make the commitment. The tone might be very businesslike, but note that both partners were still very satisfied after 7 years of marriage.

Compare their story to that told by another couple, Jake and Alisha. Alisha described the circumstances and feelings that first drew them together:

> Getting interested in each other? We were interested. We were two hurt people thrown together that needed somebody's help. Well, really he needed somebody to talk to, and I was willing to listen at that time, to his problems....He says he was in between women, so he was using me to get rid of these other women. But that I didn't mind too much. Like I said, I had just been dumped. I had my own life in order. I was getting it in order, and I needed a male who was my friend.

Jake also emphasized their feelings toward each other in describing how they first became interested:

> I got interested in her because of the women that I...had at the time, she was the more consistent. That was one of the best traits about her. I mean, aside from the fact that she could talk and had personality. I mean, most of the women I met...most of them have personalities, but most of the time, hers [Alisha's] was more even keel. It wasn't so much like a serious roller coaster ride. Like "I hate you today. I love you tomorrow. I hate you today. I love you to death." It was kinda like, you know, nice. And I needed a little calmness, cause I was seriously between these people who had

me real insecure. If I walked out of the room, it was frazzle city. So finally came time to deal with that part, and I didn't have to call her [Alisha] every day, saying "Baby, I love you; baby, I love you."

Jake and Alisha's emphasis on their feelings and emotions toward each other might sound more like a conventionally romantic narrative. Such an emphasis on connections and the state of the relationship, however, may not be the most comfortable stance toward the relationship for some males. Note that by Year 7, this couple was relatively dissatisfied with their relationship. One gets the sense that Jake might have found that marriage in fact required a little more "Baby, I love you" than he was prepared for. For men, negotiating a relationship where there is a good balance between agentic and communal needs seems to be important.

We do not see parallel findings for the wives' well-being. Women seem to have slightly clearer memories for early relationship events than do men. With these clearer memories, women may be somewhat less prone to rework the broad sweep of their past in service of current goals. More likely, however, motivations were not their key issue; a relational narrative may already serve their more relational self-concepts rather well.

SPECIFIC EFFECTS: CHANGES IN EGALITARIAN AND CONFLICT ATTITUDES AS PREDICTORS OF CHANGES IN MEMORIES

In this section, we examine how changes in particular relationship attitudes predicted more circumscribed features of the narratives.

Let us first examine changes in memories for the amount of conflict in the wedding planning. Over the shorter term, looking only at the changes from Year 1 to Year 3, exactly the sort of effects one might expect occurred. Conflict minimizers had slightly lower scores even in Year 1 than did conflict accepters, although both groups said it was very important to control your anger at this point in time. By Year 3, these small initial differences had been accentuated. Conflict minimizers appeared to have shaded their narratives in the direction of their relationship attitudes. They believed that one should always control one's anger, and they in fact described experiencing considerably less conflict during the wedding planning than they had initially indicated. Uncomfortable with conflict, they purged their narratives of any indication of such conflict over time. Conflict accepters, who became more comfortable with the notion of disagreements over time, did not show these same effects, dropping only slightly in the level of conflict they portrayed.

What is especially interesting is that these sensible effects did not seem to hold up over time. By Year 7, we see a surprising reversal. At this point, conflict accepters were actually describing less conflict in their narratives than were conflict minimizers. What is going on here? One possibility is that conflict minimizers, who have insisted over 7 years that they must control how they show their anger with their spouse, might be feeling the strain. Every couple is going to have their conflicts, their disagreements, their times when they simply want to yell at each other. Conflict accepters have overtly changed their views, and have said that controlling one's anger at all times is not actually that essential. Conflict minimizers, who continued to maintain their belief in controlling overt displays of tension, might increasingly be letting that tension seep out in more subtle ways, such as in their memories of past events. Such an interpretation is speculative.

Another possibility is that conflict minimizers who were actually successful in living up to their ideals and controlled their anger over 7 years of marriage became more sensitive over time to any indication of conflict. Wedding planning can bring out tensions in the best of couples; those who have succeeded in rarely getting angry at each other in their marriage may come to see wedding conflicts, one of their few disagreements, as relatively bad in retrospect.

Again, it should be noted that we are talking about shadings of tone and emphasis, not wholesale memory reconstruction. As an example of the sort of changes we are describing, following is an excerpt from the narrative of one couple, Ed and Jeannette, in which the wife falls into the conflict minimizer group. As a rule, Jeannette does not like conflict, but she and Ed experienced a severe stressor during the wedding planning, when Ed's friend, who was to perform the ceremony, at the last minute turned out not to be registered as a minister in the state of Michigan. As one can imagine, this caused consternation. Perhaps sensitive to his wife's dislike for disorder and conflict, Ed described the negative reactions they experienced in Year 3, but somewhat downplayed the seriousness of the situation:

> I had a friend that I grew up with, right. He's an ordained preacher, but he had left the state of Michigan before he got ordained. He was supposed to marry us, but when it come down to it, he didn't have the...we were out of his jurisdiction. We found that out at the last minute....My wife and me are more and more hysterical. Well, my future wife. My biggest problem was to keep her calm, you know, cause like I say, why worry. We'll work something out, you know. As long as you keep your head level, you know, you think about it, there's a solution to every problem.

Here, problems and tensions clearly were occurring in the wedding planning, but they were not dwelled on. In contrast, look at the same couple's story in Year 7:

> E: One thing about the wedding...I had a friend that's one of them preachers, and he was supposed to marry us. He was supposed to marry us, and we find out that he wasn't licensed in Michigan, and we found that out at the last minute....She [Jeannette] panicked, you know. She had a fit. That's one thing that I can't get out of. She panicked. It's like I tried to tell her, you know, there'll

> always be problems, and we can always find a solution. We can always find a solution to the problem, you know, but still, she panicked...
> J: *Frantic.* Not panicked, but frantic.
> E: Eventually we worked it out, you know. I talked to another friend, and I forgot that his father was a preacher.
> J: His mother made him go ask him....She said, "Ed, you better marry this girl. If not, she's gonna have a fit."

The tensions Ed and Jeannette experienced were much more obvious in this Year 7 story. Perhaps if they seldom showed their negative emotions to each other, this one time when Jeannette was understandably stressed seemed more like a "fit," more like "panic," as time went on.

Compare these changes to changes seen next, in Angie and Chris's wedding planning narratives. They showed the opposite pattern, with their emphasis on problems in the wedding planning decreasing, not increasing, over time. In Year 3, they described the disagreements between their families over the nature of the wedding celebration in detail:

> C: What the toughest thing about all of it is, myself included and my parents, our religious beliefs. I had never been to a big wedding, and her being Polish Catholic, they have a dance, they have halls, they have all this big extravaganza, and for me, a wedding was two people, and the congregation from the church, you go in, you get married, you all meet out in the overflow room of the church building and our lobby. You have coffee or punch and a piece of cake, and everyone goes home, and you're married...and that's it. And so we had to come up with a compromise somewhere between getting her family happy and making my family happy. So I talked to my parents, and she talked to her parents, and we decided that we'd get married in our church,

but we would rent a hall and we would have…dancing and all that for her family. I felt that was right, because that's what they were used to. And so, that was hard for my parents to swallow. Both sets of parents had to go through something.

A: …Him going to a wedding where there's liquor and dancing and everything was like "Um, okay…." (chuckles). So, we both gave up a little bit, just trying to please everybody.

Angie is a conflict accepter. She became more comfortable with the notion of conflict in her relationship over time, and participated freely and easily in a narrative that spoke of conflicts and tensions. By Year 7, in contrast to Ed and Jeannette, Angie and Chris seem to have moved on. They described the same disagreement, but in a much more brief, offhand fashion:

C: So we had to decide how we were gonna do this. I wasn't really following any set religion at the time, but yet, to appease my parents, I didn't want to do anything that would hurt them. So we decided that, you know, my parents wanted to help, but they wouldn't pay for alcohol and things like that. So that's how we worked it out. We got married at my parents' church, and then we held the reception at a hall, and we had dancing and drinking….Both of our parents were real adult and mature about the whole situation. They handled it really well, and they got along. That was nice, that both sets of parents could be sociable. And it was, in the years to come it's helped too.

Angie and Chris didn't dwell on the wedding planning difficulties in Year 7, as Ed and Jeannette did. They acknowledged them, but didn't seem to feel, now that sufficient time had passed, that the conflict was any big deal. Conflict minimizers, like Jeannette, though, seemed to dwell on the difficulties more as time passed. We see similar effects when we look at the average level of tension in the early portion of the narrative. Conflict minimizers

participated in narratives wherein the tensions became stronger over time, while conflict accepters showed a drop in tensions in their Year 7 stories. Again, this effect could represent a rather psychodynamic spilling over of repressed tension from conflict minimizers, or a simple contrast effect: If they indeed displayed little tension in their day-to-day relationships, any tensions they did experience in the past might come to seem more and more unusual and worthy of exploration over time.

SUMMARY

We have seen that at both the interpersonal and the personal levels, current feelings can shape the narratives of early relationship. For men, their overall well-being was related to the motivations expressed in their narratives about their past together. Happier men reconstructed narratives where there was relatively more emphasis on agency, and less on communion or connection, as compared to less happy men. An emphasis on meeting individual needs and goals seemed to serve as a more comfortable relationship narrative mode for men, particularly African-American men, when they reconstructed their memories.

Women did not show the same effects on their motivations. Where we did see narrative shaping for women was in the area of interpersonal conflict, a topic that is often highly charged for women. Women who came to accept a certain level of conflict in their relationship, who came to believe that it was not always necessary to control their anger, seemed freer to move on and let early conflicts and tensions fade away. Ironically, women who insisted that all anger must be controlled had narratives that became more charged with tension over time, and were less able to let go of wedding planning conflicts in Year 7. If controlling emotions was a central issue to them, they continued to explore issues of tension and conflict in their narratives, perhaps seeking to understand and learn lessons from times when they were unable to live up to their own high standards.

Both sets of findings support our belief that individuals' current perspectives on their relationship can reach back and color their relationship narratives in predictable ways. Current individual feelings and attitudes play a role in reconstructing the memories that make up the narratives.

DISCUSSION QUESTIONS

1. Holmberg et al. argue that people change their memories of marriage to help uphold current experiences in their marital relationship. Have you ever experienced your own or others' recollections changing over time to uphold the current definition of a relationship?

2. Holmberg et al. describe gender differences in the ways couples recall early relationship memories. What are some of the differences they identify? Are these gender differences consistent with your own experiences?

3. What are the patterns that Holmberg et al. report regarding "conflict minimizers" and "conflict accepters" over the course of a marriage? Do you know any "conflict minimizers" or "accepters"? Do they seem to follow the patterns identified by Holmberg and colleagues?

ADDITIONAL RESOURCES

Film

"Eternal Sunshine of the Spotless Mind." 2004. A fascinating fictional tale of lovers who undergo a medical procedure to erase one another from their memories. Universal Studios.

Internet

www.eternalsunshine.com. The official website for the 2004 feature film.

http://www.youtube.com/watch?v=4-94JhLEiN0. The jubilant dancing wedding party processional from Jill Peterson and Kevin Heinze's June 2009 wedding that became an Internet sensation.

http://projects.isr.umich.edu/eym/. The website for the Early Years of Marriage longitudinal research project, on which Holmberg, Orbuch, and Veroff's research is based.

http://www.drterrithelovedoctor.com/index.html. Terri Orbuch's "The Love Doctor" site, rich with suggestions for finding happiness and success in relationships, many of which come from the Early Years of Marriage longitudinal research project.

http://www.pbs.org/wgbh/pages/frontline/shows/marriage/etc/links.html. A highly interactive and rich Frontline website dedicated to the analysis of marriage.

FURTHER READING

Gardner, Jonathan and Andrew J. Oswald. 2006. "Do Divorcing Couples Become Happier by Breaking Up?" *Journal of the Royal Statistical Society: Series A (Statistics in Society)*, 169(2): 319–36.

Holmberg, Diane and John G. Holmes. 1994. "Reconstruction of Relationship Memories: A Mental Models Approach," in Norbert Schwarz and Seymour Sudman (eds.). *Autobiographical Memory and the Validity of Retrospective Reports*, 345–68. New York: Springer-Verlag.

Orbuch, Terri L. 2009. *5 Simple Steps to Take Your Marriage from Good to Great.* New York: Random House.

Rubin, Zick, Letitia Anne Peplau, and Charles T. Hill. 1981. "Loving and Leaving: Sex Differences in Romantic Attachments." *Sex Roles,* 7(8): 821–35.

Vaughan, Diane. 1986. *Uncoupling: Turning Points in Intimate Relationships.* New York: Oxford University Press.

Veroff, Joseph, Elizabeth Douvan, and Shirley, J. Hatchett. 1995. *Marital Instability: A Social and Behavioral Study of the Early Years.* Santa Barbara, CA: Praeger Publishers.

Vinitzky-Seroussi, Vered. 1998. *After Pomp and Circumstance: High School Reunion as an Autobiographical Occasion.* Chicago: University of Chicago Press.

The Definition of the Situation

These next selections epitomize the profound relevance that "classic" research has not only for contemporary research, but for real world events as well. In fact, it was during a discussion about the relevance of the findings from the Stanford Prison Experiment to the unfathomable torture at the U.S. military prison in Abu Ghraib, Iraq, that first gave us the impetus to structure this volume as a conversation connecting classic and contemporary research and issues in social psychology.

All three entries below convey the tremendous power of the social context within which social interactions take place. These contexts profoundly shape individuals' decision-making processes and behaviors. While it is comforting to think that we have the ability to rise above situational influences, the research and military experiences described in these selections convey another story. Indeed, human "actors" look to familiar social cues, such as social hierarchies, social expectations, and social norms, to identify their own "location" and appropriate behavior within social settings. Moreover, the more unfamiliar a social setting, the more likely an individual is to seek such culturally available models in setting his or her own course of action. The college boys in the Stanford Prison Experiment drew not only on their knowledge of prison guards' and inmates' behavior but also on the obvious power differential inherent in those roles. The same is true of the real military prison at Abu Ghraib where we see the guards enacting the power of their role. In the process of exercising this power, they cast the prisoners as the Enemy Other, representing terrorism itself, and thus seemingly deserving of inhumane torture.

As you read these pieces, reflect on what factors contributed to the definition of the situation in these prisons as one in which humiliation and degradation were not only acceptable but also encouraged and sometimes rewarded.

20. The Psychology of Imprisonment: Privation, Power, and Pathology

PHILIP G. ZIMBARDO, CRAIG HANEY, W. CURTIS BANKS, AND DAVID JAFFE

Philip Zimbardo's research, conducted in 1971 with his graduate student coauthors, continues to be a perennial favorite in classrooms throughout the world. It shows how the power of the situation can literally overcome an individual's sense of self. Here, Zimbardo and his former students provide an abbreviated version of the events and findings of the Stanford Prison Experiment. Its lessons are obviously relevant today; we all engage daily in the process of role making and role taking, as we develop a shared definition of the situation in our interactions with others.

The quiet of a summer Sunday morning in Palo Alto, California was shattered by a screeching squad car siren as police swept through the city picking up college students in a surprise mass arrest. Each suspect was charged with a felony, warned of his constitutional rights, spread-eagled against the car, searched, handcuffed and carted off in the back seat of the squad car to the police station for booking. In some cases, curious neighbors who witnessed these arrests expressed sympathy and concern to the families of these unfortunate young men. Said one alarmed mother of an 18-year-old college sophomore arrested for armed robbery, "I felt my son must have done something; the police have come to get my son!"

After being fingerprinted and having identification forms prepared, each prisoner was left isolated in a detention cell to wonder what he had done to get himself into this mess. After a while, he was blindfolded and transported to the "Stanford County Prison." Here he began the induction process of becoming a prisoner—stripped naked, skin searched, deloused, and issued a uniform, bedding, soap and towel. By late afternoon when nine such arrests had been completed, these youthful "first offenders" sat in dazed silence on the cots in their barren cells trying to make sense out of these unexpected events which had transformed their lives so dramatically.

Zimbardo, Philip G., Craig Haney, W. Curtis Banks, and David Jaffe. 1975. "The Psychology of Imprisonment: Privation, Power, and Pathology," in Zick Rubin (ed.). *Doing Unto Others: Joining, Molding, Conforming, Helping, Loving*, 61–73. Englewood Cliffs, NJ: Prentice-Hall.

These men were part of a very unusual kind of prison, an experimental or mock prison, created by social psychologists for the purpose of intensively studying the effects of imprisonment upon volunteer research subjects. When we planned our two-week long simulation of prison life, we were primarily concerned about understanding the process by which people adapt to the novel and alien environment in which those called "prisoners" lose their liberty, civil rights, independence and privacy, while those called "guards" gain social power by accepting the responsibility for controlling and managing the lives of their dependent charges.

The decision to investigate this and related issues in the context of a mock prison rather than an actual one was based upon two premises. Prison systems are fortresses of secrecy, closed to impartial observation, and thereby immune to critical analysis from anyone not already part of the correctional authority. It is virtually impossible even for congressional investigating committees to have extended, truly open access to daily prison operations. Second, in any real prison, it is impossible to separate out what each individual brings into the prison from what the prison brings out in each person. When observing, for instance, a given act of violence or brutality in a prison setting, it is impossible to determine whether it is attributable to some aspect of the situation or to preexisting personality characteristics of the special population of those who become prisoners and guards.

By populating our mock prison entirely with a homogeneous group of individuals judged to be "normal-average" on a variety of personality dimensions, we were better able to assess the impact of acute situational forces upon the resulting behavior, uncontaminated by chronic personality traits typically used to "explain" prison incidents.

Our final sample of participants (10 prisoners and 11 guards) were selected from over 75 volunteers recruited through ads in the city and campus newspapers. The applicants were mostly college students from all over the United States and Canada who happened to be in the Stanford area during the summer and were attracted by the lure of earning $15 a day for participating in a study of prison life. All applicants were given an intensive clinical interview and completed an extensive background questionnaire, and we selected only those who were judged to be emotionally stable, physically healthy, mature, law-abiding citizens.

This sample of average, middle-class, Caucasian college males (there was one Oriental student) was then arbitrarily divided into two subgroups by a flip of the coin. Half were randomly assigned to role-play being guards, the others to be prisoners. Thus, there were no measurable differences between the guards and the prisoners at the start of this experiment. Although initially warned that as prisoners their privacy and other civil rights would be violated and they might be subjected to harassment, every subject was completely confident in his ability to endure whatever the prison had to offer for the full two-week experimental period.

What was most surprising about the outcome of this simulated prison experience was the ease with which sadistic behavior could be elicited from quite normal young men, and the contagious spread of emotional pathology among those carefully selected precisely for their emotional stability. Perhaps even more astonishing to us was the permeability of the boundaries between reality and delusion, between self-identity and situational role. What began as a simple academic exercise gradually became a force of monstrous proportion, generating unpredictable consequences in all those who came within the walls of this special prison.

The prison was physically constructed in the basement of Stanford University's psychology building, which was deserted after the end of the summer school session. A long corridor was converted into the prison "Yard" by partitioning off both ends. Three small laboratory rooms opening onto this corridor were made into cells by replacing their doors with metal barred ones and replacing existing furniture with three cots to a cell. Adjacent offices were refurnished as guards' quarters, interview-testing rooms, and bedrooms for the "Warden" (Jaffe) and the "Superintendent" (Zimbardo). A concealed video camera and hidden microphones recorded much of the verbal and nonverbal interactions between and among guards and prisoners. The physical environment was one in which prisoners could always be observed by the staff, the only exception being when they were secluded in solitary confinement (a small, dark storage closet, labeled "The Hole").

Anonymity was promoted through a variety of operations to minimize each prisoner's uniqueness and prior identity. Their uniforms, ID numbers, and nylon stocking caps, as well as removal of their personal effects and being housed in barren cells, all made the subjects appear similar to each other, often indistinguishable to observers, and forced upon them the situational group identity of "prisoner." Having to wear smocks, which were like dresses, without undergarments caused the prisoners to be more restrained in their physical actions and to move in ways which were more feminine than masculine. Forcing the prisoners to obtain permission from the guards for routine and simple activities such as writing letters, smoking a cigarette, or even going to the toilet elicited from them a child-like dependency.

Above all, "real" prisons are time machines for playing tricks with the human conception of time. In our windowless prison, the prisoners often did not even know whether it was day or night, or what hour it was. A few hours after falling asleep, they were rousted by shrill whistles for their "count." Over the course of the study, the duration of the counts was gradually and spontaneously increased by the guards from their initial perfunctory ten minutes to a seemingly interminable several hours. During these interactions, guards who were bored could find ways to amuse themselves, recalcitrant prisoners could be ridiculed, arbitrary rules could be enacted,

and any dissension among the prisoners could be openly exaggerated by the guards.

The guards were also "deindividuated" by virtue of wearing identical khaki uniforms and silver reflector sunglasses which made eye contact with them impossible. Their symbols of power were billy clubs, whistles, handcuffs, and the keys to the cells and the "main gate." Although our guards received no formal training from us in how to be guards, for the most part they moved with apparent ease into their roles. Movies, TV, novels, and all of our mass media had already provided them with ample models of prison guards to emulate. Just as do "real" correctional officers subjected to these very same cultural influences, our mock guards had available to them behavioral templates of what it means to be a guard, upon which they could improvise their role performances. So too, our mock prisoners had already learned to some extent from mass media and selected life experiences what were appropriate prisoner reactions.

Because we were as interested in the guards' behavior as in the prisoners', they were given considerable latitude for improvisation and for developing strategies and tactics of prisoner management. For the bulk of the time guards and prisoners interacted on the yard alone without the presence of any higher-ups. Our guards were told that they must maintain "law and order" in this prison, that they were responsible for handling any trouble which might break out, and they were cautioned as to the seriousness and potential dangers of the situation they were about to enter. Surprisingly, in most prison systems, "real" guards are not given much more psychological preparation or adequate training than this for what is one of the most complex, demanding, and dangerous jobs our society has to offer. They are expected to learn how to adjust to their new employment mostly from on-the-job experience, and from contacts with the "old bulls" during a survival-of-the-fittest orientation period.

The symbolic interaction between guards and prisoners requires each to play his own role while also forcing the others to play their roles appropriately. *You cannot be a prisoner if no one will be your guard, and you cannot be a prison guard if no one takes you or your prison seriously.* Therefore, over time a perverted symbiotic relationship developed. As the guards became more aggressive, prisoners became more passive; assertion by the guards led to dependency in the prisoners; self-aggrandizement was met with self-deprecation, authority with helplessness, and the counterpart of the guards' sense of mastery and control was the depression and hopelessness witnessed in the prisoners. As these differences in behavior, mood and perception became more evident to all, the need for the now "righteously" powerful guards to rule the obviously inferior and powerless inmates became a sufficient reason to support almost any further indignity of man against man.

> GUARD M: I was surprised at myself…I made them call each other names and clean the toilets out with their bare hands. I practically considered the prisoners cattle, and I kept thinking I have to watch out for them in case they try something.
>
> GUARD A: I was tired of seeing the prisoners in their rags and smelling the strong odors of their bodies that filled the cells. I watched them tear at each other on orders given by us. They didn't see it as an experiment. It was real and they were fighting to keep their identity. But we were always there to show them who was boss.

Because the first day passed without incident, we were surprised and totally unprepared for the rebellion which broke out on the morning of the second day. The prisoners removed their stocking caps, ripped off their numbers, and barricaded themselves inside the cells by putting their beds against the door. And now the problem was, what were we going to do about this rebellion? The guards were very much upset because the prisoners also began to taunt and curse them to their faces. When the morning shift of guards came on, they were upset at the night shift who, they felt,

must have been too permissive and too lenient or else this rebellion would not have taken place. The guards had to handle the rebellion themselves, and what they did was startling to behold.

At first they insisted that reinforcements be called in. The two guards who were waiting on stand-by call at home came in and the night shift of guards voluntarily remained on duty (without extra pay) to bolster the morning shift. The guards met and decided to treat force with force. They got a fire extinguisher which shot a stream of skin-chilling carbon dioxide and forced the prisoners away from the doors, they broke into each cell, stripped the prisoners naked, took the beds out, forced some of the prisoners who were then the ringleaders into solitary confinement, and generally began to harass and intimidate the prisoners.

After crushing the riot, the guards then decided to head off further ones by creating a privileged cell for those who were "good prisoners," then without explanation switching some of the troublemakers into it and some of the good ones out into the other cells. The prisoner ringleaders could not trust these new cellmates because they had not joined in the riot and might even be "snitches." The prisoners never again acted in unity against the system. One of the leaders of the prisoner revolt later confided:

> If we had gotten together then, I think we could have taken over the place. But when I saw the revolt wasn't working, I decided to toe the line. Everyone settled into the same pattern. From then on, we were really controlled by the guards.

It was after this episode that the guards really began to demonstrate their inventiveness in the application of arbitrary power. They made the prisoners obey petty, meaningless and often inconsistent rules, forced them to engage in tedious, useless work such as moving cartons back and forth between closets and picking thorns out of their blankets for hours on end. Not only did the prisoners have to sing songs or laugh or refrain from smiling on command, but they were also encouraged to curse and vilify each other publicly during some of the counts. They sounded off their numbers endlessly, and were repeatedly made to do pushups, on occasion with a guard stepping on them or a prisoner sitting on them.

Slowly the prisoners became resigned to their fate and even behaved in ways which actually helped to justify their dehumanizing treatment at the hands of the guards. Analysis of the tape-recorded private conversations between prisoners and of remarks made by them to interviewers revealed that 85 percent of the evaluative statements by prisoners about their fellow prisoners, were uncomplimentary and deprecating.

This result should be taken in the context of an even more surprising one. What do you imagine the prisoners talked about when they were alone in their cells with each other, given a temporary respite from the continual harassment and surveillance by the guards? Girlfriends, career plans, hobbies, politics, etc., were what we assumed would be the major topics of conversation. Not so. Their concerns were almost exclusively riveted to prison topics. Their monitored conversations revealed that only 10 percent of the time was devoted to "outside" topics. During the remaining 90 percent of the time they discussed such topics as escape plans, the awful food, grievances, or ingratiation tactics to use with specific guards. The prisoners' obsession with immediate survival concerns made talk about their past and future an idle luxury. But this exclusive focus on prison topics had a doubly negative effect upon the prisoners' adjustment. First, by voluntarily allowing prison topics to occupy their thoughts even when they did not have to continue playing their roles, the prisoners themselves extended the oppressiveness and reality of the experience. Second, since the prisoners were all strangers to each other to begin with, they could only know what the others were really like by sharing past experiences and future expectations and observing how they behaved. But what each prisoner observed was his fellow prisoners allowing the guards to humiliate them, acting like compliant sheep, carrying out mindless orders with total obedience, and even being cursed

by their fellow prisoners (at a guard's command). After days of living confined together in this tight environment, many of the prisoners did not even know the names of most of the others, where they came from, nor had even the most basic information about what they were like when they were not "prisoners." Under such circumstances, how could a prisoner have respect for his fellows, or any self-respect for what *he* obviously was becoming in the eyes of all those evaluating him?

Thus, the combination of realistic and symbolic elements in this experiment fused to create a vivid illusion of imprisonment. This illusion merged inextricably with reality for at least some of the time for every individual in the situation. It was remarkable how readily we all slipped into our roles, temporarily gave up our identities, and allowed these assigned roles and the social forces in the situation to guide, shape and eventually to control our freedom of thought and action.

A few examples will convey the extent to which a role-playing simulation experience can, under certain circumstances, become a totally involving life situation.

Prisoner 819, who had gone into a rage followed by an uncontrollable crying fit, was about to be prematurely released from the prison when a guard lined up the prisoners and had them chant in unison, "819 is a bad prisoner. Because of what 819 did to prison property we all must suffer. 819 is a bad prisoner," over and over again. When we realized 819 might be overhearing this, we rushed into the room where 819 was supposed to be resting, only to find him in tears, prepared to go back into that prison because he could not leave as long as the others thought he was a "bad prisoner." Sick as he felt, he had to prove to them he was not a "bad" prisoner. He had to be persuaded that he was not a prisoner at all, that the others were also just students, that this was just an experiment and not a prison and the prison staff were only research psychologists.

Consider our overreaction to the rumor of a mass escape plot which one of the guards allegedly overheard. It went as follows: Prisoner 8612, previously released for emotional disturbance, was only faking. He was going to round up a bunch of his friends and they would storm the prison right after visiting hours. Instead of collecting data on the pattern of rumor transmission, we made plans to maintain the security of our institution. After putting a confederate informer into the cell 8612 had occupied to get specific information about the escape plans, the Superintendent went back to the Palo Alto Police Department to request transfer of our prisoners to the old city jail. This impassioned plea was turned down at the last minute when the problem of insurance and city liability for our prisoners was raised by a city official. Angered at this lack of institutional cooperation, the staff formulated another plan. Our jail was dismantled, the prisoners, chained and blindfolded, were carted off to a remote storage room. When the conspirators arrived, they would be told the study was over, their friends had been sent home, there was nothing left to liberate. After they left, we would redouble the security features of our prison, making any future escape attempts futile. We even planned to lure ex-prisoner 8612 back on some pretext and then imprison him because he had been released on false pretenses! The rumor turned out to be just that—a full day had passed in which we collected little or no data, worked incredibly hard to tear down and then rebuild our prison. Our reaction, however, was as much one of relief and joy as of exhaustion and frustration.

Perhaps the most telling account of the insidious development of this new reality, of the gradual Kafkaesque metamorphosis of good into evil, is evident in excerpts from the diary of one of the guards, Guard A:

PRIOR TO START OF EXPERIMENT: As I am a pacifist and nonaggressive individual, I cannot see a time when I might guard and/or maltreat other living things.

AFTER ORIENTATION MEETING: Buying uniforms at the end of the meeting confirms the game-like atmosphere of this thing. I

doubt whether many of us share the expectations of "seriousness" that the experimenters seem to have.

FIRST DAY: Feel sure that the prisoners will make fun of my appearance and evolve my first basic strategy—mainly not to smile at anything they say or do which would be admitting it's all only a game.... At cell 3 I stop and setting my voice hard and low say to #5486, "what are you smiling at?" "Nothing, Mr. Correctional Officer." "Well see that you don't." (As I walk off I feel stupid.)

SECOND DAY: 5704 asked for a cigarette and I ignored him—because I am a non-smoker and could not empathize.... Meanwhile since I was feeling empathetic towards 1037, I determined not to talk with him... after we had Count and lights out [Guard D] and I held a loud conversation about going home to our girlfriends and what we were going to do to them.

THIRD DAY: (Preparing for the first Visitors' Night.) After warning the prisoners not to make any complaints unless they wanted the visit terminated fast, we finally brought in the first parents. I made sure I was one of the guards on the yard, because this was my first chance for the type of manipulative power that I really like—being a very noticed figure with almost complete control over what is said or not. While the parents and prisoners sat in chairs, I sat on the end of the table dangling my feet and contradicting anything I felt like. This was the first part of the experiment I was really enjoying.... 817 is being obnoxious and bears watching.

FOURTH DAY: ... The psychologist rebukes me for handcuffing and blindfolding a prisoner before leaving the [counseling] office, and I resentfully reply that it is both necessary security and my business anyway.

FIFTH DAY: I harass "Sarge" who continues to stubbornly overrespond to all commands. I have singled him out for special abuse both because he begs for it and because I simply don't like him. The real trouble starts at dinner. The new prisoner (416) refuses to eat his sausage...we throw him into the Hole ordering him to hold sausages in each hand. We have a crisis of authority, this rebellious conduct potentially undermines the complete control we have over the others. We decide to play upon prisoner solidarity and tell the new one that all the others will be deprived of visitors if he does not eat his dinner....I walk by and slam my stick into the Hole door...I am very angry at this prisoner for causing discomfort and trouble for the others. I decided to force feed him, but he wouldn't eat. I let the food slide down his face. I didn't believe it was me doing it. I hated myself for making him eat but I hated him more for not eating.

SIXTH DAY: The experiment is over. I feel elated but am shocked to find some other guards disappointed somewhat because of the loss of money and some because they are enjoying themselves.

We were no longer dealing with an intellectual exercise in which an hypothesis was being evaluated in the dispassionate manner dictated by the canons of the scientific method. We had to end this experiment! So our planned two-week simulation was aborted after only six days and nights.

We believe there are many significant implications to be derived from this experience, only a few of which can be suggested here.

The pathology observed in this study cannot be reasonably attributed to preexisting personality differences of the subjects, that option being eliminated by our selection procedures, and random assignment. Rather, the subjects' abnormal social and personal reactions are best seen as a product of their *transaction* with an environment whose values and contingencies supported the production of behavior which would be pathological in other settings, but were "appropriate" in this prison. Had we observed comparable reactions in a real prison, the psychiatrist undoubtedly would have been able to attribute any prisoner's behavior to character defects or personality maladjustment, while critics of the prison system would have been as quick to label the guards as "psychopathic." This tendency to locate the source of behavior disorders *inside* a particular person or group underestimates the power of situational forces to control behavior while overestimating the efficacy of personality or trait dispositions.

If, indeed, the pathology of prisons can be isolated as a product of the power relations in the social psychological structure of the institution itself, change is conceivable. Social institutions, being the creations of human beings—our little experiments in social and political control—are susceptible to modification when confronted by a human consciousness protesting their inadequacy and evils, supported by an informed electorate concerned about eliminating all forms of injustice.

DISCUSSION QUESTIONS

1. How did Phil Zimbardo, acting as the prison's superintendent, affect the power of the situational definition?
2. What would have happened if the study were allowed to continue?
3. How do you think you would have responded if you were a participant in the study as a prisoner or as a guard?
4. Was this study ethical? Why or why not? What other ways are there to study the power of the situation with less potential harm to research participants?

ADDITIONAL RESOURCES

Film

"Quiet Rage: The Stanford Prison Experiment." A 50-minute documentary about the study produced by Zimbardo.

Internet

http://www.prisonexpirement.org. An instructional site about the Stanford Prison Experiment.

FURTHER READING

Lofgren, Ovrar. 2004. "The Global Beach," in Sharon Bohn Gmelch (ed.). *Tourists and Tourism.* Long Grove, IL: Waveland Press.

Smith, H. W. 1981. "Territorial Spacing on a Beach Revisited: A Cross-National Exploration." *Social Psychology Quarterly,* 44(June): 132–6.

Zimbardo, Philip G. 2007. Experts from *The Lucifer Effect: Understanding How Good People Turn Evil.* New York: Random House.

21. When Women Abuse Power, Too

MELISSA SHERIDAN EMBSER-HERBERT
Sunday, May 16, 2004; Page B01

Melissa Sheridan Embser-Herbert is a sociologist and former army MP who has studied the role of women in the military extensively. Here she sheds light on what factors enabled women guards to participate in the torture of male prisoners at Abu Ghraib. She also considers the reasons why the knowledge that women were involved in committing such inhumane acts was shocking to so many of us.

If Pfc. Lynndie England had come home in a flag-draped coffin, killed by an Iraqi detainee, we would have been far less shocked than we are at the now-infamous image of this young woman holding a leash attached to a naked Iraqi prisoner. At least then she would have been something we're used to seeing—a woman as a victim.

In the past two weeks, I've been asked repeatedly about my reaction when I first realized that some of the soldiers abusing prisoners at Abu Ghraib were women. People want to know what I think may have motivated those young women in the photos to participate in such degrading acts. Were they trying to be accepted as "one of the boys"? Was this a way of "fitting in"?

I have to say that initially, like almost everyone else, I was shocked. I somehow thought that women couldn't, or at least wouldn't, act with such disregard for humanity. Like others,

Embser-Herbert Melissa Sheridan. May 16, 2004. "When Women Abuse Power, Too." *Washington Post,* B01.

I was taken aback, especially when I saw by their smiling faces and "thumbs up" that these women appeared to be having some fun with what was happening around them. But it didn't take me long to realize that, really, we shouldn't be all that surprised. For women, I believe, are just as vulnerable as men to the group dynamics that can make people act in ways they might not otherwise have dreamed possible.

It wasn't that long ago, during the discussion over whether women should be allowed in combat, that I was among those who expressed the view that Americans apparently weren't ready for women in body bags. Yet I now find myself thinking that maybe the average American was far more prepared for that than for a woman at the aggressor's end of what looks like torture and humiliation, especially sexual torture and humiliation. This is what's at the heart of the public response to the photos from Abu Ghraib. In short, the reversal of roles has taken us completely by surprise.

It's hardly possible to watch an evening of television without seeing women as victims. Think "Law and Order: SVU." Watch your favorite news magazine, or look closely at fashion advertising, or pick up the daily paper. Women at the receiving end of degradation and abuse are everywhere in the media. And while women may also be seen in powerful roles, rarely are they seen wielding power in a way that's intended to degrade or abuse, and even more rarely is it directed at men. When women are seen in that light, their victims are children, usually their own. Remember Susan Smith? Andrea Yates? When their victims *have* been men, the perpetrators tend to be women who are already marginalized and/or victimized by the society in which they've tried to function. Think of serial killer Aileen Wuornos.

Ultimately, the distinction between seeing men as aggressors and seeing women as aggressors is that the women are usually acting as individuals, not as part of a larger, structural arrangement of discrimination or abuse. That,

I believe, is why we find ourselves so struck by the military women at Abu Ghraib. I'm not convinced that they are sadistic and perverted individuals. They may really be "the girls next door." But whether as pawns or players, they're complicit in what appears to be an organizational failure of monstrous proportions. And we're simply not used to seeing women in that role.

That's why I believe that if England had been killed, by an Iraqi detainee—or even by an American soldier—we would have been less shocked. She would, in a sense, have filled the role expected of her as a woman in American society—far more so than does a woman in a role as prison guard in a combat zone. I say this as someone who participated in military training with a woman who was later murdered by a man with whom she was stationed. I recall quite clearly how little surprise people expressed. In fact, he seemed to think people would understand his justification. They'd been drinking, he couldn't "perform," and in her own drunkenness, she laughed. So he killed her. End of story. We're somewhat desensitized to women being on the receiving end of violence. And we are, all too unfortunately, just as desensitized to men being on the aggressor's end.

In Abu Ghraib the tables are turned. Men—men who have been characterized by many as evil, or at the least not to be trusted—are on the receiving end. And women, long held up by our society as a "kinder, gentler" class of persons, are engaging in abuse and humiliation. As a society that has—albeit misguidedly—arranged itself around perceptions of women and men as fundamentally different creatures, we are simply at a loss to understand this role inversion.

This is why we search for something specific that might have "motivated" these soldiers, women and men, as individuals, even if, as some of them claim, they were just following orders. Believing the actions of these soldiers to be the result of flawed individuals lets us conclude that we—not, of course, being so flawed—would never be guilty of such actions.

But pathologizing the individual also allows us to maintain the belief that women, as a category of persons, would generally not be a party to such crimes. Surely, we say questioningly, these people, and most assuredly these women, are exceptions. But I don't think so. Individual women in the military do, undeniably, strategize to be accepted as equals by the men with whom they serve, but it's unlikely that the women involved in this chain of events were making intentional choices, just trying to be one of the guys or fitting in.

A far more likely explanation for the behavior of everyone involved is what Stanford University psychology professor Philip Zimbardo and others have described as the "power of the situation." Women, it is my guess, like their male counterparts, were largely ill-prepared—both in terms of skills and emotions—to deal with what they faced in Abu Ghraib. Does this absolve them of responsibility? No, not at all. Does it mean that there is more to this than a few individuals with poor judgment? Absolutely.

Back in the late '70s, I went through Army basic training and military police training in a sex-integrated unit. Let me make clear, I thought it was a good idea then; I still think it's the only way to train people who will, weeks later, be serving alongside one another. But I did have one experience that, long before I reflected on it as a social psychologist, always stuck with me.

While on a field exercise, we had a mock prisoner-of-war camp in which we were randomly assigned to roles as prisoners or guards. As luck would have it, I was a prisoner and all the "guards" were men—young men. As the day wore on, they got more and more carried away with their role and started pushing the boundaries of acceptable behavior. You know—where they grabbed, how they grabbed. I recall getting fed up and reminding them that they weren't really guards, that they were crossing a line. I may have learned something about being a prisoner, but they also learned something—and I don't know that it was good—about being guards. I

believed then, as I believe now, that I wouldn't have acted the way they did. There would have been no "power of the situation"; the other male "guards" would never have tolerated, let alone encouraged, my mistreatment of their buddies. This was, after all, a training situation and they weren't "the enemy." But years later, when similar, but far more egregious, incidents occurred at the Air Force Academy, I wasn't at all surprised.

In the mid-1990s, while undergoing training allegedly designed to prepare cadets for what they might experience if captured, Elizabeth Saum was assigned the role of "prisoner." She was slapped, punched, shaken, had her pants unbuttoned, and then other cadets climbed on top of her to simulate raping her. She wasn't the only victim, but she was the one who spoke out. And, interestingly, the victims weren't all women, but apparently included anyone viewed as more vulnerable than those in charge. Ask those cadets about the use of misogyny and homophobia as tools for humiliation. Ask them about the hoods placed on the "prisoners'" heads. Ask them about the fact that at least one of the incidents was videotaped. Do you think they were surprised at the Abu Ghraib photos? Maybe at first. But I'm betting the specifics were far too familiar.

It so happens that these miscreants were men. But make these real-world rather than training situations. Change the targets of the abuse to those cast as "the other" to a much greater degree than female trainees and cadets. And add to the mix all the other things that apparently went wrong at Abu Ghraib. It should no longer surprise us that women, too, acted in ways contrary to what we would like to expect.

So how do we make sense of it all? Can we make sense of it all? We can begin by understanding that the stars did not align in such a way that a random group of sadistic individuals ended up in the same military assignment. Something much larger was at work. A combination of factors yet to be fully understood—poor leadership, inad quate prepa-ration, lack of resources, and perhaps some experienced interrogators taking advantage of inexperienced soldiers—undoubtedly contrib-uted to a situation in which individuals, female and male, made bad choices.

Just as women have proven themselves capable of leading troops in difficult situations, so have they now shown that they can become vulnerable to the power of a role, the power of wielding power. Images of a woman giving a "thumbs up" beside a hooded, naked man have highlighted the horrors of war in a way I don't believe would have happened had we seen only more traditional images of men at war. Putting a woman's face on war's brutality has, I believe, prompted a depth of discussion that might not otherwise have occurred. Ultimately, through that discussion, I expect we'll gain insight far beyond what any of us expected when we first saw the young women smiling at us from inside Abu Ghraib.

DISCUSSION QUESTIONS

1. Give an example of one or two peer pressure situations in which you made decisions or took action that was contrary to your own morals, values, and ordinary behavior. What was it about the power or definition of the situation that encouraged and allowed you to act in ways that were distinct from your typical behavior?
2. Would the treatment of prisoners have differed at Abu Ghraib if the prisoners were women or if the guards had been either all women or all men? How might a change in these gender demographics alter the definition of the situation?
3. Why are situations defined by large disparities in power conducive to using sexual humiliation as a form of torture, as was true in both the simulated prison in the Stanford Prison Experiment and the real one in Abu Ghraib?

ADDITIONAL RESOURCES

Film

"Standard Operating Procedure." April 2008. Sony Pictures.

Internet

http://www.sonyclassics.com/standardoperatingprocedure/. The official site for the 2008 Errol Morris film "Standard Operating Procedure."

FURTHER READING

Herbert, Melissa S. 1998. *Camouflage Isn't Only for Combat: Gender, Sexuality, and Women in the Military.* New York: New York University Press.

22. The Lucifer Effect

PHILIP G. ZIMBARDO

It took Philip Zimbardo more than 35 years to publish this exhaustive account of the Stanford Prison Experiment and its contemporary lessons. In the brief selections we have chosen from the preface and first chapter of his book, Zimbardo details the emotional intensity he still feels about his complicity in the abuses that took place in the Stanford Prison Experiment under his watch. His empathy for the perpetrators of abuse at the military prison in Abu Ghraib surfaced when he served as an expert witness during the trial of one of the prison guards.

I wish I could say that writing this book was a labor of love; it was not that for a single moment of the two years it took to complete. First of all, it was emotionally painful to review all of the videotapes from the Stanford Prison Experiment (SPE) and to read over and over the typescripts prepared from them. Time had dimmed my memory of the extent of creative evil in which many of the guards engaged, the extent of the suffering of many of the prisoners, and the extent of my passivity in allowing the abuses to continue for as long as I did—an evil of inaction.

I had also forgotten that the first part of this book was actually begun thirty years ago under contract from a different publisher. However, I quit shortly after beginning to write because I was not ready to relive the experience while I was still so close to it. I am glad that I did not hang in and force myself to continue writing then because this is the right time. Now I am wiser and able to bring a more mature perspective to this complex task. Further, the parallels between the abuses at Abu Ghraib and the events in the SPE have given our Stanford prison experience added validity, which in turn sheds light on the psychological dynamics that contributed to creating horrific abuses in that real prison.

A second emotionally draining obstacle to writing was becoming personally and intensely involved in fully researching the Abu Ghraib abuses and tortures. As an expert witness for one of the MP prison guards, I became more like an investigative reporter than a social psychologist. I worked at uncovering everything I could about this young man, from intensive interviews with him and conversations and correspondence with his family members to checking on his background in corrections and in the military, as well as with other military personnel who had served in that dungeon. I came to feel what it was like to walk in his boots on the Tier 1A night shift from 4 P.M. to 4 A.M. every single night for forty nights without a break.

As an expert witness testifying at his trial to the situational forces that contributed to the specific abuses he had perpetrated, I was given access to all of the many hundreds of digitally documented images of depravity. That was an ugly and unwelcomed task. In addition, I was provided with all of the then-available reports from various military and civilian investigating committees. Because I was told that I would not be allowed to bring detailed notes to the trial, I had to memorize as many of their critical features and conclusions

Zimbardo, Philip G. 2007. Abridged from "Preface" and "The Psychology of Evil: Situated Character Transformations," in *The Lucifer Effect: Understanding How Good People Turn Evil*. New York: Random House.

as I could. That cognitive challenge added to the terrific emotional strain that arose after Sergeant Ivan "Chip" Frederick was given a harsh sentence and I became an informal psychological counselor for him and his wife, Martha. Over time, I became, for them, "Uncle Phil."

I was doubly frustrated and angry, first by the military's unwillingness to accept any of the many mitigating circumstances I had detailed that had directly contributed to his abusive behavior and should have reduced his harsh prison sentence. The prosecutor and judge refused to consider any idea that situational forces could influence individual behavior. Theirs was the standard individualism conception that is shared by most people in our culture. It is the idea that the fault was entirely "dispositional," the consequence of Sergeant Chip Frederick's freely chosen rational decision to engage in evil. Added to my distress was the realization that many of the "independent" investigative reports clearly laid the blame for the abuses at the feet of senior officers and on their dysfunctional or "absentee landlord" leadership. These reports, chaired by generals and former high-ranking government officials, made evident that the military and civilian chain of command had built a "bad barrel" in which a bunch of good soldiers became transformed into "bad apples."

Had I written this book shortly after the end of the Stanford Prison Experiment, I would have been content to detail the ways in which situational forces are more powerful than we think, or that we acknowledge, in shaping our behavior in many contexts. However, I would have missed the big picture, the bigger power for creating evil out of good—that of the System, the complex of powerful forces that create the Situation. A large body of evidence in social psychology supports the concept that situational power triumphs over individual power in given contexts. I refer to that evidence in several chapters. However, most psychologists have been insensitive to the deeper sources of power that inhere in the political, economic, religious, historic, and cultural matrix that defines situations and gives them legitimate or illegitimate existence. A full understanding of the dynamics of human behavior requires that we recognize the extent and limits of personal power, situational power, and systemic power.

Changing or preventing undesirable behavior of individuals or groups requires an understanding of what strengths, virtues, and vulnerabilities they bring into a given situation. Then, we need to recognize more fully the complex of situational forces that are operative in given behavioral settings. Modifying them, or learning to avoid them, can have a greater impact on reducing undesirable individual reactions than remedial actions directed only at changing the people in the situation. That means adopting a public health approach in place of the standard medical model approach to curing individual ills and wrongs. However, unless we become sensitive to the real power of the System, which is invariably hidden behind a veil of secrecy, and fully understand its own set of rules and regulations, behavioral change will be transient and situational change illusory. Throughout this book, I repeat the mantra that attempting to understand the situational and systemic contributions to any individual's behavior does not excuse the person or absolve him or her from responsibility in engaging in immoral, illegal, or evil deeds.

One of the dominant conclusions of the Stanford Prison Experiment is that the pervasive yet subtle power of a host of situational variables can dominate an individual's will to resist. That conclusion is given greater depth in a series of chapters detailing this phenomenon across a body of social science research. We see how a range of research participants—other college student subjects and average citizen volunteers alike—have come to conform, comply, obey, and be readily seduced into doing things they could not imagine doing when they were outside those situational force fields. A set of dynamic psychological processes is outlined that can induce good people to do evil, among them deindividuation, obedience to authority, passivity in the face of threats, self-justification, and rationalization. Dehumanization is one of the central processes in the transformation of ordinary, normal people into indifferent or even wanton perpetrators of evil. Dehumanization is like a cortical cataract that clouds one's thinking and fosters the perception that other people are less than human. It makes some people come to see those others as enemies deserving of torment, torture, and annihilation.

With this set of analytical tools at our disposal, we turn to reflect upon the causes of the horrendous abuses and torture of prisoners at Iraq's Abu Ghraib Prison by the U.S. Military Police guarding them. The allegation that these immoral deeds were the sadistic work of a few rogue soldiers, so-called bad apples, is challenged by examining the parallels that exist in the situational forces and psychological processes that operated in that prison with those in our Stanford prison. We examine in depth, the Place, the Person, and the Situation to draw conclusions about the causative forces involved in creating the abusive behaviors that are depicted in the revolting set of "trophy photos" taken by the soldiers in the process of tormenting their prisoners.

HORRIFIC IMAGES OF ABUSE AT ABU GHRAIB PRISON

The driving force behind this book was the need to better understand the how and why of the physical and psychological abuses perpetrated on prisoners by American Military Police at the Abu Ghraib Prison in Iraq. As the photographic evidence of these abuses rocketed around the world in May 2004, we all saw for the first time in recorded history vivid images of young American men and women engaged in unimaginable forms of torture against civilians they were supposed to be guarding. The tormentors and the tormented were captured in an extensive display of digitally documented depravity that the soldiers themselves had made during their violent escapades.

Why did they create photographic evidence of such illegal acts, which if found would surely get them into trouble? In these "trophy photos," like the proud displays by big-game hunters of yesteryear with the beasts they have killed, we saw smiling men and women in the act of abusing their lowly animal creatures. The images are of punching, slapping, and kicking detainees; jumping on their feet; forcibly arranging naked, hooded prisoners in piles and pyramids; forcing naked prisoners to wear women's underwear over their heads; forcing male prisoners to masturbate or simulate fellatio while being photographed or videotaped with female soldiers smiling or encouraging it; hanging prisoners from cell rafters for extended time periods; dragging a prisoner around with a leash tied to his neck; and using unmuzzled attack dogs to frighten prisoners.

The iconic image that ricocheted from that dungeon to the streets of Iraq and every corner of the globe was that of the "triangle man": a hooded detainee is standing on a box in a stress position with his outstretched arms protruding from under a garment blanket revealing electrical wires attached to his fingers. He was told that he would be electrocuted if he fell off the box when his strength gave out. It did not matter that the wires went nowhere; it mattered that he believed the lie and must have experienced considerable stress. There were even more shocking photographs that the U.S. government chose not to release to the public because of the greater damage they would surely have done to the credibility and moral image of the U.S. military and President Bush's administrative command. I have seen hundreds of these images, and they are indeed horrifying.

I was deeply distressed at the sight of such suffering, of such displays of arrogance, of such indifference to the humiliation being inflicted upon helpless prisoners. I was also amazed to learn that one of the abusers, a female soldier who had just turned twenty-one, described the abuse as "just fun and games."

I was shocked, but I was not surprised. The media and the "person in the street" around the globe asked how such evil deeds could be perpetrated by these seven men and women, whom military leaders had labeled as "rogue soldiers" and "a few bad apples." Instead, I wondered what circumstances in that prison cell block could have tipped the balance and led even good soldiers to do such bad things. To be sure, advancing a situational analysis for such crimes does not excuse them or make them morally acceptable. Rather, I needed to find the meaning in this madness. I wanted to understand how it was possible for the characters of these young people to be so transformed in such a short time that they could do these unthinkable deeds.

PARALLEL UNIVERSES IN ABU GHRAIB AND STANFORD'S PRISON

The reason that I was shocked but not surprised by the images and stories of prisoner abuse in the Abu Ghraib "Little Shop of Horrors" was that I had seen something similar before. Three decades earlier, I had witnessed eerily similar scenes as they unfolded in a project that I directed, of my own design: naked, shackled prisoners with bags over their heads, guards stepping on prisoners' backs as they did push-ups, guards sexually humiliating prisoners, and prisoners suffering from extreme stress. Some of the visual images from my experiment are practically interchangeable with those of the guards and prisoners in that remote prison in Iraq, the notorious Abu Ghraib.

The college students role-playing guards and prisoners in a mock prison experiment conducted at Stanford University in the summer of 1971 were mirrored in the real guards and real prison in the Iraq of 2003. Not only had I seen such events, I had been responsible for creating the conditions that allowed such abuses to flourish. As the project's principal investigator, I designed the experiment that randomly assigned normal, healthy, intelligent college students to enact the roles of either guards or prisoners in a realistically simulated prison setting where they were to live and work for several weeks. My student research associates, Craig Haney, Curt Banks, and David Jaffe, and I wanted to understand some of the dynamics operating in the psychology of imprisonment.

How do ordinary people adapt to such an institutional setting? How do the power differentials between guards and prisoners play out in their daily interactions? If you put good people in a bad place, do the people triumph or does the place corrupt them? Would the violence that is endemic to most real prisons be absent in a prison filled with good middle-class boys? These were some of the exploratory issues to be investigated in what started out as a simple study of prison life.

DISCUSSION QUESTIONS

1. What lessons can we learn from studying the power of the situational definition over an individual's ability to make reasoned, informed decisions?
2. Zimbardo insists that while the power of the situation may overcome an individual's ability to reason well, it does not excuse an individual for engaging in reprehensible behavior. If Zimbardo asks that we hold individuals accountable for their actions, why is it important to understand the situational context within which their behavior occurs?

ADDITIONAL RESOURCES

Internet

http://www.lucifereffect.com. A site with teaching and other interactive functions to accompany Zimbardo's *The Lucifer Effect* book.

FURTHER READING

Zimbardo, Philip G. 2007. *The Lucifer Effect: Understanding How Good People Turn Evil.* New York: Random House.

Conformity and Obedience

Classic

Contemporary

The following selections illustrate the significant influence of social factors on individuals' actions. Each of these articles clearly conveys the power of the situation to contextualize and influence individuals' behaviors, attitudes, and even perceptions. We explore the common themes found across this body of research that spans nearly 40 years.

There are several commonalities among these three articles as well as some clear differences. Methodologically speaking, the authors report on findings from two experiments and one "real world" experience. Both the Asch and Milgram experiments involve the deception of research subjects, using a false research premise to conceal the actual research question. Asch and Milgram both debrief their research subjects at the conclusion of their studies, thus putting an end to the deception. While offering research subjects a framework for understanding their participation in each experiment is largely beneficial in the Asch and Milgram studies, the warfare in My Lai offers no such opportunity for debriefing. Soldiers' experiences during this village massacre are so otherworldly that they no doubt may have had difficulty integrating such horror with their overall sense of self and reality, leading to the development of psychological dysfunctions such as posttraumatic stress disorder.

Across all three articles, we see examples of some research subjects and soldiers who conform or obey orders and others who do not. Comparing those who conform to those who do not is quite an important exercise in the relevance of contemporary social psychology. Three common elements found in each situation help to explain participants' conformity: authorization, routinization, and dehumanization.

Living in a highly individuated culture, one may be all too quick to dismiss the power of the context within which an individual chooses to act. Pay attention to the social factors outlined above and others you identify yourself in your reading of these selections.

23. Effects of Group Pressure upon the Modification and Distortion of Judgments

SOLOMON E. ASCH

Solomon Asch's research on conformity to peer pressure is indeed a classic. As you reflect on this research published in 1951, pay attention to the variables that led to more or less conformity to the group's influence and reflect on how this research might generalize to contemporary situations involving peer pressure.

We shall here describe in summary form the conception and first findings of a program of investigation into the conditions of independence and submission to group pressure.

Our immediate object was to study the social and personal conditions that induce individuals to resist or to yield to group pressures when the latter are perceived to be *contrary to fact*. The issues which this problem raises are of obvious consequence for society; it can be of decisive importance whether or not a group will, under certain conditions, submit to existing pressures. Equally direct are the consequences for individuals and our understanding of them, since it is a decisive fact about a person whether he possesses the freedom to act independently, or whether he characteristically submits to group pressures.

Basic to the current approach has been the axiom that group pressures characteristically induce psychological changes *arbitrarily*, in far-reaching disregard of the material properties of the given conditions. This mode of thinking has almost exclusively stressed the slavish submission of individuals to group forces, has neglected to inquire into their possibilities for independence and for productive relations with the human environment, and has virtually denied the capacity of men under certain conditions to rise above group passion and prejudice. It was our aim to contribute to a clarification of these questions, important both for theory and for their human

Asch, Solomon E. 1951. "Effects of Group Pressure upon the Modification and Distortion of Judgments," in Harold Guetzkow (ed.). *Groups, Leadership and Men*, 177–90. Pittsburgh: Carnegie Press.

implications, by means of direct observation of the effects of groups upon the decisions and evaluations of individuals.

THE EXPERIMENT AND FIRST RESULTS

To this end we developed an experimental technique which has served as the basis for the present series of studies. We employed the procedure of placing an individual in a relation of radical conflict with all the other members of a group, of measuring its effect upon him in quantitative terms, and of describing its psychological consequences. A group of eight individuals was instructed to judge a series of simple, clearly structured perceptual relations—to match the length of a given line with one of three unequal lines. Each member of the group announced his judgments publicly. In the midst of this monotonous "test" one individual found himself suddenly contradicted by the entire group, and this contradiction was repeated again and again in the course of the experiment. The group in question had, with the exception of one member, previously met with the experimenter and received instructions to respond at certain points with wrong—and unanimous—judgments. The errors of the majority were large (ranging between ½" and 1¾") and of an order not encountered under control conditions. The outstanding person—the critical subject—whom we had placed in the position of a *minority of one* in the midst of a *unanimous majority*—was the object of investigation. He faced, possibly for the first time in his life, a situation in which a group unanimously contradicted the evidence of his senses.

The technique employed permitted a simple quantitative measure of the "majority effect" in terms of the frequency of errors in the direction of the distorted estimates of the majority. At the same time we were concerned from the start to obtain evidence of the ways in which the subjects perceived the group, to establish whether they became doubtful, whether they were tempted to join the majority. Most important, it was our object to establish the grounds of the subject's independence or yielding—whether, for example, the yielding subject was aware of the effect of the majority upon him, whether he abandoned his judgment deliberately or compulsively. To this end we constructed a comprehensive set of questions which served as the basis of an individual interview immediately following the experimental period. Toward the conclusion of the interview each subject was informed fully of the purpose of the experiment, of his role and of that of the majority. The reactions to the disclosure of the purpose of the experiment became in fact an integral part of the procedure. We may state here that the information derived from the interview became an indispensable source of evidence and insight into the psychological structure of the experimental situation, and in particular, of the nature of the individual differences. Also, it is not justified or advisable to allow the subject to leave without giving him a full explanation of the experimental conditions. The experimenter has a responsibility to the subject to clarify his doubts and to state the reasons for placing him in the experimental situation. When this is done most subjects react with interest and many express gratification at having lived through a striking situation which has some bearing on wider human issues.

Both the members of the majority and the critical subjects were male college students. We shall report the results for a total of fifty critical subjects in this experiment.

The quantitative results are clear and unambiguous.

1. There was a marked movement toward the majority. One-third of all the estimates in the critical group were errors identical with or in the direction of the distorted estimates of the majority.

2. At the same time the effect of the majority was far from complete. The preponderance of estimates in the critical group (68%) was correct despite the pressure of the majority.

3. We found evidence of extreme individual differences. There were in the critical group subjects who remained independent without exception, and there were those who went nearly all the time with the majority. One-fourth of the critical subjects was completely independent; at the other extreme, one-third of the group displaced the estimates toward the majority in one-half or more of the trials.

The differences between the critical subjects in their reactions to the given conditions were equally striking. There were subjects who remained completely confident throughout. At the other extreme were those who became disoriented, doubt-ridden, and experienced a powerful impulse not to appear different from the majority.

For purposes of illustration we include a brief description of one independent and one yielding subject.

Independent After a few trials he appeared puzzled, hesitant. He announced all disagreeing answers in the form of "Three, sir; two, sir"; not so with the unanimous answers. At trial 4 he answered immediately after the first member of the group, shook his head, blinked, and whispered to his neighbor: "Can't help it, that's one." His later answers came in a whispered voice, accompanied by a deprecating smile. At one point he grinned embarrassedly, and whispered explosively to his neighbor: "I always disagree—darn it!" During the questioning, this subject's constant refrain was: "I called them as I saw them, sir." He insisted that his estimates were right without, however, committing himself as to whether the others were wrong, remarking that "that's the way I see them and that's the way they see them." If he had to make a practical decision under similar circumstances, he declared, "I would follow my own view, though part of my reason would tell me that I might be wrong." Immediately following the experiment the majority engaged this subject in a brief discussion. When they pressed him to

say whether the entire group was wrong and he alone was right, he turned upon them defiantly, exclaiming: "You're *probably* right, but you may be wrong!" To the disclosure of the experiment this subject reacted with the statement that he felt "exultant and relieved," adding, "I do not deny that at times I had the feeling: 'to heck with it, I'll go along with the rest.'"

Yielding. This subject went with the majority in 11 out of 12 trials. He appeared nervous and somewhat confused, but he did not attempt to evade discussion; on the contrary, he was helpful and tried to answer to the best of his ability. He opened the discussion with the statement: "If I'd been the first I probably would have responded differently"; this was his way of stating that he had adopted the majority estimates. The primary factor in his case was loss of confidence. He perceived the majority as a decided group, acting without hesitation: "If they had been doubtful I probably would have changed, but they answered with such confidence." Certain of his errors, he explained, were due to the doubtful nature of the comparisons; in such instances he went with the majority. When the object of the experiment was explained, the subject volunteered: "I suspected about the middle—but tried to push it out of my mind." It is of interest that his suspicion was not able to restore his confidence and diminish the power of the majority. Equally striking is his report that he assumed the experiment to involve an "illusion" to which the others, but not he, were subject. This assumption too did not help to free him; on the contrary, he acted as if his divergence from the majority was a sign of defect. The principal impression this subject produced was of one so caught up by immediate difficulties that he lost clear reasons for his actions, and could make no reasonable decisions.

A FIRST ANALYSIS OF INDIVIDUAL DIFFERENCES

On the basis of the interview data described earlier, we undertook to differentiate and describe the major forms of reaction to the experimental situation, which we shall now briefly summarize.

Among the *independent* subjects we distinguished the following main categories:

1. Independence based on *confidence* in one's perception and experience. The most striking characteristic of these subjects is the vigor with which they withstand the group opposition.

2. Quite different are those subjects who are independent and *withdrawn*. These do not react in a spontaneously emotional way, but rather on the basis of explicit principles concerning the necessity of being an individual.

3. A third group of independent subjects manifest considerable tension and *doubt,* but adhere to their judgments on the basis of a felt necessity to deal adequately with the task.

The following were the main categories of reaction among the *yielding* subjects, or those who went with the majority during one-half or more of the trials.

1. *Distortion of perception* under the stress of group pressure. These subjects report that they came to perceive the majority estimates as correct.

2. *Distortion of judgment.* Most submitting subjects belong to this category. The factor of greatest importance in this group is a decision the subjects reach that their perceptions are inaccurate, and that those of the majority are correct. These subjects suffer from primary doubt and lack of confidence; on this basis they feel a strong tendency to join the majority.

3. *Distortion of action.* The subjects in this group do not suffer a modification of perception nor do they conclude that they are wrong. They yield because of an overmastering need not to appear different from or inferior to others, because of an inability to tolerate the appearance of defectiveness in the eyes of the group. These subjects suppress their observations and voice the majority position with awareness of what they are doing.

The results are sufficient to establish that independence and yielding are not psychologically homogeneous, that submission to group pressure (and freedom from pressure) can be the result of different psychological conditions. It should also be noted that the categories described above, being based exclusively on the subjects' reactions to the experimental conditions, are descriptive, not presuming to explain why a given individual responded in one way rather than another.

THE ROLE OF MAJORITY SIZE

To gain further understanding of the majority effect, we varied the size of the majority in several different variations. The majorities, which were in each case unanimous, consisted of 16, 8, 4, 3, and 2 persons, respectively. In addition, we studied the limiting case in which the critical subject was opposed by one instructed subject. With the opposition reduced to one, the majority effect all but disappeared. When the opposition proceeded from a group of two, it produced a measurable though small distortion, the errors being 12.8 percent of the total number of estimates. The effect appeared in full force with a majority of three. Larger majorities of four, eight, and sixteen did not produce effects greater than a majority of three.

SUMMARY

We have investigated the effects upon individuals of majority opinions when the latter were seen to be in a direction contrary to fact. By means of a simple technique, we produced a radical divergence between a majority and a minority, and observed the ways in which individuals coped with the resulting difficulty. Despite the stress of the given conditions, a substantial proportion of individuals retained their independence throughout. At the same time a substantial minority yielded, modifying their judgments in accordance with the majority. Independence and yielding are a joint function of the following major factors: (1) *The character of the stimulus situation.* Variations in structural clarity have a decisive effect: with diminishing clarity of the stimulus-conditions, the majority effect increases.

(2) *The character of the group forces.* Individuals are highly sensitive to the structural qualities of group opposition. In particular, we demonstrated the great importance of the factor of unanimity. Also, the majority effect is a function of the size of group opposition. (3) *The character of the individual.* There were wide, and indeed, striking differences among individuals within the same experimental situation.

DISCUSSION QUESTIONS

1. What factors would make participants in Asch's study more or less likely to conform to the voice of the group?
2. What accounts for the greater level of conformity, nearly double, in Milgram's study than in Asch's?
3. How do you think you would respond as a subject in Asch or Milgram's research? How about if you were a soldier in My Lai or at Abu Ghraib?

ADDITIONAL RESOURCES

Internet
http://www.psych.upenn.edu/sacsec/about/solomon.htm. The site of the Solomon Asch Center.

FURTHER READING
Levine, John M. 1999. "Solomon Asch's Legacy for Group Research." *Personality and Social Psychology Review*, 3(4): 358–64.
Thomson, Irene Taviss. 1992. "Individualism and Conformity in the 1950s vs. the 1980s." *Sociological Forum*, 7(3): 497–516.

24. Behavioral Study of Obedience

STANLEY MILGRAM

Stanley Milgram's research on obedience to authority is a staple in social psychology classes and textbooks. What is the impact of Milgram's research? Why is this study taught so frequently?

Milgram, Stanley. 1963. "Behavioral Study of Obedience." *Journal of Abnormal and Social Psychology*, 67(4): 371–78.

Obedience is as basic an element in the structure of social life as one can point to. Obedience, as a determinant of behavior, is of particular relevance to our time. It has been reliably established that from 1933 to 1945 millions of innocent persons were systematically slaughtered on command. Gas chambers were built, death camps were guarded, daily quotas of corpses were produced with the same efficiency as the manufacture of appliances. These inhumane policies may have originated in the mind of a single person, but they could only be carried out on a massive scale if a very large number of persons obeyed orders.

Obedience is the psychological mechanism that links individual action to political purpose. It is the dispositional cement that binds men to systems of authority.

It must not be thought all obedience entails acts of aggression against others. Obedience serves numerous productive functions. Indeed, the very life of society is predicated on its existence. Obedience comes easily and often. It is a ubiquitous and indispensable feature of social life.

METHOD

Subjects

The subjects were 40 males between the ages of 20 and 50, drawn from New Haven and the surrounding communities. Subjects were obtained by a newspaper advertisement and direct mail solicitation. Those who responded to the appeal believed they were to participate in a study of memory and learning at Yale University. A wide range of occupations is represented in the sample. Typical subjects were postal clerks, high school teachers, salesmen, engineers, and laborers. Subjects ranged in educational level from one who had not finished elementary school, to those who had doctorate and other professional degrees. They were paid $4.50 for their participation in the experiment. However, subjects were told that payment was simply for coming to the laboratory, and that the money was theirs no matter what happened after they arrived. Table I shows the proportion of age and occupational types assigned to the experimental condition.

Personnel and Locale

The experiment was conducted on the grounds of Yale University in the elegant interaction laboratory. (This detail is relevant to the perceived legitimacy of the experiment. In further variations, the experiment was dissociated from the university, with consequences for performance.) The role of experimenter was played by a 31-year-old high school teacher of biology. His manner was impassive, and his appearance somewhat stern throughout the experiment. He was dressed in a gray technician's coat. The victim was played by a 47-year-old accountant, trained for the role; he was of Irish-American stock, whom most observers found mild-mannered and likable.

Procedure

One naive subject and one victim (an accomplice) performed in each experiment. A pretext had to be devised that would justify the administration of electric shock by the naive subject. This was effectively accomplished by the cover story. After a general introduction on the presumed relation

Table I Distribution of Age and Occupational Types in the Experiment

Occupations	20–29 years	30–39 years	40–50 years	Percentage of total (occupations)
Workers, skilled and unskilled	4	5	6	37.5
Sales, business, and white-collar	3	6	7	40.0
Professional	1	5	3	22.5
Percentage of total (Age)	20	40	40	

Note: Total N = 40.

between punishment and learning, subjects were told:

> But actually, we know *very little* about the effect of punishment on learning, because almost no truly scientific studies have been made of it in human beings.
>
> For instance, we don't know how *much* punishment is best for learning—and we don't know how much difference it makes as to who is giving the punishment, whether an adult learns best from a younger or an older person than himself—or many things of that sort.
>
> So in this study we are bringing together a number of adults of different occupations and ages. And we're asking some of them to be teachers and some of them to be learners.
>
> We want to find out just what effect different people have on each other as teachers and learners, and also what effect *punishment* will have on learning in this situation.
>
> Therefore, I'm going to ask one of you to be the teacher here tonight and the other one to be the learner.

Subjects then drew slips of paper from a hat to determine who would be the teacher and who would be the learner in the experiment. The drawing was rigged so that the naive subject was always the teacher and the accomplice always the learner. (Both slips contained the word "Teacher") Immediately after the drawing, the teacher and learner were taken to an adjacent room and the learner was strapped into an "electric chair" apparatus.

The experimenter explained that the straps were to prevent excessive movement while the learner was being shocked. The effect was to make it impossible for him to escape from the situation. An electrode was attached to the learner's wrist, and electrode paste was applied "to avoid blisters and burns." Subjects were told that the electrode was attached to the shock generator in the adjoining room.

In order improve credibility the experimenter declared, in response to a question by the learner: "Although the shocks can be extremely painful, they cause no permanent tissue damage."

Learning task. The lesson administered by the subject was a paired-associate learning task. The subject read a series of word pairs to the learner, and then read the first word of the pair along with four terms. The learner was to indicate which of the four terms had originally been paired with the first word. He communicated his answer by pressing one of four switches in front of him, which in turn lit up one of four numbered quadrants in an answer-box located atop the shock generator.

Shock generator. The instrument panel consists of 30 lever switches set in a horizontal line. Each switch is clearly labeled with a voltage designation that ranges from 15 to 450 volts. There is a 15-volt increment from one switch to the next going from left to right. In addition, the following verbal designations are clearly indicated for groups of four switches going from left to right: Slight Shock, Moderate Shock, Strong Shock, Very Strong Shock, Intense Shock, Extreme Intensity Shock, Danger: Severe Shock. (Two switches after this last designation are simply marked XXX.)

Upon depressing a switch: a pilot light corresponding to each switch is illuminated in bright red; an electric buzzing is heard; an electric blue light, labeled "voltage energizer," flashes; the dial on the voltage meter swings to the right; various relay clicks are sounded.

The upper left-hand corner of the generator is labeled Shock Generator, Type ZLB, Dyson Instrument Company, Waltham, Mass. Output 15 Volts–450 Volts.

Details of the instrument were carefully handled to ensure an appearance of authenticity. The panel was engraved by precision industrial engravers, and all components were of high quality. No subject in the experiment suspected that the instrument was merely a simulated shock generator.

Sample shock. Each naive subject is given a sample shock on the shock generator, prior to beginning his run as teacher. This shock is always

45 volts, and is applied by pressing the third switch of the generator. The shock is applied to the wrist of the naive subject, and has its source in a 45-volt battery wired into the generator. This further convinces the subject of the authenticity of the generator.

Shock instructions. The subject is told to administer a shock to the learner each time he gives a wrong response. Moreover—and this is the key command—the subject is instructed to "move one level higher on the shock generator each time the learner flashes a wrong answer." He is also instructed to announce the voltage level before administering a shock. This serves to continually remind subjects of the increasing intensity of shocks administered to the learner. Subjects are then presented with a list and are told that:

> When you get to the bottom of the list, repeat it over again, and continue giving shocks, until the learner has learned all the pairs correctly.

The experimenter instructs the subject to,

> start from 15 volts and increase the shock level one step each time the learner gives a wrong answer.

Feedback from the victim. In all conditions the learner gives a predetermined set of responses to the word pair test, based on a schedule of approximately three wrong answers to one correct answer. In the present experimental condition no vocal response or other sign of protest is heard from the learner until Shock Level 300 is reached. When the 300-volt shock is administered, the learner pounds on the wall of the room in which he is bound to the electric chair. The pounding can be heard by the subject. From this point on, the learner's answers no longer appear on the four-way panel.

At this juncture, subjects ordinarily turn to the experimenter for guidance. The experimenter instructs the subject to treat the absence of a response as a wrong answer, and to shock the subject according to the usual schedule. He advises the subjects to allow 5–10 seconds before considering no response as a wrong answer, and to increase the shock level one step each time the learner fails to respond correctly. The learner's pounding is repeated after the 315-volt shock is administered; afterwards he is not heard from, nor do his answers reappear on the four-way signal box.

Experimenter feedback. At various points in the experiment the subject may turn to the experimenter for advice on whether he should continue to administer shocks. Or he may indicate that he does not wish to go on. It was important to standardize the experimenter's responses to these inquiries and reactions.

If the subject indicated his unwillingness to go on, the experimenter responded with a sequence "prods," using as many as necessary to bring the subject into line.

> Prod 1: Please continue, *or* Please go on.
> Prod 2: The experiment requires that you continue.
> Prod 3: It is absolutely essential that you continue.
> Prod 4: You have no other choice, you *must* go on.

The prods were always made in sequence: Only if Prod 1 had been unsuccessful, could Prod 2 be used. If the subject refused to obey the experimenter after Prod 4, the experiment was terminated. The experimenter's tone of voice was at all times firm, but not impolite. The sequence was begun anew on each occasion that the subject balked or showed reluctance to follow orders.

Special prods. If the subject asked if the learner was liable to suffer permanent physical injury, the experimenter said:

> Although the shocks may be painful, there is no permanent tissue damage, so please go on. [Followed by Prods 2, 3, and 4 if necessary.]

If the subject said that the learner did not want to go on, the experimenter replied:
Whether the learner likes it or not, you must go on until he has learned all the word pairs correctly. So please go on. [Followed by Prods 2, 3, and 4 if necessary.]

Dependent Measures

The primary dependent measure for any subject is the maximum shock he administers before he refuses to go any further. In principle this may vary from 0 (for a subject who refuses to administer even the first shock) to 30 (for a subject who administers the highest shock on the generator). A subject who breaks off the experiment at any point prior to administering the thirtieth shock level is termed a *defiant* subject. One who complies with experimental commands fully, and proceeds to administer all shock levels commanded, is termed an *obedient* subject.

Further records. With few exceptions, experimental sessions were recorded on magnetic tape. Occasional photographs were taken through one-way mirrors. Notes were kept on any unusual behavior occurring during the course of the experiments. On occasion, additional observers were directed to write objective descriptions of the subjects' behavior. The latency and duration of shocks were measured by accurate timing devices.

Interview and dehoax. Following the experiment, subjects were interviewed; open-ended questions, projective measures, and attitude scales were employed. After the interview, procedures were undertaken to assure that the subject would leave the laboratory in a state of well being. A friendly reconciliation was arranged between the subject and the victim, and an effort was made to reduce any tensions that arose as a result of the experiment.

RESULTS

Preliminary notions. Before giving an account of the experimental results, it is instructive to consider how persons predict others will perform when commanded to administer powerful shocks to another person. Fourteen Yale seniors, all psychology majors, were provided with a detailed description of the experimental situation. They were asked to reflect carefully on it, and to predict the behavior of 100 hypothetical subjects. More specifically, they were instructed to plot the distribution of obedience of "100 Americans of diverse occupations, and ranging in age from 20 to 50 years," who were placed in the experimental situation.

There was considerable agreement among the respondents on the expected behavior of hypothetical subjects. All respondents predicted that only an insignificant minority would go through to the end of the shock series. (The estimates ranged from 0 to 3 percent; i.e., the most "pessimistic" member of the class predicted that of 100 persons, 3 would continue through to the most potent shock available on the shock generator 450 volts.) The class mean was 1.2 percent. The question was also posed informally to colleagues of the author, and the most general feeling was that few if any subjects would go beyond the designation Very Strong Shock.

Result of Experiment I

Subjects accept situation. With few exceptions, subjects were convinced of the reality of the experimental situation, that they were administering shocks to another person, and the most potent shocks were extremely painful. In the post-experimental interview subjects were asked: "How painful to the learner were the last few shocks that you administered to him?" Subjects were instructed to indicate their answers on a printed 14-point scale ranging from "Not at all painful" to "Extremely painful." The modal response was 14 (Extremely painful) with the mean at 13.42.

Signs of extreme tension. Many subjects showed signs of nervousness in the experimental situation, and especially upon administering the more powerful shocks. In a large number of cases the degree of tension reached extremes that are rarely seen in sociopsychological laboratory studies. Subjects were observed to sweat, tremble, stutter, bite their lips, groan, and dig their fingernails into their flesh. These were characteristic rather than exceptional responses to the experiment.

One sign of tension was the regular occurrence of nervous laughing fits. Fourteen of the 40 subjects showed definite signs of nervous laughter and smiling. The laughter seemed entirely out of place, even bizarre. Full-blown, uncontrollable seizures were observed for three subjects. On one occasion we observed a seizure so violently convulsive that it was necessary to call a halt to the experiment. The subject, a 46-year-old encyclopedia salesman, was seriously embarrassed by his untoward and uncontrollable behavior. In the post-experimental interviews subjects took pains to point out that they were not sadistic types, and that the laughter did not mean they enjoyed shocking the victim.

Distribution of scores. It had been conjectured that persons would not, in general, agree to administer shocks beyond the level designated as Very Strong Shock.

Upon command of the experimenter, each of the 40 subjects went beyond the expected breakoff point. No subject stopped prior to administering Shock Level 20. (At this level—300 volts—the victim kicks on the wall and no longer provides answers to the teacher's multiple-choice questions.)

Of the 40 subjects, 5 refused to obey the experimental commands beyond the 300-volt level. Four more subjects administered one further shock, and then refused to go on. Two broke off at the 330-volt level, and 1 each at 345, 360, and 375 volts. Thus a total of 14 subjects defied the experimenter. It is instructive to reprint their remarks at the point of defiance, as transcribed from the tape recordings:

[0124] I think he's trying to communicate, he's knocking.... Well it's not fair to shock the guy...these are terrific volts. I don't think this is very humane....Oh, I can't go on with this; no, this isn't right. It's a hell of an experiment. The guy is suffering in there. No, I don't want to go on. This is crazy. [Subject refused to administer more shocks.]

[0123]. He's banging in there. I'm gonna chicken out. I'd like to continue, but I can't do that to a man....I'm sorry I can't do that to a man. I'll hurt his heart. You take your check....No really, I couldn't do it.

These subjects were frequently in a highly agitated and even angered state. Sometimes, verbal protest was at a minimum, and the subject simply got up from his chair in front of the shock generator, and indicated that he wished to leave the laboratory.

Of the 40 subjects, 26 obeyed the orders of the experimenter to the end, proceeding to punish the victim until they reached the most potent shock available on the shock generator. At that point, the experimenter called a halt to the session. (The maximum shock is labeled 450 volts, and is two steps beyond the designation: Danger: Severe Shock.) Although obedient subjects continued to administer shocks, they often did so under extreme stress. Some expressed reluctance to administer shocks beyond the 300-volt level, and displayed fears similar to those who defied the experimenter; yet they obeyed.

After the maximum shocks had been delivered, and the experimenter called a halt to the proceedings, many obedient subjects heaved sighs of relief, mopped their brows, rubbed their fingers over their eyes, or nervously fumbled cigarettes. Some shook their heads, apparently in regret. Some subjects had remained calm throughout the experiment, and displayed only minimal signs of tension from beginning to end.

DISCUSSION

The experiment yielded two findings that were surprising. The first finding concerns the sheer strength of obedient tendencies manifested in this situation. Subjects have learned from childhood that it is a fundamental breach of moral conduct to hurt another person against his will. Yet, 26 subjects abandon this tenet in following the instructions of an authority who has no special powers to enforce his commands. To disobey would bring no material loss to the subject; no punishment would ensue. It is clear from the remarks and outward behavior of many participants that in punishing the victim they are often acting against their own values. Subjects often expressed deep disapproval of shocking a man in the face of his objections, and others denounced it as stupid and senseless. Yet the majority complied with the experimental commands. This outcome was surprising from two perspectives: first, from the standpoint of predictions made in the questionnaire described earlier.

But the results were also unexpected to persons who observed the experiment in progress, through one-way mirrors. Observers often uttered expressions of disbelief upon seeing a subject administer more powerful shocks to the victim. These persons had a full acquaintance with the details of the situation, and yet systematically underestimated the amount of obedience that subjects would display.

The second unanticipated effect was the extraordinary tension generated by the procedures. One might suppose that a subject would simply break off or continue as his conscience dictated. Yet, this is very far from what happened. There were striking reactions of tension and emotional strain. One observer related:

> I observed a mature and initially poised businessman enter the laboratory smiling and confident. Within 20 minutes he was reduced to a twitching, stuttering wreck, who was rapidly approaching a point of nervous collapse. He constantly pulled on his earlobe, and twisted his hands. At one point he pushed his fist into his forehead and muttered: "Oh God, let's stop it." And yet he continued to respond to every word of the experimenter, and obeyed to the end.

Any understanding of the phenomenon of obedience must rest on an analysis of the particular conditions in which it occurs. The following features of the experiment go some distance in explaining the high amount of obedience observed in the situation.

1. The experiment is sponsored by and takes place on the grounds of an institution of unimpeachable reputation, Yale University. It may be reasonably presumed that the personnel are competent and reputable. The importance of this background authority is now being studied by conducting a series of experiments outside of New Haven, and without any visible ties to the university.

2. The experiment is, on the face of it, designed to attain a worthy purpose—advancement of knowledge about learning and memory. Obedience occurs not as an end in itself, but as an instrumental element in a situation that the subject construes as significant, and meaningful. He may not able to see its full significance, but he may properly assume that the experimenter does.

3. The subject perceives that the victim has voluntarily submitted to the authority system of the experimenter. He is not (at first) an unwilling captive impressed for involuntary service. He has taken the trouble to come to the laboratory presumably to aid the experimental research. That he later becomes an involuntary subject does not alter the fact that, initially, he consented to participate without qualification. Thus he has in some degree incurred an obligation toward the experimenter.

4. The subject, too, has entered the experiment voluntarily, and perceives himself under obligation to aid the experimenter. He has made a commitment, and to disrupt the experiment is a repudiation of this initial promise of aid.

5. Certain features of the procedure strengthen the subject's sense of obligation to the experimenter. For one, he has been paid for coming to the laboratory. In part this

is canceled out by the experimenter's statement that:

Of course, as in all experiments, the money is yours simply for coming to the laboratory. From this point on, no matter what happens, the money is yours.

6. From the subject's standpoint, the fact that he is the teacher and the other man the learner is purely a chance consequence (it is determined by drawing lots) and he, the subject, ran the same risk as the other man in being assigned the role of learner. Since the assignment of positions in the experiment was achieved by fair means, the learner is deprived of any basis of complaint on this count. (A similar situation obtains in Army units, in which—in the absence of volunteers—a particularly dangerous mission may be assigned by drawing lots, and the unlucky soldier is expected to bear his misfortune with sportsmanship.)

7. There is, at best, ambiguity with regard to the prerogatives of a psychologist and the corresponding rights of his subject. There is a vagueness of expectation concerning what a psychologist may require of his subject, and when he is overstepping acceptable limits. Moreover, the experiment occurs in a closed setting, and thus provides no opportunity for the subject to remove these ambiguities by discussion with others. There are few standards that seem directly applicable to the situation, which is a novel one for most subjects.

8. The subjects are assured that the shocks administered to the subject are "painful but not dangerous." Thus they assume that the discomfort caused the victim is momentary, while the scientific gains resulting from the experiment are enduring.

9. Through Shock Level 20 the victim continues to provide answers on the signal box. The subject may construe this as a sign that the victim is still willing to "play the game." It is only after Shock Level 20 that

the victim repudiates the rules completely, refusing to answer further.

These features help to explain the high amount of obedience obtained in this experiment. Many of the arguments raised need not remain matters of speculation, but can be reduced to testable propositions to be confirmed or disproved by further experiments.

The following features of the experiment concern the nature of the conflict which the subject faces.

10. The subject is placed in a position in which he must respond to the competing demands of two persons: the experimenter and the victim. The conflict must be resolved by meeting the demands of one or the other; satisfaction of the victim and the experimenter are mutually exclusive. Moreover, the resolution must take the form of a highly visible action, that of continuing to shock the victim or breaking off the experiment. Thus the subject is forced into a public conflict that does not permit any completely satisfactory solution.

11. While the demands of the experimenter carry the weight of scientific authority, the demands of the victim spring from his personal experience of pain and suffering. The two claims need not be regarded as equally pressing and legitimate. The experimenter seeks an abstract scientific datum; the victim cries out for relief from physical suffering caused by the subject's actions.

12. The experiment gives the subject little time for reflection. The conflict comes on rapidly. It is only minutes after the subject has been seated before the shock generator that the victim begins his protests. Moreover, the subject perceives that he has gone through but two-thirds of the shock levels at the time the subject's first protests are heard. Thus he understands that the conflict will have a persistent aspect to it, and may well become more intense as increasingly more powerful shocks are required. The rapidity with which

the conflict descends on the subject, and his realization that it is predictably recurrent may well be sources of tension to him.

13. At a more general level, the conflict stems from the opposition of two deeply ingrained behavior dispositions: first, the disposition not to harm other people, and second, the tendency to obey those whom we perceive to be legitimate authorities.

DISCUSSION QUESTIONS

1. Was Milgram's experiment ethical? Is it more or less ethical than Solomon Asch's research? Why or why not?
2. What are some other means of studying or addressing the questions raised by Milgram and Asch with less harmful effects on the participants?
3. What are they key variables Milgram studied in this research? What variables would you highlight in your research on obedience to authority?

ADDITIONAL RESOURCES

Film

"Obedience," by Stanley Milgram 45 minutes long. Original footage from the research.

Internet

http://www.stanleymilgram.com/. A site developed and hosted by Dr. Thomas Blass, psychologist at the University of Maryland.

http://www.milgramreenactment.org. A site developed in conjunction with a reenactment of Milgram's study at the Centre for Contemporary Art in Glasgow in February 2002.

FURTHER READING

Blass, Thomas. 2004. *The Man Who Shocked the World: The Life and Legacy of Stanley Milgram.* New York: Basic Books.

Milgram, Stanley. 1974. *Obedience to Authority: An Experimental View.* New York: Harper & Row.

25. The My Lai Massacre: A Military Crime of Obedience

HERBERT C. KELMAN AND V. LEE HAMILTON

While the events that Kelman and Hamilton describe in this harrowing piece took place in the late 1960s, their analysis of these events was not published until 1989. Although they limit their analysis to a particular massacre that took place during the Vietnam Conflict, they claim that the social influence of authorization, routinization, and dehumanization may have disastrous consequences in many social situations. As you read their article, reflect on the application of this formula to other historical and contemporary events.

Kelman, Herbert C. and V. Lee Hamilton. 1989. "The My Lai Massacre: A Military Crime of Obedience," in *Crimes of Obedience,* 1–22. New Haven, CT: Yale University Press.

March 16, 1968, was a busy day in U.S. history. Stateside, Robert F. Kennedy announced his presidential candidacy, challenging a sitting president from his own party—in part out of opposition to an undeclared and disastrous war. In Vietnam, the war continued. In many ways, March 16 may have been a typical day in that war. We will probably never know. But we do know that on that day a typical company went on a mission—which may or may not have been typical—to a village called Son (or Song) My. Most of what is remembered from that mission occurred in the subhamlet known to Americans as My Lai 4.

The My Lai massacre was investigated and charges were brought in 1969 and 1970. Trials and disciplinary actions lasted into 1971. Entire books have been written about the army's year-long cover-up of the massacre, and the cover-up was a major focus of the army's own investigation of the incident. Our central concern here is the massacre itself—a crime of obedience—and public reactions to such crimes, rather than the lengths to which many went to deny the event. Therefore this account concentrates on one day: March 16, 1968.

Many verbal testimonials to the horrors that occurred at My Lai were available. More unusual was the fact that an army photographer, Ronald Haeberle, was assigned the task of documenting the anticipated military engagement at My Lai—and documented a massacre instead. Later, as the story of the massacre emerged, his photographs were widely distributed and seared the public conscience. What might have been dismissed as unreal or exaggerated was depicted in photographs of demonstrable authenticity. The dominant image appeared on the cover of *Life:* piles of bodies jumbled together in a ditch along a trail—the dead all apparently unarmed. All were Oriental, and all appeared to be children, women, or old men. Clearly there had been a mass execution, one whose image would not quickly fade.

So many bodies (over twenty in the cover photo alone) are hard to imagine as the handiwork of one killer. These were not. They were the product of what we call a crime of obedience. Crimes of obedience begin with orders. But orders are often vague and rarely survive with any clarity the transition from one authority down a chain of subordinates to the ultimate actors. The operation at Son My was no exception.

"Charlie" Company, Company C, under Lt. Col. Frank Barker's command, arrived in Vietnam in December of 1967. As the army's investigative unit, directed by Lt. Gen. William R. Peers, characterized the personnel, they "contained no significant deviation from the average" for the time. The action at My Lai, like that throughout Vietnam, was fought by a cross-section of those Americans who either believed in the war or lacked the social resources to avoid participating in it. Charlie Company was indeed average for that time, that place, and that war.

Two key figures in Charlie Company were more unusual. The company's commander, Capt. Ernest Medina, was an upwardly mobile Mexican-American who wanted to make the army his career, although he feared that he might never advance beyond captain because of his lack of formal education. His eagerness had earned him a nickname among his men: "Mad Dog Medina." One of his admirers was the platoon leader Second Lt. William L. Calley, Jr., an undistinguished, five-foot-three-inch junior-college dropout who had failed four of the seven courses in which he had enrolled his first year. Many viewed him as one of those "instant officers" made possible only by the army's then-desperate need for manpower. Whatever the cause, he was an insecure leader whose frequent claim was "I'm the boss." His nickname among some of the troops was. "Surfside 5½," a reference to the swashbuckling heroes of a popular television show, "Surfside 6."

The Son My operation was planned by Lieutenant Colonel Barker and his staff as a search-and-destroy mission with the objective of rooting out the Forty-eighth Viet Cong Battalion from their base area of Son My village. Apparently no written orders were ever issued. Barker's superior, Col. Oran Henderson, arrived at the staging point the day before. Among the issues he reviewed with the assembled officers were some of the weaknesses of prior operations by their units, including their failure to be appropriately aggressive in pursuit of the enemy. Later briefings by Lieutenant Colonel Barker and his staff asserted that no one except Viet Cong was expected to be in the village after 7 A.M. on the following day. The "innocent" would all be at the market. Those present at the briefings gave conflicting accounts of Barker's exact orders, but he conveyed at least a strong suggestion that the Son My area was to be obliterated.

Evidence that Barker ordered the killing of civilians is even more murky. What does seem clear, however, is that—having asserted that civilians would be away at the market—he did not specify what was to be done with any who might nevertheless be found on the scene. Since Barker was killed in action in June 1968, his own formal version of the truth was never available.

Charlie Company's Captain Medina was briefed for the operation by Barker and his staff. He then transmitted the already vague orders to his own men. Charlie Company was spoiling for a fight, having been totally frustrated during its months in Vietnam—first by waiting for battles that never came, then by incompetent forays led by inexperienced commanders, and finally by mines and booby traps. In fact, the emotion-laden funeral of a sergeant killed by a booby trap was held on March 15, the day before My Lai. Captain Medina gave the orders for the next day's action at the close of that funeral. Many were in a mood for revenge.

It is again unclear what was ordered. Although all participants were still alive by the time of the trials for the massacre, they were either on trial or probably felt under threat of trial. Memories are often flawed and self-serving at such times. It is apparent that Medina relayed to the men at least some of Barker's general message—to expect Viet Cong resistance, to burn, and to kill livestock. It is not clear that

he ordered the slaughter of the inhabitants, but some of the men who heard him thought he had. One of those who claimed to have heard such orders was Lt. William Calley.

As March 16 dawned, much was expected of the operation by those who had set it into motion. Therefore a full complement of "brass" was present in helicopters overhead, including Barker, Colonel Henderson, and their superior, Major General Koster (who went on to become commandant of West Point before the story of My Lai broke). On the ground, the troops were to carry with them one reporter and one photographer to immortalize the anticipated battle.

The action for Company C began at 7:30 as their first wave of helicopters touched down near the subhamlet of My Lai 4. By 7:47 all of Company C was present and set to fight. But instead of the Viet Cong Forty-eighth Battalion, My Lai was filled with the old men, women, and children who were supposed to have gone to market. By this time, in their version of the war, and with whatever orders they thought they had heard, the men from Company C were nevertheless ready to find Viet Cong everywhere. By nightfall, the official tally was 128 VC killed and three weapons captured, although later unofficial body counts ran as high as 500. The operation at Son My was over. And by nightfall, as Hersh reported: "the Viet Cong were back in My Lai 4, helping the survivors bury the dead. It took five days. To this day, the memory of the massacre is kept alive by markers and plaques designating the spots where groups of villagers were killed, by a large statue, and by the My Lai Museum, established in 1975.

But what could have happened to leave American troops reporting a victory over Viet Cong when in fact they had killed hundreds of noncombatants? It is not hard to explain the report of victory; that is the essence of a cover-up. It is harder to understand how the killings came to be committed in the first place, making a cover-up necessary.

MASS EXECUTIONS AND THE DEFENSE OF SUPERIOR ORDERS

Some of the atrocities on March 16, 1968, were evidently unofficial, spontaneous acts: rapes, tortures, killings.

Some atrocities toward the end of the action were part of an almost casual "mopping-up," much of which was the responsibility of Lieutenant LaCross's Third Platoon of Charlie Company. All of Company C was implicated in a pattern of death and destruction throughout the hamlet, much of which seemingly lacked rhyme or reason.

But a substantial amount of the killing was *organized* and traceable to one authority: the First Platoon's Lt. William Calley. Calley was originally charged with 109 killings, almost all of them mass executions at the trail and other locations. He stood trial for 102 of these killings, was convicted of 22 in 1971, and at first received a life sentence. Though others—both superior and subordinate to Calley—were brought to trial, he was the only one convicted for the My Lai crimes. Thus, the only actions of My Lai for which *anyone* was ever convicted were mass executions, ordered and committed. We suspect that there are commonsense reasons why this one type of killing was singled out. In the midst of rapidly moving events with people running about, an execution of stationary targets is literally a still life that stands out and whose participants are clearly visible. It can be proven that specific people committed specific deeds. An execution, in contrast to the shooting of someone on the run, is also more likely to meet the legal definition of an act resulting from intent—with malice aforethought. Moreover, American military law specifically forbids the killing of unarmed civilians or military prisoners, as does the Geneva Convention between nations. Thus common sense, legal standards, and explicit doctrine all made such actions the likeliest target for prosecution.

When Lieutenant Calley was charged under military law it was for violation of the Uniform Code of Military Justice (UCMJ) Article 118 (murder). This article is similar to civilian codes in that it provides for conviction if an accused:

> without justification or excuse, unlawfully kills a human being, when he—

1. has a premeditated design to kill;
2. intends to kill or inflict great bodily harm;
3. is engaged in an act which is inherently dangerous to others and evinces a wanton disregard of human life; or
4. is engaged in the perpetration or attempted perpetration of burglary, sodomy, rape, robbery, or aggravated arson.

For a soldier, one legal justification for killing is warfare; but warfare is subject to many legal limits and restrictions, including, of course, the inadmissibility of killing unarmed noncombatants or prisoners whom one has disarmed. The pictures of the trail victims at My Lai certainly portrayed one or the other of these. Such an action would be illegal under military law; ordering another to commit such an action would be illegal; and following such an order would be illegal.

But following an order may provide a second and pivotal justification for an act that would be murder when committed by a civilian. American military law assumes that the subordinate is inclined to follow orders, as that is the normal obligation of the role. Hence, legally, obedient subordinates are protected from unreasonable expectations regarding their capacity to evaluate those orders. Thus what *may* be excusable is the good-faith carrying out of an order, as long as that order appears to the ordinary soldier to be a legal one. In military law, invoking superior orders moves the question from one of the action's consequences—the body count—to one of evaluating the actor's motives and good sense.

In sum, if anyone is to be brought to justice for a massacre, common sense and legal codes decree that the most appropriate targets are those who make themselves executioners. This is the kind of target the government selected in prosecuting Lieutenant Calley with the greatest fervor. And in a military context, the most promising way in which one can redefine one's undeniable deeds into acceptability is to invoke superior orders. This is what Calley did in attempting to avoid conviction. Since the core legal issues involved points of mass execution—the ditches and trail where America's image of My Lai was formed—we review these events in greater detail.

The day's quiet beginning has already been noted. Troops landed and swept unopposed into the village. The three weapons eventually reported as the haul from the operation were picked up from three apparent Viet Cong who fled the village when the troops arrived and were pursued and killed by helicopter gunships. Obviously the Viet Cong did frequent the area. But it appears that by about 8:00 A.M. no one who met the troops was aggressive, and no one was armed. By the laws of war Charlie Company had no argument with such people.

As they moved into the village, the soldiers began to gather its inhabitants together. Shortly after 8:00 A.M. Lieutenant Calley told Pfc. Paul Meadlo that "you know what to do with" a group of villagers Meadlo was guarding. Estimates of the numbers in the group ranged as high as eighty women, children, and old men, and Meadlo's own estimate under oath was thirty to fifty people. Meadlo himself and others testified that Meadlo cried as he fired; others reported him later to be sobbing and "all broke up." It would appear that to Lieutenant Calley's subordinates something was unusual, and stressful, in these orders.

Among the helicopters flying reconnaissance above Son My was that of CWO Hugh Thompson. By 9:00 or soon after Thompson had noticed some horrifying events from his perch. As he spotted wounded civilians, he sent down smoke markers so that soldiers on the ground could treat them. They killed them instead. He reported to headquarters, trying to persuade someone to stop what was going on. Barker, hearing the message, called down to Captain Medina. Medina, in turn, later claimed to have told Calley that it was "enough for today." But it was not yet enough.

At Calley's orders, his men began gathering the remaining villagers—roughly seventy-five individuals, mostly women and children—and herding them toward a drainage ditch. Accompanied by three or four enlisted men, Lieutenant Calley executed several batches of civilians who had been gathered into ditches.

It is noteworthy that during these executions more than one enlisted man avoided carrying out Calley's orders, and more than one, by sworn oath, directly refused to obey them.

Disobedience of Lieutenant Calley's own orders to kill represented a serious legal and moral threat to a defense *based* on superior orders, such as Calley was attempting. This defense had to assert that the orders seemed reasonable enough to carry out, that they appeared to be legal orders. Even if the orders in question were not legal, the defense had to assert that an ordinary individual could not and should not be expected to see the distinction. In short, if what happened was "business as usual," even though it might be bad business, then the defendant stood a chance of acquittal. But under direct command from "Surfside 5½," some ordinary enlisted men managed to refuse, to avoid, or at least to stop doing what they were ordered to do. As "reasonable men" of "ordinary sense and understanding," they had apparently found something awry that morning; and it would have been hard for an officer to plead successfully that he was more ordinary than his men in his capacity to evaluate the reasonableness of orders.

Even those who obeyed Calley's orders showed great stress. For example, Meadlo eventually began to argue and cry directly in front of Calley. Pfc. Herbert Carter shot himself in the foot, possibly because he could no longer take what he was doing. We were not destined to hear a sworn version of the incident, since neither side at the Calley trial called him to testify.

The most unusual instance of resistance to authority came from the skies. CWO Hugh Thompson, who had protested the apparent carnage of civilians, was Calley's inferior in rank but was not in his line of command. He was also watching the ditch from his helicopter and noticed some people moving after the first round of slaughter—chiefly children who had been shielded by their mothers' bodies. Landing to rescue the wounded, he also found some villagers hiding in a nearby bunker. Protecting the Vietnamese with his own body, Thompson ordered his men to train their guns on the Americans and to open fire if the Americans fired on the Vietnamese. He then radioed for additional rescue helicopters and stood between the Vietnamese and the Americans under Calley's command until the Vietnamese could be evacuated. He later returned to the ditch to unearth a child buried, unharmed, beneath layers of bodies. In October 1969, Thompson was awarded the Distinguished Flying Cross for heroism at My Lai, specifically for the rescue of children. Four months earlier, at the Pentagon, Thompson had identified Calley as having been at the ditch.

By about 10:00 A.M., the massacre was winding down. The remaining actions consisted largely of isolated rapes and killings, "clean-up" shootings of the wounded, and the destruction of the village by fire. We have already seen some examples of these more indiscriminate and possibly less premeditated acts. By the 11:00 A.M. lunch break, when the exhausted men of Company C were relaxing, two young girls wandered back from a hiding place only to be invited to share lunch. This surrealist touch illustrates the extent to which the soldiers' action had become dissociated from its meaning. An hour earlier, some of these men were making sure that not even a child would escape the executioner's bullet. But now the job was done and it was time for lunch—and in this new context it seemed only natural to ask the children who had managed to escape execution to join them. The massacre had ended. It remained only for the Viet Cong to reap the political rewards among the survivors in hiding.

The army command in the area knew that something had gone wrong. Direct commanders, including Lieutenant Colonel Barker, had

firsthand reports, such as Thompson's complaints. Others had such odd bits of evidence as the claim of 128 Viet Cong dead with a booty of only three weapons. But the cover-up of My Lai began at once. The operation was reported as a victory over a stronghold of the Viet Cong Forty-eighth.

My Lai might have remained a "victory" but for another odd twist. A soldier who had not even been at the massacre, Ronald Ridenhour, talked to several friends and acquaintances who had been. Ridenhour's growing conviction that a massacre—or something close to it—had occurred was reinforced by his own travel over the area by helicopter soon after the event. My Lai was desolate. He gradually concluded that someone was covering up the incident within the army and that an independent investigation was needed.

At the end of March 1969, he finally wrote a letter detailing what he knew about "Pinkville." The letter was sent to thirty individuals—the president, Pentagon officials, and some members of the Senate and House. Ridenhour's congressman, fellow Arizonian Morris Udall, gave it particular heed. The slow unraveling of the cover-up began. During the following months, the army in fact initiated an investigation but carried it out in strict secrecy. Ridenhour, convinced that the cover-up was continuing, sought journalistic help and finally, by coincidence, connected with Seymour Hersh. Hersh followed up and broke the story, which eventually brought him a Pulitzer Prize and other awards for his investigative reporting. The cover-up collapsed, leaving only the question of the army's resolve to seek justice in the case: Against whom would it proceed, with how much speed and vigor, and with what end in mind?

William Calley was not the only man tried for the events at My Lai. The actions of over thirty soldiers and civilians were scrutinized by investigators; over half of these had to face charges or disciplinary action of some sort. Targets of investigation included Captain Medina, who was tried, and various higher-ups, including General

Koster. But Lieutenant Calley was the only person convicted, the only person to serve time.

The core of Lieutenant Calley's defense was superior orders.

Lieutenant Calley steadfastly maintained that his actions within My Lai had constituted, in his mind, carrying out orders from Captain Medina. Both his own actions and the orders he gave to others (such as the instruction to Meadlo to "waste 'em") were entirely in response to superior orders. He denied any intent to kill individuals and any but the most passing awareness of distinctions among the individuals: "I was ordered to go in there and destroy the enemy. That was my job on that day. That was the mission I was given. I did not sit down and think in terms of men, women, and children. They were all classified the same, and that was the classification that we dealt with, just as enemy soldiers."

A jury of combat veterans proceeded to convict William Calley of the premeditated murder of no less than twenty-two human beings. (The army, realizing some unfortunate connotations in referring to the victims as "Oriental human beings," eventually referred to them as "human beings.") Regarding the first specification in the murder charge, the bodies on the trail, he was convicted of premeditated murder of not less than one person. (Medical testimony had been able to pinpoint only one person whose wounds as revealed in Haeberle's photos were sure to be immediately fatal.) Regarding the second specification, the bodies in the ditch, Calley was convicted of the premeditated murder of not less than twenty human beings. Regarding additional specifications that he had killed an old man and a child, Calley was convicted of premeditated murder in the first case and of assault with intent to commit murder in the second.

Lieutenant Calley was initially sentenced to life imprisonment. That sentence was reduced: first to twenty years, eventually to ten (the latter by Secretary of Defense Callaway in 1974). Calley served three years before being released on bond. The time was spent under house arrest in his apartment, where he was able to receive visits from his girlfriend. He was granted parole on September 10, 1975.

SANCTIONED MASSACRES

The slaughter at My Lai is an instance of a class of violent acts that can be described as sanctioned massacres: acts of indiscriminate, ruthless, and often systematic mass violence, carried out by military or paramilitary personnel while engaged in officially sanctioned campaigns, the victims of which are defenseless and unresisting civilians, including old men, women, and children. Sanctioned massacres have occurred throughout history. Within American history, My Lai had its precursors in the Philippine war around the turn of the century and in the massacres of American Indians. Elsewhere in the world, one recalls the Nazis' "final solution" for European Jews, the massacres and deportations of Armenians by Turks, the liquidation of the kulaks and the great purges in the Soviet Union, and more recently the massacres in Indonesia and Bangladesh, in Biafra and Burundi, in South Africa and Mozambique, in Cambodia and Afghanistan, in Syria and Lebanon. Sanctioned massacres may vary on a number of dimensions. For present purposes, however, we want to focus on features they share. Two of these are the *context* and the *target* of the violence.

Sanctioned massacres tend to occur in the context of an overall policy that is explicitly or implicitly genocidal: designed to destroy all or part of a category of people defined in ethnic, national, racial, religious, or other terms. Such a policy may be deliberately aimed at the systematic extermination of a population group as an end in itself, as was the case with the Holocaust during World War II. In the Nazis' "final solution" for European Jewry, a policy aimed at exterminating millions of people was consciously articulated and executed and the extermination was accomplished on a mass-production basis through the literal establishment of a well-organized, efficient death industry. Alternatively, such a policy may be aimed at an objective other than extermination—such as the pacification of the rural population of South Vietnam, as was the case in U.S. policy for Indochina—but may include the deliberate decimation of large segments of a population as an acceptable means to that end.

Central to U.S. strategy in South Vietnam were such actions as unrestricted air and artillery bombardments of peasant hamlets, search-and-destroy missions by ground troops, crop destruction programs, and mass deportation of rural populations. These actions (and similar ones in Laos and Cambodia) were clearly and deliberately aimed at civilians and resulted in the death, injury, and/or uprooting of large numbers of that population and in the destruction of their countryside, their source of livelihood, and their social structure. These consequences were anticipated by policymakers and indeed were intended as part of their pacification effort; the actions were designed to clear the countryside and deprive guerrillas of their base of operations, even if this meant destroying the civilian population. Massacres of the kind that occurred at My Lai were not deliberately planned, but they took place in an atmosphere in which the rural Vietnamese population was viewed as expendable and actions that resulted in the killing of large numbers of that population as strategic necessities.

A second feature of sanctioned massacres is that their targets have not themselves threatened or engaged in hostile actions toward the perpetrators of the violence. The victims of this class of violence are often defenseless civilians, including old men, women, and children. By all accounts, at least after the first moments at My Lai, the victims there fit this description, although in guerrilla warfare there always remains some ambiguity about the distinction between armed soldiers and unarmed civilians. As has often been noted, U.S. troops in Vietnam had to face the possibility that a woman or even a child might be concealing a hand grenade under clothing.

In searching for a psychological explanation for mass violence under these conditions, one's first inclination is to look for forces that might impel people toward such murderous acts. Can we identify, in massacre situations, psychological forces so powerful that they outweigh the moral restraints that would normally inhibit unjustifiable violence?

In sum, the occurrence of sanctioned massacres cannot be adequately explained by the existence of psychological forces—whether these be characterological dispositions to engage in murderous violence or profound hostility against the target—so powerful that they must find expression in violent acts unhampered by moral restraints. Instead, the major instigators for this class of violence derive from the policy process. The question that really calls for psychological analysis is why so many people are willing to formulate, participate in, and condone policies that call for the mass killings of defenseless civilians. Thus it is more instructive to look not at the motives for violence but at the conditions under which the usual moral inhibitions against violence become weakened. Three social processes that tend to create such conditions can be identified: authorization, routinization, and dehumanization. Through authorization, the situation becomes so defined that the individual is absolved of the responsibility to make personal moral choices. Through routinization, the action becomes so organized that there is no opportunity for raising moral questions. Through dehumanization, the actors' attitudes toward the target and toward themselves become so structured that it is neither necessary nor possible for them to view the relationship in moral terms.

Authorization

Sanctioned massacres by definition occur in the context of an authority situation, a situation in which, at least for many of the participants, the moral principles that generally govern human relationships do not apply. Thus, when acts of violence are explicitly ordered, implicitly encouraged, tacitly approved, or at least permitted by legitimate authorities, people's readiness to commit or condone them is enhanced. That such acts are authorized seems to carry automatic justification for them. Behaviorally, authorization obviates the necessity of making judgments or choices. Not only do normal moral principles become inoperative, but—particularly when the actions are explicitly ordered—a different kind of morality, linked to the duty to obey superior orders, tends to take over.

In an authority situation, individuals characteristically feel obligated to obey the orders of the authorities, whether or not these correspond with their personal preferences. They see themselves as having no choice as long as they accept the legitimacy of the orders and of the authorities who give them. Individuals differ considerably in the degree to which—and the conditions under which—they are prepared to challenge the legitimacy of an order on the grounds that the order itself is illegal, or that those giving it have overstepped their authority, or that it stems from a policy that violates fundamental societal values. Regardless of such individual differences, however, the basic structure of a situation of legitimate authority requires subordinates to respond in terms of their role obligations rather than their personal preferences; they can openly disobey only by challenging the legitimacy of the authority. Often people obey without question even though the behavior they engage in may entail great personal sacrifice or great harm to others.

An important corollary of the basic structure of the authority situation is that actors often do not see themselves as personally responsible for the consequences of their actions. Again, there are individual differences, depending on actors' capacity and readiness to evaluate the legitimacy of orders received. Insofar as they see themselves as having had no choice in their actions, however, they do not feel personally responsible for them. They were not personal agents, but merely extensions of the authority. Thus, when their actions cause harm to others, they can feel relatively free of guilt. A similar mechanism operates when a person engages in antisocial behavior that was

not ordered by the authorities but was tacitly encouraged and approved by them—even if only by making it clear that such behavior will not be punished. In this situation, behavior that was formerly illegitimate is legitimized by the authorities' acquiescence.

In the My Lai massacre, it is likely that the structure of the authority situation contributed to the massive violence in both ways—that is, by conveying the message that acts of violence against Vietnamese villagers were *required*, as well as the message that such acts, even if not ordered, were *permitted* by the authorities in charge. The actions at My Lai represented, at least in some respects, responses to explicit or implicit orders. Lieutenant Calley indicated, by orders and by example, that he wanted large numbers of villagers killed. Whether Calley himself had been ordered by his superiors to "waste" the whole area, as he claimed, remains a matter of controversy. Even if we assume, however, that he was not explicitly ordered to wipe out the village, he had reason to believe that such actions were expected by his superior officers. Indeed, the very nature of the war conveyed this expectation. The principal measure of military success was the "body count"—the number of enemy soldiers killed—and any Vietnamese killed by the U.S. military was commonly defined as a "Viet Cong." Thus, it was not totally bizarre for Calley to believe that what he was doing at My Lai was to increase his body count, as any good officer was expected to do.

Even to the extent that the actions at My Lai occurred spontaneously, without reference to superior orders, those committing them had reason to assume that such actions might be tacitly approved of by the military authorities. Not only had they failed to punish such acts in most cases, but the very strategies and tactics that the authorities consistently devised were based on the proposition that the civilian population of South Vietnam—whether "hostile" or "friendly"—was expendable. Such policies as search-and-destroy missions, the establishment of free-shooting zones, the use of antipersonnel weapons, the bombing of entire villages if they were suspected of harboring guerrillas, the forced migration of masses of the rural population, and the defoliation of vast forest areas helped legitimize acts of massive violence of the kind occurring at My Lai.

Some of the actions at My Lai suggest an orientation to authority based on unquestioning obedience to superior orders, no matter how destructive the actions these orders call for. Such obedience is specifically fostered in the course of military training and reinforced by the structure of the military authority situation. It also, reflects, however, an ideological orientation that may be more widespread in the general population.

Routinization

Authorization processes create a situation in which people become involved in an action without considering its implications and without really making a decision. Once they have taken the initial step, they are in a new psychological and social situation in which the pressures to continue are powerful. Many forces that might originally have kept people out of a situation reverse direction once they have made a commitment (once they have gone through the "gate region") and now serve to keep them in the situation. For example, concern about the criminal nature of an action, which might originally have inhibited a person from becoming involved, may now lead to deeper involvement in efforts to justify the action and avoid negative consequences.

Despite these forces, however, given the nature of the actions involved in sanctioned massacres, one might still expect moral scruples to intervene; but the likelihood of moral resistance is greatly reduced by transforming the action into routine, mechanical, highly programmed operations. Routinization fulfills two functions. First, it reduces the necessity of making decisions, thus minimizing the occasions in which moral questions may arise. Second, it makes it easier to avoid the implications of the action, since the actor focuses on the details of the job rather than on its meaning. The latter effect is more readily achieved among those who participate in sanctioned massacres from a distance—from their desks or even from the cockpits of their bombers.

Routinization operates both at the level of the individual actor and at the organizational level. Individual job performance is broken down into a series of discrete steps, most of them carried out in automatic, regularized fashion. It becomes easy to forget the nature of the product that emerges from this process. When Lieutenant Calley said of My Lai that it was "no great deal," he probably implied that it was all in a day's work. Organizationally, the task is divided among different offices, each of which has responsibility for a small portion of it. This arrangement diffuses responsibility and limits the amount and scope of decision making that is necessary. There is no expectation that the moral implications will be considered at any of these points, nor is there any opportunity to do so. The organizational processes also help further legitimize the actions of each participant. By proceeding in routine fashion—processing papers, exchanging memos, diligently carrying out their assigned tasks—the different units mutually reinforce each other in the view that what is going on must be perfectly normal, correct, and legitimate. The shared illusion that they are engaged in a legitimate enterprise helps the participants assimilate their activities to other purposes, such as the efficiency of their performance, the productivity of their unit, or the cohesiveness of their group.

Normalization of atrocities is more difficult to the extent that there are constant reminders of the true meaning of the enterprise. Bureaucratic inventiveness in the use of language helps to cover up such meaning. For example, the SS had a set of *Sprachregelungen,* or "language rules," to govern descriptions of their extermination program. The code names for killing and liquidation were "final solution," "evacuation," and "special treatment." The war in Indochina produced its own set of euphemisms, such as "protective reaction," "pacification," and "forced-draft urbanization and modernization." The use of euphemisms allows participants in sanctioned massacres to differentiate their actions from ordinary killing and destruction and thus to avoid confronting their true meaning.

Dehumanization

Authorization processes override standard moral considerations; routinization processes reduce the likelihood that such considerations will arise. Still, the inhibitions against murdering one's fellow human beings are generally so strong that the victims must also be stripped of their human status if they are to be subjected to systematic killing. Insofar as they are dehumanized, the usual principles of morality no longer apply to them.

Sanctioned massacres become possible to the extent that the victims are deprived in the perpetrators' eyes of the two qualities essential to being perceived as fully human and included in the moral compact that governs human relationships: *identity*—standing as independent, distinctive individuals, capable of making choices and entitled to live their own lives—and *community*—fellow membership in an interconnected network of individuals who care for each other and respect each other's individuality and rights. Thus, when a group of people is defined entirely in terms of a category to which they belong, and when this category is excluded from the human family, moral restraints against killing them are more readily overcome.

Dehumanization of the enemy is a common phenomenon in any war situation. Sanctioned massacres, however, presuppose a more extreme degree of dehumanization, insofar as the killing is not in direct response to the target's threats or provocations. It is not what they have done that marks such victims for death but who they are—the category to which they happen to belong. They are the victims of policies that regard their systematic destruction as a desirable end or an acceptable means. Such extreme dehumanization becomes possible when the target group can readily be identified as a separate category of people who have historically been stigmatized and excluded by the victimizers; often the victims belong to a distinct racial, religious, ethnic, or political group regarded as inferior or sinister. The traditions, the habits, the images, and the vocabularies for dehumanizing such groups are already well established and can be drawn upon when the groups are selected for massacre. Labels help deprive the victims of identity and community, as in the epithet "gooks" that was commonly used to refer to Vietnamese and other Indochinese peoples.

The dynamics of the massacre process itself further increase the participants' tendency to dehumanize their victims. Those who participate as part of the bureaucratic apparatus increasingly come to see their victims as bodies to be counted and entered into their reports, as faceless figures that will determine their productivity rates and promotions. Those who participate in the massacre directly—in the field, as it were—are reinforced in their perception of the victims as less than human by observing their very victimization. The only way they can justify what is being done to these people—both by others and by themselves—and the only way they can extract some degree of meaning out of the absurd events in which they find themselves participating is by coming to believe that the victims are subhuman and deserve to be rooted out. And thus the process of dehumanization feeds on itself.

DISCUSSION QUESTIONS

1. What are some contemporary examples of the ways in which authorization, routinization, and dehumanization work together to create a context for committing "crimes of obedience," as discussed by Kelman and Hamilton?

2. How can we counter the forces of authorization, routinization, and dehumanization to prevent such acts against humanity?

ADDITIONAL RESOURCES

Internet

http://www.pbs.org/wgbh/amex/Vietnam/trenches/my_lai.html. An "American Experience" PBS website featuring "Vietnam Online."

FURTHER READING

Kelman, Herbert C. and V. Lee Hamilton. 1989. *Crimes of Obedience: Toward a Social Psychology of Authority and Responsibility.* New Haven, CT: Yale University Press.

Helping and Altruism

Each of the following articles shows how social factors affect helping behavior in emergency or other tragic circumstances. While many people would claim that they would offer assistance to anyone in need, the real world and experimental data discussed here give us reason to think otherwise. We may be comforted to know that Piferi and colleagues' findings show altruistic motivations in helping behavior. Cuddy and et al.'s findings are contradictory; documenting that helping behavior may be egotistically motivated.

With research stemming from three major national tragedies—the public murder of Kitty Genovese, the terrorist attacks of September 11, 2001, and the devastation of Hurricane Katrina—these scholars explore the factors that lead to action versus inaction in times of dire need. In each of the three crisis situations, strangers had the opportunity to help other strangers. How might the motivation to help and helping behavior itself be impacted by closer relationships, such as those between acquaintances, family or friends?

The research methods used in these articles raise another question. Latané and Darley report on several contrived laboratory experiments in which they could directly see research subjects' action or inaction. By contrast, Cuddy et al. and Piferi et al. discuss the subjects' self-reported motivations and helping activities. How might self-reported data differ in validity and reliability from experimental data?

Ultimately, the research discussed in these articles gives us further insight into how a person's definition of a situation influences decisions about how to act in it. Moreover, the recent string of major disasters not discussed here gives us further opportunity to explore helping behavior. The 2008 earthquakes in Myanmar and China, the I-35W bridge collapse in Minneapolis, Minnesota, in 2007, and the end-of-the-year Indian Ocean tsunami in 2004 all bring to mind images of human loss and heroism.

26. Social Determinants of Bystander Intervention in Emergencies

BIBB LATANÉ AND JOHN M. DARLEY

Kitty Genovese was brutally attacked and ultimately murdered in the residential neighborhood of Kew Gardens, in Queens, New York, on March 13, 1964. Latané and Darley's research on helping behavior was motivated by a desire to understand the bizarre behavior of 38 people who did not intervene to assist her. Such inaction, initially labeled the Genovese syndrome, was coined the *bystander effect* by Latané and Darley. Is their research about the diffusion of responsibility as relevant today as it was in the 1970s?

Most psychologists would agree that men will go to the aid of others even when there is no visible gain for themselves. At least, most would have agreed until a March night in 1964. That night, Kitty Genovese was set upon by a maniac as she returned home from work at 3:00 A.M. Thirty-eight of her neighbors in Kew Gardens came to their windows when she cried out in terror, but none came to her assistance, even though her stalker took over half an hour to murder her. No one even so much as called the police.

Since we started our research on bystander response to emergencies, we have heard about dozens of such incidents. We have also heard many explanations to account for the surprising failure of bystanders to intervene in emergencies—failures which suggest that we no longer care about the fate of our neighbors.

But can this be so? We think not. Although it is unquestionably true that the witnesses in the incidents above did nothing to save the victim, "apathy," "indifference," and "unconcern" are not

Latané, Bibb and John M. Darley. 1970. "Social Determinants of Bystander Intervention in Emergencies," in Jacqueline Macaulay and Leonard Berkowitz (eds.). *Altruism and Helping Behavior: Social Psychological Studies of Some Antecedents and Consequences*, 13–27. New York: Academic Press.

entirely accurate descriptions of their reactions. The 38 witnesses of Kitty Genovese's murder did not merely look at the scene once and then ignore it. Instead they continued to stare out of their windows at what was going on. Caught, fascinated, distressed, unwilling to act but unable to turn away, their behavior was neither helpful nor heroic; but it was not indifferent or apathetic either.

Actually, it was like crowd behavior in many other emergency situations; car accidents, drownings, fires, and attempted suicides all attract substantial numbers of people who watch the drama in helpless fascination without getting directly involved in the action. Are these people alienated and indifferent? Are the rest of us? Obviously not. It seems only yesterday we were being called overconforming. But why, then, do we not act?

Paradoxically, the key to understanding these failures of intervention may be found exactly in the fact that so surprises us about them: so many bystanders fail to intervene. If we think of 38, or 11, or 100 individuals, each looking at an emergency and callously deciding to pass by, we are horrified. But if we realize that each bystander is picking up cues about what is happening and how to react to it from the other bystanders, understanding begins to emerge. There are several ways in which a crowd of onlookers can make each individual member of that crowd less likely to act.

DEFINING THE SITUATION

Most emergencies are, or at least begin as, ambiguous events. A quarrel in the street may erupt into violence or it may be simply a family argument. A man staggering about may be suffering a coronary, or an onset of diabetes, or he simply may be drunk. Smoke pouring from a building may signal a fire, but on the other hand, it may be simply steam or air conditioner vapor. Before a bystander is likely to take action in such ambiguous situations, he must first define the event as an emergency and decide that intervention is the proper course of action.

In the course of making these decisions, it is likely that an individual bystander will be considerably influenced by the decisions he perceives other bystanders to be taking. If everyone else in a group of onlookers seems to regard an event as nonserious and the proper course of action as nonintervention, this consensus may strongly affect the perceptions of any single individual and inhibit his potential intervention.

The definitions that other people held may be discovered by discussing the situation with them, but they may also be inferred from their facial expressions or behavior. A whistling man with his hands in his pockets obviously does not believe he is in the midst of a crisis. A bystander who does not respond to smoke obviously does not attribute it to fire. An individual, seeing the inaction of others, will judge the situation as less serious then he would if alone.

But why should the others be inactive? Probably because they are aware that other people are also watching them. The others are an audience to their own reactions. Among American males, it is considered desirable to appear poised and collected in times of stress. Being exposed to the public view may constrain the actions and expressions of emotion of any individual as he tries to avoid possible ridicule and embarrassment. Even though he may be truly concerned and upset about the plight of a victim, until he decides what to do, he may maintain a calm demeanor.

If each member of a group is, at the same time, trying to appear calm and also looking around at the other members to gauge their reactions, all members may be led (or misled) by each other to define the situation as less critical than they would if alone. Until someone acts, each person sees only other nonresponding bystanders and is likely to be influenced not to act himself. A state of "pluralistic ignorance" may develop.

It has often been recognized that a crowd can cause contagion of panic, leading each person in the crowd to overreact to an emergency to the detriment of everyone's welfare. What we suggest here is that a crowd can also force inaction on its members. It can suggest by its passive behavior that an event is not to be reacted to as an emergency, and it can make any individual uncomfortably aware of what a fool he will look for behaving as if it is.

WHEN THERE'S SMOKE, THERE'S (SOMETIMES) FIRE

In this experiment we presented an emergency to individuals either alone or in groups of three. It was our expectation that the constraints on behavior in public combined with social influence processes would lessen the likelihood that members of three-person groups would act to cope with the emergency.

College students were invited to an interview to discuss "some of the problems involved in life at an urban university." As they sat in a small room waiting to be called for the interview and filling out a preliminary questionnaire, they faced an ambiguous but potentially dangerous situation. A stream of smoke began to puff into the room through a wall vent.

Some subjects were exposed to this potentially critical situation while alone. In a second condition, three naive subjects were tested together. Since subjects arrived at slightly different times, and since they each had individual questionnaires to work on, they did not introduce themselves to each other or attempt anything but the most rudimentary conversation.

As soon as the subjects had completed two pages of their questionnaires, the experimenter began to introduce the smoke through a small vent in the wall. The "smoke," copied from the famous Camel cigarette sign in Times Square, formed a moderately fine-textured but clearly visible stream of whitish smoke. It continued to jet into the room in irregular puffs, and by the end of the experimental period, it obscured vision.

All behavior and conversation were observed and coded from behind a one-way window (largely disguised on the subject's side by a large sign giving preliminary instructions). When and if the subject left the experimental room and

reported the smoke, he was told that the situation "would be taken care of." If the subject had not reported the smoke within 6 minutes from the time he first noticed it, the experiment was terminated.

The typical subject, when tested alone, behaved very reasonably. Usually, shortly after the smoke appeared, he would glance up from his questionnaire, notice the smoke, show a slight but distinct startle reaction, and then undergo a brief period of indecision, perhaps returning briefly to his questionnaire before again staring at the smoke. Soon, most subjects would get up from their chairs, walk over to the vent and investigate it closely, sniffing the smoke, waving their hands in it, feeling its temperature, etc. The usual Alone subject would hesitate again, but finally would walk out of the room, look around outside, and, finding somebody there, calmly report the presence of the smoke. No subject showed any sign of panic, most simply said: "There's something strange going on in there, there seems to be some sort of smoke coming through the wall...." The median subject in the Alone condition had reported the smoke within 2 minutes of first noticing it. Three-quarters of the 24 people run in this condition reported the smoke before the experimental period was terminated.

In contrast, subjects in the three-person-group condition were markedly inhibited from reporting the smoke. In only 38 percent of the eight groups in this condition did even one person report. Of the 24 people run in these eight groups, only one person reported the smoke within the first 4 minutes before the room got noticeably unpleasant.

The results of this study clearly support the prediction. Groups of three naive subjects were less likely to report the smoke than solitary bystanders. Our predictions were confirmed—but this does not necessarily mean that our explanation of these results is the correct one. Several alternative explanations center around the fact that the smoke represented a possible danger to the subject himself as well as to others in the building. For instance, it is possible that the subjects in groups saw themselves as engaged in a game of "chicken" in which the first person to report would admit his cowardliness. Or it may have been that the presence of others made subjects feel safer, and thus reduced their need to report.

To rule out such explanations, a second experiment was designed to see whether similar group inhibition effects could be observed in situations where there is no danger to the individual himself for not acting. In this study, male Columbia University undergraduates waited either alone or with a stranger to participate in a market research study. As they waited they heard a woman fall and apparently injure herself in the room next door. Whether they tried to help and how long they took to do so were the main dependent variables of the study.

THE FALLEN WOMAN

Subjects were telephoned and offered $2 to participate in a survey of ease and puzzle preferences conducted at Columbia by the Consumer Testing Bureau (CTB), a market research organization. When they arrived, they were met at the door by an attractive young woman and taken to the testing room. On the way, they passed the CTB office, and through its open door they were able to see a desk and bookcase piled high with papers and filing cabinets. They entered the adjacent testing room, which contained a table and chairs and a variety of games, and they were given questionnaires to fill out. The representative told subjects that she would be working next door in her office for about 10 minutes while they were completing the questionnaire and left by opening the collapsible curtain which divided the two rooms. She made sure that subjects were aware that the curtain was unlocked and easily opened and that it provided a means of entry to her office. The representative stayed in her office, shuffling papers, opening drawers, and making enough noise to remind the subjects of her presence. Four minutes after leaving the testing area, she turned on a high fidelity stereophonic tape recorder.

The Emergency

If the subject listened carefully, he heard the representative climb up on a chair to reach for a stack of papers on the bookcase. Even if he were not listening carefully, he heard a loud crash and a scream as the chair collapsed and she fell to the floor. "Oh, my God, my foot...I...I...can't move...it. Oh...my ankle," the representative moaned. "I...can't get this...thing...off me." She cried and moaned for about a minute longer, but the cries gradually got more subdued and controlled. Finally she muttered something about getting outside, knocked over the chair as she pulled herself up and thumped to the door, closing it behind her as she left. The entire incident took 130 seconds.

The main dependent variable of the study, of course, was whether the subjects took action to help the victim and how long it took them to do so. There were actually several modes of intervention possible: a subject could open the screen dividing the two rooms, leave the testing room and enter the CTB office by the door, find someone else, or most simply, call out to see if the representative needed help. In one condition, each subject was in the testing room alone while he filled out the questionnaire and heard the fall. In the second condition, strangers were placed in the testing room in pairs. Each subject in the pair was unacquainted with the other before entering the room and they were not introduced.

Since 70 percent of Alone subjects intervened, we should expect that at least one person in 91 percent of all two-person groups would offer help if members of a pair had no influence upon each other. In fact, members did influence each other. In only 40 percent of the groups did even one person offer help to the injured woman. Only eight subjects of the 40 who were run in this condition intervened. This response rate is significantly below the hypothetical baseline ($p < .001$). Social inhibition of helping was so strong that the victim was actually helped more quickly when only one person heard her distress than when two did.

When we talked to subjects after the experiment, those who intervened usually claimed that they did so either because the fall sounded very serious or because they were uncertain what had occurred and felt they should investigate. Many talked about intervention as the "right thing to do" and asserted they would help again in any situation.

Many of the noninterveners also claimed that they were unsure what had happened (59%), but had decided that it was not too serious (46%). A number of subjects reported that they thought other people would or could help (25%), and three said they refrained out of concern for the victim—they did not want to embarrass her. The important thing to note is that noninterveners did not seem to feel that they had behaved callously or immorally. Their behavior was generally consistent with their interpretation of the situation. Subjects almost uniformly claimed that in a "real" emergency they would be among the first to help the victim.

Other studies we have done show that group inhibition effects hold in real life as well as in the laboratory, and for members of the general population as well as college students. When bystanders to an emergency can see the reactions of other people, and when other people can see their own reactions, each individual may, through a process of social influence, be led to interpret the situation as less serious than he would if he were alone, and consequently be less likely to take action.

These studies, however, tell us little about the case that stimulated our interest in bystander intervention: the Kitty Genovese murder. Although the 38 witnesses to that event were aware, through seeing lights and silhouettes in other windows, that others watched, they could not see what others were doing and thus be influenced by their reactions. In the privacy of their own apartments, they could not be clearly seen by others, and thus inhibited by their presence. The social influence process we have described above could not operate. Nevertheless, we think that the presence of other bystanders may still have affected each individual's response.

DIFFUSION OF RESPONSIBILITY

In addition to affecting the interpretations that he places on a situation, the presence of other people can also alter the rewards and costs facing an individual bystander. Perhaps most importantly, the presence of other people can reduce the cost of not acting. If only one bystander is present at an emergency, he carries all of the responsibility for dealing with it; he will feel all of the guilt for not acting; he will bear all of any blame others may level for nonintervention. If others are present, the onus of responsibility is diffused, and the individual may be more likely to resolve his conflict between intervening and not intervening in favor of the latter alternative.

When only one bystander is present at an emergency, if help is to come it must be from him. Although he may choose to ignore them out of concern for is personal safety, or desire "not to get involved," any pressures to intervene focus uniquely on him. When there are several observers present, however, the pressures to intervene do not focus on any one of the observers; instead, the responsibility for intervention is shared among all the onlookers and is not unique to any one. As a result, each may be less likely to help.

Potential blame may also be diffused. However much we wish to think that an individual's moral behavior is divorced from considerations of personal punishment or reward, there is both theory and evidence to the contrary.

Finally, if others are known to be present, but their behavior cannot be closely observed, any one bystander may assume that one of the other observers is already taking action to end the emergency. If so, his own intervention would only be redundant—perhaps harmfully or confusingly so. Thus, given the presence of other onlookers whose behavior cannot be observed, any given bystander can rationalize his own inaction by convincing himself that "somebody else must be doing something."

These considerations suggest that even when bystanders to an emergency cannot see or be influenced by each other, the more bystanders who are present, the less likely any one bystander would be to intervene and provide aid. To test this suggestion, it would be necessary to create an emergency situation in which each subject is blocked from communicating with others to prevent his getting information about their behavior during the emergency.

A FIT TO BE TRIED

A college student arrived in the laboratory, and was ushered into an individual room from which a communication system would enable him to talk to other participants (who were actually figments of the tape recorder). Over the intercom, the subject was told that the experimenter was concerned with the kinds of personal problems faced by normal college students in a high-pressure, urban environment, and that he would be asked to participate in a discussion about these problems. To avoid embarrassment about discussing personal problems with strangers, the experimenter said, several precautions would be taken. First, subjects would remain anonymous, which was why they had been placed in individual rooms rather than face-to-face. Second, the experimenter would not listen to the initial discussion himself, but would only get the subject's reactions later by questionnaire.

The plan for the discussion was that each person would talk in turn for 2 minutes, presenting his problems to the group. Next, each person in turn would comment on what others had said, and finally there would be a free discussion. A mechanical switching device regulated the discussion, switching on only one microphone at a time.

The Emergency

The discussion started with the future victim speaking first. He said he found it difficult to get adjusted to New York and to his studies. Very hesitantly and with obvious embarrassment, he mentioned that he was prone to seizures, particularly when studying hard or taking exams. The other people, including the one real subject, took their turns and discussed similar problems (minus the proneness to seizures). The naive subject talked last in the series, after the last pre-recorded voice.

When it was again the victim's turn to talk, he made a few relatively calm comments, and then, growing increasingly loud and incoherent, he continued:

> I er I think I I need er if if could er er somebody er er er er er er er give me a little er give me a little help here because I er I'm er er h-h-having a a a a real problem er right now and I er if somebody could help me out it would er er s-s-sure be sure be good... because er there er er a cause I er I uh I've got a a one of the er sic... er er things coming on and and and I could really er use some help so if somebody would er give me a little h-help uh er-er-er er er c-could somebody er er help er uh uh uh (chocking sounds).... I'm gonna die er er I'm... gonna die er help er er seizure (chokes, then quiet).

The major independent variable of the study was the number of people the subject believed also heard the fit. The subject was led to believe that the discussion group was one of three sizes: a two-person group consisting of himself and the victim; a three-person group consisting of himself, the victim and the other person; or a six-person group consisting of himself, the victim, and four other persons.

The major dependent variable of the experiment was the time elapsed from the start of the victim's seizure until the subject left his experimental cubicle. When the subject left his room, he saw the experimental assistant seated at the end of the hall, and invariably went to the assistant to report the seizure. If 5 minutes elapsed without the subject's having emerged from his room, the experiment was terminated.

Eighty-five percent of the subjects who thought they alone knew of the victim's plight reported the seizure before the victim was cut off; only 31 percent of those who thought four other bystanders were present did so. Everyone of the subjects in the two-person condition, but only 62 percent of the subjects in the six-person condition ever reported the emergency. To do a more detailed analysis of the results, each subject's time score was transformed into a "speed" score by taking the reciprocal of the response time in seconds and multiplying by 100. Analysis of variance of these speed scores indicates that the effect of group size was highly significant and all three groups differed significantly one from another.

Subjects, whether or not they intervened, believed the fit to be genuine and serious. "My God, he's having a fit," many subjects said to themselves (and we overheard via their microphones). Others gasped or simply said, "Oh." Several of the male subjects swore. One subject said to herself, "It's just my kind of luck, something has to happen to me!" Several subjects spoke aloud of their confusion about what course of action to take: "Oh, God, what should I do?"

When those subjects who intervened stepped out of their rooms, they found the experimental assistant down the hall. With some uncertainty but without panic, they reported the situation. "Hey, I think Number 1 is very sick. He's having a fit or something." After ostensibly checking on the situation, the experimenter returned to report that "everything is under control." The subjects accepted these assurances with obvious relief.

Subjects who failed to report the emergency showed few signs of the apathy and indifference thought to characterize "unresponsive bystanders." When the experimenter entered her room to terminate the situation, the subject often asked if the victim was all right. "Is he being taken care of?" "He's all right, isn't he?" Many of these subjects showed physical signs of nervousness; they often had trembling hands and sweating palms. If anything, they seemed more emotionally aroused than did the subjects who reported the emergency.

Why, then, didn't they respond? It is not our impression that they had decided not to respond. Rather, they were still in a state of indecision and conflict concerning whether to respond or not. The emotional behavior of these nonresponding subjects was a sign of their continuing conflict, a conflict that other subjects resolved by responding.

The fit created a conflict situation of the avoidance-avoidance type. On the one hand, subjects worried about the guilt and shame they would feel if they did not help the person in distress. On the other hand, they were concerned not to make fools of themselves by overreacting, not to ruin the ongoing experiment by leaving their intercoms, and not to destroy the anonymous nature of the situation, which the experimenter had earlier stressed as important. For subjects in the two-person condition, the obvious distress of the victim and his need for help were so important that their conflict was easily resolved. For the subjects who knew that there were other bystanders present, the cost of not helping was reduced and the conflict they were in was more acute. Caught between the two negative alternatives of letting the victim continue to suffer or rushing, perhaps foolishly, to help, the nonresponding bystanders vacillated between them rather than choosing not to respond. This distinction may be academic for the victim, since he got no help in either case, but it is an extremely important one for understanding the causes of bystanders' failures to help.

CONCLUSION

We have suggested two distinct processes which might lead people to be less likely to intervene in an emergency if there are other people present than if they are alone. On the one hand, we suggested that the presence of other people may affect the interpretations each bystander puts on an ambiguous emergency situation. If other people are present at an emergency, each bystander will be guided by their apparent reactions in formulating his own impressions.

Even if an individual does decide that an emergency is actually in process and that something ought to be done, he still is faced with the choice of whether he himself will intervene. Here again, the presence of other people may influence him—by reducing the costs associated with nonintervention. If a number of people witness the same event, the responsibility for action is diffused, and each may feel less necessity to help.

Our studies suggest that situational factors, specifically factors involving the immediate social environment, may be of greater importance in determining an individual's reaction to an emergency than such vague cultural or personality concepts as "apathy" or "alienation due to urbanization." They suggest that the failure to intervene may be better understood by knowing the relationship among bystanders rather than that between a bystander and the victim.

DISCUSSION QUESTIONS

1. Latané and Darley provide us with an analysis of very few structural variables other than group size. What influence might a victim or bystander's race, class, and gender have on helping behavior? How might these elements of stratification go into shaping the definition of the situation? (Take their experimental scenario of the "fallen woman," for example.)

2. Give an example of an emergency situation in which you looked to others for help in defining a situation and deciding how to respond. Did you agree or disagree with others' definition of the situation and their actions?

3. Latané and Darley make the case that it is more difficult to define the situation when interacting with others than when acting alone. Why might this be so?

4. The dial 9-1-1 emergency response system was put into place in the United States in 1968, following the development of similar systems throughout western Europe in the 1930s and 1940s. How might the ease of calling for help via systems such as 9-1-1 and the availability of cell phones affect helping/bystander behavior in situations such as the Kitty Genovese attack and murder?

ADDITIONAL RESOURCES

Film

"History's Mysteries—Silent Witness: The Kitty Genovese Murder." 2001. A one-hour History Channel Documentary.

"The Human Behavior Experiments." 2006. A one-hour Sundance Channel documentary featuring compelling contemporary research on the bystander effect and the power of the situation as well as the classic research of Latané and Darley, Philip Zimbardo, and others. A must see! http://www.sundancechannel.com/films/500013451.

Radio

"Remembering Kitty Genovese." A National Public Radio piece on the 40th anniversary of Kitty's murder: http://www.npr.org/templates/story/story.php?storyId=l763547.

Internet

http://www.newsday.com/community/guide/lihistory/ny-history-hs818a,0,7944135.story. A summary of the events of Kitty Genovese's murder and prosecution of her perpetrator, Winston Moseley.

http://www.oldkewgardens.com/ss-nytimes-3.html. A deep and rich website dedicated to the neighborhood where Kitty Genovese's murder took place, Kew Gardens. This website provides much criticism of the reporting and analysis of her murder.

FURTHER READING

Latané, Bibb and John M. Darley. 1970. *The Unresponsive Bystander: Why Doesn't He Help?* New York: Appleton-Century-Crofts.

Rosenthal, A. M. 1999. *Thirty-Eight Witnesses: The Kitty Genovese Case.* Berkeley: University of California Press.

Simpson, Brent and Rob Willer. 2008. "Altruism and Indirect Reciprocity: The Interaction of Person and Situation in Prosocial Behavior." *Social Psychology Quarterly,* 37–52.

27. Aid in the Aftermath of Hurricane Katrina: Inferences of Secondary Emotions and Intergroup Helping

AMY J. C. CUDDY, MINDI S. ROCK, AND MICHAEL I. NORTON

Cuddy and colleagues draw the startling conclusion that helping behavior is grounded in egotism rather than altruism. In short, their findings provide evidence that we are most likely to help those who are most like us. Why might individualizing or humanizing the "Other" give us the ability to empathize and help with "their" plight?

Perhaps the most shocking development in the aftermath of the Hurricane Katrina disaster was the sluggish and inadequate response to victims who were clearly in dire need of assistance. Even after extensive mainstream news coverage of the miserable conditions at the Convention Center and Superdome in New Orleans, days passed before water, food, and medical supplies were delivered and before victims were finally evacuated. Michael Brown, the Director of the Federal Emergency Management Agency, famously joked in emails about how his clothing looked on television as he failed to respond to emails which—with increasingly frantic tones—described the unfolding crisis. Why was Brown's response, and the response of others responsible for handling the crisis, so muted and delayed? Was there something about those responsible for helping that impeded the helping response? Was there something about those who needed help that failed to motivate those responsible to engage? We suggest that it was a combination of the two: the particular mix of those responsible for helping and those in need of help obstructed the realization of an adequate helping response.

Specifically, this research examines how differences in observers' beliefs about the emotional anguish of victims may have contributed to the

Cuddy, Amy J. C., Mindi S. Rock, and Michael I. Norton. 2007. "Aid in the Aftermath of Hurricane Katrina: Inferences of Secondary Emotions and Intergroup Helping." *Group Processes & Intergroup Relations,* 10(1): 107–18.

inadequate response following Hurricane Katrina, whose victims disproportionately were black, Latino, and poor. After encountering tremendous stress and loss, many of the victims were likely experiencing complex and intense emotions such as grief, mourning, and dismay. We propose that the modal consumer of news coverage of Katrina—middle-class white Americans—failed to perceive Katrina victims as experiencing those emotions, and that this denial enervated the overall helping response.

People are more likely to help an ingroup member than an outgroup member. The present research aims to shed light on why people display an intergroup helping bias, by examining how people's inferences about the emotional states of victims may both trigger and impede helping responses to outgroups. We emphasize the role of intergroup bias in this process, predicting that: (a) people will perceive outgroup victims as experiencing less emotional anguish than ingroup victims (both whites observing black victims, and non-whites observing white victims); and (b) these differences will predict willingness to come to the aid of members of outgroups.

ASCRIBING EMOTIONS TO INGROUPS VERSUS OUTGROUPS

How are emotions ascribed to ingroups and outgroups? A recent social psychological account comes from the social identity perspective, uniting the concepts of ingroup favoritism and subjective essentialism. Social psychologists describe how people are motivated to reserve the 'uniquely human' essence for ingroups and to withhold it from outgroups. This phenomenon—'infrahumanization'—involves ascribing greater intelligence and language competency to ingroups, while denying outgroups those same competencies.

Infrahumanization also involves attributing to outgroups less capacity for feeling a full range of emotions. This theoretical approach differentiates primary emotions, such as pleasure, fear, and rage, from secondary emotions, such as admiration,

resentment, and disappointment. The former are believed to be experienced by both human and non-human animals; the latter are believed to be experienced exclusively by humans. Perceivers associate primary emotions, which do not impart a human essence, equally with ingroups and outgroups. However, perceivers consistently associate more uniquely human (i.e., secondary) emotions with ingroups than with outgroups.

EMOTION INFERENCES AND INTERGROUP HELPING

How might these differences in inferred emotional states relate to intergroup behavior, in this case helping responses to Katrina victims? We propose that humanization (i.e., inferences of higher secondary emotions) of individual outgroup victims promotes intergroup helping by personalizing and increasing the perceived similarity to the outgroup member. First, people are more generous toward personalized victims than they are toward aggregated victims. For example, using personalizing (i.e., humanizing) information to single out an individual child with cancer, rather than referring to a group of children with cancer, greatly increases donations to cancer funds. Second, and more pertinent to the present research, both empathizing with an outgroup and actively considering an outgroup member's point of view can ameliorate intergroup relations and facilitate intergroup helping. Empathy is elicited, in part, by viewing the other as similar to the self or the ingroup. Similarly, by creating an overlap between the self and the outgroup, perspective-taking increases perceived similarity and encourages helping responses to outgroup members.

SUMMARY OF HYPOTHESES

The present study tested two hypotheses. First, we predict that participants will infer higher secondary emotions about the states of individualized *in*group victims than about individualized *out*group victims, but will not differentiate ingroup and outgroup victims on inferences of primary emotions. Second, we predict that participants who infer lower secondary emotions will be less likely to report intentions to help with Katrina relief efforts.

METHOD

Participants

Participants for the main study were recruited at a New Brunswick, New Jersey train station during morning rush hour approximately two weeks after Hurricane Katrina. The experimenters approached participants and asked, "Would you be willing to complete a short survey about Hurricane Katrina for $2?" Participants who complied with the request were given a letter-sized self-addressed stamped envelope, which contained the two-page questionnaire and two $1 bills.

The experimenters distributed 238 questionnaires, 116 (49%) of which were completed and returned. Of those 116 participants, 51% were female; 53% were white, 16% were black, 19% were Asian or Asian-American, 8% were non-white Latino; the remaining 4% responded "other" or did not provide race information. Given our focus on a particular intergroup context, we excluded from the analyses the 25 participants who did not self-identify as black, white, or Latino, reducing our data analysis n to 91 (62 white non-Latino participants, 29 black and non-white Latino participants). We combined black and Latino participants because these were the two groups who were disproportionately harmed by Hurricane Katrina, and because our subsample of black participants was not sufficient alone for the analyses.

Materials and Procedure

Participants read a fictionalized news story about a mother who had lost a child during Hurricane Katrina. We manipulated race by using names more common to black Americans or white Americans.

The victim's surname, Johnson, was held constant across conditions. The story began, 'Two weeks after the storm, Tanesha/Amanda Johnson

has yet to hear word about her 2-year-old son, Tyrell/Joshua, who was with his uncle when Hurricane Katrina hit.' In about 200 words, the article goes on to describe the mother's efforts to find her lost child. We avoided using quotes or descriptions that conveyed information about the victim's emotional state. The child's fate was left unresolved.

On the next page, participants read, 'The following questions concern how Tanesha/Amanda Johnson might have been feeling at the time this story was reported. In your opinion, how much was Tanesha/Amanda Johnson feeling each of the following emotions?' Participants rated the seven secondary emotions (grief, sorrow, mourning, anguish, guilt, remorse, resentment) and the seven primary emotions (confusion, pain, distress, fear, panic, anger, rage), on a 5-point scale (1 = not at all to 5 = extremely).

On the final page, participants were asked whether they intended to volunteer their time to Hurricane Katrina relief efforts (yes/no), and whether they had already volunteered (yes/no).

RESULTS

Inferred Emotions

Each emotion item was weighted by its rating on the continuous primary/secondary scale, which was centered around the median, from the preliminary study data. From the weighted scores, we created composite measures of primary ($\alpha = .82$) and secondary ($\alpha = .80$) emotions.

We submitted the primary and secondary emotions scales to a 2 (Victim Race: Black, White) × 2 (Participant Race: White, Black/Latino) multivariate analysis of variance (ANOVA). There were no main effects of Victim Race or Participant Race on either of the emotions scales. As expected, the Victim Race × Participant Race interaction was not significant for the primary emotions scale ($F(1,91) = 1.96$, ns); participants did not differentiate ingroup victims from outgroup victims when inferring primary emotions. However, the critical

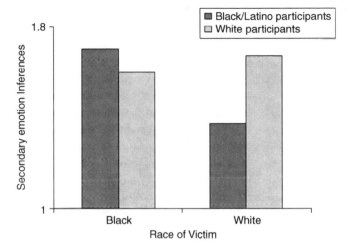

Figure1 Inferences of secondary emotions by participant race and victim race ($F(1,91)=5.62, p=.02$).

Victim Race × Participant Race interaction for the secondary emotions scale was significant ($F(1,91) = 5.62$, $p = .02$). As shown in Figure 1, the interaction took on the expected form, suggesting that participants made lower secondary emotion inferences for outgroup victims than for ingroup victims.

Intensions to Help

We predicted that inferences of higher secondary emotions about outgroup victims would relate to greater intentions to help Hurricane Katrina victims.

DISCUSSION

The present study provides several novel and intriguing findings. First, when observing the aftermath of a real-life natural disaster, perceivers infra-humanized outgroup victims, denying them the same complexity of emotions that they believed ingroup victims would experience in the same situation. Specifically, people inferred that an individual outgroup victim felt less anguish, via the experience of secondary emotions such as grief, mourning, remorse, and sorrow, than an individual ingroup victim. People did not differentiate ingroup and outgroup victims on

inferences of primary emotions, such as fear and sadness, as expected. These findings extend prior infra-humanization research by demonstrating that infra-humanization is not limited to the attribution of emotions as general group traits, but also manifests in inferences of others' emotional states, and that perceivers infra-humanize individualized outgroup members, just as they infra-humanize aggregated outgroups and depersonalized outgroup members.

This research also provides initial evidence that the infra-humanization of outgroup victims has some bearing on how they are treated. Lower inferences of secondary emotions—but not primary emotions—about victims related to reduced intentions to volunteer for Hurricane Katrina relief efforts. This moves beyond a simple empathy → helping link, demonstrating the importance of distinguishing primary from secondary emotions. The results imply that empathizing with a victim's experience of primary emotions (e.g. fear) does not lead to greater helping, but empathizing with a victim's experience of secondary emotions (e.g. mourning) does. It is also important to emphasize that group context (i.e. intergroup vs. intragroup) moderated this relationship; the relationship was significant for intergroup conditions, but not for intragroup conditions. In other words, inferring lower secondary emotions about ingroup victims does not relate to helping intentions, but inferring lower secondary emotions about outgroup victims does. To our knowledge, this is the first demonstration of a link between infra-humanization of outgroup victims and helping.

Although the predicted Participant Race × Victim Race interaction was significant for inferences of secondary emotions, Black/ Latino participants clearly infra-humanized White victims more than White participants infra-humanized Black victims. Our post hoc, perhaps cynical, interpretation of this result concerns the intensive media focus on racism that followed Hurricane Katrina, and which seemed to peak during data collection for this study. This unusual attention to the alleged effects of racism may have temporarily sensitized White people to expressions of racism, creating a vigilance to avoid such expressions. Unfortunately, this kind of sensitivity tends to be ephemeral, so we suspect that follow-up studies would reveal significant infra-humanization in both directions. Moreover, others have shown that racial and ethnic minority group members express stronger outgroup stereotypes and greater intergroup bias than majority group members. Two explanations have been offered for this difference. First, it has been attributed to differences in social desirability concerns, such that White people in the United States are more concerned about appearing racist than members of U.S. racial minority groups. Second, the difference has been attributed to a greater focus on color-blindness and assimilationist thinking by majority group members versus a greater emphasis on multiculturalism by minority group members.

FUTURE DIRECTIONS

If infrahumanization of outgroups reduces intergroup helping, then future research should strive to identify the conditions that cause perceivers to *humanize* outgroups, which should *promote* intergroup helping. Emphasizing intergroup similarities has proven to be an effective intervention for improving intergroup relations in some contexts. Taking that idea a step further, priming an inclusive identity (i.e. supplanting 'us' vs. 'them' with just 'us') can activate helping responses toward people formerly seen as outgroup members, even in real emergencies. Thus, evidence suggests that emphasizing intergroup similarity could increase the extent to which perceivers infer secondary emotions: from outgroup victims, thereby improving the likelihood of intergroup helping.

The present research suggests that intergroup helping is associated with inferences about the human emotions of those in need. Teaching people to humanize outgroups has even been proposed as an effective tool in healing the wounds of past intergroup conflict and reducing the chance of future intergroup conflict. To the extent that individuals perceive members of outgroups as either similar to themselves, or as experiencing secondary emotions, or both, the tepid response to tragedies when victims are seen as outgroups might be improved.

DISCUSSION QUESTIONS
1. Cuddy et al. claim that minority group members hold stronger ingroup/outgroup distinctions than majority group members. What might account for this difference that is so apparent in their research on interracial empathy?
2. How do Cuddy et al. define the term "infrahumanization," and what role does it play in situations that provide opportunities to help similar or dissimilar others?
3. What role may ingroup/outgroup separation have played in the murder of Kitty Genovese or in the behavior of subjects in Latané and Darley's experiments?

ADDITIONAL RESOURCES

Film

"Inside Hurricane Katrina: A Comprehensive Analysis of the Damage Caused by Nature's Fury."
2006. A National Geographic documentary.

"When the Levees Broke: A Requiem in Four Acts." 2006. An HBO documentary written and
directed by Spike Lee. http://www.hbo.com/docs/programs/whentheleveesbroke/.

Internet

http://understandingkatrina.ssrc.org/. A Social Science Research Council website dedicated to
understanding the impact of Hurricane Katrina from the perspective of social scientists.

http://www.census.gov/Press-Release/www/2005/katrina.htm. A site created by the U.S. Census
Bureau to document the many demographic disparities revealed by Hurricane Katrina.

http://www.asanet.org/cs/root/leftnav/execoffice/hurricane_katrina. A site created by the
American Sociological Association documenting many resources about natural disasters.

FURTHER READING

Johnson, Monica Kirkpatrick, Timothy Beebe, Jeylan T. Mortimer, and Mark Snyder. 1998.
"Volunteerism in Adolescence: A Process in Perspective." *Journal of Research on Adolescence*,
8(3): 309–32.

Piliavin, I. M., J. Rodin, and Jane A. Piliavin. 1969. "Good Samaritanism: An Underground
Phenomenon?" *Journal of Personality and Social Psychology*, 13: 289–99.

28. Giving to Others during National Tragedy: The Effects of Altruistic and Egoistic Motivations on Long-Term Giving

RACHEL L. PIFERI, REBECCA L. JOBE, AND WARREN H. JONES

Piferi and colleagues explore short- and long-term disaster relief efforts associated with the attacks of
September 11, 2001. Their research was motivated by a desire to understand why people help strangers. Do you think their findings also help us understand helping behavior when the targets are people
we love?

On September 11, 2001, the United States of America was abruptly and harshly attacked by terrorists. This attack resulted in the deaths of thousands of people in New York City, Washington, DC, and Pennsylvania. In the days following the event, many Americans donated their time, money, goods, and support to those who were affected by the attack. The American Red Cross reported

Piferi, Rachel L., Rebecca L. Jobe, and Warren H. Jones. 2006. "Giving to Others during National Tragedy: The
Effects of Altruistic and Egoistic Motivations on Long-Term Giving." *Journal of Social and Personal Relationships*,
23(1): 171–84.

goals of the study
not expecting to find prayer

that twice as many individuals donated blood in the 1-month period following September 11 than normally donated blood. Monetary donations to the September 11 Fund reached US$115 million by the end of September 2001.

While thousands of people were killed on September 11, most Americans did not personally know any of the victims. Thus, for many of the individuals who gave aid, their support was given to help individuals they did not know. The goal of the current study was to understand motivations for giving support to strangers during this time of great suffering. Also, this study examined the relationship between motivation for giving to others and giving over time. This examination of interpersonal relationships and helping behavior in a real world event adds to our knowledge of helping behavior within distant social relationships.

RESEARCH ON HELPING BEHAVIOR

Within the study of interpersonal relationships, many researchers have studied helping behavior and altruism. The early literature on this topic is dominated by debates over the definition of altruism. Among such definitions are other-oriented behaviors that involve self-sacrifice, caring for another's interest without concern for oneself, and helping that is motivated by another's need.

Recent research has focused on an examination of the motivations for helping others. At the core of this research is the debate over altruistic and egoistic motivations. Altruistic helping has been defined as behavior motivated by the desire to increase another's welfare, while egoistic giving has been defined as motivated by the desire to reduce one's own personal distress or to receive rewards for giving. Much of the research on motivations for giving has centered around the empathy–altruism hypothesis. According to the empathy–altruism hypothesis, focusing on the perspective of a person in need creates feelings of empathetic concern and leads to altruistic motivations to reduce the distress of the person in need. When focusing on

the person in need leads to a self-oriented focus and desire to reduce personal distress, then helping is a result of egoistic motivations to reduce one's own personal discomfort. In more than 20 experiments, Batson and colleagues have shown that empathy promotes altruistic motivation to help. They have concluded that some, but not all, helping behavior is motivated for the purpose of increasing the recipient's welfare.

By contrast, many researchers have proposed that egoistic motivations underlie many seemingly altruistic acts. Although empathy does increase helping, they contend that increasing empathy also increases personal feelings of sadness or distress. Thus, in their negative-state relief model, Cialdini and his colleagues propose that individuals are motivated to help in order to relieve their own personal discomfort with the event and not to increase the welfare of the other person. Furthermore, it has been shown that providing support does make helpers feel better and rewards them for giving. Thus, people may be motivated to help in order to reduce the negative emotions that have resulted from someone else's distress.

One common resolution to these contradictory findings is to acknowledge that there are two basic reactions to another person's need: personal distress and empathic concern. And, as seen by the plethora of research on both sides of the issue, both personal distress (self-oriented reactions to another's need) and empathetic concern (other-oriented reactions to another's need) can motivate an individual to give aid to someone who is in need. Although many laboratory experiments have yielded evidence in favor of both egoistic and altruistic motives of giving, fewer non-laboratory studies have been conducted to investigate motivations for giving. The present study examines motivations for giving within the context of a real-world, non-laboratory event.

GOALS OF THE PRESENT STUDY

The current study was conducted to examine giving behavior over time and motivations for giving aid following the terrorist attacks on the United States on September 11, 2001. Participants were surveyed regarding their giving immediately following the event and 1 year later. Due to the magnitude of the event, it was hypothesized that participants would report being greatly affected by the attacks on the United States on September 11, 2001. Given the significance of the event, it was hypothesized that many individuals would report providing aid immediately following the attacks. Furthermore, it was hypothesized that both egoistic and altruistic motivations for giving would be reported. We suspected that individuals would provide support in an effort to reduce their own sense of personal distress and in an effort to alleviate the distress of those involved. We further hypothesized that over time, emotional distress over the event would decrease. We suspected that this decrease in personal distress would be accompanied by a decrease in giving over time for those who report egoistic motives for providing aid. Furthermore, we hypothesized that sustained giving would be related to other-focused, altruistic motives rather than to egoistic motives. Those who gave support with a focus on the recipients' welfare would continue to give support even when their personal distress diminished.

METHOD

Participants

Three hundred and forty three participants (114 males; 229 females) completed a survey immediately following the terrorist attack on the United States. Participants' ages ranged from 18 to 58 years old (*M* = 20.0, *SD* = 3.8). Of the 343 participants, 308 were Caucasian, 25 were African American, three were Hispanic American, four were Asian American, one selected the category other races, and two did not report race.

Participants were recruited from classes at the University of Tennessee. Only 25 participants of the original 343 participants (7%) reported knowing someone who resided in New York City or Washington, DC and who thus were possibly personally affected by the events.

A subset of the original participant pool completed a 1-year follow-up survey of giving behavior following September 11. Of the original participants, 148 were contacted to participate in a follow-up study. Of those 148 participants, 105 (71%) completed the follow-up survey (42 males; 63 females). Demographic and personality variables of the subset did not differ from the original sample.

Procedure

In December of 2001, participants were recruited to participate in a study that assessed their reactions to the events of September 11. Participants completed a survey that included personality inventories and measures of coping. In addition to these scales, the survey asked participants to rate how emotionally affected they were by the events of September 11. Participants were asked to rate their emotional affectedness on a 5-point response format verbally anchored at the extremes by 'not at all affected' to 'extremely affected'. In addition, participants were asked if they gave any aid/support to the individuals affected by the terrorist attacks. When participants responded with 'yes' they were also asked the questions, 'What did you give?' and 'Why did you give these things?'

In December of 2002, participants were contacted via electronic mail and asked to complete a brief follow-up survey about their current reactions to the events of September 11, 2001. They were asked to rate how emotionally affected they *currently were* concerning the terrorist attacks of September 11, 2001. As in the initial data collection, the response categories ranged from 1 ('not at all affected') to 5 ('extremely affected'). Participants were also asked if they had given any support or aid to those involved in the terrorist attacks during *the past 2 months*. Finally, they were asked to report what they had given in the previous 2 months.

RESULTS

Content Coding of Open-Ended Questions

Prior to analyzing the predictors of giving, the responses to the open-ended questions were categorized. Three raters (2 males; 1 female) were given each participant's unedited response to the questions 'What have you given?' and 'Why have you helped?' The answers to these two questions were given to the raters separately from each other so that all responses to these two questions were coded independent of each other. The coders were instructed to classify each participant's responses into the categories described below.

Coding of the help given. In order to categorize the reported assistance given, four categories were logically derived prior to reading responses: money, blood, goods (i.e., food, clothing), and other. Following the raters' categorization of items into these four categories, the 'other' category was coded again for any other major category of support that was not foreseen prior to reading the responses. Follow-up analyses of the 'other' category revealed another distinct category of support that was reported: prayer. Therefore, the items were coded into five categories: money, blood, goods, prayer and other.... In some instances (77 of 211 participants), participants reported that they gave multiple items. The responses of participants who provided multiple items were coded into multiple groups.

Coding of motivations for giving. In order to categorize motivations for giving, five motivational categories were logically derived based on responses given by the participants and based on previous research on motivations for giving: personal distress (giving in order to relieve your own discomfort), other-focused giving (giving in order to relieve another's discomfort), reciprocal giving (giving because you want someone to give to you later), social responsibility (giving because it is the right thing to do as part of society), and kinship (family, friends). Based on the qualitative

responses provided by many participants, a sixth motivation classification was added after reading participants' responses: patriotism. Due to the nature of this event, many participants reported that they gave aid in order to show their allegiance to the United States or to show the terrorists that they are a part of a strong, united country.

Motivations for giving. Participants who provided support immediately following the event were also asked to provide their motivation for giving. Of the 211 participants who reported giving aid in response to the terrorist attacks, 164 participants (78%) answered the question, 'Why did you give these things?' The raters coded the motivations without awareness of participants' responses to other items in the questionnaire. Results indicated that personal distress was the most frequently reported motivation for providing support. In answering the question, 56 of the participants (34%) reported that they gave aid in order to feel better about/relieve personal pain due to the event. Thirty-six of those providing help (22%) reported that they gave aid because they would expect someone to help them in a similar situation (reciprocal altruism). Thirty-two of the help providers (19.5%) reported other-focused motives for providing support (e.g., because they were suffering). Thirty-two participants (19.5%) reported patriotism as their motive for giving. Twenty-four participants (15%) reported that it was their duty to give to others in need (social responsibility) and 19 participants (11.7%) reported that they gave support because they knew someone involved (kinship).

EMOTIONAL AFFECTEDNESS AND GIVING 1 YEAR LATER

In order to compare giving immediately following the event and 1 year following the event, we reanalyzed the data from the sample collected immediately following 9/11 with only the 105 participants who completed the follow-up. Of the 105 participants who completed the survey at Time 2, 71 individuals (68%) reported that they

Table I Motivations for Giving Immediately after the Event and 1 Year Later

Motivation	Participants giving support immediately	Participants giving support 1 year later	Participants not giving support 1 year later	% still giving after 1 year
Other-focused	20	16	4	80%
Relief of personal distress	23	5	18	22%
Reciprocal giving	14	6	8	43%
Social responsibility	12	2	10	17%
Patriotism	13	4	9	31%
Kinship	7	3	4	43%

Note. Total participants = 105.

had given some form of aid immediately following the events of September 11. This is similar to the percentage of individuals from the entire sample (62%).

While 67% of these 105 participants reported giving immediately following the terrorist attack, only 30% (*n* = 31) reported giving any support during the months of September to December of 2002 (1 year after the event). Of the 31 participants who reported giving aid 1 year later, 19 were female and 12 were male. The support provisions reported by participants included money (*n* = 14), prayer (*n* = 14), and other activities like attending rallies, buying 9–11 t-shirts, and attending a charity concert (*n* = 3). No one reported donating blood 1 year following the event.

The decline in giving (62% vs. 31%) is accompanied by a decline in emotional affectedness.

MOTIVATION FOR GIVING AS A PREDICTOR OF SUSTAINED GIVING

Among the 105 participants who completed the follow-up, motivations for giving were consistent with the results of the entire sample of 343 participants. We hypothesized that sustained giving would be related to the original motivation for giving support. Thus, we investigated the motives for giving immediately following the events of September 11 among the 31 participants who reported giving aid 1 year later. Of these 31 respondents, 16 (51%) reported other-focused motives for giving aid immediately, 6 individuals (19.3%) reported reciprocal altruism motives

immediately, 5 individuals (16%) reported that they gave immediately in order to relieve personal distress, 4 individuals (12.9%) reported patriotism as their motive for giving immediately, 3 individuals (9.7%) reported kinship motives for giving immediately, and 2 participants (6.4%) reported that they gave immediately because of social responsibility (see Table I).

To examine this another way, we also computed percentages of individuals in each motivational category that reported giving 1 year later. Of the individuals reporting an altruistic motivation originally, 80 percent reported giving following 1 year, while only 22 percent of those reporting egoistic motivations originally were still giving following one year. Percentages of participant giving after 1 year for each motivational category can be seen in Table I.

DISCUSSION

Altruism and giving behavior has been studied extensively in laboratory and field experiments, however, a majority of the research has been conducted in controlled settings. The current study examined giving behavior by strangers to examine what kind of aid was given after September 11, what the motivations for giving were, and what traits and/or motivations predicted immediate and sustained giving (one year after the event). As hypothesized, we found that our sample was highly emotionally affected by the events on September 11. Also as hypothesized, a majority of respondents gave some kind of support immediately to those directly affected by the 9/11 attacks. The three most common forms of support were giving money, prayer, and donating blood.

In addition, the present study examined predictors of giving. These predictors included how emotionally affected one was by the events of 9/11, individual coping styles, trait empathy, having a giving personality, and motivations for giving support. Analyses revealed that trait cognitive empathy, the tendency to give support to others under stress, how emotionally affected one was by the events, and scoring low on the use of drugs when stressed created a model that predicted giving immediately after the event. These traits combined only accounted for 9 percent of the variance in immediate giving and they did not predict sustained giving.

In determining the predictors of sustained giving, the motivations for giving support originally were also examined. Originally, it was hypothesized that various motivations for giving would emerge. And, as hypothesized, many motivations emerged that reflected both egoistic and altruistic themes. Strong support exists for an egoistic model of support provisions in that reducing one's own distress was the most frequently reported reason for giving support. It was the primary motivator immediately after the event for 34 percent of the participants. Altruistic motivations were reported by almost 20 percent of participants. And, nearly 20 percent of participants said that helping the victims of 9/11 was a way to demonstrate patriotism, which may be unique to this type of situation. The remaining participants reported reciprocal, kinship, or social responsibility motives for giving.

While personal distress was a primary motivator immediately after the event, examination of these motivations revealed that only the other-focused motive was related to reported giving 1 year after the event. It was originally hypothesized that a reduction in emotional arousal to the event would coincide with a reduction in giving over time. As expected, both emotional affectedness and giving were lower 1 year after the event than immediately after the event. Also

as expected, individuals who said they gave support in order to reduce personal distress were less likely to report giving support 1 year after the event than individuals who reported giving support to help reduce the recipient's distress. Consistent with egoistic models, if personal distress is the motivation for giving, giving will stop when personal distress has diminished as was found among egoistic givers in this study. By contrast, individuals who reported giving for altruistic reasons also said they were giving 1 year after the event and after personal distress had lessened. Therefore, altruistic motivations seem to be related to sustained giving, whereas immediate giving may be due to one of several motivations.

In the current study, participants who reported empathic motivations (concern for the other person's welfare) reported giving both immediately after the events of September 11 and 1 year later. This is in contrast to the individuals who reported less empathic motivations for giving (focused on personal distress or civic responsibility). These individuals with little empathic concern reflected in their qualitative responses gave immediately after the events of September 11, but were not giving support 1 year later. In the weeks following the events of September 11, accounts of the attacks dominated American news and public discourse. In those months, it was very difficult to escape the pictures, stories, and events of that day. However, as time passed, coverage of the event was reduced and it became easier to escape the event. Therefore, 1 year later when escape was easier then, it was found that primarily individuals with empathetic (other-focused) motives were giving support.

Another important finding from this study of giving to others is the inclusion of prayer as a form of support. Although we anticipated certain support provisions actually reported (e.g., money, donating blood), we were surprised to see that prayers were listed by participants as a type of support that they provided. Prayer is not a behavior that is typically included in social support provision scales, but appeared in this study on the open-ended question about support. Prayer is a behavior that is being performed with the purpose of helping those in need. Therefore, in a study of intended helping behaviors, it is a relevant behavior to consider. Prayer may be more relevant in studies of traumatic events where the effects last over time when compared with minor events. And, the support given during traumatic events may be more likely to include prayer due to the seriousness and uncontrollable nature of the event. In any case, future research should examine further prayer as a possible form of social support.

STRENGTHS AND LIMITATIONS OF THE PRESENT STUDY

The current study adds to the literature on helping behavior within distant social relationships. One strength of the current study is the focus on an actual event in which helping behavior was initiated by the studied individuals. Instead of the traditionally manipulated laboratory environment, this study examined helping in an ecologically valid event. This focus on a genuine event allowed us to examine actual giving in a situation of strong need.

While studying a naturally occurring phenomenon adds to the strength of this research study, it also serves as a limitation. Unlike laboratory studies, the current study relies on participant self-report of both helping and motivations. In many of the controlled laboratory studies, motivations and empathy have been experimentally manipulated, and, in doing so, researchers can be fairly certain of the motivations present. In the current study, the only way to determine motivations for giving is to ask the participants. And, whenever self-report is utilized, it can be argued that the responses provided by the participants may not be accurate representations of true motivation. However, despite the limitations of self-report, the nature of the study requires the use of self-reported motivation. Furthermore, through the use of open-ended self-report questions, this study has revealed information that would not have emerged without its use.

DIRECTIONS FOR FUTURE RESEARCH

This study extends the research on helping behavior. Through the use of an open-ended question about support given, a unique form of helping has been identified. Research on social support and helping behavior does not typically include prayer as a form of support. This research area may benefit from the consideration of prayer as a form of intended social support provisions. It seems probable that this type of assistance is more likely to occur in traumatic events than in daily events that require assistance. Also, it is possible that helping from a distance is limited and that prayer is a type of assistance that can be given from afar. This issue of prayer as a form of helping should be studied further.

In addition to the future study of prayer as a helping behavior, research should be directed towards the issue of helping by strangers versus acquaintances or friends. The current study examines helping over time by strangers. This research is similar to laboratory studies in which helping behavior is examined within a stranger social relationship. Future research should examine sustained helping and motivations for helping by individuals who do not personally know the individuals in need and helping by those who do personally know the individuals in need. Through this examination, researchers can determine if and how a personal relationship with the individual in need moderates the relationship between motivations and sustained giving.

CONCLUSION

In conclusion, this study has examined helping behavior following a real world event. The terrorist attack on the United States on 9/11 resulted in the deaths of thousands of people in New York City, Washington, DC, and Pennsylvania. It also resulted in many acts of helping behavior. In the days, months, and years following the event, many Americans have donated their time, money, goods, and support to those who were affected by the attack. And, while thousands of people were killed on September 11, most Americans did not personally know the individuals affected. Thus, for many of the individuals who gave aid, their support was given to help individuals whom they did not know. The goal of the current study was to understand motivations for giving support to strangers during this time of great suffering. This study suggests that both egoistic and altruistic motivations for giving support to strangers coexist. Furthermore, by examining giving behavior over time, this study showed that altruistic motivations for giving seem to be more predictive of sustained giving than egoistic motivations. While much of the research on motivations for giving has been done in the laboratory, this study has examined these themes across time in a traumatic, national event. It seems as if giving to others during a national tragedy is both egoistic and altruistic, but that long-term giving is primarily motivated by an empathic focus on those in need.

DISCUSSION QUESTIONS

1. Piferi et al. identify six different motivations for giving. What are these motives?
2. Have you ever donated money, time, or other resources to a cause? If so, which of Piferi et al.'s six motivations for giving best fit your motives? Was your giving ever sustained over a period of time? Again, why so or why not?
3. Piferi et al. argue that sustained giving is grounded in altruistic motivations rather than egoistic ones. Why do they think this is true?

ADDITIONAL RESOURCES

Film

"9/11—The Filmmakers' Commemorative Edition." 2002. A film that began as a documentary about a New York firefighter in training that ended up capturing the attacks on the World Trade Center from a firefighter's perspective.

"Fahrenheit 9/11." 2004. Written and directed by Michael Moore: http://www.fahrenheit911.com/.

"In Memoriam: New York City, 9/11/01." 2002. An HBO documentary detailing the events and rebuilding after the September 11 attacks.

"World Trade Center." 2006. Written and directed by Oliver Stone: www.wtcmovie.com.

Internet

http://www.9–llcommission.gov/. A website created by the National Commission on Terrorist Attacks upon the United States (also known as the 9/11 Commission).

http://www.academicinfo.net/usa911.html. A scholarly website dedicated to comprehensive documentation of the effects of the September 11, 2001, attacks.

FURTHER READING

Friend, David. 2007. *Watching the World Change: The Stories Behind the Images of 9/11*. New York: Picador USA.

Smelser, Neil J. and Faith Mitchell. 2002. *Terrorism: Perspectives from the Behavioral and Social Sciences*. Washington, D.C.: National Academies Press. (A National Academy of Science report that is available in PDF form online: http://www.nap.edu/catalog.php?record id=10570.)

Group Process and Performance

Just as group structures and processes affect individual members, individual participants' power, status, and level of attraction to a group influence group dynamics and
performance. These next selections explore how people relate to one another in groups,
including group identity formation, group cohesion, and intergroup conflict.

Sherif's research shows that cooperative and competitive relationships with
out-groups influence ingroup identity arid performance. The campers in Sherif's
study identified strongly with their own ingroup members when competing against
a clearly defined outgroup. During this competitive phase, ingroup members frequently defined outgroup members by inciting stereotypes. However, when the boys
were required to work cooperatively with outgroup members to reach their goals, a
different dynamic appeared. Their level of ingroup identification weakened as their
identification with outgroup members strengthened. Patterns of stereotyping others
based on cues of social status, such as gender or leadership roles, are also seen in
Fine's research.

Technological innovation has had a dramatic impact on group dynamics in recent
years. What features of virtual interaction, where members never meet face-to-face,
affect group identity formation, process, and performance? Fine's research on fantasy
role play (FRP) gaming predates the complex, multicontinent online gaming that is
wildly popular today. Even so, his research about the social worlds created by players of

the first FRP games such as Dungeons and Dragons gives us insight into the parallels and divergences between fantasy and reality worlds.

As you read the following selections, reflect on your own experiences in groups. What factors considered in these selections make groups attractive to you? What social processes contribute to groups' effectiveness in achieving their goals? What social processes or individual characteristics contribute to the emergence of seemingly "natural" group leaders and followers?

29. Superordinate Goals in the Reduction of Intergroup Conflict

MUZAFER SHERIF

Sherif presents us with a classic experiment in small group dynamics. Using 11- to 12-year-old boys as subjects, he explores three phases of group interaction: (1) the creation of ingroup cohesion, (2) the creation of intergroup conflict through competition, and (3) the reduction of intergroup conflict through a cooperative reward structure. Sherif found that the boys' ability to identify with outgroup members increased their willingness to work with them. However, the boys needed to experience their similarity with outgroup members directly, rather than just being told about it, for that commonality to produce a change in attitude and behavior.

The behavior by members of any group toward another group is not primarily a problem of deviate behavior. If it were, intergroup behavior would not be the issue of vital consequence that it is today. The crux of the problem is the participation by group members in established practices and social-distance norms of their group and their response to new trends developing in relationships between their own group and other groups.

A RESEARCH PROGRAM

A program of research has been under way since 1948 to test experimentally some hypotheses derived from the literature of intergroup relations. The first large-scale intergroup experiment was carried out in 1949, the second in 1953, and the third in 1954. The conclusions reported here briefly are based on the 1949 and 1954 experiments and on a series of laboratory studies carried out as co-ordinate parts of the program.

The methodology, techniques, and criteria for subject selection in the experiments must be summarized here very briefly. The experiments were carried out in successive stages: (1) groups were formed experimentally; (2) tension and conflict were produced between these groups by introducing conditions conducive to competitive and reciprocally frustrating relations between them; and (3) the attempt was made toward reduction of the intergroup conflict. This stage of reducing tension through introduction of superordinate goals

Sherif, Muzafer. 1958. Abridged from "Superordinate Goals in the Reduction of Intergroup Conflict." *American Journal of Sociology,* 63: 349–56.

was attempted in the 1954 study on the basis of lessons learned in the two previous studies.

At every stage the subjects interacted in activities which appeared natural to them at a specially arranged camp site completely under our experimental control. They were not aware of the fact that their behavior was under observation. No observation or recording was made in the subjects' presence in a way likely to arouse the suspicion that they were being observed.

The production of groups, the production of conflict between them, and the reduction of conflict in successive stages were brought about through the introduction of problem situations that were real and could not be ignored by individuals in the situation. For example, the problem of getting a meal through their own initiative and planning was introduced when participating individuals were hungry.

The subjects were selected by rigorous criteria. They were healthy, normal boys around the age of eleven and twelve, socially well adjusted in school and neighborhood, and academically successful. They came from a homogeneous sociocultural background and from settled, well-adjusted families of middle or lower-middle class and Protestant affiliations. No subject came from a broken home. The mean I.Q. was above average. The subjects were not personally acquainted with one another prior to the experiment. Thus, explanation of results on the basis of background differences, social maladjustment, undue childhood frustrations, or previous interpersonal relations was ruled out at the beginning by the criteria for selecting subjects.

The first stage of the experiments was designed to produce groups with distinct structure (organization) and a set of norms which could be confronted with intergroup problems. The method for producing groups from unacquainted individuals with similar background was to introduce problem situations in which the attainment of the goal depended on the co-ordinated activity of all individuals. After a series of such activities, definite group structures or organizations developed.

The results warrant the following conclusions for the stage of group formation: When individuals interact in a series of situations toward goals which appeal to all and which require that they co-ordinate their activities, group structures arise having hierarchical status arrangements and a set of norms regulating behavior in matters of consequence to the activities of the group.

Once we had groups that satisfied our definition of "group," relations between groups could be studied. Specified conditions conducive to friction or conflict between groups were introduced. This negative aspect was deliberately undertaken because the major problem in intergroup relations today is the reduction of existing intergroup frictions. The factors conducive to intergroup conflict give us realistic leads for reducing conflict.

A series of situations was introduced in which one group could achieve its goal only at the expense of the other group—through a tournament of competitive events with desirable prizes for the winning group. The results of the stage of intergroup conflict supported our main hypotheses. During interaction between groups in experimentally introduced activities which were competitive and mutually frustrating, members of each group developed hostile attitudes and highly unfavorable stereotypes toward the other group and its members. In fact, attitudes of social distance between the groups became so definite that they wanted to have nothing further to do with each other. This we take as a case of experimentally produced "social distance" in miniature. Conflict was manifested in derogatory name-calling and invectives, flare-ups of physical conflict, and raids on each other's cabins and territory.

Increased solidarity forged in hostile encounters, in rallies from defeat, and in victories over the out-group is one instance of a more general finding: Intergroup relations, both conflicting and harmonious, *affected the nature of relations within the groups involved.* Altered relations between groups produced significant changes in the status arrangements *within* groups, in some instances resulting in shifts at the upper status levels or even a change in leadership. Always, consequential intergroup relations were reflected in new group values or norms which signified changes in practice, word, and deed within the group. Counterparts of this finding are not difficult to see in actual and consequential human relations. Probably many of our major preoccupations, anxieties, and activities in the past decade are incomprehensible without reference to the problems created by the prevailing "cold war" on an international scale.

REDUCTION OF INTERGROUP FRICTION

A number of the measures proposed today for reducing intergroup friction could have been tried in this third stage. A few will be mentioned here, with a brief explanation of why they were discarded or were included in our experimental design.

1. Disseminating favorable information in regard to the out-group was not included. Information that is not related to the goals currently in focus in the activities of groups is relatively ineffective, as many studies on attitude change have shown.

2. In small groups it is possible to devise sufficiently attractive rewards to make individual achievement supreme. This may reduce tension between groups by splitting the membership on an "every-man-for-himself" basis. However, this measure has little relevance for actual intergroup tensions, which are in terms of group membership and group alignments.

3. The resolution of conflict through leaders alone was not utilized. Even when group leaders meet apart from their groups around a conference table, they cannot be considered independent of the dominant trends and prevailing attitudes of their membership. If a leader is too much out of step in his negotiations and agreements

with out-groups, he will cease to be followed. It seemed more realistic, therefore, to study the influence of leadership within the framework of prevailing trends in the groups involved. Such results will give us leads concerning the conditions under which leadership can be effective in reducing intergroup tensions.

4. The "common-enemy" approach is effective in pulling two or more groups together against another group. This approach was utilized in the 1949 experiment as an expedient measure and yielded effective results. But bringing some groups together against others means larger and more devastating conflicts in the long run. For this reason, the measure was not used in the 1954 experiment.

5. Another measure, advanced both in theoretical and in practical work, centers around social contacts among members of antagonistic groups in activities which are pleasant in themselves. This measure was tried out in 1954 in the first phase of the integration stage.

6. As the second phase of the integration stage, we introduced a series of superordinate goals which necessitated co-operative interaction between groups.

The social contact situations consisted of activities which were satisfying in themselves—eating together in the same dining room, watching a movie in the same hall, or engaging in an entertainment in close physical proximity. These activities, which were satisfying to each group, but which did not involve a state of interdependence and co-operation for the attainment of goals, were not effective in reducing intergroup tension. On the contrary, such occasions of contact were utilized as opportunities to engage in name-calling and in abuse of each other to the point of physical manifestations of hostility.

The ineffective, even deleterious, results of intergroup contact without superordinate goals have implications for certain contemporary learning theories and for practice in intergroup relations. Contiguity in pleasant activities with members of an out-group does not necessarily lead to a pleasurable image of the out-group if relations between the groups are unfriendly. Intergroup contact without superordinate goals is not likely to produce lasting reduction of intergroup hostility.

INTRODUCTION OF SUPERORDINATE GOALS

After establishing the ineffectiveness, even the harm, in intergroup contacts which did not involve superordinate goals, we introduced a series of superordinate goals.

The problem situations were varied in nature, but all had an essential feature in common—they involved goals that could not be attained by the efforts and energies of one group alone and thus created a state of interdependence between groups: combating a water shortage that affected all and could not help being "compelling", securing a much-desired film, which could not be obtained by either group alone but required putting their resources together; putting into working shape, when everyone was hungry and the food was some distance away, the only means of transportation available to carry food.

The introduction of a series of such superordinate goals was indeed effective in reducing intergroup conflict: (1) when the groups in a state of friction interacted in conditions involving superordinate goals, they did co-operate in activities leading toward the common goal and (2) a series of joint activities leading toward superordinate goals had the cumulative effect of reducing the prevailing friction between groups and unfavorable stereotypes toward the out-group.

These major conclusions were reached on the basis of observational data and were confirmed by sociometric choices and stereotype ratings administered first during intergroup conflict and again after the introduction of a series of superordinate goals.

Friendship preferences shifted from almost exclusive preference for in-group members toward increased inclusion of members from the "antagonists." Since the groups were still intact following co-operative efforts to gain superordinate goals, friends were found largely within one's group. However, choices of out-group members grew, in one group, from practically none during intergroup conflict to 23 percent. The findings confirm observations that the series of superordinate goals produced increasingly friendly associations and attitudes pertaining to out-group members.

Observations made after several superordinate goals were introduced showed a sharp decrease in the name-calling and derogation of the out-group common during intergroup friction and in the contact situations without superordinate goals. At the same time the blatant glorification and bragging about the in-group, observed during the period of conflict, diminished. These observations were confirmed by comparison of ratings of stereotypes (adjectives) the subjects had actually used in referring to their own group and the out-group during conflict with ratings made after the series of superordinate goals. Ratings of the out-group changed significantly from largely unfavorable ratings to largely favorable ratings. The proportions of the most unfavorable ratings found appropriate for the out-group—that is, the categorical verdicts that "all of them are stinkers" or "...smart alecks" or "...sneaky"—fell, in one group, from 21 percent at the end of the friction stage to 1.5 percent after interaction oriented toward superordinate goals. The corresponding reduction in these highly unfavorable verdicts by the other group was from 36.5 to 6 percent.

Our findings demonstrate the effectiveness of a series of superordinate goals in the reduction of intergroup conflict, hostility, and their by-products. They also have implications for other measures proposed for reducing intergroup tensions.

It is true that lines of communication between groups must be opened before prevailing hostility can be reduced. But, if contact between hostile groups takes place without superordinate goals, the communication channels serve as media for further accusations and recriminations. When contact situations involve superordinate goals, communication is utilized in the direction of reducing conflict in order to attain the common goals.

Favorable information about a disliked out-group tends to be ignored, rejected, or reinterpreted to fit prevailing stereotypes. But, when groups are pulling together toward superordinate goals, true and even favorable information about the out-group is seen in a new light. The probability of information being effective in eliminating unfavorable stereotypes is enormously enhanced.

When groups co-operate in the attainment of superordinate goals, leaders are in a position to take bolder steps toward bringing about understanding and harmonious relations. When groups are directed toward incompatible goals, genuine moves by a leader to reduce intergroup tension may be seen by the membership as out of step and ill advised. The leader may be subjected to severe criticism and even loss of faith and status in his own group. When compelling superordinate goals are introduced, the leader can make moves to further co-operative efforts, and his decisions receive support from other group members.

In short, various measures suggested for the reduction of intergroup conflict—disseminating information, increasing social contact, conferences of leaders—acquire new significance and effectiveness when they become part and parcel of interaction processes between groups oriented toward superordinate goals which have real and compelling value for all groups concerned.

DISCUSSION QUESTIONS

1. Sherif discusses how to bring about group cohesion and group identity formation. He also explores how to develop and resolve intergroup conflict. What are some of your own experiences with croup cohesion building? (Have you participated in any team-building or ice breaker exercises when a group first comes together?) Have you experienced any of the processes Sherif describes when engaging in intergroup competition?
2. Are Sherif's findings applicable to the reduction of current conflicts between groups? What about large-scale, ongoing conflicts, such as that between the Palestinians and Israelis or the Shias and Sunnis?

ADDITIONAL RESOURCES

Internet

http://www.muskingum.edu/~psych/psycweb/history/sherif.htm. A biographical site documenting Sherif's vast influence in the field of social psychology.

FURTHER READING

Granburg, Donald and Gian Sarup (eds.). 1992. *Social Judgment and Intergroup Relations: Essays in Honor of Muzafer Sherif.* New York: Springer.

Ridgeway, Cecilia, Joseph Berger, and Leroy Smith. 1985. "Nonverbal Cues and Status: An Expectation States Approach." *American Journal of Sociology,* 90: 955–78.

Sherif, Muzafer. 1988. *The Robbers Cave Experiment: Intergroup Conflict and Cooperation.* Middleton, CT: Wesleyan University Press.

30. Shared Fantasy: Role Playing Games as Social Worlds

GARY ALAN FINE

While Gary Alan Fine's research on fantasy role-playing (FRP) games was conducted in the 1970s and 1980s, its findings remain highly relevant to the contemporary scene. The University of Chicago Press seemed to agree, touting it as "one of the most accurate descriptions available of an often misunderstood subculture" when it published the paperback edition of *Shared Fantasy* in 2002. What was it that Fine identified, nearly 30 years ago, that still makes this work "contemporary" in its insights about the wildly popular leisure activity of FRP games?

Fantasy role-playing games are cultural systems. They are finely woven worlds of magic and belief. They have social structure, norms, values, and a range of cultural artifacts, which if not physically real, are real to those who participate in them, and presumably (if I can stretch the metaphor) are real to the characters that inhabit these fantasy worlds. In their extent they differ from many cultural systems, but in the seriousness with which the culture is created they are not so different from many microcultural systems.

FANTASY IDIOCULTURES

Every group develops a culture which I have termed its idioculture. An idioculture is a system of knowledge, beliefs, behaviors, and customs peculiar to an interacting group to which members refer and employ as the basis of further interaction. Members recognize that they share experiences and that these experiences can be referred to with the expectation that they will be understood by other members, and can be employed to construct a shared universe of discourse.

Gaming groups are particularly amenable to analysis as idiocultures in that they explicitly deal with the construction of a shared culture through game events. Gaming groups develop a culture for members within the game itself, and simultaneously as a friendship group they develop traditions. These two levels are not isolated from each other—the within-game cultural content can affect the friendship culture and vice versa. Playing together, through the development of shared community, promotes the establishment of a social group even after the game.

STRUCTURE AND FANTASY GAMERS

Even though this is a relatively small social scene, considerable fragmentation exists. Although the number of hard-core fantasy role-play gamers probably does not exceed 5,000 persons, schisms are common. I noted in Chapter 1 the strident criticism between Gary Gygax of TSR Hobbies and the amateur gaming magazines. Even those who contribute to these amateur magazines are internally split, as a result of personality or gaming orientation.

The gaming world is not made up of individuals who love and respect each other. Gamers have their own styles of playing and their own moral standards; those who cross these boundaries may be attacked in the gaming press.

THE REFEREE AND GROUP LEADER

The most obvious example of status in the gaming world is the power and prestige accorded

Fine, Gary Alan. 1983. Abridged from Chapters 4 and 5 of *Shared Fantasy: Role Playing Games as Social Worlds*. Chicago: University of Chicago Press.

referees. I have noted that the referee is referred to (jokingly, but significantly) as "God." Within the structure of the game world he *is* God. More to the point, outside the game this individual is likely to have high status.

This parallel between the referee's position in the game and his position in the group is not surprising in light of the requirements for being a good referee. Most important is a knowledge of the game and its rules. This requires that the referee have gaming experience; often he is an older group member. The imagination, role flexibility, intelligence, and verbal skills that are characteristic of many referees are also related to high status generally. When I first attended the Golden Brigade club it was clear that the regular referees were accorded high status. These young men collected names and addresses of new players for the club's membership list, and I subsequently learned they were the officers of the club. Within a few weeks I could recognize a clear status hierarchy, a supposition verified by other club members. Whenever the two highest status members would agree to referee (which they did not do frequently, having their own private gaming groups), other referees participated in their games. On the nights that one of these high-status individuals was to referee the attendance might be 50 percent above normal.

Similar preferential treatment determines who will referee. Although all referees gain status because of their structural role, some referees are recognized as being better than others, and players change referee during a game if a more talented referee arrives.

The power of the referee is supported, at least in the Golden Brigade, by the fact that the leading referees are good friends—a consequence of having played together. Thus three components of the interaction system support each other—the friendship ties among the central members, the structural position of the referee, and the experience and competence of the referee as a gamer.

THE STATUS SYSTEM OF GAME PLAYERS

In addition to the status accorded referees, a differentiated (although not entirely stable) status hierarchy defines the players as well. A general status hierarchy transcends gaming groups, and this hierarchy influences the game being played.

The referee generally heeds high-status players while ignoring those with less status. In practice this means helping high-status characters while letting low-status characters fend for themselves. Players in all groups vie for the attention of the referee with questions and comments about the game structure, but the referee responds to players depending on his evaluation of them.

Occasionally several players roll simultaneously, and generally the roll of the player with the highest status is accepted, unless the referee announces that he deliberately chose the best dice roll. High-status players most often roll dice for the group decisions (a result of their characters' usually leading the party). While less experienced players might out of fairness be given the responsibility of rolling the dice to increase their otherwise modest participation, this rarely happens. High-status players also often sit next to the referee. This places the less skilled players at the opposite end of the table, making it difficult for them to hear, to ask questions, and to participate. Of course status changes as the new player gains in experience, becomes one of the regulars, and learns how to referee.

Special treatment. The group's social structure is not only reflected in the differential power of members, but may also lead to a referee's or player's giving special treatment to his friends and their characters.

All games at the Golden Brigade are supposedly "open," in that theoretically anyone can participate in any game, with the size of the group the only basis for exclusion. In fact, games can be manipulated so that only "desirable" players get to play. This is done by not "officially" starting the game until enough desirable players arrive so that the game can then be closed without its ever having been "open," informing low-status players that the game is "filled" but allowing others to join.

Players often make charges of favoritism against referees, and a frustrated player can use the rhetoric of favoritism to alter the balance of power, whether or not such a charge is valid. For example:

> Bobby was refereeing *C & S* for the first time. Throughout the game it was apparent that he was paying special attention to Brian and Andy, his two best friends, and was ignoring the rest of the players. Don became particularly annoyed at this favoritism, and criticized it openly. Once when Bobby went off to talk privately with Brian and Andy, Don commented to the rest of us: "This game is shit." [Field notes]

Players recognize that favoritism is common, but the acceptance of it depends on who is giving preference to whom. In the example above Don challenged Bobby for favoring relatively low-status players and ignoring him (a high-status player).

Clique members are likely to give each other special treatment when they play with outsiders:

> Ted, George, and I have become quite good friends; the effects of this friendship can be seen in a game which Mark referees. Two other players were hobbits, and Ted was an elf. As Ted is rather quiet, he did not participate much. At various points George and I say that Ted should roll to see if his elf could detect any secret doors in the dungeon, instead of the hobbits. (Both character types have the ability to do this, so this was reasonable in terms of the game). On some occasions Ted did roll, gaining experience points. [Field notes]

Friendships do affect game-related behavior, a finding that is consistent with the nonrational ordering of reward systems in everyday life, but here transcending the real world and affecting the content of fantasy.

AGE AND FANTASY GAMING

During much of the period in which I participated at the Golden Brigade, the casual observer would have been struck by the wide diversity of the players' ages on any given evening. Originally the Golden Brigade was attended primarily by older adolescents and young adults, but a newspaper article publicizing the club broadened its appeal to youngsters interested in science fiction and fantasy. Thus the small, tight-knit group rapidly gained members, several of whom were preadolescents. The tenor of the club began to change with the influx of young members (aged ten to sixteen), inexperienced at fantasy gaming and without background in war gaming. To an outsider the setting may have seemed a rare example of multi-age play (as several parents believed). However, the older players became annoyed at the change in membership and consequent change in the level of sophistication of the games.

The older players resented that they were being used as "babysitters" by parents who wanted to "dump" their children for the evening. On one occasion a player made this point explicitly, if jokingly, to a parent:

> Sam's mother came for him at about midnight. Howard, who has been refereeing this thirteen-year-old all night, said to her jokingly, "We should charge you $1.50 an hour for babysitting." She attempts to maintain a good face on what she seemed to recognize was resentment on Howard's part, saying: "He is too old for that." [Field notes]

Older players would groan when they saw a station wagon pull up at the Golden Brigade, because it meant another load of children for them to teach the game to and referee patiently.

Within six months after the original article (June), the players at the Golden Brigade had changed almost completely, with the median age decreasing from about twenty to fifteen. Of the five high-status referees who figured in the earlier research (December), by June only one attended regularly. Players who still participated were becoming increasingly dissatisfied with the club. Both Don and Brian claimed that the problem was "the type of people who come now," not the number of people. The reference was to the younger players.

In an informal meeting late in June the older players attempted to reassert their right to play sophisticated scenarios without being compelled to simplify them for the younger players. The outcome of this gathering was to reorganize the club by having a "central attraction" game each week, in which participation was limited to those who knew how to play. A list of featured games was prepared and posted at the local game shop, and it was hoped that this system would bring back some of the older players.

Although this system provided some stability, ensuring that someone would be prepared to referee, it did not bring back the older players. The younger players still attended, and now defined themselves as knowing how to play the game. With some of the college students out of town for the summer and with high scholars and junior high school students able to stay out late on weekends, the average age of players decreased still further.

In late July, Don approached me (as a regular and older player) to ascertain my opinion of placing an age limit on club participation. I tried to be noncommittal, but not negative. Later I overheard Don talking to several of the other regulars about the same matter. He informed me that several former regulars would no longer attend because of the presence of young gamers. In two weeks he informed players that the officers (it was not clear who these individuals were) had decided that henceforth there would be a 9:30 P.M. curfew for anyone under sixteen. Don presented two rationales for this action, neither of which mentioned the dissatisfaction of the older gamers at the way the club had "degenerated." He claimed that the club was "not a babysitting agency," and further that the club might be held responsible if something happened to one of the younger

players after dark. He noted that Minneapolis had an official curfew for children under sixteen of 10:00 P.M., and the 9:30 gaming curfew would allow these players to reach home by 10:00. In fact, this curfew is never enforced. The rule obviously was designed to protect the interests of the older players, rather than stemming from a concern for the welfare of the younger players. Eventually the rules were modified so that younger players could stay until 10:00 P.M., and that the curfew would be disregarded if a player had written permission from a parent. However, the ruling had its desired effect as many of the younger players (especially those under fourteen) stopped attending, as parents were pointedly informed of the decision.

This decision restored the control of the older players, and eventually they let some younger players stay later, because the presence of these few younger players was no longer perceived as a problem.

Don's decision to press the issue generated some hard feelings in the younger players and their friends. Jerry (eighteen, but a close friend of Ted, fifteen) bitterly remarked that he disliked Don's autocratic attitudes: "He thinks he's always right, and that everyone else is always wrong. People who are always wrong, like me, don't like that" [field notes]. However, despite the discontent of the younger players and their friends with the decision and with Don's attitude, the policy remained in force.

What is it about age that makes this variable so important among all the others that might be used to differentiate players (e.g., social class, residence, or social dominance)? Obviously it is not chronological age itself that is crucial, but those attributes that are correlated with age.

The examples of the social structure presented here emphasize that gaming groups are social worlds with status systems, with status assigned to individuals and classes of individuals. What is significant about the gaming world as a social system is that not only does a social structure exist that incorporates players' natural interactions with each other, but a social structure also exists in the fantasy world, as characters form adventure parties, and these parties must negotiate a social order through the positions of characters in the fantasy world.

STRUCTURE AND FANTASY GAMING

Fantasy gaming is designed to be cooperative, unlike most games, in which competition is central. Players claim there are no losers, and that everyone can win. The game pits the players against the fantasy world created by the referee. Ignoring the rivalry between players and the referee, games are designed so that all players can participate in a spirit of cooperation.

The existence of social stratification among players suggests that this picture of intragame harmony is an ideal, but is somewhat misleading as a depiction of game reality. Although cooperation is emphasized in many parties, one finds rivalries among players, a leadership structure, and the mirroring of the external social structure within the fantasy reality.

COOPERATION AND RIVALRY AMONG CHARACTERS

The rhetoric of gamers stresses that intraparty cooperation is an important feature of fantasy role-playing.

The greatest unity in a party occurs when players are facing a foe whom they all must attack to stay alive, that is, when they have a superordinate goal. Ill-will and rivalries emerge immediately *after* adventures, especially when dividing up indivisible spoils (such as magic swords or magical amulets) and making new plans.

The rivalries that emerge from intraparty interaction are of two types: *role rivalries,* in which *characters* rival each other because of the characters' interests, and *personal rivalries,* in which the rivalries stem not from the positions of the characters but from the positions of the players. The first type of cooperative breakdown is legitimate in the game, if rare; the latter type is in theory inappropriate but occurs often. On occasion these personal rivalries are masked as role rivalries, with rival players attempting to construct a reasonable rationale as to why their characters could be competitive.

LEADERSHIP

Just as the gaming subsociety has a decision-making structure, there is a need for the establishment of decision-making procedures within each game. As discussed above, characters may have quite different goals within a game, so mechanisms for determining what action the party will take needs to be agreed upon—explicitly on occasion, but more often implicitly. Four approaches to leadership may be delineated: (1) the single leader, (2) task specialization, (3) group consensus, and (4) anarchy. These styles are ideal types that rarely occur in their pure form, but as ideal types they correspond to leadership styles in other collective task-oriented situations.

The single leader. Many parties, oriented to killing monsters and gaining treasure, opt for a single leader, a person who is known as the "caller" since he is supposed to "call out" to the referee what the party is doing. This method of decision-making is particularly evident at tournaments in which players give the task of successful adventuring precedence over the socioemotional rewards of gaming.

A leader must not be too autocratic or his group will rebel at his directions. The legitimate decision-making power of the caller must be recognized by the other players. In other words, the caller must receive his authority from the members of the party. Authority can be imposed democratically by a collective decision; it may emerge naturally, with one player recognized as most competent to lead the group through adventures; or it may emerge from the social order of the game with the player whose *character* has the highest prime requisites, highest level, or the highest leadership skill or charisma becoming the group leader. Players who attempt to assume leadership of the party without these attributes are frequently rebuffed by the other members of the group.

The major virtue of the single-leader model is that, aside from its obvious efficiency, this individual can reconcile the conflicting interests of players and characters in way that, if done well, can increase enjoyment for all.

Yet there are problems in a group led by single leader. Obviously there are difficulties when the leader doesn't know the rules well, but dissatisfaction and dissension also occur when a dominant player "assumes" the leadership of a group and will not accept feedback. A third difficulty with a single leader is in ensuring the involvement of all players. A party with a single leader can disintegrate into the involvement of only one player, while the others only observe.

Task specialization. Some of the problems inherent in the single-leader model can be dealt with by establishing a division of labor in the party. This division of labor is typically based on the specific strengths of the characters, which often are related to the interests of the players who role-play these characters.

Characters and players have interests and strengths related to the game structure, and a successful party should have a range of character types and player types. To be successful a party needs a mix of characters types in order to ensure that the full range of powers will protect the party. One player suggests:

> Have a combined arms operation, more or less. Like you don't go down [in a dungeon] with everybody a fighter, because if you come up against a monster that uses magic, you're wiped out before you get close enough to attack. You also don't go down there with a lot of magic users, because if somebody surprises you right next to you, you're almost certainly dead, because the magic user doesn't have any armor. [Personal interview]

When a party is composed of equally skilled players and of characters with different specializations, this model of leadership is effective. However, this presupposes that all players recognize the expertise of the other players and characters; unfortunately, this is not always the case—other members of the party sometimes feel that they are equally expert, and show no reluctance in claiming this expertise.

Consensual leadership. Many groups attempt to operate with democratic leadership and the free flow of ideas. In this model all players have a right to suggest what a character or the party as a whole should do; eventually through discussion a consensus will emerge. In theory the majority chooses the plan that seems to be the most practical for the group. In reality the idea chosen often depends on whomever is the most insistent at the moment, or on friendship patterns in real life or power relations in the group.

The consensual model is often found when a game is small and informal, and achieving task goals is secondary to having a good time.

When consensus can emerge easily, this is a desirable model of gaming. Yet it almost requires a small group of good friends who have considerable informal social control over each other, so that it becomes more important to give in when facing the opposition of the group than to continue holding a position.

Group anarchy. Groups that do not opt for a formal procedure of decision-making leave themselves open to anarchy if the structure of the group prevents consensus from emerging—typically when the group is large, when there is no accepted leader, when players do not know each other well, and when characters have markedly different goals in the game. Pure anarchy does not occur very often, because players typically know each other well, and mechanisms of informal social control constrain the actions of group members.

Whatever leadership strategy is decided upon (and whatever its effectiveness), players must select some mechanism by which they can organize the adventures of their characters. Since characters cannot animate themselves, decision-making is ultimately grounded in the "real world," although the fiction remains that the decisions exist on the characters' level of existence. These decisions, like group decisions generally, are affected by participants' statuses. In addition, the particular features of the fiction of danger and the need for quick response in crises often lead to players' desiring to reify their decision-making structure, thus creating the illusion of immediate response. Both the age and homogeneity of players influence the content of the decision-making structure that can be produced by players.

THE STRUCTURE OF PARTIES AND THE REFLECTION OF REAL LIFE

Relationships in gaming parties tend to reflect relationships in the real world. This suggests that affective ties are difficult to transform radically in fantasy. Stated differently, fantasy is constrained by social structure. On occasion siblings decide that they will be brothers in the adventuring band. Similarly, in one game an unmarried couple played in our group—the man played a male human, the woman a female elf. During the course of the game he spent the night in her tent, even though relations between humans and elves are rare (or impossible) in fantasy literature. Yet a real-world assignation was reflected in the gaming tryst. Close friendships may also be reflected in the optional decisions that players make concerning their characters.

Players who have a hostile relationship in the real world may find themselves bickering or fist-fighting in fantasy.

Thus hostile relationships as well as friendships become part of the gaming structure. When there is no congruence between the personal relations and game relations the situation is inherently unstable.

It is important for the effectiveness of the game structure that the status characteristics of players be positively correlated with the status characteristics of their characters. In situations in which the characters are not rolled up anew, this typically poses no problem because the more experienced players have more experienced characters, who are the natural leaders of the party. However, on occasion alterations are made in a character's attributes in order to bring them in line with the abilities of the character's animator.

Players sometimes convince other players to accord them special treatment in keeping with their personal status. For example, Don asked me, when it was my character's duty to stand guard one night, to wake his character up first, even before my character awakened the "leader" of the party. This was seen as a legitimate request because Don had a higher group status than Brian, the party's official leader.

Finally, the referee, through his discretionary authority, can alter a character's status to correspond to his status within a group or his relationship with the referee. Typically this is achieved by giving a player more authority than his character would "naturally" deserve within the fantasy scenario:

> [This referee] favors his friends a lot.... For example, once we were playing in his campaign, and a character I had in *Traveller* had a social level of sixteen, and one of his friend's character had a social level of nine, and his friend's character got a ship [usually reserved for] royalty, and I didn't. [Personal interview]

Obviously the social relations of players as persons influence their relations as fantasy characters. While there is an informal perception that it is legitimate to kill gorgons, harpies, chimeras, and manticores, it is considered improper for a fourteen-year-old to lead a party of adventurers in which there are twenty-year-olds. Maturity is a variable so central to these players that it is virtually impossible to transcend it even in fantasy (i.e., an immature person cannot play a mature character and so cannot lead a party). Fantasy content can only be organized within the limits of what is seen as possible in terms of the expression of players' characteristics. Fantasy is constrained by members' perceptions of what variables cannot be transcended by players and their characters under any circumstances (e.g., intelligence and maturity). These perceptions organize the display of power in these fantasy worlds. Fantasy role-play gaming provides a socially structured world in both the relationships among players and in the relationships among characters. Even in players' wildest flights of imagination we find the obdurate social reality of the "real world."

DISCUSSION QUESTIONS

1. Most role playing games are no longer played face-to-face and "around the table," as in Fine's study, but across continents and cultural divides. How has the introduction of online gaming altered the experience of role-playing games?
2. Given that they are often played across continents, how might massively multiplayer online role-playing games affect globalization, such as global communication and cultural homogenization?

ADDITIONAL RESOURCES

Film
"Second Skin." 2008. A documentary about how people's lives are affected by playing massively multiplayer online games (MMOGs), including World of Warcraft, Second Life, and EverQuest.

Internet
http://www.secondskinfilm.com/home.html. The official site for the 2008 documentary "Second Skin."

Radio
"Go Get a (Virtual) Life." August 31, 2007. A "Talk of the Nation, Science Friday" program produced by National Public Radio about the attraction of online gaming and virtual identities. The interactive website has several good links: http://www.npr.org/templates/story/story.php?storyId=14087749.

FURTHER READING

Cole, Helena and Mark Griffiths. 2007. "Social Interactions in Massively Multiplayer Online Role-Playing Gamers." *CyberPsychology & Behavior,* 10(4): 575–83.

Fine, Gary Alan. 1983. *Shared Fantasy: Role Playing Games as Social Worlds.* Chicago: University of Chicago Press.

Taylor, T. L. 2006. *Play between Worlds: Exploring Online Game Culture.* Cambridge, MA: MIT Press.

PART IV

Constructing a Social Self

The Social Self

The "self" is a core concept within social psychology. It dates back to the field's earliest roots in the work of philosophical pragmatists, including John Dewey and William James. These next selections, by Cooley, Mead, and Hellenga, explore the process by which individuals develop and express their sense of self in particular social contexts.

Charles Horton Cooley's work on "The Social Self" was published in 1902 in *Human Nature and the Social Order*. This book is still considered one of the most influential contributions to understanding the development of the self. George Herbert Mead's 1934 publication of *Mind, Self, and Society* drew heavily upon Cooley's earlier writings to extend a symbolic and social interpretation of how the self develops. In her research on adolescents and the Internet, Kate Hellenga illustrates the enduring relevance of Cooley's and Mead's early nineteenth-century theories to contemporary analysis of the social self in "virtual" social environments such as Facebook, MySpace, YouTube, and Twitter.

As you read the following selections, reflect on how frequently an unknown or unseen social "Other" (such as "Society says" or "They believe") impacts one's sense of self in various social contexts.

31. The Social Self

CHARLES HORTON COOLEY

In 1905, Charles Horton Cooley was one of the founding members of the American Sociological Society, now known as the American Sociological Association. He served as the Society's eighth president in 1918. In the following selection from *Human Nature and the Social Order,* Cooley outlines his theory of "the looking-glass self," a self that is experienced in one's imagined reflected appraisal from others. A succinct way to summarize this theory is in the saying, "I am that which I think you think I am."

There is no sense of "I," as in pride or shame, without its correlative sense of you, or he, or they. Even the miser gloating over his hidden gold can feel the "mine" only as he is aware of the world of men over whom he has secret power; and the case is very similar with all kinds of hid treasure. Many painters, sculptors, and writers have loved to withhold their work from the world, fondling it in seclusion until they were quite done with it; but the delight in this, as in all secrets, depends upon a sense of the value of what is concealed.

In a very large and interesting class of cases the social reference takes the form of a somewhat definite imagination of how one's self—that is any idea he appropriates—appears in a particular mind, and the kind of self-feeling one has is determined by the attitude toward this attributed to that other mind. A social self of this sort might be called the reflected or looking-glass self.

As we see our face, figure, and dress in the glass, and are interested in them because they are ours, and pleased or otherwise with them according as they do or do not answer to what we should like them to be; so in imagination we perceive in another's mind some thought of our appearance, manners, aims, deeds, character, friends, and so on, and are variously affected by it.

A self-idea of this sort seems to have three principal elements: the imagination of our appearance to the other person; the imagination of his judgment of that appearance, and some sort of self-feeling, such as pride or mortification. The comparison with a looking-glass hardly suggests the second element, the imagined judgment, which is quite essential. The thing that moves us to pride or shame is not the mere mechanical reflection of ourselves, but an imputed sentiment, the imagined effect of this reflection upon another's mind. This is evident from the fact that the character and weight of that other, in whose mind we see ourselves, makes all the difference with our feeling.

Cooley, Charles Horton. 1902. "The Social Self," in *Human Nature and the Social Order.* New York: Charles Scribner's Sons.

The process by which self-feeling of the looking-glass sort develops in children may be followed without much difficulty. Studying the movements of others as closely as they do they soon see a connection between their own acts and changes in those movements; that is, they perceive their own influence or power over persons. The child appropriates the visible actions of his parent or nurse, over which he finds he has some control, in quite the same way as he appropriates one of his own members or a plaything, and he will try to do things with this new possession, just as he will with his hand or his rattle. A girl six months old will attempt in the most evident and deliberate manner to attract attention to herself, to set going by her actions some of those movements of other persons that she has appropriated. She has tasted the joy of being a cause, of exerting social power, and wishes more of it. She will tug at her mother's skirts, wriggle, gurgle, stretch out her arms, etc., all the time watching for the hoped-for effect. These performances often give the child, even at this age, an appearance of what is called affectation, that is, she seems to be unduly preoccupied with what other people think of her. Affectation, at any age, exists when the passion to influence others seems to overbalance the established character and give it an obvious twist or pose.

The young performer soon learns to be different things to different people, showing that he begins to apprehend personality and to foresee its operation. If the mother or nurse is more tender than just she will almost certainly be "worked" by systematic weeping. It is a matter of common observation that children often behave worse with their mother than with other and less sympathetic people.

A child obviously and simply, at first, does things for effect. Later there is an endeavor to suppress the appearance of doing so; affection, indifference, contempt, etc., are simulated to hide the real wish to affect the self-image. It is perceived that an obvious seeking after good opinion is weak and disagreeable.

This disturbance of our equilibrium by the outgoing of the imagination toward another person's point of view means that we are undergoing his influence. In the presence of one whom we feel to be of importance there is a tendency to enter into and adopt, by sympathy, his judgment of ourself, to put a new value on ideas and purposes, to recast life in his image. With a very sensitive person this tendency is often evident to others in ordinary conversation and in trivial matters. By force of an impulse springing directly from the delicacy of his perceptions he is continually imagining how he appears to his interlocutor, and accepting the image, for the moment, as himself. If the other appears to think him well-informed on some recondite matter, he is likely to assume a learned expression; if thought judicious he looks as if he were, if accused of dishonesty he appears guilty, and so on. In short, a sensitive man, in the presence of an impressive personality, tends to become, for the time, his interpretation of what the other thinks he is. It is only the heavy-minded who will not feel this to be true, in some degree, of themselves. Of course it is usually a temporary and somewhat superficial phenomenon; but it is typical of all ascendency, and helps us to understand how persons have power over us through some hold upon our imaginations, and how our personality grows and takes form by divining the appearance of our present self to other minds.

There is a vague excitement of the social self more general than any particular emotion or sentiment. Thus the mere presence of people, and an awareness of their observation, often causes a vague discomfort, doubt, and tension. One feels that there is a social image of himself lurking about, and not knowing what it is he is obscurely alarmed. Many people, perhaps most, feel more or less agitation and embarrassment under the observation of strangers, and for some even sitting in the same room with unfamiliar or uncongenial people is harassing and exhausting.

Many people of balanced mind and congenial activity scarcely know that they care what others think of them, and will deny, perhaps with indignation, that such care is an important factor in what they are and do. But this is illusion. If failure or disgrace arrives, if one suddenly finds that the faces of men show coldness or contempt instead of the kindliness and deference that he is used to, he will perceive from the shock, the fear, the sense of being outcast and helpless, that he was living in the minds of others without knowing it, just as we daily walk the solid ground without thinking how it bears us up.

It is true, however, that the attempt to describe the social self and to analyze the mental processes that enter into it almost unavoidably makes it appear more reflective and "self-conscious" than it usually is. Thus while some readers will be able to discover in themselves a quite definite and deliberate contemplation of the reflected self, others will perhaps find nothing but a sympathetic impulse, so simple that it can hardly be made the object of distinct thought. Many people whose behavior shows that their idea of themselves is largely caught from the persons they are with, are yet quite innocent of any intentional posing; it is a matter of subconscious impulse or mere suggestion. The self of very sensitive but non-reflective minds is of this character.

DISCUSSION QUESTIONS

1. Cooley identifies three specific elements that are a part of the looking-glass self. Name these elements and provide an example of how they work together to create a sense of self.
2. Cooley claims that we are all affected by the process of the looking-glass self whether we know it or not. Can you recognize how the looking-glass self plays a part in your own life? Provide an example or two.

ADDITIONAL RESOURCES

Internet

http://www.asanet.orq/cs/root/leftnav/governance/past_officers/presidents/charles_h_cooley.
    A biographical site documenting Cooley's contributions to the fields of sociology and social psychology.

FURTHER READING

Cooley, Charles Horton. 1902. *Human Nature and the Social Order.* New York: Charles Scribner's Sons.

Yabiku, Scott T., William G. Axinn, and Arland Thornton. 1999. "Family Integration and Children's Self-Esteem." *American Journal of Sociology,* 104: 1494–524.

32. Play, the Game, and the Generalized Other

GEORGE HERBERT MEAD

The following excerpt comes from Mead's most famous work, *Mind, Self, and Society,* a collection of students' notes and unpublished manuscripts that was published after his death in 1931. Several of Mead's key contributions are contained within this brief selection, including his discussion of the "play" and "game" stages of self-development, his concept of "the generalized other," and the "I" and the "me."

We were speaking of the social conditions under which the self arises as an object. In addition to language we found two illustrations, one in play and the other in the game, and I wish to summarize and expand my account on these points. I have spoken of these from the point of view of children. The pure play attitude in which little children play at being a parent, at being a teacher—vague personalities that are about them and which affect them and on which they depend. These are personalities which they take, roles they play, and in so far control the development of their own personality. This outcome is just what the kindergarten works toward. It takes the characters of these various vague beings and gets them into such an organized social relationship to each other that they build up the character of the little child. The very introduction of organization from outside supposes a lack of organization at this period in the child's experience. Over against such a situation of the little child, we have the game as such.

The fundamental difference between the game and play is that in the latter the child must have the attitude of all the others involved in that game. The attitudes of the other players which the participant assumes organize into a sort of unit, and it is that organization which controls the response of the individual. The illustration used was of a person playing baseball. Each one of his own acts is determined by his assumption of the action of the others who are playing the game. What he does is controlled by his being everyone else on that team, at least in so far as those attitudes affect his own particular response. We get then an "other" which is an organization of the attitudes of those involved in the same process.

The organized community or social group which gives to the individual his unity of self may be called "the generalized other." The attitude of the generalized other is the attitude of the whole community. Thus, for example, in the case of such a social group as a ball team, the team is the generalized other in so far as it enters—as an organized process or social activity—into the experience of any one of the individual members of it.

There are two general stages in the full development of the self. At the first of these stages, the individual's self is constituted simply by an organization of the particular attitudes of other individuals toward himself and toward one another in the specific social acts in which he participates with them. But at the second stage in the full development of the individual's self that self is constituted not only by an organization of these particular individual attitudes, but also by an organization of the social attitudes of the generalized other or the social group as a whole to which he belongs.

Mead, George Herbert. 1934. "The Self," in *Mind, Self, and Society.* Chicago: University of Chicago Press.

Such is the process by which a personality arises. I have spoken of this as a process in which a child takes the role of the other, and said that it takes place essentially through the use of language. Language in its significant sense is that vocal gesture which tends to arouse in the individual the attitude which it arouses in others, and it is this perfecting of the self by the gesture which mediates the social activities that gives rise to the process of taking the role of the other. In play the child does definitely act out the role which he himself has aroused in himself. It is that which gives, as I have said, a definite content in the individual which answers to the stimulus that affects him as it affects somebody else. The content of the other that enters into one personality is the response in the individual which his gesture calls out in the other.

What goes to make up the organized self is the organization of the attitudes which are common to the group. A person is a personality because he belongs to a community, because he takes over the institutions of that community into his own conduct. The structure, then, on which the self is built is this response which is common to all, for one has to be a member of a community to be a self.

THE "I" AND THE "ME"

We have discussed the social foundations of the self, and hinted that the self does not consist simply in the bare organization of social attitudes. We may now explicitly raise the question as to the nature of the "I" which is aware of the social "me." I do not mean to raise the metaphysical question of how a person can be both "I" and "me," but to ask for the significance of this distinction from the point of view of conduct itself. Where in conduct does the "I" come in as over against the "me"? If one determines what his position is in society and feels himself as having a certain function and privilege, these are all defined with reference to an "I," but the "I" is not a "me" and cannot become a "me." We may have a better self and a worse self, but that again is not the "I" as over against the "me," because they are both selves. The "I" does not get into the limelight; we talk to ourselves, but do not see ourselves. The "I" reacts to the self which arises through the taking of the attitudes of others. Through taking those attitudes we have introduced the "me" and we react to it as an "I."

The simplest way of handling the problem would be in terms of memory. I talk to myself, and I remember what I said and perhaps the emotional content that went with it. The "I" of this moment is present in the "me" of the next moment. There again I cannot turn around quick enough to catch myself. I become a "me" in so far as I remember what I said. If you ask, then, where directly in your own experience the "I" comes in, the answer is that it comes in as a historical figure. It is what you were a second ago that is the "I" of the "me." It is another "me" that has to take that role. You cannot get the immediate response of the "I" in the process. The "I" is in a certain sense that with which we do identify ourselves.

The "I" is the response of the organism to the attitudes of the others; the "me" is the organized set of attitudes of others which one himself assumes. The attitudes of the others constitute the organized "me," and then one reacts toward that as an "I." I now wish to examine these concepts in greater detail.

The "I," then, in this relation of the "I" and the "me," is something that is, so to speak, responding to a social situation which is within the experience of the individual. It is the answer which the individual makes to the attitude which others take toward him when he assumes an attitude toward them. Now, the attitudes he is taking toward them are present in his own experience, but his response to them will contain a novel element. The "I" gives the sense of freedom, of initiative. The situation is there for us to act in a self-conscious fashion. We are aware of ourselves, and of what the situation is, but exactly how we will act never gets into experience until after the action takes place.

Such is the basis for the fact that the "I" does not appear in the same sense in experience as does the "me." The "me" represents a definite organization of the community there in our own attitudes, and calling for a response, but the response that takes place is something that just happens. The above account gives us, I think, the relative position of the "I" and "me" in the situation, and the grounds for the separation of the two in behavior. The two are separated in the process but they belong together in the sense of being parts of a whole. They are separated and yet they belong together. The separation of the "I" and the "me" is not fictitious. They are not identical, there is always a distinction between the "I" and the "me." The "I" both calls out the "me" and responds to it. Taken together they constitute a personality as it appears in social experience. The self is essentially a social process going on with these two distinguishable phases.

We have discussed the self from the point of view of the "I" and the "me," the "me" representing that group of attitudes which stands for others in the community, especially that organized group of responses which we have detailed in discussing the game on the one hand and social institutions on the other. In these situations there is a certain organized group of attitudes which answer to any social act on the part of the individual organism. In any co-operative process, such as the family, the individual calls out a response from the other members of the group. Now, to the extent that those responses can be called out in the individual so that he can answer to them, we have both those contents which go to make up the self, the "other" and the "I." The distinction expresses itself in our experience in what we call the recognition of others and the recognition of ourselves in the others. We cannot realize ourselves except in so far as we can recognize the other in his relationship to us. It is as he takes the attitude of the other that the individual is able to realize himself as a self.

DISCUSSION QUESTIONS

1. Mead identifies the "play" and "game" stages as two distinct processes of childhood development of the self. What does he mean by "play" and "game," and how do these stages differ from one another? Can you illustrate "play" and "game" stages from your own experiences or your observations of others?

2. Mead also defines the "generalized other" as a key concept in the development of a social sense of self. What is the "generalized other," and how does it relate to the "play" and "game" stages?

3. Finally, Mead discusses two interwoven aspects of self: the "I" and the "me." Which one is the more personal and which is the more social aspect of the self? Provide an example of how your own "I" and "me" have been in dialogue with one another in deciding how to respond to an ethical dilemma.

ADDITIONAL RESOURCES

Internet

http://plato.Stanford.edu/entries/mead/. A biographical website from Stanford University's Philosophy Department detailing key events in Mead's life and his major theoretical contributions.

FURTHER READING

Blumer, Herbert. 1966. "Sociological Implications of the Thought of George Herbert Mead." *The American Journal of Sociology*, 71(5): 535–44.

Mead, George Herbert. 1934. *Mind, Self, and Society*. Chicago: University of Chicago Press.

33. Social Space, the Final Frontier: Adolescents on the Internet

KATE HELLENGA

Adolescents prefer computers to other media and spend an increasing amount of their social time interacting online in "virtual" communication with others who are often unknown to them. In this fascinating article, Hellenga discusses how online social interactions are changing the very experience of adolescence and development of the sense of self.

The following chapter was researched and written in 2000–2001 and published in 2002. It is presented here, followed by an epilogue addressing the potential impact of developments in Internet access [written specifically for this volume].

The rapid growth of the Internet has engendered both optimism and concern about the potential impact of new communication technologies on our collective social future.

The democratization of information is another boundary shift made possible by the Internet. In the near future, some say, Internet access will be so cheap as to become universal. When that happens, previously disenfranchised individuals and communities will gain what has been denied them for so long, the powers of knowledge and widespread communication; the pedagogy of the oppressed can be made real in the virtual world. For adolescents, this positive vision might include increased self-esteem and a sense of "voice" for marginalized youth and communities, a stronger sense of global culture, a greater interest in worldwide politics and events, or a sharpened ability to see connections among superficially disparate issues (e.g., feminism and Green politics).

Internet optimists focus on the increased social connections made possible by online communication, while Internet pessimists attend more to the ways that online activity will dehumanize us, damaging or diminishing existing, offline social connections. Thus we are warned of the dangers of computer-mediated connections: the decrease in social skills and intimacy, the potential for misinformation and exploitation, and the possibilities of Internet addiction. Skeptics point out the ease with which one can adopt a false identity and with which government entities and corporations can follow the electronic tracks made by individuals who believe their Internet conversations and Web explorations are private. From this perspective, adolescents who spend too much time online run the risks of losing their friends, their mental health, or their social skills, being made prey to all manners of exploitation and falsehood, or even becoming online addicts or delinquents.

Adolescents may be particularly likely to encounter the rewards and risks of Internet activity. Adolescence is a stage of life generally understood to represent a shift from immersion in the family to increasing connections with the larger social world, from parent-defined to self and peer-influenced identity and values. Given the developmental task of negotiating a relationship with "the wider world," adolescents may be disproportionately affected by current and future changes in communication technologies, which make available increasing amounts and types of information and which increase contacts with a variety of cultures, personal styles, and values.

Hellenga, Kate. 2002; 2007. "Social Space, the Final Frontier: Adolescents on the Internet," in Jeylan Mortimer and Reed Larson (eds.). *The Changing Adolescent Experience: Societal Trends and the Transition to Adulthood in the 21st Century,* 208–49. Cambridge: Cambridge University Press. With updated epilogue written for this volume in 2007.

How accurate are the reward- and risk-focused assessments of the Internet's impact, and how will adolescents' experience of themselves and their world be affected by their online interactions? To begin answering these questions, we first need to know how adolescents use media in general, and how they use computers and the Internet in particular. Research suggests adolescents are indeed making use of the Internet, especially those functions allowing for interpersonal connection and conversation. The social space created by the Internet has unique qualities which do, indeed, present both risks and rewards for adolescent users. I will address these aspects of Internet activity in the second section of the chapter, and I will close with a set of predictions about the likely directions that adolescents' Internet use, and its effects, will take in years to come.

ADOLESCENT INTERNET USE

Current trends in computer access and Internet growth suggest that many adolescents will have access to the Internet in the near future. However, rates of growth and access differ markedly across class and ethnicity within nations, and across nations and geographic regions worldwide. This paper focuses on adolescents' home computer use and Internet access, on the assumption that use at home is more likely to represent freely chosen activity types than school or public terminal use might.

Observing current trends in adolescents' adoption and use of the Internet provides a focus for discussing future uses and their effects.

Adolescents use computers and prefer them to other media; young people are rapidly claiming the new technology as their own.

When teens get online, they are likely to spend time "going places" on the Internet and "talking to people." This is congruent with the concept of adolescence as a time of exploring the world and social relationships.

A closer analysis of adolescents' online activities suggests that the Internet's social functions in particular are attractive to teenagers. Their strong involvement in chat rooms may be a harbinger of things to come as Internet access increases and adolescents familiarize themselves with this new territory. Teenagers may be especially drawn to chat rooms, which combine direct, immediate interaction with relative anonymity for users, allowing risk-free observation and practicing of social skills. These unique social conditions also hold great potential for changing the experience of adolescence.

We might predict that the average adolescent of the future will spend much more time online than is currently the case and may replace some daily activities with Internet use. Today's "average" adolescents use chat rooms and e-mail more than any other Internet function (excluding information searches), implying a specific attraction for the social connections potential of the Internet. As social explorers seeking to develop their own identities and connect to a world beyond the family, adolescents will probably continue to seek new social experiences and information online. We can more fully grasp the impact, and the potential risks and rewards, of the interplay between adolescent development and Internet activity if we have some idea of what online life can be like.

THE INTERNET AS A UNIQUE SOCIAL SPACE

The Internet has evolved and has been conceptualized thus far as a reality which is separate from our everyday lives; discussions of "cyberspace" and "virtual reality" suggest that one can "enter" the Internet world thus leaving everyday life behind. It seems unlikely that those individuals who constitute and create the social world of the Internet are suddenly freed of their usual complement of values and behavioral norms. However, online interaction does present certain freedoms and opportunities which are generally unavailable in more traditionally created social connections. Current and future adolescents will be spending at least some of their time interacting with others in a "place" which imposes very few limits on speech, behavior, or relationships. The Internet has many liberties, each of which is likely to attract and affect teenagers in different ways.

Freedom from External Controls

Cyberspace is a place of anarchy. In spite of the role of the U.S. government in developing the technology, the Internet has become a decentralized and user-controlled communications medium. The Net was originally developed by the government and by universities, to be used primarily for military research and exchange of research information. Thus, early personal uses (e.g., e-mail and chat, newsgroups) subverted the Net's original purpose by taking advantage of the absence of absolute authority and defined laws of use.

Because the Internet is still relatively new and very large, adolescents can participate in activities their parents have neither heard of nor imagined, and can feel like a part of something separate from their parents' influence.

Freedom to Explore Sexuality

The proliferation of sexual content and activity on the Internet is potentially appealing to adolescents, and a source of concern for the adults who guide their development. Taking advantage of the relative freedom of cyberspace, and the apparent willingness of some subset of the population to pay for the privilege of viewing sexually explicit materials, numerous entrepreneurs set up pornography sites. In addition, a subset of newsgroups have emerged which offer sexually explicit stories and/or downloadable digitized photographs of pornographic materials.

The prevalence of pornographic materials on the Web can be a problem even for teenagers who do not intentionally seek them out. The very openness and freedom that allow teens to learn about sexuality online may also foist sexual content upon unwary and naive youth. Filtering software is designed to prevent these problems, but these programs and services have inconsistent success in preventing access to pornography. They may also intentionally or inadvertently filter out non-pornographic material such as family planning and sexual health. With the new federal mandate for libraries and schools to use filtering software, American adolescents' access to sexual material, whether pornographic or educational, may be quite limited for a time. However, pornography will likely continue to proliferate on the Web, and interested adolescents will probably continue to seek out or unexpectedly encounter online sexual material. Online filtering is a clumsy method for addressing this important issue, and the Internet is highly resistant to outright censorship. These factors, combined with adults' interest in guiding young people's introduction to sexuality, may hasten a shift from traditional but uncomfortable silences to more direct personal and cultural conversations about pornography and sexuality.

It is possible for adolescents (and others) to engage in sexual activity online; in addition to chat rooms devoted to "dating" and in some cases to more explicit sexual conversation, users have the opportunity to create a "private chat room" where they can converse unobserved by the rest of the chat room members. Data are not yet available concerning the extent to which adolescents seek sexual information and contact online. However, this life stage is associated with sexual maturation, along with curiosity and concern about sex and relationships. As noted previously, adolescents currently favor social uses of the Internet, such as e-mail and chat. In combination, these characteristics provide ample motivation and opportunity for sexual exploration online. Whether or not teens are more likely than other age groups to engage in this activity, its impact may be stronger for adolescents and young adults who have only limited life (or sexual) experience in which to ground their online experiences.

Freedom to Explore Identity and Political Action

The Internet may spark a new wave of political activism among young people. Consciousness raising groups in the 1960s and 1970s combined the personal and the political in building a feminist social/political movement, and grass-roots organizing was the modus operandi of young people's political change efforts during that era. Now the Internet has become a "meeting place" and a worldwide bulletin board for a vast array of cultural subgroups, political movements, and members of minority groups who would not normally have access to other people "like them." Personal and organizational Web pages, as well as topic-oriented support groups (both newsgroups and chat rooms), provide a variety of ways in which people can share information and support with a much wider network of people than they might otherwise be able to approach.

As adolescents explore their own values and identities, and struggle with issues that may not be easily discussed with parents or peers (e.g., sexuality, depression, and suicidality), Internet communication can provide information and emotional support in a relatively safe and anonymous way. OutProud (www.queer.com, www.outproud.org), for instance, is a site developed by the National Coalition for Gay, Lesbian, Bisexual, and Transgender Youth. The Web site offers an archive of coming out stories, publications discussing sexual orientation-related issues, lists of resources across the country, and perhaps most importantly, a message board. In the "high school" forum, discussion topics include gay-straight alliances, social activities, lesbian student rights, and "queers should be shot," in which several homophobic statements have been posted and subsequently refuted by other readers.

Adolescents are already seeking social contact and information online, using chat rooms, e-mail, and WWW information searches. Once familiar with the Internet-based tools of connection and activism, adolescents are likely to begin creating online spaces for themselves, rather than waiting passively for desired forums to appear. Ethnic and sexual identities may be strengthened and established through online contacts, adding a new facet to the already complex picture of adolescent development and acculturation. It appears that the gay/lesbian/bisexual/transgendered community has already recognized the benefits offered by online communication, and is becoming a leader in Internet activism and support. Other traditionally oppressed or voiceless groups are also claiming space online. Online support groups and information will have an enormous positive impact on Internet-savvy teenagers in decades to come. Young people who have no other avenues for discussing issues of identity and bigotry will be most likely to benefit. They will also be most vulnerable, to misinformation and rhetoric masquerading as fact. This is a common problem on the Net, a forum largely devoid of content control and verification. As with pornography, the decades to come will likely require educators and parents to engage in direct, open conversation about historically uncomfortable or taboo topics, to support teens as they encounter the Internet's flood of information, opinion, and rhetoric.

Freedom of Self-Presentation

My description of the Internet as a social realm has focused thus far on those aspects of the online "world" which parallel more familiar, "real-life" cultural and individual experiences. Clearly, though, the Internet is not simply a new location to which people can go and do the same things they have always done. Internet communication is qualitatively distinct from other forms of communication, even while it shares some features with those older forms (e.g., the text-only format of e-mail, Internet chat, and letter writing). Social relationships online are based in exchanges of text. Multimedia interaction, whether in games or in video conferencing, is a recent development, but technological limitations on bandwidth and (therefore) on speed of transmission make these forms somewhat unsatisfying at this point. Most multiuser adventure-type games are text-based, combining elements of storytelling, role-playing games, and social interaction. It is the combination of text-only communication and mutual anonymity that makes the Internet a truly unique social space.

Interaction on the Web can include elements of both letter-writing and telephone conversations. However, online interactions have a very different "flavor" from more traditional modes of long-distance contact, because one can communicate with complete anonymity to unknown numbers of unknown others.

Identity-play on the Net is often done consciously and for fun; individuals must actively choose to represent their gender, personality, interests, or conversational style in a particular way. Perhaps the power to choose and inhabit a different persona can be beneficial to adolescents. Net relationships are relatively risk free, and the consequences of various behaviors can be seen or experienced virtually, without affecting the person's offline life. This safe form of identity-exploration will become more common as adolescents gain access to and comfort with the social world of the Internet.

Adolescents who become familiar with the Internet will have access to a new realm of possibilities for behavior, learning, and social contact. The liberties presented here combine aspects of "real-life" behavior, such as theft, sexual experimentation, social support, and identity exploration, with unique features of life online: decentralized or nonexistent government, anonymity, and rapid access to vast numbers of people and quantities of information. To some degree, then, online adolescent behavior will parallel "real-life" behavior from pre-Internet eras. A small group of teens will find ways to misbehave and test limits, though the limits are likely in many cases to be set by their parents rather than by online authorities. Many adolescents will use the Internet primarily for e-mail and chat; they may talk only with friends from school, but over time they will probably make friends online with young people from other places. Gathering information about sensitive topics in private, or claiming a different identity for an online conversation, will appeal to teenagers' interest in discovering the world beyond their own family, and discovering their own values and self-image.

At the same time, longstanding approaches to the protection of young people from uncomfortable or confusing issues are likely to lose their effectiveness. Online exploration can expose adolescents to numerous viewpoints not generally shared in their own families or communities. Current trends toward more direct, open discussion of difficult issues, such as drug use and sexuality, will continue as concerned adults seek new ways to guide adolescents' exploration of behavior and values.

EFFECT OF ONLINE INTERACTION ON SOCIAL RELATIONSHIPS

The Internet is a "social space" whose customs and capacities combine unique freedoms with features of more traditional social systems. This combination of familiar and unfamiliar conditions can be fertile ground for changes in social behavior, norms and culture, both on- and off-line. Adolescents are already making the Internet a regular part of their learning and social lives; they will pioneer some of these new ways of thinking and being. Their online activity will, and already does, call into question the ownership of knowledge, the nature of platonic and romantic relationships, and the constitution and permanence of identity. These online differences will have a distinct and perhaps greater impact for adolescents, whose chief developmental task may be to learn about and experience a world outside the limits of adult supervision and family life. To assess the effects of online social experiences on adolescents in the future, we must consider specific social activities as they are carried out online.

Appearance, Gender, and Race

An adolescent whose social time is spent online will still encounter the constructions of gender and ethnicity so common, and to some so objectionable, in offline/face-to-face interaction.

However, as Internet communication becomes more common, it is possible that people will develop separate sets of expectations and behaviors for their interactions on- and offline. In this "separate worlds" scenario, one would attend to a speaker's gender or skin color, in face-to-face interaction, because of cultural habit and the human tendency to seek visual categorization cues. This same person might then go online and engage in a discussion or an interactive game, and never think to question the gender or race of the other participants; these cues may become irrelevant over time in our Internet communications.

One source of this irrelevancy is the somewhat superficial nature of many online connections; newsgroup participants may become familiar with each others' verbal styles, but may never know the details of their lives. Thus questions about race or gender might be set aside until an interaction becomes more personal and connected: when a discussion moves people from acquaintance into friendship. Gender will, of course, always be more obvious online for those people using their real names, but even this may be confounded as the online population becomes more international in character. Furthermore, the relative unimportance of gender to online interaction may lead to diminished interest in that categorization.

Even with separate sets of expectations and curiosities for on- and offline communication, it is quite likely that online communication styles will increasingly influence offline interactions. The direction of influence appears to be largely unidirectional at this time, from traditional to newer modes (e.g., online resumes look very much like paper resumes; online newspapers have only begun to look different from their doorstep counterparts). As Internet communication becomes more familiar, the influence may work in both directions, thus leading people to question the importance of gender and race to their categorizations of people in their day to day lives.

Deception and Exploitation

Computer-mediated communication's capacity for "identity play" has negative connotations as well. Online interaction has great potential for deception, especially regarding one's own identity. In single interactions or posts to newsgroups, misrepresenting one's identity is probably harmless, unless it involves claiming another's identity.

Although online activity could increase vulnerability to this type of attention simply by increasing the numbers of people with whom youth have contact, these risks may be reduced in the future by adolescents' increasing familiarity with the unique qualities of online interaction. Computer-mediated communication (CMC) provides limited cues for assessing trustworthiness, or any other characteristic. Online interaction plays havoc with typical human approaches to social connections. Removing important sources of information such as vocal register and body language make it even harder to assess another person's character. This may be less of a problem for adolescents in the future, accustomed as they will be to the differences between Internet and face-to-face interactions. To the extent that these low expectations for trust imply the adoption of self-protective behaviors, young people in years to come may be less likely than their current-day counterparts to be deceived or exploited, and less traumatized when those problems do occur.

Online Socialization and Communication Skills

CMC offers the possibility of "lurking" (reading the messages posted without adding any messages of your own) on newsgroups. Lurking provides a chance to observe the social terrain, learn some of the customs, and decide whether the current discussion is too hostile, too boring, or too cliquish to be an appropriate point of entry. This might be contrasted with a high school party or dance, at which a "wallflower" would be noticeably disadvantaged. By lurking, an adolescent could simply observe and learn from the interactions of others, without ever participating directly, just as young people seek information about social interaction through observing adults around them (parents, siblings, movie and television characters, teachers, strangers).

Online communication may eventually serve as a "socialization ground" for adolescents, especially those who are shy or uncomfortable with their peers in face-to-face interaction. This text-based social learning may not be beneficial. Consider the adolescent who creates and enjoys a strong persona online, who feels confident and assertive in his or her newsgroup communication. She or he may have plenty of practice in verbal argumentation and discussion, but still have no idea how to read social cues such as boredom, interest, or flirtation. Unlike direct involvement, the vicarious learning provided by lurking in online conversation may actually discourage offline social interactions, because the risks are so much higher.

The Nature of Intimacy and Dating Online

Although one may be able to find solace or social support online, it is a matter of debate whether these connections constitute intimacy, or in what way time spent online affects overall social connectedness.

Online dating may provide adolescents some shelter from the perceived risks of face-to-face relationships. Online dating may be so transient that "breakups" are not a possibility, because "breakup" implies commitment that may not be a goal in this context. If online breakups do occur, they may be less painful than the face-to-face version. They are not witnessed by the couple's peers, nor do they necessarily imply a failing of either person's "true self" to be a worthy partner. Furthermore, they do not presage a long, lonely wait for a new relationship to arise; chat room connections are made quickly, unhindered by the appearance-focus and inhibition of face-to-face relationships. The Internet is providing a forum in which adolescents can move beyond traditionally defined "intimacy" and "dating," creating relationships for their own sake. If this were to become a trend in adolescent relationships, it would provide teens in the future a clearer perspective (compared to current-day or past adolescents) on the nature and desirable qualities of intimate relationships. Having relationships "just for fun" would allow

practice in the skills of communicating to make a relationship work, without the pressures of long-term commitment and sexual contact.

EPILOGUE, 2007

Mutual Transformations: Adolescent Settlers on the Internet's Social Frontiers

Increased Access, Stable Disparities

In the fast-changing world of the Internet, five years is an extremely long time. Since the researching and publication of the "Social Space" chapter (above), the Internet ("the Net") and the World Wide Web ("the Web") have become integral parts of many people's daily lives in developed countries. In the United States, most advertising includes reference to a Web address (URL), business cards routinely include e-mail addresses, and online conversation and collaboration is not only commonplace but expected.

While access and overall use continue to increase, the Digital Divide remains. In sum, Internet access has increased across the board in the United States, and race/ethnicity alone has little influence on whether a child has Internet access on a typical day. However, race/ethnicity, median community income and parental education level (perhaps a proxy for family income) all affect the chances of a child using the Net in public, versus private, settings. Assuming the most common (and no-cost) sites are schools and libraries, it is likely that the amount of time young people spend, and the things they do there, will be significantly different at public access sites.

Increased Variety and Ease of Communication

Along with increasing Internet accessibility, recent years have shown expansions in the types of activities and communication formats available to the average Web user. Internet Relay Chat (IRC), an early Net medium for synchronous online talk, was unknown to the average personal computer user of previous years. Several websites now offer free, user-friendly instant messaging (IM) programs for registered users; users can customize the program with "avatars" (often cartoon-like images, sometimes animated, representing the user), photographs, and personalized "away messages." IM also allows sharing of URLs, photographs, files, music, and live Web-camera images. Similarly, chat rooms and online communities are much more easily accessible.

Perhaps the most striking change, however, is the ease with which an average user can create, format, and edit a personalized website, complete with photos, animated images, customized access control (to allow or disallow particular people from viewing or commenting on the content), and social networking capabilities (e.g., allowing access to one's own site, searching others' sites, publicly acknowledging one's online friends). The most popular of these sites, Facebook and MySpace, are clearly targeted at teenagers and young adults. Facebook, launched in 2003, is now the sixth most-trafficked website on the Internet, accounting for 1 percent of all Internet time; its user base has more than doubled in the past six months, from 7.5 million in July 2006 to nearly 18 million in January 2007.

There Be No Adults Here?

If the Internet is a familiar, comfortable and interesting space for teens to spend time, meet one another and express themselves, we can easily see the parallels between online and offline modes of expression. IM is augmenting, and in some cases supplanting, telephone communication, chat rooms and e-mail; it allows teens to "talk" while doing homework, watching television, listening to music, and/or talking to multiple others online, on the phone, or in person. MySpace and Facebook offer teens the opportunity to post photos and text, to personalize their sites with design and format elements, and to get comments from acquaintances or strangers. In this sense, these sites make public what might have been more private in the past, combining and publicizing elements of school-locker decoration, posters on the bedroom wall, conversations with friends,

public display of social connections and cliques, and personal diaries (this last being true also of freestanding blogs). From an adult perspective, users of these sites appear ignorant of, or oblivious to, the ramifications of publicly posting details of identity and casual activity (e.g., getting drunk, "hooking up," skipping classes). This may be a function of the "typical" adolescent oblivion to all things outside one's own social world; it may also be an outgrowth of the thoroughness with which teens have claimed the Internet as an extension of their own social space.

Putting One's Self "Out There" Online

Adolescents' use of the Net and the Web continues to demonstrate their marked interest in using its tools for direct communication, as well as claiming and transforming its unique formats and settings to communicate in-process and sometimes fluid identities, to expand and maintain social group connections, and to make contact with ideas, information and people unavailable in their offline lives. The Internet offers adolescents another venue for social exposure, and as they settle in this new social frontier, they transform its spaces; on a small scale, by creating their own websites and images, and on a larger scale, by influencing the creation, marketing and availability of new functions and sites. Socially speaking, the Net provides increased social exposure with decreased social awkwardness and discomfort. In response, adolescents have translated their offline methods of identity exploration into online formats. Offline diaries are augmented by online, public blogs and journals. Offline personal spaces, decorated with pictures of self, family, friends, personal heroes and crushes, become personal websites, available just to friends or to the entire online populace. The daily drama of friends, cliques, party invitations and gossip is performed and reified online. Deception and outright pretense may be rare, but teens can and will use online spaces to experiment with alterations in personality and social behavior, and to observe others' interactions from a socially safe distance.

DISCUSSION QUESTIONS

1. This article was originally published in 2002 with an update written in 2007. Given the rapid pace of change in online social networking applications, much has changed even since Hellenga's 2007 update. What are some examples of these changes and how might they affect one's sense of self? (For example, Twitter was not widely used in 2007.)
2. What are some of the social norms of Internet social spaces such as Facebook and MySpace? How did you become aware of what is considered normative or deviant in these online environments?
3. Provide examples from your own online experiences of times your own presentation of self or interaction with others has surprised you or differed from your typical everyday face-to-face interactions.
4. How do attributes such as gender, race, and appearance affect how people identify themselves and interact online?

ADDITIONAL RESOURCES

Film

"Frontline: Growing up Online." 2008. A documentary of children growing up using Internet technology. http://www.pbs.org/wgbh/pages/frontline/kidsonline/.

Internet

http://www.pbs.org/wgbh/pages/frontline/kidsonline/. "Frontline's" interactive website about "Growing up Online."

http://www.pbs.org/wgbh/pages/frontline/kidsonline/interviews/pascoe.html. "Frontline" interview with sociologist C. J. Pascoe about kids growing up online.

http://www.pewinternet.org/Presentations/2009/Teens-and-the-internet.aspx. A project of the Pew Research Center, the Pew Internet, and the American Life Project's website details research findings about how teens use the Internet and other technology.

Radio

"A Facebook Tale: Founder Unfriends Pals on Way Up." Program on National Public Radio's "All Things Considered," July 19, 2009, featuring Ben Mezrich, author of *Accidental Billionaires: The Founding of Facebook.* http://www.npr.org/templates/story/story.php?storyId=106742510.

FURTHER READING

Johnson, Steven. June 15, 2009. "How Twitter Will Change the Way We Live (in 140 characters or less)." *Time,* 32–7. http://www.time.com/time/business/article/0,8599,1902604,00.html.

Levy, Steven. August 20–7, 2007. "Facebook Grows Up." *Newsweek,* 41–6. http://www.newsweek.com/id/32261.

Mezrich, Ben. 2009. *Accidental Billionaires: The Founding of Facebook.* New York: Doubleday.

Reiss, Spencer. 2006. "His Space." *Wired.* www.wired.com/wired/archive/14.07/murdoch_pr_html.

Deviance and Labeling

Medical sociologists studies the institution of medicine itself, including the hierarchical structures in hospitals and other settings in which health interventions and healing take place. Medical sociologists have come to recognize that health and disease are not absolute, universal phenomena. Instead, the definition of what constitutes health, illness and both "normal" and "abnormal" behavior is an historically situated social process. Such definitions are important elements of social control.

These next selections highlight the role of medicine in defining and responding to social deviance. In his 1975 article on the medicalization of deviant behavior, Conrad details how children's behavior became the purview of medicine and pharmacists. As a result, a large portion of contemporary children are diagnosed with mental illness and treated pharmacologically.

Rosenhan, in his brilliant 1973 research, illustrates the power of psychiatric diagnostic labels and the ramifications of such diagnoses. Gagné and colleagues carry over this analysis of psychiatric labeling in their contemporary study of transsexuals coming to terms with gender identities that challenge the most basic of social norms.

34. On Being Sane in Insane Places

DAVID L. ROSENHAN

David Rosenhan and his colleagues discovered the "stickiness" of labels when they sought admission to (and release from) a dozen U.S. psychiatric institutions in the early 1970s. In the context of hospital psychiatric wards, their everyday behaviors and personal histories were interpreted as evidence of their mental illness.

If sanity and insanity exist, how shall we know them?

The question is neither capricious nor itself insane. However much we may be personally convinced that we can tell the normal from the abnormal, the evidence is simply not compelling. It is commonplace, for example, to read about murder trials wherein eminent psychiatrists for the defense are contradicted by equally eminent psychiatrists for the prosecution on the matter of the defendant's sanity. More generally, what is viewed as normal in one culture may be seen as quite aberrant in another. Thus, notions of normality and abnormality may not be quite as accurate as people believe they are.

To raise questions regarding normality and abnormality is in no way to question the fact that some behaviors are deviant or odd. But normality and abnormality, sanity and insanity, and the diagnoses that flow from them may be less substantive than many believe them to be.

At its heart, the question of whether the sane can be distinguished from the insane (and whether degrees of insanity can be distinguished from each other) is a simple matter: do the salient characteristics that lead to diagnoses reside in the patients themselves or in the environments and contexts in which observers find them? From the formulators of the recently revised *Diagnostic and Statistical Manual* of the American Psychiatric Association, the belief has been strong that patients present symptoms, that those symptoms can be categorized, and, implicitly, that the sane are distinguishable from the insane. More recently, however, the view has grown that psychological categorization of mental illness is useless at best and downright harmful, misleading, and pejorative at worst. Psychiatric diagnoses, in this view, are in the minds of the observers and are not valid summaries of characteristics displayed by the observed.

Gains can be made in deciding which of these is more nearly accurate by getting normal people (i.e., people who do not have, and have never suffered, symptoms of serious psychiatric disorders) admitted to psychiatric hospitals and then determining whether they were discovered to be sane and, if so, how. If the sanity of such pseudopatients were always detected, there would be prima facie evidence that a sane individual can be distinguished from the insane context in which he is found. Normality (and presumably abnormality) is distinct enough that it can be recognized wherever it occurs, for it is carried within the person. If, on the other hand, the sanity of the pseudopatients were never discovered, serious difficulties would arise for those who support traditional modes of psychiatric diagnosis. Given that the hospital staff was not incompetent, that the pseudopatient had been behaving as sanely as he had been outside of the hospital, and that it had never been previously

Rosenhan, David L. 1973. "On Being Sane in Insane Places." *Science,* 179(4070): 250–8.

suggested that he belonged in a psychiatric hospital, such an unlikely outcome would support the view that psychiatric diagnosis betrays little about the patient but much about the environment in which an observer finds him.

This article describes such an experiment. Eight sane people gained secret admission to 12 different hospitals.

PSEUDOPATIENTS AND THEIR SETTINGS

The eight pseudopatients were a varied group. One was a psychology graduate student in his 20's. The remaining seven were older and "established." Among them were three psychologists, a pediatrician, a psychiatrist, a painter, and a housewife. Three pseudopatients were women, five were men. All of them employed pseudonyms, lest their alleged diagnoses embarrass them later. Those who were in mental health professions alleged another occupation in order to avoid the special attentions that might be accorded by staff. With the exception of myself (I was the first pseudopatient and my presence was known to the hospital administrator and chief psychologist and, so far as I can tell, to them alone), the presence of pseudopatients and the nature of the research program was not known to the hospital staffs.

The settings were similarly varied. In order to generalize the findings, admission into a variety of hospitals was sought. The 12 hospitals in the sample were located in five different states on the East and West coasts.

After calling the hospital for an appointment, the pseudopatient arrived at the admissions office complaining that he had been hearing voices. Asked what the voices said, he replied that they were often unclear, but as far as he could tell they said "empty," "hollow," and "thud." The voices were unfamiliar and were of the same sex as the pseudopatient. The choice of these symptoms was occasioned by their apparent similarity to existential symptoms. Such symptoms are alleged to arise from painful concerns about the perceived meaninglessness of one's life. It is as if

the hallucinating person were saying, "My life is empty and hollow." The choice of these symptoms was also determined by the *absence* of a single report of existential psychoses in the literature.

Beyond alleging the symptoms and falsifying name, vocation, and employment, no further alterations of person, history, or circumstances were made. The significant events of the pseudopatient's life history were presented as they had actually occurred. Relationships with parents and siblings, with spouse and children, with people at work and in school, consistent with the aforementioned exceptions, were described as they were or had been. Frustrations and upsets were described along with joys and satisfactions. These facts are important to remember. If anything, they strongly biased the subsequent results in favor of detecting sanity, since none of their histories or current behaviors were seriously pathological in any way.

Immediately upon admission to the psychiatric ward, the pseudopatient ceased simulating *any* symptoms of abnormality. In some cases, there was a brief period of mild nervousness and anxiety, since none of the pseudopatients really believed that they would be admitted so easily. Indeed, their shared fear was that they would be immediately exposed as frauds and greatly embarrassed. Moreover, many of them had never visited a psychiatric ward; even those who had, nevertheless had some genuine fears about what might happen to them. Their nervousness, then, was quite appropriate to the novelty of the hospital setting, and it abated rapidly.

Apart from that short-lived nervousness, the pseudopatient behaved on the ward as he "normally" behaved. The pseudopatient spoke to patients and staff as he might ordinarily. Because there is uncommonly little to do on a psychiatric ward, he attempted to engage others in conversation. When asked by staff how he was feeling, he indicated that he was fine, that he no longer experienced symptoms. He responded to instructions from attendants, to calls for medication (which was not swallowed), and to dining-hall instructions. Beyond such activities as were available to him on the admissions ward, he spent his time writing down his observations about the ward, its patients, and the staff. Initially these notes were written "secretly," but as it soon became clear that no one much cared, they were subsequently written on standard tablets of paper in such public places as the dayroom. No secret was made of these activities.

The pseudopatient, very much as a true psychiatric patient, entered a hospital with no foreknowledge of when he would be discharged. Each was told that he would have to get out by his own devices, essentially by convincing the staff that he was sane. The psychological stresses associated with hospitalization were considerable, and all but one of the pseudopatients desired to be discharged almost immediately after being admitted. They were, therefore, motivated not only to behave sanely, but to be paragons of cooperation. That their behavior was in no way disruptive is confirmed by nursing reports, which have been obtained on most of the patients. These reports uniformly indicate that the patients were "friendly," "cooperative," and "exhibited no abnormal indications."

THE NORMAL ARE NOT DETECTABLY SANE

Despite their public "show" of sanity, the pseudopatients were never detected. Admitted, except in one case, with a diagnosis of schizophrenia, each was discharged with a diagnosis of schizophrenia "in remission." The label "in remission" should in no way be dismissed as a formality, for at no time during any hospitalization had any question been raised about any pseudopatient's simulation. Nor are there any indications in the hospital records that the pseudopatient's status was suspect. Rather, the evidence is strong that, once labeled schizophrenic, the pseudopatient was stuck with that label. If the pseudopatient was to be discharged, he must naturally be "in remission"; but he was not sane, nor, in the institution's view, had he ever been sane.

The uniform failure to recognize sanity cannot be attributed to the quality of the hospitals, for, although there were considerable variations among them, several are considered excellent. Nor can it be alleged that there was simply not enough time to observe the pseudopatients. Length of hospitalization ranged from 7 to 52 days, with an average of 19 days.

Finally, it cannot be said that the failure to recognize the pseudopatients' sanity was due to the fact that they were not behaving sanely. It was quite common for the patients to "detect" the pseudopatients' sanity. During the first three hospitalizations, when accurate counts were kept, 35 of a total of 118 patients on the admissions ward voiced their suspicions, some vigorously. "You're not crazy. You're a journalist, or a professor [referring to the continual note-taking]. You're checking up on the hospital." The fact that the patients often recognized normality when staff did not raises important questions.

THE STICKINESS OF PSYCHODIAGNOSTIC LABELS

Having once been labeled schizophrenic, there is nothing the pseudopatient can do to overcome the tag. The tag profoundly colors others' perceptions of him and his behavior.

Once a person is designated abnormal, all of his other behaviors and characteristics are colored by that label. Indeed, that label is so powerful that many of the pseudopatients' normal behaviors were overlooked entirely or profoundly misinterpreted. Some examples may clarify this issue.

Earlier I indicated that there were no changes in the pseudopatient's personal history and current status beyond those of name, employment, and, where necessary, vocation.

As far as I can determine, diagnoses were in no way affected by the relative health of the circumstances of a pseudopatient's life. Rather, the reverse occurred: the perception of his circumstances was shaped entirely by the diagnosis. A clear example of such translation is found in the case of a pseudopatient who had had a close relationship with his mother but was rather remote from his father during his early childhood. During adolescence and beyond, however, his father became a close friend, while his relationship with his mother cooled. His present relationship with his wife was characteristically close and warm. Apart from occasional angry exchanges, friction was minimal. The children had rarely been spanked. Surely there is nothing especially pathological about such a history. Indeed, many readers may see a similar pattern in their own experiences, with no markedly deleterious consequences. Observe, however, how such a history was translated in the psychopathological context, this from the case summary prepared after the patient was discharged.

> This white 39-year-old male...manifests a long history of considerable ambivalence in close relationships, which begins in early childhood. A warm relationship with his mother cools during his adolescence. A distant relationship to his father is described as becoming very intense. Affective stability is absent. His attempts to control emotionality with his wife and children are punctuated by angry outbursts and, in the case of the children, spankings. And while he says that he has several good friends, one senses considerable ambivalence embedded in those relationships also....

The facts of the case were unintentionally distorted by the staff to achieve consistency with a popular theory of the dynamics of a schizophrenic reaction. Nothing of an ambivalent nature had been described in relations with parents, spouse, or friends. To the extent that ambivalence could be inferred, it was probably not greater than is found in all human relationships. It is true the pseudopatient's relationships with his parents changed over time, but in the ordinary context that would hardly be remarkable—indeed, it might very well be expected. An entirely different meaning would have been ascribed if it were known that the man was "normal."

All pseudopatients took extensive notes publicly. How was their writing interpreted? Nursing records for three patients indicate that the writing was seen as an aspect of their pathological behavior. "Patient engages in writing behavior" was the daily nursing comment on one of the pseudopatients who was never questioned about his writing. Given that the patient is in the hospital, he must be psychologically disturbed. And given that he is disturbed, continuous writing must be a behavioral manifestation of that disturbance, perhaps a subset of the compulsive behaviors that are sometimes correlated with schizophrenia.

A psychiatric label has a life and an influence of its own. Once the impression has been formed that the patient is schizophrenic, the expectation is that he will continue to be schizophrenic. When a sufficient amount of time has passed, during which the patient has done nothing bizarre, he is considered to be in remission and available for discharge. But the label endures beyond discharge, with the unconfirmed expectation that he will behave as a schizophrenic again. Such labels, conferred by mental health professionals, are as influential on the patient as they are on his relatives and friends, and it should not surprise anyone that the diagnosis acts on all of them as a self-fulfilling prophecy. Eventually, the patient himself accepts the diagnosis, with all of its surplus meanings and expectations, and behaves accordingly.

DISCUSSION QUESTIONS

1. Cross-cultural differences exist in definitions of "normal" and "deviant" behavior. What behaviors are considered "normal" or "deviant" in your own culture? How did you learn to recognize these distinctions?

2. Similarly, there are cross-cultural differences in what is considered "sane" and "insane." How do we come to define *insanity* or *sanity* within a given cultural context? Do definitions of *sanity* or *insanity* change over time?

3. If Rosenhan were to conduct his study today, do you think there would be significant differences in the findings? If so, what differences would you expect and why? If not, why do you expect a similar outcome?

ADDITIONAL RESOURCES

Film

"One Flew Over the Cuckoo's Nest." 1975. This classic film stars Jack Nicholson as a psychiatric patient who challenges the rules and shakes things up after being admitted to a psychiatric ward.

Internet

http://www.law.Stanford.edu/directory/profile/52/David%20Rosenhan/. Rosenhan's profile at Stanford University, where he holds a joint emeritus appointment in the School of Law and Department of Psychology.

FURTHER READING

Becker, Howard S. 1963. *Outsiders: Studies in the Sociology of Deviance.* New York: Free Press.

Cockerham, William C. 2005. *Sociology of Mental Disorder,* 7th edition. Englewood Cliffs, NJ: Prentice Hall.

Goffman, Erving. 1959. "The Moral Career of the Mental Patient." *Psychiatry,* 22(2): 123–42.

Goffman, Erving. 1961. *Asylums.* Garden City, NY: Doubleday.

Rosenthal, Robert and Lenore Jacobson. 1968. "The Oak School Experiment," in *Pygmalion in the Classroom: Teacher Expectation and Pupils' Intellectual Development,* 61–71. New York: Holt, Rinehart and Winston.

Scheff, Thomas. 1966. *Being Mentally Ill: A Sociological Theory.* New York: Aldine Publishing.

Szasz, Thomas S. [1963] 1984. *Mental Illness: Foundations of a Theory of Personal Conduct.* New York: Harper Perennial.

Szasz, Thomas S. 1997. *The Manufacture of Madness: A Comparative Study of the Inquisition and Mental Health Movement.* Syracuse, NY: Syracuse University Press.

35. The Discovery of Hyperkinesis: Notes on the Medicalization of Deviant Behavior

PETER CONRAD

In 2004, Peter Conrad received the Leo G. Reeder Award from the American Sociological Association for his distinguished contributions to medical sociology. In this article, he explores how medicine acts as an agent of social control by diagnosing and treating hyperkinesis in children. Conrad shows how children's "deviant" behavior became defined as the concern of medical doctors, pharmacists, teachers, and politicians in the second half of the twentieth century.

INTRODUCTION

The increasing medicalization of deviant behavior and the medical institution's role as an agent of social control has gained considerable notice. By medicalization we mean defining behavior as a medical problem or illness and mandating or licensing the medical profession to provide some type of treatment for it. Examples include alcoholism, drug addiction and treating violence as a genetic or brain disorder. This redefinition is not a new function of the medical institution: psychiatry and public health have always been concerned with social behavior and have traditionally functioned as agents of social control.

This paper describes how certain forms of behavior in children have become defined as a medical problem and how medicine has become a major agent for their social control since the discovery of hyperkinesis. By discovery we mean both origin of the diagnosis and treatment for this disorder; and discovery of children who exhibit this behavior.

THE MEDICAL DIAGNOSIS OF HYPERKINESIS

Hyperkinesis is a relatively recent phenomenon as a medical diagnostic category. Only in the past two decades has it been available as a recognized diagnostic category and only in the last decade has it received widespread notice and medical popularity. However, the roots of the diagnosis and treatment of this clinical entity are found earlier.

Hyperkinesis is also known as minimal brain dysfunction, hyperactive syndrome, hyperkinetic disorder of childhood, and by several other diagnostic categories. Although the symptoms and the presumed etiology vary, in general the behaviors are quite similar and greatly overlap. Typical symptom patterns for diagnosing the disorder include: extreme excess of motor activity (hyperactivity); very short attention span (the child flits from activity to activity); restlessness; fidgetiness; often wildly oscillating mood swings (he's fine one day, a terror the next); clumsiness; aggressive-like behavior; impulsivity; in school he cannot sit still, cannot comply with rules, has low frustration level; frequently there may be sleeping problems and acquisition of speech may be delayed. Most of the symptoms for the disorder are deviant behaviors. It is six times as prevalent among boys as among girls. We use the term hyperkinesis to represent all the diagnostic categories of this disorder.

Conrad, Peter. 1975. "The Discovery of Hyperkinesis: Notes on the Medicalization of Deviant Behavior." *Social Problems,* 23(1): 12–21.

THE DISCOVERY OF HYPERKINESIS

It is useful to divide the analysis into what might be considered *clinical factors* directly related to the diagnosis and treatment of hyperkinesis and *social factors* that set the context for the emergence of the new diagnostic category.

Clinical Factors

In the middle 1950s a new drug, Ritalin, was synthesized, that has many qualities of amphetamines without some of their more undesirable side effects. In 1961 this drug was approved by the F.D.A. for use with children. Since this time there has been much research published on the use of Ritalin in the treatment of childhood behavior disorders. This medication became the "treatment of choice" for treating children with hyperkinesis.

Since the early sixties, more research appeared on the etiology, diagnosis and treatment of hyperkinesis. There had been increasing publicity of the disorder in the mass media as well. The *Reader's Guide to Periodical Literature* had no articles on hyperkinesis before 1967, one each in 1968 and 1969 and a total of forty for 1970 through 1974 (a mean of eight per year).

Now hyperkinesis has become the most common child psychiatric problem; special pediatric clinics have been established to treat hyperkinetic children, and substantial federal funds have been invested in etiological and treatment research. Outside the medical profession, teachers have developed a working clinical knowledge of hyperkinesis' symptoms and treatment; articles appear regularly in mass circulation magazines and newspapers so that parents often come to clinics with knowledge of this diagnosis. Hyperkinesis is no longer the relatively esoteric diagnostic category it may have been twenty years ago, it is now a well-known clinical disorder.

Social Factors

The social factors affecting the discovery of hyperkinesis can be divided into two areas: (1) The Pharmaceutical Revolution; (2) Government Action.

1. *The Pharmaceutical Revolution.* Since the 1930's the pharmaceutical industry has been synthesizing and manufacturing a large number of psychoactive drugs, contributing to a virtual revolution in drug making and drug taking in America.

Until the early sixties there was little or no promotion and advertisement of any of these medications for use with childhood disorders. Then two major pharmaceutical firms (Smith, Kline and French, manufacturer of Dexedrine and CIBA, manufacturer of Ritalin) began to advertise in medical journals and through direct mailing. Most of this advertising of the pharmaceutical treatment of hyperkinesis was directed to the medical sphere; but some of the promotion was targeted for the educational sector also. This promotion was probably significant in disseminating information concerning the diagnosis and treatment of this newly discovered disorder. The use of psychoactive medications for the treatment of persons who are mentally ill has undoubtedly increased the confidence in the medical profession for the pharmaceutical approach to mental and behavioral problems.

2. *Government Action.* There have been at least two significant governmental reports on treating school children with stimulant medications for behavior disorders.

The Congressional Subcommittee on Privacy chaired by Congressman Cornelius E. Gallagher held hearings on the issue of prescribing drugs for hyperactive school children. In general, the committee showed great concern over the facility in which the medication was prescribed; more specifically that some children at least were receiving drugs from general practitioners whose primary diagnosis was based on teachers' and parents' reports that the child was doing poorly in school. There was also a concern with the absence of follow-up studies on the long-term effects of treatment.

The Health Education and Welfare committee (HEW) was a rather hastily convened group of professionals (a majority were M.D.'s) many of whom already had commitments to drug treatment for children's behavior problems. They recommended that only M.D.'s make the diagnosis and prescribe treatment, that the pharmaceutical companies promote the treatment of the disorder only through medical channels, that parents should not be coerced to accept any particular treatment and that long-term follow-up research should be done. This report served as blue ribbon approval for treating hyperkinesis with psychoactive medications.

DISCUSSION

How does deviant behavior become conceptualized as a medical problem? We assume that before the discovery of hyperkinesis this type of deviance was seen as disruptive, disobedient, rebellious, anti-social or deviant behavior. Perhaps the label "emotionally disturbed" was sometimes used, when it was in vogue in the early sixties, and the child was usually managed in the context of the family or the school or in extreme cases, the child guidance clinic. How then did this constellation of deviant behaviors become a medical disorder?

Only in the late fifties were both the diagnostic label and the pharmaceutical treatment available. The pharmaceutical revolution in mental health and the increased interest in child psychiatry provided a favorable background for the dissemination of knowledge about this new disorder. The latter probably made the medical profession more likely to consider behavior problems in children as within their clinical jurisdiction.

There were agents outside the medical profession itself that were significant in "promoting" hyperkinesis as a disorder within the medical framework: the pharmaceutical companies and the Association for Children with Learning Disabilities.

The pharmaceutical companies spent considerable time and money promoting stimulant medications for this new disorder. From the middle 1960's on, medical journals and the free "throwaway" magazines contained elaborate advertising for Ritalin and Dexedrine. These ads explained the utility of treating hyperkinesis and urged the physician to diagnose and treat hyperkinetic children.

The pharmaceutical firms also supplied sophisticated packets of "diagnostic and treatment" information on hyperkinesis to physicians, paid for professional conferences on the subject, and supported research in the identification and treatment of the disorder. Clearly these corporations had a vested interest in the labeling and treatment of hyperkinesis.

The medical model of hyperactive behavior has become very well accepted in our society. Physicians find treatment relatively simple and the results sometimes spectacular. Hyperkinesis minimizes parents' guilt by emphasizing "it's not their fault, it's an organic problem" and allows for nonpunitive management or control of deviance. Medication often makes a child less disruptive in the classroom and sometimes aids a child in learning. Children often like their "magic pills" which make their behavior more socially acceptable and they probably benefit from a reduced stigma also. There are, however, some other, perhaps more subtle ramifications of the medicalization of deviant behavior.

THE MEDICALIZATION OF DEVIANT BEHAVIOR

Medicalization of mental illness dates at least from the seventeenth century. In recent years alcoholism, violence, and drug addiction as well as hyperactive behavior in children have all become defined as medical problems, both in etiology or explanation of the behavior and the means of social control or treatment.

There are many reasons why this medicalization has occurred. Much scientific research, especially in pharmacology and genetics, has become technologically more sophisticated, and found more subtle correlates with human behavior.

Alcoholism is no longer sin or even moral weakness, it is now a disease. Alcoholics are no longer arrested in many places for "public drunkenness," they are now somehow "treated," even if it is only to be dried out. Hyperactive children are now considered to have an illness rather than to be disruptive, disobedient, overactive problem children. They are not as likely to be the "bad boy" of the classroom; they are children with a medical disorder. Clearly there are some real humanitarian benefits to be gained by such a medical conceptualization of deviant behavior. There is less condemnation of the deviants (they have an illness, it is not their fault) and perhaps less social stigma. In some cases, even the medical treatment itself is more humanitarian social control than the criminal justice system.

There is, however, another side to the medicalization of deviant behavior. The four aspects of this side of the issue include (1) the problem of expert control; (2) medical social control; (3) the individualization of social problems; and (4) the "depoliticization" of deviant behavior.

1. *The problem of expert control.* The medical profession is a profession of experts; they have a monopoly on anything that can be conceptualized as illness.

    By defining a problem as medical it is removed from the public realm where there can be discussion by ordinary people and put on a plane where only medical people can discuss it.

2. *Medical social control.* Defining deviant behavior as a medical problem allows certain things to be done that could not otherwise be considered; for example, the body may be cut open or psychoactive medications may be given. This treatment can be a form of social control.

    These forms of medical social control presume a prior definition of deviance as a medical problem. Psychosurgery on an individual prone to violent outbursts requires a diagnosis that there was something wrong with his brain or nervous system. Similarly, prescribing drugs to restless, overactive and disruptive school children requires a diagnosis of hyperkinesis. These relatively new and increasingly popular forms of social control could not be utilized without the medicalization of deviant behavior.

3. *The individualization of social problems.* The medicalization of deviant behavior is part of a larger phenomenon that is prevalent in our society, the individualization of social problems. We tend to look for causes and solutions to complex social problems in the individual rather than in the social system. Rather than seeing certain deviant behaviors as symptomatic of problems in the social system, the medical perspective focuses on the individual diagnosing and treating the illness, generally ignoring the social situation.

    Hyperkinesis serves as a good example. Both the school and the parents are concerned with the child's behavior; the child is very difficult at home and disruptive in school. No punishments or rewards seem consistently to work in modifying the behavior; and both parents and school are at their wits' end. A medical evaluation is suggested. The diagnoses of hyperkinetic behavior lead to prescribing stimulant medications. The child's behavior seems to become more socially acceptable, reducing problems in school and at home.

    But there is an alternate perspective. By focusing on the symptoms and defining them as hyperkinesis we ignore the possibility that behavior is not an illness but an adaptation to a social situation. It diverts our attention from the family or school and from seriously entertaining the idea that the "problem" could be in the structure of the social system. And by giving medications we are essentially supporting the existing systems and do not allow this behavior to be a factor of change in the system.

4. *The depoliticization of deviant behavior.* Depoliticization of deviant behavior is a result of both the process of medicalization and individualization of social problems.

By defining the overactive, restless and disruptive child as hyperkinetic we ignore the meaning of behavior in the context of the social system. If we focused our analysis on the school system we might see the child's behavior as symptomatic of some "disorder" in the school or classroom situation, rather than symptomatic of an individual neurological disorder.

DISCUSSION QUESTIONS

1. "Hyperkinesis" is a synonym for which common contemporary "disorder" in children? Do you personally know someone who has a diagnosis of hyperkinesis?

2. Conrad argues that diagnosing children with hyperkinesis individualizes a social problem while ignoring larger social issues that might cause the behaviors that we label as "hyperkinetic." What social conditions might lead to hyperactive behavior in children? Might altering these social conditions lead to a decrease in the diagnosis of hyperkinesis? Why or why not?

3. Conrad and other medical sociologists argue that the social control of deviance has shifted over time from the purview of religion, to law, and, finally, to medicine (Conrad and Schneider, 1992). Provide one or two examples of deviant behaviors that were previously considered a sin or a crime but are now characterized as an illness.

ADDITIONAL RESOURCES

Film

"The Merrow Report: Attention Deficit Disorder: A Dubious Diagnosis?" 1995. A 60-minute documentary by John Merrow, broadcast on PBS. http://www.pbs.org/merrow/guides/addvg.html.

Internet

http://www.add.org/. The Attention Deficit Disorder Association focuses on attention deficit disorder (ADD) and attention deficit/hyperactivity disorder (ADHD) in adults.

http://borntoexplore.org/. Born to Explore contends that diagnoses of ADD are rarely valid and that there are several environmental sources that may lead to behaviors associated with ADD.

http://www.brandeis.edu/departments/sociology/conrad.html. Conrad's profile at Brandeis University, where he holds an appointment in the Department of Sociology.

http://www.nimh.nih.gov/health/topics/attention-deficit-hyperactivity-disorder-adhd/index.shtml. The website of the National Institute of Mental Health, featuring ADHD.

Radio

http://www.npr.org/templates/story/story.php?storyId=102118230. "Talk of the Nation," March 19, 2009. Host Neal Conan interviews actors Cynthia Nixon and Josh Stamberg about their ADHD off-Broadway comedy called "Distracted." Seventeen minutes.

FURTHER READING

Conrad, Peter. 2005. "The Shifting Engines of Medicalization." *Journal of Health and Social Behavior,* 46(March): 3–14.

Conrad, Peter. 2007. *The Medicalization of Society: On the Transformation of Human Conditions into Treatable Disorders.* Baltimore, MD: Johns Hopkins University Press.

Conrad, Peter and Joseph W. Schneider. [1980] 1992. *Deviance and Medicalization: From Badness to Sickness.* Philadelphia, PA: Temple University Press.

Szasz, Thomas S. 1971. "The Sane Slave: An Historical Note on the Use of Medical Diagnosis as Justificatory Rhetoric." *American Journal of Psychotherapy,* 25: 228–39.

Zola, Irving. 1972. "Medicine as an Institution of Social Control." *Sociological Review,* 20(November): 487–504.

see pg 251

36. Coming Out and Crossing Over: Identity Formation and Proclamation in a Transgender Community

PATRICIA GAGNÉ, RICHARD TEWKSBURY, AND DEANNA McGAUGHEY

In their study of 65 male-to-female transsexuals, Gagné and her colleagues explore the continued expansion of medical social control over behavior and identity into the twenty-first century. Transsexuality, considered an "ultimate" form of deviance by some, challenges the very foundations of social stability and selfhood that rest on gender differentiation.

In this article, we examine the coming-out experiences of a nonrandom sample of individuals who were members of the transgender community at the time we solicited volunteers for our project. Persons who enact alternative gender presentations or who have internalized alternative gender identities are referred to as "transgenderists."

Although barriers to self-awareness and acceptance are declining, transgenderists continue to grapple with many of the issues that confronted sexual minorities in the United States prior to the 1970s. For example, within the transgender community, the declassification of transsexualism as a psychiatric diagnosis has been hotly debated, with those seeking to challenge medical definitions arguing that it should be removed from the *Diagnostic and Statistical Manual of Mental Disorders* (DSM-IV) and those still seeking access to hormones and sex reassignment surgery (SRS) arguing that being diagnosed transsexual is the only way they may become the women they truly are. In other words, they must "confess" their transsexualism in ways that adhere to medical models in order to proceed from one sex to the other. Rather than choosing to live as feminine males, they opt to cross over to full-time womanhood. They deem feminine behavior in masculine attire to be highly inappropriate.

Gagné, Patricia, Richard Tewksbury, and Deanna McGaughey. 1997. "Coming out and Crossing over: Identity Formation and Proclamation in a Transgender Community." *Gender & Society,* 11(4): 478–508.

METHOD

We completed 65 semistructured, in-depth, tape-recorded interviews with masculine-to-feminine individuals from several points along the transgender spectrum. All volunteers in our sample were members of the transgender communities through which we recruited volunteers for our study.

Our research was conducted over a one-year period, spanning 1994 and 1995. Early in the research process, we made a conscious decision to include all masculine-to-feminine transgenderists who volunteered.

We solicited volunteers through 14 transgender support groups, transgender online services, and by responding to personal ads in a national transgender publication. People in every region of the contiguous 48 states volunteered for interviews, making our research national in scope. Participants resided in large urban areas, small towns, suburbs, and rural areas. Our sample includes 4 African Americans, 2 Asians, 1 Hispanic, and 58 Whites. Participants ranged in age from 24 to 68 years, with a mean age of 44. Occupationally, they were diverse with jobs ranging from doctors, airline pilots, computer systems analysts, engineers, college professors, school teachers, enlisted members of the military, police officers, welders, mechanics, food service and clerical workers, and janitors. Although our sample was occupationally diverse, the majority was well educated and had long employment histories in the skilled trades and professions. Most members of our sample were either employed or voluntarily unemployed (i.e., retired or student) at the time we talked with them. Nonetheless, one postoperative and eight preoperative transsexuals were unemployed, and the majority of those who lived full-time as the gender into which they were not assigned at birth were vastly underemployed.

To provide the greatest reliability among interviews, all but one were conducted by the first author. Where distance precluded a face-to-face meeting, interviews were conducted over the telephone. They were organized such that, after background information on age, education, occupational history, and family was gathered, respondents were encouraged to tell their life stories as they pertained to their transgendered feelings and experiences. Respondents were guided through several areas of inquiry, including their earliest transgender experiences or feelings; being discovered cross-dressed; acquiring girls' or women's clothing, makeup, and wigs; learning about and refining a feminine appearance or persona; participating in transgender support groups or on-line communities; finding therapists and surgeons and experiences with the medical community; identifying and labeling emotions, feelings, behaviors, and identity; telling others; transformations or stability in sexual fantasy, behavior, and identity; and political and gender attitudes. Interviews ranged from 45 minutes to 8 hours in length, averaging about three hours.

FINDINGS

Early Transgendered Experiences

In early childhood, cross-dressing and cross-gender behavior appear to have been tolerated. However, as children advanced beyond the "toddler" stage, they were pressured by adults and other children to recognize and adhere to traditional conceptualizations of gender and conform to masculine stereotypes. Pressures to conform to the gender binary were often based on homophobic assumptions about gender "deviants." For example, a nonoperative transsexual said,

> Around the time I was 9 or 10 years old, there was one boy in the neighborhood...[who] was never allowed to spend the night at my house...All he would tell me is, "My dad won't let me." One afternoon I approached his dad about it.... This man turned an incredible red-purple color and shaking and pointing a finger in my face [said], "Because you're a fucking queer!" I didn't know what those words meant, but it was real clear from his body language that whatever those words were tied to was not OK.

The pressure to adhere to the masculine stereotype was strong, and many in our sample tried to conform.

After an initial period of confusion about sex and gender, most children recognized that cross-dressing and feminine behavior were deviant and, therefore, they tried to repress it and keep it secret. This suggests that as children begin to understand the binary gender system, they become ashamed of feminine or transgendered feelings, learn to hide their behaviors, and become confused about who they are and how they fit into the world. Many in our sample talked about becoming addicted to alcohol or drugs later in life, in an effort to numb the emotional pain they experienced and to repress the "true self," which did not fit and, therefore, needed to be repressed. Throughout adolescence and adulthood, most went through periods of "purging," when they would stop engaging in transgendered behavior and throw out feminine clothing, makeup, and wigs. Despite the stigma attached to transgenderism, however, the need to "be themselves" was strong. Even as they tried to stop, and as their feminine attributes were criticized and sanctioned, they found it impossible to stop and learned to become more and more secretive. For example, a preoperative transsexual explained,

> I was being beat up, called sissy....I didn't feel normal. I felt like, "Why are you doing this? This isn't right. You're a boy." But I couldn't stop. The curiosity kept drawing me to it and I kept doing it. I felt guilty and I always thought after I...took the clothes off, "I'm not going to do this anymore. This is silly." A few days later...I was back doing it again.

Coming Out to One's Self

For many transgendered individuals, coming to terms with identity is driven by three factors: (1) events that inform them that to feel as they do is "wrong" (discussed above), (2) finding that there are names for their feelings, and (3) learning that there are others who have had similar experiences.

When individuals fail to adhere to the gender binary, they are often told they are wrong or bad, so they tend to initially think of themselves as sick or deviant. Until they find similar others who have rejected stigma, self-blame and the internalization of deviance are common. As the transgenderists in our sample became aware that there were others in the world like them, they experienced a sense of self-recognition, and most quickly aligned themselves with new potential identities. The refinement and adoption of relatively stable identities occurred within the possibilities offered by the transgender subculture, which has been heavily influenced by medical models of transgenderism.

Most transsexuals and a minority of the cross-dressers in our sample reported being labeled "sissies" by parents, siblings, and school mates. The difference in experiences may be due to the fact that transsexuals reported an overwhelming urge to be feminine at all times, whereas cross-dressers could more easily segment the feminine self away from public scrutiny. Those labeled "sissy" or "girl-like" experienced extreme stigmatization, isolation, and at times abuse. Derogative comments from family members seemed to affect the self-esteem and self-concept more than insults from peers or other nonrelatives. One nonoperative transsexual married to a woman recounted how her parents and friends pressured her to be more masculine. She said,

> The kids in the neighborhood that I wanted to be friends with...were the girls....I wanted my own doll and remember the boys in the neighborhood seemed to have a real problem with that....In that same time period, my dad came into my bedroom one night and he took all the dolls out of my bed. He said I could keep the animals but the dolls had to go because, "You're a little boy and little boys don't sleep with dolls."

Even with such social sanctions, the feelings persisted. Their struggles with identity and relationships arose from society's sanctions.

Throughout childhood, adolescence, and early to mid adulthood most transgenderists in our study experienced shame and confusion for not being "right." Role models who challenged binary conceptualizations of gender were largely unavailable.

Finding others who felt as they did helped to alleviate, but not remove, the sense of isolation experienced by transgendered individuals. Nonetheless, through such initial exposures, many individuals learned that there were alternatives to living in confusion and shame, if one was willing to transform (either temporarily or permanently) to the other gender. Simply learning that SRS was possible led some to reconfigure their identities and reassess their place in the world. While available role models and medical procedures may not dictate identity changes, they do provide alternatives that contribute to identity clarification.

Finally, in today's information age, on-line computer services appear to be emerging as a primary location for finding both virtual and real mentors. It was common for transgenderists who deciphered and accepted their identities in the 1990s to have done so with the assistance of on-line bulletin boards and personal conversations with already-identifying transgenderists. Here, in the privacy of one's home or work area, contacts could be made that allowed both experimentation with identities and informational inquiries that did not jeopardize existing identities or social, occupational, and familial relationships.

Coming Out to Others

Simply discovering (quasi-)similar others is not all that is needed for the transgendered individual to complete the coming-out process. Rather, finding a symbolic role model provides initial validation of a newly emergent identity and potential avenues to find further sources of external validation. The sources of validation that are most important for the stabilization of identity are the significant others in one's life and the community of similar others.

Accepting an identity for one's self was one thing; proclaiming and working to get others to accept it was quite different. Going public with a transgendered identity could be an intimidating experience, to say the least. For a minority, finding a community of similar others gave individual cross-dressers the support they needed to explore their identity as transgendered individuals and to later inform spouses or other significant others.

According to the accounts of those who have proclaimed their transgender identities to significant others, the fears about negative reactions were largely exaggerated, but not altogether unwarranted. Less than one-fourth of all persons interviewed for this project reported that their first experience of coming out to someone else lead to a negative reaction. This was related to several factors. First, transgenderists had exaggerated fears about the reactions of most significant others. Second, most individuals were actually successful at controlling knowledge of their transgenderism. They consciously selected individuals to come out to who were, in fact, sympathetic to the alternative identity. Those who received negative reactions to their proclamations were least likely to have gathered information or to have laid the necessary groundwork. Instead, they simply announced the new identity.

The arena where transsexuals were least likely to receive positive reactions was at work. Although there were a few people who were permitted to transition on the job, it was more common for transsexuals to be fired, demoted, pressured to quit, and harassed by other workers. Frequently, the loss of professional identity and income came at the same time that relationships with old friends and family members were being risked and sometimes lost.

Resolution of Identity

Within the transgender community, a desire to pass and blend into society sometimes introduced tensions and additional levels of hierarchy and structure. Those who sought to pass, and believed they had the ability to do so, sometimes believed that varying statuses of achievement (passing ability) were important. Some passable transgenderists, therefore, viewed those who could not pass as liabilities. Being seen with a detectable transgenderist was believed to bring suspicion and possible detection to those who would otherwise pass. Once again, a transsexual showed her aptitude for clear expression when she explained her withdrawal from a local support group because, "I didn't feel the group gave me anything. I was too far ahead of them.... We're still friends, but I won't walk down the street with them."

For both those who were not seeking to pass when in public, the most common, overwhelming desire was to simply be accepted. To "blend in" to society as a woman was something most transgenderists, especially transsexuals, saw as an ultimate goal. The ultimate resolution was an identity that was not wrapped in the language of transgenderism. To be known as simply just another person was desirable.

Despite one's own aspirations for individual identity and ability to blend socially, there was a sense of community among the vast majority of transgenderists that facilitated a desire to work with others and to contribute to the developmental processes of other community members. Helping others transform appears to be an important

final "step" in the transformation process. Once a stable identity as "woman" has been established, many leave the community.

CONCLUSION

Individuals who attempt to challenge the binary conceptualization of sex and gender, by living androgynously between genders, are likely to be ridiculed and stigmatized.

As we have shown, the recognition, exploration, establishment, and final resolution of an identity outside cultural understandings is a difficult, complex, and for some, impossible process. Despite the policing of gender that was experienced by the transgenderists in our sample, the need to express a "true self" was an overwhelming urge that could not be denied. Although many tried to hide their femininity through hypermasculine activity or self-isolation, and most tried to deny transgendered feelings and urges, all eventually found the urge to "be themselves" overwhelmingly undeniable. Only when they discovered that there were others like them were they able to begin to make sense of what they were experiencing and who they were. Entering into a community of supportive others allowed for an exploration and resolution of identity.

DISCUSSION QUESTIONS

1. Gender is often considered the "great divide" with a vast ocean of difference separating girls from boys and women from men in a way that seems "natural." In what ways do the social institutions of religion, government, and medicine serve to uphold this division of gender?

2. Gagné et al. identify how the medicalization of transsexuality alleviates stigma and yet presents barriers to accessing resources for sex reassignment. What did you learn about the medical treatment and diagnosis of transsexuality by reading the article? What part does medicine play, if any, in the "coming out" experience of transsexuals?

3. How might transsexuality be responded to differently if the responsibility for addressing this form of "deviance" was assigned to a different social institution, such as religion or government?

ADDITIONAL RESOURCES

Film

"Transamerica." 2005. A stunning feature-length film starring Felicity Huffman as a preoperative male-to-female transsexual who discovers that she is the father of a teenage son.

Internet

http://www.ifge.org/. The International Foundation for Gender Education advocates for freedom of gender expression for all people. They publish a quarterly magazine called *Transgender Tapestry*. http://www.ifge.org/tgmag/tgmagtop.htm.

http://www.transgenderlaw.org/. The Transgender Law and Policy Institute, a nonprofit organization that advocates for transgender dignity and civil rights.

http://www.wpath.org/. The World Professional Association for Transgender Health, Inc. (formerly known as the Harry Benjamin International Gender Dysphoria Association). This organization serves as the primary governing body over sex reassignment surgery, publishing the internationally recognized Standards of Care for Gender Identity Disorders, as well as overseeing the criteria for gender identity disorder diagnosis in the *Diagnostic and Statistical Manual* of the American Psychiatric Association.

http://wpath.org/Documents2/socv6.pdf. *The Standards of Care for Gender Identity Disorders*, sixth version (2001), published by the World Professional Association for Transgender Health, formerly known as the Harry Benjamin International Gender Dysphoria Association.

FURTHER READING

Adams, Mary Louise. 2005. "'Death to the Prancing Prince': Effeminacy, Sport Discourses and the Salvation of Men's Dancing." *Body & Society*, 11(4): 63–86.

Gagné, Patricia and Richard Tewksbury. 1998. "Conformity Pressures and Gender Resistance among Transgendered Individuals." *Social Problems*, 45(1): 81–101.

Gagné, Patricia and Richard Tewksbury. 1999. "Knowledge and Power, Body and Self: An Analysis of Knowledge Systems and the Transgendered Self." *The Sociological Quarterly*, 40(1): 59–83.

Gagné, Patricia and Richard Tewksbury (eds.). 2002. *Advances in Gender Research: Gendered Sexualities* (Volume 6). Stamford, CT: JAI Press.

Maguen, Shira, Julian C. Shipherd, Holly N. Harris, and Lisa P. Welch. 2007. "Prevalence and Predictors of Disclosure of Transgender Identity." *International Journal of Sexual Health*, 19(1): 3–13.

Mason-Schrock, Doug. 1996. "Transsexuals' Narrative Construction of the 'True Self.'" *Social Psychology Quarterly*, 59(3): 176–92.

Tewksbury, Richard and Patricia Gagné (eds.). 2007. *Deviance and Deviants: An Anthology*. New York: Oxford University Press.

Stigma

Classic

Contemporary

The following articles draw on interviews with members of stigmatized groups: women who abort a pregnancy, wheelchair users, and persons with AIDS. While there are clear similarities across various forms of stigma, those who have a visible difference, such as wheelchair users, experience their discrediting attribute whenever they are out in public. In cases of "invisible" stigma, such as women who abort a pregnancy or individuals who are HIV positive or who have AIDS, concealing their difference is possible in many circumstances.

In attempting to manage their own and others' emotional responses to their "deviance," people who are stigmatized engage in an array of strategies to reclaim identities that are sullied by their disreputable characteristic.

In his research on people living with AIDS, Sandstrom examines the pressure to maintain the secrecy of an invisible stigma. He also describes behavioral strategies to diminish the evidence of difference. Similarly, Zimmerman conveys the complex means through which women come to terms with their choice to have an abortion.

As Cahill and Eggleston point out, using a wheelchair in public elicits a different set of complications: interacting with "helpful walkers," who are often unsure how to socialize with people who have a visible disability.

"the man involved in the pregnancy" - Not father of the baby [handwritten annotation]

37. Passage Through Abortion: The Personal and Social Reality of Women's Experiences

MARY K. ZIMMERMAN

Zimmerman documents the long-term experiences of forty women who have an abortion, from the point they decide to have the procedure to how their identities and relationships are affected long after their pregnancy is aborted.

INTRODUCTION

We are interested in the ways the women interpreted their abortions as well as in the significance these interpretations held for their immediate social worlds and for the continuing social patterns of their lives.

ARRANGING THE ABORTION

Once the abortion decision was made, the women scheduled their abortions almost immediately. The abortions of most of the women studied (35 of 40) were performed at one of the two freestanding, specialized clinics in a neighboring city.

The clinic alternative was selected primarily because an abortion there cost approximately $400 less than the same procedure in the hospital. The women whose pregnancies had advanced beyond 13 weeks were forced to use Clinic A since none of the other facilities would perform an abortion on a woman more than 12 weeks

pregnant. In addition to cost and the length of the pregnancy, some women mentioned other social and medical concerns which influenced them in their choice of facility.

One such concern was for privacy. A few of the women mentioned the "social protection" they gained by having their abortion in an out-of-town clinic:

[The social workers at Midville Clinic] has told me I could have it here and have Doctor Doe do it, but I decided to go to the city instead. I thought that maybe—Doctor Doe is a very good friend of [my fiancé's] family, you know, and I didn't really—it wasn't that I was scared he would tell, but I didn't want to put myself in that position...they see him socially and we have seen him a couple of times. We have gone out to dinner with [my fiancé's] family, and the doctor and his family would have been there, too, and I just felt like that would be an uncomfortable position and so I just decided to go to the city.

Zimmerman, Mary K. 1977. Abridged from "Having the Abortion" and "Moving On: Restructuring Social Worlds and Establishing Closure," in *Passage through Abortion: The Personal and Social Reality of Women's Experiences*. New York: Praeger.

Coming to the clinic here [Midville] I thought, "Oh, I just hope there is nobody that knows my mother," you know, here that would tell her. And then I thought, if I had to go to Midville Hospital or something, I know there is someone somewhere that is going to know and is going to tell. And so, when I did get to go to the city, I was relieved by the fact that there is probably no one down there that would know me.

INITIAL PERCEPTIONS OF THE ABORTION FACILITY

The women who went to the local hospital took for granted that it was an appropriate medical setting for their abortions. They had no problem in establishing its legitimacy. That was not the case for the women who went to the freestanding clinics. While they had not questioned the clinic's appropriateness at the time of making the appointment, on the day of the abortion questions commonly arose. The two freestanding clinics were very different in terms of location, physical structure of the building, and inside atmosphere. These differenced appeared to influence the women to view one clinic more suspiciously than the other.

The stigma associated with abortion was illuminated when the women were confronted with having to define and interpret the clinic setting. The clinics were unfamiliar and, for many of the women, unexpected in appearance and atmosphere. Over half the women going to the freestanding clinics (19 of 35) initially perceived them in terms of illegitimacy and the deviant imagery of the abortion stereotype. Specifically, these women described the clinics in terms of two central themes: the impersonal, mass-production image associated with an "abortion mill," and the haphazard, unsanitary medical image associated with a quack abortionist.

The majority of women who perceived the abortion facility as an illegitimate or otherwise inappropriate place were clients of Clinic A rather than Clinic B.

Perceptions of Clinic A

The descriptions of Clinic A patients often began with a description similar to this one:

The one I went to is right down there in the middle of nowhere, down in the boonies. (Could you describe the building?) It was a big, old brown brick building setting down in among a bunch of trees right at the end of a street. It didn't even look anything like a hospital. It was just stuck down there.

The meaning or interpretation underlying this description became clear when this woman was asked how she had reacted to this particular clinic setting. She said, "I thought, 'Oh, my God!'" Her exclamation is further clarified by the comments of several other clients of Clinic A:

We was looking for this big hospital...when we saw it we almost fainted...I said, "Wow, that looks like my junior high." It was just a little brick building and I thought, "Gosh." (What was going through your mind?) I was scared. "How could they do this to us? Send us to such a little place."...and then, on the way there, it was on a dirt road and...the houses around there were kind of poverty like, you know. I don't know, I expected a big, white hospital with all these guys walking around in white suits, white overcoats, and all.

It was such an old dilapidated building to me. I was expecting like Midville Hospital or something like that and it was just very different and I was scared. Maybe I would go in there and there would be cockroaches running around or something...maybe I wasn't going to have the kind of care that I had thought I was going to have...that's like the impression my mother had always made on me. It kind of made me think, "Well, abortions are something you just don't talk about, so maybe that's why they are sending me back here to this old, dilapidated building. Maybe just to keep hush-hush," you know, and that sort of thing.

The wide discrepancy between these women's expectations and the actual appearance of the clinic not only led them to question the medical care they would receive but it also encouraged them to think in images of crime. The following comments, for example, include the words "prison" and "jail":

(Can you remember how you reacted to the drive up there and seeing the clinic for the first time?) The drive didn't bother me but the clinic looked like a jail or something to me. It kind of scared me because it looked so—I don't know—looked so icky really...You see on all these movies about how they did it in strange ways with knives and stuff, and that's what it made me think of...something the law didn't know about—against the law. They did it unlawfully, you know, and you could get disease in about three seconds. That's what it reminded me of...I don't know how to explain it—it just looked like not the right thing to do.

To me it looked like a prison. It had bars on the windows and I didn't like it at all. I thought, "Boy, that's really a great place to go."...I was thinking, "I wonder what kind of medical facilities they've got," you know. "Is it such a grubby place that all it is is a doctor who isn't even qualified?" And I was thinking, "It looks like a prison."...it was all bricked up. It just looked terrible to me. Here I am used to Midville Hospital, a nice, clean hospital...and there it was run-down in one of the run-down sections of town....

Clinic A was located in a predominantly black neighborhood. This aspect of the setting added further to many of the women's anxieties. It became even more salient to their illegitimate definition of the clinic as they entered and observed black staff members:

I tell you, when we came, all we could see outside, playing ball, everywhere, on the first floor, was just colored people...It kind of scared me to think, "I'm going to go in this hospital and there's going to be all these colored people."...

(What happened when you went in?) I almost cried. I mean, I've always been raised in small towns where there are no black people, and I

walked in and all there were there black people. And I thought—you think when you see black people—to me, I saw the black people as meaning that they're doing it unlawfully. "It's going to be a black doctor." That's the first thing that I thought—that this doctor is going to be a black doctor. I kept thinking about that....

I thought it was some quack's place—a bunch of quacks in there...Then I got in there and all I saw was colored on the first floor, and oh, boy.

In summary, two-thirds (16 of 24) of the women having their abortions scheduled for Clinic A initially questioned the clinic's legitimacy. They quickly associated the small size and old age of the clinic building and the low-income, black neighborhood surrounding it with the abortion stereotype left over from the illegal period—the notion of an abortion mill run by unqualified personnel under medically dangerous conditions. These perceptions provided an extreme contrast to the women's original expectations of a large, modern hospital, similar to the one in Midville.

The women reported that their initial interpretation of their abortion facility left them extremely apprehensive. Nevertheless, they stayed. None of the women left until the abortion had been performed. One way that they have tried to justify an otherwise apparently deviant situation was to consider the fact that they had been referred by a legitimate, professional health clinic, a clinic they trusted. The comments of one woman reflect the usefulness of this notion in coping with her fear:

I had to sit there and convince myself that I knew [that] the [social worker]—maybe not her, but that the public health department clinic was not going to send me or anybody else to a place that wasn't medically capable and OK and everything....I just sat there and kept saying..."I just don't believe they would do that." So I felt better.

Perceptions of Clinic B
Enthusiasm was absent from even the most favorable of the initial reactions to Clinic A. First

perceptions of that clinic were most frequently negative, neutral at best. Perceptions of Clinic B, on the other hand, were generally more positive. A particularly favorable comment from one Clinic B woman illustrates this point:

> It was just great. I can't say enough good things about it…and, you know, the building is just a beautiful, normal building. It could be anywhere…. The whole setting was really nice…It was almost to the point of being plush….

The favorable reaction to Clinic B becomes clearer when directly compared to the reaction to Clinic A. While only 8 of the 24 women going to Clinic A (33%) initially perceived it as a legitimate medical facility, 8 of the 11 women going to Clinic B (73%) did so. Even among those who questioned the legitimacy of Clinic B, the degree to which they considered the clinic problematic was much less than among those who questioned the legitimacy of Clinic A:

> (Was there anything about the clinic [B] that was different than you expected?) Well, the building wasn't as bad. The counselor [at Midville Clinic] said it was in the basement of the building and that sounded to me really—well, I didn't want some place raunchy…. And then, when we saw it, it didn't look like a medical building. (How was your husband reacting to the building?) He was very suspicious. He said if it was too bad, we'd leave. But when we went inside it was OK.

> …the outside of the place was like a motel or an apartment and [my boyfriend] goes, "I don't think we should go in there. I don't want you hurt." And I said, "No, let's just go on down," and it was just like an office building. I mean, I thought I was in a doctor's office….

Both these women's adverse interpretations were immediately altered and the deviant image normalized as soon as they entered the clinic. This was not the case for women entering Clinic A.

Entering the Clinic

Entering the clinic provided the women with new observations which either confirmed or refuted their first interpretations of the clinic. Most of the women going to Clinic B had already perceived the clinic as legitimate; seeing the inside simply confirmed this interpretation. The few who had suspicions about Clinic B quickly altered their view upon entering and seeing the interior and the staff. Although the legitimacy of Clinic B was quickly established, the legitimacy of Clinic A was more difficult for the women to ascertain. As we have pointed out, many of those initially interpreting Clinic A as illegitimate apparently had their perceptions validated when they entered the clinic on the first floor. Several of these women, however, altered their view when they went upstairs and began preparations for the abortion:

> …when I got to walking around the place and finding out that everything was all right, then I knew it *would* be all right. When they started doing actual tests on me and stuff, then I knew everything was all right.

Racial stereotyping was again the basis for changing interpretations in some of these cases:

> The first floor scared me…because everybody I saw was colored. Everybody! I didn't see one white person except the girls that were waiting to go, too. And then I got upstairs and I was so relieved. I just felt so much better…I got upstairs and I saw some white people and it was real clean and real bright and cheerful and it really helped. It made me feel a lot better.

> …it didn't bother me anymore after I got upstairs. I saw a bunch of white nurses and I was so happy to see them—it didn't bother me that much after I got upstairs….

Although some women altered their interpretation of Clinic A and defined it as legitimate upon beginning their abortion procedure, others did not. For them, their initial perceptions were confirmed.

Rather than the "normal" functioning of the clinic being an affirmation of legitimacy, for these women it evoked the image of the abortion mill:

> That's all they did there. It was like a slaughter house.

> ...I felt like I was being pushed through, you know, "Next please, next please, next please," because they asked you all these questions....I felt like I was a cow getting ready to get butchered; I really did.

One reason for this imagery was the fact that Clinic A, like many much larger hospitals, had the various routes the women were supposed to take mapped out along the hallways with a series of colored lines. While this practice is common, it is interesting to see how the women interpreted it in the context of an already problematic situation:

> ...they had all of these little arrows on the floor pointing which way to go...and it made me think like they do this every day, you know, and there were hundreds of girls...I didn't like the arrows on the floor. It made it seem like they were packing us all in and standing in line and getting it done and then walking out.

> After you go in the admissions office, they say follow the green line upstairs and around; and then after you pay the rest of your money, they say follow the red line around. You are just following a bunch of lines....It was kind of like an assembly line.

THE ABORTION PROCEDURE: PATIENTS' PERSPECTIVES

On the whole the women viewed the abortion procedures as "easier" than they had originally thought. For the most part, this view was a result of the simplicity of the vacuum aspiration technique:

> ...it was a lot easier than I thought it was going to be...It was easier, a lot easier. I was, you know, imagining all sorts of wild things—I thought it would take a half hour or an hour and they would have to put you out and you would be in intensive care for a couple of hours...It was so easy and I was glad.

> The operation itself was easier than I expected...because, you know, I had psyched myself up to where I thought it was going to be a major operation. They were going to cut me open and everything, but it just seemed a lot easier.

> It went a lot better, I think, than I had really thought—heard—maybe expected it to go. I had expected a lot of pain. Even though the social worker here had told me, "It's not painful," I had really expected a lot.

The entire abortion procedure took from five to six hours in the clinic setting and an hour or two longer for those in the hospital. Most of this time, however, was devoted to preparation and recovery. The vacuum aspiration technique itself (the same at all facilities) was done within a few minutes. As an example, the woman who had her abortion in a doctor's office reported that she was there only for an hour or so—quite a contrast to the length of time required at the other locations.

Observing Other Patients

Almost all of the women who had clinic abortions had some observations to make about the other women there. The most common observation concerned the number of patients at the clinic:

> I don't think I really expected to see that many women there in the same situation as I was....

> I didn't expect that many girls to be there. I really didn't. I thought I would go in and a doctor would meet me and take me up and I would have it done and then—you know, I just thought it was me and I was the only one; and it turned out that there was a lot more girls there than I expected....

When asked how they reacted to the other women, responses were varied. Several women said that the other patients made them realize that they were not alone:

> ...it made me feel a lot better because I knew I wasn't so unusual—I kind of felt like a criminal, you know, going in and having it done.

I couldn't imagine that there were going to be that many girls that were going to be there.... (How did that make you feel when you saw all those girls?) I wasn't alone. I didn't feel alone anymore.

Some women expected more blacks to be there than were there. Others commented on the fact that the presence of "older" and married women surprised them; one of these women was herself "older" and married. One of the women who expected to see more blacks was herself black. Of the other patients, another woman said:

> I was surprised. Most of them looked like decent people....I don't know...maybe something I had already preconceived in my mind...it was going to be a little stranger....

This tendency to view fellow patients as morally inferior was consistent with many of the women's preabortion attitudes. They reported having stigmatized or looked down on women having abortions. It is interesting that these women tended to continue to see themselves as "different" from the others even when they were in the very same situation.

Perhaps more important for our analysis than the perceived qualities of others was the very fact that each woman who went the specialized clinic route was very observant of other patients and actively tried to place herself with respect to them.

The Abortion

Let us now consider the actual moments when the abortion was performed. For the women at Clinic B, the procedure went quickly and smoothly:

> Then I went in for the abortion. It took about ten minutes. They explained to me everything they were doing as they went through the abortion. I had a hold of this lady's [counselor's] hand and I was just squeezing it as hard as I could....

> When you laid down for the procedure—I mean, they tried to do everything in the world to keep you from thinking about it, that it was going to hurt or anything. She [counselor] came up and took my hand, this young girl that was one of the girls I talked to and she just said, "Squeeze my hand as hard as you want to," and I said, "Well, I don't really want to do that. Just keep talking to me because if I don't think about pain then I won't have as much." (Did you?) No, not a lot. It was just a little bit. It wasn't really a pain. It was just kind of a little uncomfortable feeling. And it was a woman doctor—which was another thing which made me feel comfortable, I think. She was very nice.

Several other women, like this one, commented favorably about having a woman doctor. They also, like Clinic A women, were particularly comforted by having the counselor there with them.

Clinic B women reported no disruptive elements during the performance of their abortions. The women at Clinic A, on the other hand, some of whom still questioned it as a legitimate medical facility, reported some disruption. One cause cited was the rock music which played during the procedure:

> ...I was real quiet and real calm on the inside and then, when I went into the operating room, they had this real loud music going...That automatically got me off balance because I completely had my mind geared in another direction and I never did adjust to that situation....(Did you have any physical discomfort?) Umm, it seemed like there was more pressure than I had thought there would be...that kind of took me off guard a little. But she [counselor] stood right beside me and held my hand and she told me everything that he was going to do...I liked her talking to me to keep my mind off that lousy music....

Another source of disruption among the still suspicious group was the physician:

> I was scared still...I remember what happened, but I was just kind of in a daze. It scared me when the doctor walked in because he was a little, short doctor and he had one of those things around his head....I don't know what

you call them, but he came in there and it reminded me of some old movie. You know, where the doctor comes in, some quack or something. Then, I got kind of shaky....

As pointed out at the beginning of this section, the vacuum aspiration procedure was generally reported to be much easier to go through than the women had originally thought. The emotional nature of the procedure varied. Many of the women spoke of the aspiration matter-of-factly, reporting no particular emotional reactions. Another woman's account, however, does reveal the emotional nature of the experience:

> ...they prepared me, put my legs up and everything, and it was a while before they went to work on me, but they finally started...I was kind of nervous, but I kept taking deep breaths, trying to be calm...well, I was calm up to where he started dilating and that hurt, so I was hanging on to her [counselor]. That hurt. And then, when they started the suction bit, that's what got to me. It was kind of sad....

After the abortion was completed, the women were taken to a recovery room which was usually shared with one woman or more. They spent approximately an hour in this room. The last person quoted above continues:

> ...then, when they got all done and everything, they took me into the recovery room and I felt fine....(Did you still feel sad?) Oh, yes. I really felt sad....I was laying there and there was another girl in there, one other girl. There were about six beds. I was facing her and she was having bad cramps and everything and I didn't feel like saying anything. I just lay there. I was sad and finally I was talking to her about it and asking her how she felt. And she was all right and everything, and I was thinking about it and I told her I thought it was sad and I started crying. I could have flooded out the place, only I kept thinking, "This is silly."

The impact of being grouped together—specifically, the influence of other patients on the woman's thinking and behavior—is further evidenced in another account:

> I laid down and they gave me a Coke and some crackers and put the heating pad on me and I was just sitting there looking around at the walls, and I looked at the girl that was supposed to go in next, and she just started crying her eyes out. She was crying real hard and that just hit me and I started crying. I cried for a little while and I almost fell asleep...then I had my hour and it was up....

The relevance to dissonance starts here

AFTER THE ABORTION: TROUBLED OR UNTROUBLED

In the hours and first few days following the abortion, slightly more than half the women (21) reported that they were completely untroubled by the abortion and feeling fine:

> Oh, I felt great...It didn't bother me at all. [My husband] said, "My God, you act like you've never been through it." No, I felt super. I didn't have any trouble at all.

> I felt great....When I come out of there, man, I was on top of the world. I didn't feel down. I didn't feel guilty. I didn't feel nothing.

The women were advised to rest for several days after the abortion before resuming their normal activities. Most reported they rested for a day or two. Some went back to their normal routines the very next day:

> ...I went right back to work. I was in pain while I was at work, but yet I didn't say anything. I'm sure I probably did things that I shouldn't have done, but I had to because I didn't want to tell anybody.

A typical comment made by these women was that their experience was something they tended to block out, something that seemed almost as though it had never happened:

> ...it just doesn't seem like it happened. It just seems like part of my life that never did

happen. I came home and lay down and went to sleep, got up and got my daughter and went to the grocery store, came home and watched TV and went to bed....It seemed like those few hours I was down there never really existed, even though they did. I guess you just try and put them out of your mind. I guess that's what I did. You know, I just went about the rest of the day just like I would any other Saturday. I slept for about an hour, but I felt real good. (Did you go to work then on Monday?) Yes.

I kind of guess I blocked it out of my mind. I remembered what happened, but...I guess I just didn't want to think about it and I still don't, I guess, connect it—to really sit down and connect my being pregnant with what I did. In my mind, I never really connected my being pregnant with what I did. In my mind, I never really connected one with the other.

While some in the untroubled group felt this sense of unreality about their abortions, others reported that they became more interested in the general topic of abortion than before. They often were more receptive to media coverage for example:

I don't tune it out. I am usually more interested in it now. We had to do a research paper at school and I was going to do it on abortion, but I couldn't—that was kind of obvious and my boyfriend would have gotten mad at me if I would have done it. It interests me more whenever something comes up about it or I read something about it. I just see the word "abortion" and right away I read it.

In contrast to those who were untroubled, the remaining 19 women reported some troubled thoughts following their abortions. The nature of these thoughts varied. One woman reported that she was very sad. Another woman reported she felt "empty":

...everything was over with and I felt relieved, but then I felt-wow, I felt so empty. I just wanted to—ugh, I feel like crying thinking about it....I just couldn't stand that. It still bothers me.

Reflecting some of these same feelings, another woman spoke in terms of a reaction to the abortion which appears to resemble mourning:

...I started crying in the wheelchair. Then the nurse bent over me and was really concerned with physical hurting, if I was all right and nothing was wrong with me physically. I said, "No, I'm sad" and "Just leave me alone," because that feeling—if the mother can't care, who can? Or if she can't—somebody has to cry....I was just going through a period of, you know, decently I can show some grief just to be decent. Nobody else seemed to be decent about that at all, to me. There was just no decency.

Women who reported no trouble or disruption after the abortion were nevertheless concerned about stigma and were carefully maintaining secrecy. Troubled women were even more concerned about the morality and appropriateness of what they had done. They, too, did not tell others; however, their primary orientation was toward coping with the abortion and their own doubts:

It's not very pleasant, really...it's kind of something I'd just as soon forget. I mean, I'll always remember it, but I'd just as soon forget. (How was that week right after?) I had some, I don't know—I was thinking—some nights, you know how you just sit and think? You shouldn't do that sometimes, but I'd just sit and think about it and it would upset me....I don't know, it was just like, "Why did I do it?"

(How did you feel afterwards?) I felt relieved. Later on in the day I had mixed feelings—by the time I got home I had mixed feelings...but then I got a hold of myself somewhat and I realized that this was a decision I had made and I had to learn to make decisions and stick to them....It's kind of sad, but I try to think of abortion as little as possible....

The questioning of the abortion and the accompanying emotions had diminished somewhat by the time of the interview, six to ten weeks after the abortion. The feelings had not disappeared completely, but most women thought about it less frequently and with less intense feeling:

> It's a lot easier to discuss now than it was, but it's something that I can't put completely out of my mind and have no emotional reactions to because to me it was very important. It was something that was very hard.

For the troubled group, as we have pointed out, coping was very important. These women were walking a thin moral line. With their abortions still problematic in their minds, the slightest event could further disrupt their post-abortion lives. Thus, in contrast to the untroubled group, these women tried to avoid the subject of abortion as much as possible:

> ...when I hear things, I don't know whether it's in my conscience or what, but whenever I hear things like on the news about abortion, I kind of block it out. I don't even listen to it. (And if you are reading something?) No, I don't even read anything. I just don't care to know about it....

> Well, I kind of avoid it just because I don't want to think about it. I know how I feel now and I don't feel guilty and I could change to think that I did the wrong thing....

The vulnerability of these women to information or events which would throw their past abortion into further question is well illustrated in the following comment:

> (Have you thought about it much since you had the abortion?) Every now and then I started thinking—well, once especially when I saw—I was in a bookstore and I saw on the front of a magazine a picture of a 16-week-old fetus. It was on the cover of *Time* magazine. It was about abortion and I thought, "My God," because they told me if I was to see it right then it would look like a blood clot...that had really helped a lot, too, in making my decision because I couldn't think of it as a little person, you know. But then, I saw that picture and it kind of upset me for a while, but I just said,

> "Don't think about it." (In what way did it upset you?) That it looked so much like a human. It looked so developed. I mean, when they had said it just looked like a blood clot, I thought it was kind of like when you break a chicken egg, you know. You can see the little white part that is supposed to be a chicken but you don't think you are killing a chicken or something. You just eat the egg. (Did it put doubts in your mind then or...?) Oh, a little bit. I wondered about—since I believe in God, I wondered if it was the right thing to do. But I just said, "Well, if it was the wrong thing to do, I'll pay." But while I'm here on earth, I'd just as soon not think about it and not let it bother me.

In another case, the woman's efforts to define the abortion as appropriate and to forget it, moving on to other things, were disrupted by the man involved in the pregnancy. Although they had ended their relationship, he continued to contact her:

> (In the period after the abortion, up until now, have you thought about it much?) No, I just want to block it out of my mind. (Can you always do that?) No....Well, the only way it pops up, you know, is if me and my girlfriend starts talking about it or if my ex-boyfriend calls and gives one of his prank telephone calls. (What does he do?) Oh, he'll call up and call me a murderer and things like that. (Does he still do that?) Yes, except for lately I haven't been at home when he's called—somehow, I've been dodging it.

For another woman, the source of disruption was high school peers:

> I've been having troubles, emotional problems...like when I came back to school they had stuff all over the bathroom walls like, "Jane Jones goes to bed with guys and then has abortions." And so, I was real upset...I was just walking down the halls real fast. I was practically crying....

She claimed not to have told any of these persons but speculated that perhaps her boyfriend had.

In summary, for those women already troubled by their abortion, the hostile reaction of others caused even more disruption. The woman was vulnerable to adverse reactions at the same time that she was trying to reduce the doubts and other problematic aspects of the abortion in order to achieve some degree of closure. This situation characterized most of the troubled group. Despite this, only two of the women reported that they definitely regretted the abortion. For most, rather, the issue was one of moral uncertainty—of struggling to define the abortion as a proper act. In short, the abortion remained somewhat ambiguous and unsettling for the troubled women; for those untroubled, it was a closed issue.

TELLING OTHERS AFTERWARD

As might be expected from the analysis just presented, very few of the women had told any additional persons about their abortion by the time of the interview. This fact simply underscores the general aura of deviance which they felt surrounded their abortion and their care to avoid being stigmatized. One woman, when asked if she were worried about anyone finding out, replied, "A little bit, because I'm afraid they would think less of me...it bothers me."

Interestingly, most of the unmarried women said they would consider it important for their future husband to know that they had an abortion:

> I'd make it a point to tell him because I think it's—he's going to have to—he's going to be my husband and I think it's something he ought to know. I think that both people ought to be truthful with each other and tell each other everything. I think it's only fair.

When asked if they would consider ever telling their children, the women almost all replied, "No"; that is, unless one of their children got into a similar situation.

To conclude this section on the abortion procedure, a summary offered by one of the women interviewed seems particularly appropriate:

> (What kind of experience was it?) That's hard in a way-there were so many feelings all in this. Well, it was an *experience* I must admit. It

wasn't as bad as I expected really. It was—I can't explain it. It was weird. It was so quick. It's something that when it comes to deciding to have an abortion and you're there and you're going to do it, OK, you get there and you do it. You know, it's got to be done, so you go through with it. And after it's over, it's a relief, but yet it's a feeling of emptiness. You don't want to go through it again...but I do, I feel like I've learned a lot. I don't know how exactly....

After the abortion, each woman's task was to reduce its problematic aspects so that she could establish a stable foundation from which to move on. For some this task was more difficult than for others, reflecting the differences between disruptive and smooth abortion passages.

CHANGES IN SOCIAL RELATIONSHIPS

One way of looking at the impact of abortion on the social worlds of the women is to examine what happened to their relationships with others from the time they first suspected pregnancy to the post abortion interview. Of particular interest throughout this study has been whether or not the various phases of the abortion process were "smooth" or "disruptive"—whether or not, in other words, the abortion could be sociologically termed a "crisis." Thus, in examining any changes which might have occurred in the women's social relationships, we will focus on disruptions.

For purposes of analysis, we can separate the study group into two categories. One refers to women who experienced either no changes or who experienced only positive changes (changes which brought them closer) in their relationships with others. The second refers to women who experienced disruptions—relationships either broken off or substantially dissolved.

Disruption in Relationships

Slightly more than half of the women (22, or 55%) had a disruption in at least one social relationship central to their lives. For 20 of these 22 women, disruption occurred in the termination of their relationship with the man involved in the pregnancy. Some of these relationships were terminated by him, usually before the abortion. In others, the break was initiated by the woman, usually after the abortion—for example:

> I just don't want to have any more to do with him.... I just told him that this just wasn't going to work.... He really didn't know why I didn't want to see him anymore, but I just didn't want to mess with him anymore.

> I'm saying I'm dating other people now, but he doesn't like to accept the fact.... I guess through this we got to know each other better and I realized some things that I didn't want to put up with in the future....

Frequently, the involvement and intimacy fostered by the pregnancy and abortion experience appeared to demand more intensity and commitment than the relationship could provide. This is illustrated by the following description of a relationship disintegrating after the abortion:

> (What happened between you two?) That's kind of—I don't really know. It got to the point where he was just—it's like he had been through all of this stuff with me and we weren't really getting along that well. He wanted me, or thought he did, but he also wanted out—he wanted his freedom now. He had had enough of close contact. He didn't want to admit it that he wanted to cut it off. He wanted to let it ride and wanted me to say, "Okay, whatever you say. If you don't want to see me tonight, fine," which I did. And then I started getting upset again, and we just had a lot of conflicts because he didn't want to see me as much and I still wanted to see him. He was starting to feel really guilty about it—about getting me pregnant—I thought maybe for a while we could both have a certain amount of freedom and still continue to date, but that didn't work either because I couldn't do it. We had to totally cut it off and be totally away from each other. So one night he called me up and... I said, "Well, look, just come over for an hour...and that will be it." And it was just like we both knew that it was

going to be the end, finish, we were going to cut it off.... We just couldn't do it.... We both felt it. There were things just beyond our control. You know, if I hadn't gotten pregnant, things might have been different; but, as far as things went, we both had so many emotional upsets, and this is all we have been thinking about for three or four weeks. So we just said, "Well, there is nothing we can do," and we never really said, you know, "Well, why don't we quit dating." I just said, "It's really tough," and he said, "Yes, I know," and I said, "I don't want to start crying," and he said, "Don't, because I will," and it was really strange. So after that, he avoided me in school. He would park on the other side of school...I don't know where things are with him right now. My girlfriend says I should realize that it is over and go on, but I can't do it. There is just...we went through so much together....

The disintegration of the relationship with the man was not the only disruption. Two women reportedly each experienced a severe break with her sister as a result of the abortion:

> With my sister-in-law, there is no difference in our relationship; but my sister-she doesn't call or come over or anything. She just lives across the street, but I never see her....

In both cases, the sisters were morally opposed to abortion.

In addition, three women experienced disintegrating relationships with friends who were opposed to the abortion and in three other cases women reported that they were no longer as close to their parents as they had been. Two of these women moved out of their parents' home after the abortion. As one woman explained, "I just don't want to stay there."

Maintaining and Cementing Relationships
While 55 percent experienced disruption in relationships, 45 percent (18 women) reported either no change or else a positive change in relationships with other persons. These other persons varied among parents, siblings, friends, and male

partners. The positive change or increased closeness in the relationship was frequently attributed to "sharing" or to having confided in the other person.

Since the males involved in the pregnancy were almost always told (and told early), sharing and confiding particularly involved them. As we have illustrated, the abortion process frequently demanded too much from these relationships, resulting in their termination. In other cases, however, the relationships were already at a high level of intensity and commitment. The passage through abortion had the effect of strengthening or "cementing" them—at least, from the viewpoint of the women. For example:

> I think that was the first time he ever actually has been concerned about me—*really* concerned. And I think the whole thing brought us closer because we had been through all of this soul-searching and had gone through the whole thing together. I think that it made us even closer than we were before.

Only six of the women reported no change at all in their relationships. Three women, on the other hand, reported a major change. In two cases, the change was marriage, one a few days before the abortion and one soon after. The fact that the abortion precipitated the wedding was apparent:

> It must have been during that week after the abortion. I decided—I was sad; and, besides that, it saddened me that my boyfriend had to leave again…and so I said, "This is ridiculous," and so that's when I decided I wanted to get married then.

The third woman moved in with her boyfriend after her abortion and, at the same time, set a wedding date for several months ahead.

DEVIANCE, RESPONSIBILITY, AND THE ABORTION

Throughout their abortion passage and into the postabortion period the women in this study were confronted with a discrepancy. Their view of themselves as "moral" persons was inconsistent with having an abortion, defined as immoral or wrong by the community (according to the women). In order to reduce this discrepancy and to establish closure on their abortion experience, the women adopted several ways of coping. As we have seen, they tended to carefully select and limit the people who knew about the abortion. After the abortion, their relationships with others were "adjusted" to eliminate persons who provided further disruption. Finally, they had to adopt a verbal stance on their abortion—a definition or interpretation of the situation. These ways of coping, if successful, would enable the women to move on into new experiences relatively free of unresolved questions about their abortion.

In this section, we consider the verbal positions taken by the women. It might be argued that, because abortion was recognized by the women as a deviant act within their community, they might have thought and spoken less highly of themselves afterward. Only one woman in the study, however, made any comment to this effect:

> …at first I thought, "Wow," you know, "I'm just not a good girl. I'm just another girl." I don't know. (Did you feel that it lowered you?) Yeah, it did. It still does make me feel that way.

Most of the women, rather than accept the deviant implications that abortion held for them, appeared to continue to view themselves as "moral" persons, just as they were before the abortion. They were able to do this by using a particular verbal strategy when thinking and talking about their abortion.

A verbal strategy in coping with the aforementioned discrepancy could either accept or reject the committed act as deviant. The implication of deviance disappears if the act is considered to be "normal." The implications remain if the act is considered to be deviant *unless* the person is able to relieve herself of personal responsibility. Thus, the woman had two ways to retain her "moral" status, her self-worth: (1) she could reject the deviance of abortion, or (2) she could admit it, at the same time denying her own responsibility in having the abortion.

Overwhelmingly, the women in this study chose the latter strategy. Two-thirds of the women made statements in which they portrayed themselves as having "no choice" in the matter of abortion, being "forced" to have the abortion:

It was like I knew what I had to do and I was dead set on doing it, but I didn't want to. It was like I was being forced to do something, but that I didn't want to.

You know, at this point in my life and everything else, that's the only way. As far as I'm concerned, I don't see any other way—that there could be any other way....I don't think it will bother me too much because it was the only way out and you have to accept that.

I was frightened of the abortion. And I was also sad as far as the child was concerned. I could feel for the part that would have been me. But, as far as circumstances go, I had no choice.

Personal responsibility is the underlying theme in these comments. By portraying themselves as having no alternative other than abortion, these women guided others toward viewing them as victims rather than as perpetrators of the abortion. Responsibility for the act was abrogated.

The ultimate success of such a strategy is, of course, dependent upon the audience and the credibility of the woman's claim. Since so many of the women chose to deny personal responsibility rather than challenge the deviant definition of abortion, we can suggest that this was the approach that they perceived others could best accept. In other words, it appears that the women interpreted that it would be more effective for them to claim no responsibility—that they had no alternative in choosing abortion—than it would have been for them to claim that abortion is an acceptable act.

Two additional aspects of the women's postabortion comments support this view. First, while many women claimed to be more "understanding" as a result of their abortion experience, it can be suggested that perhaps their underlying abortion attitudes retained at least some of their earlier restrictiveness. If so, then this would certainly support the view that they did not significantly challenge or refute the notion of abortion as a deviant act. The woman quoted below became pregnant when she failed to take her birth control pills regularly. Her postabortion attitudes toward others who might be in her situation revealed that she continued to stigmatize some women having abortions:

I think after having my abortion I can say that my views have changed some. I still don't believe in just going out and getting pregnant, having an abortion...just because you're too stupid or lazy to practice birth control. I think it all depends on each person's reason. I know each person thinks they've got a good reason. Everybody's got a different reason. Some of them are a little bit stronger than others; some of them are just weak reasons, because they don't want the baby.

Second, the women's comments concerning the nature of the fetus and the issue of whether or not abortion constitutes an act of killing also suggested that it was difficult for many of them to think of abortion as a nondeviant act.

Out of ethical concerns for the women and the deeply sensitive moral issues involved, the women interviewed for this study were not asked specifically about this topic. Nevertheless, only one-third of the women avoided the issue altogether. The remaining two-thirds offered their views.

While it is a central argument of many people who support abortion, and might be thought to characterize women who themselves have abortions, only 15 percent of the women interviewed made statements explicitly stating a belief that the fetus was *not* a person or human life:

I just personally don't look at a little fetus as being a person, and I don't agree with the argument that it is manslaughter. I just don't agree with that.

When you are that far along, I don't really feel—I feel that it's something there, but I don't really feel that it's a life yet....I don't feel that it is really a human life that early.

I can't go along with the idea that from the moment of conception this is a person.

On the other hand, and of central concern to the point being made, nearly one-fourth of the study group took the position in their comments that the fetus was, indeed, a life or baby or person. They also in many cases explicitly stated the related idea that abortion constitutes an act of killing that life:

I just felt like I was killing something.

I thought it was terrible, taking a life. Something that is alive. You can't say that it's not because it is. No matter how small it is, it's still alive, and the thought of killing something like that just kind of makes you sick...you're killing something.

We both realize that we've done something wrong, something immoral. It goes against our beliefs—taking a life is wrong.

I didn't want to have the feeling of killing the baby and that's what I felt like.

In addition, another 25 percent expressed confusion and their inability to completely come to terms with the question of the fetus:

...I was brought up in the Church and I know that, as far as God and in the religious way, that it is wrong. Because that is taking a life—which I didn't really feel like—well, I don't know. I'm still kind of mixed-up about that, too—whether it was a life or whether not.

What these statements reveal is that the notion of abortion as deviance was central in the women's thinking as they attempted to establish closure. Certainly, by denying full responsibility for their actions, they could protect their identity from stigma to some extent. How successful this will be in the long run is another question. Again, we conclude that many of these women were holding an acceptable definition of their abortion situation together with very fragile fabric. Of perhaps even more significance is the fact that, because of this fragility, a future disruption might throw the whole situation into question once again. The full problematic nature of the abortion would be reexposed.

For many of these women, the establishment of closure was enhanced by viewing the self as somehow "different" as a result of the abortion experience. In the majority of these cases, the changes were perceived as minor ones.

DISCUSSION QUESTIONS

1. Zimmerman published this research in 1977. What was the historical context of abortion in mid-1970s America?
2. How do the women in Zimmerman's study cope with the stigma of having an abortion? How does the experience differ for women who go to Clinic A versus Clinic B for the procedure?
3. If Zimmerman were to conduct her research today, do you think there would be significant differences in her findings? If so, what differences would you expect and why? If not, why do you expect a similar outcome? Put another way, what, if anything, has changed with regard to abortion since 1977?
4. Do you know someone who has considered having, or who has had, an abortion? If so, how is her experience similar to or different from the women in Zimmerman's research?

ADDITIONAL RESOURCES

Film

"If These Walls Could Talk." 1996. A riveting 97-minute HBO home video starring Demi Moore, Sissy Spacek, and Cher as three women dealing with unplanned pregnancies in the 1950s, 1970s, and 1990s.

"The Last Abortion Clinic." 2005. A 60-minute PBS "Frontline" documentary featuring access to abortion in the southern region of the United States. http://www.pbs.org/wgbh/pages/frontline/clinic/etc/synopsis.html.

Internet

http://www.guttmacher.org/sections/abortion.php. The Guttmacher Institute provides a site with comprehensive contemporary and historical data on abortion in several countries.

http://www.nlm.nih.gov/medlineplus/abortion.html. This is MEDLINE Plus's information clearinghouse site about abortion. This website is sponsored by the U.S. National Library of Medicine and the National Institutes of Health.

http://www.prochoice.org/. The National Abortion Federation is the professional association of abortion providers.

FURTHER READING

Casper, Monica J. 1998. *The Making of the Unborn Patient: A Social Anatomy of Fetal Surgery.* Rutgers, NJ: Rutgers University Press.

Faundes, Anibel and Jose S. Barzelatto. 2006. *The Human Drama of Abortion: A Global Search for Consensus.* Nashville, TN: Vanderbilt University Press.

Wicklund, Susan and Alan Kesselheim. 2007. *This Common Secret: My Journey as an Abortion Doctor.* New York: Public Affairs, A member of the Perseus Books Group.

Zimmerman, Mary K. 1977. *Passage through Abortion: The Personal and Social Reality of Women's Experiences.* New York: Praeger.

" surface act ".
" interactional place "   " micropolitical costs "

38. Managing Emotions in Public: The Case of Wheelchair Users

SPENCER E. CAHILL AND ROBIN EGGLESTON

Cahill, an able-bodied sociologist, and Eggleston, a social work graduate student who uses a wheelchair, conducted a fascinating ethnographic study of how wheelchair users cope with having a visible stigma. Both authors used wheelchairs in public to gather data for this research.

Social life is at least as emotionally as physically challenging for wheelchair users. The vagaries of fate have left them in an emotionally vulnerable and volatile social position. Both "helping" professionals and caring acquaintances alternately encourage them to accept their disability and to

Cahill, Spencer E. and Robin Eggleston. 1994. "Managing Emotions in Public: The Case of Wheelchair Users." *Social Psychology Quarterly,* 57(4): 300–12.

rise above it, stirring conflicting feelings of shameful inadequacy and prideful self-confidence.

The public lives of wheelchair users are no less stormy. More of them are making this discovery as they frequent public places more often than in the recent past, but students of social life have shown little interest in the lessons that wheelchair users are learning. Even the few students of social life who have paid some attention to wheelchair users' public experiences have lumped them with widely dissimilar categories of people under the general heading of the "stigmatized." Unquestionably there are revealing parallels between the public treatment of wheelchair users, persons with other disabilities, and those with otherwise "spoiled identities," but wheelchair users' distinctive experiences may be especially instructive. We explore that possibility here by focusing exclusively on wheelchair users' experiences in public places such as shopping malls, restaurants, grocery stores, and city sidewalks.

THE INSTRUCTION OF WHEELCHAIR USE AND USERS

Our collective interest in wheelchair users' public experiences grew out of conversations between the first author and second author, who has used an electrically powered wheelchair as her principal mode of public mobility. At the urging of the first author, she started to make field notes of her daily participant observation of the social life of a wheelchair user. Those notes provided the basis for an earlier article (Eggleston, 1992) and inspired a more extensive study of wheelchair users' experiences in public places.

While the second author continued to make notes of her public experiences, the first author supplemented these with field notes that he made when using a wheelchair in public places for the specific purpose of participant observation. His experiences included short trips along city sidewalks, excursions to shopping malls, and a visit to a restaurant in the company of the second author and another regular wheelchair user. We also collected and read wheelchair users' autobiographical accounts. In addition, we collectively conducted and recorded interviews with seven women and five men who regularly use a wheelchair in public places.

Although admittedly this was a convenience sample, they were as diverse a group of wheelchair users as we could find. They ranged from 11 to 62 years of age, had been using a wheelchair for as little as three months or as long as 50 years, and had a variety of diagnosed medical conditions including cerebral palsy (2), multiple sclerosis (3), muscular dystrophy (1), traumatic brain injury (1), and paraplegia resulting from spinal injury (4) and viral infection (1). Five were employed in such varied jobs as college professor and stock clerk; the rest were currently unemployed, including a full-time student, two retired schoolteachers, and a retired store clerk. Our conversations with them lasted from one and one-half to four hours and yielded 150 single-spaced pages of transcript.

We repeatedly reviewed and compared information from these varied materials, both during and after collection. Although initially we did not intend to focus on the emotional challenges of public wheelchair use, emotional dilemmas loomed large in our own and our informants' accounts and in the published accounts of other wheelchair users' public experiences. Gradually we became convinced that those dilemmas contained a revealing story about the place of wheelchair users in public life, about contemporary public life more generally, and about interpersonal processes of emotion management. The following analysis tells that story.

THE EMOTIONAL DEMANDS OF PUBLIC WHEELCHAIR USE

For many wheelchair users, the very decision to venture into public places is emotionally turbulent. The desire for autonomy and for the many pleasures that only public places offer collides with fears—among others, fear of moving past and among much larger vehicles. There is the fear of upsetting others that has kept one of our informants, who recently started using a wheelchair, from using it in restaurants.

> I think it's hard for people to eat food close to people who are ill. There's something about the process of eating that makes people even more uptight about disease. My rolling in probably wouldn't affect people in that way, but in the back of my mind I'm afraid it would. I'll have to get over that.

Wheelchair users also fear, with justification, being an embarrassing and embarrassed public spectacle.

Humoring Embarrassment

Like those whom one of our informant calls "stand-up people," wheelchair users face a variety of embarrassing possibilities whenever they venture into public places. For any number of familiar reasons, they may lose control over self or situation, falling short of what is generally expected of competent public actors. Wheelchair users, however, face a number of uniquely embarrassing contingencies because the physical environment, both natural and constructed, is unfriendly to their mode of mobility. Rain and snow can leave them immobile and embarrassingly in need of rescue. Doorway thresholds, uneven sidewalks, and unanticipated depressions at the bottom of curb cuts may cause a wheelchair to tip over, leaving its occupant embarrassingly sprawled on the ground. Crowded and narrow passage ways may make it nearly impossible for wheelchair users to avoid knocking merchandise off shelves, rolling into standing strangers, or struggling to maneuver around tight corners in front of anxiously paralyzed bystanders. Although wheelchair users do not welcome such discomfort, many become quite adept at easing the "disease" of potentially embarrassing situations because they face them so often.

Humor is the most common and perhaps most effective strategy that wheelchair users employ for this purpose. As Goffman suggests, laughing at or joking about embarrassing events reduces their seriousness and thereby lessens potentially embarrassing concern about them. Laughter and humor are also means of allaying anxiety, which can serve a dual definitional purpose. A wheelchair user's potentially embarrassing situation often provokes anxiety in witnesses to her or his plight. Defining the situation as laughable can ease everyone's particular "dis-ease," as the second author learned when shopping at a clothing store.

> I wheeled up to the entrance to a dressing room while my friend held a number of garments. I forgot to set the brakes on my chair, so when I started to raise myself up with my crutches the chair went rolling backwards while I went falling forward onto the floor. My friend stood there with this look of alarm until I started laughing. The two of us started laughing, and then a saleswoman came rushing over: "My goodness, are you all right?" I answered "Yes, I'm fine" while still laughing. Her facial expression went from alarm to unconcern in a flash, once she realized we were laughing.

Through incidents like this, wheelchair users acquire the experiential wisdom that a sense of humor is "a tremendous asset":

> ...if you can laugh at yourself, no matter what.... And if it's funny to me first, then my feelings aren't hurt. And you don't feel self-conscious because you can laugh with me.

As this 60-year-old woman had learned from countless falls in public places, laughter can both prevent and relieve hurt feelings, anxious self-consciousness, and the contagious "dis-ease" of embarrassment.

On the other hand, humor sometimes has the opposite effect. A woman who had been using a wheelchair in public for only six months told us of her recent experience in a shopping mall bathroom:

> There was a whole line of people waiting to get into these two stalls. It was packed. And I'm trying to back up and not doing a very good job of it and having to start over again, bumping into

the washbasin. I finally get myself around, with all these people obviously watching me. There was dead silence. So I finally got myself out, and I looked up at all these people and I went "Now, I would like a big round of applause, please." Nobody did anything. It was like you can't make a joke about this stuff. I thought "Give me a break."

This incident illustrates one of the emotional dilemmas that wheelchair users face when in public places: they must attempt to remain poised and good-humored in frustrating and potentially embarrassing circumstances without thereby increasing others' already considerable discomfort at those circumstances. In public places they often have the double duty of managing both their own and others' emotions.

Wheelchair users commonly assume this double duty when the recipients of young children's incivil attentions as often they are. On one occasion, for example, one of our informants drove us to a shopping mall in her van. We were all using wheelchairs and had to take turns using the power lift to exit the van. As we were doing so, a girl approximately four years old, whose hand was being held by a young woman, approached.

The girl stared in awe while the young woman pulled her by the hand and studiously avoided glancing in our direction. We just as studiously avoided glancing in their direction. As they passed us, the girl loudly asked: "Mommy, what's wrong with those people? What's wrong with those people?" The girl's mother quickened their collective pace and did not reply until well out of the range of our hearing.

Although the tactic of "tactful blindness" served us well in this instance, wheelchair users often do not find it so easy to ignore young children's uncivil attentions.

This is clearly the case when wheelchair users are interrogated by curious children, as often happens, about their unusual mode of mobility and physical condition. All but one of our informants report that they gladly answer such young

interrogators' questions. One informant, whose left leg had been amputated, had an uncommon sense of humor, but his openness with young children was not unusual.

Kids go "Where's your leg?" "It's gone. If you find it, I'll give you fifty cents. I've been looking for that damn thing all week." "Can I see it?" "Sure." I take my pants up, show the stump. "Wow, it's gone. You're not sitting on it." "Yep, it's gone." They're frank. They're very candid.

Inquisitive children's accompanying adult caretakers, however, seldom appreciate their young charges' candor. As the man quoted above reported, "The parents turn blue. They turn shades of pink and red. I have to protect the kids from the parents. They want to jerk them away." Other informants reported similar experiences.

And children, you find that they come up and ask "How come you're in that chair? You mean you can't walk? Really?" But if there's an adult with them, they tend to pull the child back. "Oh now, don't disturb her." And I say "They're not disturbing me."

If our informants are at all representative, most wheelchair users not only graciously endure and satisfy young children's uncivil curiosity when in public places. They also attempt to manage the embarrassment and (sometimes the wrath) of those curious children's adult caretakers in the interest of child protection. Whatever emotion work is done is usually done by them.

In both our own and our informants experience, most adults accord wheelchair users the surface acceptance of civil inattention in public places. Wheelchair users commonly resolve the emotional dilemmas of their public lives in this way. They expressively mask their own emotions so as to manage others'. They cover their embarrassment with good humor, relieving witnesses' emotional discomfort. They hide resentment behind calm graciousness, saving forward strangers the embarrassment that would be caused by expressing such resentment. Even when wheelchair users feel fully justified in their emotional reactions, their public expression often contrasts sharply with their private feelings. The example of righteous anger suggests some reasons why.

Embarrassing Anger

Apparently uncomfortable salesclerks may busy themselves folding merchandise as if a potential customer in a wheelchair were invisible. Restaurant personnel may huddle behind a wheelchair user, close enough to let her overhear their discussion of "where to put her." All kinds of service workers may treat a wheelchair user's walking companions as his or her spokespersons and caretakers. Sometimes they return change to such companions after receiving payment from the wheelchair user, or ask her companions "And what would she like?"

Such nonperson treatment often provokes wheelchair users' anger but seldom the expression of that anger. As one of our informants told us, "I just want to reach out and grab a hold of them and shake them for all they're worth. But I just sit back, and I grit my teeth." Our informants report that they usually try to respond to nonperson treatment not with anger but with calm reminders of their presence and ability to speak for themselves. They also report that this strategy is usually effective in eliciting an embarrassed apology and more civil treatment.

Yet no matter how common and how effective such gentle reminders are, wheelchair users sometimes reveal their anger at nonperson treatment through hostile comments and tone. When a waiter asked the wife of one of our informants whether "he will be getting out of the chair," our informant sarcastically replied "Yes, *he* will." Such hostile expressions can be even more effective than calm reminders in eliciting embarrassed apologies, but at the expense of leaving the wheelchair user feeling embarrassed and guilty about his or her lack of emotional poise. These contradictions lead to conflicting feelings of justifiable anger and guilt at expressing the anger. Wheelchair users

are not alone in experiencing such contradictory feelings in public or elsewhere.

Private guilt and embarrassment are not the only potentially unwelcome consequences of wheelchair users' public expressions of anger. Rather than eliciting embarrassed apologies, their anger may be returned, as one of our informants learned when she protested a robustly walking man's choice of parking places.

> I've had a guy park in a handicapped parking spot, and I've gone up and said: "Look, do you realize you're parked in a handicapped parking spot?" And he said "I know it, and I'm sick of you people getting all the good spots. It's reverse discrimination. I'm sick of being discriminated against." "Well," I said, "I'm going to call the police and you can tell your story to them." And he says, "Go ahead. I've had it. It's about time."

Although this man moved his car when our informant wheeled to the nearest public telephone, it was a harder-won moral victory than she had anticipated.

The angry protests by self-appointed defenders of wheelchair users' public privileges are no less instructive in this regard. One of our informants, who drove a car with hand controls that was otherwise unremarkable, told us of the following public encounter:

> I pull the car into a handicapped place, and this car pulls up alongside me with two young women in it. One of them leans over and says, "You know you're in a handicapped place." And I said, "Yes, I'm disabled." And then she says "You don't look disabled." And I don't usually do this kind of thing, but I just said "What does disabled look like?" And they just drove off. Maybe I shouldn't have done that, but it was one of those days.

The informant's hostile retort and the tinge of guilt he apparently felt as a result illustrate both the possible subjective costs and the interpersonal risks of publicly expressing anger. This is one horn of an emotional dilemma that wheelchair users often face in public. Should they suppress their righteous anger and forgo the satisfaction that its expression often brings, or should they assume the costs and risks of expression? As suggested previously, our informants, like the second author, commonly resolve this dilemma in favor of suppression—if not of their anger, then at least of expression.

That decision, however, does not always save wheelchair users from the embarrassing public scenes that angry protests can create. Their walking companions see to that, as a 34-year-old paraplegic woman explains.

> After thirteen and a half years you've heard just about everything, so it's like "Oh, you know." But it's my friends who [say] "Can you imagine the nerve? Let's get out of here." They've actually made me leave. My ex-boyfriend, we got up from the table and walked out . . . it started when they didn't know where to put me, and then the waitress ignored me. And he had just had it. He said "We're out of here." I said "Don't make an issue out of it." "The issue's made." Got my purse, got my coat, and we started to leave. We had the manager on our coattails. I think that's more embarrassing.

Walkers who befriend and accompany wheelchair users in public are apparently no exception. Their easy susceptibility to moral outrage may lead to public scenes that their wheelchair-using companions would just as soon avoid. As if their occasional nonperson treatment were not painful enough, wheelchair users also must sometimes bear the embarrassment of their defenders' self-righteous zeal.

Wheelchair users' experiences with public anger are not unique. Regardless of our mode of mobility, public expressions of anger are risky: they can provoke angry retaliation and create embarrassing scenes. For most of us, much of the time, those potential costs seem to outweigh whatever personal satisfaction we might gain by expressing our righteous rage. Consequently we "surface act" (Hochschild, 1979, p. 558) so as to prevent our anger from reaching the surface. Thus, public appearances of emotional indifference are

sometimes just that—appearances. Wheelchair users' experiences in public places remind us of how much emotion work may be invested in maintaining those appearances.

Ingratiating Sympathy

Prevailing expression rules, possible retaliation, and potential embarrassment are not the only deterrents to wheelchair users' public expression of righteous anger. They also know that they cannot afford to alienate the walkers who populate the public places they frequent. Experience has taught them that their uncooperative bodies and, more commonly, the unfriendliness of the physical environment to their mode of mobility sometimes leave them hopelessly dependent on others' sympathetic assistance. They may need waiters to move chairs away from a table so that they can wheel their own under it, or to store their wheelchair after transferring to a chair with legs. Often they must rely on strangers to fetch items from shelves that are either too high or too low for them to reach. They may wheel down a curb cut on one side of a street only to find a curb on the other side, over which anonymous passersby must help them if they are to continue along their intended path. Like one of our informants, they may find themselves in a restaurant or bar without "handicap accessible" toilet facilities and themselves without same-sexed companionship, and thus may require the assistance of total strangers to use those much-needed facilities. Or, like another of our informants, they may need to flag down a passing motorist on a city street to help them replace a foot on the footrest of their wheelchair after it has been dislodged by an involuntary spasm. These are only a few of the circumstances in which wheelchair users find themselves requiring the sympathetic assistance of walkers with whom they are unacquainted.

Whatever its form, that assistance qualifies as sympathetic. The assistance that walkers sometimes provide wheelchair users in public places involves empathetic role-taking and is a culturally recognized expression of sympathy, even if not motivated by sincere "fellow-feeling" or senti-ment. Regardless of the motivation, its provision stirs emotions.

Although many wheelchair users do not hesitate to ask for assistance when they need it, they are as aware of, and as strongly committed to, prevailing sympathy etiquette as other rules of feeling and expression. Therefore they often find themselves torn between concern about making excessive claims on others' sympathy and their immediate need for sympathetic assistance. Guilt is the typical result.

> If I'm in the grocery store, and I need some-thing, and I ask somebody to get it [I say] "Oh, I'm sorry." And I find myself making excuses, saying things like "Oh, it's just not been my day" or "it seems everything I want today is up too high." I feel like I'm putting people out of their way. I feel like I'm imposing on someone to ask for help.

This wheelchair user's sensitivity to the sacrifices of sympathetically helpful strangers is not unusual. Wheelchair users often are forced to request sym-pathetic assistance from strangers in order to con-tinue on their daily rounds, but still feel a pang of guilt when doing so. Those who have some choice may feel somewhat more than a guilty pang, as the first author learned when using a wheelchair in public places. Wherever someone opened a door or performed some other minor service, this author felt like a shameless fraud who was exploit-ing strangers' kindness. One of our informants, who could walk short distances with the aid of a cane, often experienced similar feelings:

> I've had people do double and triple takes when I get up out of my wheelchair....Sometimes when I'm using my chair in a grocery store and I can't reach something, I get up; sometimes I ask people to get it for me. I mean, that's where I feel like a fraud, because I can get up. But if I get up, then I feel like a fraud because people can tell that I'm using a wheelchair but I don't need to—I mean, I don't *have* to.

To avoid such a perception and the resulting guilt, they may take needless risks and expend needless

energy rather than requesting even minor aid from strangers. The micropolitical benefits of such dogged self-reliance may also help to compensate for inefficient expenditures of time, energy, and personal safety.

Even if wheelchair users defiantly refuse to pay the subjective price of guilt when requesting and accepting sympathetic assistance, they pay an interpersonal price. And deferential gratitude is the only emotional currency with which wheelchair users can repay gifts of sympathetic assistance from strangers whom they are unlikely to encounter in the future.

Wheelchair users often pay that price cheer-fully when they require and request sympathetic assistance, but those are not the only occasions on which they are expected to pay it. Walkers who are unknown to wheelchair users provide sympa-thetic assistance not only when it is requested, but also when it is not. The first author learned this in the opening moments of his first public appear-ance in a wheelchair.

> I got the chair unfolded and assembled and started wheeling down the hallway. As I was approaching the door, a woman walked along-side my chair and asked: "Are you going that way?" Assuming that she meant toward the door, I answered "Yes." She gracefully moved in front of me and opened the first of the double doors. I thanked her. She then just as gracefully opened the outer door once I was through the first, and again I thanked her.

From all reports, this is not an unusual experi-ence for wheelchair users. Walkers often quicken or slow their pace so as to be in a position to open and hold doors for wheelchair users whom they do not know. They offer to push occupied wheelchairs up steep inclines, and sometimes begin to do so without warning. Also, they volunteer to fold and load wheelchairs into their users' cars and vans. These are only a few examples of the unsolicited assistance that wheelchair users report receiving from strang-ers in public places. Such tenderness and help have a price, however.

Unsolicited acts of sympathetic assistance place wheelchair users under no less of obligation than acts that are requested. It is still generally expected that the recipient will repay the granter with "deferential gratitude," and the micropolitical cost of that repayment may be even greater than for requested acts of sympathetic assistance.

This is not to say that wheelchair users never appreciate unsolicited offers and acts of sympathetic assistance. One of our informants reports that he adjusts the speed of his wheelchair in relation to the reflections of approaching walkers in glass doors so as to ensure that they will reach the door slightly before him and will open and hold it for him voluntarily. At times he is more than willing to absorb the micropolitical losses caused by accepting such a minor expression of sympathetic kindness, and he is not alone.

Yet neither he nor other wheelchair users appreciate all the unsolicited assistance that sympathetic walkers shower on them. Sometimes they resent the costs in definitional authority or in mere time and energy that such acts of kindness impose. In the 1970s, for example, one of our informants was mistaken for a wounded veteran of the Vietnam war by a bouncer at a popular country and western bar. Before our informant could correct the misidentification, the bouncer carried him and his chair past the long queue of people awaiting admittance to the bar, forcibly removed some patrons from a table, and then offered the table to our informant and his companions. When the bouncer left to order "drinks on the house," our informant's wife wisely advised him, "Don't you dare tell him you're not a vet." For the rest of the evening, our informant and his companions were held hostage to the bouncer's definition of the situation, and had to feign knowledge of Vietnamese geography. Another informant reports that bartenders routinely refuse to accept payment for his drinks, insisting that his "money's no good here." A relatively well-paid civil servant, our informant resented the definitional implication that he was unable to pay his own way, but sometimes "let it go because they just wouldn't take my money." At

times, too, unsolicited assistance merely makes wheelchair users' lives more difficult, as when walkers insist on helping a wheelchair user disassemble, fold, and load the wheelchair into a car or van, taking twice as long to do so as the user commonly takes and sometimes damaging the wheelchair in the process.

Even more maddening are those occasions on which self-appointed benefactors bear some responsibility for the wheelchair user's plight. One of our informants reported that she called a restaurant to inquire if it was accessible to wheelchair users. After being assured that it was, she made reservations for the following evening.

> [W]e got there only to find that they had four or five steps, and there was no way I was going to get up there. So the owner of the restaurant and several of the male kitchen help came out and just picked my chair right up. They made every effort, once I got there, to help, which was really nice, but at the same time I was not happy after what they'd told me…I get embarrassed when people make too much fuss over me.

This embarrassed and unhappy, if not angry, woman never returned to the restaurant in question. Yet on the evening of her first and only visit, she graciously thanked its owner and his employees for helping her over, through, and out of a predicament into which he had lured her. Her apparently insincere expression of seemingly undeserved gratitude is not aberrant among wheelchair users who receive unsolicited and unwelcome acts of sympathetic assistance. Here again, wheelchair users' public expression and their private feelings often contrast sharply.

At least our informants often express gratitude for unsolicited offers and acts of assistance even when they are unneeded, unwelcome, inconvenient, embarrassing, and demeaning. They know all too well the consequences of not doing so: their self-appointed benefactors, as well as those who witness his or her charity, are likely to judge them harshly for any hint of ingratitude. One of our informants learned this on his first trip to a highly recommended barbershop.

I drove over there and got out of my car and wheeled my wheelchair up to the door. I opened the door and prepared to go in, and one of the two barbers came out and grabbed my handles. Now, as I've said, I like to do and insist on doing things for myself, but this fellow would not let go of the handles. I had my brakes on, preventing him from pushing me, but he insisted that he was going to push me over the threshold....And finally...I forget what he said, but I asked for an apology. And he said "Okay, I apologize, but you have a chip on your shoulder, don't you?"

For many wheelchair users on many occasions, thankful and deferential acceptance of such charitable acts may seem less micropolitically costly than being judged ungrateful, testy, and uncivil.

Even when wheelchair users are willing to pay the price of such harsh judgments rather than cooperating in diminishing the interactional place, another consideration often prevents them from doing so: they feel a sense of responsibility toward other wheelchair users and worry that their example might influence how other wheelchair users are treated in the future.

I have people falling all over themselves trying to help me. It used to bother me, but, god, the older you get the less it does. But I know a lot of people it does. I've got one friend that's at the point of almost being rude. This is bad because it sets a bad example. That person in the future may not be quite so willing to help the next person who really needs it.

As in this woman's case but not her friend's, the contradiction between a wheelchair user's immediate micropolitical interests and the presumably greater interests of his or her "real group" often blocks the wheelchair user's expression of his or her subjective emotional reactions to unsolicited and unwelcome offers and acts of assistance. He or she consequently sacrifices interactional place for the presumably greater good of those who share the stigma of moving through public places in a sitting position.

THE WAGES OF PUBLIC ACCEPTANCE

Wheelchair users are at least as different as the walkers whom they encounter in public. Like a number of our informants, some have no visible disability apart from their wheelchair use. Like other of our informants, some have amputated or apparently atrophied limbs, slurred speech, and obvious difficulty controlling their limb, neck, and facial muscles. Although walkers undoubtedly treat wheelchair users with visibly different disabilities differently, our diverse informants' reports of their public treatment, as well as the autobiographical reports that we read, were remarkably similar.

According to those reports, wheelchair users still must endure being treated like children in public places. Sometimes they are treated as open persons who can be addressed at will about their condition and the technical means of their mobility. At other times they are discussed and talked past as if absent. Although wheelchair users often depend on others' friendly assistance when the physical features of public places prove difficult to negotiate, most take pains to avoid exhausting the goodwill and sympathy of those who move through public places in a standing position. The above discussion demonstrates that wheelchair users more than reciprocate walkers for their assistance.

As in their relations with acquaintances, wheelchair users commonly assume primary responsibility for alleviating whatever strain occurs in their public relations with strangers. In the preceding examination of wheelchair users' emotionally charged experiences in public places, we illustrated some of the ways in which they do so. They laughingly make themselves butts of jokes so as to ease others' anxious discomfort with the wheelchair users' own potentially embarrassing plight. They are tactfully blind to young children's intrusive stares, tactfully deaf to such children's tactless remarks, and responsive to young interrogators' questions. Their poised example in such circumstances often counteracts the embarrassed "dis-ease" and sometimes anger of these children's adult caretakers, to the benefit of all concerned. Wheelchair users may remain poised even in the face of nonperson treatment, and may attempt to calm their companions' moral outrage. Thus they prevent embarrassing scenes that would engulf not only the guilty and the wronged but innocent bystanders as well. Again, when wheelchair users must impose on strangers' sympathy for minor acts of public aid, they often reciprocate with overgenerous remedial offerings and deferential gratitude. They may even accept unneeded and unwanted assistance with a gracious smile and hearty thanks so as not to offend their self-appointed benefactors or discourage them from assisting others in the future. In most of these cases, wheelchair users suppress the expression of their private feelings so as not to provoke or hurt others' feelings. Sometimes they also lower their interactional standing in the process.

Thus wheelchair users more than reciprocate the public acceptance and assistance that others grant them with considerable emotion work and micropolitical sacrifices. That work and those sacrifices profit the walkers whom they encounter in public. As some of our informants' comments indicate, they are keenly aware of the public favors that they do for helpful walkers.

> I just resign myself to the fact that people like to help you. They really get a joy out of it. You can see it in their faces. I say hey, if they're willing to help regardless of how it hurts, let them. Let them help. They think they're doing me a favor. People are always running over, and I let them. They seem happy. It makes them feel good.

Perhaps wheelchair users who frequent public places still are sometimes treated as children because the attention-attracting assistance they sometimes must request, but more often receive, overshadows all the interactional and identificatory assistance they give others. Yet one can easily discern wheelchair users' efforts and sacrifices on others' behalf by looking beyond the glare of physical feats and into the emotional and micropolitical shadows of public encounters. In those shadows wheelchair users stand tall, supporting the emotional weight of public tranquility and their public benefactors' moral identities.

PUBLIC LIFE AND EMOTION MANAGEMENT

Wheelchair users are not the only ones who manage both their own and others' emotions in public places. Walkers who encounter wheelchair users in public undoubtedly sometimes avoid expressing their own private anxieties, aversion, admiration, or sympathetic concern out of concern for the wheelchair users' feelings. It is also doubtful that public encounters between unacquainted walkers and wheelchair users are unusual in this respect. Our public etiquette would seem to proscribe the public expression of emotions that are prescribed by our feeling rules, and public life is often emotionally provocative. Although strangers in public places may take pains to avoid physical contact with one another, nonetheless they touch one another emotionally in a variety of ways. They are touched embarrassingly by one another's presumed judgments as well as by one another's embarrassment. They are caressed reassuringly by others' averted gaze and pinched with fear by others' stares. Others' slights and impositions touch them with anger, and they feel a touch of guilt over their own anger. They touch one another sympathetically when requesting and providing minor acts of public aid, and repay such gifts touchingly in a variety of emotional currencies.

Yet whatever our mode of public mobility, we commonly appear emotionally reserved in public places. We mask our own emotions so as not to excite others'. We manage our own expression and thereby others' feelings. We surface act so as to sustain the tranquil exterior of public life and to avoid being swept away by its emotionally turbulent undercurrents. As suggested by the example of wheelchair users, this is part of the implicit social bargain of contemporary public life.

DISCUSSION QUESTIONS

1. Cahill and Eggleston identify three key emotional demands on people who use wheelchairs in public. What are these demands?
2. Have you ever used a wheelchair? Do you know someone who uses a wheelchair? If so, can you relate to the emotional demands identified by Cahill and Eggleston?
3. What do Cahill and Eggleston mean when they refer to "helpful walkers"? Have you ever been or witnessed a "helpful walker"?

ADDITIONAL RESOURCES

Film

"Murderball." 2005. An 88-minute documentary about wheelchair users who play full contact rugby.

Internet

http://www.disabledandproud.com/. Disabled and Proud is one of many websites documenting pride in disability.

http://www.wsusa.org/. Wheelchair Sports USA was founded in 1956 to promote and organize athletes who use wheelchairs, many of whom are veterans of war.

http://www.apparelyzed.com/support/sport/xtreme_wheelchair_sports.html. Extreme Wheelchair Sports. This site promotes information on intense sports for wheelchair users.

Radio

http://www.kfai.org/disabledand proud. "Disabled and Proud" is an ongoing weekly radio show on Twin Cities–based KFAI, Radio without Boundaries. The show airs Tuesdays, 7–7:30 P.M. Central Standard Time.

FURTHER READING

Cahill, Spencer E. and Robin Eggleston. 1995. "Reconsidering the Stigma of Physical Disability: Wheelchair Use and Public Kindness." *The Sociological Quarterly*, 36(4): 681–98.

Eggleston, Robin. 1992. "The Everybody Sociology of the Differently-Abled." *Politeia: Skidmore's Student Journal of Academic Opinion*, 25:30–41.

Goffman, Erving. [1956] 1982. *Interaction Ritual*. New York: Random House.

Heatherton, Todd F., Robert E. Kleck, Michelle R. Hebl, and Jay G. Hull (eds.). 2003. *The Social Psychology of Stigma*. New York: Guilford Press.

Hochschild, Arlie Russell. 1979. "Emotion Work, Feeling Rules, and Social Structure." *American Journal of Sociology*, 85(3):551–75.

Hochschild, Arlie Russell. 1990. "Ideology and Emotion Management: A Perspective and Path for Future Research," in Theodore Kemper (ed.). *Research Agendas in the Sociology of Emotions*, 117–42. Albany, NY: SUNY Press.

39. Confronting Deadly Disease: The Drama of Identity Construction among Gay Men with AIDS

KENT L. SANDSTROM

In this moving piece written close to the onset of HIV infection and AIDS in the United States, Sandstrom draws on 56 interviews with 19 gay men who are HIV positive or who have AIDS. Sandstrom received the Herbert Blumer Award from the Society of Symbolic Interaction for best graduate student paper for an earlier version of this article.

The phenomenon of AIDS (acquired immunodeficiency syndrome) has been attracting increased attention from sociologists.

Despite this growing interest in the social and psychosocial dimensions of AIDS, little attention has been directed toward the processes of social and self-interaction by which individuals acquire and personalize an AIDS-related identity. Further, given the stigmatizing implications of AIDS, there has been a surprising lack of research regarding the strategies of stigma management and identity construction utilized by persons with this illness.

This article presents an effort to address these issues. It examines the dynamics of identity construction and management which characterize the everyday lives of persons with AIDS (PWAs).

METHOD AND DATA

The following analysis is based on data gathered in 56 in-depth interviews with 19 men who had been diagnosed with HIV (human immunodeficiency virus) infections. On the average, each individual was interviewed on three separate occasions and each of these sessions lasted from 1 to 3 hours. The interviews were guided by 60 open-ended questions and were audiotaped. Most interviews took place in the participants' homes. However,

a few participants were interviewed in a private university office because their living quarters were not conducive to a confidential conversation.

Participants were initially recruited through two local physicians who treat AIDS patients and through a local self-help organization that provides support groups and services for people with HIV infections. Those individuals who agreed to be interviewed early in the study spoke with friends or acquaintances and encouraged them to become involved. The majority of interviews were thus obtained through "snowball" or chain-referral sampling.

All respondents were gay males who lived in a metropolitan area in the Midwest. They varied in age, income, and the stage of their illness. In age, they ranged from 19 to 46 years, with the majority in the 28 to 40 age bracket. Six persons were currently employed in professional or white-collar occupations. The remaining 13 were living marginally on Social Security or disability benefits.

ON BECOMING A PWA: THE REALIZATION OF AN AIDS IDENTITY

For many of these men, the transformation of physical symptoms into the personal and social reality of AIDS took place most dramatically when they received a validating diagnosis from

Sandstrom, Kent L. 1990. "Confronting Deadly Disease: The Drama of Identity Construction among Gay Men with AIDS." *Journal of Contemporary Ethnography,* 19(3): 271–94.

a physician. The following account reveals the impact of being officially diagnosed:

> She [the doctor] said, "Your biopsy did come out for Kaposi's sarcoma. I want you to go to the hospital tomorrow and to plan to spend most of the day there." While she is telling me this, the whole world is buzzing in my head because this is the first confirmation coming from outside as opposed to my own internal suspicions. I started to cry—it [AIDS] became very real… *very real.*…
>
> Anyway, everything started to roller coaster inside me and I was crying in the office there. The doctor said "You knew this was the way it was going to come out, didn't you?" She seemed kind of shocked about why I was crying so much, not realizing that no matter how much you are internally aware of something, to hear it from someone else is what makes it real. For instance, the first time I really accepted being gay was when other people said, "You are gay!"… It's a social thing—you're not real until you're real to someone else.

This quote illustrates the salience of social processes for the validation and realization of an identity—in this case, an AIDS-related identity. Becoming a PWA is not simply a matter of viral infection, it is contingent on interpersonal interaction and definitions. As depicted in the quote, a rather momentous medical announcement facilitates a process of identity construction which, in turn, entails both interpersonal and subjective transformation. Within the interpersonal realm, the newly diagnosed "AIDS patient" is resituated as a social object and placed in a marginal or liminal status. He is thereby separated from many of his prior social moorings. On the subjective level, this separation produces a crisis, or a disruption of the PWA's routine activities and self-understanding. The diagnosed individual is prompted to "make sense" of the meaning of his newly acquired status and to feel its implications for future conceptions and enactments of self.

PERSONALIZING THE ILLNESS: SELF-FEELINGS EVOKED BY AIDS

As he interprets and responds to the meaning of his condition, the diagnosed individual *personalizes* it, adjusting it to the distinctive features of his life (e.g., his work situation, family history, personal relationships, character traits, and access to resources). Certain self-feelings and psychic reactions are especially important in this personalizing process. For example, PWAs may feel anguished about the loss of their future, the loss of a highly valued job, or by a diminished sense of sexual desirability. They may also feel troubled by their loss of everyday skills or opportunities and their lack of involvement in normal interaction.

Feelings of guilt can also be induced by an AIDS diagnosis. These feelings have several sources and dimensions. For instance, PWAs may feel guilty about the possibility that they infected their sexual partner(s). They may also feel guilty about the anguish, grief, or suffering that their diagnoses provoke among partners, friends, or family members. Furthermore, they may experience identification guilt because they are members of groups which are stigmatized by cultural conceptions, media accounts and conservative religious doctrines. These stigmatizing perspectives are sometimes internalized by PWAs and may lead them to (consciously or unconsciously) interpret their condition as a kind of punishment. Such a reaction is illustrated in the following remarks:

> In the beginning, it [AIDS] triggered feelings that had to do with…well, I hesitate to say this but it was like I deserved this [illness]. This is exactly what I deserved! I've heard other gay men talk about the same thing like "God, we've tried to live such a decent life and we're being punished." We made that connection of somehow being punished…and even if we didn't come right out and say it was punishment or something, what we said or what I said was "Well, God's trying to tell us something here."

Finally, due to the fatality of this disease, being informed that one has AIDS can also elicit strong feelings of death anxiety:

> After the doctor told me that I had Kaposi's sarcoma, I was really in bad shape.... I don't mean to be melodramatic but something inside me was saying "Holy shit, you're going to die! No you're not going to just die but you're going to die very soon!"

THE LIMINAL SITUATION OF THE PWA: CONSTRAINTS AND OPPORTUNITIES

As an individual enters into and personalizes the status of being a PWA, he finds his life characterized by ambiguity. The manifestations and consequences of his HIV infection are unclear and unpredictable. He is uncertain about what specific symptoms will be triggered by his illness, how he will feel from day to day, how much longer he can expect to live, and whether or not he will be able to live with dignity.

In the social realm, the experience of the PWA is especially ambiguous. Given the fear and mystery that surround AIDS, responses of others to his diagnosis can range from avoidance, hostility, and rejection to empathy and support. Regardless of the specific reactions of others, a shift or rupture occurs in the individual's social location. The PWA is not only separated from his previous social anchorages but he is not clearly linked to any new ones. Also, given the diverse and competing social definitions of AIDS, he is not provided with a precise indication of his current status.

Most important, recently diagnosed PWAs encounter both the constraints and opportunities that go along with their liminal social situation. On one hand, their liminal location can intensify problematic self-feelings and provoke a sense of confusion about the implications of their illness. Further, the ambiguous social meaning of their condition makes it more difficult for them to enact an AIDS-related identity. That is, although

PWAs are provided with a medical designation, they are not given a clear idea of what role or set of behavioral expectations correspond to this identity. They subsequently have few practical guidelines for constructing a meaningful course of action.

In their ongoing efforts to construct and negotiate a viable identity, PWAs must grapple with a number of stigmatizing reactions and interpersonal dilemmas.

INTERPERSONAL DILEMMAS ENCOUNTERED BY PWAS

Stigmatization

Stigmatization is one of the most significant difficulties faced by people with AIDS as they attempt to fashion a personal and social meaning for their illness. The vast majority of our informants had already experienced some kind of stigma because of their gay identities. When they were diagnosed with AIDS, they usually encountered even stronger homophobic reactions and discreditation efforts. An especially painful form of stigmatization occurred when PWAs were rejected by friends and family members after revealing their diagnosis. Many respondents shared very emotional accounts of how they were ostracized by parents, siblings, or colleagues. Several noted that their parents and family members had even asked them to no longer return home for visits. However, rejections were not always so explicit. In many cases, intimate relationships were gradually and ambiguously phased out rather than abruptly or clearly ended.

A few PWAs shared stories of being stigmatized by gay friends or acquaintances. They described how some acquaintances subtly reprimanded them when seeing them at gay bars or repeatedly reminded them to "be careful" regarding any sexual involvements. Further, they mentioned that certain gay friends avoided associating with them after learning of their AIDS-related diagnoses. These PWAs thus experienced the problem of being "doubly stigmatized," that is, they were devalued within an already stigmatized group, the gay community.

PWAs also felt the effects of stigmatization in other, more subtle ways. For example, curious and even sympathetic responses on the parts of others, especially strangers, could lead PWAs to feel discredited. One PWA, reflecting on his interactions with hospital staff, observed:

> When they become aware [of my diagnosis], it seemed like people kept looking at me...like they were looking for something. What it felt like was being analyzed, both physically and emotionally. It also felt like being a subject or guinea pig...like "here's another one." They gave me that certain kind of look. Kind of that look like pity or that said "what a poor wretch," not a judgmental look but rather a pitying one.

An experience of this nature can precipitate a crisis of identity for a person with AIDS. He finds himself being publicly stigmatized and identified as a victim. Such an identifying moment can seriously challenge prior conceptions of self. That is, it can lead a PWA to internalize stigmatizing social attributions or it can incite him to search for involvements and ideologies which might enable him to construct a more desirable AIDS identity.

FEARS OF CONTAGION AND DEATH ANXIETY

Fears of contagion present another serious dilemma for PWAs in their efforts to negotiate a functional social identity. These fears are generated not only by the fact that people with AIDS are the carriers of an epidemic illness but also because, like others with a death taint, they are symbolically associated with mass death and the contagion of the dead. The situation may even be further complicated by the contagion anxiety which homosexuality triggers for some people.

In general, others are tempted to withdraw from an individual with AIDS because of their fears of contracting the virus. Even close friends of a PWA are apt to feel more fearful or distant

toward him, especially when first becoming aware of the diagnosis. They may feel anxious about the possibility of becoming infected with the virus through interactions routinely shared with him in the past (e.g., hugging and kissing). They may also wish to avoid the perils of being stigmatized themselves by friends or associates who fear that those close to a PWA are a potential source of contagion.

This death-related contagion anxiety often results in increased strain and distance in a PWA's interactions with friends or family members. It can also inhibit the level of openness and intimacy shared among fellow PWAs when they gather together to address issues provoked by their diagnoses. Responses of grief, denial, and anxiety in the face of death make in-depth discussions of the illness experience keenly problematic. According to one respondent:

> Usually no one's ever able to talk about it [their illness and dying] without going to pieces. They might start but it only takes about two minutes to break into tears. They might say something like "I don't know what to do! I might not even be here next week!" Then you can just see the ripple effect it has on the others sitting back and listening. You have every possible expression from anger to denial to sadness and all these different emotions on people's faces. And mostly this feeling of "what can we do? Well...Nothing!"

PROBLEMS OF NORMALIZATION

Like others who possess a stigmatizing attribute, people with AIDS come to regard many social situations with alarm and uncertainty. They soon discover that their medical condition is a salient aspect of all but their most fleeting social encounters. They also quickly learn that their diagnosis, once known to others, can acquire the character of a *master status* and thus become the focal point of interaction.

In light of this, one might expect PWAs to prefer interaction contexts characterized by "closed" awareness. Their health status would be unknown to others and they would presumably encounter fewer problems when interacting. However, when in these situations, they must remain keenly attuned to controlling information and concealing attributes relevant to their diagnosis. Ironically, this requirement to be dramaturgically "on" may give rise to even more feelings of anxiety and resentment.

The efforts of persons with AIDS to establish and maintain relationships within more "open" contexts are also fraught with complications. One of the major dilemmas they encounter is how to move interactions beyond an atmosphere of fictional acceptance. A context of fictional acceptance is typified by responses on the part of others which deny, avoid, or minimize the reality of an individual's diagnosis. In attempting to grapple with the management of a spoiled identity, PWAs may seek to "break through" relations of this nature. In doing so, they often try to broaden the scope of interactional involvement and to normalize problematic elements of their social identity.

Yet even if a PWA attains success in "breaking through," it does not necessarily diminish his interactional difficulties. Instead, he can become caught in an ambiguous dilemma with respect to the requisites of awareness and normalization. Simply put, if others begin to disregard his diagnosis and treat him in a normal way, then he faces the problem of having to remind them of the limitations to normalcy imposed by this condition. The person with AIDS is thus required to perform an intricate balancing act between encouraging the normalization of his relationships and ensuring that others remain sensitized to the constraining effects of such a serious illness. These dynamics promote the construction of relationships which, at best, have a qualified sense of normalcy. They also heighten the PWAs sense that he is located in an ambiguous or liminal position.

AVOIDING OR MINIMIZING DILEMMAS

In an attempt to avoid or defuse the problematic feelings, attributions, and ambiguities which arise

in their ongoing interactions, PWAs engage in various forms of identity management. In doing so, they often use strategies which allow them to minimize the social visibility of their diagnoses and to carefully control interactions with others. These strategies include *passing, covering, isolation,* and *insulation.*

The particular strategies employed vary according to the progression of their illness, the personal meanings they attach to it, the audiences serving as primary referents for self-presentations, and the dynamics of their immediate social situation.

PASSING AND COVERING

As Goffman (1963) noted in his classic work on stigma, those with a spoiled identity may seek to pass as normal by carefully suppressing information and thereby precluding others' awareness of devalued personal attributes. The PWAs we interviewed mentioned that "passing" was a maneuver they had used regularly. It was easily employed in the early stages of the illness when more telltale physical signs had not yet become apparent and awareness of an individual's diagnosis was confirmed to a small social circle.

However, as the illness progresses, concealing the visibility of an AIDS-related diagnosis becomes more difficult. When a person with AIDS begins to miss work frequently, to lose weight noticeably, and to reduce his general level of activity, others become more curious or suspicious about what ailment is provoking such major changes. In the face of related questions, some PWAs elected to devise a "cover" for their diagnosis which disguised troubling symptoms as products of a less discrediting illness.

One informant decided to cover his AIDS diagnosis by telling co-workers that he was suffering from leukemia:

> There was coming a point, I wasn't feeling so hot. I was tired and the quality of my life was decreasing tremendously because all of my free time was spent resting or sleeping. I was still

keeping up with work but I thought I'd better tell them something before I had to take more days off here and there to even out the quality of my life. I had already had this little plan to tell them I had leukemia...but I thought how am I going to tell them, what am I going to tell them, how am I going to convince them? What am I going to do if someone says, "You don't have leukemia, you have AIDS!"? This was all stuff clicking around in my mind. I thought, how could they possibly know? They only know as much as I tell them.

This quote reveals the heightened concern with information control that accompanies decisions to conceal one's condition. Regardless of the psychic costs, though, a number of our informants opted for this remedial strategy. A commonly used technique consisted of informing friends, parents, or co-workers that one had cancer or tuberculosis without mentioning that these were the presenting symptoms of one's AIDS diagnosis. Covering attempts of this kind were most often employed by PWAs when relating to others who were not aware of their gay identity. These relationships were less apt to be characterized by the suspicions or challenges offered by those who knew that an individual was both gay and seriously ill.

ISOLATION AND INSULATION

For those whose diagnosis was not readily visible, dramaturgical skills, such as passing and covering, could be quite useful. These techniques were not so feasible when physical cues, such as a pale complexion, emaciated appearance, or facial lesion made the nature of a PWA's condition more apparent. Under these circumstances, negotiations with others were more alarming and they were more likely to include conflicts engendered by fear, ambiguity, and expressions of social devaluation.

In turn, some PWAs came to view physical and social isolation as the best means available to them for escaping from both these interpersonal difficulties and their own feelings of ambivalence. By withdrawing from virtually all interaction, they sought to be spared the social struggles and

psychic strains that could be triggered by others' recognition of their condition.

Nonetheless, this strategy was typically an unsuccessful one. Isolation and withdrawal often exacerbated the feelings of alienation that PWAs were striving to minimize in their social relationships. Moreover, their desire to be removed from the interactional matrix was frequently overcome by their need for extensive medical care and interpersonal support as they coped with the progressive effects of the illness.

Given the drawbacks of extreme isolation, a number of PWAs used a more selective withdrawal strategy. It consisted of efforts to disengage from many but not all social involvements and to interact regularly with only a handful of trusted associates (e.g., partners, friends, or family members). Emphasis was placed on minimizing contacts with those outside of this circle because they were likely to be less tolerant or predictable.

PWAs engaging in this type of selective interaction tried to develop a small network of intimate others who could insulate them from potentially threatening interactions. Ideally, they were able to form a reliable social circle within which they felt little need to conceal their diagnosis. They could thereby experience some relief from the burden of stigma management and information control.

BUILDING AND EMBRACING AN AIDS IDENTITY

Strategies such as passing, covering, isolation, and insulation are used by PWAs, especially in the earlier stages of their illness, to shield themselves from the stigma and uncertainty associated with AIDS. However, these strategies typically require a high level of personal vigilance, they evoke concerns about information control, and they are essentially defensive in nature. They do not provide PWAs with a way to reformulate the personal meaning of their diagnosis and to integrate it with valued definitions of self.

In light of this, most PWAs engage in more active types of *identity work* to gain a greater sense of mastery over their condition and to make better use of the behavioral possibilities arising from their liminal condition.

The most prominent type of identity work engaged in by the PWAs we interviewed was embracement. Among the PWAs involved in this study, embracement was promoted and reinforced through participation in local AIDS-related support groups.

SUPPORT GROUPS AND ASSOCIATIONAL EMBRACEMENT

The vast majority of respondents in this study became involved in PWA support groups in order to better address the crisis elicited by their illness and to find new forms of self-expression. They typically joined these groups within a few months of receiving their diagnosis and continued to attend meetings on a fairly regular basis.

By and large, support groups became the central focus of identity work and repair for PWAs. These groups were regarded as a valuable source of education and emotional support that helped individuals to cope better with the daily exigencies of their illness. At support group meetings, PWAs could exchange useful information, share feelings and troubles, and relate to others who could see beyond the negative connotations of AIDS.

Support groups also facilitated the formation of social ties and feelings of collective identification among PWAs. Within these circles, individuals learned to better nurture and support one another and to emphasize the shared nature of their problems. Feelings of guilt and isolation were transformed into a sense of group identification:

> I spend almost all of my time with other PWAs. They're my best friends now and they're the people I feel most comfortable with. We support one another and we know that we can talk to each other any time, day or night.

For some PWAs, especially those with a troubled or marginal past, support group relationships provided an instant "buddy system" that was used to bolster feelings of security and self-worth. Recently formed support group friendships even took on primary importance in their daily lives. Perhaps because of the instability and isolation which characterized their life outside of support groups, a few of these PWAs tended to exaggerate the level of intimacy which existed in their newly found friendships. By stressing a romanticized version of these relationships, they were able to preserve a sense of being cared for even in the absence of more enduring social connections.

IDENTITY EMBRACEMENT AND AFFIRMATION

Most of the PWAs we interviewed had come to gradually affirm and embrace an AIDS-related identity. Participation in a support group exposed them to alternative definitions of the reality of AIDS and an ongoing system of identity construction. Hence, rather than accepting public imputations which cast them as "AIDS victims," PWAs learned to distance themselves from such designations and to avow more favorable AIDS-associated identities. In turn, the process of *identity embracement* was realized when individuals proudly announced that they were PWAs who were "living and thriving with the illness."

Continued associations with other PWAs could also promote deepening involvement in activities organized around the identity of being a person with AIDS. A case in point is provided by a man who recounted his progression as a PWA:

> After awhile, I aligned myself with other people with AIDS who shared my beliefs about taking the active role. I began writing and speaking about AIDS and I became involved in various projects. I helped to create and promote a workshop for people with AIDS....I also got involved in organizing a support group for family members of PWAs.

As involvement in AIDS-related activities increases, embracement of an AIDS-centered identity is likely to become more encompassing. In some cases, diagnosed individuals found themselves organizing workshops on AIDS, coordinating a newsletter for PWAs, and delivering speeches regularly at schools and churches. Virtually all aspects of their lives became associated with their diagnosis. Being a PWA thus became both a master status and a valued career. This process was described by a person who had been diagnosed with AIDS-related complex (ARC) for two years:

> One interesting thing is that when you have AIDS or ARC and you're not working anymore, you tend to become a veteran professional on AIDS issues. You get calls regularly from people who want information or who want you to get involved in a project, etc. You find yourself getting drawn to that kind of involvement. It becomes almost a second career!

This kind of identity embracement was particularly appealing for a few individuals involved in this study. Prior to contracting an AIDS-related infection, they had felt rejected or unrecognized in many of their social relationships (e.g., family, work, and friendships). Ironically, their stigmatized AIDS diagnosis provided them with an opportunity for social affirmation. It offered them a sense of uniqueness and expertise that was positively evaluated in certain social and community circles (e.g., public education and church forums). It could even serve as a springboard for a new and more meaningful biography.

IDEOLOGICAL EMBRACEMENT: AIDS AS A TRANSFORMING EXPERIENCE

One of the most prominent subcultural interpretations of AIDS highlighted the spiritual meaning of the illness. For PWAs embracing this viewpoint, AIDS was symbolically and experientially inverted from a "curse" to a "blessing" which promoted a liberating rather than a constricting form of identity transformation. The following remarks illustrate this perspective:

> I now view AIDS as both a gift and a blessing. That sounds strange, I suppose, in a limited

context. It sounds strange because we [most people] think it's so awful, but yet there are such radical changes that take place in your life from having this illness that's defined as terminal. You go through this amazing kind of *transformation*. You look at things for the first time, in a powerful new way that you've never looked at them before in your whole life.

A number of PWAs similarly stressed the beneficial personal and spiritual transitions experienced as a result of their diagnosis. They even regarded their illness as a motivating force that led them to grapple with important existential questions and to experience personal growth and change that otherwise would not have occurred.

These individuals placed a premium on disseminating information about AIDS and promoting a level of public awareness which might inhibit the further transmission of this illness. Some felt that their diagnosis had provided them with a unique opportunity to help and educate others. They subsequently displayed a high level of personal sacrifice and commitment while seeking to spread the news about AIDS and to nurture those directly affected by this illness. Most crucially, their diagnosis provided them with a heightened sense of power and purpose:

> Basically I feel that as a person with ARC I can do more for humanity in general than I could ever do before. I never before in my life felt like I belonged here. For the most part, I felt like I was stranded on a hostile planet—I didn't know why. But now with the disease and what I've learned in my life, I feel like I really have something by which I can help other people. It gives me a special sense of purpose.

> I feel like I've got a mission now and that's what this whole thing is about. AIDS is challenging me with a question and the question it asks is: If I'm not doing something to help others regarding this illness, then why continue to use up energy here on this earth?

Most PWAs realized their condition offered them an opportunity to experience both psychological and social power. They subsequently accentuated the empowering dimensions of their lived experience of AIDS and linked these to an encompassing metaphor of transformation.

SUMMARY AND CONCLUSIONS

People with AIDS face many obstacles in their efforts to construct and sustain a desirable social identity. In the early stages of their career, after receiving a validating diagnosis, they are confronted by painful self-feelings such as grief, guilt, and death anxiety. These feelings often diminish their desire and ability to participate in interactions which would allow them to sustain favorable images of self.

PWAs encounter additional difficulties as a result of being situated (at least initially) as liminal persons. That is, their liminal situation can heighten negative self-feelings and evoke a sense of confusion and uncertainty about the social implications of their illness. At the same time, however, it releases them from conventional roles, meanings, or expectations and provides them with a measure of power and maneuverability in the processes of identity construction.

In turn, as they construct and negotiate the meaning of an AIDS-related identity, PWAs must grapple with the effects of social reactions such as stigmatization, counterfeit nurturance, fears of contagion, and death anxiety. These reactions both elicit and reinforce a number of interactional ambiguities, dilemmas, and threats to self.

In responding to these challenges, PWAs engage in various types of identity management and construction. On one hand, they may seek to disguise their diagnoses or to restrict their social and interactional involvements. PWAs are most likely to use such strategies in the earlier phases of the illness. The disadvantage of these strategies is that they are primarily defensive. They provide PWAs with a way to avoid or adjust to the effects of problematic social reactions, but they do not offer a means for affirming more desirable AIDS-related identities.

On the other hand, as their illness progresses and they become more enmeshed in subcultural networks, most PWAs are prompted to engage in forms of identity embracement which enable them to actively reconstruct the meaning of their illness and to integrate it with valued conceptions of self. In essence, through their interactions with other PWAs, they learn to embrace affiliations and ideologies which accentuate the transformative and empowering possibilities arising from their condition. They also acquire the social and symbolic resources necessary to fashion revitalizing identities and to sustain a sense of dignity and self-worth.

Ultimately, through their ongoing participation in support networks, PWAs are able to build identities which are linked to their lived experience of AIDS. They are also encouraged to actively confront and transform the stigmatizing conceptions associated with this medical condition. Hence, rather than resigning themselves to the darker implications of AIDS, they learn to affirm themselves as "people with AIDS" who are "living and thriving with the illness."

DISCUSSION QUESTIONS

1. Sandstrom identifies four key strategies employed by persons with AIDS to minimize the visibility of their illness. What are these strategies and how do they work?
2. Similar to Zimmerman's findings on women's experiences with abortion, Sandstrom discovers that persons with AIDS often experience rejection from family and friends. How is the stigma associated with AIDS similar to and different from the stigma associated with having an abortion?

3. Much has changed in the treatment and experience of HIV and AIDS since Sandstrom published this article in 1990. While it is no longer considered a "death sentence" to receive an HIV-positive diagnosis, the demands of a lifetime of intensive medications and debilitating side effects remain strong. How might changes in the treatment of HIV and AIDS affect the stigma associated with the virus and syndrome?

4. Do you know someone who is HIV positive or who has AIDS? If so, have you witnessed the identity distancing and embracement documented by Sandstrom?

ADDITIONAL RESOURCES

Film

"The Age of AIDS." A PBS "Frontline" documentary of the 25-year international history of the disease. http://www.pbs.org/wgbh/pages/frontline/aids/.

"Angels in America." 2003. An HBO film version of playwright Tony Kushner's award-winning epic AIDS drama, starring Al Pacino, Meryl Streep, and Emma Thompson. http://www.hbo.com/films/angelsinamerica/.

"Common Threads: Stories from the Quilt." 1989. A 79-minute documentary of the history of AIDS in the United States and the development of the Names Quilt. Narrated by Dustin Hoffman with music by Bobby McFerrin, this Academy Award–winning film tells the profoundly touching and political story of AIDS through the lives of those most deeply affected by it.

"Longtime Companion." 1990. A 96-minute film directed by Norman René that chronicles the impact of living with AIDS on one's closest relationships.

Internet

http://www.alternativesmagazine.com/15/hill.html. 2000. A provocative article by Daniel Hill detailing the gay male underground phenomenon of "bug chasing" by those who seek to become HIV positive.

http://www.avert.org/. Avert.org is an international charity dedicated to documenting and eradicating HIV and AIDS.

http://www.cdc.gov/hiv/default.htm. The Centers for Disease Control and Prevention's website dedicated to HIV and AIDS education and prevention.

http://www.unaids.org/en/. The United Nations AIDS website dedicated to international AIDS education and prevention.

FURTHER READING

Brown, Lisanne, Kate Macintyre, and Lea Trujillo. 2003. "Interventions to Reduce HIV/AIDS Stigma: What Have We Learned?" *AIDS Education and Prevention*, 15(1): 49–69.

Deacon, Harriet, Stephney Inez, and Sandra Prosalendis. 2005. *Understanding HIV/AIDS Stigma: A Theoretical and Methodological Analysis*. Cape Town: Human Science Research Council Press.

Grodeck, Brett and Daniel S. Berger. 2007. The *First Year: HIV: An Essential Guide for the Newly Diagnosed*. Cambridge, MA: Da Capo Press.

Kroeger, Brooke. 2003. *Passing: When People Can't Be Who They Are*. New York: Public Affairs, A member of the Perseus Books Group.

Valdiserri, Ronald O. 2002. "HIV/AIDS Stigma: An Impediment to Public Health." *American Journal of Public Health,* 92(3): 341–2.

Weitz, Rose. 1990. "Living with the Stigma of AIDS." *Qualitative Sociology,* 13(1): 23–38.

Social Structure and Social Psychology

V.A. Race and Ethnicity

V.B. Social Class

V.C. Gender

"Actually, Lou, I think it was more than just my being in the right place at the right time. I think it was my being the right race, the right religion, the right sex, the right socioeconomic group, having the right accent, the right clothes, going to the right schools..."

Race and Ethnicity

We have included four selections in this section: two classics about the experience of racism from the perspective of black men and two contemporary pieces about "ethnic" cosmetic surgery and the pressure of those with dark skin to conform to a white ideal.

Du Bois, who was born 34 years before Hughes but died just 4 years before him, wrote about a "double consciousness" and "the veil" experienced by people whose race and ethnicity are deemed "a problem." Hughes was multiracial himself, having black, Native American, Jewish, and Scottish heritage. He described the rule of hypodescent, also known as the "one drop" rule, and the complexity of a multiracial identity.

While Du Bois wrote about *The Souls of Black Folk*, Hughes documented the Harlem Renaissance in which he participated. Hughes helped to articulate the meaning of white privilege and "whiteness" itself in publications such as *The Ways of White Folks* (1934).

In their contemporary research, Kaw and Thompson and Keith write about the continued ostracism experienced by racial and ethnic minorities, echoing themes established in the earlier work of Du Bois and Hughes.

40. The Souls of Black Folk

W. E. B. DU BOIS

In 1909, William Edward Burghardt Du Bois served as one of the founding members of the National Association for the Advancement of Colored People (NAACP). A sociologist, historian, and civil rights activist, Du Bois continued to serve the NAACP as a member of its board of directors from 1910 to 1934. This excerpt from *The Souls of Black Folk* is one of his best known contributions to ongoing discussions about racism.

I

Of Our Spiritual Strivings

BETWEEN me and the other world there is ever an unasked question: unasked by some through feelings of delicacy; by others through the difficulty of rightly framing it. All, nevertheless, flutter round it. They approach me in a half-hesitant sort of way, eye me curiously or compassionately, and then, instead of saying directly, How does it feel to be a problem? they say, I know an excellent colored man in my town.

Being a problem is a strange experience—peculiar even for one who has never been anything else, save perhaps in babyhood. It is in the early days of rollicking boyhood that the revelation first bursts upon one, all in a day, as it were. I remember well when the shadow swept across me. I was a little thing, away up in the hills of New England, where the dark Housatonic winds between Hoosac and Taghkanic to the sea. In a wee wooden school-house, something put it into the boys' and girls' heads to buy gorgeous visiting-cards—ten cents a package—and exchange. The exchange was merry, till one girl, a tall newcomer, refused my card,—refused it peremptorily, with a glance. Then it dawned upon me with a certain suddenness that I was different from the others; shut out from their world by a vast veil. I had thereafter no desire to tear down that veil, to creep through; I held all beyond it in common contempt, and lived above it in a region of blue sky and great wandering shadows. That sky was bluest when I could beat my mates at examination-time, or beat them at a foot-race, or even beat their stringy heads. Alas, with the years all this fine contempt began to fade; for the worlds I longed for, and all their dazzling opportunities, were theirs, not mine. But they should not keep these prizes, I said; some, all, I would wrest from them. Just how I would do it I could never decide: by reading law, by healing the sick, by telling the wonderful tales that swam in my head,—some way.

After the Egyptian and Indian, the Greek and Roman, the Teuton and Mongolian, the Negro is a sort of seventh son, born with a veil, and gifted with second-sight in this American world—a world which yields him no true self-consciousness, but only lets him see himself through the revelation of the other world. It is a peculiar sensation, this double-consciousness, this sense of always looking at one's self through the eyes of others, of measuring one's soul by the tape of a world that looks on in amused contempt and pity.

The history of the American Negro is the history of this strife—this longing to attain self-conscious manhood, to merge his double self into a better and truer self. In this merging he wishes neither of the older selves to be lost. He would not Africanize America, for America has too much to teach the world and Africa. He would not bleach his Negro soul in a flood of white Americans,

Du Bois, W. E. B. 1903. "Of Our Spiritual Strivings," in *The Souls of Black Folk*. 1–12. New York: Bantam.

for he knows that Negro blood has a message for the world. He simply wishes to make it possible for a man to be both a Negro and an American, without being cursed and spit upon by his fellows, without having the doors of Opportunity closed roughly in his face.

The facing of so vast a prejudice could not but bring the inevitable self-questioning, self-disparagement, and lowering of ideals which ever accompany repression and breed in an atmosphere of contempt and hate. Whisperings and portents came borne upon the four winds: Lo! we are diseased and dying, cried the dark hosts; we cannot write, our voting is vain; what need of education, since we must always cook and serve? And the Nation echoed and enforced this self-criticism, saying: Be content to be servants, and nothing more; what need of higher culture for half-men? Away with the black man's ballot, by force or fraud—and behold the suicide of a race!

Will America be poorer if she replaces her brutal dyspeptic blundering with light-hearted but determined Negro humility? or her coarse and cruel wit with loving jovial good-humor? or her vulgar music with the soul of the Sorrow Songs?

Merely a concrete test of the underlying principles of the great republic is the Negro Problem, and the spiritual striving of the freedmen's sons is the travail of souls whose burden is almost beyond the measure of their strength, but who bear it in the name of an historic race, in the name of this the land of their fathers' fathers, and in the name of human opportunity.

DISCUSSION QUESTIONS

1. Du Bois claims that it is difficult to be both a Negro and an American. When you are asked to envision an American, who comes to mind first? What is their race or ethnicity?
2. Are blacks or other people of color ever considered truly American? How might the requirements for "being American" differ for women versus men and for people of various social classes and ethnicities?
3. Du Bois published this piece more than a century ago. Is it still relevant today? How so or why not?
4. Du Bois addresses how it feels "to be a problem." Have you ever felt the "shadow" of "being a problem" sweep across you or others you know?

ADDITIONAL RESOURCES

Film

"The Two Nations of Black America: Booker T. and W.E.B." 1998. A PBS "Frontline" program about the opposing philosophies of Booker T. Washington and W.E.B. Du Bois. http://www.pbs.org/wgbh/pages/frontline/shows/race/etc/road.html.

Internet

http://www.cnn.com/2009/HEALTH/07/23/doctors.attitude.race.weight/index.html. A CNN video featuring recent research on racial inequities in health care.

http://www.naacp.org/about/history/dubois/index.htm. A comprehensive biography of Du Bois published by the National Association for the Advancement of Colored People.

http://www.theatlantic.com/unbound/flashbks/black/mcgillbh.htm. Du Bois' final interview, published in *The Atlantic* in 1965.

FURTHER READING

Ciccariello-Maher, George. 2009. "A Critique of Du Boisian Reason: Kanye West and the Fruitfulness of Double Consciousness." *Journal of Black Studies,* 39(3): 371–401.

Du Bois, W. E. B. 1903. *The Souls of Black Folk.* New York: Bantam.

Falcon, Sylvanna M. 2008. "Mestiza Double Consciousness: The Voices of Afro-Peruvian Women on Gendered Racism." *Gender & Society,* 22(5): 660–80.

Gates, Henry Louis, Jr. (ed.). 2007. *The Oxford W.E.B. Du Bois: 19-Volume Set.* New York: Oxford University Press.

Lewis, David Levering. 1994. *W.E.B. Du Bois, 1868–1919: Biography of a Race.* New York: Henry Holt.

Lewis, David Levering (ed). 1995. *W.E.B. Du Bois: A Reader.* New York: Henry Holt.

Lewis, David Levering. 2001. *W.E.B. Du Bois, 1919–1963: The Fight for Equality and the American Century.* New York: Henry Holt.

Rabaka, Reiland. 2007. "The Souls of White Folk: W.E.B. Du Bois's Critique of White Supremacy and Contributions to Critical White Studies." *Journal of African American Studies,* 11(1): 1–15.

41. That Powerful Drop

LANGSTON HUGHES

In 1943, Hughes created the character Jesse B. Simple—an affable uneducated black man from Harlem who spouted racially conscious plain truths about life from his barstool. "That Powerful Drop" is one of many dialogues written by Hughes that features Simple.

Leaning on the lamp post in front of the barber shop, Simple was holding up a copy of the *Chicago Defender* and reading about how a man who looks white had just been declared officially colored by an Alabama court.

"It's powerful," he said.

"What?"

"That one drop of Negro blood—because just *one* drop of black blood makes a man colored. *One* drop—you are a Negro! Now, why is that? Why is Negro blood so much more powerful than any other kind of blood in the world? If a man has Irish blood in him, people will say, 'He's *part* Irish.' If he has a little Jewish blood, they'll say, 'He's *half* Jewish.' But if he has just a small bit of colored blood in him, bam!—'He's a Negro!' Not, 'He's *part* Negro.' No, be it ever so little, if that blood is black, *'He's a Negro!'* Now, that is what I do not understand—why our *one* drop is so powerful. Take paint—white will not make black *white.* But black will make white *black.* One drop of black

Hughes, Langston. 1958. "That Powerful Drop," in *The Langston Hughes Reader,* 201. New York: Harold Ober Associates Incorporated.

in white paint—and the white ain't white no more! Black is powerful. You can have ninety-nine drops of white blood in your veins down South—but if that other *one* drop is black, shame on you! Even if you look white, You're black. That drop is really powerful. Explain it to me. You're colleged."

"It has no basis in science," I said, "so there's no logical explanation."

"Anyhow," said Simple, "if we lived back in fairy tale days and a good fairy was to come walking up to me, the very first thing I would wish would be:

THAT ALL WHITE FOLKS WAS BLACK

Then nobody would have to bother about white blood and black blood any more.

DISCUSSION QUESTIONS

1. What is the "powerful drop" to which Hughes refers? Is it culturally relevant today? For all people who are multiracial or just for some?
2. In this piece, Hughes' character Simple wishes that all white people were black so that no one would have to worry about black and white blood. Why do you think Simple wishes for this rather than wishing that all black people were white or that all people were the same color?
3. If the entire world "became black," as Simple desires, would there indeed be no "problems of blood" or would the shade of one's skin tone become significant?

ADDITIONAL RESOURCES

Film

"Cora Unashamed." 2000. A PBS "Masterpiece Theatre American Collection" production of Hughes' story of an African American domestic worker in the Depression-era Midwest.

"I'm Biracial, Not Black Damn It." 2009. An extraordinary documentary about the lives and experiences of biracial and multiracial Americans. http://videoproduction.battlecatt.com/index.php?/component/option,com_seyret/Itemid,5/id,9/task,videodirectlink/.

Internet

http://www.kansasheritage.org/crossingboundaries/page6el.html. A biography of Langston Hughes, who was raised in Kansas, published by the Kansas Heritage Group.

http://www.nytimes.com/interactive/2008/03/18/us/politics/20080318_OBAMA_GRAPHIC.html#. *The New York Times'* transcript and video of Barack Obama's speech on race, delivered March 18, 2009, in Philadelphia.

http://www.pbs.org/wgbh/masterpiece/americancollection/cora/index.html. The website for the Masterpiece Theatre film "Cora Unashamed" features numerous resources about Hughes and his work.

http://www.ronmccurdy.com/about_hudges_project.htm. The Langston Hughes Project is a multimedia performance of Hughes' epic poem "Ask Your Mama: Twelve Moods for Jazz," with music composed by Hughes.

http://spencer.lib.ku.edu/exhibits/langston/author.htm. A page from the Kenneth Spencer Research Library of the University of Kansas dedicated to the publications of Langston Hughes.

FURTHER READING

Doane, Ashley W. and Eduardo Bonillia-Silva. 2003. *White Out: The Continuing Significance of Racism.* New York: Routledge.

Frazier, Sundee. 2002. *Check All That Apply: Finding Wholeness as a Multiracial Person.* Downers Grove, IL: InterVarsity Press.

Fulbeck, Kip. 2006. *Part Asian, 100% Hapa.* San Francisco: Chronicle Books.

Gaskins, Pearl Fuyo (ed.). 1999. *What Are You? Voices of Mixed Race Young People.* New York: Henry Holt & Co.

Hughes, Langston. 1934. *The Ways of White Folks.* New York: Knopf.

Hughes, Langston. 1958. *The Langston Hughes Reader.* New York: Harold Ober Associates Incorporated.

Hughes, Langston. 1961. *The Best of Simple.* New York: Hill and Wang.

McLaren, Joseph. 1997. *Langston Hughes: Folk Dramatist in the Protest Tradition, 1921–1943.* Santa Barbara, CA: Greenwood Press.

Middleton, Richard T., IV. 2008. "Institutions, Inculcation, and Black Racial Identity: Pigmentocracy vs. the Rule of Hypodescent." *Social Identities,* 14(5): 567–85.

Root, Maria P. P. (ed.). 1996. *The Multiracial Experience: Racial Borders as the New Frontier.* Newbury Park, CA: Sage Publications.

Spencer, Rainier. 2004. "Assessing Multiracial Identity Theory and Politics: The Challenge of Hypodescent." *Ethnicities,* 4(3): 357–79.

42. Medicalization of Racial Features: Asian American Women and Cosmetic Surgery

EUGENIA KAW

In 1991, when she was a graduate student, Kaw was awarded the Steven Polgar Prize in medical anthropology from the American Anthropological Association for a previous version of this article. Drawing on interviews with plastic surgeons and Asian American women who have undergone cosmetic surgery, Kaw illustrates how medical intervention can play a powerful role in racial identity negotiation.

Throughout history and across cultures, humans have decorated, manipulated, and mutilated their bodies for religious reasons, for social prestige, and for beauty. In the United States, permanent alteration of the body for aesthetic reasons has become increasingly common. The cosmetic surgery industry, a $300 million per year industry, has been able to meet an

Kaw, Eugenia. 1993. "Medicalization of Racial Features: Asian American Women and Cosmetic Surgery." *Medical Anthropology Quarterly,* 7(1): 74–89.

increasingly wide variety of consumer demands. Now men, too, receive services ranging from the enlargement of calves and chests to the liposuction of cheeks and necks. Most noticeably, the ethnic composition of consumers has changed so that in recent years there are more racial and ethnic minorities.

The types of cosmetic surgery sought by women in the United States are racially specific. Like most white women, Asian American women who undergo cosmetic surgery are motivated by the need to look their best as women. White women, however, usually opt for liposuction, breast augmentation, or wrinkle removal procedures, whereas Asian American women most often request "double-eyelid" surgery, whereby folds of skin are excised from across their upper eyelids to create a crease above each eye that makes the eyes look wider. Also frequently requested is surgical sculpting of the nose tip to create a more chiseled appearance, or the implantation of a silicone or cartilage bridge in the nose for a more prominent appearance. In 1990, national averages compiled by the American Society of Plastic and Reconstructive Surgeons show that liposuction, breast augmentation, and collagen injection were the most common surgical procedures among cosmetic patients, 80 percent of whom are white. Although national statistics on the types of cosmetic surgery most requested by Asian Americans specifically are not available, data from two of the doctors' offices in my study show that in 1990 eyelid surgery was the most common procedure undergone by Asian American patients (40% of all procedures on Asian Americans at one doctor's office, 46% at another), followed by nasal implants and nasal tip refinement procedures (15% at the first doctor's office, 23% at the second). While the features that white women primarily seek to alter through cosmetic surgery (i.e., the breasts, fatty areas of the body, and facial wrinkles) do not correspond to conventional markers of racial identity, those features that Asian American women primarily seek to alter (i.e., "small, narrow" eyes and a "flat" nose) do correspond to such markers.

My research focuses on the cultural and institutional forces that motivate Asian American women to alter surgically the shape of their eyes and noses. I argue that Asian American women's decision to undergo cosmetic surgery is an attempt to escape persisting racial prejudice that correlates their stereotyped genetic physical features ("small, slanty" eyes and a "flat" nose) with negative behavioral characteristics, such as passivity, dullness, and a lack of sociability. With the authority of scientific rationality and technological efficiency, medicine is effective in perpetuating these racist notions. The medical system bolsters and benefits from the larger consumer-oriented society not only by maintaining the idea that beauty should be every woman's goal but also by promoting a beauty standard that requires that certain racial features of Asian American women be modified. Through the subtle and often unconscious manipulation of racial and gender ideologies, medicine, as a producer of norms, and the larger consumer society of which it is a part encourage Asian American women to mutilate their bodies to conform to an ethnocentric norm.

Social scientific analyses of ethnic relations should include a study of the body. As evident in my research, racial minorities may internalize a body image produced by the dominant culture's racial ideology and, because of it, begin to loathe, mutilate, and revise parts of their bodies. Bodily mutilation and adornment are symbolic mediums most directly and concretely concerned with the construction of the individual as social actor or cultural subject.

METHOD AND DESCRIPTION OF SUBJECTS

In this article I present findings of an ongoing ethnographic research project in the San Francisco Bay Area begun in April 1991. I draw on data from structured interviews with physicians and patients, medical literature and newspaper articles, and basic medical statistics. The sample of informants for this research is not random in the strictly statistical sense since informants were difficult to locate. In the United States, both clients and their medical practitioners treat the decision to undergo cosmetic surgery as highly confidential, and practitioners do not reveal the names of patients without their consent. In an effort to generate a sample of Asian American woman informants, I posted fliers and placed advertisements in various local newspapers for a period of at least three months, but I received only one reply. I also asked doctors who had agreed to participate in my study to ask their Asian American patients if they would agree to be interviewed. The doctors reported that most of the patients preferred not to talk about their operations or about motivations leading up to the operation. Ultimately, I was able to conduct structured, open-ended interviews with eleven Asian American women, four of whom were referred to me by doctors in the study, six by mutual acquaintances, and one through an advertisement in a local newspaper. Nine have had cosmetic surgery of the eye or the nose; one recently considered a double-eyelid operation; one is considering a double-eyelid operation in the next few years. Nine of the women in the study live in the San Francisco Bay Area, and two in the Los Angeles area. Five had their operations from the doctors in my study, while four had theirs in Asia—two in Seoul, Korea, one in Beijing, China, and one in Taipei, Taiwan. Of the eleven women in the study, only two, who received their operations in China and in Taiwan, had not lived in the United States prior to their operations. The two who had surgery in Korea grew up in the United States; they said that they decided to go to Korea for their surgeries because the operations were cheaper there than in the United States and because they felt doctors in Korea are more "experienced" since these types of surgery are more common in Korea than in the United States. The ages of the women in the study range from 18 to 71; one woman was only 15 at the time of her operation.

In addition to interviewing Asian American women, I conducted structured, open-ended interviews with five plastic surgeons, all of whom practice in the Bay Area. Of the eleven doctors I randomly selected from the phone book, five agreed to be interviewed.

Since the physicians in my study may not be representative of plastic surgeons, I reviewed the plastic surgery literature. To examine more carefully the medical discourse on the nose and eyelid surgeries of Asian American women, I examined several medical books and plastic surgery journals dating from the 1950s to 1990. I also reviewed several news releases and informational packets distributed by such national organizations as the American Society of Plastic and Reconstructive Surgeons, an organization that represents 97 percent of all physicians certified by the American Board of Plastic Surgery.

To examine popular notions of cosmetic surgery and, in particular, of how the phenomenon of Asian American women receiving double-eyelid and nose-bridge operations is viewed by the public and the media, I referenced relevant newspaper and magazine articles.

For statistical information, I obtained national data on cosmetic surgery from various societies for cosmetic surgeons, including the American Society of Plastic and Reconstructive Surgeons. Data on the specific types of surgery sought by different ethnic groups in the United States, including Asian Americans, are missing from the national statistics. At least one public relations coordinator told me that such data are quite unimportant to plastic surgeons. To compensate for this, I requested doctors in my study to provide me with data from their clinics. One doctor allowed me to review his patient files for basic statistical information. Another doctor allowed his office assistant to give me such information, provided that I paid his assistant for the time she had to work outside of normal work hours reviewing his patient files. Since cosmetic surgery is generally not covered by medical insurance, doctors often do not record their patients' medical information in their computers; therefore, most doctors told me that they have very little data on their cosmetic patients readily available.

MUTILATION OR A CELEBRATION OF THE BODY?

Although it is at least possible to imagine race-modification surgery as a *rite de passage* or a bid for incorporation into the body and race norms of the "dominant" culture, my research findings lead me to reject this as a tenable hypothesis. Here I argue that the surgical alteration by many Asian American women of the shape of their eyes and nose is a potent form of self, body, and society alienation. Mutilation, according to *Webster's*, is the act of maiming, crippling, cutting up, or altering radically so as to damage seriously essential parts of the body. Although the women in my study do not view their cosmetic surgeries as acts of mutilation, an examination of the cultural and institutional forces that influence them to modify their bodies so radically reveals a rejection of their "given" bodies and feelings of marginality. On the one hand, they feel they are exercising their Americanness in their use of the freedom of individual choice. Some deny that they are conforming to any standard—feminine, Western, or otherwise—and others express the idea that they are, in fact, molding their own standards of beauty. Most agreed, however, that their decision to alter their features was primarily a result of their awareness that as women they are expected to look their best and that this meant, in a certain sense, less stereotypically Asian. Even those who stated that their decision to alter their features was personal, based on individual aesthetic preference, also expressed hope that their new appearance would help them in such matters as getting a date, securing a mate, or getting a better job.

For the women in my study, the decision to undergo cosmetic surgery was never purely or mainly for aesthetic purposes, but almost always for improving their social status as women who are racial minorities. For example, "Jane," who underwent double-eyelid and nose-bridge procedures at the ages of 16 and 17, said that she thought she should get her surgeries "out of the way" at an early age since as a college student she has to think about careers ahead:

> Especially if you go into business, whatever, you kind of have to have a Western facial type and you have to have like their features and stature—you know, be tall and stuff. In a way you can see it is an investment in your future.

INTERNALIZATION OF RACIAL AND GENDER STEREOTYPES

The Asian American women in my study are influenced by a gender ideology that states that beauty should be a primary goal of women. They are conscious that because they are women, they must conform to certain standards of beauty. "Elena," a 20-year-old Korean American said, "People in society, if they are attractive, are rewarded for their efforts . . . especially girls. If they look pretty and neat, they are paid more attention to. You can't deny that." "Annie," another Korean American who is 18 years old, remarked that as a young woman, her motivation to have cosmetic surgery was "to look better" and "not different from why [other women] put on makeup." In fact, all expressed the idea that cosmetic surgery was a means by which they could escape the task of having to put makeup on every day. As "Jo," a 28-year-old Japanese American who is thinking of enlarging the natural fold above her eyes, said, "I am still self-conscious about leaving the house without any makeup on, because I feel just really ugly without it. I feel like it's the mask that enables me to go outside."

The need to look their best as women motivates the Asian American women in my study to undergo cosmetic surgery, but the standard of beauty they try to achieve through surgery is motivated by a racial ideology that infers negative behavioral or intellectual characteristics from a group's genetic physical features. All of the women said that they are "proud to be Asian American" and that they "do not want to look white." But the standard of beauty they admire and strive for is a face with larger eyes and a more prominent nose. They all stated that an eyelid without a crease and a nose that does not project indicate a certain "sleepiness," "dullness," and "passivity" in a person's character. "Nellee," a 21-year-old Chinese American, said she seriously considered surgery for double eyelids in high school so that she could "avoid the stereotype of the 'Oriental bookworm'" who is *dull* and doesn't know how to have fun." Elena, who had double-eyelid surgery two years ago from a doctor in my study, said, "When I look at Asians who have no folds and their eyes are slanted and closed, I think of how they would look better more *awake*." "Carol," a 37-year-old Chinese American who had double-eyelid surgery seven years ago, and "Ellen," a 40-year-old Chinese American who had double-eyelid surgery 20 years ago, both said that they wanted to give their eyes a "more spirited" look. "The drawback of Asian features is the puffy eyes," Ellen said. "Pam," a Chinese American aged 44, who had had double-eyelid surgery from another doctor in my study two months earlier, stated, "Yes. Of course. Bigger eyes look prettier. . . . Lots of Asians' eyes are so small they become little lines when the person laughs, making the person look *sleepy*." Likewise, Annie, who had an implant placed on her nasal dorsum to build up her nose bridge at age 15, said:

> I guess I always wanted that *sharp* look—a look like you are smart. If you have a roundish kind of nose, it's like you don't know what's going on. If you have that sharp look, you know, with black eyebrows, a pointy nose, you look more *alert*. I always thought that was cool. [emphasis added]

Clearly, the Asian American women in my study seek cosmetic surgery for double eyelids and nose bridges because they associate the features considered characteristic of their race with negative traits.

These associations that Asian American women make between their features and personality characteristics stem directly from stereotypes created by the dominant culture in the United States and by Western culture in general, which historically has wielded the most power and hegemonic influence over the world. Asians are rarely portrayed in the U.S. popular media and then only in such roles as Charlie Chan, Suzie Wong, and "Lotus Blossom Babies" (a.k.a. China Doll, Geisha Girl, and shy Polynesian beauty). They are depicted as stereotypes with dull, passive, and nonsociable personalities. Similar stereotypes of the stoic Asian also exist in East and Southeast Asia, and since many Asian Americans are immigrants or children of recent immigrants from Asia, they are likely to be influenced by these stereotypes as well. U.S. magazines and films have been increasingly available in many parts of Asia since World War II. Racial stereotypes of Asians as docile, passive, slow witted, and unemotional are internalized by many Asian American women, causing them to consider the facial features associated with these negative traits as defiling.

Undergoing cosmetic surgery, then, becomes a means by which the women can attempt to permanently acquire not only a feminine look considered more attractive by society, but also a certain set of racial features considered more prestigious. For them, the daily task of beautification entails creating the illusion of features they, as members of a racial minority, do not have. Nellee, who has not yet undergone double-eyelid surgery, said that at present she has to apply makeup every day "to give my eyes an illusion of a crease. When I don't wear makeup I feel my eyes are small." Likewise, Elena said that before her double-eyelid surgery she checked almost every morning in the mirror when she woke up to see if a fold had formed above her right eye to match the more prominent fold above her left eye: "[on certain mornings] it was like any other day when you wake up and don't feel so hot, you know. My eye had no definite folds, because when Asians sleep their folds change in and out— it's not definite." The enormous constraints the women in my study feel with regard to their Asian features are apparent in the meticulous detail with which they describe their discontent, as apparent in a quote from Jo who already has natural folds but wants to enlarge them: "I want to make an even bigger eyelid [fold] so that it doesn't look slanted. I think in Asian eyes this inside corner of the fold [she was drawing on my notebook] goes down too much."

The women expressed hope that the results of cosmetic surgery would win them better acceptance by society. Ellen said that she does not think her double-eyelid surgery "makes me look too different," but she nonetheless expressed the feeling that now her features will "make a better impression on people because I got rid of that sleepy look." She says that she will encourage her daughter, who is only 12 years old, to have double-eyelid surgery as she did, because "I think having less sleepy-looking eyes would help her in the future with getting jobs." The aesthetic results of surgery are not an end in themselves but rather a means for these women as racial minorities to attain better socioeconomic status. Clearly, their decisions to undergo cosmetic surgery do not stem from a celebration of their bodies.

MEDICALIZATION OF RACIAL FEATURES

The Western medical system is a most effective promoter of the racial stereotypes that influence Asian American women, since medical knowledge is legitimized by scientific rationality and technical efficiency, both of which hold prestige in the West and increasingly all over the world. According to my Asian American informants who had undergone cosmetic surgery, their plastic surgeons used several medical terms to problematize the shape of their eyes so as to define it as a medical condition. For instance, many patients were told that they had "excess fat" on their eyelids and that it was "normal" for them to feel dissatisfied with the way they looked. "Lots of Asians have the same puffiness over their eyelid, and they often feel better about themselves after the operation," the doctors would assure their Asian American patients.

The doctors whom I interviewed shared a similar opinion of Asian facial features with many

of the doctors of the patients in my study. Their descriptions of Asian features verged on ideological racism, as clearly seen in the following quote from "Dr. Smith."

The social reasons [for Asian Americans to want double eyelids and nose bridges] are undoubtedly continued exposure to Western culture and the realization that the upper eyelid *without* a fold tends to give a *sleepy* appearance, and therefore a more *dull* look to the patient. Likewise, the *flat* nasal bridge and *lack of* nasal projection can signify *weakness* in one's personality and by *lack of* extension, a *lack of force* in one's character. [emphasis added]

By using words like "without," "lack of," "flat," "dull," and "sleepy" in his description of Asian features, Dr. Smith perpetuates the notion that Asian features are inadequate. Likewise, "Dr. Khoo" said that many Asians should have surgery for double eyelids since "the eye is the window to your soul and having a more open appearance makes you look a bit brighter, more inviting." "Dr. Gee" agreed:

I would say 90% of people look better with double eyelids. It makes the eye look more spiritually alive.... With a single eyelid frequently they would have a little fat pad underneath [which] can half bury the eye and so the eye looks small and unenergetic.

Such powerful associations of Asian features with negative personality traits by physicians during consultations can become a medical affirmation of Asian American women's sense of disdain toward their own features.

Medical books and journals as early as the 1950s and as recent as 1990 abound with similar metaphors of abnormality in describing Asian features. The texts that were published before 1970 contain more explicit associations of Asian features with dullness and passivity.

In published texts, doctors write about Asians' eyes and noses as abnormal even when they are careful not to associate negative personality traits with these features. In the privacy of their clinics, they freely incorporate both metaphors of abnormality and the association of Asian features with negative characteristics into medical discourse, which has an enormous impact on the Asian American patients being served.

The doctors' scientific discourse is made more convincing by the seemingly objective manner in which they behave and present themselves in front of their patients in the clinical setting. They examine their patients as a technician diagnosing ways to improve a mechanical object. With a cotton swab, they help their patients to stretch and measure how high they might want their eyelids to be and show them in a mirror what could be done surgically to reduce the puffy look above their eyes. The doctors in my study also use slides and Polaroid pictures to come to an agreement with their patients on what the technical goals of the operation should be. The sterile appearance of their clinics, with white walls and plenty of medical instruments, as well as the symbolism of the doctor's white coat with its many positive connotations (e.g., purity, life, unaroused sexuality, superhuman power, and candor) reinforce in the patient the doctor's role as technician and thus his sense of objectivity. One of my informants, Elena, said that, sitting in front of her doctor in his office, she felt sure that she needed eyelid surgery: "[Dr. Smith] made quite an impression on me. I thought he was more than qualified—that he knew what he was talking about."

With its authority of scientific rationality and technical efficiency, medicine effectively "normalizes" not only the negative feelings of Asian American women about their features but also their ultimate decision to undergo cosmetic surgery. For example, "Dr. Jones" does not want to make her patients feel "strange" or "abnormal" for wanting cosmetic surgery. All the doctors in my study agreed that their role as doctor is to provide the best technical skills possible for whatever service their patients demand, not to question the motivation of their patients. Her goal, Dr. Jones said, is "like that of a psychiatrist in that I try to make patients feel better about themselves." She

feels that surgeons have an advantage over psychiatrists in treating cosmetic surgery patients because "we…help someone to change the way they look…psychiatrists are always trying to figure out why a person wants to do what they want to do." By changing the patients' bodies the way they would like them, she feels she provides them with an immediate and concrete solution to their feelings of inadequacy.

Dr. Jones and the other doctors say that they only turn patients away when patients expect results that are technically impossible, given such factors as the thickness of the patient's skin and the bone structure. "I turn very few patients away," said Dr. Khoo. And "Dr. Kwan" notes

> I saw a young girl [a while back] whose eyes were beautiful but she wanted a crease....She was gorgeous! Wonderful! But somehow she didn't see it that way. But you know, I'm not going to tell a patient every standard I have of what's beautiful. If they want certain things and it's doable, and if it is consistent with a reasonable look in the end, then I don't stop them. I don't really discuss it with them.

Like the other doctors in my study, Dr. Kwan sees himself primarily as a technician whose main role is to correct his patient's features in a way that he thinks would best contribute to the patient's satisfaction. It does not bother him that he must expose an individual, whom he already sees as pretty and not in need of surgery, to an operation that is at least an hour long, entails the administering of local anesthesia with sedation, and involves following risks. He finds no need to try to change his patients' minds. Likewise, Dr. Smith said of Asian American women who used to come to him to receive really large double eyelids: "I respect their ethnic background. I don't want to change them drastically." Yet he would not refuse them the surgery "as long as it was something I can accomplish. Provided I make them aware of what the appearance might be with the changes."

Though most of my Asian American woman informants who underwent cosmetic surgery recovered fully within six months to a year, with only a few minor scars from their surgery, they nonetheless affirmed that the psychologically traumatic aspect of the operation was something their doctors did not stress during consultation. Elena said of her double-eyelid surgery: "I thought it was a simple procedure. He [the doctor] should have known better. It took at least an hour and a half.... And no matter how minor the surgery was, I bruised! I was swollen." Likewise, Annie could remember well her fear during nose surgery. Under local anesthesia, she said that she was able to witness and hear some of the procedures.

> I closed my eyes. I didn't want to look. I didn't want to see like the knives or anything. I could hear the snapping of scissors and I was aware when they were putting that thing [implant] up my nose. I was kind of grossed out.

By focusing on technique and subordinating human emotions and motivations to technical ends, medicine is capable of normalizing Asian American women's decision to undergo cosmetic surgery.

MUTUAL REINFORCEMENT: MEDICINE AND THE CONSUMER-ORIENTED SOCIETY

The medical system bolsters and benefits from the larger consumer-oriented society by perpetuating the idea that beauty is central to women's sense of self and also by promoting a beauty standard for Asian American women that requires the alteration of features specific to Asian American racial identity. All of the doctors in my study stated that a "practical" benefit for Asian American women undergoing surgery to create or enlarge their eyelid folds is that they can put eye makeup on more appropriately. Dr. Gee said that after double-eyelid surgery it is "easier" for Asian American women to put makeup on because "they now have two instead of just one plane on which to apply makeup." Dr. Jones agreed that after eyelid surgery Asian

American women "can do more dramatic things with eye makeup." The doctors imply that Asian American women cannot usually put on makeup adequately, and thus, they have not been able to look as beautiful as they can be with makeup. By promoting the idea that a beautiful woman is one who can put makeup on adequately, they further the idea that a woman's identity should be closely connected with her body and, particularly, with the representational problems of the self. By reinforcing the makeup industry, they buttress the cosmetic surgery industry of which they are a part. A double-eyelid surgery costs patients $1,000 to $3,000.

The medical system also bolsters and benefits from the larger consumer society by appealing to the values of American individualism and by individualizing the social problems of racial inequality. Dr. Smith remarked that so many Asian American women are now opting for cosmetic surgery procedures largely because of their newly gained rights as women and as racial minorities:

> Asians are more affluent than they were 15 years ago. They are more knowledgeable and Americanized, and their women are more liberated. I think in the past many Asian women were like Arab women. The men had their foot on top of them. Now Asian women do pretty much what they want to do. So if they want to do a surgery, they do it.

Such comments by doctors encourage Asian American women to believe that undergoing cosmetic surgery is merely a way of beautifying themselves and that it signifies their ability to exercise individual freedom.

Ignoring the fact that the Asian American women's decision to undergo cosmetic surgery has anything to do with the larger society's racial prejudice, the doctors state that their Asian American women patients come to cosmetic surgeons to mold their own standards of beauty. The doctors point out that the specific width and shape the women want their creases to be or the specific shape of nose bridges they want are a matter of personal style and individual choices. Dr. Smith explains:

> We would like to individualize every procedure. There is no standard nose we stamp on everybody so that each patient's need is addressed individually. My goal is to make that individual very happy and very satisfied.

Dr. Kwan also remarked, "I think people recognize what's beautiful in their own way." In fact, the doctors point out that both they and their Asian American patients are increasingly getting more sophisticated about what the patients want. As evidence, they point to the fact that as early as a decade ago, doctors used to provide very wide creases to every Asian American patient who came for double eyelids, not knowing that not every Asian wanted to look exactly Caucasian. The doctors point out that today many Asian American cosmetic surgery patients explicitly request that their noses and eyelids not be made to look too Caucasian.

CONCLUSION

Cosmetic surgery on Asian American women for nose bridges and double eyelids is very much influenced by gender and racial ideologies. My research has shown that by the conscious or unconscious manipulation of gender and racial stereotypes, the American medical system, along with the larger consumer-oriented society of which it is a part, influences Asian American women to alter their features through surgery. With the authority of scientific rationality and technological efficiency, medicine is effectively able to maintain a gender ideology that validates women's monetary and time investment in beauty even if this means making their bodies vulnerable to harmful and risky procedures such as plastic surgery. Medicine is also able to perpetuate a racial ideology that states that Asian features signify "dullness," "passivity," and "lack of emotions" in the Asian person. The medicalization of racial features, which reinforces and normalizes Asian American women's feelings of inadequacy, as well as their decision to undergo cosmetic surgery, helps to bolster the consumer-oriented society of which medicine is a part and from which medicine benefits.

Given the authority with which fields of "expert" knowledge such as bio-medicine have come to define commonsense reality today, racism and sexism no longer need to rely primarily on physical coercion to legal authority. Racial stereotypes influence Asian American women to seek cosmetic surgery. Yet, through its highly specialized and validating forms of discourse and practices, medicine, along with a culture based on endless self-fashioning, is able to motivate women to view their feelings of inadequacy as individually motivated, as opposed to socially induced, phenomena, thereby effectively convincing them to participate in the production and reproduction of the larger structural inequalities that continue to oppress them.

DISCUSSION QUESTIONS

1. What are the ethical implications of having "ethnic" versus other forms of cosmetic surgery? What are examples of other "ethnic" cosmetic surgeries beyond those documented in Kaw's research?
2. How might the motivations of Jewish women to have their noses "bobbed" to appear "less Jewish" differ from those of Asian American women who undergo cosmetic eye surgery? Do you think that these women experience different consequences, with respect to their identities or others' "reflected appraisals"?

ADDITIONAL RESOURCES

Film

"Never Perfect." 2007. A film by Regina Park that documents a young Vietnamese-American woman's journey through plastic surgery in her quest for self-acceptance.

Internet

http://www.cosmeticsurgery.org/. The website of The American Academy of Cosmetic Surgery.

http://www.ienhance.com/swan-premiere.asp. I Enhance, a cosmetic surgery site, provides an in-depth summary of the 2004 cosmetic surgery/beauty contest reality television program "The Swan." "The Swan" featured a racially diverse group of self-proclaimed "ugly ducklings" who underwent a three-month cosmetic surgery and fitness training makeover, followed by a beauty contest whose winner was crowned "The Swan."

http://www.youtube.com/watch?v=cPV7ztzJQpo. A segment from The Swan Pageant Finale, featuring the winners from each weekly episode of the reality TV program competing against one another in evening gown, swimsuit, and lingerie contests to be crowned the winning "swan" of the season.

http://www.neverperfectthemovie.com/. The website for Regina Park's 2007 film "Never Perfect."

http://www.plasticsurgery.org/. The website of The American Society of Plastic Surgeons.

http://www.tcm.com/2008/aif/index.jsp. Turner Classic Movie's website "Race & Hollywood: Asian Images in Film."

FURTHER READING

Davis, Kathy. 2003. *Dubious Equalities and Embodied Differences: Cultural Studies on Cosmetic Surgery.* Lanham, MD: Rowman & Littlefield.

Gilman, Sander. 1998. *Creating Beauty to Cure the Soul: Race and Psychology in the Shaping of Aesthetic Surgery.* Durham, NC: Duke University Press.

Gimlin, Debra. 2007. "Accounting for Cosmetic Surgery in the USA and Great Britain: A Cross-Cultural Analysis of Women's Narratives." *Body & Society,* 13(1): 41–60.

Grimes, Pearl E. (ed.). 2007. *Aesthetics and Cosmetic Surgery for Darker Skin Types.* Philadelphia: Lippincott, Williams, & Wilkins.

Morgan, Kathryn Pauly. 1991. "Women and the Knife: Cosmetic Surgery and the Colonization of Women's Bodies." *Hypatia,* 6(3): 25–53.

Pitts-Taylor, Victoria. 2007. *Surgery Junkies: Wellness and Pathology in Cosmetic Culture.* New Brunswick, NJ: Rutgers University Press.

Sullivan, Deborah A. 2000. *Cosmetic Surgery: The Cutting Edge of Commercial Medicine in America.* New Brunswick, NJ: Rutgers University Press.

Zhou, Min. 2004. "Are Asian Americans Becoming 'White'?" *Contexts,* 3(1): 29–37.

43. The Blacker the Berry: Gender, Skin Tone, Self-Esteem, and Self-Efficacy

MAXINE S. THOMPSON AND VERNA M. KEITH

Drawing on data from the National Survey of Black Americans, Thompson and Keith assess the impact that skin tone has on African Americans' sense of self. Their findings show that the experience of skin tone differs by gender and social class, and that one's conformity to traditional roles of masculinity and femininity affects one's sense of self as well.

No longer an unspoken taboo, color prejudice within the African American community has been a "hot" topic of talk shows, novels, and movies and an issue in a court case on discrimination in the workplace.

Skin color is highly correlated with other phenotypic features—eye color, hair texture, broadness of nose, and fullness of lips. Along with light skin, blue and green eyes, European-shaped noses, and straights as opposed to "kinky" hair are all accorded higher status both within and beyond the African American community. Colorism embodies preference and desire for both light skin as well as these other attendant features. Hair, eye color, and facial features function along with color in complex ways to shape opportunities, norms regarding attractiveness, self-concept, and overall body image. Yet, it is color that has received the most attention in research on African Americans. Ethnographic research suggests that the research focus on skin color is somewhat justified. For example, it played the central role in determining membership in the affluent African American clubs.

Although colorism affects attitudes about the self for both men and women, it appears that these effects are stronger for women than men. There is very little empirical research on the relationship between gender, skin color, and self-concept

development. In this article, we evaluate the relative importance of skin color to feelings about the self for men and women within the African American community.

Using an adult sample of respondents who are representative of the national population, we examine the relationship of skin tone to self-concept development. We examine the way in which gender socially constructs the impact of skin tone on self-concept development.

SKIN TONE AND GENDER

Issues of skin color and physical attractiveness are closely linked and because expectations of physical attractiveness are applied more heavily to women across all cultures, stereotypes of attractiveness and color preference are more profound for Black women. The "what is beautiful is good" stereotype creates a "halo" effect for light-skinned persons. The positive glow generated by physical attractiveness includes a host of desirable personality traits. Included in these positive judgments are beliefs that attractive people would be significantly more intelligent, kind, confident, interesting, sexy, assertive, poised, modest, and successful, and they appear to have higher self-esteem and self-worth. Frequent exposure to negative evaluations can undermine a woman's sense of self.

Thompson, Maxine S. and Verna M. Keith. 2001. "The Blacker the Berry: Gender, Skin Tone, Self-Esteem, and Self-Efficacy. *Gender & Society,* 15(3): 336–57.

Several explanations are proffered for gender differences in self-esteem among Blacks. One is that women are socialized to attend to evaluations of others and are vulnerable to negative appraisals. Women seek to validate their selves through appraisal from others more than men do. And the media has encouraged greater negative self-appraisals for dark-skinned women. A second explanation is that colorism and its associated stressors are not the same for dark-skinned men and women. For men, stereotypes associated with perceived dangerousness, criminality, and competence are associated with dark skin tone, while for women the issue is attractiveness. Educational attainment is a vehicle by which men might overcome skin color bias, but changes in physical features are difficult to accomplish. Third, women may react more strongly to skin color bias because they feel less control of their lives. Black women face problems of racism and sexism, and when these two negative status positions—being Black and being female—combine with colorism, a triple threat lowers self-esteem and feelings of competence among dark Black women.

CONCEPTUAL ARGUMENT

Skin Tone and Self-Evaluation

In our society, dark-skinned men and women are raised to believe that "light" skin is preferred. They see very light skinned Blacks having successful experiences in advertisements, in magazines, in professional positions, and so forth. They are led to believe that "light" skin is the key to popularity, professional status, and a desirable marriage. Colorism may lead to negative self-evaluations among African Americans with dark skin.

Self-evaluations are seen as having two dimensions, one reflecting the person's moral worth and the other reflecting the individual's competency or agency (Gecas, 1989). The former refers to self-esteem and indicates how we feel about ourselves. The latter refers to self-efficacy and indicates our

belief in the ability to control our own fate. These are two different dimensions in that people can feel that they are good and useful but also feel that what happens to them is due to luck or forces outside themselves.

Self-esteem and skin tone. Self-esteem consists of feeling good, liking yourself, and being liked and treated well. Self-esteem is influenced both by the social comparisons we make of ourselves with others and by the reactions that other people have toward us (i.e., reflected appraisals). The self-concept depends also on the attributes of others who are available for comparison. Self-evaluation theory emphasizes the importance of consonant environmental context for personal comparisons; that is, Blacks will compare themselves with other Blacks in their community. Consonant environmental context assumes that significant others will provide affirmation of one's identity and that similarity between oneself and others shapes the self. Thus, a sense of personal connectedness to other African Americans is most important for fostering and reinforcing positive self-evaluations.

Self-efficacy and skin tone. Self-efficacy is the belief that one can master situations and control events. Performance influences self-efficacy such that when faced with a failure, individuals with high self-efficacy generally believe that extra effort or persistence will lead to success. However, if failure is related to some stable personal characteristic such as "dark skin color" or social constraints such as blocked opportunities resulting from mainstreaming practices in the workplace, then one is likely to be discouraged by failure and to feel less efficacious than his or her lighter counterparts. Self-efficacy results not primarily from beliefs or attitudes about performance but from undertaking challenges and succeeding. Thus, darker skinned Blacks who experience success in their everyday world (e.g., work, education, etc.) will feel more confident and empowered.

DATA AND METHOD

The Sample

Data for this study come from the National Survey of Black Americans (NSBA). The sample for the survey was drawn to ensure that every Black household in the United States had an equal probability of being selected for the study. Within each household in the sample, one person age 18 or older was randomly selected to be interviewed from among those eligible for the study. Only self-identified Black American citizens were eligible for the study. Face-to-face interviews were carried out by trained Black interviewers, yielding a sample of 2,107 respondents.

RESULTS

We see that skin tone has a significant positive effect on self-efficacy for both men and women. A lighter complexion is associated with higher feelings of perceived mastery. Among men, each incremental change in skin color from dark to light is associated with a .33 increment in self-efficacy; for women, changes in skin color are associated with a .18 increment in self-efficacy. Thus, the skin tone effect on self-efficacy is much stronger for men. In fact, the coefficient for the skin tone effect in the equation predicting self-efficacy for men is almost twice that of the coefficient for women.

The pattern of skin tone effects for men and women begins to diverge when the sociodemographic variables are added.

DISCUSSION

The data in this study indicate that gender—mediated by socioeconomic status variables such as education, occupation, and income—socially constructs the importance of skin color evaluations of self-esteem and self-efficacy. Self-efficacy results not primarily from beliefs or attitudes about performance but rather reflects an individual's competency or agency from undertaking challenges and succeeding at overcoming them. Self-esteem consists of feeling good about oneself

and being liked and treated favorably by others. However, the effect of skin color on these two domains of self is different for women and men. Skin color is an important predictor of perceived efficacy for Black men but not Black women. And skin color predicts self-esteem for Black women but not Black men. This pattern conforms to traditional gendered expectations. The traditional definitions of masculinity demand men specialize in achievement outside the home, dominate in interpersonal relationships, and remain rational and self-contained. Women, in contrast, are expected to seek affirmation from others, to be warm and nurturing. Thus, consistent with gendered characteristics of men and women, skin color is important in self-domains that are central to masculinity (i.e., competence) and femininity (i.e., affirmation of the self).

Turning our attention to the association between skin color and self-concept for Black men, the association between skin color and self-efficacy increases significantly as skin color lightens. And this is independent of the strong positive contribution of education—and ultimately socioeconomic status—to feelings of competence for men. We think that the effect of skin tone on self-efficacy is the result of widespread negative stereotyping and fear associated with dark-skinned men that pervade the larger society and operates independent of social class. As a consequence, employers exclude "darker" African American men from employment and thus block their access to rewards and resources.

While skin color is an important predictor of self-efficacy for African American men, it is more important as a predictor of self-esteem for African American women. These data confirm much of the anecdotal information from clinical studies of clients in psychotherapy that have found that dark-skinned Black women have problems with self-worth and confidence. Our findings suggest that this pattern is not limited to experiences of women who are in therapy but that colorism is part of the everyday reality of Black women. Black women expect to be judged by their skin tone. No doubt messages from peers, the media, and family show a preference for lighter skin tones.

The relationship between skin color and self-esteem among African American women is moderated by socioeconomic status. For example, there is no correlation between skin color and self-esteem among women who have a more privileged socioeconomic status. Consequently, women who are darker and "successful" evaluate themselves just as positively as women of a lighter color. On the other hand, the relationship between skin color and self-esteem is stronger for African American women from the less privileged socioeconomic sectors. In other words, darker skinned women with the lowest incomes display the lowest levels of self-esteem, but self-esteem increases as their skin color lightens. Why does skin color have such importance for self regard in the context of low income or poverty? Low income shapes self-esteem because it provides fewer opportunities for rewarding experiences or affirming relationships. In addition, there are more negative attributes associated with behaviors of individuals from less privileged socioeconomic status than with those of a more prestigious one. For example, the derisive comment "ghetto chick" is often used to describe the behaviors, dress, communication, and interaction styles of women from low income groups. Combine stereotypes of classism and colorism, and you have a mixture

that fosters an undesirable if not malignant context for self-esteem development. An important finding of this research is that skin color and income determine self-worth for Black women and especially that these factors can work together. Dark skin and low income produce Black women with very low self-esteem. Accordingly, these data help refine our understanding of gendered racism and of "triple oppression" involving race, gender, and class that places women of color in a subordinate social and economic position relative to men of color and the larger white population as well. More important, the data suggest that darker skinned African American women actually experience a "quadruple" oppression originating in the convergence of social inequalities based on gender, class, race, and color.

Finally, the data indicate that self-esteem increases as skin color becomes lighter among African American women who are judged as having "low and average levels of attractiveness." That physical attractiveness influenced feelings of self-worth for Black women is not surprising. Women have traditionally been concerned with appearance, regardless of ethnicity. Indeed, the pursuit and preoccupation with beauty are central features of female sex-role socialization. Our findings suggest that women who are judged "unattractive" are more vulnerable to color bias than those judged attractive.

DISCUSSION QUESTIONS

1. Thompson and Keith write about the concept of "colorism." What does colorism mean? How is colorism similar to or different from the concept of racism?
2. Thompson and Keith write about "blue vein societies." What are or were these societies? Do they still exist today?
3. Thompson and Keith note that black women and men are affected by colorism in different ways. What are these differences?
4. What connections do you see between this article and Kaw's piece about Asian American women who have cosmetic surgery? What connections do you see between Thompson and Keith's observations and Hughes' piece on the "one drop" rule?

ADDITIONAL RESOURCES

Film
"School Daze." The 1988 musical drama written, directed by, and starring Spike Lee features the social division by skin color and social class among blacks as its primary theme. 120 minutes.

Internet
http://www.icpsr.umich.edu/cocoon/ICPSR/SERIES/00164.xml. The Program for Research on Black Americans at the University of Michigan's Institute for Social Research conducted the National Survey of Black Americans, on which Thompson and Keith's research is based.

http://www.rcgd.isr.umich.edu/prba/nsal.htm#background. The National Survey of American Life: Coping with Stress in the 21st Century is follow-up research conducted by the Program for Research on Black Americans at the University of Michigan's Institute for Social Research.

FURTHER READING

Byrd, Ayana D. and Lori L. Tharps. 2002. *Hair Story: Untangling the Roots of Black Hair in America.* London: Macmillan.

Davis, Kathy. 2003. "Surgical Passing: Or Why Michael Jackson's Nose Makes 'Us' Uneasy." *Feminist Theory,* 4(1): 73–92.

Gecas. Viktor. 1989. "The Social Psychology of Self-Efficacy." *Annual Review of Sociology,* 15: 291–316.

Glenn, Evelyn. 2009. *Shades of Difference: Why Skin Color Matters.* Stanford, CA: Stanford University Press.

Hunter, Margaret. 2007. "The Persistent Problem of Colorism: Skin Tone, Status, and Inequality." *Sociology Compass,* 1(1): 237–54.

Mullane, Deirdre. 1993. *Crossing the Danger Water: Three Hundred Years of African-American Writing.* New York: Anchor.

Segura, Denise. 1986. "Chicanas and Triple Oppression in the Labor Force," in Teresa Cordova and The National Association of Chicana Studies Editorial Committee's *Chicana Voices: Intersections of Class, Race and Gender.* Austin, TX: Center for Mexican American Studies.

Thurman, Wallace. 1929. *The Blacker the Berry: A Novel of Negro Life.* New York: Macmillan.

Wright, Marguerite A. 2000. *I'm Chocolate, You're Vanilla: Raising Healthy Black and Biracial Children in a Race-Conscious World.* San Francisco: Jossey-Bass.

Social Class

We have become accustomed to conversations about gender and, to a lesser degree, race in our college classrooms and in the larger society. Discussions about social class are less prominent, and perhaps more uncomfortable, because we aspire as a nation to be "classless," with equal rights and opportunities for all. When social class is discussed, it is often conflated with issues of race and gender. In this section, we pay tribute to social class as one of the most important components of social structure, with broad consequences for group dynamics, social relationships, and personality.

The next selections explore the impacts of socioeconomic status on parenting, educational experiences, and aspirations over the life course.

In his article about differences between working- and middle-class parents, Kohn assesses how parenting values vary by social class. Nearly 40 years later, Aries and Seider take up the issue of social class and education, comparing lower-income students' transition from high school to college at a state school versus an elite private one. McLeod's research on the achievement-related goals of high school boys in a housing project highlights racial differences in expectations and in the boys' coping strategies.

44. Social Class and Parental Values

MELVIN L. KOHN

Melvin Kohn studied the values of 400 white parents living in Washington, D.C. His groundbreaking study identified differences in working- and middle-class parents' judgments about the most important traits to be developed in their children, as well as value differences held by mothers and fathers, and values that varied by the gender of their child.

We undertake this inquiry into the relationship between social class and parental values in the hope that a fuller understanding of the ways in which parents of different social classes differ in their values may help us to understand why they differ in their practices. This hope, of course, rests or two assumptions: that it is reasonable to conceive of social classes as subcultures of the larger society, each with a relatively distinct value-orientation, and that values really affect behavior.

SAMPLE AND METHOD OF DATA COLLECTION

Washington, D.C.—the locus of this study—has a large proportion of people employed by government, relatively little heavy industry, few recent immigrants, a white working class drawn heavily from rural areas, and a large proportion of Negroes, particularly at lower economic levels. Generalizations based on this or any other sample of one city during one limited period of time are, of course, tentative.

Our intent in selecting the families to be studied was to secure approximately two hundred representative white working-class families and another two hundred representative white middle-class families, each family having a child within a narrowly delimited age range. We decided on fifth-grade children because we wanted to direct the interviews to relationships involving a child old enough to have a developed capacity for verbal communication.

The sampling procedure involved two steps: the first, selection of census tracts. Tracts with 20 percent or more Negro population were excluded, as were those in the highest quartile with respect to median income. From among the remaining tracts we then selected a small number representative of each of the three distinct types of residential area in which the population to be studied live: four tracts with a predominantly working-class population, four predominantly middle-class, and three having large proportions of each. The final selection of tracts was based on their occupational distribution and their median income, education, rent (of rented homes), and value (of owner-occupied homes). The second step in the sampling procedure involved selection of families. From records made available by the public and parochial school systems we compiled lists of all families with fifth-grade children who lived in the selected tracts. Two hundred families were then randomly selected from among those in which the father had a "white-collar" occupation and another two hundred from among those in which the father had a manual occupation.

In all four hundred families the mothers were to be interviewed. In every fourth family we scheduled interviews with the father and the fifth-grade child as well.

Kohn, Melvin. 1959. "Social Class and Parental Values." *American Journal of Sociology,* 64: 337–51.

When interviews with both parents were scheduled, two members of the staff visited the home together—a male to interview the father, a female to interview the mother. The interviews were conducted independently, in separate rooms, but with essentially identical schedules. The first person to complete his interview with the parent interviewed the child.

Our inquiry was limited to the values that parents would most like to see embodied in their children's behavior. We asked the parents to choose, from among several alternative characteristics that might be seen as desirable, those few which they considered *most* important for a child of the appropriate age. Specifically, we offered each parent a card listing 17 characteristics that had been suggested by other parents, in the pretest interviews, as being highly desirable. Then we asked: "Which three of the things listed on this card would you say are the *most* important in a boy (or girl) of (fifth-grade child's) age?" The selection of a particular characteristic was taken as our index of value.

CLASS AND VALUES

Middle- and working-class mothers share a broadly common set of values—but not an identical set of values by any means. There is considerable agreement among mothers of both social classes that happiness and such standards of conduct as honesty, consideration, obedience, dependability, manners, and self-control are highly desirable for both boys and girls of this age.

Popularity, being a good student (especially for boys), neatness and cleanliness (especially for girls), and curiosity are next most likely to be regarded as desirable. Relatively few mothers choose ambition, ability to defend one's self, affectionate responsiveness, being liked by adults, ability to play by one's self, or seriousness as highly desirable for either boys or girls of this age. All of these, of course, might be more highly valued for children of other ages.

Although agreement obtains on this broad level, working-class mothers differ significantly from middle-class mothers in the relative emphasis they place on particular characteristics. Significantly fewer working-class mothers regard happiness as highly desirable for *boys*. Although characteristics that define standards of conduct are valued by many mothers of both social classes, there are revealing differences of emphasis here too. Working-class mothers are more likely to value obedience; they would have their children be responsive to parental authority. Middle-class mothers are more likely to value both consideration and self-control; they would have their children develop inner control and sympathetic concern for other people. Furthermore, middle-class mothers are more likely to regard curiosity as a prime virtue. By contrast, working-class mothers put the emphasis on neatness and cleanliness, valuing the imaginative and exploring child relatively less than the presentable child.

Middle-class mothers' conceptions of what is desirable for boys are much the same as their conceptions of what is desirable for girls. But working-class mothers make a clear distinction between the sexes: they are more likely to regard dependability, being a good student, and ambition as desirable for boys and to regard happiness, good manners, neatness, and cleanliness as desirable for girls.

What of the *fathers'* values? Judging from our subsample of 82 fathers, their values are similar to those of the mothers. Essentially the same rank-order of choices holds for fathers as for mothers, with one major exception: fathers are not so likely to value happiness for their daughters.

Middle-class parents (fathers as well as mothers) are more likely to ascribe predominant importance to the child's acting on the basis of internal standards of conduct, working-class parents to the child's compliance with parental authority.

CLASS, SUBCULTURE, AND VALUES

In discussing the relationship of social class to values we have talked as if American society were composed of two relatively homogeneous groups, manual and white-collar workers, together with their families. Yet it is likely that there is considerable variation in values, associated with other bases of social differentiation, *within* each class. If so, it should be possible to divide the classes into subgroups in such a way as to specify more precisely the relationship of social class to values.

Consider, first, the use we have made of the concept "social class." Are the differences we have found between the values of middle- and working-class mothers a product of this dichotomy alone, or do values parallel status gradations more generally? An examination of the choices made by mothers in each stratum indicates that variation in values parallels socioeconomic status rather closely:

1. The higher a mother's status, the higher the probability that she will choose consideration, curiosity, self-control, and (for boys) happiness as highly desirable; curiosity is particularly likely to be chosen by mothers in the highest stratum.
2. The lower her status, the higher the probability that she will select obedience, neatness, and cleanliness; it appears, too, that mothers in the lowest stratum are more likely than are those in the highest to value *honesty.*

Mothers' values also are directly related to their own occupational positions and educational attainments, independently of their families' class status.

So, too, for mothers' educational attainments: a middle-class mother of *relatively* low educational attainment (one who has gone no further than graduation from high school) is less likely to value curiosity and more likely to value (for girls) neatness and cleanliness. A working-class mother of *relatively* high educational attainment (one who has at least graduated from high school) is more likely to value self-control for boys and both consideration and curiosity for girls.

INTERPRETATION

Our first conclusion is that parents, whatever their social class, deem it very important indeed that their children be honest, happy, considerate, obedient, and dependable.

The second conclusion is that, whatever the reasons may be, parents' values are related to their social position, particularly their class position.

There still remains, however, the task of interpreting the relationship between parents' social position and their values. In particular: What underlies the differences between the values of middle- and of working-class parents?

One relevant consideration is that some parents may "take for granted" values that others hold dear. For example, middle-class parents may take "neatness and cleanliness" for granted, while working-class parents regard it as highly desirable. But what does it mean to say that middle-class parents take neatness and cleanliness for granted? In essence, the argument is that middle-class parents value neatness and cleanliness as greatly as do working-class parents but not so greatly as they value such things as happiness and self-control. If this be the case, it can only mean that in the circumstances of middle-class life neatness and cleanliness are easily enough attained to be of less immediate concern than are these other values.

A second consideration lies in the probability that these value-concepts have differing meanings for parents of different cultural backgrounds. For example, one might argue that honesty is a central standard of conduct for middle-class parents because they see honesty as meaning truthfulness; and that it is more a quality of the person for working-class parents because they see it as meaning trustworthiness. Perhaps so; but to suggest that a difference in meaning underlies a difference in values raises the further problem of explaining this difference in meaning.

It would be reasonable for working-class parents to be more likely to see honesty as trustworthiness. The working-class situation is one of less material security and less assured protection from the dishonesty of others. For these reasons, trustworthiness is more at issue for working-class than for middle-class parents.

Both considerations lead us to view differences in the values of middle- and working-class parents in terms of their differing circumstances of life and, by implication, their conceptions of the effects that these circumstances may have on their children's future lives. We believe that parents are most likely to accord high priority to those values that seem both *problematic,* in the sense that they are difficult of achievement, and *important,* in the sense that failure to achieve them would affect the child's future adversely. From this perspective it is reasonable that working-class parents cannot afford to take neatness and cleanliness as much for granted as can middle-class parents. It is reasonable, too, that working-class parents are more likely to see honesty as implying trustworthiness and that this connotation of honesty is seen as problematic.

These characteristics—honesty and neatness—are important to the child's future precisely because they assure him a respectable social position. Just as "poor but honest" has traditionally been an important line of social demarcation, their high valuation of these qualities may express working-class parents' concern that their children occupy a position unequivocally above that of persons who are not neat or who are not scrupulously honest. These are the qualities of respectable, worthwhile people.

So, too, is obedience. The obedient child follows his parents' dictates rather than his own standards. He acts, in his subordinate role as a child, in conformity with the prescriptions of established authority.

Even in the way they differentiate what is desirable for boys from what is desirable for girls, working-class mothers show a keen appreciation of the qualities making for respectable social position.

The characteristics that middle-class parents are more likely to value for their children are internal standards for governing one's relationships with other people and, in the final analysis, with one's self. It is not that middle-class parents are less concerned than are working-class parents about social position. The qualities of person that assure respectability may be taken for granted, but in a world where social relationships are determinative of position, these standards of conduct are both more problematic and more important.

The middle-class emphasis on internal standards is evident in their choice of the cluster of characteristics centering around honesty; in their being less likely than are working-class parents to value obedience and more likely to value self-control and consideration; and in their seeing obedience as inconsistent with both consideration and curiosity. The child is to act appropriately, not because his parents tell him to, but because he wants to. Not conformity to authority, but inner control; not because you're told to but because you take the other person into consideration—these are the middle-class ideals.

These values place responsibility directly upon the individual. He cannot rely upon authority, nor can he simply conform to what is presented to him as proper. He should be impelled to come to his own understanding of the situation. He is to govern himself in such a way as to be able to act consistently with his principles. The basic importance of relationship to self is explicit in the concept of self-control. It is implicit, too, in consideration—a standard that demands of the individual that he respond sympathetically to others' needs even if they be in conflict with his own; and in the high valuation of honesty as central to other standards of conduct: "to thine own self be true."

Perhaps, considering this, it should not be surprising that so many middle-class mothers attribute first-rank importance to happiness, even for boys. We cannot assume that their children's happiness is any less important to working-class mothers than it is to middle-class mothers; in fact, working-class mothers are equally likely to value happiness for *girls.* For their sons, however, happiness is second choice to honesty and obedience. Apparently, middle-class mothers can afford instead to be concerned about their son's happiness. And perhaps they are right in being concerned. We have noted that those middle-class mothers who deem it most important that their sons outdistance others are especially likely to be concerned about their sons' happiness; and even those mothers who do not are asking their children to accept considerable responsibility.

DISCUSSION QUESTIONS

1. What attributes do working-class and middle-class parents consider "most important" in rearing their children? How are parents in the two classes different? How are they similar?
2. How do you think the value differences between working-class and middle-class parents influence children's future achievement and aspirations?
3. What values did your parents or caregivers focus on most when you were growing up? Can you relate these values to the working- or middle-class values identified by Kohn?
4. Kohn studied only urban white families. Do you think his findings would be different if he had included rural and more racially diverse families?

ADDITIONAL RESOURCES

Film

"People Like Us: Social Class in America." This PBS documentary explores how social class, race, and gender intersect via profiles of Americans from a variety of social class backgrounds. 120 minutes. http://www.pbs.org/peoplelikeus/film/index.html.

Internet

http://www.pbs.org/peoplelikeus/film/index.html . The website for "People Like Us: Social Class in America" includes interactive features and video shorts to help assess and learn about people's experiences, attitudes, and beliefs related to socioeconomic status.

Radio

National Public Radio's "This American Life" features a program on the Harlem Children's Zone. September 26, 2008. http://www.thisamericanlife.org/Radio_Episode.aspx?episode=364.

FURTHER READING

Kiyosaki, Robert T. and Sharon Lechter. 1998. *Rich Dad, Poor Dad: What the Rich Teach Their Kids about Money that the Poor and Middle Class Do Not.* New York: Warner Business Books.

Kohn, Melvin. 1980. "Job Complexity and Adult Personality," in Neil J. Smelser and Erik H. Erikson (eds.). *Themes of Work and Love in Adulthood.* 193–212. Boston: Harvard University Press.

Lareau, Annette. 2002. "Invisible Inequality: Social Class and Childrearing in Black Families and White Families." *American Sociological Review,* 67(5): 747–76.

Lareau, Annette. 2003. *Unequal Childhoods: Class, Race, and Family Life.* Berkeley: University of California Press.

45. The Interactive Relationship Between Class Identity and the College Experience: The Case of Lower Income Students

ELIZABETH ARIES AND MAYNARD SEIDER

Aries and Seider conducted interviews with 30 lower-income college students near the beginning of their college careers. They note fascinating differences in the feelings of inferiority, inadequacy, exclusion, and powerlessness experienced by lower-income students who attended an elite college versus those who attended a state school. Cultural and economic capital took very different forms in these two higher education contexts.

Prestigious colleges and universities in the United States have become increasingly concerned that the students they are educating come disproportionately from upper-income families.

As prestigious colleges commit themselves to seeking greater economic diversity among their student body, attention must be paid to the challenges as well as the benefits for low income students who enter elite colleges. A college education indeed broadens an individual's employment opportunities and opportunities for self-development, but comes not without personal costs. For lower income students, many of whom represent the first generation in their family to attend college, entrance to college means an encounter with faculty and students from very different class backgrounds than their own.

We sought to understand how class-based aspects of identity shape the college experience, and how the college experience influences the class-based aspects of identity of lower income students. We highlight the ways that institutional variability (i.e., the type of college one attends) shapes that relationship. It is not uncommon for students entering college to feel intimidated, uncertain of the competition and concerned about how they will adjust to their new circumstances. But lower income students at prestigious liberal

arts colleges face an additional set of challenges, as they lack the financial resources (or "economic capital") and cultural capital (Bourdieu, 1977) of their more affluent counterparts.

We expected that lower income elite college students would experience greater social difficulties than state college students due to greater disparities in economic and cultural capital between students at the elite college than at the state college. Our interest was in examining how social context can play an important role in making salient the absence of economic and cultural capital of lower income students. One's economic and cultural capital take on meaning within a social context, a dimension that has received insufficient attention in previous research.

The experience of a college education brings opportunities for growth and development, as students acquire more knowledge, encounter new people, ideas and values. But for lower income students an additional dimension of the growth and development that occurs is the acquisition of new forms of cultural capital that affluent students already possess. Movement between classes challenges and changes self-identities and relationships and involves changes in judgment, taste, opinions, preferences and practices. We expect that lower income students at both the

Aries, Elizabeth and Maynard Seider. 2005. "The Interactive Relationship Between Class Identity and College Experience: The Case of Lower Income Students." *Qualitative Sociology*, 28(4): 419–43.

elite and state college would acquire new forms of cultural capital at college, but lower income students at the elite college would experience greater changes due to exposure to many highly affluent students and to greater resources and opportunities.

METHOD

Participants

We interviewed a total of 30 lower income students, including 15 students who attended a highly selective liberal arts school (labeled Little Ivy), and 15 students who attended a state college (State College), as part of a larger study of social class and identity. We recognized that age, race and gender would influence the college experience of lower income students. Given that the experiences of lower income students who are African-American, Hispanic, Asian and white may differ from one another, we decided to hold race constant and to restrict our sample to students who were white. Students at Little Ivy were all of traditional college age, so we limited our sample at State College to students of traditional age as well. The groups were equally balanced by gender.

Family incomes for all but one of the State College group were under $50,000. One third had a father and 27 percent had a mother who had completed college, and 60 percent were first generation college students. These demographic data correlate well with entering State College students as a whole. Parental education and family income for the Little Ivy sample was slightly higher than for the State College sample: half of the mothers and of fathers had completed college, and a third of the participants were first generation college students. Parental incomes were less than $60,000, with half the students reporting parental incomes between $20,000 and $49,999. These Little Ivy sample data also correlate well with the Little Ivy population of entering low income white students from families with incomes under $60,000.

While we began our study using a simple income measure as an indicator of class, as we analyzed our sample we noted differences in parental education, differences that we would have to take into account, particularly since we are interested in the role of "cultural capital" in student adjustment and identity. Thus, we have taken into account the fact that only one-third of our Little Ivy sample is first generation, while 60 percent of our State College sample fits that category. (These differences should not be surprising. For low income students to make it to Little Ivy it helps having a parent or parents who have had the college experience, have the "right" vocabulary, know the differences between elite and non-elite colleges, and can help navigate the hurdles of the college application process.) Therefore we have tried to determine if the additional cultural capital (measured by parental education) that some lower income students bring to their college campuses makes a significant difference in their college experiences.

Procedure

At Little Ivy, all white first and second year students receiving financial aid whose family incomes were less than $50,000 received a letter from the Director of Financial Aid saying they qualified for a study on identity, and were asked to contact the researchers if they were interested in participating. When this did not produce a large enough sample, a second letter went out to all white first and second year students whose parental incomes were less than $60,000. With this second letter, a "lower income" sample was constituted. Since State College students differed very little in family income, and those incomes were comparable to the Little Ivy "lower income" sample, there was no need to draw a stratified sample, and all participants were simply recruited from compulsory social science or introductory sociology classes. On both campuses, participants received $20 in compensation for participation in an interview, which ranged from 1 to 2 hours.

Interview

Interviews were conducted by the authors, who are both white and in their mid to late 50's. The female author is from an upper middle class family, and the male author from a working class family. Both authors conducted roughly half of the interviews at each of the schools. The interviews were conducted either in empty study rooms or faculty offices. Students were interviewed in the spring semester of either their first or second year of college. A year after the initial interview we re-contacted our participants, and 60 percent agreed to return for a second interview, which ranged from 30 minutes to one hour.

We used semi-structured interviews because we wanted to provide the participants the opportunity to reflect on the ways in which social class had an impact on their identities, their interactions with others, and their college experiences.[1] Since relatively little work has been done with college students asking them to discuss their

---

[1] We asked students the following questions: What differences has social class made in the things you do? What things are made easier or harder? On a day-by-day basis, how much thought do you give to your social class? Are there contexts in which it becomes salient? Would you say your social class is expressed in the way you present yourself physically, in your clothing, hairstyle, cosmetics, the way you interact with others? Was class ever a factor in your interactions on campus? Has there ever been an incident here on campus where you felt your class position caused you to be left out, put down, dismissed, or discriminated against? Do you feel your college experiences have changed the way you see the world, the way you think about things, your attitudes, your tastes, your values? How have these changes affected your relationships with friends at home? Do you find yourself changing your language or dress when you go home? What happens if you don't switch language or dress? Have the changes you've made brought you closer, or made you more distant from friends at home? How have your experiences at college affected your relationships with parents?

class background, and since we were well aware of the often taboo strictures against discussing class, we wanted to provide students with a comfortable and open setting to reflect on their biographies.

Interviews were tape recorded and transcribed to permit later coding. Both authors read all the transcripts. The first author went through the transcripts and identified statements as falling into one of the following three categories: reactions to lack of cultural or economic capital; changes caused by the college experience; and ways of coping with class-based discontinuity. From those statements the first author then identified themes. The second author responded to and modified the themes identified by the first author.

RESULTS

Lower-Income Students Who Come to College Lacking the Cultural and Economic Capital of Middle and Upper-Middle Class Students

Little Ivy

Differences in the economic capital of the affluent and lower income students became salient to the lower income students upon arrival at college. The economic capital of the affluent students stood out in their possessions, in their electronic equipment (e.g., large screen televisions, stereos, computers), dorm furnishings (e.g., leather couches, designer bedding), designer clothes, expensive cars, and in the money they spent on possessions (e.g., CDs, DVDs, videos, clothes), meals off campus at expensive restaurants, and vacations (e.g., to Europe, Caribbean resorts, family estates). For the lower income students, their lack of such possessions and the money required for such lifestyles seemed clear markers of their difference. The lower income students made many references to the possessions and lifestyles of the affluent students. Despite the fact that many of these students had a parent who had completed college, their lack of economic capital proved highly salient to them.

Carl[2] grew up in a single parent home with his mother who had a college degree but worked as a secretary. Carl had attended a public magnet school that included students from some very wealthy backgrounds, and as Carl described himself:

> I was always the different kid who didn't have the right equipment....I felt I didn't have the right clothes, and I was made fun of for having dirty old holey sneakers, or just not the right clothes, especially in elementary school and middle school....[At Little Ivy] I came with just clothes and a toothbrush where others came with computers, televisions, video games, etc....I didn't have a winter coat. You don't need a winter coat in [my home town] and those are expensive. I didn't have the money for that. I didn't have very warm clothes at all. I didn't have a computer. I didn't think I needed a computer. I can use the ones here in the computer lab.

Allen's parents had both completed college but his father was forced into early retirement from his white-collar job, and his mother subsequently retired, so their family income had dropped significantly. Allen was struck by students who "just blow $500 shopping on-line or something just like [on] impulse;" Marie, raised by an immigrant mother and grandmother, neither of whom had completed college, was told growing up that she was "on the low end of the spectrum" and "there's other people who are going to think that they're better than you." Marie was aware that there were "certain ways to show off you're rich, like wear little Tiffany necklaces." Kate, a first generation college student with two working parents said, "I think most of my friends here are upper, upper middle, upper class. The presence

_____
[2] We have used pseudonyms throughout to protect students' confidentiality.

of wealth is felt a lot more here than I've ever experienced."

As the lower income students discussed the ways in which they differed from the affluent students, the following themes emerged, capturing negative feelings based on class-based differences: inadequacy, inferiority, intimidation, exclusion and powerlessness.

Inadequacy, Inferiority and Intimidation. A number of the lower income students worried about their self-presentation and focused in particular on inadequacies of their linguistic competence, e.g., their inability to articulate their ideas clearly, deficiencies in their grammar, their regional accents. These problems seemed particularly acute for the first generation students lacking in cultural capital. When speaking up in class some students worried that their speech would mark them as less intelligent than the other students. Ann, the daughter of blue collar immigrants and a first generation student, commented on her own anxiety: "In class I have all these ideas sometimes and saying them is like, 'What did I just say? I must have come across like an idiot!' So I don't think I'm very eloquent."

The language of home was often not the language spoken in the academy. Sarah, a first generation college student whose parents worked blue-collar jobs remarked, "The people I'm used to at home are very different in just grammar." Several lower income students became aware of their regional accents, which they found to be devalued in the college context. Speech, then, proved to be a marker of class background that could cause others to look down upon lower income students, an aspect of self that made them feel inadequate.

Lower income students, and in particular first generation students, came to view their own parents through a new lens as they compared their parents to the parents of the affluent students, and the differences seemed associated with deficiency. Their parents had less education, and their parents' occupations held less status and prestige. Sarah spoke of having a hard time telling people about her dad's blue-collar job as a mechanic "when they say [their] father is a doctor, or [their] father is a writer." She described her parents as "not like" Little Ivy in "their level of education, the way they speak," and confessed that "it was always kind of weird for them to come here. It seemed like they didn't belong."

The education and skills of the parents of the affluent students enabled them to be resources for their children in ways that the parents of the lower income students were not. According to Ann, a first generation student, "People on my floor talk about their mothers being professors and editing their papers, and part of me is just like 'I feel awful, why couldn't I have had that?'"

 Exclusion. Many lower income students felt their class backgrounds made it difficult for them to connect to the wealthy students. While the first generation students were more likely to express feelings of inadequacy, inferiority and intimidation, feelings of exclusion were not exclusive to first generation lower income students. As Rob phrased it:

> I would love to be friends with [wealthy students], but I do feel I am excluded based on class…One of the first nights I got here I tried to meet people. There was a party in my dorm on the second floor. I didn't realize it was a rich white kids' party. Everyone was giving me one-word answers, turning their face and that made me feel kind of crummy that night.

It was not just that more affluent students failed to include them; the lower income students often found it difficult to bridge the gulf. For Paul, simply knowing he was around wealthier people caused him to be "deaf and dumb." He went on to say:

> There is just such immaterial knowledge. [Wealthy students] know that they make up a certain subset of the population, and that they have a certain niche, and it fosters in them a really unique bond between each other and excludes you. They can be totally friendly with

me, not hostile or anything like that, but it excludes me in ways. It's attitude and personality. The way you react to everything. The way that we look at a sporting event on television, like a basketball game. I know a lot about basketball and I enjoy it. I am like this passive fan where my roommate and his friends talk about prior games that they have been to, players they have met, training in a gym with one player on the opposing team. Just being part of that and feeling much more involved in that team or event in a way that I wasn't.

Some of the tastes and preferences of the lower income students differed from those of the wealthy students, and led to their exclusion. Peter grew up in a blue-collar family, and remembers living on food stamps for several years. Despite the fact that his mother later achieved a graduate degree and currently works as a scientist, Peter reported feeling "slightly left out when they talk about skiing, musicals, etc., because I haven't been exposed to that.…I like classical music once in a while, but I don't enjoy it or I wouldn't choose to go to the opera. I'd go bowling ten times instead." Wealth and leisure give one the opportunity to explore the arts and intellectual realms not directly relevant to job opportunities, and many lower income students have developed different preferences and values based on necessity.

The ongoing lifestyles of the affluent students required resources that the lower income students did not possess, and that also led to their exclusion. Lower income students could not afford to accompany their friends on trips abroad for spring break, or to go to dinners at high priced restaurants. Some Little Ivy students reported that they never went out to eat, or if they accompanied others to restaurants, they hid their lack of resources by not ordering anything. While the cultural signals of the affluent students may have been sent unconsciously, the unintended consequences remained.

Powerlessness. One lower income student spoke of being rendered powerless socially because of his lack of economic resources, a requirement for shaping social life. Carl described:

> ...the system of drinking [at Little Ivy], that you host and you provide and nobody ever gives you any money towards it. You host and people get some sort of power by buying the keg. People who have a lot of money to throw lots of parties and have provided all the resources of alcohol and marijuana, and people get a sense of power from that.

While lower income students might be included in these parties, the organization of social life required resources they did not possess.

Lower income students also felt greater powerlessness relative to the affluent students in determining their own futures. The affluent students could plan on future careers that required graduate degrees without having to worry about the costs of further education, while the lower income students felt constrained by their financial need. Karen, a second generation college student, had planned to go to graduate school, but her father had recently gone on disability and faced a future of expensive medical care. She said: "It makes me feel that these financial concerns are shaping my future goals and not necessarily shaping the rest of [the other students' goals]."

State College

Because our State College sample was not surrounded by highly affluent students, class-based differences did not generally seem salient to them. The State College students did not make comments about markedly different material possessions from other students, and made no mention of students who went out to expensive dinners, made extravagant purchases, or took trips abroad for spring break. They did not seem particularly aware of their speech (e.g., ability to express themselves, grammar, or regional accents); most had not gone out of state to college and thus were not in contact with students speaking in different regional accents. They had less reason to feel excluded and intimidated, and never mentioned

feeling powerless. In the few instances where working class students at State College spoke of interactions with more affluent students, they were cognizant, however, of being judged as less adequate. Chris, a first generation college student whose father was disabled and often unemployed, and whose mother was unemployed due to illness, spoke of having a roommate from an "upper-level class" who, because of his money, "thinks he's just way better than everyone."

While many State College students volunteered that their clothes reflected their social class position, they did not see their clothes as a marker differentiating them from other students on campus. Many State College students spoke of not having "a lot of new clothes," or designer clothes. Elena, a second-generation student said, "I don't really dress in name brand clothes. I go to Goodwill a lot." Craig, a first generation student, reported, "I don't wear Gucci or Armani or what not." While their clothes marked their exclusion from the affluent classes, they did not symbolize their exclusion from other students on campus.

New Forms of Capital that Lower Income Students Develop at College

Little Ivy

Since coming to college, many Little Ivy students described changes that had occurred in their language, dress, and behavior, in their self-confidence and self-respect, and in their understanding of their position in the world.

Language, Dress, Behavior

Regardless of the educational level of their parents, the experience of being at Little Ivy was marked for lower income students by the assimilation of aspects of speech, attire and behavior commonly associated with the middle and upper classes. As Carl remarked:

> Part of what [Little Ivy] does is socialize people into the wealthy elite. And so I dress differently. I speak differently. I'm more articulate than [my mother]....My education

has given me the ability to adjust to situations rationally.... Freshman year it was people telling me on my floor, friends of mine, what to wear, how to dress, how to act in certain social circumstances. And there's this whole culture that goes along with [Little Ivy] that's very different from my friends at the state university and that culture. And so there is a tension between who I have been and who I want to be. I think I'm part of a different social class than I came in here with, I was socialized to be part of.

The changes were motivated, in part, by students' desires to win acceptance in this new environment. Rob spoke of being highly aware of "people's criticisms, the desire to fit in and please people." Sarah commented, "I would probably say that people of my class would say that I look kind of preppy or probably not in their social class. I think I kind of try to fit in to what a [Little Ivy] student is like to some extent."

Self-Confidence, Self-Respect, and Position in the World

Perhaps the most significant changes that accompanied the acquisition of middle class cultural capital were the attainment of new forms of self-confidence and self-respect that came along with diminished feelings of difference, inadequacy and exclusion. Based on their academic performance, some students in fact recognized that their academic talents measured up to that of the affluent students. Rob, who spoke of feelings of inferiority when he initially arrived on campus, discovered that his academic work was equal to that of other students. He noted with pride that he no longer thought of himself "as less capable than anyone on this campus."

Little Ivy opened up opportunities that put lower income students on a new trajectory into society. Several lower income students spoke of feeling they inhabited a new position in relation to the world around them. Peter recognized that "I am one of the people that might be making big decisions in the future." Paul reported having "more

self respect and optimism. I don't use drugs. I look more up instead of down." Reflecting on how things might have been different had he gone to a state college, Allen said, "I think that my ambitions and prospects would probably be a lot less than they are now. There wouldn't be as much opportunity to get into medical school; there wouldn't be connections with the alumni....I would be thinking a lot more practical in a state college."

State College

State College students had less to say about the acquisition of new forms of cultural capital (e.g., changes in language, dress or behavior) although some students articulated these changes. Tom, whose parents both had college degrees, knew that his "vocabulary has grown as a side effect of all that I've learned at college. I think I talk with bigger words." Tom went on to say, "I feel that I can present myself decently well now in a situation where I would need to." Craig, a first generation student, noted the changes that had occurred in the way he constructed an argument. His opinions were now grounded in knowledge he had acquired.

> Me and my dad sometimes if we get into a discussion, we almost always have different opinions on the subject. And I feel my opinion comes more from my education in college than from anything else. I feel everything I opinionate is from what I've learned from courses I've taken, and I think it's different for him. I think he makes his opinions based on his experiences.

Explicit statements about increased self-confidence and self-respect were lacking, although such feelings are implicit in the above statements.

Coping with Class-Based Discontinuity

For some students the discontinuity between their pre-college careers and their college experiences proved difficult, but many students successfully found ways to cope with the shift. The changes that had occurred made it hard for a number of students to maintain connections with family and friends at home. Others found the college experience allowed aspects of self to flourish for the first time. Many students found ways to compartmentalize old and new aspects of self so that they could coexist. Some were able to bring new aspects of self into their old relationships. Many class-based aspects of self were not repudiated. Rather, the college experience led to increased pride among lower income students in their class-based characteristics.

Little Ivy

Maintaining Prior Relationships. Some students spoke of discontinuities with friends at home due to their acquisition of middle class cultural capital. The educational opportunity afforded to them changed students' perceptions of the world and their place in it. Broader options had opened to them; they had developed new priorities, perspectives, values, and greater engagement with an intellectual world. Yet some students found it difficult to bridge the gap and bring new aspects of self into their old relationships.

Marie remarked, "My friends who stayed home and went to local college really didn't have this kind of eye opening experience that I had coming here. I can't even describe it to them, so there is a sort of difference between us as I have this new perspective on things." Rob remarked, "Since my priorities have sort of changed, I feel maybe a degree of separation with some friends because their priorities are different. As far as my priorities go, there are not a lot of people [at home] who share the same kind of desires." Carl spoke of being "ripped" from his home community and put in a "totally new environment, all these new experiences, all these new ideas, new people, new social interactions." He said,

> I sometimes have to think about my values and how I want to live in the world because I am confronted with this multiplicity of social interactions. Now I have the options to choose. How am I going to live? A lot of my friends at

home have never been pushed to think about that. My education is very central to my identity, and the more educated I get, the more difficult it is to share certain parts of me and certain sides of me. I can't talk to my friends about a book.

Carl added that he maintained his relationships to friends at home by mostly going out to drink with them.

For some students, it was not clear whether they would be able to maintain their connections to parents and friends. Marie, for example, said, "I think that [my mother and I] are going to keep growing farther and farther apart." Thinking about distance from friends at home, Allen said, "There is a greater distance; our lives are beginning to take shape in a direction. I am not really upset about it. I really loved coming to college. I just didn't want to be home. I never looked back."

While most of the lower income students experienced difficulties maintaining prior relationships, a few did not attribute the difficulties to their college experience. Sarah drifted away from friends at home, but said, "I think that we weren't true friends to begin with. They were the kind of people you hang out with in high school." Paul experienced a certain distance from friends, but that had always been true. "I was always the smart one."

Avoiding Judgments. A number of lower income students struggled with avoiding judgments of those they had left behind. These feelings emerged regardless of whether their parents were college educated. These judgments appeared to accompany the acquisition of new knowledge and the development of a more critical perspective. Paul worried that the college experience had made him look down upon "dumb people. It has probably made me an intolerant person." Naomi commented that being around "so many intellectual people" makes it easy for her to forget that everyone is not like Little Ivy professors and students, and she worried "you fall into sort of a trap" of being judgmental that she tried to avoid. "I try to stay away from a superior role."

Students also struggled over negative judgments of their parents and over feelings of betrayal. New opportunities have opened up to them, and some would no longer consider following their parents' footsteps in the occupational world. Their parents, too, worried about them becoming judgmental. Allen noted, "My mom seems to think that I am becoming in her words 'a snob.' "

Coping Strategies. Lower income students used a number of strategies to cope with the discontinuities between former and newly acquired aspects of self. Some students compartmentalized different parts of the self, keeping them separate but allowing them to co-exist. They described code switching as they moved back and forth from home to college, i.e., using different modes of speech in each setting. They noted they faced criticism for using too large a vocabulary when talking with people at home. As Allen said, "If I use a big word, it's like 'Oh, Mr. Smarty Pants over here.' I try not to show off my vocabulary."

Code switching helped them to manage the tensions between past and present aspects of self, and appeared to be carried out unconsciously.

Pride in Class-Based Character Traits. Although lower income students did take on aspects of middle class culture, parts of their class backgrounds remained firmly rooted in their identities and were affirmed with pride. Just as the homeless accepted and asserted their street role identities, so too did the lower income students affirm aspects of their class identities. In fact, many of our lower income students expressed pride in the character traits their class backgrounds had given them, particularly when they contrasted themselves to some of the very affluent students. Lower income students did not want to take on all aspects of the upper middle class.

The lower income students, regardless of the level of education of their parents, highlighted the positive virtues gained from their class position,

enabling them to feel the self-respect and dignity that derived from their class backgrounds. They expressed gratitude for the character traits they attributed to their class experience: they had become independent and self-reliant, had learned to appreciate things because they had been given less, and they could understand and empathize with a broad range of humanity. They came to affirm and value these aspects of their identities. As Rob remarked, "When we didn't have money it was really hard. I am not upset with anything that has happened in my life. If anything, I think it has made me a better person. Having my experiences has been an advantage."

Independence and Self-Reliance. Many lower income students seemed shocked by the lack of independence and self-reliance that some of their affluent counterparts exhibited. Marie remarked,

> I remember, especially as a freshman, that people didn't know how to open up bank accounts, didn't know how to do their own laundry, didn't ever cook for themselves back home. People get into car accidents here and their parents pay for it. That would never have happened back home. People pay for their own car crashes. You took more responsibility for your own actions whereas here Mom and Dad can come in and fix them.

Mike, a first generation college student with a blue-collar father and a lower level white-collar mother, said,

> My roommate, basically his whole life has been centered on [the upper east side of Manhattan]. The only trips they make are to [the Hamptons] or up to Westchester. Watching him here, he is so helpless. He admits it himself. He can't do a darn thing. In our freshman year he would wash his clothes and took them wet from the washing machine and put them in his laundry bag and just left them there. He had no idea.

Appreciation. While lower income students did not possess a lot of material resources, they learned to curb their desires, and to appreciate what they did have. According to Peter, "From a very early age I understood that we didn't have very much so I didn't want much. I never missed anything." They felt that if they made a purchase they appreciated it more because they worked hard to get it. Allen felt that his class background made him value opportunities more. "I kind of latch on to them, like I don't want to lose this. I don't know, I just feel like I treat them with more care than somebody else would."

Understanding and Empathy. The lower income students felt that their class upbringing had given them the ability to understand, relate to and empathize with a broad range of individuals, qualities they believed some of the affluent students lacked. Naomi felt "almost grateful that I haven't had a really very easy childhood economically" because it made her "appreciate the struggles that people have." Sarah referred to her ability to "adapt to situations more easily, or understand different kinds of people ... [with] the background that I have, as opposed to kids growing up that kind of have everything. It's harder for them to really understand other people I think sometimes." Marie was stunned when others in her tutoring seminar

> were worrying about how to relate to kids in [a nearby economically depressed city]. How do I get along with these kids? That shocked me. Do you think they are aliens or something? These are kids: be natural, make them laugh. Maybe I still don't see myself as a [Little Ivy] kid.

Peter realized that many of the affluent students had a very different outlook on life than he did, and felt that "they have no clue as to what 90% of the people in this country live with."

The lower income Little Ivy students had worked minimum wage summer jobs (e.g., waitress, toll collector). They identified and empathized with workers on campus; they knew what working such jobs entailed. At Little Ivy they encountered some affluent students who would

not have ever considered working such "inferior" jobs, and who showed insensitivity to people in these positions. Kate had been a waitress in the summers, one of the few opportunities available to her in her hometown.

> I remember one of my first experiences [at Little Ivy] with a kid that lived upstairs from me, and [his family vacationed] where I live in the summer. He went to summer there all through his life. And I waitressed at this little restaurant, and he had been coming in apparently. One day he came down and he said, "Haven't you ever thought of getting a real job?" And I just kind of looked at him like, I'm not even going to listen to you because he's working at this big firm or something in New York city and in [my state], I'm sure you're aware, you don't have those opportunities.

Marie felt embarrassed when she saw the workers in the dining hall wiping the tables and cleaning up after the students. She was not accustomed to being waited upon, cleaned up after, and did not share a sense of entitlement to these services. While many other students seemed oblivious to the services that were being performed for them, she identified with the workers' position, and felt embarrassed by her superior status relative to these workers. "It makes me ashamed that we didn't clean up after ourselves. They are sort of degraded doing this work and I wonder if some of the other kids feel that way, if they have ever been in that position."

State College

Like their Little Ivy counterparts, some State College students struggled with bridging differences in knowledge, modes of thinking, perspectives, and priorities as they moved between college and home, and they, too, seemed concerned about making critical judgments of those they have left behind. Craig said,

> Not to downgrade [my parents] or anything, it's just that nobody ever went to college. I

think I know too much for them and they don't understand my point of view because they don't know where I'm coming from, and what I've been exposed to through school. From my opinion, they might just be scared to start talking to me because they might just feel inferior. They might think I'm a little cocky about that opinion.

Aspects of who he had become were left out in his relationship to his parents. As with Little Ivy students, one solution to these tensions was to compartmentalize, and express different aspects of self with parents and professors. Craig sought out professors to talk over ideas he could not discuss with his family.

For the most part, however, the State College students talked less of difficulties in bridging the gap between home and school than did the Little Ivy students. While Little Ivy students all lived on campus, as did almost all of the State College students we interviewed, the State College students lived closer to home, and remained more connected to their childhood friends. Most did not speak of a new social distance from friends at home. Few of the State College students spoke of shifts in language or dress as they moved from college to home. Students who spoke of code-switching referred primarily to age-based aspects of speech. They spoke primarily of not being as "well-spoken" among friends or cleaning up their language when speaking with younger siblings.

While many lower income Little Ivy students expressed pride in their class-based aspects of self, which derived from a comparison with affluent students who lacked their independence, self-reliance, empathy and understanding, these types of comments did not emerge in the interviews with the State College students. The latter expressed an acceptance of their class position, and pride in the character traits it had given them, but their pride derived from comparing themselves with a generalized concept of those who were more affluent, and those who had less than they did.

DISCUSSION AND CONCLUSION

Our interviews with lower income students revealed that the type of college one attends differentially influences the relationship between class identity and the college experience. Lower income students at a prestigious private college faced more class-related challenges and difficulties than students at the state college, despite the fact that they came to college with greater cultural capital than the state college students. The disparities of wealth between students at the prestigious college heightened awareness of social class, whereas greater homogeneity in class backgrounds at the state college made class less salient. Our direct comparison of elite and state college students demonstrates the importance of social context (i.e., of the type of institution one attends) in shaping the class-based experience of identity for lower income students and in understanding the meaning that cultural capital may have for individuals.

The first generation students who entered the elite college with the least cultural capital evidenced the greatest initial feelings of intimidation, discomfort, inadequacy, and deficiency. As to the issue of exclusion and powerlessness, lower income students at the elite college displayed roughly similar feelings regardless of the educational background of their parents. Our study points to the importance of looking at both economic and cultural capital in an analysis of social class in a college setting.

Our data also highlight the importance of returning to Bourdieu's original definition of cultural capital as encompassing skills and abilities (1977). When speaking of their lack of cultural capital, students at the elite college referred to competencies and "immaterial knowledge" such as not possessing the "right" linguistic skills, the proper forms of dress, knowledge of how to act in certain social situations, and the strategies and contacts used to procure summer jobs. These were important aspects of cultural capital that differentiated them from affluent students upon entry to college.

Lower income students at both schools, regardless of the educational backgrounds of their parents, struggled with class-based discontinuities between their pre-college identities and their evolving identities. They spoke of acquiring new ways of dressing, speaking and behaving. They worried, for example, about how to be different from parents and friends at home without being judgmental. These issues were heightened for the elite college students who had moved further from home, and whose anticipated college degrees put them on a trajectory for greater upward mobility.

The findings of this study have important implications for faculty and administrators at prestigious colleges and universities, where disparities in wealth among students are great. As these schools commit themselves to recruiting more low-income students, and to counteracting the reproduction of social advantage, attention must be paid to how to best support and incorporate lower income students into the life of these campuses. The problems are particularly acute for first generation students, most lacking in cultural capital, who experience the greatest degree of inadequacy, inferiority and intimidation. Lower income students will need to find new bases of support and to develop a class analysis of their experience by linking themselves with others who share their class backgrounds.

Ironically enough, our research demonstrates that for low income students to move from the margins and to become fully integrated into elite colleges and universities, those institutions may need to nurture and support working-class-based clubs or organizations, in the same way that they have fostered the development of similar groups based on gender, sexual orientation, ethnicity and race. Beyond that, institutions of higher education must create a climate where class can be acknowledged and openly discussed.

DISCUSSION QUESTIONS

1. What are some of the key markers of social class identified by Aries and Seider? Have you noticed other signifiers of social class in your daily life?
2. What differences do Aries and Seider find between lower-income college students at "Little Ivy" and those attending a state school?
3. How would you respond to some of Aries and Seider's interview questions? For example, on a day-to-day basis, how much thought do you give to your social class? Are there contexts in which your social class becomes more or less salient?
4. What is the concept of "code switching" mentioned by Aries and Seider? Have you ever used this method of identity negotiation? If so, how, why, and where?

ADDITIONAL RESOURCES

Internet

http://www.firstinthefamily.org/. First in the Family has resources for first-generation high school and college students to help make the transition easier and the experience more successful.

http://ies.ed.gov/pubsearch/pubsinfo.asp?pubid=98082. The U.S. Department of Education's report "First Generation Students: Undergraduates Whose Parents Never Enrolled in Postsecondary Education" is accessible on the Institute of Education Services website.

Radio

http://www.npr.org/tcmplates/story/story.php?storyId=l0089929. "Challenges Face First-Generation Students." A May 2007 "Morning Edition" story featuring a Missouri community college support group that assists students whose families may not understand the challenges associated with attending college.

FURTHER READING

Aronson, Pamela. 2008. "Breaking Barriers or Locked Out? Class-Based Perceptions and Experiences of Postsecondary Education." *New Directions for Child and Adolescent Development*, (119): 41–54.

Bourdieu, Pierre. 1977. "Cultural Reproduction and Social Reproduction," in Jerome Karabel and Albert Henry Halsey (eds.). *Power and Ideology in Education*, 487–511. New York: Oxford University Press.

Choy, Susan P. 2001. *Students Whose Parents Did Not Go to College: Postsecondary Access, Persistence, and Attainment* (NCES 2001–126). Washington, DC: U.S. Department of Education, National Center for Education Statistics.

Jones, Sandra J. 1998. "Subjectivity and Class Consciousness: The Development of Class Identity." *Journal of Adult Development*, 5(3): 145–62.

Orbe, Mark P. 2008. "Theorizing Multidimensional Identity Negotiation: Reflections on the Lived Experiences of First Generation College Students." *New Directions for Child and Adolescent Development*, (120): 81–95.

Warburton, Edward C., Rosio Bugarin, and Anne-Marie Nunez. 2001. "Bridging the Gap: Academic Preparation and Postsecondary Success of First-Generation Students." *Education Statistics Quarterly*, 3(Fall): 73–7.

46. Teenagers in Clarendon Heights: The Hallway Hangers and the Brothers

JAY MACLEOD

Jay MacLeod conducted field research in the 1980s with teenage boys in an inner city housing project that he dubbed "Clarendon Heights." In this excerpt from his book, *Ain't No Makin' It*, MacLeod describes at length two primary groups in this housing development with highly divergent identities, coping strategies, and trajectories of attainment.

On any given day, except during the coldest winter months, the evening hours in Clarendon Heights are filled with activity. At one end of the housing development, elderly women sit on wooden benches and chat. In the center of the project, children play street hockey, kickball, stickball, or football, depending on the season. At the other end, teenage boys congregate in

MacLeod, Jay. 2008. "Teenagers in Clarendon Heights: The Hallway Hangers and the Brothers," in *Ain't No Makin' It: Leveled Aspirations in a Low-Income Neighborhood*, 3rd edition. 25–49. Boulder, CO: Westview Press.

the stairwell and on the landing of one of the entries—doorway #13.

THE HALLWAY HANGERS: "YOU GOTTA BE BAD"

This doorway and the area immediately outside it are the focus of activity for the Hallway Hangers, one of the two main peer groups of high-school-age boys living in Clarendon Heights. Composed of a core of eight youths, but including up to ten additional people who are loosely attached to the group, the Hallway Hangers are tough, streetwise, individuals who form a distinctive subculture. Except for Boo-Boo, who is black, and Chris, who is of mixed racial parentage, the Hallway Hangers are white boys of Italian or Irish descent. The eight members considered here range in age from sixteen to nineteen. Five have dropped out of school, two graduated last year, and one continues to attend high school. They all smoke cigarettes, drink regularly, and use drugs. All but two have been arrested. Stereotyped as "hoodlums," "punks," or "burnouts" by outsiders, the Hallway Hangers are actually a varied group, and much can be learned from considering each member.

Frankie, the acknowledged leader of the Hallway Hangers, is of only medium height and weight, but his fighting ability is unsurpassed among teenagers in Clarendon Heights. Missing two front teeth from one of his few unsuccessful encounters, Frankie maintains a cool, calculating demeanor that only occasionally gives way to his fiery temper. He commands the respect of the other boys because he is a natural leader and because he comes from a family that is held in high esteem by the city's underworld. His brothers have been involved in organized crime and have spent time in prison; four of them were incarcerated at the time I conducted my research. Although Frankie is the ringleader of the Hallway Hangers, he has never been arrested—no small feat considering the scope of the group's criminal activity.

Whereas Frankie combines physical toughness and mental acuity, Slick, although no weakling, clearly possesses an abundance of the latter attribute. Very articulate and perceptive, Slick scored high on standardized tests and fared well in school when he applied himself (he dropped out last year). Slick gets along well on the street, where his quick wit and sharp tongue are major assets. Although his status falls short of Frankie's, Slick is accorded much respect by the other boys of Clarendon Heights.

As Slick is known for the strength of his intellect, Shorty is known for his physical toughness. When a teacher at the local high school remarked, "What makes someone tough has nothing to do with size or even muscle—it's the fear factor. If someone's fearless, crazy, he'll do anything," he doubtless had Shorty in mind. As his nickname implies, Shorty is small, but well built. His temper is explosive, and under the influence of alcohol or drugs, he has been known to accost strangers, beat up friends, or pull a knife on anyone who challenges him. On one occasion, he repeatedly stabbed himself in the head in a fit of masochistic machismo. Although Frankie and Slick also consider themselves alcoholics, Shorty's drinking problem is more severe. The county court ordered him to a detoxification center—an arrangement Shorty has slyly managed to avoid.

Like the other three boys, Chris is a self-professed alcoholic who also admits to being dependent on marijuana. Chris's father (who does not live at home) is black, and his mother is white, which gives Chris an ethnic heritage that makes his acceptance by the rest of the Hallway Hangers difficult. A tall, very slender youth, Chris is loud and talkative but without the self-confidence and poise of Slick or Frankie. He is often the object of the other boys' abuse, both verbal and physical, but nevertheless has some stature in the group largely because of his loyalty and sense of humor.

Boo-Boo, the other black member of the Hallway Hangers, is a tall, quiet, dark-skinned youth. His serious nature makes him a less frequent target of abuse, which begins as playful racial barbs but often degenerates into downright racial animosity. Like Chris, Boo-Boo is a follower. A sincere and earnest boy, his general demeanor is at odds with the violence and bluster that characterize the group as a whole. Nevertheless, Boo-Boo has been known to fight—and quite effectively—when seriously antagonized and generally is held in moderate esteem by the rest of the boys.

Like Boo-Boo, Stoney is a bit of a loner. The only Hallway Hanger to hold stable employment, Stoney works full time in a pizza shop. His regular income, which he recently used to buy a car, earns him a measure of deference from the other boys, but Stoney lacks the cockiness and bravado necessary for high stature within the group. Skinny and averse to street fights, Stoney perpetually but ineffectively strives to rid himself of the label "pussy." Stoney does share with the other boys an enthusiasm for beer and drugs; he has been arrested for possession of mescaline and is psychologically dependent on marijuana. He has a steady girlfriend (another anomaly for the Hallway Hangers, who generally reject serious relationships in favor of more casual romantic encounters) with whom he spends much of his time, but Stoney still values the friendship of the Hallway Hangers and remains an integral member of the group.

Steve, Slick's younger brother, is the stereotypical project youth. Constantly on the lookout for a free ride, Steve is insolent and loud but lacks his brother's sophistication. He is courageous, full of energy, and fights well, but Steve is not particularly popular with the other boys, who tolerate him as Slick's brother and as a person who can be counted on for support and loyalty in the most trying situations. Steve is the only Hallway Hanger still in school; he expects to graduate in two years.

In contrast to Steve, Jinks is a sensitive, shy boy who shares with Stoney and Chris a psychological dependence on marijuana. Although he is considered immature and is taunted as a "mama's boy" by some of the Hallway Hangers, Jinks seems to have inner reserves of confidence and self-esteem that protect his ego from such assaults. Lighthearted and understanding of others, Jinks is the only white member of the Hallway Hangers who is not overtly racist. Although he takes a good deal of abuse from the others, especially Frankie and Shorty, Jinks's acceptance as a bona fide member of the group is beyond question.

These boys come together in the late afternoon or early evening after dinner and "hang" in doorway #13 until late at night. They come to "see what's up," to "find out what's goin' down," to "shoot the shit," and, generally, to just pass the time. Smelling of urine, lined with graffiti, and littered with trash and broken glass, this hallway is the setting for much playful banter, some not so playful "capping" (exchange of insults), and an occasional fight. The odors of cigarette smoke, beer, and marijuana are nearly always present. During the weekend, there may be a case or two of beer, a nearly constant circulation of joints, and some cocaine, mescaline, or "angel dust" (PCP). Late at night, one occasionally stumbles upon a lone figure shooting up heroin.

In an inversion of the dominant culture's vocabulary and value scheme, the subculture of the Hallway Hangers is a world in which to be "bad" is literally to be good. A common characteristic of lower-class teenage peer cultures, this emphasis on being bad is inextricably bound up with the premium put on masculinity, physical toughness, and street wisdom in lower-class culture. Slick, in articulating the prominence of this value for the Hallway Hangers, states in definite terms what being bad often involves.

SLICK: You hafta make a name for yourself, to be bad, tough, whatever. You hafta be, y'know, be with the "in" crowd. Know what I mean? You hafta—it's just all part of growing up around here—you hafta do certain things. Some of the things you hafta do is, y'know, once in awhile you hafta, if you haven't gotten into a fight, if you have a fight up the high school, you're considered bad. Y'know what I mean? If you beat, someone up up there, especially if he's black, around this way...if you're to be bad, you hafta be arrested. You hafta at least know what bein' in a cell is like.

Thus, good grades in school can lead to ostracism, whereas time spent in prison earns respect. To be bad is the main criterion for status in this subculture; its primacy cannot be overemphasized, and its importance is implied continually by the boys.

For the Hallway Hangers, being bad entails the consumption of alcohol and the use of drugs on a regular basis. The boys are intoxicated for a good portion of almost every weekend and drink heavily during the week. During the summer, the level of drinking reaches staggering proportions, often involving the consumption of two or more "beer balls" (the equivalent of two and half cases of beer pressurized into a plastic ball about two feet in diameter) a day for a group of eight or ten boys. Most of these boys began drinking beer regularly at the age of thirteen or fourteen; their preferences now include whiskey and Peppermint Schnapps.

The Hallway Hangers also began smoking marijuana when they were twelve or thirteen years old, a tendency that has led many to use an assortment of heavier drugs as well. Most of them describe stages in their adolescence during which they used PCP, mescaline, valium, or THC (the chief intoxicant in marijuana). Having moderated what they now see as their youthful enthusiasm for different drugs, the Hallway Hangers generally limit themselves to marijuana and cocaine. All the Hallway Hangers smoke a great deal of marijuana; Chris, Jinks, and Stoney acknowledge their dependence on the drug. Marijuana joints circulate in doorway #13 almost as often as cans of beer, and all admit they get high before and during school.

Obviously, underage drinking and drug use are illegal, and the Hallway Hangers have made their share of trips to the police station and the courthouse. Stoney has three convictions, twice for possession of narcotics and once for passing stolen property. Boo-Boo has been arrested for "hot boxes" (stolen cars). Chris has assault with a deadly weapon in addition to some less serious convictions on his record. Shorty has been to court for larceny, assault with a deadly weapon, and other less substantial crimes. One of the older teenagers on the fringes of the Hallway Hangers was convicted of rape and sentenced to eighteen months in the maximum security state prison after his sophomore year in high school.

These, of course, represent only the crimes at which the Hallway Hangers have been caught. Their criminal activity is actually much more widespread. Those trusted by the Hallway Hangers are occasionally approached with offers for good deals on bicycles, stereo equipment, or musical instruments, all of which have been stolen. Chris makes serious money dealing drugs. Other Hallway Hangers make small amounts of cash selling drugs to friends and acquaintances.

Jimmy Sullivan, an experienced and perceptive teacher of the adjustment class in which Frankie, Shorty, and Steve are, or were at one time, enrolled, gives a good description of the Hallway Hangers' criminal careers.

JS: One thing about these kids: Crime pays, and they know it....It's so easy to go over to the hallowed halls across the street there [a large university] and pick up a bike. I know three or four stores in the city that will pay thirty to forty dollars for a good bike, no questions asked. They'll turn it over for a hundred fifty or two hundred bucks. What do these kids need money for? What do they care about? Beer, sneakers, joints. They're not going to work when they can make easy money through virtually riskless criminal enterprises. Only suckers are gonna work for that. As long as their expectations stay low and they only need a hundred bucks a week—as Steve said, "All I want is my beer money"—they're all set. Up to when they're seventeen years old there's no risk. But when they turn about eighteen, the peer group doesn't accept that anymore. If they could go on stealing bikes for the rest of their lives, I think they would. But when you're seventeen or eighteen and someone says, "Hey man, where'd you get the cash?" it's unacceptable to say, "Oh, stealing bikes, man." You've got to be into cars, dealing drugs, or holding people up. That's when the risk and fear start coming into it. For many of them, the easiest route is to get a job. Of course, some of them don't, and they end up in jail.

Like many urban slums, the teenage underworld of Clarendon Heights is characterized by predatory theft, and some of the Hallway Hangers specialize in "cuffing" drugs, stolen merchandise, and money off those who themselves are involved in illegal activity. Shorty and Frankie have sold hundreds of fake joints, robbed other drug pushers, and forced younger or less tough boys to give them a share of their illegal income. The consensus among the Hallway Hangers is that this type of thievery is morally more defensible than conventional theft. More importantly, there is less risk of detection, for the authorities are unlikely to become involved.

An important characteristic of the subculture of the Hallway Hangers is group solidarity. Membership in the Hallway Hangers involves a serious commitment to the group: a willingness to put out for others and to look out for the rest of the group's well-being as well as one's own. This loyalty is the glue that holds the group together, and honoring it is essential. The requirements and limits of this commitment to the group are seldom expressed, but are such that Slick would not leave Shorty "hanging with the cops," even though to stay with Shorty resulted in his own arrest.

SHORTY: See, that's how Slick was that day we were ripping off the sneakers [from a nearby factory]. He figured that if he left me that would be rude, y'know? If he just let me get busted by myself and he knew I had

a lot of shit on my head, that's what I call a brother. He could've. I could've pushed him right through that fence, and he coulda been *gone*. But no, he waited for me, and we both got arrested. I was stuck. My belly couldn't get through the fucking hole in the fence.

This cohesion between members of the Hallway Hangers is a striking characteristic of their subculture and one to which they constantly draw attention. Not only are they proud of their adoption of communitarian values, but they also see their "brotherhood" as inconsistent with conventional middle- and upper-class attitudes.

Daily life for the Hallway Hangers is marked by unrelieved boredom and monotony. The boys are generally out of work, out of school, and out of money. In search of employment or a "fast buck on the street," high or drunk a good deal of the time, many are preoccupied with staying out of prison—a struggle some already have lost—and with surviving from one day to the next.

SLICK: All through the teenage years around here, you hafta learn to survive, before you learn to do anything else.
SHORTY: Nobody learns anything from school around here. All it is is show how to survive and have money in your pocket.
SLICK: You hafta learn how to survive first.
SHORTY: This is the little ghetto.
SLICK: Y'know, you hafta learn how to survive; if you can't survive, especially around here, that's why you see so many people who are just down and out. It's tough. That's what it is. It's tough.

Growing up in Clarendon Heights is indeed tough, and the frustrations of project life find release through the racist attitudes held by the boys. Racism among members of the Hallway Hangers runs very deep. Frankie and Shorty are violent in their prejudice against black people, while Slick, Steve, and Stoney are racist in a less strident manner. Only Jinks has a measure of empathy and respect for blacks.

According to the Hallway Hangers, their antipathy toward blacks stems from an incident in the early 1970s. At that time, a full-scale riot erupted in Clarendon Heights between the project's mostly white residents and black youths from the predominantly black Emerson Towers housing project a half mile away. The conflict lasted several days and involved the National Guard and riot police. Frankie describes how this event crystallized his own racist attitudes.

Although both Chris and Boo-Boo are full members of the Hallway Hangers, their position often seems tenuous because of their race. Both take a lot of ribbing for their skin color. Chris routinely is referred to as nigs, nigger, breed, half-breed, or oreo; Boo-Boo gets less direct abuse but is the butt of racist jokes and occasional taunts. Both tend to deal with it in the same way: They "play it off" make a joke of it, or ignore it.

> JM: So you naturally hung with Frankie and them. Are there any problems with you being black?
> BOO-BOO: No. They say things but they're just fooling around. I take it as a joke. They're just fooling around. It doesn't bother me at all. If they hit me or something, that's a different story.

Chris occasionally will play along with the other Hallway Hangers by agreeing with their racist statements and denigrating other blacks.

One balmy night in late autumn, I walked into doorway #13 at about eleven o'clock to find Frankie, Chris, and two older guys on the fringes of the Hallway Hangers, Joe and Freddy, smoking a joint and drinking beer. I struck up a conversation with Frankie, but I was interrupted by Joe, a twenty-three-year-old man whose six-foot frame boasts a lot more brawn than mine. "Hey Jay," he said in a mocking, belligerent tone, glancing sharply up at me from his two empty six packs of Miller, "You're a fucking nigger. You're a nigger. You play basketball with the niggers. You talk like

a nigger. You're a fucking nigger." This reference to a basketball game a few days earlier in which I played with the Brothers demanded a response that would not provoke a fight but would allow me to maintain some poise and dignity in front of the others. (I had learned long since that to confront the Hallway Hangers' racism was a fruitless exercise and not particularly conducive to entry into the group.) In the end, although I escaped with my pride and body intact, Chris was not so lucky. The exchange that followed highlights his deep ambivalence toward his ethnic identity.

> JOE: Did you hear me? I said you're a nigger, a motherfucking nigger.
> JM: What, you'd rather play four on six? It's not my fault we won; maybe it's yours.
> JOE: You're a nigger, a fucking nigger. You act like a nigger.
> JM: You must be really rat-assed drunk or that must be really good herb, cuz it isn't that fucking dark in here. My skin looks white to me.
> FRANKIE: (*in an attempt to steer the conversation away from confrontation*) No, really though Jay, you don't have to have black skin to be a nigger.
> CHRIS: Yeah, look at me. My skin is black, right? But I ain't a nigger. I ain't. It's not cool. The Brothers, I don't like them. I ain't like them. I ain't a nigger.
> FRANKIE: Chris, you're a fucking nigger.
> CHRIS: No, I ain't, Frankie. You know that.

Chris will go so far as to shout racial epithets at fellow blacks and to show enthusiasm for fighting with the Hallway Hangers against other black youths.

Much of this attitude, however, is expedient posturing that enables Chris to maintain his sometimes tenuous status in the group. His real feelings are quite different.

> CHRIS: I've lived here for fourteen years. I've always hung with these guys. I dunno, maybe it's cuz I never knew many black people back then. These guys are all right

though. They fuck with me some, but not like with some kids. I mean, after fourteen fucking years you get used to them calling you nigger every ten minutes. It doesn't do no good to get upset. I just let it slide. Fuck it. I've gotten used to it. I'm glad you're not prejudiced though. The only time they get real bad is when they've been drinking; then I gotta watch myself, I know how these guys think. That's something too—understanding how they think. I've been here fourteen fucking years, and I know how these motherfuckers think. Like, I can tell when they're gonna fuck with me. When they're trashed, they'll be looking at me a certain way and shit. Then another one will do it. I get the fuck out of there because I know they're gonna fuck with me. Yeah, when they're drunk, they'll get like that. Fucking assholes. But when they haven't been pounding the beers, they're the most dynamite people around. Really.

The rest of the Hallway Hangers are quick to deny any animosity toward Chris.

Nevertheless, outright hostility toward Chris does come to the surface at times, especially when people are under the influence of alcohol or drugs. It seems that whenever Chris threatens the status of others in the group with his street hockey ability, his knack for making a fast buck selling drugs, or his success with girls, racial antagonism comes to the fore. One particular incident is illustrative of this dynamic. Frankie and I were talking in the doorway when we noticed two white girls giving Chris a few lines of cocaine on the landing above us. As they came down the stairs on their way out, Frankie demanded in a very abrasive tone, "What are you getting that fuckin' *nigger* high for? You don't fucking do that." As the door slammed behind them, Frankie muttered, "They want to suck his black cock, that's why Fuckin' cunts."

Although the Hallway Hangers attribute their racist attitudes to the riots that occurred in Clarendon Heights during their childhoods,

such an explanation cannot account for the racial antagonism that gave rise to the riots in the first place. Racism in Clarendon Heights is a complex phenomenon that does not lend itself to easy interpretation or explanation. Nevertheless, in the attitudes and comments of the Hallway Hangers, it is possible to discern evidence in support of the proposition that racism in lower-class communities stems from competition for scarce economic resources. The perceived economic threat blacks pose to the Hallway Hangers contributes to their racism. The racial prejudice of the Hallway Hangers, a subject of academic interest in its own right, also has important ramifications for social reproduction. We see how it not only harms blacks but is ultimately self-destructive as well.

Although the Hallway Hangers can be hostile to Boo-Boo and Chris, their real racial venom is directed against the Brothers, the black peer group at Clarendon Heights. Interestingly, when considering each member of the Brothers individually, the Hallway Hangers admit respect and esteem for a number of them. Considered as a group, however, there is little feeling aside from bitter racial enmity. As with Chris, the enmity is at its sharpest when the Brothers are perceived as threatening in some way.

THE BROTHERS: CONSPICUOUS BY THEIR CONVENTIONALITY
In contrast to the Hallway Hangers, the Brothers accommodate themselves to accepted standards of behavior and strive to fulfill socially approved roles. It is the white peer group from Clarendon Heights that is at odds with mainstream American culture. Nonconformity fascinates the sociologist, and if undue attention is given to the distinctive cultural novelty of the Hallway Hangers, it should be borne in mind that the Brothers also pose an interesting and in many ways exceptional case. However, because my primary interest is the role that aspirations play in social reproduction, and because the Hallway Hangers undergo the process of social reproduction in a unique fashion, my emphasis in both

the presentation of ethnographic material and in its analysis inevitably falls on the Hallway Hangers.

The most obvious difference between the two peer groups is in racial composition: The Brothers have only one white member. When one considers that this peer group emerges from the same social setting as do the Hallway Hangers, other striking differences become apparent. Composed of a nucleus of seven teenagers and expanding to twelve at times, this peer group is not a distinctive subculture with its own set of values defined in opposition to the dominant culture. The Brothers attend high school on a regular basis. None of them smokes cigarettes, drinks regularly, or uses drugs. None has been arrested.

Craig is a quiet, tall, dark-skinned youth with a reserved manner and easy smile, except on the basketball court. A graceful athlete, he is on the varsity basketball team at the high school. He moved to the projects six years ago and was one of a few black children to attend the neighborhood grammar school. His family is tightly knit; he lives with his parents, four brothers and sisters, and two stepsiblings. Self-assured and agreeable, Craig maintains a leadership role in the peer group, although such status demarcations are much less clearly defined among the Brothers than among the Hallway Hangers.

In contrast to Craig, Super is a fiery, loud, yet often introspective lad who, despite his medium size, never backs down from a fight. Hesitant in speech and uncomfortable with written material, Super struggles in the classroom. He is, however, a natural athlete. His speed, quickness, and agility lend themselves to football and basketball but his carefree attitude toward sport and his flare for flashy moves do not sit well with high school coaches and have prevented success in these areas at the varsity level. Super's home life is turbulent; his temper, apparently, is matched by his father's, and the confrontations between father and son have prompted Super to leave home for safer environs for a week or two on at least three occasions.

Originally from the Dominican Republic, Juan is the only Brother to have finished school, but he currently is unemployed. He is slight of build, a sincere and sensitive youth. Juan speaks in somewhat broken English, was not particularly successful in school, and is not a good athlete. His loyalty, kind manner, and sense of fair play, however, are attributes that have earned him respect. Such remarks as these are-typical of him: "Yup," he said, as he left one evening to meet his girlfriend, "there's the three things everyone needs—a job, a car, and a girl. And the girl's the most important. Because otherwise you'd be lonely. You need someone to talk to and somebody to love." In a neighborhood notorious for its toughness, such a comment is remarkable for its honesty and tenderness.

Mokey is a quick-tempered boy whose impatience with others often borders on insolence. Stocky and of medium height, Mokey commits himself with vigor and enthusiasm to whatever he is pursuing but has difficulty sustaining this drive for an extended period of time. One week he is enthused about his prospects on the school football team, but two weeks later he has quit the squad and exhibits a newfound zeal for track and field. Full of energy and constantly on the move, Mokey chafes against the tight rein his mother keeps on him but generally accedes to her wishes. When necessary, his father, who does not live with the family, is called in to straighten out any problems.

James, a junior at the high school, is very small for his age. He manages to compensate for his diminutive size, however, with a quick and caustic tongue. He is not as well integrated into the group as the other boys, perhaps because of a long, involved relationship with a girl that recently ended. A year ago, James was a fixture in one of the city's video arcades during school hours; now he attends school every day as well as on Thursday evenings to make up for failed subjects. This turnabout resulted from a serious talk with his father, whose presence in the household is sporadic. James's wit, sense of humor, and toughness have earned him the esteem of the Brothers.

Derek is Boo-Boo's half brother. The two boys have different friends, interests, and attitudes and are not particularly close, but they do maintain an amiable cordiality outside their home, which is a considerable achievement in view of the animosity between the Brothers and Hallway Hangers. Their paths parted when, as a third grader, Derek's scholastic achievements enabled him to secure a government scholarship to a prestigious private school. Derek attended Barnes Academy through the eighth grade with great success; his grades were good, and he had many friends. Nevertheless, he decided to attend the city high school, where he has continued his academic achievement. Although lacking in athletic prowess, Derek is admired by the other boys for his scholastic success and personal motivation.

Mike is the sole white member of the Brothers. He lives with his mother and grandmother and rules the household. His large frame and strength have made him a valuable asset to the high school's football, wrestling, and track and field squads. His athletic ability and an aversion to drugs and alcohol inculcated by his mother as well as a strong and lasting friendship with Super all account for Mike's allegiance to the Brothers. He is subject to some abuse from his white peers on this account but seems to take their ribbing in stride.

The Brothers, in contrast to the Hallway Hangers, are not a distinctive subculture with its own set of shared values. The Brothers accept the dominant culture's definitions of success and judge themselves by these criteria. A night in the city jail would permanently tarnish a Brother's reputation rather than build it up. In the eyes of the Brothers, John Grace, the bartender who was involved in the Shootout in Clarendon Heights, only would be worthy of disdain, and perhaps pity, rather than the respect Frankie accords him. While the Hallway Hangers have little concern for the judgments of the dominant culture, the Brothers become uncomfortable and embarrassed when recounting disciplinary problems they have had at home or in school. Such a "confession" for a member of the Hallway Hangers, on the other hand, might be accompanied by laughter and a sense of triumph.

Just as the Brothers accept the values of the dominant culture, their behavior generally conforms to societal expectations. Whereas the Hallway Hangers are conspicuous in their consumption of cigarettes and beer, the Brothers reject both. Although many of the Brothers drink beer in moderation every once in a while at a party or on a similar occasion, their consumption of alcohol is very limited. Likewise, although most of the Brothers have tried marijuana, they rarely smoke it, and they never use other drugs.

The Brothers are uncomfortable with simply "hanging"; they cannot tolerate such inactivity. They often can be found playing basketball in the park or the gym. If a pick-up game of basketball cannot be mustered in the immediate neighborhood, they often will walk a half mile to the Salvation Army gym or another housing project. Energetic and spirited, the Brothers dislike the idleness of the Hallway Hangers.

> DEREK: I would never hang with them. I'm not interested in drinking, getting high, or making trouble. That's about all they do.... I don't like to just sit around.

Although the Brothers do not adopt those practices that symbolize rejection of authority or basic societal values, their peer group does have its own distinctive attributes. The Brothers carry themselves in ways familiar to most urban black Americans, although somewhat scaled down. Their style of dress, mode of speech, and form of greeting clearly set them apart from other residents of Clarendon Heights. However, the caps, neck chains, and open shirts so prevalent among teenagers in the predominantly black sections of the city are lacking among the Brothers, whose residency in a white neighborhood has important implications for much more than their dress.

Athletics is one activity into which the Brothers channel their energies. Many excel in organized youth, church, and school basketball leagues as well as in regular pick-up games. Mike,

Super, and Mokey also play on the school football team. Only Juan and Derek are not good athletes, and even they maintain an interest in sports, often rounding out the teams for a pick-up game of basketball.

Girls also claim much of the Brothers' time. A frequent topic of conversation, their interest in girls seems much more widespread than is the case for the Hallway Hangers. While the Hangers tend to go out with girls on a casual basis (typically for a weekend), the Brothers often have steady girlfriends, with whom they are constantly speaking on the phone, to whose house they are forever headed, and about whom they always are boasting. Whereas the Hallway Hangers focus on their beer and drugs, the Brothers have their basketball and girlfriends.

Since Juan bought an old worn-out Vega for two hundred dollars and fixed it up complete with paint job and functioning engine, cruising the streets also has become a favorite pastime for the Brothers. It gives them access to the "Port" and the "Coast," the black sections of the city. Considering the tense racial atmosphere of the Clarendon Heights community, it is no wonder that the Brothers do not spend as much time in the vicinity of the Heights as the Hallway Hangers do and instead prefer the black neighborhoods.

In addition to being the objects of many of the Hallway Hangers' racist slurs and insults, the Brothers suffer from even more substantive racial abuse. Super tells how the windows in his family's car have been broken year after year and how one morning last spring he awoke to find "KKK" drawn in spray paint on the side of the car. Juan recounts with anger accompanied by matter-of-fact acceptance how his mother was taunted by some members of the Hallway Hangers, which led his father into a confrontation with them. His father was lucky to escape unharmed from the ensuing argument. Juan has a measure of understanding for the Hallway Hangers: "When they call me a nigger, I usually don't let it bother me none. They drunk or high, y'know. They don't

know what they're doing." In his freshman year of high school, however, Juan was beaten up by Shorty for no apparent reason; he still bears the scar on his lip from the fight, and the memory of it burns in his mind, fueling the resentment he feels toward the Hallway Hangers.

Although the Brothers are not submissive in the face of racial animosity from the Hallway Hangers, they are outnumbered and outmatched, and they usually find it expedient to walk away before a confrontation explodes into a street fight. They are accustomed to the violent racial prejudice of the Hallway Hangers. In fact, Craig, instead of being upset that a simple basketball game threatened to erupt into a racial brawl, merely commented, "That was good of Shorty to come over and tell us we better leave before his friends start all sorts of trouble." Although the Brothers are hesitant to answer openly the insults of the Hallway Hangers, they do vent their contempt for the Hallway Hangers in private discussions.

JUAN: I don't like their attitude, their gig, what they do.... They'll be there, hanging in front of the Heights, fighting and arguing and stuff like that.... It wasn't until I moved here that I heard the word "nigger." I had heard about people in the projects; I knew they'd be a pain in the ass sometimes.... I swear, if I ever see one of them touching my mother or doing something to my car, I don't care, I'll kill them. Cuz I don't like none of them. I'm afraid I'm gonna hurt one of them real bad. Every time I hear them call me nigger, I just don't say anything, but I can't take the pressure of people getting on my case every time, y'know?

CRAIG: I don't know why they just hang out there being crazy and getting drunk and bothering people. Maybe cuz they need attention or something. They got nuttin' better to do so they might as well cause trouble so people will think they're bad and stuff. They're just lazy. They wanna take the easy way out—that is, hang around outside all day.

JAMES: They're not gonna get anywhere except for standing at that same corner going *(imitating someone who is very benumbed)*, "Hey man, got some pot, man? Hey Frank, let's get high."

DEREK: We just have different attitudes. We like to stay away from the projects as much as possible, or they'll give us trouble. That's about all they do: make trouble.

SUPER: They smoke reefer; they drink. They ain't friendly like people, y'know what I'm sayin'? They go around the street laughing at people, ragging them out, y'know what I mean? They just disrespect people.

MIKE: They're just a bunch of fuck-ups.

Such perceptions are often voiced by the Brothers. The situation between the two peer groups, however, is not one of constant strife. Rather, there is a constant underlying tension that surfaces occasionally—often during basketball games or when the Hallway Hangers have been drinking excessively—but that threatens to erupt into considerable violence.

Aside from racial factors, the character of the two peer groups differs markedly in other ways. The Brothers have no pecking order based on fighting ability. Although Craig is generally respected most, there is no hierarchy in the group, hidden or otherwise; the Brothers do not playfully abuse each other, physically or verbally. Loose and shifting cliques develop among the members and sometimes encompass outsiders. Friendships wax and wane according to the season and the extracurricular activities and responsibilities of the boys. During the winter, for example, Craig is so tied up with the basketball team that he effectively drops out of the group, and his best friend, Super, becomes closer to Derek and Mokey. During the school day, the Brothers often see little of each other and, once out, invariably break up into smaller friendship groups, coming all together only once in while. In short, the Brothers are no more than a peer group, whereas the Hallway Hangers are a much more cohesive unit with its own subculture.

The Hallway Hangers, who reject the values of the dominant culture and subscribe to their own distinctive cultural norms, have a sense of solidarity that is noticeably absent from the Brothers' peer group. Internal cohesion and the adoption of communitarian values, in which the Hallway Hangers take pride, are missing among the Brothers. Although all the Brothers would support each other in a fight, the ties that bind them are not as strong and are not as strongly affirmed as those that bind the Hallway Hangers.

The Brothers do not compare themselves to members of the upper classes, nor do they feel as keenly the stigma or shame associated with life in public housing.

Daily life for the Brothers is far less circumscribed than it is for the Hallway Hangers. Active, enthusiastic, and still in school, the Brothers are not preoccupied with mere survival on the street. Their world extends into the classroom and onto the basketball court, and it extends into the home a great deal more than does the world of the Hallway Hangers.

DISCUSSION QUESTIONS

1. Describe the primary characteristics of the Hallway Hangers and the Brothers. How are they similar to and different from one another?

2. The boys in both groups are in their late teens at the time of interview. What do you foresee as unfolding for members of each group as they move forward into adulthood? Do you expect the groups' members to remain in contact with one another? Why or why not?

3. What makes the Hallway Hangers a more cohesive group than the Brothers?

4. How do Black and biracial boys gain and sustain membership in the White, racist Hallway Hangers' group?

5. What role might parents or caregivers play in shaping the identities and activities of the Hallway Hangers and the Brothers?

ADDITIONAL RESOURCES

Film

"A&E Investigative Reports: Wage Slaves: Not Getting by in America." 2002. Originally shown on cable television's A&E network, and now available on DVD, this documentary features *Nickel and Dimed* author Barbara Ehrenreich trying to make a living on minimum wage. 100 minutes.

Internet

http://www.apa.org/pi/ses/homepage.html. The website of the American Psychological Association's Office on Socioeconomic Status.

http://www.census.gov/. The website of the United States Census Bureau has numerous reports regarding socioeconomic status, income, and poverty.

http://www.time.com/time/photogallery/O, 29307,1626519_13736_64,00.html. "What the World Eats" is a photo essay by Peter Menzel and Faith D'Alusio that depicts families from 24 countries with their budgets and groceries for the week.

Radio

National Public Radio's Michele Norris interviews Peter Menzel and Faith D'Alusio about their book, *Hungry Planet: What the World Eats.* "All Things Considered." November 9, 2005. http://www.npr.org/templates/story/story.php?storyId=5005952.

FURTHER READING

Chambliss, William J. 1973. "The Saints and the Roughnecks." *Society,* 11(1): 24–31.

Coles, Robert, Randy Testa, and Michael H. Coles (eds.). 2001. *Growing Up Poor: A Literary Anthology.* New York: New Press.

Ehrenreich, Barbara. 2002. *Nickel and Dimed: On (Not) Getting by in America.* New York: Holt Paperbacks.

MacLeod, Jay. 2008. *Ain't No Makin' It: Leveled Aspirations in a Low-Income Neighborhood,* 3rd edition. 25–49. Boulder, CO: Westview Press.

Menzel, Peter and Faith D'Alusio. 2008. *What the World Eats.* Berkeley, CA: Tricycle Press.

Moore, Valerie Ann. 2002. "The Collaborative Emergence of Race in Children's Play: A Case Study of Two Summer Camps." *Social Problems,* 49(1): 58–78.

Scott, Kimberly A. 2003. "In Girls, Out Girls, and Always Black: African-American Girls' Friendships." *Sociological Studies of Children and Youth,* 9: 179–207.

Shipler, David K. 2005. *The Working Poor: Invisible in America.* Vintage.

New York Times, The. 2005. *Class Matters.* New York: Times Books.

Gender

Utilizing participant observation, interviews, surveys, and archival research, the authors of the next selections study the ways that gender, power, and identity intersect.

In her classic study of men and women in corporations, Kanter shows how gender, power, credibility, and leadership intersect in the business world. Williams, who draws on Kanter's concept of tokenism, explores the same issues, but focuses on men who work in traditionally female-dominated fields. Shapiro's research on drag kings helps to broaden the focus beyond gender and work by exploring how conscious performances of gender impact one's sense of self.

Put another way, Kanter studies women who do "men's work," Williams studies men who do "women's work," and Shapiro, by studying drag performances, questions the very categories of "woman" and "man" and the gender structure upon which much of social life is based.

47. Men and Women of the Corporation

ROSABETH MOSS KANTER

In the 1970s, Rosabeth Moss Kanter undertook a groundbreaking study of women who worked in corporations. Conducting field research, surveys, interviews, and archival research with the women and men of "Industrial Supply Corporation" (INDSCO), Kanter paints a portrait of differences in power masquerading as differences in gender.

Every day a large proportion of all Americans don their figurative white collars and go to work in offices, where they take their stations in the administrative machines that run large organizations.

Large organizations not only dominate economic and political life; they also control most of the jobs. The possibilities people experience in work, then, are often limited by the job structure made available by the design of large organizations. Both men and women work in large organizations, then, but their experiences are shaped by very different distributions across administrative positions.

Sex polarization and sex segregation of occupations is a fact of the American work world. Women populate organizations, but they practically never run them.

The exact proportion of men and women in management positions varies from industry to industry. There has been virtually no room for women in the management of construction, mining, and oil companies, basic industrial goods manufacturing, and production—or in top management in general. Women have had more opportunities in certain other fields: education, the arts, social service, retail trade, office management, personnel work, advertising, public relations, and staff support positions.

Even in areas decreed by tradition to encompass "female concerns," such as the service

fields, and in areas where the workers are largely women, managers are still overwhelmingly likely to be men.

SCIENTIFIC MANAGEMENT AND THE IMAGE OF MANAGERS

Management found its first prophet in Frédérick Winslow Taylor, the steel company engineer turned management consultant, and its theory in Taylor's "scientific management." Taylor gave a name and rationale to the concept of the rational manager who made decisions based on logical, passionless analysis.

Taylor's premise was the application of the systematic analysis of science, to management methods, emphasizing routines, order, logic, production planning, and cost analysis. His ideas influenced task specialization, time and motion studies, and assembly line philosophies.

Although the specifics of Taylor's thought were not necessarily adopted, his general ideas influenced managerial thinking and helped create what has become known as "classical" administrative theory.

Early management theory thus developed rationality as the central ideal of the organization and the special province of managers. Organizations were considered tools for generating rational decisions and plans. Workers were motivated to participate on utilitarian grounds and could contribute specific skills, but the real

Kanter, Rosabeth Moss. 1977. Abridged from "Men and Women of the Corporation: The Population" and "Power," in *Men and Women of the Corporation.* New York: Basic Books.

effectiveness of the organization was seen to lie in the efforts of management to design the best way for individuals to fit together in an overall scheme. The rationality of the formal organization was thought to arise not so much from the nature of its participants as from the superiority of the plan created by management. This design could minimize the non-rational, efficiency-undermining feature of human beings to the extent that the participants consented to the authority up the line. The very design of organizations thus was oriented toward and assumed to be capable of suppressing irrationality, personality, and emotionality.

A "masculine ethic" can be identified as part of the early image of managers. This "masculine ethic" elevates the traits assumed to belong to some men to necessities for effective management: a tough-minded approach to problems; analytic abilities to abstract and plan; a capacity to set aside personal, emotional considerations in the interests of task accomplishment; and a cognitive superiority in problem-solving and decision-making. These characteristics supposedly belonged to men; but then, practically all managers were men from the beginning. However, when women tried to enter management jobs, the "masculine ethic" was invoked as an exclusionary principle.

The first thrust in management theory—planning and decision-making to order the tasks and functions of an impersonal bureaucracy—put the "rational man" into management.

HUMAN RELATIONS IN INDUSTRY

Human relations theories have made inroads, adding what some have called a "feminized" element to the old "masculine ethic," and new forms of organization, such as team-oriented matrix and project management systems, are in use in many organizations. Yet for most of the twentieth century a "masculine ethic" of rationality dominated the spirit of managerialism and gave the manager role its defining imaged. It told men how to be successful as men in the new organizational worlds of the twentieth century.

Such an image also provided a rationale for where women belonged in management. If they belonged at all, it was in people-handling staff functions such as personnel, where their emotional fine-tuning, according to the stereotype in operation, was more appropriate than in decision-making functions. Personnel staff are like the social workers of management.

If women have been directed into the "emotional" end of management, they have also been excluded from the centers of power in management for the same reason. Perhaps the most pervasive stereotype of women in organizations is that they are "too emotional," whereas men hold the monopoly on rational thought. Women represent the antithesis of the rational manager. Male managers in the corporation I studied expressed the fear that a woman would cry in their office or fly off the handle if they criticized her, so they avoided giving negative reactions to women, whether secretaries or colleagues. The women who could get in were the ones who could demonstrate the ability to "think like a man."

While management was being defined as a "masculine" pursuit, more routine office chores were being "feminized."

THE EVOLUTION OF OFFICE WORK FOR WOMEN

Women did not always dominate the clerical labor force; office work in the nineteenth century was first a male preserve.

The rise in the employment of women in the office around the turn of the century was dramatic, and it corresponded to a large decrease in "household occupations" (servants, dressmakers and seamstresses outside of factories, and laundresses). The growth of modern administration brought women into domination in the office but left them absent in management. Whereas factory jobs were divided between men and women, clerical jobs rapidly became the work almost exclusively of women.

Popular images changed along with the labor force shifts, promoting the "feminization" of the clerical labor force that was occurring. In 1900 the *Ladies Home Journal* was urging women to stay out of offices, but by 1916 the same magazine was glorifying the feminine traits of stenographers: their ability to radiate sympathetic interest, agreeableness, courtesy. Magazine fiction began to build romantic stories around the young girl working in an office who would find her true love, leaving at that point, of course, to get married. Office work was acceptable to the extent that women emphasized their femininity rather than their skills and saw it as clearly subordinate to the ultimate goal of marriage.

While the secretarial image was taking shape, the organization of office work was also developing. The increased use of office machines as well as the expansion of the office affected the arrangement of tasks. Specialists in the running of one machine or the processing of one kind of paperwork developed, working factory-style at row after row of desks supervised by office managers. Secretarial work was divided into two kinds: marriage-like and factory-like. The elite corps of private secretaries were directly attached to one or more bosses for whom they did a variety of tasks and from whom they derived status. Other secretarial work was done in steno and typing pools whose occupants were little more than extensions of their machines—and highly replaceable at that. The contrast in the privileges, rewards, and status of these two types of work enhanced the desirability of the private secretarial position, making it seem the culmination of a clerical worker's aspirations.

Although the reporting arrangements and personnel policies around secretaries were formalized in large organizations, the actual content of a secretary's role, beyond the basics like typing, was defined by a relationship to a specific boss. Here the fact that most secretaries were female helped shape or reinforce the definition of the secretarial role. Men type and run machines too, and they often act in a service-like capacity for bosses. However, the nature of the secretarial role, as found in practically all large organizations, is

heavily bound up with the feminization of the occupation.

Men and women of the corporation, then, relate to each other and to their work through jobs that are often sex-segregated and laden with idealized images of the capacities of the people in them. These views define the principal players. The stage setting is an industrial giant like Industrial Supply Corporation.

Industrial Supply Corporation: The Setting

Industrial Supply Corporation (INDSCO) is not a real name, but it is a very real place. Some of the details of its existence are disguised, too, to protect confidentiality, but the overall picture is true to the life of this organization, as it revealed itself through surveys, interviews, meetings, and documents in the 1970s.

INDSCO was one of those hybrid firms that grew during the first great wave of corporate mergers at the beginning of the century, a conglomerate that developed out of a number of smaller companies employing new technology and later diversified. Consolidation of the loose divisions comprising the corporation took place after World War II, especially in the 1960s. INDSCO is one of the world's largest producers of industrial goods, a multinational on the *Fortune* magazine list of 500 leading industrial firms; its stock is actively traded. It dominates two or three of its markets (including areas in which it supplies its major competitors) but competes with a range of firms, including smaller ones, in other markets.

Power

Somewhere behind the formal organization chart at INDSCO was another, shadow structure in which dramas of power were played out. An interest in corporate politics was a key to survival for the people who worked at INDSCO.

For the people called "leaders," power was supposedly an automatic part of their functioning. They were given the formal titles of leadership (director, manager, supervisor), and they were expected to aid the mobilization of others toward the attainment of objectives. They had responsibility for results, and they were accountable for what got done, but as everyone knew, power did not necessarily come automatically with the designation of leaders, with the delegation of formal authority. People often had to get it not from the official structure but from the more hidden political processes.

Power begets power. People who are thought to have power already and to be well placed in hierarchies of prestige and status may also be more influential and more effective in getting the people around them to do things and feel satisfied about it. Thus, people who look like they can command more of the organization's resources, who look like they can bring something that is valued from outside into the group, who seem to have access to the inner circles that make the decisions affecting the fate of individuals in organizations, may also be more effective as leaders of those around them—and be better liked in the process.

Twenty INDSCO executives in a sample of managers reached the same conclusion when asked to define the characteristics of effective managers. The question of the relative importance of "people sensitivity," as they put it, provoked considerable debate. Finally, they agreed that "credibility" was more important than anything else. "Credibility" was their term for competence plus power— the known ability to get results. People with credibility were listened to, their phone calls were answered first, because they were assumed to have something important to say. People with credibility had room to make more mistakes and could take greater risks because it was believed that they would produce. They were known to be going somewhere in the organization and to have the ability to place their people in good jobs. They could back up their words with actions. Thus, the ultimate in credibility in the corporate bureaucracy was "the guy who doesn't have to make recommendations; he comes out with a *decision* and all supporting material. Everyone else just says yes or no...."

For people at INDSCO, having a powerful boss was considered an important element in career progress and the development of competence, just as lack of success was seen as a function of working under a dead-ender. People wanted to work for someone on the move who had something to teach and enough power to take others along. A secretary recalled, "I came in looking for a place to stake out my career. I was first assigned to work for a man who was a dowdy dresser and never cleaned his shoes. (I have a thing about men and shoes. How they take care of their shoes is a good sign of other things.) The whole atmosphere in the group made it clear that people were going nowhere. It was not businesslike. So I said to myself, 'He's going nowhere. I'd better change.' And he did go nowhere." One of INDSCO's highest ranking women said, "I had to learn everything myself. So did men. Lots of people go into managerial jobs without any training. I had to model myself after my boss. If the boss is good, okay. If not, that can be terrible. It's better to get a boss who is successful in the organization's terms." In response to a question about what is "helpful" in manager, a sales worker wrote, "He sees a subordinate's growth as in his interest. He is confident, capable, and conveys a sense that he will be promoted. Clichés like 'being on a winner's team' have taken on new meaning for me...Unhelpful managers are uncertain of themselves, their abilities, present position, or future." An older executive commented, "It's a stroke of luck to get an opportunity to work for someone who's a mover and demonstrate performance to him because astute managers look for good workers and develop them." There was much agreement among managers that people were more likely to emerge with "manager quality" if they worked for the right boss. "Right" meant high credibility. Credibility meant power.

CYCLES OF POWER AND POWERLESSNESS

Power rises and falls on the basis of complex exigencies: the organizational situation, environmental pressures, the simultaneous actions of others. However, in terms of individual behavior at least, power is likely to bring more power, in ascending cycles, and powerlessness to generate powerlessness, in a descending cycle. The powerful have "credibility" behind their actions, so they have the capacity to get things done. Their alliances help them circumvent the more restricting aspects of the bureaucracy. They are able to be less coercive or rules-bound in their exercise of leadership, so their subordinates and clients are more likely to cooperate. They have the security of power, so they can be more generous in allowing subordinates power of their own, freedom of action. We come full circle. The powerful are not only given material and symbolic advantage but they are also provided with circumstances that can make them more effective mobilizers of other people. Thus they can accomplish and, through their accomplishments, generate more power. This means they can build alliances, with other people as colleagues rather than threats, and through their alliances generate more power.

The powerless are caught in a downward spiral. The coping mechanisms of low power are also those most likely to provoke resistance and further restriction of power. The attitudes of powerlessness get translated downward, so that those under a low-power leader can also become ineffective. There was this vicious circle at INDSCO: A young trainee was assigned to a "chronic complainer" of a manager, who had had organizational problems and had fallen well below the level of peers in his cohort. The trainee was talented but needed to be channeled. The manager's negativism began to transfer down to the trainee, and the young man started to lose his motivation. Nothing was done to correct the atmosphere. He became less motivated and more critical of the organization. He vented his hostility in nonconformist ways (long hair, torn clothes, general disrespect for people and things). Then people began to reinforce his negativity by focusing on what they observed: he's a "wise guy." They observed the symptoms but never looked at the real problem: the manager's situation. Finally, the trainee resigned just before he would have been terminated. Everyone breathed a sigh of relief that the "problem" was gone. The manager lost even more credibility. This just reinforced his negativity and his coerciveness.

Since the behavioral responses of the powerless tend to be so ineffective as leadership styles, it would be the last rather than the first solution of most organizations to give such ineffective people more power or more responsibility. Yet all the indicators point to the negative effects of behavior that come from too little power, such as rules-mindedness and close supervision. Chris Argyris has noted that alienation and low morale accompany management's praise for the reliable (rules-obedient) rather than the enterprising (risk-taking) worker. Studies have shown that turnover varies with the degree to which supervisors structure tasks in advance and demand compliance, absenteeism with the tendency of supervisors to be "directive" and maintain close and detailed control. So perhaps it is meaningful to suggest interrupting the cycle of powerlessness: to empower those in low-power situations by increasing their opportunities and their latitude rather than to continue to punish them for their ineffectiveness, reinforcing their powerless state of mind.

"Power" in organizations, as I am using the term, is synonymous with autonomy and freedom of action. The powerful can afford to risk more, and they can afford to allow others their freedom. The bureaucratic machinery of modern organizations means that there are rather few people who are really powerful. Power has become a scarce resource that most people feel they lack. Although the scramble for political advantage still distinguishes relative degrees of power, the organization places severe limits on everyone's freedom of action. The powerful get more, but they still share some of the mentality of powerlessness.

And women, in large hierarchical organizations, are especially often caught in the cycles of powerlessness.

WOMEN AND POWER IN ORGANIZATIONS

My analysis of the importance of power in large organizations and the behavioral consequences of powerlessness for management styles can help to explain some familiar clichés about women's lack of potential for organizational leadership: "no one wants to work for a woman" and "Women are too rigid and controlling to make good bosses anyway."

Preference for Men = Preference for Power

There is considerable evidence for a general cultural attitude that men make better leaders. A large number of studies have concluded that neither men nor women want to work for a woman (although women are readier to do so than men). In the survey of nonexempts at INDSCO, these workers overwhelmingly agreed with the statement that "men make better supervisors." And they did so while also rejecting the idea that it was "unacceptable" or "unfeminine" for a woman to be a manager. Women managers were aware of this attitude. One woman at INDSCO showed me a poster which she considered indicative; it was large and painted in dark, rather foreboding tones. Most of the poster was taken up by the head of a man wearing a workman's cap; he was saying furtively into a telephone, "I just quit. The new boss is a woman."

Yet when it comes to evaluating concrete leadership styles, as used by men or by women outside of organizations, research has found that there is no strong preference for men or general tendency to perceive men and women differently. In one study subjects were asked to make judgments about male and female leaders exhibiting a variety of styles. The evaluations of men and women did not differ significantly on most variables, including such critical ones as "production emphasis," but there was a tendency to give higher ratings to men than to women when they "initiated structure" and higher ratings to women than men when they showed "consideration," demonstrating some propensity for raters to "reward" people for sex-stereotypical behavior. Another study used a different set of categories but had nearly identical results. Students and bank supervisors judged stories involving male and female leaders using four different styles. The "reward" style was rated somewhat more effective when used by men, but the "friendly-dependent" style (which the researchers hoped would capture a female stereotype) was rated high for *either* sex when used with the opposite sex. The use of "threat" was considered ineffective for both sexes, though there was a slight but not significant tendency to let men get away with it more than women. And women are slightly more accepting of the idea of women supervisors and managers than are men. Thus, sex preferences in general seem to play only a very small role, if any, in responding to the style of any specific leader.

If the much greater desire for men as leaders in organizations does not reflect real sex differences in style and strategy, what does it reflect? As we have seen, people often prefer the *powerful* as leaders. Thus, a *preference for men is a preference for power,* in the context of organizations where women do not have access to the same opportunities for power and efficacy through activities or alliances.

As in the old cliché, everyone likes a winner; in large organizations at least, people would rather work for winners than losers. Perhaps a preference for male managers reflects a "bet" that men are more likely to emerge as winners and power-holders than women. In the great corporate contest, then, subordinates may be "betting" on who is going to be a winner when they respond differently to the idea of women or men as bosses. It is as though followers extend "credit" in the present for imagined future payoffs. This is reminiscent of the Mark Twain tale of the Englishman with the million-pound note. He made a bet with a wealthy man that he could live well forever just on the strength of the note and without using it. Credit was given to him; people vied with each other to supply his wants; and they graciously picked up the bills. He became wealthy and successful—and he never had to cash in the million-pound note. The power that devolved on star performers backed by sponsors at INDSCO worked in much the same way. The problem with women was that, first, there were doubts about how far they could go in the corporation, and second, a widespread belief that women could only be individual "movers"—that is, even if they moved, they could not take anyone else with them.

But power wipes out sex. A woman who does acquire power stops arousing the same level of concern about whether or not she will be wanted as a leader. People who want to attach themselves to power may not even notice sex. On one occasion, a senior INDSCO salesman told a long story to colleagues about a problem with a "very, very smart, tough-minded" president of a small company. The president had made good friends among a number of senior INDSCO people and therefore managed to get all kinds of concessions. The salesman had to bring this to an end, as well as tell this very powerful client that there would be no credit for the material that had failed when her customers, in turn, used it. . . . It took a long time for the audience to this story to realize that the salesman was saying "she." Some even interjected comments using "he." The salesman presented the story with such awe of the powerful customer that sex made no difference. He said later that she was someone he would eagerly work for.

The "Mean and Bossy Woman Boss" Stereotype

Abuse of power is only the first in a long list of negative characteristics attributed to women managers over the last few decades by those who don't want them.

Stereotypes persist even in the face of evidence negating them. The *real* extent of bossiness

among women in authority in organizations may have little to do with the persistence of the stereotype, but this particular portrait has one very important characteristic: *It is a perfect picture of people who are powerless. Powerlessness tends to produce those very characteristics attributed to women bosses.*

A careful look at comparisons between men and women supposedly in the same position shows that what looks like sex differences may really be power differences. It has been hard to test this directly, partly because there are so few women managers, especially in the same organizational positions as men.

The difference in atmosphere in the woman-run departments can be traced directly to differences in organizational power of the men and women leaders, although the author of the research did not see this. Mobility prospects, the likelihood that department heads would be moving up in the system, were strikingly different for the men and women in this set of high schools.

Women at INDSCO in exempt positions where they had organizational accountability or leadership responsibilities were differentially in the most powerless situations. They were primarily first-line supervisors of secretaries or clerical workers or they held staff jobs in personnel or public relations functions. There were no other women with line responsibilities and no women above grade 14, with the exception of a senior researcher. They were more likely to lack powerful alliances, and they reported constantly having to fight off the tendency for the organization to "protect" them by encapsulating them in safe situations. Statistics on the distributions of men and women in organizational functions make clear how common this situation is. Women, when they do achieve managerial or leadership positions, are clustered in the low-power situations. It should not be surprising if they adopt the behavior of the powerless.

It is not only their own relative power that determines the behavior of managers but also the behavior and feeling of powerlessness of those above and below. The relationship with their own superiors is important in shaping the responses of those who supervise too closely. One such generalization about where most women bosses are found is that they are located in tightly supervised and rules-conscious hierarchies. The "female" professions, like nursing, social work, and primary school teaching, all feature close supervisory hierarchies and concern with detail, Government agencies, where more women managers are found than in private business, epitomize bureaucracy in civil service structure, endless red tape, and concern with rules and regulations. Women managers in these settings are likely to themselves be subject to bossy bosses and may take this restriction of their power out on their own subordinates, perpetuating the style downward. Simultaneously, they learn bossiness as a leadership style from their own role models. In corporations like INDSCO, where women managers are so rare as to be tokens, they themselves may watched more closely, so that again the restriction of their own latitude of conduct may be transmitted to subordinates.

Simultaneously, powerless feelings of subordinates are translated upward to leaders. Most women managers are likely to manage relatively powerless subordinates: clerical workers, women factory workers, low-level personnel. Powerless subordinates may take out their own frustration in resistance to their managers, provoking them to adopt more coercive styles. The powerless may also resent a boss's advantage, particularly if they think that they could just as easily be the boss. One woman at INDSCO who had not attended college was forthright about her hostility toward "credentialed" women brought in to manage her department as a result of affirmative action efforts, while she was still held back. She resented the special treatment they were getting.

Women who are jealous of another woman's promotion and try to let her know she's really no better than they may instead provoke her to try to demonstrate her superiority and her control. This is the "lording it over us" behavior some women have complained of in women bosses. From the subordinate's perspective, it is hard to be generously happy about the success of someone getting a chance denied to you. From the boss's perspective, it is hard to share power with people who resent you. The combination of these two viewpoints produces controlling, directive bosses.

Furthermore, people who feel vulnerable and unsure of themselves, who are plunged into jobs without sufficient training or experience, regardless of the official authority they are given, are more likely to first adopt authoritarian-controlling leadership styles. The behavior attributed to women supervisors is likely to be characteristic of new and insecure supervisors generally. Without the experience or confidence to permit the minor deviations from the rules that in fact make the system work and without enough knowledge and faith in outcomes to loosen control, new managers may be prone to be too directive, controlling, and details-oriented.

In a variety of ways, then, powerlessness stemming from organizational circumstance breeds a particular leadership style caricatured in the stereotype of the bossy woman. This style reflects the situation more than sex, however—if the stereotype carries even a grain of truth—for men who are powerless behave in just the same ways.

The problem of power thus is critical to the effective behavior of people in organizations. Power issues occupy center stage not because individuals are greedy for more, but because some people are incapacitated without it.

DISCUSSION QUESTIONS

1. Kanter conducted this research in the 1970s. What, if anything, has changed regarding gender and power in corporations (and elsewhere) since then? Put another way, if Kanter were to conduct her study today, would her findings differ? If so, how and why?

2. How does Frederick Taylor's "scientific management" relate to the gendered division of labor in today's corporations?

3. What does Kanter mean by the phrase "the masculine ethic"? How is it related to a gendered division of power in the world of work?

4. What work have women typically done at American corporations? How does this history affect the current gendered power structure in business?

ADDITIONAL RESOURCES

Internet

http://www.ibiblio.org/eldritch/fwt/taylor.html. A biographical website about Frederick Winslow Taylor, founder of "scientific management."

http://www.pbs.org/wgbh/theymadeamerica/whomade/taylor_hi.html. A PBS website dedicated to documenting people "Who Made America," including a profile of Frederick Taylor.

http://blogs.harvardbusiness.org/kanter/. Rosabeth Moss Kanter's blog, hosted by the Harvard Business School, where she holds the Ernest L. Arbuckle Professorship.

http://drfd.hbs.edu/fit/public/facultyInfo.do?facInfo=bio&facEmId=rkanter. Kanter's biography on the Harvard Business School's website.

FURTHER READING

Broadbridge, Adelina and Jeff Hearn. 2008. "Gender and Management: New Directions in Research and Continuing Patterns in Practice." *British Journal of Management,* 19(suppl): S38–49.

Collinson, David L. and Jeff Hearn. 1996. "Men Managing Leadership? Men and Women of the Corporation Revisited." *The International Review of Women and Leadership,* 1(2): 1–24.

Hearn, Jeff and David Collinson. 2006. "Men, Masculinities and Workplace Diversity/Diversion: Power, Intersection, and Paradoxes," in Alison M. Konrad, Pushkala Prasad, and Judith Pringle (eds.). *Handbook of Workplace Diversity,* 299–322. Newbury Park, CA: Sage Publications.

Kanter, Rosabeth Moss. 1977. *Men and Women of the Corporation.* New York: Basic Books.

Marshall, Judi. 1995. "Gender and Management: A Critical Review of Research." *British Journal of Management,* 6(suppl): S53–62.

Morrison, Ann M. and Mary A. von Glinow. 1990. "Women and Minorities in Management." *American Psychologist,* 45(2): 200–08.

Taylor, Frederick W. 1911. *The Principles of Scientific Management.* New York: W.W. Norton & Co.

48. Still a Man's World: Men Who Do Women's Work

CHRISTINE L. WILLIAMS

Drawing on Kanter's concept of tokenism outlined in her 1970s research, Christine Williams conducted interviews with 27 men and 23 women who work in the fields of nursing, elementary education, librarianship, and social work.

This book challenges stereotypes about men who do "women's work" through case studies of men in four predominantly female occupations: nursing, elementary school teaching, librarianship, and social work. I show that men maintain their masculinity in these occupations, despite the popular stereotypes. Moreover, male power and privilege is preserved and reproduced in these occupations through a complex interplay between gendered expectations embedded in organizations, and the gendered interests workers bring with them to their jobs. Each of these occupations is "still a man's world" even though mostly women work in them.

I selected these four professions as case studies of men who do "women's work" for a variety of reasons. First, because they are so strongly associated with women and femininity in our popular culture, these professions highlight and perhaps even exaggerate the barriers and advantages men face when entering predominantly female environments. Second, they each require extended periods of educational training and apprenticeship, requiring individuals in these occupations to be at least somewhat committed to their work (unlike those employed in, say, clerical or domestic work). Therefore I thought they would be reflective about their decisions to join these "nontraditional" occupations, making them "acute observers" and, hence, ideal informants about the sort of social and psychological processes I am interested in describing. Third, these occupations vary a great deal in the proportion of men working in them. Although my aim was not to engage in between-group comparisons, I believed that the proportions of men in a work setting would strongly influence the degree to which they felt accepted and satisfied with their jobs.

I traveled across the United States conducting in-depth interviews with seventy-six men and twenty-three women who work in nursing, teaching, librarianship, and social work. Like the people employed in these professions generally, those in my sample were predominantly white (90%). Their ages ranged from twenty to sixty-six, and the average age was thirty-eight. I interviewed women as well as men to gauge their feelings and reactions to men's entry into "their" professions. Respondents were intentionally selected to represent a wide range of specialties and levels of education and experience. I interviewed students in professional schools, "front line" practitioners, administrators, and retirees, asking them about their motivations to enter these professions, their on-the-job experiences, and their opinions about men's status and prospects in these fields.

RIDING THE GLASS ESCALATOR

Men earn more money than women in every occupation—even in predominantly female jobs (with the possible exceptions of fashion modeling and prostitution). Men outearn women in

Williams, Christine L. 1995. Abridged from "Gendered Jobs and Gendered Workers" (selection from pp. 1–19) and "Riding the Glass Escalator" and "Masculinity in 'Feminine' Occupations," in *Still a Man's World: Men Who Do Women's Work*. Berkeley: University of California Press.

teaching, librarianship, and social work; their salaries in nursing are virtually identical. The ratios between women's and men's earnings in these occupations are higher than those found in the "male" professions, where women earn 74 to 90 percent of men's salaries. That there is a wage gap at all in predominantly female professions, however, attests to asymmetries in the workplace experiences of male and female tokens. These salary figures indicate that the men who do "women's work" fare as well as, and often better than, the women who work in these fields.

Although men certainly contribute to their own professional standing through their personal effort, they face organizational pressures in these occupations that affect their success, independent of their ambition and effort. Men sometimes encounter prejudice, and even discrimination in these occupations. But unlike women in nontraditional occupations, the consequences of this prejudice actually can benefit men.

HIRING DECISIONS

Contrary to the experience of many women in the male-dominated professions, many of the men and women I spoke to indicated that there is a *preference* for hiring men in these four occupations. A Texas librarian at a junior high school said that his school district "would hire a male over a female":

[CW: Why do you think that is?]

Because there are so few, and the…ones that they do have, the library directors seem to really…think they're doing great jobs. I don't know, maybe they just feel they're being progressive or something, [but] I have had a real sense that they really appreciate having a male, particularly at the junior high….As I said, when seven of us lost our jobs from the high schools and were redistributed, there were only four positions at junior high, and I got one of them. Three of the librarians, some who had been here longer than I had with the school district, were put down in elementary school as librarians. And I definitely think that being male made a

difference in my being moved to the junior high rather than an elementary school.

Many of the men perceived their token status as males in predominantly female occupations as an *advantage* in hiring and promotions. When I asked an Arizona teacher whether his specialty (elementary special education) was an unusual area for men compared to other areas within education, he said,

Much more so. I am extremely marketable in special education. That's not why I got into the field. But I am extremely marketable because I am a man.

In several cases, the more female the specialty, the greater the apparent preference for men. For example, when asked if he encountered any problem getting a job in pediatrics, a Massachusetts nurse said,

No, no, none.…I've heard this from managers and supervisory-type people with men in pediatrics: "It's nice to have a man because it's such a female-dominated profession."

Hiring decisions are often based on supervisors' stereotypes of appropriate roles for men and women. Frequently these stereotypes benefit men, as was the case with one Massachusetts librarian. He was one of only two men in his first paraprofessional library job, which sparked controversy among the agency's higher administration:

I found out after I'd been hired, that there were serious questions raised about…what my then supervisor—a woman librarian—had done because she was hiring two men essentially for clerical duties and that just went against the grain of everything that the people had seen before. They were used to men supervising the women in clerical jobs. But the idea of having a woman, and then sitting two men down in the secretarial pool under her supervision really made it difficult.

His supervisor's boss intervened and promoted him to a supervisory position—before he completed his professional training. He explained,

He [the supervisor's boss] tended to move people not on the basis of their credentials so much as on the kind of skills and interests and impetus that they showed, and his own feelings about what they were capable of doing.

He believed that he was promoted to his first professional position to satisfy the administration's sense of "appropriate" jobs for men and women.

Some men described being "tracked" into practice areas within their professions which were considered more legitimate for men. For example, one Texas man described how he was pushed into administration and planning in social work, even though "I'm not interested in writing policy; I'm much more interested in research and clinical stuff." A nurse who is interested in pursuing graduate study in family and child health in Boston said he was dissuaded from entering the program specialty in favor of a concentration in "adult nursing." And a kindergarten teacher described his difficulty finding a job in his specialty after graduation: "I was recruited immediately to start getting into a track to become an administrator. And it was men who recruited me. It was men that ran the system at that time, especially in Los Angeles."

This tracking may bar men from the most female-identified specialties within these professions. But men are effectively being "kicked upstairs" in the process. Those specialties considered more legitimate practice areas for men also tend to be the most prestigious, and better-paying specialties as well. For example, men in nursing are overrepresented in critical care and psychiatric specialties, which tend to be higher paying than the others.

A distinguished kindergarten teacher, who had been voted citywide "Teacher of the Year," described the informal pressures he faced to advance in his field. He told me that even though people were pleased to see him in the classroom, "there's been some encouragement to think about administration, and there's been some encouragement to think about teaching at the university level or something like that, or supervisory-type position."

The effect of this "tracking" is the opposite of that experienced by women in male-dominated occupations. Researchers have reported that many women encounter "glass ceilings" in their efforts to scale organizational and professional hierarchies. That is, they reach invisible barriers to promotion in their careers, caused mainly by the sexist attitudes of men in the highest positions. In contrast to this "glass ceiling," many of the men I interviewed seem to encounter a "glass escalator." Often, despite their intentions, they face invisible pressures to move up in their professions. Like being on a moving escalator, they have to work to stay in place.

A public librarian specializing in children's collections (a heavily female concentration) described an encounter with this "escalator" in his very first job out of library school. In his first six-months' evaluation, his supervisors commended him for his good work in storytelling and related activities, but they criticized him for "not shooting high enough":

Seriously. That's literally what they were telling me. They assumed that because I was a male—and they told me this—and that I was being hired right out of graduate school, that somehow I wasn't doing the kind of management-oriented work that they thought I should be doing. And as a result, really they had a lot of bad marks, as it were, against me on my evaluation. And I said I couldn't believe this!

Throughout his ten-year career, he has had to struggle to remain in the children's collections.

SUPERVISORS AND COLLEAGUES: THE WORKING ENVIRONMENT

A major difference in the experience of men and women in nontraditional occupations is that men are far more likely to be supervised by a member of their own sex. In each of the four professions I studied, men are overrepresented in administrative and managerial capacities, or, as in the case of nursing, the organizational hierarchy is governed by men. For example, 15 percent of all elementary school teachers are men, but men make up over 80 percent of all elementary school principals and 96 percent of all public school superintendents and assistant superintendents. Likewise, over 40 percent of all male social workers hold administrative or managerial positions, compared to 30 percent of all female social workers. And 50 percent of male librarians hold administrative positions, compared to 30 percent of female librarians, and the majority of deans and directors of major university and public libraries are men. Thus, unlike women who enter "male fields," the men in these professions often work under the direct supervision of other men.

Many of the men interviewed reported that they had good rapport with their male supervisors. It was not uncommon in education, for example, for the male principal to informally socialize with the male staff, as a Texas special education teacher describes:

> Occasionally I've had a principal who would regard me as "the other man on the campus" and "it's us against them," you know? I mean, nothing really that extreme, except that some male principals feel like there's nobody there to talk to except the other man. So I've been in that position.

These personal ties can have important consequences for men's careers. For example, one California nurse, whose performance was judged marginal by his nursing superiors, was transferred to the emergency room staff (a prestigious promotion) due to his personal friendship with the physician in charge. And a Massachusetts teacher acknowledged that his principal's personal interest in him landed him his current job:

> [CW: You had mentioned that your principal had sort of spotted you at your previous job and had wanted to bring you here [to this school]. Do you think that has anything to do with the fact that you're a man, aside from your skills as a teacher?]
>
> Yes, I would say in that particular case, that was part of it.... We have certain things in common, certain interests that really lined up.

> [CW: Vis-à-vis teaching?]
>
> Well, more extraneous things—running specifically, and music. And we just seemed to get along real well right off the bat. It is just kind of a guy thing; we just liked each other....

Interviewees did not report many instances of male supervisors discriminating against them, or refusing to accept them because they were male. Indeed, these men were much more likely to report that their male bosses discriminated against the *females* in their professions. When asked if he thought physicians treated male and female nurses differently, a Texas nurse said:

> I think yeah, some of them do. I think the women seem like they have a lot more trouble with the physicians treating them in a derogatory manner. Or, if not derogatory, then in a very paternalistic way than the men [are treated]. Usually if a physician is mad at a male nurse, he just kind of yells at him. Kind of like an employee. And if they're mad at a female nurse, rather than treat them on an equal basis, in terms of just letting their anger out at them as an employee, they're more paternalistic or there's some sexual harassment component to it.

A Texas teacher perceived a similar situation where he worked:

> I've never felt unjustly treated by a principal because I'm a male. The principals that I've seen that I felt are doing things that are kind of arbitrary or not well thought out are doing it to everybody. In fact, they're probably doing it to the females worse than they are to me.

However, one nurse did tell me about an exception to this generally favorable treatment. During the fire drills at a Catholic hospital where he worked (which was administered by men), the male nurses were required "to report to the site of the fire with the maintenance department and housekeeping," while the female nurses were required to "stay on the floor and close the doors and make sure that everything is out of the hall." The administrators assumed that the men, and not the women, could help combat fires—a distinction that hardly favored the men.

There are also indications that supervisors treat openly gay men less favorably than straight men. For example, a nurse in Texas told me that one of the physicians he worked with would prefer to staff the operating room with male nurses exclusively—as long as they were not gay. And a Massachusetts social worker told me that he was passed over for promotion because he did not seem masculine enough:

> They were going to hire a social worker and I sort of thought for sure I would get that job, but in fact I did not get that job. They wanted somebody more assertive, more aggressive.... I am someone who is pretty even-keeled, soft-spoken, and often that gets interpreted, particularly by men, as being ineffectual, and that is what happened there.... It was a group of men who were interviewing me and they felt that I couldn't, sort of, be more male-like.... I mean, they didn't say it, but that's my interpretation of it.

Thus, although in general, respondents believed that male supervisors treated men more favorably than they treated women, there were some notable exceptions to this rule.

Although I did not interview many supervisors, I did include twenty-three women in my sample to ascertain their perspectives about the presence of men in their professions. All of the women I interviewed claimed to be supportive of their male colleagues, but some conveyed ambivalence. For example, a social work professor said she would like to see more men enter the social work profession, particularly in the clinical specialty (where they are underrepresented). She said she would favor affirmative action hiring guidelines for men in the profession, and yet, she resented the fact that her department hired "another white male" during a recent search. I confronted her about this apparent ambivalence:

> [CW: I find it very interesting that, on the one hand, you sort of perceive this preference and perhaps even sexism with regard to how men

are evaluated and how they achieve higher positions within the profession, yet, on the other hand, you would be encouraging of more men to enter the field. Is that contradictory to you, or...?]
>
> Yeah, it's contradictory.

A similar feeling was related to me by another social worker. After she described the meteoric rise of a young man in the agency where she works, I asked whether she thought the women workers facilitated men's advancement in any way. She said,

> Absolutely. I think the women expect the men to come in and pass them by. These are older women. They expect the young white male to exceed them, and they give them a hand up. I don't hear any anger. I hear them slapping them on the back: "Go on, Charlie! You're twenty-nine; isn't that cute? I'm fifty-nine; my son is your age. Charlie's going to make it to the top."
>
> [CW: Do you think that's different from the younger women that you see?]
>
> I think maybe we're a little more skeptical, angry, and resentful. And we're more apt to try to be peers with these guys. But you can see how it sets up for some anger. We all have the same student loans. Women actually have more work at home.

Men's reception by their female colleagues is thus somewhat mixed. It appears that women are generally eager to see men enter "their" occupations, and the women I interviewed claimed they were supportive of their male peers. Indeed, several men agreed with this social worker that their female colleagues had facilitated their careers in various ways (including college mentorship). At the same time, however, women often resent the apparent ease with which men seem to advance within these professions, sensing that men at the higher levels receive preferential treatment, and thus close off advancement opportunities for women.

But this ambivalence does not seem to translate into the "poisoned" work environment described by many women who work in male-dominated occupations. Among the male interviewees, there were no accounts of sexual harassment (indeed, one man claimed this was a disappointment to him!). However, women do treat their male colleagues differently on occasion. It is not uncommon in nursing, for example, for men to be called upon to help catheterize male patients, or to lift especially heavy patients. Some librarians also said that women asked them to lift and move heavy boxes of books because they were men. And male teachers occasionally confront differential treatment as well, as described by this Texas teacher:

> As a man, you're teaching with all women, and that can be hard sometimes. Just because of the stereotypes, you know. I'm real into computers…, and all the time people are calling me to fix their computer. Or if somebody gets a flat tire, they come and get me. I mean, there are just a lot of stereotypes. Not that I mind doing any of those things, but it's…you know, it just kind of bugs me that it is a stereotype— "A man should do that." Or if their kids have a lot of discipline problems, that kiddo's in your room. Or if there are kids that don't have a father in their home, that kid's in your room. Hell, nowadays that'd be half the school in my room. [laughs] But you know, all the time I hear from the principal or from other teachers, "Well, this child really needs a man…a male role model." [laughs] So there are a lot of stereotypes that…men kind of get stuck with.

Another stereotype confronting men, in nursing and social work in particular, is the expectation that they are better able than women to handle aggressive individuals and diffuse violent situations. An Arizona social worker who was the first male caseworker in a rural district, described this preference for men:

> They welcomed a man, particularly in child welfare. Sometimes you have to go into some tough parts of towns and cities, and they felt it was nice to have a man around to accompany them or be present when they were dealing with a difficult client. Or just doing things that males can do. I always felt very welcomed.

But this special treatment bothered some respondents: Getting assigned all the violent patients or discipline problems can make for difficult and unpleasant working conditions.

Furthermore, women's special treatment of men sometimes enhanced—rather than detracted from—the men's work environments. One Texas librarian said he felt "more comfortable working with women than men" because "I think it has something to do with control. Maybe it's that women will let me take control more than men will." Several men reported that their female colleagues often cast them into leadership roles. For example, this special education teacher who "team teaches" with a female, told me,

> We have an inside joke in our room because we have a lot of problems that we have to take care of, whether it's budget problems or whatever. She [the other teacher] says, "Jerry, we have a problem, and I need you to do your male bonding [with the principal]." [laughs] Jokingly. But then again, not so jokingly.
>
> [CW: Because she thinks maybe you can get further with him than…?]
>
> And if it's true or not, we don't know, but we joke about it. And underneath it all, it may not be as big a joke as we think. Whether it's because I can come in and talk basketball and small talk, you know what I mean? Over my partner who is not able to do that because she doesn't feel comfortable….It sounds awful! [laughs]….I think it's that way because I feel more comfortable approaching him. I think I can go in and say, "Hey, Stan, I need some help, this is a screwy situation."

Not all of the men I interviewed liked being cast into leadership roles, but it did enhance their authority and control in the workplace. In subtle (and not-so-subtle) ways, then, this differential treatment contributed to the "glass escalator" confronting these men in nontraditional professions.

Even outside of work, most of the men interviewed said they felt fully accepted by their female colleagues. They were usually included in informal social occasions with the women—even though this sometimes meant attending baby showers or Tupperware parties. Many of the men said that they declined offers to attend these events because they were not interested in "women's things," although several others claimed to attend everything. The minority men I interviewed seemed to feel the least comfortable in these informal contexts. One social worker in Arizona was asked about socializing with his female colleagues:

[CW: For example, if all the employees were going to get together to have a party, or celebrate a bridal shower or whatever, would you be invited along with the rest of the group?]

They would invite me, I would say, somewhat reluctantly. Being a black male, working with all white females, it did cause some outside problems. So I didn't go to a lot of functions with them....

[CW: You felt that there was some tension there on the level of your acceptance?]

Yeah. It was OK working, but on the outside, personally, there was some tension there. It never came out, that they said, "Because of who you are we can't invite you" [laughs], and I wouldn't have done anything anyway. I would have probably respected them more for saying what was on their minds. But I never felt completely in with the group.

Some single men also said they felt uncomfortable socializing with their married female colleagues because it gave the "wrong impression." But in general, the men said that they felt very comfortable around their colleagues, and they described their workplaces as very congenial for men.

The interviews suggest that the working environment encountered by "nontraditional" male workers is quite unlike that faced by women who work in traditionally male fields. Because it is not uncommon for men in predominantly female professions to be supervised by other men, they tend to have closer rapport and more intimate social relationships with people in management. These ties can facilitate men's careers by smoothing the way for future promotions. Relationships

with female supervisors were also described for the most part in positive terms, although in some cases, men perceived an "old girls'" network in place that excluded them from decision making. But in sharp contrast to the reports of women in nontraditional occupations, men in these fields did not complain of feeling discriminated against because they were men. If anything, they felt that being male was an asset that enhanced their career prospects.

Those men interviewed for this study also described congenial workplaces, and a very high level of acceptance from their female colleagues. The sentiment was echoed by women I spoke to who said that they were pleased to see more men enter "their" professions. Some women, however, did express resentment over the "fast-tracking" that their male colleagues seem to experience. But this ambivalence did not translate into a hostile work environment for men: Women generally included men in their informal social events and, in some ways, even facilitated men's careers. By casting men into leadership roles, presuming they were more knowledgeable and qualified, or relying on them to perform certain critical tasks, women unwittingly contributed to the "glass escalator effect" facing men who do "women's work."

HEGEMONIC MASCULINITY IN FEMALE OCCUPATIONS

Waiting for a scheduled interview with a librarian, I had a chance to peruse the various clippings and announcements posted on his office door. In the center was a cartoon drawing of an enormous, brutish, muscular man labeled "Conan the Librarian" (a takeoff on "Conan the Barbarian"). There was to be little doubt that the man behind the door was masculine.

Men use several different strategies to "maintain" hegemonic masculinity in female occupations. Men distinguish themselves from women in the workplace by segregating themselves into certain male-identified specialties, emphasizing the masculine elements of the job, pursuing higher administrative positions, and disassociating from

Summary so far

their work altogether. Each of these strategies enables men to maintain a sense of themselves as different from and better than women—thus contributing to the gender system that divides men from women in a way that privileges men.

Sex Segregation

Certain specialties contain higher percentages of men than others. For example, it is more common to find male nurses in hospital emergency rooms and psychiatric wards than in obstetrical wards. Men are more likely to teach in the higher grades in elementary schools, whereas 98 percent of kindergarten teachers are women. School librarianship is also an overwhelmingly female specialty (over 95% female), but men make up over a third of all academic librarians. And caseworkers in social-work agencies are mostly women, while administrators and managers in those agencies are mostly men.

Several of the men I interviewed claimed that they entered their particular specialties precisely because they contained more men. For example, one man left his job as a school social worker to work in a methadone drug treatment program because "I think there was some macho shit there [in myself], to tell you the truth, because I remember feeling a little uncomfortable there...; it didn't feel right to me." Another social worker told me, "I think one of the reasons personally for me that I moved to corrections—and I think it was real unconscious—was the conflict [over masculinity]. I think corrections...is a little more macho than like if I worked in a child guidance clinic like I used to." For both of these men, specializing in "male-identified" areas helped them resolve inner conflicts about masculinity caused by being male in a predominantly female occupation.

The social workers I interviewed seemed much more self-consciously aware of specialization as a strategy for maintaining masculinity than members of the other professional groups (probably as a result of their professional training). Other men in the study were not quite so articulate in describing their psychological needs to differentiate from

women, but they often made it clear during the course of the interviews that their specialties were chosen in part because they felt they were more appropriate for men. For instance, a psychiatric nurse chose his specialty "because psych is pretty easy for me. That's what I scored the highest in on the boards. And there's a lot more males, I think, in psych than on the floors...." And this sixth grade teacher explained his preference for teaching the upper grades:

> I felt I had a little more of an affinity for that age level. I could go down to fifth, but below fifth, they're just a little too cutesy, a little too young, and I get a little tired of explaining things seven or eight times....I did [substitute teaching in] second grade three different times, and after that I said, "No more primaries." I think it was like that movie with Arnold Schwarzenegger, *Kindergarten Cop*: You think you have everything under control and things just fall apart....I think at that age, the kids relate more effectively to a woman, you know, the mother figure. Cause that's more of a significant person in their lives at that age. That's the way I see it. And I think, I assume that's why you don't see so many men teaching those grades.

It is significant that this teacher identifies with Arnold Schwarzenegger, an emblem of masculinity in our culture. This is how hegemonic masculinity works: It is not necessarily what men are, but a symbolic form that men are motivated to support. Arnold Schwarzenegger is a physically strong, stoic, and unambiguously heterosexual movie star. By identifying with him and his inability to control a kindergarten class, this teacher establishes a sense of himself as powerful and in control since he teaches the *sixth* grade—even though this is also a traditionally female occupation.

Stratification within these professions is due in part to the "glass escalator": Men are channeled into specialties considered more legitimate for men, and many of them are complicit with this process. Internal stratification is due to a combination of organizational pressures and individual motives. This point was nicely summarized in an interview with a female social worker. When asked if her agency assigned men and women to different jobs, she quipped, "They'd never give some big buck a juvenile job unless he wants it. And if he wants it, he wouldn't say it anyways."

Emphasizing the Masculine

Specializing in male-identified areas is perhaps the most obvious way that men can differentiate themselves from women. However, even those who work in the more "traditional" female specialties can distinguish the work they do from "women's work" by highlighting the masculine aspects of their specialties. School and public librarians, for example, can identify with automating the library catalogue and other computer work that they do. One public librarian specializing in cataloging believes that advanced technology was the key to attracting him as well as other men to the profession.

> After automation became part of the profession, more and more men are coming. I think that men are looking more for prestigious careers, and automation has given that to the profession. Not just organizing books, but applying technology in the process.

Another approach to emphasizing the masculine is to focus on the prestige of one's workplace. A California teacher who described his institution as "the top flight elementary school in the country" said,

> It makes you feel good about your job. It makes you, as a male, feel like it's okay to be a teacher, because this is a highly prestigious institution in the world of private schools.

Other men focused on the power and authority of their particular job specialties. Describing a previous job in Children's Protective Services (a heavily female specialty), this Arizona social worker said,

> Child welfare is an area in social work where you balance a helping role with a social control role. Going out to people's homes, I almost wore two hats: a social worker and an authority figure, someone with some enforcement power....I carried a certain amount of professional and legal authority with me....I literally had the authority to take people's kids out of their homes.

In addition, a few men emphasized the physical aspects of their work. A former teacher at a school for autistic children explained that men were needed for "restraining" the children, some of whom were "very, very violent." And a public librarian specializing in children's collections described a distinctive reading style he observed among the few male storytellers in town:

> I guess you could say, maybe in some sense, we're real physical in our storytimes, you know, the way we interact with the kids. I don't mean...I mean, these days, you have to be very careful touching children, of course....I don't mean real touchy-feely, but I mean...you just get a real physical sense of the story.

Thus, men can identify with the technical or physical aspects of their jobs, or emphasize the special prestige or power that accrue to them because of their specific institutions. In all of these ways, men can highlight the components of their jobs that are consistent with hegemonic masculinity, thus maintaining a sense of themselves as "masculine" even though they work in nontraditional occupations.

This particular strategy of "emphasizing the masculine" is used when dealing with individuals outside the workplace. Some men told me that in certain contexts they rename their work to give it a more masculine, and hence more legitimate, connotation. For example, one social worker in private practice calls himself a "psychotherapist." A teacher tells those he meets at parties that he is "in education." A nurse introduces himself to new patients as "a former Vietnam combat nurse." And a librarian told me that he is always selective about the contexts in which he reveals his occupation:

> At a "redneck" bar, I wouldn't sit down and drink a couple of beers and announce to the

guy next to me with his gimme cap, "Hello, I'm a school librarian." He wouldn't care and he wouldn't be able to even think about a job like that. So it really depends on the audience. But the people I socialize with are people who are extremely understanding.

For these men, "naming" the occupation to the "wrong" audience could be threatening, so they rename their work, or describe it to "outsiders" in more masculine, and hence, more acceptable language.

This strategy of "emphasizing the masculine" also is employed by some men in their dealings with their female colleagues at work. Some men occasionally set themselves apart from women by refusing to participate in certain "feminine" activities. One teacher, for example, described how the only male teacher she worked with was very selective about his participation in school functions:

> Roland does fix all the projectors and he runs around…and sets up science kits and stuff, but he's volunteered for that. There are other things that he claims he can't do as well.…He never wants to be on a social committee, for example, or get plants when someone's ill, or collect for cards, for whatever reasons. Even picking up the staff room—he jokes that he has to have a cleaning lady at his house so he certainly doesn't want to be on the cleanup detail at school. So there are things that he doesn't do. But he makes up in other ways, because that's what he's gifted in and good at.

> [CW: And the teachers feel fine about that?]

> Oh, yeah.

In another example, a social worker who enjoyed socializing with his female colleagues (they even threw him a wedding shower) drew the line at bringing a covered dish to the office "pot luck" parties:

> I told them I wasn't making any. We have pot lucks for our Christmas party, and picnics for the [foster] children. But I informed them that now that I'm married, I had no intention

of changing that either. I bring potato chips or Kool-Aid, something that's very easy and takes no work. The rest of the women make something.

These are subtle ways that men can informally set themselves apart from their female colleagues. By picking and choosing among various informal activities in the workplace, men can carve a "masculine" niche for themselves among their female peers.

Administration and Higher Educational Credentials

A third distancing strategy is to define the present occupation as a way station for future jobs that are more lucrative, prestigious, or challenging (and thus more legitimate for men). Men who use this strategy do not identify with their current jobs, but see them as laying the groundwork for future jobs. For instance, a teacher told me that he chose to start his career in elementary school to "learn the basics of human nature," and then move up to junior high, and ultimately high school (where there is a much larger proportion of men). Others saw their professions as "springboards" to other careers. An Arizona nurse, for example, who saw "nursing as a backup," hoped in the future to work in the biomedical engineering profession.

Aspiring to the top rungs of the profession was an especially common distancing strategy. Men described future plans to become "director of a branch library" (children's librarian), "director of a home for the aged" (floor nurse), or a "principal of a school" (fourth grade teacher). These areas were all explicitly defined as more appropriate for men, and they are also viewed as more prestigious and powerful than rank-and-file jobs.

As is the case in most professions, advancement to these top positions often requires higher educational preparation beyond the entry-level credential. Men are more likely than women to seek postgraduate degrees in these occupations. Indeed, men received nearly half of the doctorates awarded in education and library science in 1988.

This discrepancy in the representation of men and women in postcredential degree programs is due to a number of factors. First, men are often encouraged to "aim high" by mentors simply because they are men. A Massachusetts nurse was told by his first clinical instructor in his associate degree (ADN) program,

> "You've got to go on. You *have* to go on...past the ADN," she said. "You have to; you are a man." She said, "You have to get more men into the profession; we need men."

Thus, men may receive more encouragement than women to reach the top of their professions.

A second reason for men's overrepresentation among higher degree recipients and administrative officeholders involves men's and women's different family obligations. Women often shoulder the primary responsibility for household care, even when they are employed full-time. This frees up married men to dedicate themselves more exclusively to pursuing higher educational credentials and higher administrative positions. I interviewed three men whose spouses were in the same profession as they, and each had a higher degree than his wife. A doctoral student in library science, who met his wife in the master's degree program, explained why he pursued an advanced degree and she did not:

> I realized that I have the responsibility to become the provider at home....She thought that if she were comfortable, if she found a nice [work] environment, she didn't need to go further [with her education]. She didn't have to push harder....And during the time we were in college, the family was growing. So the demand for her to stay at home and care for the kids was growing, too.

Thus, men have more opportunities and receive more encouragement than women to seek the top positions in these occupations. But aside from these two structural reasons, men often have personal motives, linked to their desire to be masculine, to strive for the top. Achieving success is a way they can maintain their masculinity in a female occupation. For example, a social worker employed in the mental health services department of a large urban area, reflected on his move into administration:

> The more I think about it, through our discussion, I'm sure that's a large part of why I wound up in administration. It's okay for a man to do the administration. In fact, I don't know if I fully answered a question that you asked a little while ago about how did being male contribute to my advancing in the field. I was saying it wasn't because I got any special favoritism as a man, but...I think...because I'm a man, I felt a need to get into this kind of position. I may have worked harder toward it, may have competed harder for it, than most women would do, even women who think about doing administrative work.

For many men, pursuing administrative positions is a way of "distancing" themselves from women, carving a masculine niche for themselves, and thus establishing more legitimacy for their presence in these female occupations.

Part of what motivates this particular strategy for maintaining masculinity is competition with other men. A clinical social worker at a university hospital described why he decided to pursue a doctorate:

> First of all, even though most of the social workers there were women, most of the people [at the hospital where he worked] were men, especially the psychiatrists and psychologists....Most of my friends were...male...who were psychology or psychiatry interns or residents....And I think it just got to me, or motivated me, or a sense of competition, or something, but seeing each new cohort move on to getting their degree and moving on to something bigger and better, I just felt that I ought to do the same....I decided to apply either to law school or for a doctorate in social work or psychology.

Those men I interviewed who worked alongside other professional men with better paid and more prestigious credentials felt an enormous amount of pressure to advance their own education. A former Licensed Vocational Nurse (LVN) who was taken under the wing of a prominent research physician explained why he was motivated to eventually pursue a master's degree in nursing:

> Because I was always working with people with Ph.D.'s, with M.D.'s, or with RN behind their name— BSN, MSN [Bachelor's and Master's of Science in Nursing]—it really served as a catalyst. That was it, I had to get back to school.

This nurse's experience illustrates the combination of organizational pressures and individual desires motivating many men in these professions. His pursuit of higher degrees was motivated in part by the unusual opportunity he was given to publish and do research as an LVN, and in part by his personal desire to make himself an equal to the other men at work. Greater opportunities for men, combined with their psychological desire to identify with the higher-status males (and disassociate from women) encourage them to strive for advancement instead of remaining, as another director of social work services put it, "just a social worker."

Of course, women also pursue advanced degrees and careers in administration. But the women I interviewed did not pursue advanced degrees as a distancing strategy. This emphasis on competing for prestige was missing from their accounts of their motivations. Indeed, in one case, a respondent entered a doctoral program because she thought that college teaching would be more accommodating to her family obligations:

> If I look back, I think that really the most satisfying times in my career was when I had my master's degree and I supervised in child welfare....I think I saw coming back to get my Ph.D. as a way to teach at the university level and have a different, more flexible schedule when I was raising my child. I really kind of looked at it as the means to have a certain kind of lifestyle.

It is not the case that women in these professions lack ambition, or that they "fear success."

Rather, my interviews suggest that many men in these professions are "hyperambitious" in part because of their psychological need to distance themselves from the work of women. Pursuing higher degrees and administrative positions are strategies they use to reproduce masculinity in female occupations.

Disassociation

The final distancing strategy used by the men in this study was disassociation from their work. Some men feel little or no connection to their jobs: They either fell into their professions with little forethought or planning, or they became gravely disaffected by their work once they began their careers. For example, a public librarian explained why he chose his profession:

> I sort of thought that it wouldn't be too stressful, it wouldn't be too hard. You could go anywhere in the country you wanted to and get a job. To a small town or something, which certainly has an appeal. Since there's a lot of women, you could do things like take a year off and come back, and people wouldn't look at your résumé and say, "What is that? What is this year off?" And you wouldn't be required to climb a career ladder.

This man described himself as entirely lacking in ambition and enthusiasm for the librarianship profession, and mocked others who took their jobs more seriously.

Similarly, a teacher told me that he got his teaching certificate in college because "it was always something I figured I could fall back on. Or if I moved, I could always get a teaching position if something else didn't work out." Currently he is working on a second degree to become an exercise physiologist, and he plans to continue teaching "only as long as it takes me to get out of there."

Part of this disassociation strategy is to condemn or deride others who are in the profession—particularly other men. A public librarian described his male co-workers as "a bit old ladyish because they've worked in reference a long time. I don't know if that's because of their personality or working in a job so many years. Just being sort of nervous." He explained that he has remained in the same position for nineteen years only because he loves living in Cambridge—not because of his job. And a social worker who periodically leaves his profession to pursue other interests (including a yearlong stint as a card dealer in Atlantic City), described his male colleagues in less-than-glowing terms:

> I grew up in the world of work, business, the bottom line. There is not that kind of account-ability in social work. My stereotype of men coming into social work is maybe this is easier, they don't want to face the real world where you're going to be held accountable.

By condemning the profession—and the other men in it—men can distance themselves from their work, and preserve a sense of themselves as different and better than those employed in these professions.

Sometimes this disassociation strategy is directed toward gay men in these professions. Some straight men deride their gay colleagues, blaming them for the poor status of their work. Several of the men I interviewed did make it perfectly clear that they were straight, apparently to distinguish themselves from their gay colleagues (and the gay stereotype about men who work in these professions). Since heterosexuality is a key component of hegemonic masculinity, this disassociation strategy allows men to maintain a sense of themselves as appropriately masculine even though they work in predominantly female jobs.

Thus, men can use several strategies to maintain their masculinity in these female occupations: They can differentiate themselves from women by specializing in certain male-identified areas, by emphasizing masculine components of their jobs, by aspiring to higher administrative positions, and by disassociating from their professions altogether. Each of these strategies entails establishing difference from and superiority over women. Thus, paradoxically, men in nontraditional occupations can and do actually support hegemonic masculinity, and end up posing little threat to the social organization of gender.

CONCLUSION

Men working in traditionally female occupations symbolize a challenge to—if not an outright rejection of—masculinity. Picture a male nurse, librarian, elementary school teacher, or social worker. The image that comes to mind is probably not a hypermasculine Rambo-type of man, but a softer, more effeminate man.

Men who work in nursing, teaching, librarianship, and social work have a lot at stake in maintaining their masculinity. The economic and status advantages men receive in these occupations may be contingent on successfully presenting an image of themselves as both different from and better than women. And for many men, establishing a subjective sense of their masculine identity requires that they distinguish themselves from women.

For the men in these occupations, convincing themselves and others that they are appropriately masculine is an uphill battle because of the stereotypes that surround men who do "women's work." Men in more traditional "male" occupations probably face a less formidable struggle to demonstrate that they are masculine. Occupational segregation historically has been a guaranteed means used by men to maintain their masculinity. This has been one of the reasons why men have been very reluctant to allow women into their occupations: The prospect of job integration threatens men because it challenges their automatic claims to privilege that they have been socialized to desire, and which many expect as their birthright.

The men in these female occupations may be in the vanguard of looking for ways to be "men" in integrated workplaces. Their strategies for doing this vary, but each enables them to maintain an image of themselves as different from women and superior to them. Ironically, they support "hegemonic masculinity" in spite of their nontraditional roles.

DISCUSSION QUESTIONS

1. What does Williams mean by the terms "glass escalator" and "glass ceiling"? How are they related to one another?
2. What does Williams mean by the term "hegemonic masculinity"? How is this form of masculinity apparent in your own life?
3. Williams describes four strategies that men who do "women's work" use to distance themselves from being labeled feminine or gay. What are they?

ADDITIONAL RESOURCES

Film

"North County." 2005. Starring Charlize Theron, this gripping film documents one of the first major successful sexual harassment lawsuit in the United States. The film follows the story of women who broke gender stereotypes and barriers by working in northern Minnesota iron mines. 126 minutes.

Internet

http://www.thp.org/what_we_do/program_overview/empowering_women?gclid=CJuy–97-Qo5wCFdoU5wodJ1UANg. The Hunger Project is an international organization that empowers women and men to end poverty. This link features an article on "Empowering Women as Key Change Agents."

http://www2.asanet.org/sectionsexgend/. The website of the Sex and Gender Section of the American Sociological Association.

http://www.nytimes.com/2009/01/30/us/politics/30ledbetter-web.html. The Lilly Ledbetter Fair Pay Act was the first piece of legislation signed by President Barack Obama in January 2009. This legislation is dedicated to eradicating pay discrimination based on gender.

FURTHER READING

Maume, David J., Jr. 1999. "Glass Ceilings and Glass Escalators: Occupational Segregation and Race and Sex Differences in Managerial Promotions." *Work and Occupations,* 26(4): 483–509.

Pierce, Jennifer. 1996. *Gender Trials: Emotional Lives in Contemporary Law Firms.* Berkeley: University of California Press.

Reskin, Barbara and Heidi Hartmann. 1986. *Women's Work, Men's Work: Sex Segregation on the Job.* Washington, DC: National Academies Press.

Reskin, Barbara and Patricia Roos. 1990. *Job Queues, Gender Queues: Explaining Women's Inroads into Male Occupations.* Philadelphia, PA: Temple University Press.

Simon, Robin W. and Leda E. Nath. 2004. "Gender and Emotion in the United States: Do Men and Women Differ in Self-Reports of Feelings and Expressive Behavior?" *American Journal of Sociology,* 109: 1137–76.

Thorne, Barrie. 1993. *Gender Play: Girls and Boys in School.* New Brunswick, NJ: Rutgers University Press.

Williams, Christine L. 1989. *Gender Differences at Work: Women and Men in Nontraditional Occupations.* Berkeley: University of California Press.

Williams, Christine L. 1995. *Still a Man's World: Men Who Do Women's Work.* Berkeley: University of California Press.

Williams, Christine L. 2006. *Inside Toyland: Working, Shopping, and Social Inequality.* Berkeley: University of California Press.

Wingfield, Adia Harvey. 2009. "Racializing the Glass Escalator: Reconsidering Men's Experiences with Women's Work." *Gender & Society,* 23(1): 5–26.

Observational posture

49. Drag Kinging and the Transformation of Gender Identities

EVE SHAPIRO

As a member of the Santa Barbara, California–based drag king performance troupe, Disposable Boy Toys, Eve Shapiro conducted field research and interviews with 28 of its members. A previous version of this article was awarded the Graduate Student Paper Award from the Sexualities Section of the American Sociological Association in 2005.

This article is based on a case study of the Santa Barbara-based drag troupe, Disposable Bay Toys (DBT), undertaken between July 2002 and September 2004. I conducted semistructured interviews with 28 of 31 current and past members. Participants ranged in age from 17 to 34, with 23 identifying as white, 1 as Black, 1 as Asian/Pacific Islander, and 3 as multiracial. Participants described coming from or living in a range of class positions from poor to upper middle class. Interviews lasted between one and a half and three and a half hours, with 23 conducted in person and 5 over the phone. Interviews were recorded and transcribed.

Throughout the article, I refer to performers using their drag names and corresponding gender pronouns regardless of their gender identity out of drag. I chose to use the troupe's and the performers' real drag names instead of pseudonyms because DBT's distinctive style and national recognition made the group easily recognizable. In addition, each member chose to use his or her drag name in publications, and the group as a whole asked to be identified.

I also analyzed documents from DBT and from an annual conference called the International Drag King Extravaganza. In addition, I undertook content analysis of 200 hours of video-recorded drag performances from DBT between 2000 and 2004. Finally, I conducted participant observation from June 2002 to September 2004 at meetings, rehearsals, workshops, and performances. Throughout the research, I was an active member of DBT.

When I conceived this case study, I engaged in ongoing conversations with other DBT members about the research methods, data collection, and ethics. My insider status granted me significant access and rapport with the group. As an insider, I was privy to all group activities and was able to unobtrusively collect unique and nuanced data. I was also part of group disagreements and divisions. My existing relationships with other members, both friendly and contentious, affected

Shapiro, Eve. 2007. "Drag Kinging and the Transformation of Gender Identities." *Gender & Society,* 21(2): 250–71.

the content and analysis of interviews. In light of this, I actively worked to recognize my own bias and effect on the group. I paid particular attention to what members assumed I knew, what they were willing and/or hesitant to share with me, and how I affected group decisions, processes, and outcomes. In every case, I have tried to corroborate my analyses with those made by other members in interviews and recorded in field notes. Simultaneously, my sociological training enriched my experience and allowed me to draw theoretical conclusions based on the data I collected.

DISPOSABLE BOY TOYS

When DBT was founded, it was one of a handful of drag troupes, many of which existed in towns similar to Santa Barbara in size and university affiliation. Between its debut in May 2000 and its last performance in August 2004, DBT grew from a five-person drag king group to a self-titled "political feminist collective." While several other troupes, such as H.I.S. Kings from Columbus, Ohio, worked collectively or engaged in politicized performance, DBT's explicit feminist and political mission was distinctive.

The group was composed of drag kings, transgender kings and queens (transgender-identified performers, performing masculinity or femininity), and bio-queens (women performing femininity). The group lip-synched and danced to numbers that conveyed messages about sexism, racism, body size, and militarism. Performances also critiqued binary categories of masculinity/femininity and gay/straight through numbers about transsexual, genderqueer, and fluid identities. Performances took place in queer spaces (such as gay bars and gay/lesbian pride festivals) as well as at straight progressive events (such as living wage marches and community fundraising events). The group often performed benefit shows for political and community organizations. Paid performances at universities and bars cost anywhere from $200 to $1,800 per show.

DBT members were short and tall, fat and thin, masculine and feminine, newly out and firmly queer identified, although most were young, white, and middle class. Reasons for joining DBT were remarkably consistent. Most talked about joining because they were searching for a queer and/or transgender positive community in Santa Barbara, an opportunity to perform, or because their friends were involved in DBT. Seven members joined DBT calling themselves activists, but no one joined the group to do political work around gender. No members suggested they joined out of a desire for gender identity transformation. As the group grew, it became more diverse in terms of age, education, and class, but the group was consistently described by members and audiences as predominantly white, middle class, and affiliated with the University of California, Santa Barbara.

Toward the end of 2003, seven members moved away from Santa Barbara or left the group because of disagreements, and remaining members held several months of intense group discussions about unequal leadership within the group and ongoing tensions about racial diversity and the politics of performance. During the next few months, members stopped volunteering for shows. As is the case in many organizations, DBT ended with a whimper. Without any formal disbanding, the group never performed together as DBT after August 2004.

As the DBT group developed, it created a structure that encouraged community formation. From the start, the group rehearsed all numbers collectively, relied on consensus decision-making processes, pooled group earnings, and spent time in group retreats and social events. The group developed a strong collective identity. DBT incorporated the performance of femininity by female performers and came to define drag as any intentional performance of gender. DBT shows typically included both verbal and performed challenges to gender. For example, one typical Saturday night show at the local queer bar began with a tall drag queen's stepping up to the stage. She began, "Hi! I'm Summer's Eve, and we are the Disposable Boy Toys." Summer's Eve appeared both female bodied and feminine. The crowd rushed the stage and began clapping. She continued, "We're a political feminist collective of drag kings and queens. Are you ready for a great show?" As the music swelled, eight performers dressed as cheerleaders stepped on stage and began lip-synching to female vocals from the popular 1980s song "Hey Mickey." Performers doing classic cheerleading moves included "women" with facial hair, "men" in outfits that revealed breasts, butch women, effeminate men, and a range of other genders. By the end of the song, the conventionally feminine-appearing performers revealed that they were wearing boy's underwear stuffed with socks to mimic male genitalia, and the masculine-appearing performers were flirting with each other. The number made an explicit effort to portray a wide range of genders that were incongruent with both the performers' gender identities and their bodies.

What emerged in studying DBT is that participation in the troupe fostered gender shifts among most members. By "gender identity shifts," I mean both coming to a new gender identity and defining or understanding a preexisting gender identity in new ways. While 25 members identified exclusively as female when they joined DBT, only 16 did so during interviews. Instead, members came to call themselves genderqueer, female-to-male (FTM), and transgender. "Genderqueer" was used to claim a gender outside of the male/female, masculine/feminine binaries and was defined by participants as male, female, and in between. The term "FTM" was used by individuals who identified as moving from a feminine to a masculine gender identity or from a female to a male body. An FTM transsexual was changing the physical body as well as gender, while an FTM transgendered individual identified as masculine and with a male sex category but was not necessarily taking steps to alter his body. Finally, the term "transgender" was used broadly to refer to a wide range of gender nonconformity, including genderqueer and FTM identities.

FINDINGS

Expanding the Borders of Gender Identity

When asked how DBT affected performers, many claimed that their gender identities changed because of participation. As T. Drake, who was one of the founders of DBT and transgender identified, explained, "doing drag gave me a way to open the door on gender discussions with myself and with others....DBT opened the door in a huge way because drag was the closest thing to what I was feeling and what I was wanting to live."

For some members, the environment of gender exploration led them not to transgender identities but to new femininities, and others came to identify as genderqueer and/or as gender outlaws, a move seen as both a political act and as resistance to gender norms. While some members became more visibly gender transgressive, others like Kentucky Fried Woman, who remained femme presenting, expanded the meaning of gender transgression—what she and others called a genderqueer identity—to include conscious and politicized gender play. She stated, "I do identify as genderqueer now. I believe that me and the people I perform with in Santa Barbara and here [in Seattle], my friends, my community, we're gender outlaws. We refuse to be placed in a box that says this is what we're born as, this is what we are. We play with it."

When asked whether and how their gender shifted over time, DBT members described the development of a nuanced sense of identity. Participants who previously identified with the categories of male and female began naming themselves as located somewhere on a continuum of masculinities and femininities. For example, when describing how DBT affected him, Vance Jett commented, "When I joined DBT, I found more of my masculine side; [now] I identify more with masculinity than femininity." Members described how they differed from normative gender identities. For some members who claimed a "radical femininity," doing gender was a political act of queering femininity and honoring the history of femmes in queer communities. On stage and off, these members worked to politicize femme identity. For example, in "Drive," two feminine women engaged in sexually explicit activities while lip-synching to a song about lesbian desire. Summer's Eve, a femme-identified woman, felt that this number challenged social norms by performing femme-on-femme desire and an empowered female sexuality. For others, queer femininity was a genderqueer identity, a reference to the transgressive performance of high femininity (defined by the group as extremely feminine dress and makeup). Kentucky Fried Woman, for example, argued in her interview that high femininity was equally as socially transgressive as female masculinity because of sexism, especially within queer communities. Members also discussed expanding "doing female" to include androgyny and argued that the category female is much larger than what is conventionally considered feminine. Dylan, who identified as a dyke and almost always performed masculinity, commented, "I have a really androgynous gender. For me, it's more powerful and expansive to say I'm female and look at all these things I can do....Female doesn't mean you're bound to anything." For Dylan, and other members of DBT, drag was one way to unbraid gender and sex and broaden the meaning of "woman."

Many participants described a range of female masculinities, including butch and masculine woman. Some participants drew connections to histories of butchness, and others saw maintaining a female body as a political act. Nate Prince, a butch-identified member who was sometimes assumed to be transgender, talked about a solo performance he created to female vocals. "I did the India Arie song ["Video"] to say I don't wear pantyhose, I don't shave my legs all of the time, and I don't look like a supermodel, but I'm still a woman. I wore my boxers and [men's undershirt]

and showed 'here are ways to be a woman.'" Similarly, numbers such as "I Think We're Alone Now," which featured a romance between an FTM and a butch, linked female bodies with different masculine gender identities on stage and simultaneously reinforced these possibilities off stage. This number was an effort to distinguish between butch women and FTM men. During the creation of this number, Holden Thicke and Roman Hands expressed a desire to reflect their own sex and gender negotiations as transgendered and butch-identified individuals.

Many women performers went from naming themselves simply "female" to claiming a radical femininity, described as "chosen," "proud," and "transgressive." Similarly, a number of participants came to resist singular gender classification and prefaced naming with "if I have to choose," or "I guess I am." Regardless of identity, members described gender as a conscious act and explained these gender shifts as outcomes of participation in DBT. Summer's Eve noted, "We joke in DBT about drag being the gateway drug for gender regardless of what that gender is. Some members came into a masculine butch, some members came into a female-identified butch, and some members came into fiercely femme." Participation in DBT facilitated identity exploration during adulthood.

Opportunities for Enactment

Perhaps the most important function DBT provided for members was being a place to try on, practice, and enact different genders. The opportunity for enactment was a significant collective mechanism for gender identity shifts. In DBT, members could try on a variety of genders, and many members who entered DBT with narrow ideas about what they could perform broadened their repertoire over time. Twenty-one participants performed both masculinity and femininity at least once. Indeed some members performed both femininity and masculinity in the same show, quickly changing back and forth between numbers.

In a workshop on transgender and drag at the International Drag King Extravaganza, Damien Danger described how the chance to enact a diverse array of genders in DBT affected him profoundly: "When I first started doing drag it was a replication of what I thought masculinity was and that was a white, heterosexual masculinity. As I did drag more, these definition all changed. Race, class, sexuality all intersect in your drag performance. As you learn about those things in drag, some people, including myself have been able to take those and apply the same theories and questions to your own body." All members highlighted this type of gender play and the effect it had on how they thought about gender regardless of their gender identity. For some members, these opportunities for enactment amplified or shifted existing gender identities. Summer's Eve, a femme-identified participant, remarked that doing drag allowed her to explore a variety of femininities that, in turn, affected the lived femininity she expressed. She elaborated: "I no longer need to perform high femme [an identity associated with exaggerated femininity] in my daily life because I have a place to perform it. I get to be much more relaxed because my sense of self comes from my community as opposed to society at large."

The combination of a close-knit supportive community in general and social support for members' gender choices in particular created a space that validated individuals' gender identities. Because DBT provided recognition for members' chosen gender identities, participants were able to navigate more hostile social environments, as femmes as well as transgender and genderqueer individuals.

CONCLUSIONS

Doing drag in a group with an oppositional collective identity, feminist political commitment, and collective organizational practices can harness drag's disruptive power. Members saw DBT as the central catalyst for their own and others' identity shifts. Before participation in the group, 25 members admitted embracing hegemonic gender identities with only 3 members identifying as transgender or genderqueer. After participating in DBT, members described gender as a range of masculinities and femininities and claimed complex sets of gender identities. All but 5 members described a significant identity shift around gender, whether that was within or across the gender binary.

In this drag troupe, the mechanisms that supported identity shifts included the imaginative possibility of gender as fluid and mutable, information and resources that educated members about gender identities and services, opportunities for enactment of a variety of masculinities and femininities, and social support for members' chosen genders. These mechanisms affected all members of the drag troupe to varying degrees, regardless of whether they maintained their existing gender identities, took on additional more fluid identities, or came out as transgender.

My findings suggest that it is organizational context and ideology that contains the potential for challenging gender on the individual and societal level. Given this, my conclusions are generalizable not to all drag performance but rather to performance groups that share these group characteristics. Future research on other performance groups as venues for identity transformation would be fruitful.

DISCUSSION QUESTIONS
1. What does Shapiro mean by the term "gender binary"?
2. Have you ever felt constrained by gender norms or expectations? If so, how?
3. Shapiro claims that we all "perform" gender, participating in "putting on" portrayals of femininity and masculinity in our daily lives. Discuss situations you have

encountered when you have been conscious of your own gender "performance" in the presence of others.

4. What do Shapiro's interviewees mean by the term "gender outlaw"?

ADDITIONAL RESOURCES

Internet

http://www.dckings.com/Pages/aboutus1.html. The website for the world's longest performing drag king troupe, the DC Kings.

http://www.disposableboytoys.com/. The website for the drag king troupe Shapiro performed with and studied, the Disposable Boy Toys.

http://idke.info/. The website for the International Drag King Extravaganza, an organization that has been in operation since 1999.

http://www.cnn.com/video/#/video/health/2009/07/25/lkl.transgenders.long.cnn?iref= videosearch. July 25, 2009. This "Larry King Live" episode about transsexuality is called "Born in the Wrong Body."

http://www.slate.com/id/2180294/. December 19, 2007. *Slate* journalist Emily Yoffe discusses her transition to drag king performer Johnson Manly, with the assistance of the DC Kings, in her article and video entitled "Man Made: My Short Life as a Drag King."

FURTHER READING

Butler, Judith. 1990. *Gender Trouble: Feminism and the Subversion of Identity.* New York: Routledge.

Butler, Judith. 1993. *Bodies That Matter: On the Discursive Limits of Sex.* New York: Routledge.

Devor, Holly 1999. *FTM: Female-to-Male Transsexuals in Society.* Bloomington: Indiana University Press.

Green, Jamison. 2004. *Becoming a Visible Man.* Nashville, TN: Vanderbilt University Press.

Halberstam, Judith. 1998. *Female Masculinity.* Durham, NC: Duke University Press.

Kimmel, Sara B, et al. 2004. "Measuring Masculine Body Ideal Distress: Development of a Measure." *International Journal of Men's Health,* 3(1): 1–10.

Rupp, Leila and Verta Taylor. 2003. *Drag Queens at the 801 Cabaret.* Chicago: University of Chicago Press.

Tewksbury, Richard. 1994. "Gender Construction and the Female Impersonator: The Process of Transforming 'He' to 'She.'" *Deviant Behavior: An Interdisciplinary Journal,* 15(11): 27–43.

Troka, Donna, Kathleen LeBesco, and Jean Noble (eds.). 2003. *The Drag King Anthology.* New York: Harrington Park Press.

West, Candace and Sarah Fenstermaker. 1995. "Doing Difference." *Gender & Society,* 9(1): 8–37.

West, Candace and Don Zimmerman. 1987. "Doing Gender." *Gender & Society,* 1(2): 125–51.

PART VI

Changing Worlds, Changing Selves

Global and Postmodern Identities

With vast changes in technology and the economy over the last century, we have increasingly become a mobile and global world society. These next selections explore the roles that immigration, transition to adulthood, and social ostracism play in the development of social structure and identity.

In his classic 1908 essay on being an outsider, German sociologist Georg Simmel writes a poignant and timeless description of people who are considered strangers or foreigners. Extending Simmel's concept to immigration, Yen Le Espiritu studies how second-generation Filipino Americans cope with the conflicts and contradictions of living between two cultures. Douglas Hartmann and Teresa Swartz develop several of the concepts introduced by Espiritu in their research on the changing transition to adulthood. Like Espiritu, Hartmann and Swartz conduct in-depth interviews with youth to examine how young people today experience this transition.

50. The Stranger

GEORG SIMMEL

Georg Simmel was one of the founders of German sociology. Born in Berlin in 1858, Simmel was known to possess many of the qualities of "the stranger" that he describes in his famous essay. He lived and worked as a scholar but was denied true membership, or professorial ranking, at the University of Berlin, where he was a lecturer. Despite these challenges, Simmel was a prolific writer and much beloved teacher.

The stranger being discussed here, not in the sense often touched upon in the past, as the wanderer who comes today and goes tomorrow, but rather as the person who comes today and stays tomorrow. He is, so to speak, the *potential* wanderer: although he has not moved on, he has not quite overcome the freedom of coming and going. He is fixed within a particular spatial group, or within a group whose boundaries are similar to spatial boundaries. But his position in this group is determined, essentially, by the fact that he has not belonged to it from the beginning, that he imports qualities into it, which do not and cannot stem from the group itself.

The unity of nearness and remoteness involved in every human relation is organized, in the phenomenon of the stranger, in a way which may be most briefly formulated by saying that in the relationship to him, distance means that he, who is close by, is far, and strangeness means that he, who also is far, is actually near. For, to be a stranger is naturally a very positive relation; it is a specific form of interaction. The stranger, like the poor and like sundry "inner enemies," is an element of the group itself. His position as a full-fledged member involves both being outside it and confronting it. The following statements, which are by no means intended as exhaustive, indicate how elements which increase distance and repel, in the relations of and with the stranger produce a pattern of coordination and consistent interaction.

Throughout the history of economics the stranger everywhere appears as the trader, or the trader as stranger. As long as economy is essentially self-sufficient, or products are exchanged within a spatially narrow group, it needs no middleman: a trader is only required for products that originate outside the group. Insofar as members do not leave the circle in order to buy these necessities—in which case *they* are the "strange" merchants in that outside territory—the trader *must* be a stranger, since nobody else has a chance to make a living.

This position of the stranger stands out more sharply if he settles down in the place of his activity, instead of leaving it again: in innumerable cases even this is possible only if he can live by intermediate trade. Trade can always absorb more people than primary production; it is, therefore, the sphere indicated for the stranger, who intrudes into a group in which the economic positions are actually occupied—the classical example is the history of European Jews. The stranger is by nature no "owner of soil"—soil not only in the physical, but also in the figurative sense of a life-substance which is fixed, if not in a point in space, at least in an ideal point of the

Simmel, Georg. 1950. "The Stranger," in Kurt Wolff (trans., ed.). *The Sociology of Georg Simmel,* 402–08. New York: Free Press.

social environment. Although in more intimate relations, he may develop all kinds of charm and significance, as long as he is considered a stranger in the eyes of the other, he is not an "owner of soil." Restriction to intermediary trade, gives him the specific character of mobility. If mobility takes place within a closed group, it embodies that synthesis of nearness and distance which constitutes the formal position of the stranger. For, the fundamentally mobile person comes in contact, at one time or another, with every individual, but is not organically connected, through established ties of kinship, locality, and occupation, with any single one.

Another expression of this constellation lies in the objectivity of the stranger. He is not radically committed to the unique ingredients and peculiar tendencies of the group, and therefore approaches them with the specific attitude of "objectivity." But objectivity does not simply involve passivity and detachment; it is a particular structure composed of distance and nearness, indifference and involvement.

Objectivity is by no means nonparticipation, but a positive and specific kind of participation-just as the objectivity of a theoretical observation does not refer to the mind as a passive *tabula rasa* on which things inscribe their qualities, but on the contrary, to its full activity that operates according to its own laws, and to the elimination, thereby, of accidental dislocations and emphases, whose individual and subjective differences would produce different pictures of the same object.

Objectivity may also be defined as freedom: the objective individual is bound by no commitments which could prejudice his perception, understanding, and evaluation of the given. The freedom, however, which allows the stranger to experience and treat even his close relationships as though from a bird's-eye view, contains many dangerous possibilities. In uprisings of all sorts, the party attacked has claimed, from the beginning of things, that provocation has come from the outside, through emissaries and instigators.

Insofar as this is true, it is an exaggeration of the specific role of the stranger: he is freer practically and theoretically; he surveys conditions with less prejudice; his criteria for them are more general and more objective ideals; he is not tied down in his action by habit, piety, and precedent.

Finally, the proportion of nearness and remoteness which gives the stranger the character of objectivity, also finds practical expression in the more abstract nature of the relation to him. That is, with the stranger one has only certain more general qualities in common, whereas the relation to more organically connected persons is based on the commonness of specific differences from merely general features. In fact, all somehow personal relations follow this scheme in various patterns. They are determined not only by the circumstance that certain common features exist among the individuals, along with individual differences, which either influence the relationship or remain outside of it.

The stranger is close to us, insofar as we feel between him and ourselves common features of a national, social, occupational, or generally human, nature. He is far from us, insofar as these common features extend beyond him or us, and connect us only because they connect a great many people.

A trace of strangeness in this sense easily enters even the most intimate relationships. In the stage of first passion, erotic relations strongly reject any thought of generalization: the lovers think that there has never been a love like theirs; that nothing can be compared either to the person loved or to the feelings for that person. An estrangement—whether as cause or as consequence, it is difficult to decide—usually comes at the moment when this feeling of uniqueness vanishes from the relationship. A certain skepticism in regard to its value, in itself and for them, attaches to the very thought that in their relation, after all, they carry out only a generally human destiny; that they experience an experience that has occurred a thousand times before; that, had they not accidentally met their particular partner, they would have found the same significance in another person.

Something of this feeling is probably not absent in any relation, however close, because what is common to two is never common to them alone, but is subsumed under a general idea which includes much else besides, many *possibilities* of commonness. No matter how little these possibilities become real and how often we forget them, here and there, nevertheless, they thrust themselves between us like shadows, like a mist which escapes every word noted, but which must coagulate into a solid bodily form before it can be called jealousy. In some cases, perhaps the more general, at least the more insurmountable, strangeness is not due to different and ununderstandable matters. It is rather caused by the fact that similarity, harmony, and nearness are accompanied by the feeling that they are not really the unique property of this particular relationship: they are something more general, something which potentially prevails between the partners and an indeterminate number of others, and therefore gives the relation, which alone was realized, no inner and exclusive necessity.

On the other hand, there is a kind of "strangeness" that rejects the very commonness based on something more general which embraces the parties. The relation of the Greeks to the Barbarians is perhaps typical here, as are all cases in which it is precisely general attributes, felt to be specifically and purely human, that are disallowed to the other. But "stranger," here, has no positive meaning; the relation to him is a non-relation; he is not what is relevant here, a member of the group itself.

As a group member, rather, he is near and far *at the same time,* as is characteristic of relations founded only on generally human commonness. But between nearness and distance, there arises a specific tension when the consciousness that only the quite general is common, stresses that which is not common. In the case of the person who is a stranger to the country, the city, the race, etc., however, this non-common element is once more nothing individual, but merely the strangeness of origin, which is or could be common to many strangers. For this reason, strangers are not really conceived as individuals, but as strangers of a particular type: the element of distance is no less general in regard to them than the element of nearness.

This form is the basis of such a special case, for instance, as the tax levied in Frankfort and elsewhere upon medieval Jews. Whereas the *Beede* [tax] paid by the Christian citizen changed with the changes of his fortune, it was fixed once for all for every single Jew. This fixity rested on the fact that the Jew had his social position as a *Jew,* not as the individual bearer of certain objective contents. Every other citizen was the owner of a particular amount of property, and his tax followed its fluctuations. But the Jew as a taxpayer was, in the first place, a Jew, and thus his tax situation had an invariable element. This same position appears most strongly, of course, once even these individual characterizations (limited though they were by rigid invariance) are omitted, and all strangers pay an altogether equal head-tax.

In spite of being inorganically appended to it, the stranger is yet an organic member of the group. Its uniform life includes the specific conditions of this element. Only we do not know how to designate the peculiar unity of this position other than by saying that it is composed of certain measures of nearness and distance. Although some quantities of them characterize all relationships, a *special* proportion and reciprocal tension produce the particular, formal relation to the "stranger."

DISCUSSION QUESTIONS

1. Simmel describes "the stranger" in a variety of ways. Describe your understanding of Simmel's "stranger" in your own words.
2. Whom did Simmel identify as "the stranger" in this essay?
3. Simmel published his essay "The Stranger" in his influential book *Sociology: Investigations on the Forms of Sociation* (1908) more than 100 years ago. In what ways does "the stranger" appear in today's global, capitalist society? Put another way, who are today's strangers?
4. Can society exist without "strangers"? How do you think Simmel would respond to this question? How is your response similar to or different from Simmel's?

ADDITIONAL RESOURCES

Internet

http://www.kporterfield.com/aicttw/articles/boardingschool.html. This website documents the tragic American history of American Indians' forced assimilation via "boarding schools" meant to erase their cultural differences from European Americans.

http://socio.ch/sim/bio.htm. This website features a nicely detailed biography of Georg Simmel.

Radio

http://www.npr.org/templates/story/story.php?storyId=16516865&ps=rs. May 12, 2008. This National Public Radio "Morning Edition" show features a chilling two-part story called "American Indian Boarding Schools Haunt Many."

FURTHER READING

Anzaldúa, Gloria. 1999. *Borderlands: The New Mestiza,* 2nd edition. San Francisco: Aunt Lute Press.

MacCannell, Dean. 1973. "Staged Authenticity: Arrangements of Social Space in Tourist Settings." *American Journal of Sociology,* 79(3): 589–603.

Ritzer, George and Allan Liska. 1997. "'McDisneyization' and 'Post-Tourism': Complementary Perspectives on Contemporary Tourism," in Chris Rojek and John Urry (eds.). *Touring Cultures: Transformations of Travel and Theory,* 97–109. New York: Routledge.

Stouffer, Samuel A. 1955. "Is There a National Anxiety Neurosis?" in *Communism, Conformity, and Civil Liberties Study,* 58–88. New York: Doubleday & Company.

Trask, Haunani-Kay. 1999. "Lovely Hula Hands: Corporate Tourism and the Prostitution of Hawaiian Culture," in *From a Native Daughter: Colonialism and Sovereignty in Hawaii,* 179–97. Honolulu: University of Hawaii Press.

Wolff, Kurt Wolff (trans., ed.). *The Sociology of Georg Simmel,* 402–8. New York: Free Press.

51. "What of the Children?" Emerging Homes and Identities

YEN LE ESPIRITU

Espiritu's research focuses on the strategies that second-generation Filipino Americans develop to find their place between two competing cultures. She conducted interviews with forty 17- to 35-year-olds who were children of Filipino immigrants living in San Diego, California, supplemented by statistical analysis of the Children of Immigrants Longitudinal Study in San Diego.

When asked why they chose to move their families from the Philippines to the United States, Filipino immigrant parents would say, "We did it for the children." In the United States, they believe, their children would have better health care, education, and job opportunities. Even when immigrant parents desired to return to the Philippines permanently, their children's welfare often mandated against such a move. This chapter discusses what it is like to grow up as young Filipinos in San Diego, paying particular attention to contestations over terms of inclusion, to instances of cross-group alliances, and to the constant transformation of ethnic identities. The point of my analysis is not to determine the extent to which second-generation Filipino Americans have retained their "original" culture or adopted the "American" culture. Rather, my interest is in the strategies these Filipino Americans have used to construct distinct new cultures and subcultures and to rework dominant ideologies about their place in the United States. In addition to my interview data, this chapter draws on quantitative data from the Children of Immigrants Longitudinal Study (CILS) conducted in San Diego in 1992 and again in 1995.

GROWING UP FILIPINO: "I DIDN'T FIT IN"

The CILS data indicate that of the approximately eight hundred Filipino high school students surveyed in 1995, close to two-thirds reported that they had experienced racial and ethnic discrimination. Among those suffering discrimination, it is important to note, their own race or nationality were the overwhelming forces perceived to account for that unfair treatment. My interviews with forty children of Filipino immigrants, ranging in age from seventeen to thirty-five, corroborate these findings: the majority related that they were ignored, teased, harassed, or ostracized by their peers because of their perceived racial difference. At the same time, reflecting the complexities of identities and identifications in contemporary United States, many Filipino San Diegans have ongoing relations—both cooperative and antagonistic—with multiple racial and ethnic groups. According to the 1995 CILS data, about 90 percent of the students surveyed stated that they had Filipino friends. But their circle of friends also included other racial and ethnic groups: more than 40 percent reported having (non-Filipino) Asian friends; about a quarter had Latino friends; 18 percent had white friends; and close to 4 percent had African American friends. These data suggest that white American culture, while still prominent, is no longer the only point of reference from which young Filipino Americans construct their identities. Not surprisingly, the family's choice of residence

Espiritu, Yen Le. 2003. "'What of the Children?' Emerging Homes and Identities" (selection from pp. 179–204), in *Home Bound: Filipino American Lives Across Cultures, Communities, and Countries*. Berkeley: University of California Press.

and school plays a major role in structuring the children's friendship patterns.

Multiracial Neighborhoods

Reflecting the long history of racial and class segregation in San Diego, multiracial neighborhoods house primarily working-class families, including a high number of Navy families. According to the 1992 CILS data, 43 percent of the respondent's fathers and 2.8 percent of the mothers were in either blue-collar or low-wage service jobs, and more than 50 percent of the fathers worked for or were retired from the U.S. Navy. In these neighborhoods, Filipino youngsters mingle and collide with other Filipinos as well as with those in other groups of color. Arturo Caponong, son of a U.S. Navy steward, had fond memories of his tight-knit Filipino neighborhood in National City, where he lived until he was thirteen: "All my friends were Filipino. We were a close community. It was almost like that one street, you know, maybe a strip of eight to ten houses, it was like a gigantic family.... All my friends' parents, I would call aunt or uncle. And they would know like each other's parents."

In Arturo's neighborhood, many of the mothers also had the same jobs, providing yet another bond for these families: "And the moms, they had this carpool thing going from National City to the job.... They all worked in assembly line-type jobs. They all carpool together, and they eat their lunch together. They would all come over when we have a birthday party or some celebration." These Filipino Navy families also shared other rituals, such as weekly trips to church and the commissary. According to Jovy Lopez, "It used to be a joke; most of the Filipinos are Catholics so we'd go to church and then after church you would see the same families at the commissary and the Navy Exchange and you would see them and they would look at you and acknowledge you."

These Filipino events pull the second generation into a Filipino-centered universe in which they can "hang out" with other Filipinos, eat Filipino food, enjoy Filipino music, and listen to spoken Tagalog, even if they themselves cannot speak it. For many young Filipinas, these get-togethers provided a meaningful space to discuss their lives as daughters of immigrant parents. Mona Ampon cherished the times that she shared with other Filipinas: "There was really a comfortable feeling because you ate the same food and you stay up late and watch videos and talk…because you know your parents are playing mah-jongg and socializing with their friends." These late-night talks invariably pivoted around the young women's often-stormy relationships with their parents—a forum to vent their frustrations over the numerous restrictions on their autonomy and mobility. For Mona, "trading stories" with like-minded Filipinas helped her to weather the difficult teen years:

> I was just really in a rebellious stage, you know, and I just thought that my parents were being really unfair. I was very policed by my parents. That was one thing that was good about having other Filipino women, you know, when we had these little get-togethers, we always talked about these kinds of stuff. You know, things like "if my parents ever found out this and that, this is what they would do.…" Talking about those kinds of things and sharing our upbringing. That really helped.

As these narratives suggest, the family and community get-togethers thrive because they nurture and reinforce Filipino claims to "community" and "home." But Grace Espartero, a multiracial Filipina, did not feel "at home" at these Filipino get-togethers. Grace's father was a Filipino immigrant and her mother a third-generation white American. Her paternal grandparents disapproved of the interracial marriage and often slighted Grace's mother at family functions. As the following excerpt indicates, Grace felt excluded because she was perceived to be "not Filipino enough":

> I hated going to my father's side. I saw them not real often, like Easter, Christmas, and there are a whole bunch of birthdays.…It was

always uncomfortable because...I wasn't that close like everybody else who would go there all the time. Most of my cousins, I don't know who they are. They all knew each other....I felt uncomfortable because I was half white too 'cuz I could see how they treated my mom, and her reactions were like a fight, and then I'd see that and I'd feel like they were doing that to me, too. I think also because I didn't understand what they were saying 'cuz they had very heavy accents, and it used to make me uncomfortable because I didn't know how to answer them. Just the fact that I didn't know all the cultures...and I thought if I did something wrong they would get really mad.

Henry Aguilar, who is gay, also felt uneasy at Filipino functions because his gayness often collided with the group's notion of what constituted Filipinoness:

It's really hard. I'm still finding it hard to go out to a Filipino gathering knowing that a lot of people would probably reject me if they find out that I am gay, because there aren't too many liberal-minded Filipinos out there. I mean, I can tell because when I go to my sister's party, a lot of Filipino guys who gather around drinking and talking about girls and all that and I can very much tell that if I say something about my lover, they will just stop the conversation or talk about something else.

Tension also emerged between Philippine-born and U.S.-born Filipinos. Dario Villa, who immigrated to San Diego at the age of seventeen, reported that he faced "overt racism" from the local Filipino Americans:

When we arrived in San Diego in 1976, I attended Montgomery High School in South San Diego. I was happy to be there because I saw many Filipino faces that reminded me of home....To my surprise, I offended many Filipinos because I was an "FOB"—"fresh off the boat." I was ridiculed because my accent reminded them of their parents. It was their shame coming out at my expense. I was a reminder of the image they hate, part of themselves. The overt racism from the Filipino Americans broke my heart....So I

had very few Filipino friends in high school, not because I didn't want to be friends with them, but because they didn't want to be friends with somebody who was their own but not really theirs.

U.S.-born Eleonor Ocampo admitted that in her quest to fit in with the high school crowds, she would harass the recently immigrated Filipinos:

In high school, we were at an age where we didn't want to be seen as the FOB, fresh-off-the-boat type of stereotype. And we were so bad that we would tease people who recently immigrated who had an accent. They would be, like, speaking the language and we would be, like, walking down the hall, "Why don't you guys learn English?" We would be as rude as that.

Joseph Gonzalez likewise acknowledged that he and his friends used to snub the "FOBs":

"The people who were fresh from the Philippines, we did not hang around them at all. I had this unfortunate belief that the newcomers were not as good as the people who were born here: they talked weird; they didn't understand the language; they dressed differently."

Grace, Henry, and Dario's vexed relationships with other Filipino Americans underscore the larger argument that I wish to make in this book: home, however nurturing and comforting, is by definition a place that is established as the exclusive domain of a few. In these cases, Filipinoness is defined as the exclusive domain of monoracial, heterosexual, and English-speaking Filipinos; all others, by definition, are constructed to be outside these carefully drawn and maintained boundaries.

The majority of the young Filipinos I interviewed, especially the women, reported that their parents forbade them to befriend African Americans. Eleonor Ocampo confided, "It's like an understood silence in my family; don't ever cross the line and marry an African American. It just saddens me because of the perception that my parents have of African Americans as being on welfare and lazy and crimes and gangs."

The above narratives suggest the following: all-Filipino and cross racial friendships emerged in part out of shared experiences within the racial economy of the United States. Although personal affinities drew young people together, it was their families' racial and economic subordination that landed them in the same neighborhoods and schools. But the narratives also indicate that shared experiences with subordination do not always produce meaningful friendships and alliances. Thus some Filipinos adopt anti-black and anti-Latino racism in an effort to secure ethnic inclusion for themselves. For their part, U.S.-born Filipinos, African Americans, and Mexican Americans taunt Dario, Nicholas, Mary, and Cecilia in part because they have internalized the anti-Asian and anti-immigrant rhetorics and practices that characterize so much of the culture and social structure in the United States.

White-Dominated Neighborhoods

A sizeable proportion of the post-1965 Filipino immigrants in San Diego are college-educated professionals who end up in the U.S. middle class. Of the students sampled for CILS, 30 percent of their fathers and almost 50 percent of their mothers had at least a college degree or more. The proportion of parents in white-collar occupations matches closely their educational attainment, with almost 60 percent of the mothers and 40 percent of the fathers in white-collar positions. Additionally, almost 75 percent of those sampled come from families that own their home, a strong indicator of middle-class status.

This is not to say that Filipino suburbanites are wholly isolated from other Filipinos. Although they may not live in immigrant neighborhoods, many actively maintain social ties with friends and kin through membership in various professional and alumni organizations and through family get-togethers in both the United States and the Philippines. However, from the perspective of the second generation, these "ethnic events" are periodic, brief, and disconnected from their otherwise white-dominated environment. As

Armando Alvarez explained, "Being Filipino was an event, it was going to a party on the weekend with my parents and eating Filipino food; that's when I was a Filipino. It was periodic and external.... We only associated with Filipinos, mostly my parents' friends, two, three, or maybe four times a year. The rest of the year, it didn't come into play."

In this largely white environment, young Filipinos reported that they were often teased, harassed, or excluded from social cliques and events. Pablo Barcenas remembered that he had to learn early on to fend off racial insults:

> I grew up in a neighborhood that was primarily white. I went to an all-white school. They always made fun of me and this other Chinese kid. It was really stereotypical jokes. I guess at the time, I just kinda had to play it off just like a survival thing because, you know, I was just by myself. But the jokes, when you're a kid, they hurt. Like my eyes aren't even slanted, but they'd always give the Japanese eye thing, they'd always called me a "Nip" or a "Chink" or something.

In high school, not fitting in extended to dating. "I was attracted, I remember, to white girls," said Joseph. "But the Anglo girls really didn't accept me. That was what started my feelings of lower self-esteem. I was small and I was not white. So the girls were not attracted to me. That was a big issue for me."

To counter the social costs of being racially different, many young Filipino Americans strove to be "average American teenagers": to speak only English, to date and associate primarily with whites, and to slight Filipino culture. Joseph Gonzalez detailed his efforts "to be white":

> I tried whatever I could to assimilate like the other Anglos. I did a lot of Anglo things like surfing, skiing, and I listened to not real Filipino-type music. I did a lot of things that were almost anti-Filipino. I didn't hang around Filipinos. I didn't join Filipino organizations. And I really missed out. I really did, because I didn't have any real, real, true friends that

could understand my culture. I was just setting myself up for being left out. And even the types of girls that I would go after were not the ones that would be attracted to me.

When Mona Ampon moved to the other side of town and attended a white-majority high school, she too developed an "identity crisis": "I had this identity crisis where I just wanted to be white. I guess the feeling of just wanting to be accepted. I started to recognize that, you know, people who were white who had blond hair and blue eyes were popular. And that's what you want to be, you want that attention." Mona plotted to join the popular groups:

What you had to do to be popular was basically you had to hang out with people who were white and they were usually wealthy, like they lived in the gated community. And they were the ones who threw the parties. So I joined the tennis team. Going through the tennis team, I met those girls and because I was playing really well, they wanted to practice with me. And that's where I started to be invited to parties. I remember trying to wear all the same brand-name clothes and stuff like that. I feel so sorry for my parents because, like, we used to go to these outlet stores and I made them wait, like, in these three-hour lines to get into the stores to buy me those clothes.

Even though Mona was invited to the parties, she never felt included: "During my senior year, I just got tired of the social scene because I was always getting hurt, you know, because I would think that these people were my friends and then they would talk behind my back."

A small group of Filipino Americans eventually managed to penetrate the all-white cliques, through honors courses, through sports, or through other school activities such as the school band and yearbook club. But most were forced to set aside their Filipino selves in the process. Raul Calderon related how he lost touch with his Filipino side during high school:

In high school, most of my friends were white. So, say my friends were having a party, I really

couldn't invite my cousins because they are not used to hanging out with white people. And they really couldn't invite me to their parties 'cause I wasn't used to hanging out with Filipinos. So at that point there was kind of a tension between me and some of my cousins. Some of them are very Filipino centered and some have only black friends.

In the same way, Pablo Bacenas felt "out of place" at all-Filipino events:

When I went to this dance, it was all Filipino. I felt so out of place. I felt really weird. I have never seen so many young Filipinos in my life. It was just a funny feeling. I think I was just making the whole thing really hard on myself, like, I didn't talk to anyone. I wasn't sure what to say. I guess I must have thought that I was supposed to act this way or something. I felt maybe there was something lacking in what I knew about myself. I stayed the whole dance, but I didn't dance. In my mind, I pictured they could pick me out of the whole crowd that I was different, that I was a little more like whiter, Americanized, or something.

In the following narrative, Joey Laguda details how excruciating it was for U.S.-born Filipinos like himself to strike a balance between the Filipino and white groups:

I remember in high school I stopped a fight between the Filipinos that just moved to the States and some white people. That was really weird. I remember telling the Filipinos to knock it off. I said, "You make us all look bad" because I worked hard at that time to integrate myself, to make sure that there is no difference between Filipinos and white people. I didn't want to be associated with any negative feedback like, "Oh, Filipinos hate white people." But I saw both sides. I could see that it was hard for the new Filipinos to fit in. I see my brothers [who were born in the Philippines] having a hard time fitting in and having language barriers.

For Joey, being in the middle was more than he could handle:

Basically, it was so much going back and forth that sometimes I lost myself. What the hell are these Filipinos doing? What the hell are these white people doing? So I was bouncing back and forth, and in trying to understand, I got caught up in a lot of things....Since I wasn't a part of either group, I didn't quite fit in either model. I got really lost and I got involved in alcohol, drugs, and gangs. I just got into it, basically trying to understand what didn't really make much sense.

Although these personal narratives document on the individual level an acceptance of the given rules of U.S. society, they are important because they are part of a dialogue of domination. They reveal that young Filipinos live within and in tension with a racist system that defines white middle-class culture as the norm.

For these young Filipino Americans, repeated encounters with the inequalities of a race-based social world at first puzzled and wounded them but ultimately led them to reconsider their relationship to and understanding of their assigned place in U.S. society—and in so doing, to act.

LANGUAGE AND CULTURE: "NOBODY TALKS ABOUT FILIPINOS"

When Joey Laguda was in elementary school, his friends used to think he was Chinese. When he told them that he was Filipino, they were puzzled: "What is a Filipino?" The invisibility of Filipino Americans in U.S. culture prompts at least one second-generation Filipina to exclaim, "Nobody ever talks about Filipinos." As evident in the accounts of racism above, young Filipinos were repeatedly mistaken for Chinese, Japanese, and even Mexican. Armando Alvarez's experience is typical: "In my high school, they didn't know how to discriminate against me. They called me like Kung Fu. They called me Tojo because of World War II, and they called me VC because of the Vietnam War, and things like that." While these mistakes may reflect genuine ignorance, they also are symptomatic of a society that is racialized and yet indifferent to or contemptuous of the racial differences and hybridization among its peoples.

School curriculum also marginalizes the experiences of U.S. Filipinos. No matter where young Filipinos attended school, whether in underresourced or affluent school districts, they seldom learned about Filipino American or Philippine history in their classes. High school senior Lisa Graham hungered for more information on the Philippines and Filipino culture:

> I want to learn more about Filipino culture, but I don't know how to go about it. I wish they would teach that kind of stuff in school because it would make things a lot easier. But if you want to learn about the Filipino culture, you have to go do your own research on your own time. In school, they don't really teach us about the Philippines. Once in a while in world history, the teacher will mention the Philippines. That class usually puts me to sleep, but when the teacher says anything about the Philippines, I wake up. I am interested. I want to know more about the Philippines, because it has something to do with me.

Many young Filipinos I interviewed also complained that even in their homes, "nobody talks about Filipinos." With some bitterness, Armando Alvarez told of what he perceived to be a "cultural void" in his family:

> Not much was going on at my house. Nothing. It wasn't made explicit that Filipino culture is something that we should retain, that we should hold on to, as something that's valuable. There wasn't that sense that we should keep the language. So you don't really get taught, you know. And I found that to be a real common experience among Filipinos my age. Our parents don't realize that we don't know anything about the old country: Who was the first president, when was Independence Day, who was Jose Rizal?

On the issue of language, Filipino children of immigrants are unequivocally moving toward being monolingual, that is, speaking English only. Many of the young Filipinos I interviewed deeply regretted their inability to speak a Filipino language. As Agnes Gonzalez stated, "I want to be a Filipina, but

I can't really say that I am a true Filipina because I don't know how to speak the language. I wish my parents had taught me." And Lisa Graham reported, "Once in a while, I would ask my mom how to say this and that in Tagalog. I always hear her talking Tagalog on the phone. I wish there were a Tagalog class at school so I could learn."

CLAIMING HOME: "I AM AMERICAN!"
"You're not American," her friend said. But Grace Espartero defiantly shot back, "I too am. I was born here. I *am* American!" This too-familiar exchange encapsulates the failure of U.S. citizenship to guarantee truly equal rights to all the nation's citizenry. Like other Asian Americans, Filipino Americans—even as U.S. born citizens—continue to be constructed as different from, and as other than, Americans of European origin. Many young Filipinos, like Juanita Domingo, understood full well the bounds of U.S. citizenship:

> You can't really ever be looked upon as completely American just because of what you look like, even though you were born here, even though you grew up here, even though you speak English very well. The first impression a person is going to have is that you don't belong here because of how you look.

According to Ruby Partido, her racial awareness began in her senior year in high school when an academic counselor discouraged her from applying to the University of California. An active and above-average high school student, Ruby was baffled by the counselor's advice: "I remember coming home crying. My self-confidence was really low." When Ruby asked her friends about their experiences with the same counselor, she discovered that while her white friends received ample information on colleges and scholarships, her Filipino friends were advised against applying to prestigious universities—even though they had higher grades. "It started clicking in my head. They are picking us out just because we are not white. This was the first time that I ever started getting any sense of awareness, or consciousness,

that I am different." For Leah Dullas, anti-Filipino racism targeted her body:

> One time, I was walking with a friend of mine and it was late, getting kind of dark, and there were these couple of guys and you could tell they had been drinking whatever, and so we walked by and they were like, "I hear Oriental girls give a good time," and I was just like, "Oh, my God!" I was ready just to blow up, but I was also so scared so we just walked away and ignored them. It was so sexist and so racist.

The ability to name racism provides young Filipinos with a frame of reference not only for understanding contemporary incidents but also for reinterpreting childhood episodes. Noting that the experience of racism is cumulative, Armando Alvarez revealed, "My personal understanding of things in the present has allowed me to give names and labels to my experiences in the past. Before, I could only describe it as a 'weird experience.' I didn't understand why they didn't like me, why they kept calling me Jap or Gook when I am Filipino."

Mindful that outsiders generally lump all Asians together, many Filipino American activists herald their common fate to build political unity with other Asian Americans. Nicholas Santos described the impact on his identity of lumping all Asians together:

> Growing up, I never saw myself as Asian. When I thought of Asian, it was like the Chinese, Japanese, you know. But eventually, I think my experiences sort of helped me to understand that I have this racial uniform. I've been called, ya know, Chink, Jap. Most of the times I have been called a Chink. So I would look in the mirror and say, "Humph, maybe I do look Chinese! Maybe I do look Asian!"

Similarly, Ella Labao recounted how she developed her Asian American consciousness:

> Not until I became a freshman at San Diego State did I really get involved in the Asian American Student Alliance. I met some friends in some of my classes and we got to be really good friends.

A lot of them are Japanese descent. We went to a statewide Asian American Conference, and it was a really good experience. I learned a lot about being Asian American. Just to put it bluntly, we all are going through the same thing and we are all Asian American; we are all minorities here. You know, we're all striving for the same thing. Just because you're Filipino American, Chinese American, Japanese American, whatever, we're all Asian American.

Other Filipino Americans attributed their racial consciousness to their friendships with Latinos and African Americans. As Maria Galang put it, "I think my racial consciousness was raised because I hung around more with blacks in high school." Jovy Lopez attributed her current commitment to racial justice to her early friendships with Latino neighbors and classmates: "I guess it made me more culturally aware and sensitive than some people who only grew up among one race." In the same way, Nicholas Santos credited his African American friends with sharpening his racial awareness: "In some ways they were demything me. Like, one time, I told a black friend, 'Larry, I want to be a doctor or an astronaut.' And he said, 'You believe that shit? I mean, how do you know that white America is not putting something on you?' And I certainly got a lot out of that. To be careful of trusting the establishment." Nicholas identified the organic links between Filipino Americans and African Americans:

I realized that what it is to be Filipino American was closer to the African American experience. I think it was Kareem Adbul Jabar who wrote that he refused to join the Olympic team to represent America because he didn't want to play for a country that was not his country. But then his mentor told him, "Don't you ever say that America is not your country because your forefathers' sweat, blood, and tears went into this land, into making it what it is now." So now when people tell me, "Go back to where you came from," I always think to myself, "Wait a minute, who planted the fields of Hawaii? Who built the canneries in Alaska? Filipinos did. So

don't tell me that I can't stay here. I have a stake here." So there were those parallel experiences that I felt comfortable in claiming or understanding. I can never be black, but it is comforting to know that I am not alone.

African American history of racial struggles was thus central to Nicholas's claim for full citizenship rights for him and his children:

I want my [future] children to realize that this is their country, that historically the Filipinos, the *manongs*, the field workers…helped build America and that is our heritage. Nobody can tell me to go back to where I came from because as far as I am concerned, this is my home. I have a stake in this country in that I like to see it get better, get more humane, get more kind.

As Nicholas suggested, to stake a claim in the United States, one must fight for a "better, more humane, and more kind" society. Many young Filipino activists did just that. Equal opportunities for education topped their agenda as they tutored and organized "college days" for underrepresented high school students, fought for the admission and retention of students of color on college campuses, and demanded an education that was more relevant and accessible to their communities. For Ruby Partido, working for the Student Affirmative Action/Economic Opportunity Program (SAA/EOP) on her college campus sensitized her to issues of student retention and multiculturalism and helped forge her identity as a student of color: "I was out there on the front line, you know, helping students of color pass classes and talk out their problems." Samantha Reyes attributed her activism to her relationship with her African American roommate and to the racially charged atmosphere of her college campus:

It was gradual, my becoming active. My roommate, she is an African American, and I learned a lot from her about the civil rights movement, about the things that she learned in high school that I didn't learn. I felt so dumb compared to her because she was so much more aware. And

I started taking classes, and we discussed issues of race in terms of what teachers are teaching, the lack of offerings in African American classes, Asian American Studies classes. I really wanted to become involved. It was something I needed to claim for myself. So I got involved. And we wanted to make sure that there was more hiring of women professors and more hiring of professors to teach ethnic studies courses or just to have more Asian American and African American professors, Hispanic professors, more gay and lesbian professors.

As young Filipino activists fought for social justice in the United States, their thoughts often turned to the Philippines, with how to help with the social struggles there. Eleonor Ocampo described the strong responsibility she felt toward the Philippines:

> I would say that the Philippines has a special place in my heart because that's where my roots are. I think there is a stronger sense of hurt when I see, like, when I saw a film in an urban planning class about the development of the international workforce, it has a segment on the Philippines, and you know, I saw what they did to the women workers. And I was ready to cry because, you know, I am fighting for so much here, for Asian Americans in America, but yet there is a sense of helplessness that I can't go back and make a difference for my people, the Filipino people. So, I would jockey back and forth between…Asian American issues versus Asian and Filipino issues. Do I stay within the confines of North America, or do I take a second look at what's going in the government back home and the people back home? Where can I best be of help? I don't really know much about the Philippines, a land that is so far away, but yet I know that's where my heart truly is.

Few Filipino Americans took the next step to join the social movements in the Philippines.

However, the majority of the Filipino activists I interviewed made peace with themselves by focusing their energy on the local struggles. As Arturo Coponong related, "Two years ago I was leaning toward living in the Philippines. And helping out the people there. But then I realized that I probably could be of better use if I stay here and help out the Filipinos that are here." Even for Maricela Rebaya, who planned to return to the Philippines "to help the people," the move would only be temporary: "When I finish college, one of my goals is to bring something back to the Philippines and maybe work there or something. To help the people. But I probably don't want to live there because I can do more if I am here."

The multiple subject positions of second-generation Filipino Americans remind us that identities are not fixed or singular, but multiple, overlapping, and simultaneous and that they reflect events both in the United States as well as in the "home country." Filipino immigrant children thus live with paradoxes. They feel strong symbolic loyalty to the Philippines, but they know very little about it and have little contact with their parents and other adults who might educate them about it. They feel pressured to become like "Americans," but their experiences as racialized subjects leave them with an uneasy relationship with both Filipino and U.S. culture. They display the visible markers of assimilation yet remain ferociously nationalist. Their case thus demonstrates the impossibility both of complete assimilation within U.S. society and of a return to the Philippines for these youths. In the end, for many second-generation Filipino Americans, *here* is home—at least for now. They have claimed this space; it is theirs. As Jovy Lopez exclaimed, "This is the country that I was born in, and it's my country too. It's just as much my country as anyone else's. This *is* my home."

DISCUSSION QUESTIONS

1. According to Espiritu's research, why do most Filipinos immigrate to the United States?
2. Espiritu describes key differences in the experience of Filipino youth who were born in the United States and those who immigrate to the United States during their youth. What are some of these distinctions?
3. What is an "FOB," and what role does this concept play in the lives of Filipino Americans and how they relate to one another?
4. Identify at least three strategies Filipino American youth use to fit into American society.
5. How do these coping strategies change as the youth transition from high school to college?

ADDITIONAL RESOURCES

Film

"Filipino Americans: Discovering Their Past for the Future." 1994. This documentary details the 400-year history of Filipino immigration to the United States from the late 16th century to the early 21st century. Analysis includes the significant contributions Filipinos have made to American culture. 54 minutes. http://www.nationalvideo.com/filip.html.

A PBS "Point of View" feature, "Kelly Loves Tony" (1998) is the story of a young and unlikely Southeast Asian American couple trying to make a go of it despite the challenges they face. This is a moving tale about second-generation immigrants moving between social worlds. 57 minutes. http://www.pbs.org/pov/kellylovestony/.

Internet

http://cmd.princeton.edu/data%20CILS.shtml. The website for The Children of Immigrants Longitudinal Study, housed by the Center for Migration and Development at Princeton University.

http://www.filameda.org/Film.htm. The Filipino American Educators of San Diego County sponsor a Filipino language movement to preserve Filipino language and culture in the United States.

http://www.filipinoamericanlibrary.org/. The website for the Filipino American Library, located in Los Angeles.

http://www.fanhs-national.org/. The website for the Filipino American National Historical Society.

http://www.migrationinformation.org/Feature/display.cfm?id=445. The website for the Migration Information Source, featuring a 2006 article, "The Second Generation in Early Adulthood: New Findings from the Children of Immigrants Longitudinal Study."

http://www.migrationpolicy.org/. The website for the Migration Policy Institute.

http://www.youtube.com/watch?v=nX08a6HYttw. Author Sandra Cisneros describes the inspiration for her stirring novel *The House on Mango Street*.

FURTHER READING

Cisneros, Sandra. 1991. *The House on Mango Street*. London: Vintage (Random House).

Espiritu, Yen Le. 2003. *Home Bound: Filipino American Lives Across Cultures, Communities, and Countries*. Berkeley: University of California Press.

Kasinitz, Philip, John Mollenkopf, and Mary C. Waters. 2004. "Worlds of the Second Generation," in *Becoming New Yorkers*, 1–19. New York: Russell Sage.

Lee, Yueh Ting, et al. 2002. "Attitudes Toward U.S. Immigration Policy: The Roles of In-Group-Out-Group Bias, Economic Concern, and Obedience to Law." *The Journal of Social Psychology*, 142(5): 617–34.

Okamura, Jonathan. 1998. *Imagining the Filipino American Diaspora: Transnational Relations, Identities, and Communities.* New York: Routledge.

52. The New Adulthood? The Transition to Adulthood from the Perspective of Transitioning Young Adults

DOUGLAS HARTMANN AND TERESA TOGUCHI SWARTZ

Hartmann and Swartz base their research on in-depth interviews with 54 participants in the University of Minnesota's longitudinal Youth Development Study. They note significant generational shifts in conceptions of adulthood between the interviewees and their parents.

In recent years, social scientists from numerous fields have argued that the transition to adulthood has become more complicated, multifaceted, and extended than ever before, so much so that they believe it is best understood as a distinct phase in the life course. But, while scholars have learned a great deal about the various pathways and structural forces that define this new "young" or "emerging" adulthood, we know much less about how it is understood and experienced by the young people actually living through the stage. What do "transitioning" young adults know and think about themselves and their lives as they move into "traditional" adult roles, those of worker, partner/spouse, and parent? Are they aware of the ways in which their experiences are different from their parents? Do they think of themselves as being in a distinct life phase or period? Do they assign any particular meaning and significance to it? What challenges and obstacles do they believe stand in their way? How do they understand their lives and adulthood more generally?

Research on these more subjective, culturally oriented questions has so far been dominated by psychologists. Sociologists have begun to re-examine these claims in the past few years, focusing especially on the salience and timing of traditional, more socially oriented markers of adulthood.

Although such work lays an important foundation, further research remains to flesh out these broad-brush renderings of subjective states and personal perceptions of young adults in the transition to adulthood. Even more important, we need to gather data on their broader, more

Hartmann, Douglas and Teresa Toguchi Swartz. 2007. "The New Adulthood? The Transition to Adulthood from the Perspective of Transitioning Young Adults," in Ross Macmillan (ed.). *Constructing Adulthood: Agency and Subjectivity in Adolescence and Adulthood. Advances in Life Course Research,* 11: 253–86.

synthetic views about adulthood and young adulthood taken as a whole: how do they conceptualize young adulthood in their own terms? Do they really see it as a new and distinct phase in the life course? What is meaningful or significant about it? How do they understand the relationship of this part of life to more traditional conceptions of adulthood? The goal of this paper is to draw on a new battery of intensive, life history interviews we conducted with selected participants in the University of Minnesota's longitudinal Youth Development Study (YDS) to generate some answers to these questions and in doing so to cultivate a deeper and broader understanding of the challenges and possibilities of the transition to adulthood that emerge when we take subjective states and cultural meaning worlds seriously.

SAMPLE AND METHOD

Young adults interviewed for this chapter are all long-term participants of the YDS. The YDS has followed a panel of young people from St. Paul, Minnesota since 1987. The initial YDS sample was drawn randomly from a list of ninth grade students attending public schools (1,138 students and their parents consented to participate, including 128 Hmong families). The first data collection took place in the Spring of 1988 (1,105 students completed the first-wave surveys) when most panel members were 14 and 15 year old. Parents also completed surveys during the first year and four years later. The panel included teenagers of diverse social backgrounds although because the sample was drawn in the public schools, it does not represent the more affluent residents of the city who send their children to private or parochial schools.

The panel has been followed via annual surveys in all years (with the exception of 1996 and 2001) since 1988, which have enabled us to monitor their aspirations and plans with respect to future work and education, as well as family formation; their investment in work and education, and the quality of their occupational experiences. In addition to this survey data, several subsamples of participants were interviewed in early adulthood. We drew participants for our current project from three specific batteries of earlier interviews. The first was a 1999–2000 study of some 69 YDS respondents who were interviewed regarding their work experiences and occupational choice. Twenty-four of these respondents, spread across each of the three career-decision trajectories, were re-interviewed for the present project.

The second interview-based study we used to draw our current sample consisted of 31 YDS female respondents who had indicated on their surveys that they had received AFDC during the previous five years. These young women were interviewed in 1999 about their experiences while receiving welfare. For the current study, 20 of these women were re-interviewed. The final subsample of research participants were drawn from the 42 Hmong YDS subjects who responded to the 2000 YDS survey. Five Hmong men and five Hmong women were interviewed for a total of 10 Hmong respondents. About half of these respondents had been interviewed previously regarding their educational, work, and family experiences. Although the other half had not been interviewed previously, they were recruited for this qualitative study to increase the number of Hmong participants, and thus enhance our understanding of the experiences of young Hmong immigrants as they move into adulthood in Minnesota.

The 54 in-depth, semistructured interviews were conducted during the summer and fall of 2001 by Swartz and YDS collaborator, Lorie Grabowski. They averaged between 1½ and 2 hours in length and took place in a convenient location for participants, often in their homes or local coffee shops, and less often at their workplace. All interviews were tape recorded, and descriptive and analytic field notes were written up by the interviewers to provide the necessary context information and to facilitate ongoing analysis. Interview tapes were transcribed and coded by a team of research assistants using the qualitative analysis software package Atlas.ti and working under the supervision of Hartmann and Swartz.

YOUNG ADULTHOOD AS A PACKAGE

Our first and arguably single most important finding is that, contrary to the claims of psychologists, our respondents' conceptions of their emerging adult status and of adulthood more generally remain very much tied to traditional social roles and demographic markers. When we asked them questions about the timing of their own entry into adulthood, we got rich personal narratives that consistently harkened back to specific markers and traditional demographic indicators. For instance, when asked whether he thought of himself as an adult, John, a White college-educated man from working-class origins, exclaimed, "I try not to a whole lot!," but then went on to explain that he indeed thought of himself as an adult because "[I'm] 29. I have a full time job, I earn a decent wage, I own my own car, I have a fiancée, I'm looking at buying a house." For John, age and traditional markers of adulthood were important to his perception of himself as an adult.

Some of our respondents pegged their "emerging adulthood" to a single moment or marker, such as child-bearing, setting up a household, or landing a job as might be the case when answering a standard survey. Twenty-nine-year-old Jake laughed when asked if he thought of himself as an adult. "Most of the time," he said hesitantly. When asked when he started thinking of himself as an adult, Jake, an attorney working for a large firm in downtown Chicago, said that it was on launching his law career, "Probably when I started working at a law firm, once I was out of school." Similarly, Scott, an undercover police officer, suggested age and work as important to his self-perception of being adult. "Probably mid-twenties....It's about the time I became a cop and I had to get pretty serious...the job kind of dictated that, you get more responsibilities." Having children in their teens or early twenties was experienced by many women in our sample as pushing them abruptly into adulthood. For instance, Alicia, a biracial poor mother of three, remembered first considering herself an adult during her senior year of high school—"right after I had my kid....I had no choice. I had to take care of [her], that's my responsibility."

Even those who had a conception of themselves as grown-up in many respects sometimes experienced their adult status as limited when they had not yet achieved or had lost an adult role that they themselves or others defined as a central marker of adulthood. For instance, although Kate, the young college-educated mother introduced earlier, considered herself to be an adult she felt her adult status was challenged by the fact that she now worked as a cashier at a pizza place. Even Jake, our attorney, insisted, "There are now degrees of adults." While he believed his position in the law firm legitimately granted him status as an adult where "I can behave the same in a courtroom as someone who's 50 or 60," he still hesitated to confidently declare himself an adult. Instead, his single status (when he wanted to be married) and his residence in a trendy urban apartment (when he wanted to own a home in the suburbs) limited his own sense of himself as fully adult in the way he wanted to be. "I'm not a settled adult," he said resigning himself to his perception that he had yet to realize his view of adulthood, which consisted of a constellation of adult roles, rather than achieving a single marker.

The key point here is that when asked to talk about their adulthood in their own terms, young adults used the language of independence, maturity, autonomy, and responsibility, but almost always tied these concepts to social roles and statuses, experiences with others, and involvement in other and often new social positions and relationships. What is more, many of our respondents appeared to experience, understand, and explain these more abstract attributes and qualities only insofar as they were tied to concrete social roles and experiences. Indeed, more than a few respondents resorted to individualistic qualities such as "independence" or "maturity" only after coming at a loss for words when they were prompted to describe the characteristics they believed defined adulthood.

BEING POSITIVE ABOUT THE PROCESS

It is important to emphasize that our respondents thought about and understood their early adulthood not only as a cluster of social roles and individualistic attributes but also as an ongoing, dynamic process. For these young people, adulthood was not a stagnant state that they had (or had not yet) achieved, but something they were constantly growing into or becoming. For instance, Julia, an occupational therapist, told us that she started thinking of herself as an adult as soon as she turned 20 years old but that it really didn't take hold until much later in her twenties. "I think just more independence and being away from family and having that independence and making my own decisions. I think that continued to grow, that feeling, that maybe it wasn't quite as strong [at first]." Asked about people her age who she believed were successful, a florist we named Trina talked about those who were striving to be more financially independent, to do things they want to do, and to cultivate loving personal relationships. "I don't expect everything to happen overnight. It's kind of like small steps every day." "In my mind," she explicitly concluded, "it's all kind of a process."

Several young women who had retreated from the workforce in order to stay home with young children also experienced young adulthood as nonlinear, but for them there was no sense of regret or remorse about back-sliding. Indeed, for women with young children early adulthood was a time when they felt the need to prioritize competing adult roles. Self-described stay-at-home mothers described moving out of full-time or career-oriented work in order to focus on childrearing (even while several still earned income through part-time or in-home work) as "embracing family responsibilities." These women did not expect to stay home for most of their adult lives, but planned to do so

temporarily while their children were young. For example Tricia, a stay-at-home mother and in-home day care provider, planned to earn a bachelor's degree once her children enter school and hopes to eventually launch an undefined career: "When I'm all done having babies, when all of my kids are in school all day, so first grade and older, I'm going to school part-time at night. So…when all my kids are in school, I'll finish up whatever I have to do to get my degree and then I'll get a job outside the home." Kate, the college graduate who was working as a cashier at a pizza place (for the family-friendly flexible hours while her daughters were small), still expected to go to graduate school to become a school librarian when her children were a little older. She envisioned that her work hours as a school librarian would parallel her children's school and vacation schedules, thus allowing her to balance work and family obligations. Adulthood, for these young mothers, was a long and open-ended process that would take shape as their work and family roles unfolded for years to come.

The fact that our respondents experienced this early adulthood as a process—gradual, multifaceted, open-ended, and even erratic—will not be particularly surprising for scholars who have been tracking the variable and uneven attainment of traditional adulthood markers for young people in this cohort. But what is of interest here is how our young folks understand and evaluate this process in contrast to the experts.

For instance, after several years of practicing law focused on corporate litigation, Jake contemplated a career move because he "would feel better about myself doing [something other] than defending a large company, and a lot of times the frivolous law suits, where it's larger companies fighting each other." In order to feel "a passion for what I'm doing," Jake sought more intrinsically meaningful work. This liberal-leaning young attorney hoped to spend his energies working for the U.S. Attorney's office or another entity, which he saw as defending the common good or those with less power. Jake did not feel trapped in a career trajectory that left him unfulfilled, but felt empowered to fashion his work life to reflect his values and interests. He also believed that his talent, education, and experience would enable him to successfully make such a change.

Optimism about the future came from the overwhelming majority of our respondents, even those who had experienced hardships as children or in adolescence. For the most part, even the more challenged young adults believed that hard work and determination would eventually pay off for them. Bo, for instance, a 30-year-old White man from a lower class family, remained very optimistic about his work future even though he had spent most of his teen years and early adulthood in dead-end, low-wage work, sometimes unable to even afford food and rent. At the time of his interview, Bo had recently been laid off from a factory job and was using his time on unemployment insurance to go to community college, hoping to eventually earn a business degree to develop a well-paying business career. When asked about the likelihood that he would achieve his ambitions, Bo replied: "I think having the credentials to be able to get a job, I think is a huge part of it and I think work ethic is a big part of it too. If I have to do something completely different tomorrow, as long as I'm willing and able to work at it, I think I will be fine."

As a single man with no dependents, Bo felt he could make sacrifices now to achieve his future goals. Poorer respondents with little education and who faced daily responsibilities for providing for dependents may have been optimistic about changing to better jobs and experiencing some upward mobility, but often found their options were more constrained. Lee, a Hmong working-class father who works for a utilities company, for example, imagined his future after describing his difficult employment experiences including a recent incident of racial discrimination in the workplace: "I think it might be better. When my kids grow up and I can complete my apprenticeship then bring more money, then I might be able to do a lot of things that I really want to do." For

the most part, lower and working class respondents, particularly those with dependent children who they had to continue to provide for, may have expressed optimism about financial stability and even upward mobility, but their aspirations often remained modest, for example, acquiring "clean" office jobs if they currently did manual labor, opening an in-home family day care or a foster home, or increasing the commission they received from phone solicitations or bill collections.

The most typical exceptions to the general optimism expressed by the young adults were young women who had been single, welfare-dependent mothers in their late teens and early twenties. Many who had lived through this experience were cautious about what the future might bring. They hesitated in imagining what their lives would be like beyond their continued relationships with their children. "I[t] will be me and my kids, something simple," said Alicia, a biracial, homeless mother of three. "I don't want to get my hopes too high for nothing, me and my kids and I'm not looking at a man or male figure. Just me and my kids, everything going pretty good." A White divorced mother of two put it like this: "I think it is going to be crazy because my kids are going to be teenagers. I think there is definitely going to be stressful points, but I think it is going to be wonderful." While few expressed outright pessimism, several balked at sharing definite plans or hopes for the future many seemed to feel they had little control over. As Tasha, a single African-American mother of three, explained: "I have no idea because I like taking one day at a time and it's hard to [predict] the future because I don't want to disappoint myself. If I don't try and predict and say what I think should happen then I won't disappoint myself." Similarly, when asked what she thought her life would be like in five years, Gina, a White mother of one with a second on the way, replied: "I don't even know. I don't even know. I'm having a kid, I know that one. So hopefully I'll have a kid and things will get easier, that's all I'm hoping for. I don't know, I just want things to get easier, that's all I'm hoping for." Talk of returning to school to meet long-term goals or of changing careers to more meaningful or lucrative work was less prevalent in their descriptions of their imagined future. Like their peers, these young women experienced young adulthood as indeterminate and changing, and expected this to continue in the future. However, more than in the other groups we spoke with these women anticipated this unpredictability as potentially bringing future hardship rather than positive prospects.

The caution of once-welfare-dependent mothers stands in stark contrast to our Hmong respondents who also had high rates of early childbirth and economic hardship. To a person, the Hmong young adults in our sample displayed an almost boundless sense of optimism about their accomplishments in life and future opportunities. Even those individuals who had come to the United States in their late teens, attained little education, and worked in low-wage work were hopeful about their futures and the futures of their children. Of course, Hmong immigrants constitute an exceptional if not extraordinary case. As refugees from Thailand (some recalled memories of escaping from war-torn Laos, crossing the Mekong River, and witnessing the deaths of family members who did not make it out successfully), their parents were mostly illiterate and essentially impoverished on their arrival in the United States. They had already survived very traumatic childhoods and had seen their fortunes increase dramatically over their lifetime. In view of this past, these Hmong young adults believed that they would continue to succeed in life, no matter what life threw their way. One young Hmong woman sums this up: "... considering all of the different things I've gone through, I would say that I've weathered [the] storm pretty well and life is full of possibilities but you have to be open to them and that's what I have always tried to do. For me, if one door closes, five or six open, and it's just a matter of realizing what's an opportunity....I know that I'm not that old but I've been through so much. I guess life is what you make it, you have to want things to make it happen."

Almost without exception, the young people we interviewed were convinced that the existence of dynamic, individualistic pathways into adulthood enabled each person to choose their own way in a manner that more accurately reflected his or her true personal desires and readiness for social roles and responsibilities. Waiting to have children until after marriage, completing education before moving on to other endeavors, or attaining financial self-sufficiency—these pathways were often seen to make adult life easier, but our respondents also insisted that this was not the case for every individual, and they certainly denied that any were moral imperatives.

This deeply held belief that variability and individuality in the transition to adulthood was preferable to a clear timetable for achieving milestones not only allows for many different pathways into adulthood. It also means that the process of discovering and developing one's adulthood can stretch much further into the life cycle than many older or more traditional Americans would ever imagine possible.

CONCLUSION AND DISCUSSION

This chapter offers two main insights into the subjective experience of the transition to adulthood, and one unresolved, albeit provocative, question. The first and most basic finding is that people in their late twenties experience the transition to adulthood as a dynamic, multi-dimensional package of new social roles and personal attributes. The second is that these young adults not only accept the open-ended, diverse, and uneven nature of this transition, they embrace it as a condition to be celebrated, valued, and perpetuated. There is some reason to believe that these two characteristics, taken together, constitute the subjective or experiential dimensions of a distinct new phase in the life course—what scholars looking at objective markers have most commonly referred to as young or early adulthood. However, a good deal of evidence also suggests that it could be that these attitudes and understandings signal a broader and deeper re-conceptualization of adulthood itself. In this view, adulthood is coming to be understood as less of a static state or a permanent status (as our respondents believe it was for those of their parents' generation) and more of an ongoing process of continued personal growth, career mobility, and the deepening and expanding of relationships with others—an ongoing process of development, achievement and discovery that extends across the life course, occurs in all domains of life, and varies from individual to individual.

The potential consequences and implications of these emerging conceptions among young people are also broad and complicated, so we conclude with two general comments. On the positive side, we believe that these results may indicate that young people moving into adulthood are uniquely situated and prepared for the changing economy and labor market and social demands that await them. It may even be that these subjective attitudes and conceptions will allow them to experience a deeper, more satisfying and meaning-filled adult life. In contrast, we are also concerned that all of this optimism about the dynamic, diverse, and extended processes of being and becoming an adult does not appear to be matched by a particularly high degree of planning and purposiveness, much less an awareness of the constraints that can make life stage transitions of any sort, not to mention life itself, challenging. Our respondents simply do not appear particularly realistic or planful about their futures. This lack of realism and planning—where subjectivity collapses into destiny instead of providing useful understanding and real agency—is particularly a concern for those individuals who come from the most vulnerable and disadvantaged places and populations in our study. We can't help but worry that as much as their optimism and pragmatism may sustain these young adults in the short run, it may not serve them well over the long haul of adult life. We may not know for sure which individuals will follow which of the many pathways into adulthood (or how successful they will be), but as sociologists we do know that these pathways tend to unfold in fairly predictable ways that tend to benefit those who are the most privileged and purposeful to begin with. We can only hope that, as cultural attitudes and understandings about adulthood and the transition to adulthood take shape in coming years, these realities, too, will be incorporated therein.

DISCUSSION QUESTIONS

1. Although Espiritu writes about immigration and Hartmann and Swartz write about transitions to adulthood, there are clear parallels between the two articles. What connections do you see between these two pieces?
2. How do the youth in Hartmann and Swartz' research describe adulthood? How does this differ from their parents' definition of "adulthood"?
3. Which of Hartmann and Swartz' interviewees are most optimistic about their future prospects? What are some explanations for their optimism?

ADDITIONAL RESOURCES

Internet

http://www.transad.pop.upenn.edu/. The website for the Network on Transitions to Adulthood.
http://www.soc.umn.edu/research/lcc/pubpaper.html. The website for the University of Minnesota's Youth Development Study.

FURTHER READING

Andrew, Megan, Jennifer Eggerling-Boeck, Gary D. Sandefur, and Buffy Smith. "The 'Inner Side' of the Transition to Adulthood: How Young Adults See the Process of Becoming an Adult." *Advances in Life Course Research,* 11: 225–51.

Arnett, Jeffrey. 2000. "Emerging Adulthood: A Theory of Development from the Late Teens through the Twenties." *American Psychologist,* 55: 469–80.

Aronson, Pamela. 2008. "The Markers and Meanings of Growing Up: Contemporary Young Women's Transition from Adolescence to Adulthood." *Gender & Society,* 22: 56–82.

Blatterer, Harry. 2007. "Adulthood: The Contemporary Redefinition of a Social Category." *Sociological Research Online,* 12(4).

Cote, James E. 2000. *Arrested Adulthood: The Changing Nature of Maturity and Identity.* New York: New York University Press.

Gergen, Kenneth. 1991. Excerpt from *The Saturated Self: Dilemmas of Identity in Contemporary Life.* New York: Basic Books.

Goldscheider, Frances, Sandra Hofferth, Carrie Spearin, and Sally Curtin. 2009. "Fatherhood Across Two Generations: Factors Affecting Early Family Roles." *Journal of Family Issues,* 30(5): 586–604.

Ross Macmillan (ed.). 2007. *Constructing Adulthood: Agency and Subjectivity In Adolescence and Adulthood. Advances in Life Course Research,* 11.

Settersten, Richard A., Jr. 2003. "Age Structuring and the Rhythm of the Life Course," in Jeylan Mortimer and Michael J. Shanahan (eds.). *Handbook of the Life Course,* 81–9. New York: Kluwer Academic/Plenum Publishers.

Shanahan, Michael J. 2000. "Pathways to Adulthood in Changing Societies: Variability and Mechanisms In Life Course Perspective," *Annual Review of Sociology,* 26: 667–92.

Shanahan, Michael J., Eric J. Porfeli, Jeylan T. Mortimer, and Lance D. Erickson, 2005. "Subjective Age Identity and the Transition to Adulthood: When Do Adolescents Become Adults?" in Richard A. Settersten, Jr., Frank F. Furstenberg, Jr., and Ruben G. Rumbaut (eds.). *On the Frontier of Adulthood: Theory, Research, and Public Policy,* 177–224. Chicago: University of Chicago Press.

Stanger-Ross, Jordan, Christina Collins, and Mark J. Stern. 2005. "Falling Far from the Tree: Transitions to Adulthood and the Social History of Twentieth-Century America." *Social Science History,* 290(4): 623–48.

Border Patrol: Insiders and Outsiders

With research that spans more than 80 years, these next selections explore the power
of prejudice, the pervasive divisions between social groups, and the lasting impact of
ingroup/outgroup distinctions.

Sociologist Emory Bogardus' Social Distance Scale, developed in the 1920s, is one
of the most enduring measures of prejudice created to date. Given the significance of
his research, it is no surprise that contemporary scholars, such as Edgell, Gerteis, and
Hartmann, draw on Bogardus' seminal work to assess discriminatory attitudes today.
Moreover, in a post-9/11 world, Weigert's research helps us understand how terrorism
affects our perceptions of and interactions with others on a daily basis.

53. A Social Distance Scale

EMORY S. BOGARDUS

Emory Bogardus was the twenty-first president of the American Sociological Society. He developed the Social Distance Scale in 1924 to measure perceived likeness or dissimilarity with members of various races, religions, and occupations. With a list of 40 races, 30 occupations, and 30 religions, Bogardus interviewed over 8,000 research subjects during his career to measure the amount of social distance between people of diverse backgrounds.

In making the social distance scale in its present form the writer prepared a list of 60 single sentence descriptions, nearly all of which were heard in ordinary conversations where a person was expressing himself about other persons. These statements represent several different types of social relationships; that is, they relate to contacts within the family, within social or fraternal groups, within neighborhoods, within churches, within schools, within play groups, within transportation groups, within occupational and business groups, within political or national groups.

One hundred persons were invited to rate each of the 60 statements according to the amount of social distance which it is judged that the statements represent. Each of the 100 persons was asked to judge the amount of social distance which he thought existed between the person making, for example, statement No. 1 and the person concerning whom it was made, from the standpoint of the first two persons involved. In the same fashion each statement was judged.

Social Distance Statements

1. "Would marry."
2. "Would be willing to have my brother or sister marry."
3. "Would be willing to have my son or daughter marry."
4. "Would have as chums."
5. "Would have a minority in my social club, fraternity, or lodge."
6. "Would have as a majority in my social club, fraternity, or lodge."
7. "Would debar from my social club, fraternity, or lodge."
8. "Would have as my regular friends."
9. "Would decline to have as friends."
10. "Would have merely as speaking acquaintances."
11. "Would decline to speak to."
12. "Would have as my guests at public dinners."
13. "Would decline to be seen with in public."
14. "Would have as my guests at private dinners."
15. "Would entertain overnight in my home."
16. "Would decline to invite to my home."
17. "Would allow one family only (of their group) to live in my city block."
18. "Would allow several families (of their group) to live in my city block."
19. "Would live surrounded by them in their neighborhood."
20. "Would rejoice when as my neighbors they gained increased social standing."
21. "Would feel disturbed when as my neighbors they gained increased social standing."

Bogardus, Emory S. 1933. "A Social Distance Scale." *Sociology and Social Research*, 17: 265–71.

22. "Would debar from my neighborhood."
23. "Would take as my guests at church."
24. "Would have a few as members of my church."
25. "Would have one-half of my church composed of their group."
26. "Would have as my pastor, or religious guide."
27. "Would have as my teachers."
28. "Would allow a few of their children to attend school with my children."
29. "Would have none of their children attend school with my children."
30. "Would have two-thirds of the school attended by my children composed of their children."
31. "Would have their children attend segregated schools."
32. "Would have my small children play with them regularly."
33. "Would have their young people as social equals for my adolescent sons and daughters."
34. "Would forbid my children from playing with their children."
35. "Would dance with in public regularly."
36. "Would dance with in private regularly."
37. "Would play bridge or golf with regularly."
38. "Would play bridge or golf with occasionally."
39. "Would decline to play bridge or golf with."
40. "Would take as guests on automobile trips."
41. "Would ride with them as their automobile guests."
42. "Would decline to ride in an automobile with them."
43. "Would have them ride in segregated sections of street cars."
44. "Would ride in same seat with them in street cars."
45. "Would have as mayors of cities in my country."
46. "Would have several of them in our Congress."
47. "Would debar them from being Congressmen."
48. "Would have as president of my country."
49. "Would have as voting citizens of my country up to 1/5 of total population."
50. "Would have as voting citizens of my country up to 1/3 of total population."
51. "Would have as voting citizens of my country up to 2/3 of total population."
52. "Would allow as visitors in my country but without citizenship rights."
53. "Would keep out of my country entirely either as visitors or citizens."
54. "Would work beside in an office."
55. "Would decline to work with in same office."
56. "Would work under as my supervisor."
57. "Would have them as my business partners."
58. "Would have them in a competitive business near my business location."
59. "Would have them in a noncompetitive business near my business location."
60. "Would debar them as competitors in my business."

Each of the 60 statements was typed on a 3 by 5 slip of paper. Each judge was given the 60 different slips of paper and asked to distribute them in seven boxes or piles representing seven different degrees of social distance. Each judge worked independently of the others.

The 100 judges included 66 faculty members and graduate students, all imbued with something of the research point of view, and 34 undergraduates. The number included 62 women and 38 men.

The seven statements are as follows:

Seven Equidistant Social Situations

1. Would marry
2. Would have as regular friends
3. Would work beside in an office
4. Would have several families in my neighborhood

5. Would have merely as speaking acquaintances
6. Would have live outside my neighborhood
7. Would have live outside my country

In administering the test the subject is given a list of 40 races, 30 occupations, and 30 religions together with the following general instructions:

General Instructions

You are urged to give yourself as complete freedom as possible. In fact, the greater the freedom you give yourself, the more valuable will be the results. Use only checkmarks or crosses.

Seven kinds of social contacts are given.

You are asked to give in every instance your first feeling reactions. Proceed through the tests without delaying. The more you "stop to think," the less valuable will be the results. Give your reactions to every race, occupation, or religion in the following lists which you have ever heard of.

Social distance means the different degrees of sympathetic understanding that exist between persons. This test relates to a special form of social distance known as personal-group distance, or the distance that exists between a person and groups, such as races, occupations, and religions.

By taking this test at intervals of six months or a year, a person can discover what some of the changes in attitudes are that he is undergoing. If given to a group at intervals, changes in group attitudes may likewise be gauged.

Specific instructions are also given as follows but are repeated at intervals so as to keep them before the subject's mind as steadily as possible.

Specific Instructions

Remember to give your first feeling reactions in every case.

Give your reactions to each race as a group. Do not give your reactions to the best or the worst members that you have known.

Put a cross after each race in as many of the seven columns as your feeling reactions dictate.

SCORING SUGGESTIONS

In scoring, the simple practice is used of adding the numbers of the columns nearest to the left which has been checked, for instance, for each race, that is, the checked column bearing the lowest number, and of adding these numbers for each race, and dividing by the total number of races that have been checked. In this way it is possible to obtain a person's racial distance quotient (Ra. D. Q.); also his occupational distance quotient (O. D. Q.), and his religious distance quotient (Re. D. Q.). By adding these and dividing by three, a number will be obtained which may be called his social distance quotient (S. D. Q.). By giving these tests to a person at intervals of perhaps six months or a year it would be possible to note changes in his attitudes.

DISCUSSION QUESTIONS

1. Bogardus used seven degrees of social distance to measure attitudes toward others. What are the seven degrees he measured?
2. When you initially read Bogardus' seven different degrees of social distance, which races, religions, and occupations came to mind first? Are you comfortable sharing your initial reactions with your classmates, or do you find yourself altering your responses to avoid potentially offending someone?
3. In this article, Bogardus describes his methods but not his results. If he were to administer the social distance scale today, what might his findings be?

4. Bogardus developed the social distance scale in 1924 and published this article in 1933. How do you think this historical context might have affected the social distance between groups?

ADDITIONAL RESOURCES

Film

"Crash." This riveting film challenges stereotypes about race and class and won the Oscar for Best Picture in 2005. 112 minutes. http://www.crashfilm.com/.

Internet

http://www2.asanet.org/governance/bogardus.html. The American Sociological Association's biographical website about Emory Bogardus.

http://www.brocku.ca/MeadProject/Bogardus/Bogardus_1925b.html. A full-text version of Bogardus' landmark 1925 publication, "Social Distance and Its Origins," which reports the original findings of his Social Distance Scale.

http://www.brocku.ca/MeadProject/Bogardus/Bogardus_1926.html. A full-text version of Bogardus' 1926 publication "Social Distance in the City," which reveals the applications of the Social Distance Scale to urban life.

http://www.usc.edu/libraries/archives/arc/findingaids/bogardus/index.html. The University of Southern California, where Bogardus founded the Department of Sociology and Social Work, houses an archive of Bogardus' work.

FURTHER READING

Bogardus, Emory S. 1925. "Social Distance and Its Origins." *Journal of Applied Sociology,* 9: 216–26.

Bogardus, Emory S. 1959. *Social Distance.* Los Angeles: University of Southern California Press.

Hughes, Gordon. 2007. "Community Cohesion, Asylum Seeking and the Question of 'the Stranger.'" *Cultural Studies,* 21(6): 931–51.

Karakayali, Nedim. 2006. "The Uses of the Stranger: Circulation, Arbitration, Secrecy, and Dirt." *Sociological Theory,* 24(4): 312–30.

Kreager, Derek A. 2008. "Guarded Borders: Adolescent Interracial Romance and Peer Trouble at School." *Social Forces,* 87(2): 887–910.

Lee, Sharon M. and Monica Boyd. 2008. "U.S. Data: Marrying Out: Comparing the Marital and Social Integration of Asians in the U.S. and Canada." *Social Science Research,* 37(1): 311–29.

McVeigh, Rory and David Sikkink. 2005. "Organized Racism and the Stranger." *Sociological Forum,* 20(4): 497–522.

Stonequist, Everett V. 1937. *The Marginal Man: A Study in Personality and Culture Conflict.* New York: C. Scribners Sons.

Wark, Collin and John F. Galliher. 2007. "Emory Bogardus and the Origins of the Social Distance Scale." *The American Sociologist,* 38(4): 383–95.

Yancey, George. 2009. "Cross racial Differences in the Racial Preferences of Potential Dating Partners: A Test of the Alienation of African Americans and Social Dominance Orientation." *The Sociological Quarterly,* 50(1): 121–43.

54. Atheists as "Other": Moral Boundaries and Cultural Membership in American Society

PENNY EDGELL, JOSEPH GERTEIS, AND DOUGLAS HARTMANN

To study Americans' acceptance of atheists, Edgell et al. draw on survey data they collected from a nationally representative sample of 2,081 people and in-depth interviews with residents of Los Angeles, Minneapolis–St. Paul, Atlanta, and Boston. A part of their broader American Mosaic Project, their research studies race and religion to gain insight into diversity and cohesion in America.

In this article, we explore Americans' attitudes toward atheists.

Using data from a new national survey, we show that Americans draw symbolic boundaries that clearly and sharply exclude atheists in both private and public life. From a list of groups that also includes Muslims, recent immigrants, and homosexuals, Americans name atheists as those least likely to share their vision of American society. They are also more likely to disapprove of their children marrying atheists. We show that these attitudes are driven by religious affiliation and involvement as well as by social context and broader moral outlook.

We show not only that atheists are less accepted than other marginalized groups but also that attitudes toward them have not exhibited the marked increase in acceptance that has characterized views of other racial and religious minorities over the past forty years. Rather than treating atheists as akin to other out-groups, we reveal the unique social and cultural bases underlying attitudes toward this group, leading us to rethink some core assumptions about Americans' increasing acceptance of religious diversity and to consider how the weakening of internal boundaries between religious groups may heighten awareness of the external boundary between the religious and the nonreligious. We argue that attitudes toward atheists clarify why and how religion forms a basis for solidarity and collective identity in American life through its historical association with morality and citizenship.

ATHEISTS AS OTHER

We argue that it is important to understand Americans' attitudes toward atheists even though they are few in number—and not an organized and self-conscious group—and even though individual atheists are not easily identified. Our focus is not on mistreatment of atheists, but on attitudes that mark them as outsiders in public and private life, that may even designate them as unworthy of full civic inclusion. For our analysis what is important is that other Americans respond to "atheist" as a meaningful category.

We assess the degree to which atheists represent a symbolic "other" against which some Americans define themselves as good people and worthy citizens. This allows us to explore what attitudes about atheists reveal regarding the nature of cultural membership and moral solidarity in American society. Do Americans feel that atheists are "like me"? Do they see them as moral people and good citizens?

We examine Americans' willingness to recognize and accept atheists in both public and private life. We asked people to say whether

Edgell, Penny, Joseph Gerteis, and Douglas Hartmann. 2006. "Atheists as 'Other': Moral Boundaries and Cultural Membership in American Society." *American Sociological Review*, 71: 211–34.

members of particular minority groups "Share your vision of American society," a question about public acceptance designed to shed light on the question of cultural membership. We also asked about willingness to accept one's own child marrying someone from a particular religious, ethnic, or other minority group—a private matter. These questions go beyond tolerance to capture the importance and nature of symbolic boundaries and the distinctions that people use to define their own identity and worth.

We find that out of a long list of ethnic and cultural minorities, Americans are less willing to accept intermarriage with atheists than with any other group, and less likely to imagine that atheists share their vision of American society. We find that Americans' willingness to draw a boundary that excludes atheists is influenced by certain demographic factors that are more generally associated with levels of tolerance, but it is also influenced by religious identity and practice, by social context and exposure to diversity, and by broader value orientations. We argue that atheists provide an important limiting case to the general narrative of increasing tolerance of religious pluralism in the United States, and that this exception is a useful lens through which to understand Americans' assumptions about the appropriate role of religion in both public and private life. We find that in private life, many Americans associate religiosity with morality and trustworthiness; religion forms a basis for private solidarity and identity. In public life, many Americans believe now that affirming a religious identity is an important way of "being American," a basis for citizenship and a source of a common American identity.

DATA AND DESIGN
Our data come from the American Mosaic Project, a multi-year, multi-method study of diversity and solidarity in American life with particular emphasis on race and religion (University of Minnesota, Minneapolis, principal investigators Hartmann, Gerteis, and Edgell). The research includes a nationally representative random-digit

dial telephone survey (N = 2081) conducted during the summer of 2003. In addition, in-depth interviews and fieldwork were conducted in four U.S. cities (Los Angeles, Minneapolis–St. Paul, Atlanta, and Boston) by a team of graduate students in the summer of 2004. For this article, we also review contemporary public discourse on atheists in American society.

The core data for this article are drawn from the telephone survey we designed and fielded through the Wisconsin Survey Center. Households were randomly selected, then respondents were randomly chosen within households. The survey, on average, took slightly more than 30 minutes to complete. Additionally, African Americans and Hispanics were over-sampled to provide complete data on these populations; to facilitate this over-sampling, the survey could also be conducted in Spanish if the respondent preferred. Two items from our survey capture one's willingness to draw boundaries separating oneself from others in both public and private life. The first question is akin to the "thermometer" questions familiar to survey researchers, where respondents are asked about various groups and asked to rate them on a scale of feelings, from 100 (very warm) to 0 (very cold). Rather than ask about feelings in general, the question we constructed and fielded asked about the degree to which members of particular groups share one's "vision of America"—the response categories were "almost completely agree," "mostly," "somewhat," and "not at all." This question was asked of all respondents. Someone who does not share your vision of American society may not value the same things about America or understand what it means to be an American citizen in the same way. A positive answer is thus an indicator of moral solidarity. In the negative answers, symbolic boundaries become visible.

The second question asked whether the respondent would approve or disapprove if his or her child wished to marry a member of each of a list of groups. This item is a standard measure of group prejudice, with reluctance to accept intermarriage typically interpreted as an indicator of underlying intolerance. The item on intermarriage with atheists was asked of half of our respondents. We interpret it here as a measure of personal trust and acceptance, an evaluation of who is thought to be capable of being caring and moral, able to make one's child happy, and to treat other family members well.

DESCRIPTIVE ANALYSIS— ATTITUDES TOWARD ATHEISTS IN PUBLIC AND PRIVATE LIFE

For both of our measures, atheists are at the very top of the list of problematic groups. Americans are less accepting of atheists than of any of the other groups we asked about, and by a wide margin.

The next-closest category on both measures is Muslims. We expected Muslims to be a lightning-rod group, and they clearly were. This makes the response to atheists all the more striking. For many, Muslims represent a large and mostly external threat, dramatized by the loss of life in the World Trade Center attacks and the war in Iraq. By contrast, atheists are a small and largely silent internal minority. When the "somewhat" and "not at all" responses are combined for the public acceptance measure, atheists (78.6%) and Muslims (77.6%) appear nearly equally problematic—the vast majority of Americans reject both groups.

One's own religious identity and involvement shape attitudes toward atheists. Church attenders, conservative Protestants, and those reporting high religious saliency are less likely to approve of intermarriage with an atheist and more likely to say that atheists do not share their vision of American society. It should surprise no one that the lowest level of rejection of atheists comes from the nonreligious, measured here as those who do not go to church, do not claim a religious identity, and report that religion is "not at all" salient to them. A notable proportion of even this group, however, does not accept atheists. About 17 percent of the nonreligious say that atheists do not at all share

their vision of America, while about one in ten indicate that they would not approve of their child marrying an atheist.

Attitudes toward atheists also are related to social location. White Americans, males, and those with a college degree are somewhat more accepting of atheists than are nonwhite Americans, females, or those with less formal education. Party affiliation matters, especially on our intermarriage item. Those in the South and Midwest are also less accepting of atheists in both public and private life than are those in the East or West. Across all of these categories, however, rates of non-acceptance of atheists range from about one in three (34%) to three in five (60%).

Across all of the groups we examined, negative attitudes toward atheists are correlated with negative views of homosexuals and, for most, Muslims; none of these correlations is large.

SUPPLEMENTAL ANALYSES AND INTERPRETATIONS

These analyses allow us to begin to identify the factors that predict the symbolic and cultural exclusion of atheists from both public and private life.

For our measure of public acceptance, the strongest effects are divided between one's own religious belief and involvement, living in a diverse community, and three of our cultural values variables. For intermarriage, religious involvement is by far the strongest predictor of attitudes, and cultural values also have large effects. It makes sense that one's own religious involvement would have the most effect on the measure of private acceptance. It also, though, affects public acceptance, highlighting the importance of the social and communal aspects of religion for attitudes toward the nonreligious.

Respondents had various interpretations of what atheists are like and what that label means. Those whom we interviewed view atheists in two different ways. Some people view atheists as problematic because they associate them with illegality, such as drug use and prostitution—that is, with immoral people who threaten respectable community from the lower end of the status hierarchy. Others saw atheists as rampant materialists and cultural elitists that threaten common values from above—the ostentatiously wealthy who make a lifestyle out of consumption or the cultural elites who think they know better than everyone else. Both of these themes rest on a view of atheists as self-interested individualists who are not concerned with the common good.

One woman, KW, a Republican in her mid-60s, told our interviewer that belief in something transcendent is necessary to move beyond "the me," the narrowly self-interested consumerism that she sees as rampant. This interview excerpt shows how she linked together the ideas of consumerism, arrogance, atheism, and American identity:

> It's that same arrogance again. I'm an American, I can do anything I want, and to heck with the rest of the world. [Interviewer: Do you see religion fitting into it very well?] These people aren't very religious, you'll notice that. There's a real, "I'm an atheist" attitude among people with major money. You don't see this nice balance...I'll say it again, some religious belief, I don't care who or what you worship, just something to give you that stability.
>
> If you're going all through life, "I'm an atheist, I don't believe in anything except the almighty dollar," this is definitely a destructive attitude and the rest of the world sees it.

In these interviews, the atheist emerges as a culturally powerful "other" in part because the category is loaded with multiple meanings. For all these respondents, atheists represent a general lack of morality, but for some, this lack was associated with criminality and its dangers to safety and public order, while for others the absence of morality was that of people whose resources or positions place them above the common standards of mainstream American life. To put it somewhat differently, atheists can be symbolically placed at either end of the American status hierarchy. What holds these seemingly contradictory views together is that the problem of the atheist was perceived to be a problem of self-interest, an excessive individualism that undermines trust and the public good. It is important to note that our respondents did not refer to particular atheists whom they had encountered. Rather they used the atheist as a symbolic figure to represent their fears about those trends in American life—increasing criminality, rampant self-interest, an unaccountable elite—that they believe undermine trust and a common sense of purpose.

CONCLUSION

The core point of this article can be stated concisely. Atheists are at the top of the list of groups that Americans find problematic in both public and private life, and the gap between acceptance of atheists and acceptance of other racial and religious minorities is large and persistent. It is striking that the rejection of atheists is so much more common than rejection of other stigmatized groups. For example, while rejection of Muslims may have spiked in post-9/11 America, rejection of atheists was higher. The possibility of same-sex marriage has widely been seen as a threat to a biblical definition of marriage, as Massachusetts, Hawaii, and California have tested the idea, and the debate over the ordination of openly gay clergy has become a central point of controversy within many churches. In our survey, however, concerns about atheists were stronger than concerns about homosexuals. Across subgroups in our sample, negative views of atheists are strong, the differences being largely a matter of degree.

We believe that in answering our questions about atheists, our survey respondents were not, on the whole, referring to actual atheists they had encountered, but were responding to "the atheist" as a boundary-marking cultural category. Unlike members of some other marginalized groups, atheists can "pass": people are unlikely to ask about a person's religious beliefs in most circumstances, and even outward behavioral signs of religiosity (like going to church) do not correlate perfectly with belief in God. Moreover, acceptance or rejection of atheists is related not only to personal religiosity but also to one's exposure to diversity and to one's social and political value orientations. So while our study does shed light on questions of tolerance, we are more interested in what this symbolic boundary tells us about moral solidarity and cultural membership. We believe that attitudes toward atheists tell us more about American society and culture than about atheists themselves, and that our analysis sheds light on broader issues regarding the historic place of religion in underpinning moral order in the United States.

If we are correct, then the boundary between the religious and the nonreligious is not about religious affiliation per se. It is about the historic place of religion in American civic culture. To be an atheist in such an environment is not to be one more religious minority among many in a strongly pluralist society. Rather, Americans construct the atheist as the symbolic representation of one who rejects the basis for moral solidarity and cultural membership in American society altogether. Over our history, other groups have, perhaps, been subject to similar moral concerns. Catholics, Jews, and communists all have been figures against which the moral contours of

American culture and citizenship have been imagined. We suggest that today, the figure of the atheist plays this role—although we emphasize that this is for contingent historical and institutional reasons, and we also emphasize that this is the case regardless of the morality and patriotism of actual atheists.

We already know that Americans draw boundaries in private life based on morality. Our findings suggest that moral boundaries are also drawn in public life, and these findings help us to understand why and how they are drawn. In this case, the symbolic boundaries drawn around atheists help us to understand the problem of moral solidarity in a diverse society. They point to a specific cultural content, and to a specific historical and institutional basis for the intersection of religion, morality, and models of the public and the private good. They shed light on the shared or fractured nature of cultural membership, and also on the content of the culture that is shared. We call for more work that investigates the range and depth of meanings associated with the term "atheist," how moral worth is linked discursively with citizenship, and how the construction of cultural membership in American society proceeds through the drawing of symbolic boundaries.

DISCUSSION QUESTIONS

1. What were the two primary questions Edgell et al. asked to assess Americans' public and private feelings about others? How are these questions similar to or different from Bogardus' Social Distance Scale?

2. What were Edgell et al.'s findings? How did their findings differ across the public and private spheres?

3. What surprised you most, if anything, about Edgell et al.'s findings?

4. Language often provides insight into a culture's beliefs about a particular topic. What are some terms in the English language used to describe an atheist or nonbeliever? What do these terms reveal about Americans' beliefs about atheists?

5. Edgell et al. suggest that future research should investigate the various meanings invoked by the term "atheist." What methods would you use to undertake this type of research? What questions would you ask and of whom?

ADDITIONAL RESOURCES

Film

"The God Who Wasn't There: A Film Beyond Belief." 2005. A documentary that critically examines fundamental Christian beliefs. 62 minutes. http://www.thegodmovie.com/.

"Religulous." 2008. A documentary featuring Bill Maher that critically explores world religions. 101 minutes. http://www.lionsgate.com/religulous/.

Internet

http://www.soc.umn.edu/research/amp.html. The website of the American Mosaic Project, the research program on which the Edgell et al. article is based.

http://www.atheists.org/. The website of the American Atheists, an organization that works to defend the rights of atheists.

http://www.atheistalliance.org/. The website of the group Atheists Alliance International.

http://www.camp-quest.org/. Camp Quest is an overnight camp for atheist youth with several locations throughout Canada, Great Britain, and the United States.

http://www.centerforinquiry.net/oncampus/. The website of the Center for Inquiry on Campus, an organization dedicated to protecting secular rights in educational settings.

Radio

http://www.npr.org/templates/story/story.php?storyId=9180871. March 28, 2007. National Public Radio's program "Fresh Air" features an interview with Oxford University Professor Richard Dawkins about his book *The God Delusion*.

FURTHER READING

Hartmann, Douglas and Joseph Gerteis. 2005. "Dealing with Diversity: Mapping Multiculturalism in Sociological Terms." *Sociology Theory*, 23(2): 218–40.

Hartmann Douglas, Xeufeng Zhang, and William Windschadt. 2005. "One (Multicultural) Nation Under God? The Changing Meanings and Uses of the Term 'Judeo-Christian' in the American Media." *Journal of Medial Religion*, 4(4): 207–34.

Jacoby, Susan. 2004. *Freethinkers: A History of American Secularism*. New York: Metropolitan.

Lofland, Lyn. 1995. "Social Interaction: Continuities and Complexities in the Study of Nonintimate Sociality." In Karen S. Cook, Gary Alan Fine, and James S. House (eds.). *Sociological Perspectives on Social Psychology*, 176–201. Boston: Allyn and Bacon.

Martin, Michael. 2002. *Atheism, Morality, and Meaning*. London: Prometheus.

McGrath, Alister. 2004. *The Twilight of Atheism: The Rise and Fall of Disbelief in the Modern World*. New York: Doubleday.

Sherkat, Darren E. 2008. "Beyond Belief: Atheism, Agnosticism, and Theistic Certainty in the United States." *Sociological Spectrum*, 28(5): 438–59.

Turner, James. 1985. *Without God, Without Creed: The Origins of Unbelief in America*. Baltimore, MD: Johns Hopkins University Press.

55. Terrorism, Identity, and Public Order: A Perspective from Goffman

ANDREW J. WEIGERT

In this article, Weigert addresses the impacts of terrorism on our daily lives. Weigert argues that the anxiety brought about by a culture of terrorism erodes the security of our identities, particularly in public spaces and during social interactions with unknown others.

September 11, 2001 brought the "Fourth Wave" of terrorism to the United States and an emerging global society. The Fourth Wave is characterized by religious legitimation, international scope, increasingly bloody tactics and weapons, and reliance on technologies of modernity, namely, communications, ease of travel and border crossings, and availability of finances and weapons of mass destruction (Jenkins, 2000; Rapoport, 1999). Research on terrorism typically covers definitional issues, typologies, causes, organizational features, recruitment strategies, and historical changes. There is some attention to social outcomes such as increased fear and anxiety and runs on guns, medicines, and gas masks. These psychological and defensive responses of individuals suggest a sociological social psychological outcome, namely, the Fourth Wave of terrorism as a "culture of terror" that threatens public order.

A defining specific difference of the Fourth Wave is the function of religious validation: The culture of terror is characterized by "sacred violence" or "apocalyptic violence" that is without historical precedent and beyond traditional limits. In the Fourth Wave, terrorism potentially reaches a global stage. All weapons are legitimate. All "others" are legitimate targets. No distinction among targets is recognized.

TERRORISM RUPTURES PUBLIC ORDER

Interactionally, terrorism is a rupture in and thus a threat to public order. The objectives of terrorism, strictly speaking, are not things or persons. The target object is the public as a whole. The public as a whole is not physically killed. Rather the public's culture is altered from one of routine awareness, security, and stability to one of unfocused alertness, vulnerability, and uncertainty about what may happen next. Terrorism is a source of anxiety and fear in public life-debilitating emotions that threaten routine situational meanings, self-understandings, and identity performances. It sows "dis-ease," the social pathology of interaction.

Debilitating emotions, along with loss of cognitive assurance and predictability, threaten the enactment of public order. Both George W. Bush and Osama bin Laden, who are not likely to agree on anything else, recognized that the events of September 11 were designed to, and to some degree caused, fear in the citizenry of the United States. Bush used democratic rhetoric in defending the "freedom of people ... to raise their children free from fear. I know many Americans feel fear today" ("Bush's Remarks," 2001, p. B6). On the other side, bin Laden used religious rhetoric to assert that "America has been filled with

Weigert, Andrew J. 2003. "Terrorism, Identity, and Public Order: A Perspective from Goffman." *Identity: An International Journal of Theory and Research*, 3(2): 93–113.

horror…and thanks be to God" ("Bin Laden's Statement," 2001, p. B7).

Faced with anxiety and fear, people take ameliorative action that may sublimate, as it were, their feeling responses. There is a run on gas masks, guns, flags, medicines, decals, yard signs, and ribbons. These actions are not likely objectively efficacious, but if they ease negative emotions, they are subjectively useful. Terrorism's lingering effects are visible in a start at a siren's wail or a jump at a commotion in a jetliner's aisle. Such responses point to cognitive and affective intimations of public disorder.

Threats to public order are realized in the corridors, media, and channels through which persons are copresent such as terminals, tunnels, bridges, roadways, or pathways. Likewise, public order is enacted through communication media such as airwaves, video frequencies, internet avenues, and the ways persons communicate and record such communications—the lifeblood of bureaucracies. Finally, public order affects channels of life-support systems such as air, water, food, soil, organisms, and chemicals. Therefore, anthrax sent through the mails or toxins placed in the water, food, or soil threaten public order based on shared bodily functions such as breathing, drinking, or eating.

In addition to physical and psychological outcomes, breaches in public order put at risk the symbolic legitimacy of the state. Indeed, "breaches of public order may be performed…as a pointed challenge to the authority of the state—symbolic acts read as a taunt" (Goffman, 1983, p. 6). Terrorist acts go beyond taunting. They endanger societal and personal identities through threats to the apparent morality of identity presentation and situational definition in face-to-face interaction that presumably reproduces cultural reality.

Interactional reenactment of the cultural norms and values assumed to underlie public order both flow from commitment to those same norms and values and simultaneously reestablish those commitments for the future. Terrorist violations of public order then potentially generate a self-fulfilling dynamic: They both contradict situational norms and values and increase the likelihood that selves will see similar situations as dangerous. Thus, terrorism weakens interactional trust and increases uncertainty, fear, or anxiety. Once situational trust is destroyed, public disorder threatens.

IDENTITY AND APPARENT MORALITY

Apparent morality warrants the promissory validity that you and I are who you and I appear to be. In a word, apparent morality underwrites identity morality. Persons in each others' presence then take identity morality as the guarantee that you will act in accord with the identity you present, and so people enroll their present identities and future selves into the course of action premised on those identities. This interactional dynamic allows a sense of secure identities throughout public situations.

Apparent morality and inferred identity morality allow the real possibility of not being who one appears to be. Inferences about identity morality and situational rights and duties mislead normals. The apparent traveler and his or her inferred identity as fellow airline passenger are really, though not apparently, false identities. There are true but hidden identities that override apparent identities, namely, terrorist and suicide, if named from the victim's frame, or hero and martyr, if named from the perpetrator's frame.

The powerful grandeur of these identities extolled at home is confirmed in the complementary but oppositional meanings given to the same deeds by the victim group. The hero or martyr is a criminal and evil doer whose motives are fanatical or insane. The two cultures frame opposed meanings: embodiment of the worst versus embodiment of the best and evil versus good (see earlier Bush and bin Laden quotes). Initial empirical studies, however, suggest that terrorists are normal, sane, and committed to their group's values. As normal humans, terrorists are as dramaturgically adept as anyone else, and their adeptness includes hiding their operant identities.

How then are victims to respond to happenings in public spaces? Unexpected happenings are after all quite routine. Goffman (1971) noted that "if a subject is to be at ease in his surroundings...he need not find that things are as he expected..., only that, howsoever they are, he can be safe in withdrawing his attention from them" (p. 310).

Once interactors take the unexpected as worthy of notice, however, ease dissipates and dis-ease, anxiety, or fear define self in situation. The negativity grows with a sense that the unexpected is somehow malevolently designed to disrupt public order and threaten a person's life. Both normal and unexpected situational elements cause self not to feel at home but to sense risk from quarters not apparent and thus all the more threatening.

SELF PROJECTED IN ACTION IS MORAL

As emphasized earlier, rules for presenting self and norms to be who one appears create conditions for self to have a hidden identity that in fact motivates unexpected action in the situation. Entering a situation with a hidden discreditable identity that motivates actions threatening others' identities presents that self with the dramaturgical task of *passing,* that is, appearing and acting as though one is as one appears when the apparent identity is false and the real identity is hidden.

So too in situations of potential terrorist presence, other selves must become "scanners of possibilities" that come with the strangers. The passer meets the profiler! Normalcy is a fragile facade as self and other interpret situations not for what is manifest but for what the manifest may hide.

Presentational skills of the passer are matched against scanning skills of profilers. Profiling is an interactional imperative for those copresent with strangers, especially if the situation may be hot with threats. As an aside, then, profiling by law enforcement agencies is an interactional

imperative put to narrower social functions of police powers.

A terrorist passer lives one life organized around the identity he or she appears to be and a second life organized around the identity he or she has within the hidden group relevant to the passer's intended course of action. The terrorist passer leads a double life in the host society—one public but false, the other secret but true.

Why get upset, even enraged, over stories of an imposter, terrorist, or seducer who successfully passes as a doctor, priest, traveler, or lover? Of course, persons touched by imposters' activities and who share waiting rooms or classrooms are offended and violated by the revelation that he or she was not who he or she appeared to be. Why does this felt sense of violation emerge? And why is the feeling shared by others who find out about the violation but were not in the interaction? Why are embarrassment, anxiety, and terror contagious beyond the situation? People feel violated because the fundamental interactional apriority and moral equation of social life is shown to be a contingent artifice of skilled performers, whether lovers or predators; that contingency and artifice inform the massively real and moral sense of who we as humans are, who others are, what we are doing now, and what we expect in the future. Recognizing instances of life's contingency and artifice is apparently threatening in itself.

Just below the surface of everyday life seethes a molten sense of a contingent moral and sacred self. Indeed, people think of someone who lacks this moral sense as a sociopath or fanatic. After all, without a moral sense any random response, hidden goal, or unannounced self is as worthy or worthless as any other, and meeting situational expectations has no greater claim on a normal's or sociopath's or terrorist's self than any other responses. The precariousness of life is not only a cognitive probability, an emotional anxiety, and an empirical contingency, but also a profound moral risk to oneself as a valued, sacred being.

IDENTITY TRANSITIVITY

Identity threats have effects across members in the victimized identity category. I refer to this process with a sensitizing concept: identity transitivity. Identity transitivity has two moments: a cognitive placement of self in an identity category including those affected by events; and an affective reaction to that placement, such as pride for positive events, shame for disgraceful deeds, or anxiety and fear for threatening acts. Identity transitivity, then, follows from recognition of kind and resultant self-feeling such as pride, shame, or anxiety. Identity transitivity offers a conceptualization for interpreting affective contagions such as embarrassment that runs through a high school audience when the student actor forgets his lines in full view.

Terrorism activates a pathway of negative identity transitivity among selves who share a membership identity with victims. Members of the nationality or group targeted by terrorists are liable to acquire felt identities as vicarious victims. Self-identification with members of a target category such as citizen, student, federal worker, ethnic group, or even passerby internalizes the threatened identity as victim. Self then feels under threat as he or she enters a public domain and commingles in a common carrier or passageway.

Groups and institutions underwrite pathways of identity transitivity to control and motivate members, clients, and related others. The logic of identity transitivity suggests how beliefs among some fundamentalist Muslim males that, as an ancient saying reflects, the honor of the family lies between the legs of its virgin women, lead to their feelings of shame and dishonor if a female is adulterous. The brother's response is to remedy his identity as dishonored family member and reacquire the collective identity of an honorable family by doing his duty and killing his adulterous sister. As "honor killing" shows, identity transitivity enmeshes us in moral dynamics flowing from those with whom we are interrelated and categorized in shared narratives.

In short, identity transitivity works systematically along social relationships and cultural categories. It illuminates age-old codes underlying such phrases applied to self as destroying family honor, disgracing the church, scandalizing the innocent, betraying the flag, and other contagious moral identities. Military, religious, educational, ethnic, and cultural institutions and groups claim the right to punish behavior by members who demean the uniform, abominate the cowl, or disgrace school colors, even if the actions are away from the base, in a bedroom, or in a bar far from campus. Institutions, groups, and properly socialized selves hold each member responsible for the honorable identities of all and the representational identity of the entity. One's shame dishonors everyone's identity: "No person is an island."

CULTURAL ASSUMPTIONS UNDERWRITE PUBLIC ORDER

Public order, then, is ultimately based on cultural understandings shared by commingling members of relevant societies. The question arises in global networks that provide the context for sacred international terrorism or arbitrary state violence whether there is universal commitment to the sacredness of each self and the security of citizens and noncombatants. These core values serve as cultural templates to judge how and when self or other fails to fulfill the moral requirements of face-to-face behavior and thus to uphold each other's sacred self. In a failed interaction, self experiences not just interrupted action and frustrated goals but also a failure at the moral core of what it means to be a person here and now, the only moment and place in which we enact common identities. Perceived interactional failures call forth ritual remedies to realign with the core values and reestablish a sense of valued self.

To the extent that each of us is a proper person enacting core values, each experiences self as validated in meaningful interaction, realigned with those values through ritual remedy if meaning is interrupted, and deeply threatened if those core values are violated and left ritually unintegrated. After the violence of Waco, Texas, Littleton, Colorado, and 9/11, even casual observation notes enhanced barriers to commingling in public spaces.

Protective devices, however, cannot warrant meaningful interaction and authentic self-presentation within public order. Sabotage and booby traps work precisely because they are premised on erroneous interpretations of appearances that hide operant identities. The actual number of casualties may in fact be quite insignificant, especially compared to other threats we routinely accept in daily life. The aim of terrorism is not to kill persons but morale.

At the heart of public order is a profound interactional paradox: The rules and expectations that generate order are the very rules and expectations that allow for hiding threats to that order. The apparentness of normal identity doubles as a mask for an operant identity. Warranting public order are, first, the moral apriority that one is who one appears to be, and second, the functional assumption that one trusts another person's appearances lead to interaction allowing every person to continue as the selves they appear to be. For example, "The person next to me looks like a passenger and I trust his appearance sufficiently to fly alongside him."

Assumptions underwriting conduct toward one another are the ties of society. Interacting selves, even strangers reenacting public order, reproduce themselves in the apparent meanings they enact. Yet, in the ritual dance of deference and demeanor, there may be a deadlier game underway, one that is known to one of the parties but hidden from the other. In such closed awareness games, a hidden terrorist self is affirmed through destruction of victim selves and threats to public order.

DISCUSSION QUESTIONS

1. In this article, Weigert describes a "fourth wave" of terrorism. What does he mean by this and what are the features of this "fourth wave"?
2. What does Weigert mean by the phrase "apparent morality"? How is apparent morality challenged by terrorism?
3. Weigert uses the term "public order" throughout his article. Provide a definition and a few examples of "public order."
4. Weigert also uses the terms "passer" and "profiler" in his article. What does he mean by each term? Who are the passers and profilers in his article?

ADDITIONAL RESOURCES

Film

"9/11 Backlash: Being Muslim in America." 2005. This documentary explores the difficulties faced by U.S. Muslims following the terrorist tacks of 9/11/01. 25 minutes.

"United 93." 2006. A major motion picture that tells the story of the hijacking of United Airlines Flight 93, which crashed in rural Pennsylvania, on September 11, 2001. 111 minutes.

Internet

http://www.fema.gov/hazard/terrorism/index.shtm. The U.S. Government's Federal Emergency Management Agency's website on terrorism.

http://www.honorflight93.org/. Flight 93 National Memorial commemorates the lives of those lost aboard United Airlines Flight 93 during the September 11, 2001, terrorist attacks.

http://www.globalgiving.com/saferworld.html. Global Giving is an Internet-based philanthropic organization created by friends and family members of those killed in the terrorist attacks of September 11, 2001.

http://www.start.umd.edu/start/. The website of the National Consortium for the Study of Terrorism and Responses to Terrorism housed at the University of Maryland and sponsored by the U.S. Department of Homeland Security.

http://www.national9llmemorial.org/site/PageServer?pagename=New_Home. The website of the National September 11 Memorial and Museum at the World Trade Center.

http://www.terrorism.com/. The website of the Terrorism Research Center.

http://www.un.org/terrorism/. This United Nations' website documents their actions to counter terrorism.

FURTHER READING

Ai, Amy L., Toni Cascio, Linda K. Santangelo, and Teresa Evans-Campbell. 2005. "Hope, Meaning, and Growth Following the September 11, 2001 Terrorist Attacks." *Journal of Interpersonal Violence,* 20(5): 523–48.

Bin Laden's Statement: "The Sword Fell." October 8, 2001. *New York Times,* B7.

Bush's Remarks on U.S. Military Strikes in Afghanistan. October 8, 2001. *New York Times,* B6.

Coryn, Chris L., James M. Beale, and Krista M. Myers. 2004. "Response to September 11: Anxiety, Patriotism, and Prejudice in the Aftermath of Terror." *Current Research in Social Psychology,* 9(12): 165–83.

Durkheim, Emile. 1951. "The Social Element of Suicide," in *Suicide.* New York: The Free Press.

Fraher, Amy L. 2004. "Flying the Friendly Skies': Why U.S. Commercial Airline Pilots Want to Carry Guns." *Human Relations,* 57(5): 573–95.

Goffman, Erving. 1971. *Relations in Public: Microstudies of the Public Order.* New York: Basic Books.

Goffman, Erving. 1983. "The Interaction Order." *American Sociological Review,* 48(1): 1–17.

Houston, Brian, Betty Pfefferbaum, and Gil Reyes. 2008. "Experiencing Disasters Indirectly: How Traditional and New Media Disaster Coverage Impacts Youth." *The Prevention Researcher,* 15(3): 14–17.

Jenkins, Brian M. 2000. "Terrorism," in Edward F. Borgotta (ed.). *Encyclopedia of Sociology,* 2nd edition, 3137–41. New York: Macmillan Reference.

Rapoport, David C. 1999. "Terrorism," in Lester Kurtz (ed.). *Encyclopedia of Violence, Peace, and Conflict,* 497–510. New York: Academic.

Rodgriguez-Carballeira, Alvaro and Federico Javaloy. 2005. "Psychosocial Analysis of the Collective Processes in the United States after September 11." *Conflict Management and Peace Science,* 22(3): 201–16.

The Power of Belief: Collective Action and Social Movements

More than 50 years apart, Festinger et al. and Preves study two divergent groups who are deeply committed to their respective causes. Festinger et al. draw our attention to groups that predict the end of the world. Over the course of history, there have been numerous predictions of a messianic era or the end of the world, yet none have come to fruition. Despite a lack of evidence for this apocalyptic thinking, many individuals and groups remain strongly convicted to such beliefs. Festinger et al. provide a fascinating theoretical explanation for this seemingly irrational behavior via the workings of cognitive dissonance.

Preves examines the social movement action of an extremely stigmatized and marginalized population: hermaphrodites. Like Festinger et al.'s subjects, the activists in Preves' research are intensely committed to their cause, yet the means by which they attempt to effect change varies dramatically over the course of just a decade. Members of a group that picketed at medical conventions, calling themselves Hermaphrodites with Attitude, came to collaborate with the very doctors they were protesting merely a few years later, creating medical language and policies that many in the movement found objectionable.

416 THE POWER OF BELIEF

The course of social movement activism is very difficult to predict, given members' interpretations of ongoing events, others' responses, available resources, the creative exercise of individual agency, and other factors. In both of these articles, the authors explore how members of social movements rationalize their actions and attract members to their cause.

56. Unfulfilled Prophecies and Disappointed Messiahs

LEON FESTINGER, HENRY RIECKEN, AND STANLEY SCHACTER

In this fascinating study of a group that proclaimed the end of the world, Festinger and colleagues find evidence in support of Festinger's cognitive dissonance theory. Mrs. Keech, the group's founder, reported that she received this prediction and other messages from aliens via "automatic writing." The aliens communicated that the believers were to be saved from a catastrophic flood by a space ship. When the flood failed to materialize, Festinger and colleagues discovered that the faith of the believers was surprisingly strengthened rather than challenged.

A man with a conviction is a hard man to change. Tell him you disagree and he turns away. Show him facts or figures and he questions your sources. Appeal to logic and he fails to see your point.

We have all experienced the futility of trying to change a strong conviction, especially if the convinced person has some investment in his belief. We are familiar with the variety of ingenious defenses with which people protect their convictions, managing to keep them unscathed through the most devastating attacks.

But man's resourcefulness goes beyond simply protecting a belief. Suppose an individual believes something with his whole heart; suppose further that he has a commitment to this belief, that he has taken irrevocable actions because of it; finally, suppose that he is presented with evidence,

unequivocal and undeniable evidence, that his belief is wrong: what will happen? The individual will frequently emerge, not only unshaken, but even more convinced of the truth of his beliefs than ever before. Indeed, he may even show a new fervor about convincing and converting other people to his view.

How and why does such a response to contradictory evidence come about? This is the question on which this book focuses.

Let us begin by stating the conditions under which we would expect to observe increased fervor following the disconfirmation of a belief. There are five such conditions.

1. A belief must be held with deep conviction and it must have some relevance to what the believer does or how he behaves.

Festinger, Leon, Henry Riecken, and Stanley Schacter. 1956. "Unfulfilled Prophecies and Disappointed Messiahs," in *When Prophecy Fails: A Social and Psychological Study of a Modern Group that Predicted the Destruction of the World,* 3–32. Minneapolis: University of Minnesota Press.

2. The person holding the belief must have committed himself to it; he must have taken some important action that is difficult to undo.

3. The belief must be sufficiently specific and concerned with the real world so that events may unequivocally refute the belief.

4. Such undeniable disconfirmatory evidence must occur and must be recognized by the individual holding the belief.

5. The individual believer must have social support. It is unlikely that one isolated believer could withstand the kind of disconfirming evidence we have specified. If, however, the believer is a member of a group of convinced persons who can support one another, we would expect the belief to be maintained and the believers to attempt to proselyte or to persuade nonmembers that the belief is correct.

These five conditions specify the circumstances under which increased proselytizing would be expected to follow disconfirmation. There have been throughout history recurring instances of social movements which do satisfy the conditions adequately. These are the millennial or messianic movements, a contemporary instance of which we shall be examining in detail.

Typically, millennial or messianic movements are organized around the prediction of some future events. Sometimes the predicted event is the second coming of Christ and the beginning of Christ's reign on earth; sometimes it is the destruction of the world through a cataclysm; or sometimes the prediction is concerned with particular occurrences that the Messiah or a miracle worker will bring about. Whatever the event predicted, the fact that its nature and the time of its happening are specified satisfies the third point on our list of conditions.

The second condition specifies strong behavioral commitment to the belief. This usually follows almost as a consequence of the situation. If one really believes a prediction (the first condition), for example, that on a given date the world will be destroyed by fire, with sinners being destroyed and the good being saved, one does things about it and makes certain preparations as a matter of course. These actions may range all the way from simple public declarations to the neglect of worldly things and the disposal of earthly possessions. Through such actions and through the mocking and scoffing of nonbelievers there is usually established a heavy commitment on the part of believers. What they do by way of preparation is difficult to undo, and the jeering of non-believers simply makes it far more difficult for the adherents to withdraw from the movement and admit that they were wrong.

Our fourth specification has invariably been provided. The predicted events have not occurred. There is usually no mistaking the fact that they did not occur and the believers know that.

Finally, our fifth condition is ordinarily satisfied—such movements do attract adherents and disciples, sometimes only a handful, occasionally hundreds of thousands.

History has recorded many such movements. From these we have chosen several relatively clear examples of the phenomena under scrutiny in an endeavor simply to show what has often happened in movements that made a prediction about the future and then saw it disconfirmed.

Ever since the crucifixion of Jesus, many Christians have hoped for the second coming of Christ, and movements predicting specific dates for this event have not been rare. But most of the very early ones were not recorded in such a fashion that we can be sure of the reactions of believers to the disconfirmations they may have experienced.

There is somewhat better documentation of millennial movements in more recent history. Such was the situation in 1533, when the end of the world was due. Many people had accepted this belief and some were even disposing of their worldly goods. What happened as the end of 1533 approached and, indeed, when 1534 arrived, without the Second Coming having materialized?

From all accounts it would seem that instead of dampening the ardor of the Anabaptists, the disconfirmation of the predicted Second Coming increased their enthusiasm and activity. They poured greater energy than ever before into obtaining new converts, and sent out missionaries, something they never had done before.

Another, and rather fascinating, illustration of the reaction to disconfirming evidence is provided by the messianic movement of which Sabbatai Zevi was the central figure. Sabbatai Zevi was born and raised in the city of Smyrna. By 1646 he had acquired considerable prestige through living a highly ascetic life and devoting his whole energy to the study of the cabala. Indeed, though he was only twenty years old, he had already gathered around him a small group of disciples. To these disciples he taught and interpreted the highly mystical writings of the cabala.

Prevalent among Jews at that time was the belief that the Messiah would come in the year 1648. His coming was to be accompanied by all manner of miracles and the era of redemption would dawn. Sometime in 1648 Sabbatai Zevi proclaimed himself as the promised Messiah to his small group of disciples. Needless to say, the year 1648 passed and the era of redemption did not dawn and the expected miracles were not forthcoming. The significant point for our interest is that it was *after* the year 1648 had passed and nothing had happened that Zevi proclaimed his messiahship to people outside his small circle of disciples.

Clearly, we may regard Zevi's later arrest as a serious disappointment to the followers of Sabbatai and a disconfirmation of his predictions. Indeed, there were evidences of shock and disappointment. But then there began to emerge the familiar pattern: recovery of conviction, followed by new heights of enthusiasm and proselytizing.

The very fact that Sabbatai was still alive was used by the Jews to argue that he was really the Messiah. When he was moved to another jail and his incarceration became milder (largely through bribery) the argument was complete. A constant procession of adoring followers visited the prison where Sabbatai held court, and a steady stream of propaganda and tales of miracles poured out all over the Near East and Europe.

The Sabbataian movement strikingly illustrates the phenomenon we are concerned with: when people are committed to a belief and a course of action, clear disconfirming evidence may simply result in deepened conviction and increased proselytizing. But there does seem to be a point at which the disconfirming evidence has mounted sufficiently to cause the belief to be rejected.

There are many more historical examples we could describe at the risk of becoming repetitive and at the risk of using highly unreliable data. Let the examples we have already given suffice.

We can now turn our attention to the question of why increased proselyting follows the disconfirmation of a prediction. How can we explain it and what are the factors that will determine whether or not it will occur?

Since our explanation will rest upon one derivation from a general theory, we will first state the bare essentials of the theory which are necessary for this derivation. The full theory has wide implications and a variety of experiments have already been conducted to test derivations concerning such things as the consequences of decisions, the effects of producing forced compliance, and some patterns of voluntary exposure to new information. At this point, we shall draw out in detail only those implications that are relevant to the phenomenon of increased proselytizing following disconfirmation of a prediction. For this purpose we shall introduce the concepts of consonance and dissonance.

Dissonance and consonance are relations among cognitions—that is, among opinions, beliefs, knowledge of the environment, and knowledge of one's own actions and feelings. Two opinions, or beliefs, or items of knowledge are *dissonant* with each other if they do not fit together—that is, if they are inconsistent, or if, considering only the particular two items, one does not follow from the other. For example, a cigarette smoker who believes that smoking is bad for his health has an opinion that is dissonant with the knowledge that he is continuing to smoke. He may have many other opinions, beliefs, or items of knowledge that are consonant with continuing to smoke but the dissonance nevertheless exists too.

Dissonance produces discomfort and, correspondingly, there will arise pressures to reduce or eliminate the dissonance. The person may try to change one or more of the beliefs, opinions, or behaviors involved in the dissonance; to acquire new information or beliefs that will increase the existing consonance and thus cause the total dissonance to be reduced; or to forget or reduce the importance of those cognitions that are in a dissonant relationship.

If any of the above attempts are to be successful, they must meet with support from either the physical or the social environment. In the absence of such support, the most determined efforts to reduce dissonance may be unsuccessful.

The foregoing statement of the major ideas about dissonance and its reduction is a very brief one and, for that reason, it may be difficult to follow. We can perhaps make these ideas clearer to the reader by showing how they apply to the kind of social movement we have been discussing, and by pointing out how these ideas help to explain the curious phenomenon we have observed.

Theoretically, what is the situation of the individual believer at the pre-disconfirmation stage of such a movement? He has a strongly held belief in a prediction—for example, that Christ will return—a belief that is supported by the other members of the movement. By way of preparation for the predicted event, he has engaged in many activities that are entirely consistent with his belief. In other words, most of the relations among relevant cognitions are, at this point, consonant.

Now what is the effect of the disconfirmation, of the unequivocal fact that the prediction was wrong, upon the believer? The disconfirmation introduces an important and painful dissonance.

The fact that the predicted events did not occur is dissonant with continuing to believe both the prediction and the remainder of the ideology of which the prediction was the central item. The failure of the prediction is also dissonant with all the actions that the believer took in preparation for its fulfillment. The magnitude of the dissonance will, of course, depend on the importance of the belief to the individual and on the magnitude of his preparatory activity.

In the type of movement we have discussed, the central belief and its accompanying ideology are usually of crucial importance in the believers' lives and hence the dissonance is very strong—and very painful to tolerate. Accordingly we should expect to observe believers making determined efforts to eliminate the dissonance or, at least, to reduce its magnitude. How may they accomplish this end? The dissonance would be largely eliminated if they discarded the belief that had been disconfirmed, ceased the behavior which had been initiated in preparation for the fulfillment of the prediction, and returned to a more usual existence. Indeed, this pattern sometimes occurs and we have seen that it did happen to the Sabbataians after Zevi himself was converted to Islam. But frequently the behavioral commitment to the belief system is so strong that almost any other course of action is preferable. It may even be less painful to tolerate the dissonance than to discard the belief and admit one had been wrong. When that is the case, the dissonance cannot be eliminated by giving up the belief.

Alternatively, the dissonance would be reduced or eliminated if the members of a movement effectively blind themselves to the fact that the prediction has not been fulfilled. But most people, including members of such movements, are in touch with reality and cannot simply blot out of their cognition such an unequivocal and undeniable fact. They can try to ignore it, however, and they usually do try. They may convince themselves that the date was wrong but that the prediction will, after all, be shortly confirmed; or they may even set another date. Or believers may try to find reasonable explanations and very often they find ingenious ones. The Sabbataians, for example, convinced themselves when Zevi was jailed that the very fact that he was still alive proved he was the Messiah. Even after his conversion some stanch adherents claimed this, too, was part of the plan. Rationalization can reduce dissonance somewhat. For rationalization to be fully effective, support from others is needed to make the explanation or the revision seem correct. Fortunately, the disappointed believer can usually turn to the others in the same movement, who have the same dissonance and the same pressures to reduce it. Support for the new explanation is, hence, forthcoming and the members of the movement can recover somewhat from the shock of the disconfirmation.

But whatever explanation is made it is still by itself not sufficient. The dissonance is too important and though they may try to hide it, even from themselves, the believers still know that the prediction was false and all their preparations were in vain. The dissonance cannot be eliminated completely by denying or rationalizing the disconfirmation. But there is a way in which the remaining dissonance can be reduced. *If more and more people can be persuaded that the system of belief is correct, then clearly it must, after all, be correct.* Consider the extreme case: if everyone in the whole world believed something there would be no question at all as to the validity of this belief. It is for this reason that we observe the increase in proselytizing following disconfirmation. If the proselytizing proves successful, then by gathering more adherents and effectively surrounding himself with supporters, the believer reduces dissonance to the point where he can live with it.

There is a type of occurrence that would indeed disprove our explanation—namely, a movement whose members simply maintained the same conviction after disconfirmation as they had before and neither fell away from the movement nor increased their proselytizing. But it is precisely such an occurrence that might very well go unnoticed by its contemporaries or

by historians and never find its way into their annals.

Since the likelihood of disproof through historical data is small, we cannot place much confidence in the supporting evidence from the same sources. The reader can then imagine the enthusiasm with which we seized the opportunity to collect direct observational data about a group who appeared to believe in a prediction of catastrophe to occur in the near future. Direct observations made before, during, and after the disconfirmation would produce at least one case that was fully documented by trustworthy data directly relevant to our purpose.

One day in late September the Lake City *Herald* carried a two-column story, on a back page, headlined: PROPHECY FROM PLANET. CLARION CALL TO CITY: FLEE THAT FLOOD. IT'LL SWAMP US ON DEC. 21, OUTER SPACE TELLS SUBURBANITE. The body of the story expanded somewhat on these bare facts:

> Lake City will be destroyed by a flood from Great Lake just before dawn, Dec. 21, according to a suburban housewife. Mrs. Marian Keech, of 847 West School street, says the prophecy is not her own. It is the purport of many messages she has received by automatic writing, she says....The messages, according to Mrs. Keech, are sent to her by superior beings from a planet called 'Clarion.' These beings have been visiting the earth, she says, in what we call flying saucers. During their visits, she says, they have observed fault lines in the earth's crust that foretoken the deluge. Mrs. Keech reports she was told the flood will spread to form an inland sea stretching from the Arctic Circle to the Gulf of Mexico. At the same time, she says, a cataclysm will submerge the West Coast from Seattle, Wash., to Chile in South America.

The story went on to report briefly the origin of Mrs. Keech's experiences and to quote several messages that seemed to indicate she had been chosen as a person to learn and transmit teachings from the "superior beings." A photograph of Mrs. Keech accompanied the story. She appeared to be about fifty years of age, and she sat poised with pad and pencil in her lap, a slight, wiry woman with dark hair and intense, bright eyes. The story was not derogatory, nor did the reporter comment upon or interpret any of the information he had gathered.

Since Mrs. Keech's pronouncement made a specific prediction of a specific event, since she, at least, was publicly committed to belief in it, and since she apparently was interested to some extent in informing a wider public about it, this seemed to be an opportunity to conduct a "field" test of the theoretical ideas to which the reader has been introduced.

In early October two of the authors called on Mrs. Keech and tried to learn whether there were other convinced persons in her orbit of influence, whether they too believed in the specific prediction, and what commitments of time, energy, reputation, or material possessions they might be making in connection with the prediction. The results of this first visit encouraged us to go on. The three of us and some hired observers joined the group and, as participants, gathered data about the conviction, commitment, and proselyting activity of the individuals who were actively interested in Mrs. Keech's ideas. We tried to learn as much as possible about the events that had preceded the news story, and, of course, kept records of subsequent developments.

DISCUSSION QUESTIONS

1. What are the five conditions outlined by Festinger et al. that coexist to increase personal conviction despite contrary evidence?
2. Have you ever encountered someone with strong commitment to their beliefs despite contrary evidence? If so, provide an example.
3. What do Festinger et al. mean by the terms "consonance" and "dissonance?" Provide examples of each.
4. According to Festinger et al., how do people attempt to decrease cognitive dissonance?

ADDITIONAL RESOURCES

Film

"2012." An epic film about the end of the world. 155 minutes. http://www.whowillsurvive2012.com/.

Internet

http://umcssa.org/2012-end-of-the-world-prophecies. This website contains several prophecies about the end of the world that are predicted to occur in the year 2012.

http://www.circleofa.org/articles/AcimStory.php. This website describes how the contemporary spiritual text *A Course in Miracles* was transcribed via the same "automatic writing" that Festinger et al.'s research subject, Mrs. Keech, used to receive messages from aliens.

http://www.endoftheworldprophecy.com/. This website for an end of the world prophecy provides biblical verses predicting the apocalypse.

http://www.saintgermainfoundation.org/. A website dedicated to the "I AM" spiritual movement of the twentieth century.

http://www.y2ktimebomb.com/. A website detailing the "Y2K" computer bug that was expected to cause mass chaos at the turn of the twenty-first century.

FURTHER READING

Bader, Chris. 1999. "When Prophecy Passes Unnoticed: New Perspectives on Failed Prophecy." *Journal for the Scientific Study of Religion,* 38(1): 119–31.

Balch, Robert W., Gwen Farnsworth, and Sue Wilkins. 1983. "When the Bombs Drop: Reactions to Disconfirmed Prophecy in a Millennial Sect." *Sociological Perspectives,* 26(2): 137–58.

Dein, Simon. 2001. "What Happens When Prophecy Really Fails: The Case of Lubavitch." *Sociology of Religion,* 62(3): 383–401.

Festinger, Leon, Henry Riecken, and Stanley Schacter. 1956. *When Prophecy Fails: A Social and Psychological Study of a Modern Group that Predicted the Destruction of the World.* Minneapolis: University of Minnesota Press.

Festinger, Leon. 1957. *A Theory of Cognitive Dissonance.* Palo Alto: Stanford University Press.

Greenwald, Anthony G. and David L. Ronis. 1978. "Twenty Years of Cognitive Dissonance: A Case Study of the Evolution of a Theory." *Psychological Review,* 85(1): 53–7.

Scott-Kakures, Dion. 2009. "Unsettling Questions: Cognitive Dissonance in Self-Deception." *Social Theory and Practice,* 35(1): 73–106.

Shaw, Eric K. 2001. "Pennies from Heaven: An integration of Cognitive Dissonance and Spiritual Frames in a Prosperity Church." *Sociological Focus,* 34(2): 213–29.

Singelenberg, Richard. 1989. ' "It Separated the Wheat from the Chaff': The '1975' Prophecy and Its Impact among Dutch Jehovah's Witnesses." *Sociological Analysis,* 50(1): 23–40.

Stone, Jon R. 2009. "Prophecy and Dissonance: A Reassessment of Research Testing the Festinger Theory." *Nova Religio: The Journal of Alternative and Emergent Religions,* 12(4): 72–90.

van Fossen, Anthony B. 1988. "How Do Movements Survive Failures of Prophecy?" *Research in Social Movements, Conflicts, and Change,* 10: 193–212.

Weiser, Neil. 1974. "The Effects of Prophetic Disconfirmation of the Committed." *Review of Religious Research,* 16(1): 19–30.

Wernik, Uri. 1979. "Cognitive Dissonance Theory, Religious Reality, and Extreme Reactionism." *The Psychohistory Review* 7(3): 22–8.

Wilson, Bryan. 1978. "When Prophecy Failed." *New Society,* 43(799): 183–4.

57. Out of the O.R. and into the Streets: Exploring the Impact of Intersex Media Activism

SHARON E. PREVES

Preves traces the tensions within and transformation of the intersex rights movement from radical activism against the medical establishment to affiliation with medical professionals. Since the publication of this article, the intersex rights movement has become even more polarized with the closure of the Intersex Society of North America in 2008 and the creation of a new label for intersex conditions, lauded by ISNA's founding director, Cheryl Chase: disorders of sex development.

INTRODUCTION

Every day babies are born with bodies that are deemed sexually ambiguous and with regularity they are surgically altered to reflect the sexual anatomy associated with "standard" female and male sex assignment. Recent estimates indicate that approximately one or two in every 2000 infants are born with anatomy that some people regard as sexually ambiguous; that is, they are born with ambiguous genitalia, sexual organs, or sex chromosomes (Blackless et al., 2000). To put these numbers in perspective, although its occurrence has only recently begun to be openly discussed, physical sexual ambiguity occurs about as often as the well-known conditions of cystic fibrosis and Down syndrome (Desai, 1997; Dreger, 1998; Roberts et al., 1998). These statistics indicate that intersexuality is far more common than is publicly recognized.

Due to the efforts of intersex activists, the frequency and medicalization of sexual ambiguity have recently become common topics of classroom and dinner table conversation. What it means to be intersexed is itself currently being redefined. Given the context of the social movements of the last 40 years it is not a surprise that many people recently began questioning the ethics and effectiveness of intersex medical sex assignment procedures. Most of these critics agree that surgical sex assignment is not in the best interest of intersexuals and that performing surgery without the patient's consent (meaning the child's consent, *not* their parents') is unethical. They argue that intersex ought to be demedicalized because it is not in itself pathological. The critics claim, rather, that the pathology lies in the social system and its strict adherence to gender and sexual binarism.

This article explores how the very definition of what it means to be intersexed has transitioned from what was once considered an obscure and shameful medical condition to a recently politicized category of identity within the past 15 years. I outline the recent mobilization of North American intersexuals and their attempts to destigmatize physical sexual variation and to transform medical practice. I also consider the intersex movement's use of mass media as a tool to reframe medical and lay conceptions of hermaphroditism, and the explosion of media coverage about intersex in recent years. Using frame analysis to understand the ways in which meanings about intersex are constructed, I examine the impact of the intersex rights movement on medical education and practice, scholarly research, and popular culture.

Preves, Sharon E. 2004. "Out of the O.R. and into the Streets: Exploring the Impact of Intersex Media Activism." *Research in Political Sociology*, 13: 179–223.

THE SEXUAL POLITICS OF MEDICAL SEX ASSIGNMENT

While being born with indeterminate sexual organs indeed problematizes a binary understanding of sex and gender, there seems to be general consensus (even among the doctors performing the "normalizing" operations) that most children with ambiguous sexual anatomy do not require medical intervention for their physiological health. Nevertheless, the majority of sexually ambiguous infants are medically assigned a definitive sex, often undergoing repeated genital surgeries and ongoing hormone treatments, to "correct" their variation from the norm.

For well over 50 years in the United States, doctors have framed intersex as a social emergency in need of immediate medical attention to mitigate the stigma that may be associated with being perceived as sexually "deviant." That is, medical treatments to surgically or hormonally alter intersexed children to appear genitally "normal" serve to erase or downplay what doctors perceive to be sexual abnormalities. Because of its association with "deviant" sexuality, medical doctors have also constructed intersex as a shameful condition, one many physicians claim (despite a lack of documentation) that will result in feelings of suicidal despair.

The medical construction of intersex as a shameful social emergency has recently begun to shift with the continued attempts at reframing intersex in a more positive and less pathological light brought about by intersex activists.

THE INTERSEX SOCIAL MOVEMENT

In the early to mid-1990s a heated debate about the medical management of intersex developed between intersex activists, scholars, and clinicians all seemingly dedicated to the same goal: destigmatizing people who are born with sexual ambiguity. Primary points of contention between these groups are whether or not most interventions are medically necessary, or whether these procedures are primarily cosmetic and potentially psychologically and physiologically harmful. This

debate is quite polarized. Many involved say there isn't sufficient evidence to warrant continued medical intervention. Others dismiss the critiques of intersex activists as representative of only an unhappy vocal minority.

A cornerstone of this debate is the popular attention many intersex groups and individuals have garnered by expressing their dissatisfaction with intersex medical intervention in such a way as to identify a unified injustice frame. These activists articulate their grievances as follows: (1) the majority of medical interventions, from a strictly physiological point of view, are not necessary for survival; (2) as a result of medical intervention, both sexual and psychological satisfaction and functioning are often impaired; and (3) for intersex individuals the lack of open discussion of their intersex status results in feelings of shame and isolation. This critique is evident in intersexuals' personal stories, many of which have been featured in popular and scholarly publications.

Despite the medical aim to surgically erase or downplay sexual ambiguity, many intersexuals are finding each other through their own activism and are attempting to reframe their difference as a source of pride. In fact, in recent years intersexuals have been implementing their own networks of support and avenues for social change at a rapid pace.

As is true with other contemporary social movements, the intersex movement has used electronic media and communications, including the Internet and electronic mail, as a primary means of participant recruitment and networking. Internet technology, with its relative accessibility, has given former patients and family members an opportunity to discuss intersex beyond the clinic, in their own homes and virtual communities. For successful mobilization of disparate individuals, such communication networks are essential. Many individuals and families have developed their own web sites that are linked to a larger support group's site, in order to tell their stories and connect with other people and families who are also connected to intersex. Given the silence and secrecy surrounding intersex, the Internet has been especially important for people to seek out others in a relatively anonymous forum.

EMERGENCE OF A KEY ADVOCACY GROUP: THE INTERSEX SOCIETY OF NORTH AMERICA

For the purposes of this article, I focus on one organization in particular, the Intersex Society of North America (ISNA), because it is the most active and visible group with regard to intersex advocacy and media action; indeed, it has become the movement's most well known representative. In addition to exploring the activism of the Intersex Society, I focus on the work of one key figure within the organization: ISNA's founding director, Cheryl Chase. As evidence of their significance, consider that ISNA and Chase had acquired so much media attention by 1998 that Chase was voted one of the one 100 "most interesting and influential gay men and lesbians in America" in *Out* magazine's top 100 people of the year (*Out*, 1998)

In addition to ISNA, a significant number of intersex support and advocacy groups formed throughout the world between 1987 and 2009.

Cheryl Chase founded the Intersex Society of North America in 1993 by publishing a letter to the editor in the July/August issue of the New York Academy of Sciences' journal, *The Sciences* (Chase, 1993, p. 3). Chase wrote this letter in response to biologist Anne Fausto-Sterling's article "The Five Sexes," which appeared in the March/April issue of the journal that same year (Fausto-Sterling, 1993). In her letter, Chase critiqued intersex medical sex assignment as "immensely destructive" raising concerns about the ethics and effectiveness of phallocentric surgical procedures that impair sexual and psychological function. In doing so, Chase paired this intersex injustice frame with ISNA's very inception. In the last line of her letter, Chase announced the formation of a support group for intersexuals called the Intersex Society of North America. At the time she wrote the letter, the Intersex Society didn't yet exist. In

actuality, the organization was formed by Chase's publication of this letter to the editor. In the signature line, Chase listed a mailing address for ISNA and she soon began receiving mail from other intersexuals throughout the world.

One of Chase's primary objectives in establishing ISNA was to document intersex people's experiences to further amplify the injustice frame she established in her letter to the editor in *The Sciences*. Fittingly, the early issues of the *Hermaphrodites with Attitude* newsletter consisted primarily of personal stories, essays, and poetry. These personal contributions provided formerly isolated individuals with the means to develop political consciousness and frame resonance about their personal experiences by connecting them to the experiences of others like themselves. The newsletter quickly extended beyond its role of providing support to formerly isolated intersexuals by becoming a source of activism and frame bridging in its own right when Chase and others began distributing the newsletter to journalists, scholars, civil rights organizers, medical doctors and others who could draw attention to ISNA's grievances and their mission to effect clinical change.

Hermaphrodites with Attitude was published on a fairly regular basis from 1994 to 1999. In addition to its newsletter, ISNA has provided other resources over the years to intersexuals and the public at large such as the former bimonthly support groups, which started in January 1995, a popular Internet website that went online in January 1996, and the once-held annual retreats that began in September 1996.

More recently, ISNA retooled itself to put forth a more professional image. This frame transformation is apparent in the organization's new newsletter format, *ISNA News*, introduced in February 2001. In addition to the newsletter's change in title, *ISNA News* moved away from the personal stories and humor that were commonplace in *Hermaphrodites with Attitude* to amplify its reporting of professional and organizational concerns such as financial reports, profiles of board members, and the continued coverage of medical conferences and research. The Intersex Society's shift in newsletter format mirrors the overarching frame realignment that has taken place within the movement, as activists and doctors have begun working alongside one another for change, rather than against each other as political adversaries. This frame transformation from ISNA being associated with an injustice frame characterized by personal medical trauma was made even more complete when Cheryl Chase stepped down as the executive director and a nonintersexed medical sociologist, Monica Casper, took the helm in January 2003. Under Casper's leadership, ISNA extended its frame to utilize Casper's networks in disability studies, and children's and women's rights arenas. After a year of service, Casper decided to step down as ISNA's executive director, effective January 2004. In a surprising turn of events, Cheryl Chase stepped back in at the beginning of 2004 to serve as ISNA's executive director once again. It is unclear at the time of this writing as to whether or not Chase's reprised role as ISNA's executive director will be to merely bridge a gap between the service of others, or if she is back as the director for the long term.

FRAMING IDENTITY: TENSIONS WITHIN THE INTERSEX MOVEMENT

As is true with other social movements, there is a diversity of groups within the intersex movement and not all agree on the goals or methods of making change. In fact, there has been considerable tension between intersex activists about the objectives and tactics of the movement, including how best to frame intersex to be most attractive to potential movement recruits and supporters. As the number of intersex groups, voices, and opinions proliferated, struggles over the methods and very purpose of the movement ensued. The very definition of what it means to be intersexed is politicized, contested, and fraught with conflict, as is the objective of mobilization. Such tensions are a predictable element of frame alignment

processes because individuals and groups bring competing ideologies to their interactions with one another.

Clearly, all of the intersex groups work toward destigmatizing intersex; however, some do this through peer support while others work toward achieving systemic social change and changes in medical education and practice. In fact, what began as a peer support movement in the late 1980s has more recently developed into an advocacy movement focused on medical, political, and cultural transformation. It was ISNA's shift away from peer support and toward political action that caused the first divide among intersex groups. This is where the story of intersex activism (and media activism in particular) becomes a story about ISNA, rather than the larger intersex movement.

The second, longer lasting split occurred as ISNA continued to associate intersex with gay, lesbian, bisexual, and transgender issues. Given that fear of sexual difference seems to drive medical sex assignment, this conflict should come as no surprise. Some of the support groups have intentionally aligned themselves with GLBT allies. Other groups, especially those run by parents of intersex children, have expressed their reticence to associate intersex with GLBT persons and concerns. In fact, in speaking with parents of intersex children, I have encountered parents' explicit efforts to sever associations between intersex and GLBT issues. Despite this clear divide among interested parties, the Intersex Society of North America has made deliberate appeals to queer activists, press outlets, and medical organizations, framing intersex as an issue of gender and sexuality from its inception in 1993. ISNA's decision to do so has no doubt increased its linkages to GLBT persons and groups, but at the same time alienated itself from the potential support of others who disagree with the organization's framing of intersex in this way.

In its infancy, ISNA's mission was divided between providing peer support to its members and its objective of medical reform. While other intersex groups chose to address the mission of providing support, ISNA ultimately decided to pursue advocacy and social change. Their political action alienated them from other activists and groups that were far less political. In fact, while I was conducting interviews with members of various intersex support groups in the late 1990s, several interviewees frequently identified themselves as non-ISNA members with a sentiment of, "You know I'm not part of that radical lobbying group, right?" More recently, when I was asked to speak about my research at an intersex support group's annual conference, I was given a list of issues to avoid, lest I present intersex as too political or too "queer" (read: "too ISNA") and end up alienating potential recruits of the group or their family members. Thus, even when activists disagree with ISNA's position, the organization maintains its central role in defining the intersex movement and its activities.

Consider the intersex groups that have formed more recently, such as Intersex Initiative Portland and Bodies Like Ours, both of which emerged in direct response to services their leaders perceived to be lacking in the work of the Intersex Society of North America. Intersex Initiative's founding director, Emi Koyama, used to be an intern and staff member at ISNA. Because of her experience working for ISNA, she saw a need to develop another intersex political action group that had the willingness to confront medical doctors the way ISNA once did, before its recent collaborative, and more palatable, approach to medicine. Her decision to form Intersex Initiative is an example of a movement participant's negative response to ISNA's "professional" frame transformation and extension through its allegiance building within medical communities. That is, Koyama was disappointed that ISNA no longer voiced its critique in the acerbic tones it once employed. Furthermore, Koyama's choice to return to the movement's earlier, more radical, frame is an example of frame amplification (or perhaps even frame resurrection). Here Koyama conveys the need to implement a radical intersex political organization

and rearticulates the movement's earlier injustice frame:

> I think of Intersex Initiative as similar to what ISNA used to be. With one foot inside the medical community, ISNA can no longer afford to take certain positions that they used to. For example, our mission statement says that we are working to end the medical abuse of intersex children, but ISNA cannot afford to use the word "abuse" to describe what happens to intersex children today—"misguided treatment" perhaps, but calling it "abuse" would instantly result in ISNA losing its ability to work with medical "experts." This is understandable, but is sometimes difficult for many people who feel that what was done to them was nothing less than "abuse." As it should be obvious, any doctor who is now on ISNA's side used to belong to the other side until three years ago. There are a lot of intersex people who are murderously angry at them, but now they see these same doctors being friendly and having dinner with ISNA, which most people understand, but still feels like a betrayal. I reactivated Intersex Initiative instead of continuing to work within ISNA because I felt that there needed to be other groups that work on the goals we share through different tactics (Personal e-mail communication. Quote used with permission).

Similarly, Bodies Like Ours was developed in response to what the founding directors saw as lacking in the larger intersex movement, and in the Intersex Society in particular. As ISNA moved toward advocacy and away from providing peer support, other groups emerged to provide support to people affected by specific diagnoses or "conditions" (e.g., the Androgen Insensitivity Support Groups). Some activists dedicated to providing support saw the need for bridge building to network people with disparate intersex diagnoses. In co-founder Betsy Driver's words,

> Eventually, we came to realize that the intersex movement needed more than just ISNA as they were focused on the policy and advocacy side. After speaking with Cheryl [Chase] about it, and tossing around ideas to expand

the movement, it became clear that there was a need for a non-condition specific peer support organization (Personal e-mail communication. Quote used with permission).

Although it is focused on support, Bodies Like Ours integrates political action into its work, such as their September 26, 2003 protest of "intersex genital mutilation" in front of the Connecticut Children's Medical Center in Hartford, after the organization's leaders learned about an upcoming intersex surgery to be performed in a teaching theater. They summarize this event on their website: "The hospital went from ignoring us early in the week to inviting us in for a future date to share the adult survivor perspective. Dr. Rink [the doctor from Indiana University who was to perform the procedure] cancelled his appearance due to the publicity surrounding our plans. Finally, we made the front page of the Hartford Courant that morning with a well-written article about intersexuality" (Altimari, 2003; Bodies Like Ours, 2004).

Despite their differences, ISNA, Intersex Initiative, and Bodies Like Ours frequently work closely with one another and have formed an allegiance to further destigmatize intersex by cosponsoring the first-ever international "Intersex Awareness Day" in 2004 (http://www.intersex-awareness-day.org).

LEARNING TO USE MEDIA AS A FORM OF ACTIVISM

The Intersex Society's early use of media as an activist tool solidified the association of intersex with GLBT issues. Using media as a tool to meet its goals, ISNA adopted the methods and networks of veteran transgender activists. Chase's vision of support was realized when ISNA held its first intersex retreat, with ten attendees, in the fall of 1996.

Chase was intentional in her use of media to record intersex grievances from the very beginning. This included videotaping ISNA's first retreat, which was later edited and broadly circulated as the medical and university teaching video

"Hermaphrodites Speak!" She also publicized intersexuals' mobilization from the outset.

While intersex is not entirely parallel to GLBT concerns, the issues connected to sexual minority status are in common. That is, intersexuals, regardless of sexual orientation or identity, nonetheless fall into socially constructed categories of "otherness" based on perceived sexual difference. Indeed ISNA aligned itself with other sexually marginalized groups from its inception, establishing long-lasting connections with other groups and their causes. Bridging the frames between GLBT and intersex groups provided much needed support to members of each community given the similarity of the groups' goals and grievances. At the same time, aligning intersex issues with other sexual minorities' compromised intersex activists' ability to establish credibility with the non-GLBT medical mainstream, who view heterosexual normalcy as one of the primary objectives of intersex medical sex assignment.

EVIDENCE OF CLINICAL REFORM

As a direct result of intersexuals' vocal critiques, clinicians have started to reform their practices—and their frames of intersex and intersex treatment—and many are now claiming to be far less eager advocates of surgical intervention on intersexed infants and children. Those who have made these changes are often physicians who have had personal interaction with adult intersexuals who are critical of medicalization. The critiques that are deemed most credible are adults' complaints of sexual dysfunction, due to medically induced nerve damage, and complaints of incorrect gender role assignment.

In addition to this emerging frame transformation within medicine, there is also an apparent shift in the way ISNA frames itself and in the way others perceive the organization. The ISNA that was once barred from attending and speaking at medical conferences is now seen as a credible advocacy organization. This shift is no doubt related to the way ISNA has transformed its approach from its once hostile anti-medical stance to working alongside clinicians to effect change.

Certainly, many clinicians have begun to listen to the concerns, experiences, and needs of intersexuals. Most importantly, some in the medical profession have begun to recognize that the "success" of sex assignment surgery should not rest on the outcome measure of gender identity alone. That is, whether or not the individual later transitions to the "other" gender should not be the only criterion for determining whether surgery is the correct approach or not. Intersex activists have pushed to broaden definitions of clinical success to include quality of life measures and measures of sexual function, family dynamics, and psychological well-being. The National Institutes of Health even issued a program announcement in 2001 for funding dedicated to new and continued research on intersex, and in May 2002 convened a committee dedicated to overseeing research on the topic. This call for more evidence and research has been echoed by many health care providers and scientists, and has resulted in some of the first follow-up studies since the inception of the "normalization" paradigm. Indeed, this call for more research indicates a shift in the intersex injustice frame and objectives of the movement, from activists' previous call to be heard to their new stance of needing more data to support their plea for surgical nonintervention. Some of the findings from this new research are just now beginning to be reported.

Even though the American Academy of Pediatrics and others may still be strong adherents of the "intersex is a social and medical emergency" paradigm, their willingness to be informed by former patient critiques is undoubtedly a dramatic shift. Instead of being relegated to "zapping" and picketing medical conventions, intersex activists are now being featured as invited keynote speakers at prominent medical conventions. For example, in May 2002, Chase addressed the First World Congress on the "Hormonal and Genetic Basis for Sexual Differentiation Disorder," informing them of the agenda of the intersex patient advocacy movement. Clearly, the intersex patients' rights and medical reform movement has garnered significant attention and has begun to effect change. As further evidence, consider the 1998 publication of the *Journal of Clinical Ethics* special issue on intersex, which brought together essays written by intersex activists, scholars, and physicians in one volume. This special issue was published in book form as *Intersex in the Age of Ethics* in 1999 (Dreger), and featured photographs of the authors on the cover. Notably, this was the first time that photographs of intersex doctors and intersex individuals appeared alongside one another without drawing attention to intersexed genitalia. In fact, by looking at the photos alone, there is no way to discern between doctor and patient; intersexed and not.

Also consider the January 2000 formation of the North American Task Force on Intersex (NATFI), which is a clear example of frame bridging that has networked previously unconnected groups to address issues of intersex clinical treatment. The task force was convened by pediatric urologist Ian Aaronson of the Medical University of South Carolina in response to the increasing debate over medical sex assignment in order to reevaluate medical care for children with ambiguous sexual anatomy. A first of its kind, the committee is comprised of specialists from various medical fields, as well as ethicists and members of intersex advocacy organizations, including former patients and critics of medical sex assignment themselves. The committee represents the first decision-making body to bring patients and doctors together to discuss the topic of medical treatment of sexual variation.

The mission of the task force is to improve the standards and experience of medical treatment for people who are subjected to sex "normalizing" procedures. In addition to establishing new medical guidelines, the group has set out to address the previously ignored legal and ethical issues of informed consent and quality of life for intersex patients following medical sex assignment.

Psychologist John Money, the now infamous psychologist who popularized the medical paradigm in question, is notably absent from the 30-person executive committee; however, strong proponents of the current medical model, including the pediatric endocrinologist Claude Migeon and the pediatric urologists John Gearhart and Antoine Khoury, may make up for his absence. In an apparent balancing act, some of the committee's members are among the most vocal critics of intersex medical management, including the Intersex Society of North America's founder Cheryl Chase and the social psychologist Suzanne Kessler. Perhaps one of the biggest indicators of change is that the primary professional medical associations that have even recently touted the merits of conventional sex assignment have signed on as supporters of the group. NATFI is endorsed by the American Academy of Pediatrics, the American Urological Association, the American Academy of Child and Adolescent Psychiatry, the American College of Medical Genetics, the Lawson Wilkins Pediatric Endocrine Society, the Society for Pediatric Urology, the Society for Fetal Urology, and the Society of Genitourinary Reconstructive Surgeons.

The American Academy of Pediatrics (AAP) is among the list of task force endorsers. Their support of this path-breaking patient-doctor dialogue comes just four years after Chase and other members of Hermaphrodites with Attitude picketed the AAP's annual conference when they were refused the opportunity to present patients' perspectives to conference goers (Fausto-Sterling, 2000b). But despite their willingness to back the efforts of the task force, the American Academy of Pediatrics published an article in July of 2000 that reaffirmed and amplified the organization's framing of intersex as a medical emergency and their commitment to prompt medical intervention. I take the following from this article, on which NATFI head Ian Aaronson is listed as a consultant:

> The birth of a child with ambiguous genitalia constitutes a social emergency. Abnormal appearance can be corrected and the child raised as a boy or a girl as appropriate. Parents should be encouraged not to name the child or register the birth, if possible, until the sex of rearing is established. Infants raised as girls will usually require clitoral reduction which, with current techniques, will result not only in a normal-looking vulva but preservation of a functional clitoris. [These children's] diagnosis and prompt treatment require urgent medical attention (American Academy of Pediatrics, 2000, p. 138).

What we see, then, is not only an escalating level of interest in intersex issues within medicine and beyond, but also an entrenchment of the controversy surrounding treatment. While mainstream media coverage focused on issues of gender and sexual identity, and helped to place intersex issues on the map, medical responses to intersex activism focused more specifically on treatment issues and physicians' role in relation to intersex conditions. What this coverage reflects is both the enduring belief among many physicians that intersex is pathological—indeed an emergency—as well as the opposing belief that intersex is simply a benign bodily variation that might warrant some intervention, but not necessarily surgery. What is striking here is that this debate has played out not only at medical conferences, but also in a more public fashion. That is, intersex in the public eye has come to represent not just a bodily condition having to do with sex and gender, but also a condition that is associated with medical controversy. Thus, while intersex is not considered exclusively pathological anymore, it is still lodged firmly within the realm of science and medicine. What people know about intersex continues to be filtered and framed through a biomedical lens.

IMPLICATIONS OF INTERSEX IDENTITY POLITICS

The possibility of developing new clinical guidelines or alternatives to the current medical treatment of intersex is expanding rapidly as a result of intersex activism and new research in this area. With this possibility on the horizon and more and more doctors coming on board to help, the intersex movement has transformed not only the way intersex is seen, but the way it has chosen to represent itself as well. That is, the activist organization that once "zapped" medical conferences is now working on building bridges and on making changes from within the medical arena. Consider ISNA's formation of a Medical Advisory Board in 2003, which currently has 25 members representing general practice, pediatric urology, pediatric endocrinology, nursing, social work, psychiatry, psychology, and bioethics. In 2003, ISNA also established their umbrella project, the Medical Education and Reform Initiative (MERI), which represents a number of ISNA's new programs, such as the Medical Advisory Board. Some of the additional projects included in the MERI initiative are the distribution of ISNA'S documentary: *First Do No Harm: Total Patient Care for Intersex,* the development of medical guidelines, replete with clinicians' and parents' handbooks, and ISNA's plan to revise textbook representations of intersex.

ISNA's move toward policy and advocacy, and away from direct peer support, was begun under Chase and intensified under Casper's brief leadership. During her time at ISNA, Casper helped to extend the intersex movement's concerns to other movements and communities such as those focused on women's health, disability rights, children's rights, sexual rights, and reproductive rights. ISNA began a strategic planning process in 2003 designed to reposition the organization vis-a-vis these communities, while strengthening its relationship to the medical profession and other health care providers.

Regardless of which direction intersex activists move politically, media activism is likely to continue to be an indispensable tool. Whole new audiences might be found by emphasizing any of the above directions. At the same time, however, activists need to balance new approaches with ongoing concerns and commitments. It would

be unfortunate if a shift in direction led to a decrease in support for intersex issues among, for example, either GLBT communities or physicians advocating non-surgical approaches. Also, as the movement has professionalized, including developing more formal relationships with the medical and legal professions, activists need to be careful to not slip into the more "radical" stance taken in the early days of the movement. With increased legitimacy comes increased responsibility to speak in more "established" ways, as Intersex Initiative founder Emi Koyama reminds us in her decision to develop an activist organization untethered to such political concerns.

CONCLUSIONS

In sum, the intersex social movement and its adversaries have engaged in meaningful framing processes that have helped to further the advancement of the movement's objectives and the medical establishment's clarification of its changing perspectives on intersex treatment.

Before intersex mobilization and political and media activism, most North Americans didn't know the meaning of the word *hermaphrodite,* let alone *intersex.* Within recent years, the topic of sexual ambiguity has been featured in national magazines, popular and educational television shows, and local news media. With the breadth of activists' important and effective efforts to demedicalize and destigmatize intersex, scholars have placed the topic of sexual ambiguity under the rubric of queer theory and gender studies. As a result, a new field of intersex studies, replete with its own canon, is currently in formation. Moreover, some university and community groups have extended the customary GLBT classification (now GLBTI) to demonstrate their inclusion of intersex issues among queer rights and politics.

The intersex movement has shaped and been reshaped by the strategic use of media activism. During the first decade of the movement's growth, key players, such as the Intersex Society of North

America and Cheryl Chase, used the media to position intersex as an important concern, and to generate public support for the movement's goals, building a bridge between those concerned with intersex and those concerned with broader themes of human and children's rights. The major accomplishment of this period was to put intersex issues on the map, making intersex injustice frames familiar to previously "unconcerned" others, and to work toward increasing public understanding and acceptance of intersex. However, because some of these strategies were learned from gender warriors and transactivists, and because intersex is culturally linked to gender and sexuality, the issue of intersex has been conflated with issues of sexuality and gender. On the one hand, this has enabled intersex activists to gain allies in GLBT communities, including the provision of crucial movement funding and mentorship. On the other hand, this attention to sex and gender has precluded others from resonating with the intersex movement's grievances and goals.

The medical profession has also been very present in media discourse about intersex. Initially weighing in on what intersex is, medical professionals subsequently began to use the media to challenge one another about appropriate means and methods of responding to intersex. In this public exchange, medical doctors have both amplified the traditional medical perspective of intersex as a "social and medical emergency" as well as articulated an emerging trend in medical education and practice towards nonsurgical intervention. The past decade has seen a quite lively debate about how intersex should be treated, with many physicians adhering to a "traditional" surgical approach, and others advocating the newer model of delayed or even no surgery. What is clear is that general media coverage of intersex helped to broaden the movement organized around intersex advocacy, which in turn helped to place the medical debate at the forefront of key intersex issues. Intersex media activism has been instrumental in destabilizing heretofore widely accepted medical practices. While intersex activists have not reached their ultimate goal of preventing surgery on all intersexed infants (in the absence of life-threatening conditions), they have been successful in putting the medical profession on the defensive, and in sparking what has become a heated and increasingly consequential controversy.

DISCUSSION QUESTIONS

1. Preves provides a definition of intersex and information about its prevalence. What is intersex and how often does this variation in anatomy occur?
2. What are the three issues held in common by intersex activists that they attempt to address with their advocacy?
3. Despite their common interests, Preves shows that intersex activists use competing methods. What seems to be the main issue causing tension between these activists who seem to have so much in common?
4. Are you aware of similar tensions in other social movements? Provide an example.
5. What do you think of the change in medical and activist language from "intersex" to "disorders of sex development?" What might account for such a dramatic shift?

ADDITIONAL RESOURCES

Film

"XXY." 2008. A powerful Argentinean film about a 15-year-old hermaphroditic girl. In Spanish with English subtitles. 86 minutes. http://www.peccadillopictures.com/View/id,68.

"Is It a Boy or a Girl?" 2000. A Discovery Channel documentary featuring Intersex Society of North America founder Cheryl Chase. 60 minutes. http://www.isna.org/videos/boy_or_girl

Internet

http://www.accordalliance.org/. The website for Accord Alliance, the nonprofit organization that developed from the Intersex Society of North America after its directors adopted the language "disorders of sex development" to describe conditions previously referred to as "intersex."

http://www.indiana.edu/~ais/html/home.html. The website for the Androgen Insensitivity Syndrome Support Group, U.S.

http://www.dsdguidelines.org/. The website for Disorders of Sex Development Guidelines, a project of the Consortium on the Disorders of Sex Development.

http://www.aboutkidshealth.ca/HowTheBodyWorks/Sex-Development.aspx?articleID=7671&categoryID=XS. This website, hosted by the Hospital for Sick Children in Toronto, provides a fascinating, interactive tutorial on intersex, female, and male sex development.

http://www.isna.org/library/hwa. All issues of the newsletter *Hermaphrodites with Attitude*, formerly published by the Intersex Society of North America, are available in PDF form via this link.

http://www.ipdx.org/. The website for Intersex Initiative.

http://www.isna.org/. The website for the now defunct Intersex Society of North America. The directors of Accord Alliance are keeping up the ISNA website as an archive.

http://www.intersexualite.org/Index.html. The website for Organisation Intersex International, a nonprofit group based in Quebec that strongly supports intersex advocacy and denounces the "nomenclature" disorders of sex development.

http://notadisorder.weebly.com/index.html. "Not a Disorder" is a blog created by the founding director of Organisation Intersex International to critique the disorders of sex development label and the closure of the Intersex Society of North America.

FURTHER READING

Altimari, Daniela. September 26, 2003. "Born Neither Girl nor Boy, They Speak Out." *Hartford Courant*, A1.

American Academy of Pediatrics, Committee on Genetics. 2000. "Evaluation of the Newborn with Developmental Anomalies of the External Genitalia." *Pediatrics*, 106(1): 138–42.

Blackless, Melanie, Anthony Charuvastra, Amanda Derryck, Anne Fausto-Sterling, K. Lauzanne, & E. Lee. 2000. "How Sexually Dimorphic Are We?" *American Journal of Human Biology*, 12(2): 151–66.

Bodies Like Ours. 2004. "Hartford Action Wrap-up." Retrieved February 15, 2004, from http://www.bodieslikeours.org/hartford03.html.

Chase, Cheryl. 1993. "Intersexual Rights. Letter to the Editor." *The Sciences*, July/August, 3.

Desai, Sindoor S. 1997. "Down Syndrome: A Review of the Literature." *Oral Surgery, Oral Medicine, Oral Pathology, Oral Radiology, and Endodontics*, 84(3): 279–85.

Dreger, Alice Domurat. 1998. *Hermaphrodites and the Medical Invention of Sex*. Cambridge, MA: Harvard University Press.

Dreger, Alice Domurat. (ed.). 1999. *Intersex in the Age of Ethics*. Frederick, MD: University Publishing Group.

Eugenides, Jeffrey. 2003. *Middlesex: A Novel*. New York: Picador USA.

Fausto-Sterling, Anne. 1993. "The Five Sexes: Why Male and Female Are Not Enough." *The Sciences*, 33(2): 20–5.

Fausto-Sterling, Anne. 2000a. *Sexing the Body: Gender Politics and the Construction of Sexuality.* New York: Basic Books.

Fausto-Sterling, Anne. 2000b. "The Five Sexes, Revisited." *The Sciences*, 40(4): 18–23.

Hillman, Thea. 2008. *Intersex: For Lack of a Better Word.* San Francisco: Manic D. Press, Inc.

Karkazis, Katrina. 2008. *Fixing Sex: Intersex, Medical Authority, and Lived Experience.* Durham, NC: Duke University Press.

Kessler, Suzanne. 1998. *Lessons from the Intersexed.* New Brunswick, NJ: Rutgers University Press.

Morland, Ian. (ed.) 2009. *GLQ: A Journal of Lesbian and Gay Studies Special Issue: Intersex and After*, 15(2).

Preves, Sharon E. 2003. *Intersex and Identity: The Contested Self.* New Brunswick: Rutgers University Press.

Roberts, Helen E., Janet D. Cragan, Joanne Cono, Muin J. Khoury, Mark R. Weatherly, and Cynthia A. Moore. 1998. "Increased Frequency of Cystic Fibrosis among Infants with Jejunoileal Atresia." *American Journal of Medical Genetics*, 78(5): 446–9.

Systma, Sharon E (ed.). 2006. *Ethics and Intersex.* New York: Springer.

"The Out 100." 1998, December/January. *Out magazine*, 102.

CPSIA information can be obtained at www.ICGtesting.com
Printed in the USA
BVOW060407160212

283076BV00003B/21/P